Places in the United States and
Canada significant in Orson Hyde's life.

ORSON HYDE

Myrtle Stevens Hyde

ORSON HYDE

The Olive Branch
of
Israel

Myrtle Stevens Hyde

Salt Lake City

Jacket and maps by Bryan Baker.

Publisher's Cataloging-in-Publication Data *(Provided by Quality Books, Inc.)*
  Hyde, Myrtle Stevens.
    Orson Hyde: the olive branch of Israel / Myrtle Stevens Hyde—1st ed.
      p. cm.
    Includes bibliographical references and index.
    LCCN: 99-067645
    ISBN: 1888106719
    1. Hyde, Orson, 1805–1878.   2. Mormons—Biography.   I. Title.
  BX8695.H87H94 2000   289.3/32092
    [B]   QBI99-1733

First Edition
Manufactured in the United States of America

(October 12, 1856)

CONTENTS

		Page
PREFACE		xi
PART ONE		
1	. . . *a marvellous work and a wonder.* . . . *(1805-1831)*	3
2	. . . *saints [and] walk.* . . . *(1831-1832)*	17
3	. . . *prepare.* . . . *(1832-1834)*	32
4	. . . *to Zion . . . a wife . . . witnesses.* . . . *(1834-1835)*	45
5	. . . *Elijah.* . . . *(1836)*	66
6	. . . *nations, and isles afar off.* . . . *(1836-1838)*	72
7	. . . *sorrow.* . . . *(1838-1839)*	95
8	. . . *toward Jerusalem.* . . . *(1839-1841)*	111
9	. . . *he shall come and pray.* . . . *(1841-1842)*	131
PART TWO		
10	. . . *Martha and Mary.* . . . *(1843)*	153
11	. . . *many things.* . . . *(1843-1844)*	162
12	. . . *foundation of apostles.* . . . *(1844-1846)*	179
13	. . . *labours, journeyings.* . . . *(1846-1848)*	206
14	. . . *gold.* . . . *(1848-1850)*	234
15	. . . *deserts and mountains.* . . . *(1850)*	258
16	. . . *gain and loss.* . . . *(1850-1852)*	272
17	. . . *went our way.* . . . *(1852)*	293
PART THREE		
18	. . . *build.* . . . *(1852-1855)*	305
19	. . . *westward.* . . . *(1855)*	325
20	. . . *Israel among the Gentiles.* . . . *(1855-1856)*	348
21	. . . *edifying and chastisement.* . . . *(1856-1860)*	364

22   . . . *increase*. . . . *(1860–1865)*   389

23   . . . *afflictions*. . . . *(1865–1867)*   412

24   . . . *no more thine enemy*. . . . *(1867–1872)*   438

25   . . . *daily walk*. . . . *(1872)*   463

26   . . . *unto the end*. . . . *(1873–1878)*   469

EPILOGUE   488

APPENDIX ONE: Was Orson Hyde a Jew?   489

APPENDIX TWO: Location of Hyde Park in Iowa   492

APPENDIX THREE: Orson Hyde's Estate   494

APPENDIX FOUR: Wives   496

BIBLIOGRAPHICAL ESSAY   508

ACKNOWLEDGMENTS   511

ABBREVIATIONS   513

NOTES   515

SELECTED BIBLIOGRAPHY   573

INDEX   589

MAPS

United States   Inside front cover

Places of consequence to Orson Hyde 1819–1831   7

A section in the north part of Kirtland, Ohio   11

Orson's 1832 mission with Samuel H. Smith   26

Zion's Camp   46

Missouri and Illinois places significant to Orson 1838–1839   106

Jerusalem and environs   132

Nauvoo and environs   164

The Council Bluffs area   209

Kanesville   235

Salt Lake City   310

MAPS (continued)

Genoa and Wassau (Washoe) Valley area   356

Sanpete Valley and area   392

Black Hawk War area south of Sanpete Valley   417

Spring City   477

England, Europe, the Holy Land, and Egypt   Inside back cover

PHOTOGRAPHS   Following page 292

Marinda Nancy Johnson Hyde

Newell K. Whitney Store

Jerusalem

Orson's portable desk

Mary Ann Price Hyde

Hyde home in Nauvoo

Joseph Smith with Church Leaders in Nauvoo

Hyde home in Kanesville

Kanesville

Kanesville

Kanesville

Orson Hyde's newspaper

Orson Hyde, probably 1851 or 1852

Orson Hyde, 1853

Hyde home in Great Salt Lake City

Great Salt Lake City, 1855

Plot of Genoa

Orson Hyde letter, 1856

Ann Eliza Vickers Hyde

Julia Thomene Reinert Hyde

Elisabeth Josephine Gallier Hyde

PHOTOGRAPHS (continued)

Hyde log home in Spring City

Sophia Margaret Lyon Hyde

Hyde rock home in Spring City

Orson Hyde, older

PREFACE

AN event in 1841 inspired the creation of this book. That year, red-haired Orson Hyde trod a pebbled path up the Mount of Olives, gazed upon the golden city of Jerusalem, and prayed, fulfilling the commission from the Almighty for which he had come. In his eloquent prayer he beseeched the Most High God that divine powers would operate to again make this Promised Land fruitful and to bring her children home.

Because his words have proved prophetic in the many decades since his entreaty, a peaceful garden on the Mount now honors him and his supplication. Civil authorities in Jerusalem invited the development of this five-acre hillside garden. During the planning I was asked, as the Hyde family genealogist, to assist in gathering contributions. The generosity of thousands of donors assured the completion of the park in 1979.

When first told about the garden, I thought that someone should write a book about Orson Hyde. The purpose of the book should be twofold. First, it should acquaint the Jews with Orson Hyde. Second, it should help people understand the devout faith that gave him the courage to leave his home and family in the United States and travel for a year and a half, with limited means, to faraway Jerusalem.

Then I was surprised to receive distinct spiritual promptings that *I* should write the book. This dismaying occurrence brought denial on my part and a great sense of inadequacy. After a time, however, my feelings changed to commitment to do whatever the assignment required. To be trusted with this sacred endeavor, I at length realized, was an honor to be revered.

During the period of seeking the pieces of Orson Hyde's story, insightful and fascinating information emerged in extraordinary scope. The scattered notes, documents, reports, articles, speeches, letters, and books, by and about this man, are from a unique missionary and pioneering time. Retrieving them from their resting places required many years and brought soul-stirring rewards. The records caused another purpose of the book to evolve: to share with readers precious details never before published.

Research revealed Orson Hyde to be a remarkable individual. Born and orphaned in Connecticut, he matured in frontier Ohio. Though his most well-known achievement is his journey to Jerusalem from Illinois, he received esteem in numerous roles. Among these are apostle in the Mormon Church, teacher, missionary (United States, Canada, and England), orator, scripturalist, editor, journalist, lawyer, judge, statesman, colonizer, administrator, husband, and father.

His religious pursuits led to various other adventures. He accomplished praiseworthy work as an editor in both England and Iowa. In 1850 his legal business brought him admittance "as an Attorney and Counsellor at law, to practice in the several Courts of Iowa." In this state he also successfully met leadership challenges during gold-rush outfitting excitement. Here, too, a President of the United States nominated him as a Supreme Court Judge for distant Utah Territory. He encountered high drama while crossing the great plains of North America five times, by horse and by wagon. He colonized in what afterward became western Nevada. Later, as an administrator and colonizer in central Utah, he was a major figure in Utah's Black Hawk Indian War.

Contrasts in Orson Hyde's life, I discovered, were more broad than most people experience, from the devastating to the sublime. Distress occasionally brought deep anguish. Pinnacles of communication with heavenly realms, on the other hand, brought supreme elation. Faltering at times in his personal commitment to the Almighty, he rallied, stronger because of his efforts to overcome lack of faith. Difficulties and spiritual sustenance, in their sequence, polished him into one of the solid foundation stones of the Lord's work on earth. Unconcerned for wealth or for praise to himself, he gave his all for the benefit of Israel—in his own time—and in time to come.

Here is Orson Hyde's amazing story.

Note: In the interest of historical accuracy when quoting original materials, any modifications are mentioned in Notes. Orson Hyde and others, while writing, occasionally used underlining for emphasis, and this is preserved in quotations.

PART ONE

(1805–1842)

Ezekiel wrote: *And the word of the Lord came unto me, saying, Son of man, prophesy against the shepherds of Israel, prophesy, and say unto them, Thus saith the Lord God unto the shepherds; . . . The diseased have ye not strengthened, neither have ye healed that which was sick, neither have ye bound up that which was broken, neither have ye brought again that which was driven away, neither have ye sought that which was lost. . . .*

For thus saith the Lord God; Behold, I, even I, will both search my sheep, and seek them out. . . . I will seek that which was lost, and bring again that which was driven away, and will bind up that which was broken, and will strengthen that which was sick.

—Ezekiel 34:1-2, 4, 11, 16

CHAPTER 1

... a marvellous work and a wonder. ... (1805-1831)

> ... the Lord said, ... Therefore, behold, I will
> proceed to do a marvellous work among this people, even
> a marvellous work and a wonder. ...
> —Isaiah 29:13, 14

ORSON again rearranged his covers as his mind examined the question keeping him awake: Was the "golden Bible" genuine? Sleep had eluded him during the night as restless thoughts evolved from inquiry to anguish. "What will now become of me," he agonized, "if perchance I have denounced the will of my Father in Heaven, and used my every effort to thwart God Almighty's plans? Oh! What will become of me if such be the case?"

In contrast to this distress, the religious gathering of the preceding 1831 spring day had been exhilarating. As in other towns, Orson Hyde, a Campbellite preacher, had been invited by people in Ridgeville, Ohio, to come and speak to them against the "golden Bible." The book was published by a new religious faction, the Mormons, who declared that Joseph Smith, a "Prophet," had translated the record from writings of ancient Israelites who came to America.

Pastor Hyde—of average height: five feet, seven and three-quarters inches—stood out in the crowd because of his red hair, "red as a fox's tail." Wearing a nicely-pressed suit, he moved with a muscular dignity that manual labor had worked into his twenty-six years.[1]

The people of Ridgeville, sturdy frontierfolk the same as Orson, had axed, sawed, and plowed to make a community among the tree-covered ridges that extended like gigantic ripples from the south shore of Lake Erie. A few bears and wolves still roamed the hilly woods, but the town boasted log cabins, frame homes, modest stores, a couple of small schools, a home post office, taverns, mills, and a new brick hotel. The settlers renewed their spiritual strength in small gatherings in homes or schools and in larger gatherings in barns or groves. The Campbellites, though a minor group, met acceptance in this frontier setting where folks drew together more by common daily pursuits than by details of religious belief. Orson pastored his own congregations in Elyria, a few miles west of Ridgeville, and in Florence, his town of residence, twenty-two miles beyond Elyria. He had become well known locally for his knowledge of scripture and for his polish as an orator.[2]

The meeting began. Orson stood confidently. The congregation saw his sincere smile and his large blue eyes in an intelligent-looking face framed by that familiar red hair (somewhat unruly), a squarish face with the jaw slightly broader than square. He had prominent eyebrows, a straight nose, and in the middle of his chin a dimple. Orson's appeal came not because of strikingly handsome features, but rather from a look and manner of well-groomed assurance and boyish openness.[3]

Earnestly Orson spoke, varying the volume and the pace of his strong voice. Praising God, he raised his arms. Quieting his words to a personal tone, he drew his hands close. Asking questions, he leaned forward. Harmony flowed between him and the people.

The Bible contained *all* that mankind needed to know in order to gain the blessings of heaven, Pastor Hyde reminded his listeners. In rich melodious phrases he recited verse after verse, his delivery as impeccable as his thoroughly brushed suit. Quoting the scriptures he loved seemed as natural to him as breathing. Carefully he rehearsed passages warning that false prophets would arise. The Mormon book, in his opinion, was an object of these warnings. Like a wolf in sheep's clothing, it was a snare to devour the Lord's flock. The Mormons proclaimed that their book contained necessary clarifications to the Bible. Absurd!

Orson related his own impressions of the Mormon volume. Here in northern Ohio the previous autumn he had conversed with four traveling Mormon missionaries. Because some of their teachings intrigued him, he "procured the book and read a portion of it." Finding its organization confusing, he decided that reading all five hundred and ninety pages would waste his time. The book, he now told his audience, was definitely fiction!

After the lengthy meeting the people congratulated Orson highly, convinced that he had "completely floored" Mormonism. When he retired to bed that night, in the home of a Ridgeville friend, Orson had no notion that his feeling of satisfaction would change.

Before trying to sleep, true to his usual practice he reviewed in his mind his sermon. As thoughts progressed, the things he had said posed disturbing questions and kept him awake. In essence he now scrutinized the criteria of false prophets, searched his experience for evidence that the "golden Bible" snared people into disobeying the Lord, analyzed the scriptures he knew so well to recall if the Almighty declared that new scriptures would *never* come to light, and wondered if the format of the new book would have been less confusing if he had read more.

During his previous discussions with the Mormon missionaries, Orson felt a vague fascination. Recognizing that these preachers lacked advanced education, he had been surprised to observe "superior wisdom and truth" in their explanations. Milo Andrus, with whose family Orson roomed in Florence, recounts his own amazement that, after hearing the missionaries,

"Brother Hyde did not question these men about their faith, [even though] he was in the habit of controverting the various preachers about the correctness of the doctrines advocated by them."[4]

Orson's own insights had been long in coming, and unlikely, considering the events of his youth. "I, Orson Hyde, son of Nathan Hyde and Sally Thorp," he tells, "was born in Oxford, New Haven County and State of Connecticut, January 8, 1805. At the age of seven years, my mother, a pious and godly woman, according to the light that then was, and member of the Methodist Episcopal Church, died soon after being delivered of a son, named Ami. [She had] given birth to eight sons and three daughters in the following order, according to my best recollection: Abijah, Harry, Laura, Nathan, Sally, Asahel, Horatio, Maria, Charles, Orson and Ami.

"My father, a boot and shoe maker by trade," Orson continues, "was a very talented man; quick, athletic, and naturally witty and cheerful. He was kind and affectionate, except when under the influence of strong drink (a habit to which he was somewhat addicted). After the death of my mother, my father enlisted into the army of the United States . . . in the war with Britain in 1812 and 1813."

Apparently the distraught father joined the army as a way to cope with losing his wife and being unable to manage everything. He dispersed the younger children, including Orson, to families who would take them. Orson saw little of his father after this. When Orson talked of those days he became melancholy: "After the death of my mother, the family was scattered abroad, and took their chances in life under no special protector or guide, save that of a kind Providence who ever watches, with care, over the lonely orphan and hears the plaintive cry of the young sparrows, bereft of their parent mother."[5]

After his mother's passing, Orson dreamed boyhood dreams of departing too. "It became my ambition to run away to sea," he later told his own son, "and eventually my pride to become an officer in the U. S. Navy; yet," he added after a pause, "Heaven had divined otherwise."[6] However, he retained his fascination for things of seas and ships.

"I was placed in the care of a [neighbor] gentleman by the name of Nathan Wheeler," Orson continues, "or rather, I fell into his hands. . . . This was a very good family, but quite penurious [miserly]. Mr. Wheeler worked me nigh unto death. I had to get up in the morning before daylight, with a lantern, and flail wheat [thresh wheat by hand] in the barn. This labor continued during the whole day, either on that particular job or other necessary work on the farm, until late at night. For my services I received my board and lodging, and a meager allotment of clothing."

To relieve drudgery Orson invented his own diversions. One prank he played that brought glee to him, and was not really harmful to any cow of Mr. Wheeler's, began by feeding a cow green apples. When she relished these and nuzzled Orson's hand for more, Orson popped an onion into her mouth, then stood back and laughed at her reaction.[7]

Life became more difficult for Orson when his guardian failed in business. Then Mr. Wheeler, with hope of bettering his condition, decided to join the surge of migration to the frontier, the Western Reserve in Ohio. "Mr. Wheeler first visited the Western Reserve by himself," Orson recounts, "purchased a farm in Kirtland, and sent for me and his nephew, Nathan Wooster, to come out the next spring."

In early spring "Mr. Wooster and myself started . . . (I then being fourteen years of age)," Orson details. "This was a hard trip for a youngster to perform on foot, with knapsack upon the back, containing clothes, bread, cheese, and dried beef for the journey, and obliged to keep up with a strong man, traveling from 30 to 38 miles per day, until we had performed the entire distance of 600 miles."

Kirtland, Ohio, in 1819, was primarily a thick forest of tall, majestic trees. In open parts, grape vines profusely intertwined saplings. Orson watched canvas-topped wagons weave around stumps that still filled the roads. He listened to the local music: the ring of axe-blows and the percussion of falling forest giants.[8]

Orson's efforts added volume to the frontier refrain. Mr. Wheeler's acreage lay on the north boundary of Kirtland, "heavily timbered," Orson relates. Trees had to be felled and sod turned for crops. This, Orson adds, "was the hardest kind of labor to prepare [the land] for cultivation."

The start of school each year made no difference to Mr. Wheeler's requirements. Orson still labored every daylight hour. He had received a beginning education in Connecticut, enough to whet his appetite for knowledge, and as he swung an ax or plowed a furrow he yearned to attend school. Not until cold weather caused a halt to most outdoor work did Mr. Wheeler allow Orson to sit in a classroom.

His first days in school, as a stranger and an orphan and starting late, bullies knocked him down, but with muscles strong he learned to punish his opponents amply while on his back on the ground. This earned him respect. His diligence in practicing lessons, plus a remarkable memory, helped him do well in penmanship, reading, grammar, and spelling. As seasons passed, with classroom days so few, he resolved that some day he would acquire advanced schooling.[9]

Because his guardian paid him no wage and discouraged education, Orson decided that his service from age seven to age eighteen would repay Mr. Wheeler sufficiently for his rearing. He would strike out for himself to earn money. As he neared eighteen, childless Mr. and Mrs. Wheeler begged him to remain on the farm, now productive, but Orson's decision held firm. The winter morning of his eighteenth birthday, January 8, 1823, he walked away from the Wheeler home to carve out his "fortune and destiny," he recounts. His "outfit and capital stock in trade" consisted of "one suit of home-made woollen clothes (butternut colored); two red flannel shirts, also home-made; two pairs of socks; one pair of coarse shoes on the feet; one old hat; and six and a quarter cents in *clean cash*."[10]

Orson's resolute strides carried him away from the Wheeler farm at the north edge of Kirtland and up a hill road for about half a mile to a small log iron foundry on the south edge of Mentor. At the foundry, owned by progressive and energetic Grandison Newell, Orson hired on for six months. He burned piles of wood to make charcoal for use in the rock blast furnace. He shoveled raw materials: charcoal, ore, and limestone. He endured the fierce heat of the furnace. And he learned to pour crucibles full of glowing, thick, liquid iron into molds for clock bells, irons, sleigh shoes, and various other articles. He saved his regular earnings of six dollars per month and also his pay for laboring extra hours. At the end of his six months he spent the sum for a good suit of clothes, new boots, and a fine hat.[11]

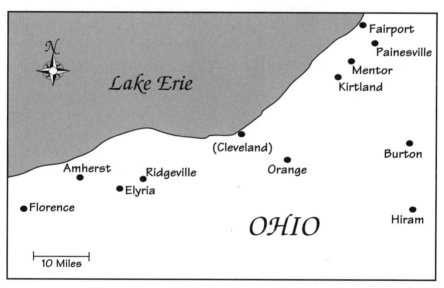

Places of consequence to Orson Hyde 1819–1831.

Orson found summer work in Kirtland at a river-powered carding mill. Here his muscles ached from the strenuous exertion of moving the huge levers of the carding machines. The machines had different-sized rotating cylinders covered with wire teeth that disentangled washed wool, cleaned out sticks and weeds, straightened the fibers, and turned out fluffy wool ready for spinning into yarn. "Being a raw hand at the business, I could not get very high wages," Orson narrates.[12]

When the carding season ended in the fall of 1823 he procured a clerking job in a store in Kirtland owned by A. Sidney Gilbert and Newel K.

Whitney. During two and a half years with them he developed a flair for dealing with the public.

The summer of 1826 he again operated carding machines. Though he was only twenty-one years of age, the mill owners hired him as foreman. They had such confidence in him that they required no financial security for his rental of the machines. Orson placed an advertisement in the newspaper in the neighboring village of Painesville. Published May 13, the notice reveals his positive personality:

> **Wool Carding.** The subscriber takes this course to inform the public that he has rented the well known Carding Machines, near Kirtland mills, heretofore occupied by Cards & Holmes, and has supplied new and superior cards from the celebrated factory of W. Wetmore & Co. and the whole Machines are in complete repair.—From the long experience of the subscriber in this business, with a machine not surpassed on the Western Reserve, he does not hesitate to give assurances to old and new customers, that Carding will be executed to their entire satisfaction. Special care & exertions will be made to accomplish this. He would recommend to his friends to forward their wool as early as they conveniently can.
>
> Terms for carding 3 cents per pound—but for prompt pay, a discount of 25 per cent will be made. Most kinds of country produce will be received in payment.
>
> **ORSON HYDE.**

"During this season," Orson narrates, "I paid my hired help, and also my rent, and cleared about 600 dollars in cash. This, I thought, was doing very well for a boy." He returned to his clerking job in the fall. In December he had not received payment from all of his carding contracts and placed another advertisement. His sense of humor shone through when he asked the editor of the newspaper to run the ad upside down. He wanted it to catch attention. The upside down ad of December 29 stated:

> **NOTICE.** The principal part of the claims due the subscriber for Carding are deposited with Messrs. N. K. Whitney & Co. to whom payment may be made till the 1st February next. For the most part of said claims, Grain will be received through the month of January, after which they will be disposed of for collection. ☞Improve the opportunity now, or ———
>
> **ORSON HYDE**

Orson clerked until the next spring, receiving moderate wages.

"Then," he continues, "business being rather slack in the store, I went to work for the same parties [Gilbert and Whitney], making pot[ash] and pearl [ash]" for the manufacture of glass and soap. His nose and eyes stung from the acrid smoke of the roaring pit fires consuming green plants, vines, and cut-down trees. His clothes became blackened with charcoal and soot from shoveling the ashes into large iron pots and from handling these pots, in which water dissolved out the valuable chemicals as it evaporated.[13]

A turning point came in 1827, the day that Orson dressed in his good clothes and attended a Methodist camp meeting. The exuberance of the speeches electrified him, and he joined the Methodists. He *wanted* religion in his life. His excitement grew as he studied the scriptures. At the formation of a group in Kirtland, he was appointed class leader.

Several months later he heard sermons by Campbellite preachers. "Being forcibly struck with the doctrine of immersion or baptism for the remission of sins," he recounts, "and many other important items of doctrine which were advocated by this new sect, and which were passed over by the Methodists as non-essentials, I left the Methodists and became a convert to this new faith."

As he listened to Campbellite preachers explain doctrine he gained a desire to do the same, but he felt a "great deficiency in learning." The time had come to use the money he had saved for education. The most dynamic Campbellite preacher in the area was Elder Sidney Rigdon. Sidney was taller than Orson by a couple of inches, and older by twelve years. His high forehead, bushy hair, and pronounced cheek bones gave emphasis to his piercing blue eyes. Orson admired Sidney's eloquent command of words and asked to be his student. Sidney consented, and Orson moved from Kirtland to the Rigdon home in neighboring Mentor. Under Sidney's direction Orson studied grammar "day and night," for months. Also, he became well acquainted with Pastor Rigdon's enthusiasm, his sometimes over-exuberance, and the occasional "wildness of his extravagant nature." Orson overlooked these quirks, realizing that everyone has quirks. Orson ever after felt deep gratitude for the "unwearied pains and care" of Sidney's tutoring.[14]

Next Orson moved to Burton, Ohio, twenty-two miles southeast of Kirtland, and paid for six months at Burton Academy (forerunner of Western Reserve University). Here he polished his oratorical skills and reviewed geography, arithmetic, and grammar.[15]

To broaden his reading he returned to Mentor and boarded for a season with Judge Orris Clapp, whose home contained the public library. Utilizing the banquet of books, Orson absorbed facts and feelings, historical and scientific and literary. Contentment in the Clapp home strengthened Orson's yearnings for a home of his own.

Judge Clapp and his son Matthew (about Orson's age) were avid Disciples, or Campbellites, and Orson delighted in hearty religious discussions with them. Orson's conviction grew that he wanted to use his education to effectively explain God's relationship with man. This in mind, he devoted consistent reading and pondering time to the Bible. The Campbellites encouraged scripture memorization, and Orson's extraordinary memory enabled him to recall and recite passages with ease.[16]

At last, after Orson had spent more than a year studying doctrine, leaders of The Disciples considered him ready to preach. In early autumn 1829 they ordained him an elder in their church. Fired by missionary enthusiasm, he traveled with Sidney Rigdon west from Kirtland to Elyria and Florence. Preaching during the fall season, they converted and baptized many people and organized several branches of the Campbellite Church before returning home to Mentor.

Eagerly, the following spring, 1830, Orson traveled west again to Elyria and Florence, and became the pastor of the branches that he and Sidney had organized. Sharing laughter, sorrows, fun, and meals with the families of his congregations made them seem his own. Gratitude filled his soul that he had saved his money for education. A long road had brought him from an uneducated orphan to Methodist class leader, then to Campbellite pastor. Now, this busy spring of 1831, he had gained the reputation of a master at delivering speeches against a strange new religious book.

During the reflective night after his successful address in Ridgeville, pondering that his efforts might be against the plans of God, Orson's anguish increased. What did that "golden Bible" contain? Had the Spirit guided his perplexing thoughts this sleepless night?

In the early morning light, objects in the room became clearly visible, and Orson reached a decision. "I, for the first time," he recounts, "thought that the Mormon Bible might be the truth of heaven; and I fully resolved before leaving the house, that I would never preach against it any more until I knew more about it, being pretty strongly convicted in my own mind that I had been doing wrong." He remembered his own remark the previous year, when he first read vague reports about the book: "Who knows but that this 'golden Bible' may break up all our religion, and change its whole features and bearing?"

After making his personal covenant in Ridgeville, Orson returned to Florence and resumed his duties as pastor and as schoolteacher. He had secured a teaching position in the fall to insure against being a financial burden to his congregations. Normally he enjoyed teaching, but after his Ridgeville speech he felt unsettled. Also, his preoccupation with Mormonism made him uneasy about what he said in sermons to his Campbellite congregations. He must do more than refrain from preaching against the new book.

To seek a resolution to his mental conflicts, Orson decided to return the forty miles east to Kirtland, which he had left three years before. Kirtland had now become a Mormon center, with Joseph Smith, spiritual and temporal leader of the group, residing there. Many of Orson's old friends, including store owners Sidney Gilbert and Newel Whitney, had joined the new religion, and other converts had moved into town. Sidney Rigdon, too, Orson's friend and teacher, had left the Campbellites and now used his persuasive and elo-quent talents for the Mormons. In Kirtland Orson could easily observe.

In Florence, Orson's acquaintances saw no sense in his decision to close his successful school and give up his career as a popular pastor. Finally, in the face of this dismay, Orson shared his insecurity about Mormonism with a few trusted friends. "My object is to get away from the prejudices of the peo-ple," he confided, imploring tolerant understanding, "and to place myself in a position where I can examine the subject without embarrassment."[17]

In northwestern Kirtland the summer of 1831, "The Corners" appeared as Orson recalled. Here on the flats near the Chagrin River the roads from Wil-loughby and from Mentor intersected. On one corner stood the clapboard store of "N. K. Whitney and Co." Yes, Newel could again use Orson as a clerk. His partner, Sidney Gilbert, had traveled to Missouri with Joseph Smith, Sidney Rigdon, and others and would remain there in the Mormon settlement to operate a new store. Employment as a clerk suited Orson's pur-poses ideally. This would be the perfect "cover" for examining Mormonism.[18]

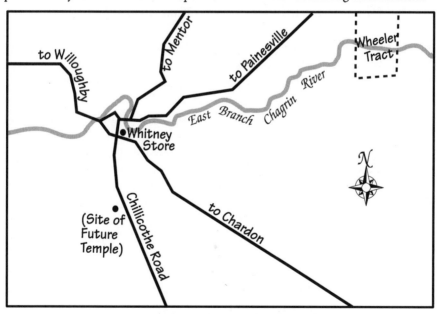

A section in the north part of Kirtland, Ohio.

Orson listened carefully as Mormon customers conversed. They accepted amazing claims of their esteemed Joseph Smith. They believed his accounts about visits to mortals by God and by angels. Mormons spoke of heavenly beings by name, like revered friends. As Orson swept floors and stocked shelves he pondered these things. At night, in his bed in the loft of the store, he read the Bible by flickering candle flame and compared its precepts with what he heard during the day. Sometimes he read until morning.[19]

Abundant Bible accounts of heavenly beings visiting earth and speaking to mortals indicated that anciently such events were considered natural. God spoke to Noah; the Lord appeared to Abraham; two angels visited Sodom; Jacob saw God face to face; an angel appeared to Moses in a flame of fire; and for Daniel, God sent an angel to shut the lions' mouths.[20] Throughout Bible times the Lord gave guidance and miraculous powers to his prophets. Noah received instructions for building the ark to save his family from the flood. Moses was told what to say to Pharaoh that the children of Israel might be freed. At Elijah's word no rain fell; and when the widow's son lay dead, at Elijah's request the Lord gave back life. Isaiah, Jeremiah, Ezekiel, and others pronounced inspired prophecies of future events.[21]

In Kirtland, Orson heard Mormons proclaim that the Almighty had restored to Joseph Smith the same powers possessed by past prophets. With these powers he, like they, directed his followers' actions and performed miracles for their benefit. He had even healed one woman's lame arm.[22]

In addition to the traditional Bible, Orson studied the "golden Bible." Bound in natural brown leather, the volume's name was stamped with gilt letters on a black leather label on the spine: Book of Mormon. Soon, the pages of Orson's copy gained a supple, friendly feel. Like the Bible that he loved and knew so well, the book contained the history of people involved with prophecies and intrigues, problems and blessings. It had liberal references to familiar Old Testament individuals, such as Adam and Abraham, and to familiar practices, such as the law of Moses. Desiring accurate insight, Orson "prayed much unto the Lord for light and knowledge, for wisdom and spirit to guide me in my . . . investigations."[23]

The narrative[24] of the Book of Mormon began in Jerusalem in the first year of the reign of Zedekiah, king of Judah (600 B.C.), and told of a prophet named Lehi, a descendant of the Joseph who was sold into Egypt. The same as to other prophets of that era, the Lord revealed to Lehi that wickedness would bring about the destruction of Jerusalem.[25] Lehi should take his family and depart. For several years they traveled and camped, then built a ship, crossed the ocean, and settled in the "choice land" later known as America. Over the centuries, Lehi's descendants were sometimes worshipful, sometimes not, and reaped due rewards the same as did Bible peoples.

Mormons claimed that a prophetic blessing pronounced by Jacob, or Israel, upon his son Joseph referred to the Book of Mormon peoples. Jacob declared, "Joseph is a fruitful bough, even a fruitful bough by a well; whose branches run over the wall" (Genesis 49:22). The well symbolized the ocean, the Mormons said, and that a branch of Joseph's descendants would "run over the wall" meant that some of his progeny would travel to a far place. America lay far from any land familiar to Jacob.

Mormons also said that the Book of Mormon fit a description given by the prophet Isaiah that a record would come forth from the earth. Isaiah prophesied: ". . . and thy voice shall be, as of one that hath a familiar spirit, out of the ground, and thy speech shall whisper out of the dust" (Isaiah 29:4).

The "familiar spirit" of the Book of Mormon indeed called to mind many prophecies in the Old Testament, notably the one about the Messiah where Isaiah said that "a virgin shall conceive, and bear a son" (Isaiah 7:14). The prophet Nephi, son of Lehi, foretold that "six hundred years from the time that my father left Jerusalem, a prophet would the Lord God raise up among the Jews—even a Messiah, or, in other words, a Savior of the world." Nephi saw in vision "a virgin most beautiful and fair" who would become "the mother of the Son of God, after the manner of the flesh" (1 Nephi 10:4, 11:13, 15, 18). The book told that signs in the western hemisphere heralded the birth of the Son of God in the land of Jerusalem. "[T]here was no darkness in all that night, but it was as light as though it was mid-day, . . . also . . . a new star did appear" (3 Nephi 1:19-21).

The book also detailed the signs of the suffering and death of the Savior in far-away Jerusalem—tempests, thunder, fire, earthquakes, and "thick darkness." Earlier a prophet named Alma had foretold this event. "[T]he Son of God suffereth according to the flesh," Alma prophesied, "that he might take upon him the sins of his people, that he might blot out their transgressions according to the power of his deliverance. . . . For . . . according to the great plan of the Eternal God there must be an atonement made, or else all mankind must unavoidably perish; . . . yea, all are fallen. . . . Therefore, it is expedient that there should be a great and last sacrifice . . . ; then shall the law of Moses be fulfilled; . . . and that great and last sacrifice will be the Son of God, yea, infinite and eternal" (Alma 7:13, 34:9, 13, 14).

The resurrected Savior visited the people in America. He prayed with them, blessed them, and healed their sick. He taught them eternal truths, that man should love God above all else and "thy neighbour as thyself" (as in Deuteronomy 6:5 and Leviticus 19:18). He told multitudes about events that would precede his glorious second coming. He also explained the resurrection, or reuniting of body and spirit separated by death, and that he, the Son of God, in overcoming death had provided that all mortals would be resurrected.

For generations after the Messiah taught them, Orson read, the people lived righteously, but eventually selfishness brought devastation. The Lord told the custodian of their records, a prophet named Mormon, to compile an abridgment of the sets of metal plates inscribed over the centuries. Obeying the Lord's command, Mormon engraved his abridgment on sheets of gold and called it the Book of Mormon. When he grew old he gave it to his son Moroni to finish. After Mormon's death Moroni added a few writings and, in about 421 A.D., buried the record in a hill near present Palmyra, New York.

Joseph Smith, Orson was told, as a lad had lived near that hill. Joseph claimed that an angel showed to him the repository of the abridgment. After a period of preparation he was allowed to remove the record from its hiding place and, with divine help, translate it.

Orson learned from his studying that the Book of Mormon contained many facets. Its teachings agreed with the teachings of the Bible. Its contents spanned centuries of time and the sagas of numerous peoples. Its integrity proclaimed that inspired men chronicled it in their own season and place.

Orson balanced his examination of Mormon teachings by listening to the opposition. From talk in the store, conversations around town, and anti-Mormon speeches in gatherings, he heard denunciations against Joseph Smith and his followers. Continuing to study, to pray, and to analyze, he remained careful to say nothing about either side.[26]

Joseph Smith and his companions returned from Missouri on August 27, 1831, and received a glad welcome in Kirtland. At last Orson met the man about whom he had heard so much. Joseph Smith radiated a magnetic aura that his height of at least six feet enhanced. Twenty-five years of age, he had broad shoulders, a full chest, trim, expressive hands, and long legs. His light brown hair complimented the fair complexion of his oval face. His forehead sloped, and his nose arched moderately. His most striking feature, his eyes—large, wide-set, and hazel-blue, with long thick lashes—conveyed inner strength, a loving nobleness. His warm smile invited friendship.

Orson listened to Joseph Smith's speeches and chatted with him in private, becoming increasingly fascinated by his thought-soaring concepts and his extraordinary experiences.[27]

Orson heard him tell the details of boyhood confusion about which church to join. This, Joseph recounted, led him to pray in a grove of trees across the field from his home.[28] After few words of supplication, though, a most unexpected thing happened. Darkness overshadowed him, and his strength dwindled. Just as he felt he would be destroyed, the ominous force withdrew. What happened next was transcendent beyond imagination:

To his incredible astonishment, light enveloped him—sublime, magnificent light—and two glorious heavenly Personages appeared.[29] They emanated incomparable love. In reply to his question, they told him to join no church, assuring that "the fulness of the gospel, [shall], at some future time, be made known to [you]."[30] They also gave him other instructions. Joseph had been visited by the Father and the Son!

After Joseph talked of his amazing experience with others, Orson learned, scorn and harassment assailed him. Orson understood why—this was a revolutionary story! Though the next few years proved difficult, Joseph refused to deny his account. His family bolstered him, but he yearned for additional divine communication, which had been promised.

Orson marveled further when he heard what Joseph claimed happened a few years after his astounding saga began. In 1823, while thinking and praying as he lay in bed, a hoped-for heavenly messenger indeed appeared, in brilliant light. This one said his name was Moroni. He disclosed joyful tidings: God would soon fulfill his covenant with ancient Israel regarding their posterity. Preparations for the Messiah's second coming were to commence. The fullness of the gospel would be preached in all nations to prepare a righteous people for the Millennium of peace. Moroni, Joseph told, quoted Old Testament prophecies, among them the words of Malachi announcing the return of "Elijah the prophet before the coming . . . of the Lord,"[31] and also the words of Isaiah proclaiming that the Lord "shall set up an ensign for the nations, and shall assemble . . . Israel."[32] Moroni said that Joseph had been chosen by God to help fulfill these prophecies.

Moroni added that a sacred history of the ancient inhabitants of the Americas had been engraved on plates of gold and long ago hidden. Joseph would be privileged to bring this history to light, if he continued faithful. In a vision he was shown a hill near his home and the location on it where a large stone marked the repository of the record.

To Orson's great absorption, Joseph's remarkable story continued that the next day he followed Moroni's directions, climbed the designated hill, and near the top recognized the rock that he had seen in vision. Digging soil and grass from its edges, he lifted it with a lever and found it to be the lid of a stone box. Inside lay the record of shining gold, a metal that would remain untarnished over the centuries. The thin gold sheets were engraved with curious marks. Rings bound them together like the leaves of a book.

Joseph started to reach into the box, but an unseen power stopped him. Then, at his side, Moroni appeared and said that Joseph must learn more before receiving the record.

And some things he was to learn that very day. Moroni bid him to look up. He did, and "the heavens . . . opened, and the glory of the Lord shone round about and rested upon him." His soul thrilled at the wondrous scene. Everywhere in the brilliant spaciousness he saw beauty and order and majesty and splendor. Light and love and peace flowed into him. He saw that "the righteous are blessed with a place in the kingdom of God where joy unspeakable surrounds them. . . . The glory of God crowns them, and they continually feast upon his goodness and enjoy his smiles."[33]

Then Moroni pointed in another direction, according to Joseph's narrative, and with somber tone said, "Look!"

Joseph turned his gaze, and he saw Satan, "the prince of darkness," with his innumerable droves of fiendish followers. Joseph recoiled. Rather than peaceful, the scene was oppressive with agitation and turmoil. Joseph's mind staggered at the vast number of the Satanic host, and he recognized the source of that suffocating power that had beset him a few years previously in the grove. Before the devilish scene closed to his view he knew the reality of the menace of evil, a monstrous force against light and truth.

Joseph said that Moroni explained, "All this is shown, . . . the glory of God and the power of darkness, that you may know hereafter the two powers and never be influenced or overcome by that wicked one." Moroni warned Joseph that by the influence of Satan, people would continue to revile him and to circulate falsehoods about him and even try to take his life. Moroni then again gave Joseph the promise that "if you are faithful, and shall hereafter continue to keep the commandments of the Lord, you shall be preserved to bring these things forth." Not only would the book come forth, he said, but the work of God would "increase the more opposed."[34] Orson carefully made no public reaction to Joseph Smith's incredulous statements, but his fascination grew.

During the next four years after seeing the gold record, Joseph continued to endure ridicule from skeptics. He was strengthened by increased knowledge of the things of God that he learned as angels visited and taught him.[35] No mortal, Orson was beginning to conclude, could fabricate the miraculous events Joseph Smith claimed had transpired; there were no inconsistencies.

Joseph said that Moroni allowed him to take the gold book home in 1827. For two challenging years, while he possessed it, trials increased. But, with guidance from Heaven, diligent effort, and aid from family and a few friends, Joseph's exertions kept the plates hidden from prying hands and eyes while he translated the ancient script into English. Joseph gave all translating credit to the gift and power of God. He finished the record in 1829.[36]

Before Joseph Smith returned the volume to Moroni, Orson also learned, eleven witnesses received the privilege to see it, and they signed written testimonies of their experience. Joseph no longer carried the burden of being alone in his claims! Twelve men, counting himself, had seen the gold plates and willingly testified this to the world.[37] Orson met and conversed with some of these men. They seemed upright and sensible, and their accounts, too, were consistent.

Orson gained profound respect for Joseph Smith as he learned Joseph's story. Observations added to this respect. Though of confident bearing, Joseph was humble. Intelligence radiated from him, but he showed no arrogance. Rather he showed kindness and consideration. Even in every-day acts he was gentle: when talking with a child or mounting his horse or walking with his wife Emma. His common title, "Brother Joseph," indicated how much people loved and admired him. Dramatic things, too, revealed his quiet strength. When confronted with malicious taunts and threats, his reactions reflected calm assurance of guidance from the Lord. Like steady Daniel of old, Joseph Smith was full of wisdom, in harmony with God, and willing, for his convictions, to face a den of lions or to walk in a fiery furnace.

. . . saints [and] walk. . . . *(1831–1832)*

> And the heavens shall praise thy wonders, O Lord: thy faithfulness
> also in the congregation of the saints. . . . Blessed is the people that
> know the joyful sound: they shall walk, O Lord, in the light of thy
> countenance.
>
> —Psalm 89:5, 15

IN late September, 1831, Orson realized that the seeds of his belief in Mormonism had matured. Planted in his heart in the springtime, cultivated and nurtured in the summer, they had blossomed and then ripened for harvest. Weeds of opposition had sprung up and been examined, then were hoed out and tossed aside to wither. He felt ready to ask for baptism, to join himself with the "Saints."

Though outsiders called them Mormons, members referred to themselves as Saints, following the pattern in the Old and the New Testaments, in the Book of Mormon, and in the revelations of the Lord to Joseph Smith. In all of these the Lord called his followers saints.[1] The Lord's church required commitment of its members, all receiving calls to serve, regardless of education or experience. Orson liked the spirit of these people and the glow in their faces. He wanted to *belong* and felt eager to receive assignments.

Sunday, October 2, Orson attended the Saints' meeting in Kirtland, discovering Sidney and the Prophet Joseph also there. Joseph Smith had moved his family to Hiram, Ohio, and his visit this day added the special vitality to the services that only his presence gave. After the meeting Orson approached him and requested baptism. Brother Joseph's smile conveyed approval. Sidney would have the honor of performing the ordinance.

Down the road from "The Corners," the Kirtland baptism place was a pool in the river held quiet by a walnut-wood dam. Friends watched Orson and Sidney step into the stilled stream together and wade into deeper water. Sidney raised his right arm, squared at the elbow, bowed his head, and pronounced: "Orson Hyde, having been commissioned of Jesus Christ, I baptize you in the name of the Father, and of the Son, and of the Holy Ghost. Amen." Sidney immersed Orson by laying him backward into the water, then lifted him up to a standing position, wet clothes clinging, and Orson wiped water from his face. This voluntary act of baptism carried with it the automatic covenant that Orson would remember the Savior at all times and serve him and keep his commandments.[2]

Orson had become familiar with baptism by immersion as a Campbellite, but their baptism, his recent studies convinced him, lacked heavenly sanction. The privilege to baptize authoritatively had been given to Joseph Smith and his assistant Oliver Cowdery in the same transcendent way as other commissions, by the visit of an angel of the Lord. The glorious being who brought this power was "John, the same that is called John the Baptist in the New Testament." John taught Joseph Smith and Oliver Cowdery that the privilege to baptize was part of the priesthood held by Aaron, the brother of Moses. John placed his hands on their heads and conferred upon them the priesthood of Aaron.[3]

Orson understood that in addition to immersion by one having proper authority, baptism contained a second part, confirmation. Joseph Smith and Oliver Cowdery had received the divine right to perform confirmations from three heavenly beings—Peter, James, and John, apostles of the Lord Jesus Christ—as part of the higher priesthood of God. This higher power was called the Melchizedek priesthood, after ancient Melchizedek, a righteous servant of the Almighty. Seated, Orson felt the light pressure of Brother Joseph's and Brother Sidney's hands on his head. With inspiring words the Prophet Joseph confirmed him a member of Christ's church and conferred upon him the gift of the Holy Ghost. This gift gave him the privilege of the help and companionship of the third member of the Godhead as long as he kept his baptismal covenant to serve the Lord. Orson had no thought that he would ever thwart this trust.[4]

Joseph Smith said that Orson had prepared himself for privileges beyond baptism, and, in a second blessing, conferred upon him the Melchizedek priesthood, with the office of elder. "Elder" had been Orson's title for two years in the Campbellite church. He had now learned that even though the Campbellites used the title, patterning their terms after those bestowed by the Savior in his church in New Testament times, their titles lacked authority. As an elder in the Church of Jesus Christ, Orson received power from heaven to act, under inspiration, in God's name.

Asked to express his feelings, Orson searched his memory and then said that now he felt ready to feed the fowls of the Lord, as in his youth he had fed the poultry of Mr. Wheeler. Crooking one arm as though holding a pan of grain, dipping into it with his free hand, and scattering imaginary kernels, he continued, "When I poured the corn upon the ground, the fowls all came together en masse, but after the corn was exhausted . . . the fowls all turned away, going in different directions, each one singing his own song. So with religion. While God poured out . . . revelation upon the ancient church, they were all united and ate the living bread, but when he withheld revelations in latter times, because of the unbelief of men, they turned and went their own course, and sung their own song, some a Methodist song, some a Baptist song, some a Presbyterian song, &c.; but if they had had revelation they would have sung one of the songs of Zion."[5]

Orson had heard Saints talk of a sacred peace that came to them after baptism and confirmation. He, however, received no special feeling, and this disappointed him. Had his analytical approach to the gospel dulled his perception of celestial quickenings?

"Not until about three days after," he recounts, "did I receive any internal evidence of the special approbation of Heaven of the course I had taken." He was in the store that evening, behind the counter. A lull in customers brought quiet. Suddenly, each cell of his body, from head to feet, seemed to expand with exhilaration, energized with a surging glow. For a brief instant his throat tightened. However, this feeling was good, he reasoned immediately. In this encompassing of sublime love he recognized the manifestation of the Holy Spirit. Now he understood the description of this sensation as the baptism by fire and also the peace which passeth understanding. He now knew of God's pleasure with his actions. "[T]he Spirit of the Lord came upon me in so powerful a manner," his narrative continues, "that I felt like waiting upon no one, and withdrew in private to enjoy the [spiritual] feast alone. This, to me, was a precious season, long to be remembered."

Eager now to share the gospel message, he felt that his old friends would want to hear it. Enthusiastically he visited among them and shared his new insights. Rather than interest, however, he encountered cold indifference. In dismay he received reactions of pity that he, a man of intelligence, had been overpowered by the Mormon delusion.[6]

His friends in the Church, on the other hand, expressed joy that he had finally joined them. October 10, eight days after his baptism, he was asked to serve as the clerk for a meeting. Two weeks later, October 25, he attended a general conference at a member's large home in Orange, Ohio, fifteen miles southwest of Kirtland. A sizeable congregation gathered, among them forty priesthood holders, mostly young men like Orson who exhibited zest for life and excitement about fresh ideas. The Prophet spoke about the sacred powers of the office of high priest in the Melchizedek priesthood, and he assured the elders in the room that they would be privileged to be ordained to this office, just as had others. Joseph Smith encouraged the brethren to express their feelings. Orson, unable to repress his fullness of heart, stood second. Sincerely he uttered his testimony. The clerk of the conference summarized: "Br. Orson Hyde said that he covenanted to give all to the Lord and be for [H]is glory, and as to all [H]is works his heart responded a hearty Amen."

In the evening a second conference session convened, and Orson was among the fifteen elders who received ordination to the office of high priest. High priests in the Church now numbered more than three dozen.

In the same evening meeting Orson accepted, gladly, his second official Church appointment. As part of a "committee of six" he received assignment to visit and teach and set in order the several branches of the Church in Ohio and to collect funds for the support of Joseph Smith and Sidney Rigdon. The daily responsibilities of these two Church leaders required many hours, leaving no opportunity to earn livelihoods. Also, the Prophet was preparing a corrected version of the Bible. Sidney acted as his scribe. This revision consumed much time, but the Lord had revealed the necessity of it, because many important principles had been removed or lost over the centuries. With his love of the Bible, Orson had high interest in the project. In today's earlier meeting Brother Joseph referred to the revision and stated that "except the church [members] receive the fulness of the Scriptures . . . they [will] yet fall."

After the meeting Oliver Cowdery prepared credentials for the "committee of six." Credentials gave the Saints evidence in writing that Orson and the five others had authority to instruct the branches of the Church and to collect donations.

Unable to absorb the profoundness of the events surrounding him, Orson set aside thoughts of the intricacies of the Church and enjoyed lighthearted banter with his companions. In the conference session the next morning he relaxed, entertained by his friend Sidney's magical voice telling of the "privileges of the Saints in these last days." Then Sidney's tone changed. He looked at Orson and others in the room who had been ordained high priests the previous evening and proclaimed that "the Lord [is] not well pleased with some of them because of their indifference to be ordained to that office."

This stung Orson, to receive an official rebuke when he had been in the Church only three weeks, but he thoughtfully analyzed his actions of the previous evening and his feelings of this morning. Sidney was right. When Sidney concluded his remarks, Orson immediately expressed his humble acceptance of the censure. After discussion of business matters, a vote chose Sidney Rigdon, Oliver Cowdery, Hyrum Smith, and Orson to address the congregation later that day. In his sermon Orson tried to be sincere. He wished no further reprimands.[7]

Orson felt honored to be one of ten brethren selected to attend a business conference the following week. The ten assembled, November 1, in Hiram, in the large, white, clapboard farmhouse where Joseph Smith and his family now resided. They were guests of John Johnson and his wife Elsa.

Orson enjoyed getting better acquainted with the Johnson family. John and Elsa Johnson, accommodating and faithful, in every way supported the Prophet Joseph. Their sons Luke (age twenty-three) and Lyman (age twenty) still lived at home, an asset to their father in his extensive farm operation. Orson had become friends with them already, and at the conference in Orange had savored their agreeable company. They had a younger brother,

Justin, age ten years. Two attractive daughters (older ones had married) added their touch of graciousness to the household: Emily, eighteen, and younger Marinda, sixteen and energetic, with hazel eyes.

In the commodious living room of the Johnson home, the big, brick-lined fireplace providing warmth, the discussion centered around publishing the revelations that Joseph Smith had received from the Lord for the guidance of the newly-restored Church. The revelations covered a broad spectrum from chastening to sublime, including present needs and instructions to specific persons; also information about the priesthood, the second coming of the Messiah, life after death, and things eternal. The compilation would be called the Book of Commandments. Orson had read many of the revelations from various copies and had heard people discuss additional ones. Having them bound together in a book would be wonderful. Orson and the others voted to publish 10,000 copies as soon as a printing press could be purchased, transported to Independence, Missouri, and assembled. The group chose Independence because the Lord had designated that it would be the center of the Church, the site of the City of Zion, foreseen in grandeur by ancient prophets.

In the afternoon meeting the Prophet asked the brethren what testimony they would be willing to attach to the Book of Commandments. Inner feelings of peace, and the hallowed sensation in the room, witnessed to them that the Lord had indeed given the revelations. The brethren stood in turn and declared this feeling of surety.

The conference ended the next day, but Orson and several of the other men yearned for the uplift to continue. They remained at the Johnson home and conversed more with the Prophet. The reward came, the expanding of mind with an abundance of ideas and reactions of wonderment. Orson basked in the honor of watching and hearing a Prophet of God, seeing the conviction in this man's expressions that told how much he loved the Lord and enjoyed teaching eternal truths. Four brethren—Orson, the Johnson brothers Luke and Lyman, and William E. M'Lellin—asked Joseph Smith to seek a revelation for them. The Prophet complied.

Orson marveled at the results of the Prophet's prayer. Joseph Smith's face took on a beautiful and glowing appearance, and his eyes sparkled. Orson listened with jubilant gladness to the words that the Prophet spoke from the Lord personally to him. "My servant, Orson Hyde," the message began, "was called by his ordination to proclaim the everlasting gospel, by the Spirit of the living God, from people to people, and from land to land, in the congregations of the wicked, in their synagogues, reasoning with and expounding all scriptures unto them. . . . Wherefore, be of good cheer, and do not fear, for I the Lord am with you, and will stand by you; and ye shall bear record of me. . . . This is the word of the Lord unto you, my servant Orson Hyde. . . . And unto you it shall be given to know the signs of the times, and the signs of the coming of the Son of Man; and of as many as the Father shall bear record, to you shall be given power to seal them up unto eternal life." Orson's soul soared.[8]

As a member of the teaching and fund-gathering "committee of six" Orson's mission companion became Hyrum Smith, the Prophet's brother. Their assignment was to visit Orson's friends in Elyria and Florence. As the two traveled and worked together, Orson's admiration grew for pleasant and agreeable Hyrum, tall and well-built like Joseph, sedate and serious, a seasoned missionary. Though near the same age, Orson looked to Hyrum like he would to a father. Hyrum taught patiently the skills required of an effective missionary for the Lord: to be humble and listen to the guidance of the Spirit.

By following Hyrum's example in allowing his practiced techniques of persuasion to be directed by inspiration, Orson had a rewarding few weeks' mission in November and early December 1831. He felt the promptings of a power higher than his own, and a hallowed peace became his.

Strengthened by this power, he endured the threats and cold taunts of the opposition. Hecklers disrupted meetings, and they scoffed as the missionaries walked the rutted roads of the area. Abusive words, Orson learned, were more a nuisance than a concern, as long as he heeded the whisperings of heavenly guidance. After one stirring meeting he was told that a few citizens had planned to ride him on a rail and had readied the rail. Fortunately, his preaching changed their minds. Before long, the missionaries baptized about fifty persons in that neighborhood.

In addition to teaching, preaching, gathering donations, baptizing, confirming, and conferring authority on other brethren, Orson and Hyrum together blessed several sick people. They anointed the heads of the distressed with consecrated oil and, laying their hands on those heads, pronounced words guided by the Holy Ghost. Feverish and dull eyes usually became bright. Stiff legs quickened as the faithful arose and walked. Orson learned that when he blessed the sick with priesthood authority, words came from his lips filled with power and conviction and miraculous promises.

In addition to other converts, many of Orson's Campbellite friends rejoiced that he and his companion brought greater gospel light to them than they had known before. Orson and Hyrum organized the new members into branches of the Church in the different towns and taught them their duties. Joyful Saints sang the songs of Zion. Their mission successful, Hyrum and Orson returned to Kirtland by December 13.[9]

Several weeks later, January 25, 1832, a conference was to be held in Amherst, near Florence and Elyria. Eager for the special feelings of oneness with the Spirit that conferences generate, Orson retraced the fifty miles of winter roads to attend. The meetings more than filled his expectations. One accomplishment was the vote to sustain Joseph Smith as "President of the

High Priesthood." This formal organization had become necessary because Church membership had grown to approximately two thousand members. A second memorable event occurred after attendees asked the Prophet to seek divine guidance in their behalf regarding missions.

The Prophet Joseph looked at each man in turn with strength and love. Yes, he said, the Lord had a message for them. The Prophet directed his scribe to be prepared to write and asked the rest of the assembly to kneel with him and pray. A silent holiness filled the room. After the prayer Joseph Smith spoke the words of the Lord in rich, vibrant tones: "Behold, . . . you should go forth and not tarry, . . . Lifting up your voices as with the sound of a trump, proclaiming the truth according to the revelations and commandments which I have given you." Orson rejoiced silently. The revelation continued, and he heard his own name: ". . . let my servant Orson Hyde and my servant Samuel H. Smith take their journey into the eastern countries [eastern United States], and proclaim the things which I have commanded them; and inasmuch as they are faithful, lo, I will be with them even unto the end." After the conference, the scribe wrote copies of the revelation and gave them to the twenty-four missionaries named by the Lord.[10]

Before leaving Amherst, members of the group received personal priesthood blessings. With the light pressure of Joseph Smith's hands on his head, Orson's consciousness ascended above earthly things. Intently he listened to the Prophet's encouraging and powerful words. Then Joseph Smith said things astounding: "In due time, thou shalt go to Jerusalem, the land of thy fathers, and be a watchman unto the house of Israel; and by thy hands, shall the Most High do a good work, which shall prepare the way, and greatly facilitate the gathering together of that people."[11]

Orson felt incredulous wonderment! Jerusalem! Jerusalem existed in a world apart from Orson's, in an ancient world alive only in a panorama of Bible figures. Bible lands seemed a million miles away. Many prophets in those ancient lands had foretold the gathering of the children of Israel to Jerusalem and its area. And he, Orson Hyde, according to modern prophetic declaration, would someday have a role in that grand enterprise! Wonder of wonders!

But, for now, he must treasure this sacred knowledge in a secluded corner of his being and concentrate on the work of the present.

February 1, 1832, Samuel H. Smith and Orson Hyde set out from Kirtland, their coats and hats providing protection from wintry blasts and falling snows, and their knapsacks heavy with copies of the Book of Mormon.[12] They were the first Mormon missionaries to be sent to Boston, Massachusetts, nearly seven hundred miles away. Thomas B. Marsh, a former Boston resident and now enthusiastic Church member, had given them names of Boston friends to contact. In New York, Connecticut, and New Hampshire, Orson hoped to visit his own brothers and sisters. Samuel H. Smith—tall like his brothers, the Prophet Joseph and Hyrum—already had extensive missionary experience. He was known for his intense devotion to the gospel, his integrity, and his deliberate manner.[13]

The two traveled "from house to house, and from village to village," obedient to the Lord's revelation at Amherst. In families and in groups they told of the restoration of the church and warned of the impending disasters that awaited the unheeding. They also shared the Book of Mormon. In his journal Orson recorded varied responses: some people "treated our message rather lightly," or "would not receive us, not hear one word"; others "gave good attention," or "received us kindly"; some bought a Book of Mormon, expressing interest.

Orson and Samuel also obeyed two other commands of the Lord: "And in whatsoever house ye enter, and they receive you, leave your blessing upon that house. And in whatsoever house ye enter, and they receive you not, ye shall depart speedily from that house, and shake off the dust of your feet as a testimony against them."[14] The elders sadly shook dust (or mud or snow) more often than they pronounced blessings. Later study indicates that the Lord gave these instructions to hurry the missionaries over the country and quickly find the people prepared to be stalwarts in the fledgling Church.

Traveling eastward along Lake Erie, Orson observed amazing changes since he had trudged this same route westward at the age of fourteen. Bridges crossed streams where he waded or swam. Houses and fields had replaced forests. Most evenings, because Orson and Samuel were ministers, a homeowner fed them a meal, conversed a while, gave them a place to sleep, and asked no charge. Occasionally the two stayed at a tavern, usually a large home where meals and beds or bedroll space could be purchased for a small fee. Most days the missionaries walked several miles and knocked on doors, but at times the Spirit directed that they tarry. They remained in the Springfield, Pennsylvania area for eleven days and elatedly performed their first baptisms. The last week in March they stayed with a Church member in Fredonia, New York, and met disappointment: "[A] number [were] almost constrained to go forward [for baptism], but for fear of persecution, they held back."[15]

The missionaries reached Buffalo, New York, at the eastern end of Lake Erie, April 8. In this bustling and prospering migration center they "found the people hard."[16]

Farther on in western New York, where Joseph Smith had lived as a youth, exaggerated tales had caused prejudice against the Mormons. "We were often rejected in the after part of the day," Orson tells, "compelling us to travel in the evening, and sometimes till people were gone to bed, leaving us to lodge where we could. We would sometimes travel until midnight or until nearly daylight before we could find a barn or shed in which we dare to lie down; must be away before discovered lest suspicion rest upon us. Would often lie down under trees and sleep in day time to make up loss. . . . When one [missionary] would be teaching in private families, the other would frequently be nodding in his chair, weary with toil, fatigue and want of sleep."[17]

On the other hand, in scattered villages Church members showed the missionaries every kindness. They organized meetings and invited their friends. For five rewarding springtime weeks midway across New York, Samuel and Orson remained among the forested hills and hollows south and east of Lake Skaneatelas, seeking new members and teaching the old members.

The last day of May they headed southeastward, Orson enthusiastic to visit his brother Asahel in Oxford, New York. The brothers had last seen each other eighteen years before, when Orson was nine. Asahel, sixteen at that time, left Connecticut to seek his fortune in the New York wilderness.

June 6, in Oxford village, the missionaries found Asahel's home. Embraces and laughter and happy hello-talk followed. Orson and Samuel relaxed with Asahel, his wife Mary, and their six children, ages twelve years to fifteen months.[18] Amid precious hours of sharing memories and news, Orson tried to tell Asahel about the restored gospel, but Asahel showed no interest. The next day Orson and Samuel arranged a meeting for the afternoon and posted notices. Asahel declined the invitation to attend.

The following morning, Friday, "[we] left brother Asahel with hearts full of grief; united with him in prayer before we left," Orson penned. "We shed many tears over each other, and I bade my brother, my own mother's child adieu, his wife and little ones farewell, to see my face no more."[19]

For the next couple of days Orson and Samuel felt no inclination or inspiration to tarry at dwelling or village. By Sunday evening they had walked sixty-seven miles. Monday brought them a ten-mile uphill hike, a thirty-five-mile coach ride over the Catskill Mountains to the town of Catskill, a ferry ride across the immense Hudson River,[20] and a five-mile walk farther to a night's rest in a tavern. Tuesday they trekked thirty more miles and that night slept in Connecticut.

In Connecticut, Orson's home state, they planned to walk south. In Woodbury they would visit his sister Sally and her husband, David Miner. In Oxford they would call on his oldest brother, Abijah. In Oxford, the area of his childhood, Orson would stand on the low hill and see "yonder the timber wherein he gathered nuts and down yonder the meadow where he hunted birds' nests and learned to be a good swimmer!" He would gaze upon the "many small farms all fenced with *rock walls* about as wide as they are high . . . built out of . . . stone [gathered] from the farm[s]" and watch the people "hoeing and farming" within those stone fences. He would see "at every farm house, large piles of stove wood chopped up the size of three tons of newly unloaded hay!" He hoped to see someone in the yard of one of those familiar houses with a "scythe and newly cut grass!" He would then be "home."[21]

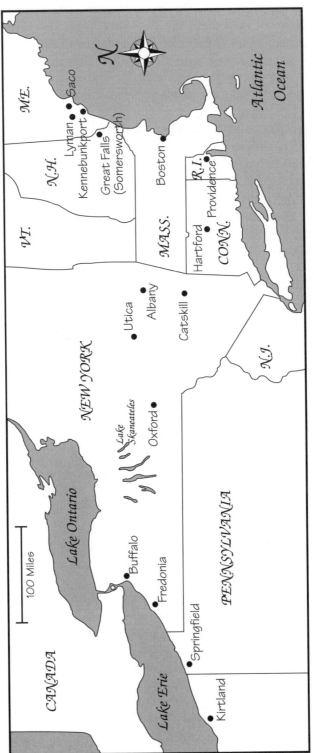

Orson's 1832 mission with Samuel H. Smith.

But destiny dealt otherwise. Spiritual inner promptings urged the missionaries to travel eastward, to "hurry on to Boston."[22] The one hundred sixty miles from western Connecticut to Boston took nine long, hot, footsore, and fatiguing summer days, with little preaching. Orson and Samuel entered the historic city June 22 and felt of the bustle that abounded from Beacon Hill to the boats in the harbor. They also observed that the bustle subsided in the grand old churches and in the central "Common" with its bridged stream and its grass, flowers, and trees.[23] Locating the addresses previously given them, the two "found the friends of Brother Thomas Marsh very glad to see us."[24] Thomas had sent a letter telling of the missionaries' pending arrival.

This reception in Boston contrasted pleasantly with past weeks. The missionaries received "invitations to visit people in different parts of the city and to hold meetings in their houses."[25] They were hosted to delicious meals and to soft beds. Several of the people had already prepared themselves for baptism; they had read the Book of Mormon and discussed gospel principles. They now rejoiced that men had come who held the priesthood. After three days, the missionaries baptized four people. In two weeks the number grew to nine, eight of them women.

The missionaries also met opposition. The priests of several churches became alarmed at their popularity and preached against them. Listening to the priests, "people began to be hardened"[26] toward the strangers from the west who told unusual things. But the work had a start.

Part of the foundation had been laid by Vienna Jacques (pronounced Jackway). Forty-four years old and wealthy, Vienna had traveled to Kirtland the previous summer to learn about Mormonism, became converted, and was baptized.[27] Since her return home she had talked of the gospel and the Book of Mormon (she brought copies from Kirtland) to her friends and her family in a wide region around Boston. She eagerly wanted all of them to listen to the missionaries. Particularly, she wanted the gospel presented to her sister, Harriet Jacques Angell, in North Providence, Rhode Island.

Samuel and Orson had been in Boston less than three weeks when they complied with Vienna's entreaties and traveled to Rhode Island. They anticipated that the Lord's desires of them in that locality would require several weeks. But in two weeks they came back. Word of their return circulated quickly, and friends gathered at a member's home early that summer evening, excited to hear why the missionaries had cut short their Rhode Island stay. Orson and Samuel related their adventures. Vienna's friends and relatives had treated them kindly, but other citizens stirred up a mob spirit. Twice the missionaries miraculously escaped being tarred and feathered. Vienna's sister's husband, William Angell, a friendly host for a few days, became angry when his wife liked their message, and he threatened to do them harm. His brother, James Angell, befriended them and helped them evade William's wrath. The missionaries baptized two men and ordained one of them to the priesthood, thus a foundation was begun. They left town in the middle of a night.

After remaining in Boston a week and baptizing seven more women, the missionaries spent three energetic weeks in towns and farming areas northeast of Boston, returning to the city occasionally. Received kindly by the people to whom friends referred them, they performed several baptisms and organized a branch of the Church.[28] During this period Orson wrote varied entries in his journal: "August 3rd: . . . Dug a good mess of clams, boiled them, and ate them." "August 7th: . . . had considerable conversation with the Editor of the paper, and he put a piece in the paper, saying: 'Let these men alone. If this work be of God ye cannot assail.'" "August 12th: . . . Had the greatest liberty and freedom of speech that I have had since I left Kirtland; subject was the 'Priesthood' – spoke about two hours." "August 16th: . . . a numerous crowd came out and fired crackers during the meeting [in the home of Vienna's brother-in-law] and made disturbance, and after the meeting the rabble set up a hue and cry through the town and round the house like a pack of grizzly wolves determined to devour us, but the Lord sent them home [with the help of the missionaries' host, who got out his gun and threatened to use it] and we returned to rest."[29]

The missionaries traveled farther north in Massachusetts, spent three successful weeks, and organized another branch. And then came the hoped for inspiration to go on to New Hampshire to visit Orson's sister, Laura North, in Great Falls.

Laura and her husband William expressed jubilant surprise at the visit by her younger brother. Orson savored the renewing of family ties and of getting acquainted with Laura's husband, her daughter, age thirteen, and her sons, ages twelve and four. William, a foreman in a large cloth factory, had influence in the community and arranged for the missionaries to conduct a meeting. Orson wrote notices announcing the time and place, and William helped post the notices around the village. Orson remembered his experience with his brother Asahel and during the day said little about his beliefs.

That evening William and Laura joined the townsfolk who crowded into the meeting hall. Orson spoke boldly and long, explaining the Book of Mormon, the restoration of eternal principles, and authority. Samuel bore solemn witness that the truth had been spoken. People crowded around the missionaries and asked questions about the gold plates. Orson and Samuel answered the questions, sold one Book of Mormon, and loaned another. When a few noisy and jesting people hurled mocking questions at them, the two men quickly, but with dignity, left the hall and returned to Laura's.

At home William made scornful and flippant objections. He could not comprehend, he said, how his wife's brother could be so misguided as to preach the nonsense sounded this night.

Disappointed, and yet trying to be true to the trust of their callings, Samuel and Orson spoke fervent testimonies of the authenticity of the Book of Mormon and the divinity of the message it contained.

Anger flushed William's face. He declared that the time had come to retire.

In their room Orson and Samuel talked quietly. Had William "rejected so much" that they should leave the house, even though night had partly passed? At length they stayed.

The next day, Sunday, William left to attend his church. Samuel left to retrieve the Book of Mormon loaned the evening before. Orson visited with Laura, his heart praying for guidance. Beginning softly, he reminded her that the Lord had shown particular respect for her, had not sent her this message by a stranger. "But," he continued, "the Lord has taken your own mother's son—dandled upon the same knee, nursed at the same breast, and like Joseph in Egypt, separated from his kinsfolk and compelled to make friends among strangers. This brother comes to you with this message in the name of the Lord!"

"If the Lord had sent you," she replied evenly, "I should think he would have prepared my heart to receive your message, which he has not done."

Orson's mind cried out in anguish, but with effort he remained calm. "Laura, do you think that God sent his Son with a message to the Jews?"

"Yes," came the reply.

"Did he, or did he not, prepare their hearts to receive it?"

Laura answered with silence.

Samuel returned to the house, as did William. Orson tried once more to reason with his brother-in-law, but in vain. William and Laura said that they considered Orson and Samuel deluded. Then William paused. Turning to Orson, he said that because Elder Hyde was Laura's brother he was welcome to remain at the house. "But," William went on, with a disdainful glance at Samuel, "I do not care to entertain your colleague!"

Orson's muscles tightened at William's words, and his heart warmed with love for Samuel. "Oh," he thought, "that you were worthy before God to entertain Brother Samuel H. Smith!" Orson said that both he and Samuel would depart. Tears welled up in Laura's eyes. Orson, too, wept, as did William and Samuel.

The missionaries walked away sadly. When Laura's home was out of sight, they stopped. Somberly and reluctantly each raised one foot at a time and shook the dust from it. Orson's heart felt pierced to the center, and he thought numbly, "The will of the Lord be done. I shall be slow to call upon any more of my relatives that I might be exempted from the duty of washing my feet against my own kindred in case of being rejected, leaving them to be warned and dealt with by strangers." Was Orson the only one in his family who would be gathered with the children of Israel?[30]

For three days the missionaries knocked on doors in New Hampshire towns and received no encouragement to tarry. September 19 they crossed the mile-wide Piscataqua River in a canoe, paddles dipping the water, and stepped ashore in the state of Maine.

Invigorated by the autumn sea breezes, they planned to travel fifty miles along the Maine coast northward to Portland. Favorable beginnings encouraged them. "Never saw better attention," Orson recorded of a meeting September 23. With more inspirational power "than ever I had before," he spoke in a meeting September 25. The lightness of the missionaries' hearts matched their packs. They had sold or given away all but one Book of Mormon. They anticipated, from their initial Maine response, to find a fruitful field for harvesting souls, even without books to leave with the people. "[O]n our return," Orson wrote in his journal, "we hope to reap from the seed now sown."[31]

But the cheering experiences, it turned out, became the exception rather than the pattern that emerged in Maine. The people were friendly, but few became excited about the gospel message. The missionaries met no violent opposition by mobs like they had in Providence, nor loud denunciations by priests like they had in Boston, but they met apathy.

This mood spread to the missionaries. September 28, in Kennebunkport, when Orson "felt low in mind and much cast down," he humbled himself "before the Lord" and asked for pardon. Two days later, in Saco, they preached twice to large, attentive congregations, and the people to whom Boston friends had sent them treated them kindly, but no one asked them to tarry. After a few days of walking in drenching rain, and slogging through sticky mud, they felt no inclination to trudge the fifteen miles farther north from Saco to Portland. Instead, October 4, they started back southward.

Retracing their path slowly, their message received more negative responses than positive. In Kennebunkport again, Orson recorded, "October 20th . . . the people came together, but [we] had no liberty, shut right up. [We] then concluded the Lord had no preaching for us to do there." They traveled on. "October 21st . . . [One woman] was afraid we were impostors, and we showed our certificate [license to preach] and then read our command [revelation from the Lord] and that seemed to take away [her and her husband's] suspicions in a measure."

Their efforts appearing fruitless, Orson and Samuel considered going directly back to Massachusetts, but inspiration whispered to travel inland. From Kennebunkport they walked through woods and by streams to isolated farms and small villages for two days before anyone consented to a meeting. Neither their host nor his neighbors asked them to preach again, but Simeon Weymouth invited them to preach the next evening in his home three miles away in Lyman.

After breakfasting and walking the three miles, they received a warm welcome at the Weymouth door. But their mouths dropped open in disbelief when they looked inside. Huge piles of corn covered the floor! All day the missionaries helped husk corn to make room for the evening meeting. They husked corn again the next day, explaining the gospel as they worked. Mr. Weymouth seemed receptive, and they preached in his home the second evening. At last, here in the Lyman area of Maine, Orson and Samuel felt encouragement about harvesting souls for the Kingdom of God.

Within two weeks they baptized five people, including Simeon Weymouth and his wife, two other women, and one other man. During the evening of November 9 they held a meeting with these new Saints, "had prayer, and a very good time; and the Lord was with us."[32]

During the meeting, however, they were startled by a woman staggering in wild-eyed and uncontrolled. A strange sensation quivered through the group. Samuel and Orson immediately recognized the woman to be possessed of evil spirits. Jumping up from their chairs, the missionaries unitedly used both physical and spiritual exertion, the laying on of hands and the voice of priesthood authority. They succeeded in casting the woman's unwelcome host from her body. As the evil spirits departed, peace and calm returned.

Orson and Samuel spent a few days teaching the Saints and preparing Brother Weymouth to receive the priesthood that he might preside over a branch and preach and baptize. They ordained him an elder November 15.

The next day the missionaries left Lyman and traveled southward, often wearing their coats. Returning to several places where they had preached two months before, and where they had hoped to "reap from the seed now sown," they met disappointment. "[T]he Priests had stirred up the people to unbelief," so no harvest was ready.[33]

November 26 they arrived back in northeastern Massachusetts, welcomed at a member's home. A message awaited them that Joseph Smith had been in Boston and left instructions that they should return to Kirtland. Thus they remained in this area for only a week, walking snowy roads as they savored visits with friends made before. They strengthened faith, taught doctrine, and explained duties. They also baptized four candidates after wading through deep snow to the nearest water and chopping a large hole in the ice.

In Boston, December 4, friendly reception pleased them, but disappointments challenged them. During their absence personal animosities had arisen among the sisters, caused by differences of opinion about Church doctrine and procedures. The missionaries remained a week, preached several times, counseled long with individuals, "baptized one," Orson recorded, "broke bread on the first day of the week, [and] settled all matters of difference pretty much."[34]

The homeward journey of almost seven hundred stagecoach and foot miles from Boston to Kirtland, via Albany and Utica, New York, took thirteen days. Coats buttoned securely against the cold, Orson and Samuel arrived in Kirtland December 22.

CHAPTER 3

... *prepare*. . . . *(1832–1834)*

> *. . . sanctify yourselves, and prepare. . . , that [you]*
> *may do according to the word of the Lord. . . .*
> —2 Chronicles 35:6

AFTER Orson returned, in December 1832, from his eastern mission, he heard reports, both sad and good, of happenings during his absence. The previous March, on a dark frosty night, several apostate Mormons and anti-Mormons burst into the John Johnson home in Hiram. They abducted the Prophet from his sleep, carried him out into a field, and tore off his clothes. They ripped long fingernail gouges in his skin, smeared his body with sticky black tar, tried to pour poison down his throat, and fled. The Prophet stumbled back home. His wife Emma, the Johnson family, and neighbors worked the remainder of the night scraping and scrubbing off the tar. Sidney fared even worse, being dragged from his home near the Johnson's, heels in the air and head bouncing over rough frozen ground. His abductors left him unconscious and bleeding when John Johnson, wielding a club, chased them off. Eventually Brother Joseph, Emma, and their child (other children had died) moved to Kirtland to a part of Newel Whitney's store. Since then, violent anti-Mormon episodes had diminished.[1]

During 1832, the Prophet Joseph had received several revelations, one of them telling that priesthood brotherhood bridged the millenniums. Adam held the priesthood. Abraham "received the priesthood from Melchizedek, who received it through the lineage of his fathers, even till . . . Adam." Moses received the priesthood "under the hand of his father-in-law, Jethro." Jethro received the priesthood through a succession of five righteous men, the first of the five having "received it under the hand of God." Because the children of Israel "hardened their hearts" in the time of Moses, the Lord allowed only the "lesser," or "Aaronic," priesthood to continue among them.

December 27, five days after his return home, Orson attended a conference of ten high priests in the translating room above Newel Whitney's store. This room is where Joseph Smith "translated," or revised, the Bible. The Prophet said he felt inspired to call this group together to unite the strength of their faith that he might receive a message the Lord had for them. All knelt and prayed silently. Arising, each expressed the sacred feelings his prayer prompted. Then the Prophet spoke, the flowing words entwining Orson's heart with golden threads spun from heaven: "Verily, thus saith the Lord unto you who have assembled yourselves together to receive his will . . . : Behold, this is pleasing . . . , and the angels rejoice over you." The phrases continued, magnificent, about the omnipotent light of Christ, about the judgment and resurrection, about the eternal laws of the universe. Joseph Smith later called this revelation the "olive leaf . . . plucked from the Tree of Paradise." Night came, and the revealed words ceased at about nine o'clock. In the subdued light Joseph Smith asked the group to return in the morning. They did, and revelation resumed. The words told of the Lord's second coming, expounded more about the resurrection, and also directed that a "solemn assembly" be conducted for "you, who are the first laborers in this last kingdom." "[Y]ou," the hallowed phrases to Orson and the others went on, "shall teach one another the doctrine of the kingdom. . . . Behold, I sent you out to testify and warn the people. . . . Therefore, they are left without excuse, and their sins are upon their own heads."

A week later, January 3, 1833, the Lord told Joseph Smith that the "solemn assembly" should be a "school of the prophets," where "the Spirit shall give utterance in all your doings . . . , that it may become a sanctuary, a tabernacle of the Holy Spirit to your edification." Not only would the brethren of the school be edified by words, the Prophet Joseph declared, but "on conditions of our obedience" the Lord "has promised us . . . a visit from the heavens to honor us with His own presence."[2]

In mid January, Joseph Smith called the school members to a preparatory meeting. At this "Conference of Twelve High Priests," he reminded Orson and the others that the Lord had declared, "And ye shall not receive any among you into this school save he is clean from the blood of this generation [free from sin]."[3] Before the school commenced, though, the Prophet said, the group needed to sound one more warning, written to the Saints who had moved out to Missouri to begin the city of Zion.

The location the Lord had revealed for building the city of Zion—Independence, Jackson County, Missouri—had surprised Orson. To him, Old Testament scriptures indicated that Zion, the place of gathering for Israel, would be Jerusalem. The Lord had clarified the terms to Joseph Smith. "[T]he land of America," the Prophet explained, "is a promised land unto . . . all the tribes of Israel" except "the tribe of Judah [who] will return to old Jerusalem." The scriptures spoke of two locations, not one.

The Zion Saints needed to repent because of personal pride resulting from success. They had cleared land, built homes, set up a printing press, and started businesses. Already they prospered more than many of their non-Mormon neighbors. Caught up in their comfort, some Church members had grown covetous, hesitant to share their goods with less fortunate Saints who arrived in their midst. And a portion of them, including some leaders, had begun to feel superior to other settlers, with no need of a prophet's direction.

The conference in Kirtland appointed Hyrum Smith and Orson to write the letter to Zion. Prayers requested that the two "might be enabled to write the mind and will of God upon this subject." They wrote a long letter, January 14, speaking for all twelve high priests. They reminded the leaders in Missouri "to call to mind the . . . Nephites, and the children of Israel rising up against their Prophets, . . . and see what befell them, and take warning before it is too late." They also reminded the Missouri Saints that "covetousness . . . ought not to be. . . . [D]o just as the Lord has commanded, . . . and then the Lord will open His coffers, and . . . wants will be liberally supplied." Explaining that they, the assembled twelve high priests, were themselves heeding a warning from the Lord, the letter went on: "[T]he Lord has commanded us . . . to write this letter." To emphasize that God's plans would be carried out, they warned: "Zion is the place where the temple will be built, and the people gathered, but all people upon that holy land being under condemnation, the Lord will cut off, if they repent not, and [He will] bring another race [group] upon it, that will serve Him."[4]

Tuesday evening the next week, January 22, 1833, the final preparatory conference for the School of the Prophets commenced, with both brethren and sisters attending. In this sacred meeting miraculous outpourings of spiritual enlightenment blessed the participants with the gift of tongues. Joseph Smith first spoke in tongues, flowing tones and inflections given him by the Spirit. Others in turn, including Orson, stood too, moved by Heavenly powers, and spoke what the Prophet had previously identified as "the pure Adamic language." Until late in the night the group spoke, sang, and prayed praises to the Lord, all in tongues.

Orson awoke early on Wednesday morning, January 23. As the Prophet had requested, he bathed, dressed in clean clothes, and refrained from eating. In the winter morning crispness, he and more than a dozen other priesthood brethren arrived at the Whitney store and ascended the stairs to a small, recently-finished room, about eleven by fourteen feet. Still scented with sawed wood and fresh paint, the room held chairs ready for them. The brick-lined fireplace radiated warmth. Again all spoke, sang, prayed, and praised God in tongues. In a vote with raised right hands, they "sustained" Joseph Smith as the president of the School of the Prophets, to commence the next day. The Prophet designated Orson Hyde as the teacher of the school.[5]

The session closed that late afternoon with the sacrament, the Lord's supper. The aroma of freshly baked bread wafted up the stairs from Emma Smith's kitchen. Wrapped in a clean cloth, the loaves were carried to the upper room. Brother Joseph knelt and blessed the bread, broke it into fist-sized pieces, and gave a warm piece to each brother. Next he blessed wine, that he had brought to the room before the gathering, and poured a glassful for each man. The brethren ate and drank, closing the day's fast. The Prophet commented that this was "the way that Jesus and his disciples partook of the bread and wine, and this was the order of the Church anciently." Already, in the latter day Church, the Lord had directed that wine was unessential to the sacrament ordinance, that water could be used if conditions dictated.[6]

Many days for the next three months, at sunrise the School of the Prophets assembled. As well as gaining enlightenment in "all things that pertain unto the kingdom of God" and in prophecies about earth's people, the Lord had directed the exploration of fields such as history, geology, geography, science, and governments. Orson lectured on various topics, Sidney at times instructed in grammar, and the Prophet Joseph taught what God and angels had revealed to him. He assured his brethren that "the operations of the Spirit upon the mind of man" pertain to matters both temporal and spiritual.

Discussions proved as important as lectures. The men in the school came with diverse experiences, and they shared their knowledge. The Lord had said of the discussions: "[L]et not all be spokesmen at once; but let one speak at a time and let all listen unto his sayings, that when all have spoken that all may be edified of all, and that every man may have an equal privilege." Also, Joseph Smith encouraged sharing thoughts and feelings, saying that it was "very common for the Holy Spirit to reveal some things to obscure individuals, that are not made known to others, hence an exchange of ideas and reflections are profitable to all."[7]

Warmth from the fireplace, and the congenial atmosphere, helped the men feel comfortable. Invigorated in mind, and refreshed with an occasional rest period of walking around, harmony prevailed. In this tranquillity Orson and his brethren shared the mellow, heady smell of their pipes and enveloped themselves in a haze of smoke, or they whittled plugs of chewing tobacco and savored the tangy taste.

February 27, Joseph Smith came from his translating room to the school, which now numbered twenty-one priesthood holders. His face radiating brilliance, he shared a revelation he had just received: "A Word of Wisdom, for the benefit of the council of high priests, assembled in Kirtland, and the church, and also the saints in Zion— . . . showing forth the order and will of God." The Prophet continued on through introductory phrases and then added, "[I]nasmuch as any man drinketh wine or strong drink among you, behold it is not good, . . . only . . . to offer up your sacraments. . . . And, behold, this should be wine, yea pure wine of the grape of the vine, of your own make."

The brethren listened intently as Joseph Smith spoke on, "And again, tobacco is not for the body, neither for the belly, and is not good for man, but is an herb for bruises and all sick cattle, to be used with judgment and skill." Astonishment was the primary reaction.

The Prophet recited the remainder of the revelation. The Lord's words instructed that people should eat wholesome herbs "with prudence and thanksgiving," flesh of beasts and fowls "sparingly," and grain as "the staff of life." To persons who heeded these admonitions, the Lord promised health and wisdom and that "the destroying angel shall pass by them, as the children of Israel, and not slay them."

Orson and the others sat in dismayed silence, fingering their pipes. They agonized, but they reached a decision and made a solemn "covenant of abstinence." In accord they tossed their pipes and tobacco into the fireplace. Small flames ate at the edges.

Later, in response to being asked if he requested the revelation, Joseph Smith admitted that he had wondered if tobacco smoking and chewing were good and had inquired. In part, his decision to ask had been influenced by his wife Emma, who tired of scrubbing the brown tobacco spots from the floor. The Lord gave a broader answer than he expected.

For a few days Orson and the others struggled to overcome the physical and mental discomforts of using no tobacco. To diminish their cravings they chewed licorice root. They strengthened their mental progress by discussing God's interest in all facets of living. They supported each other as a part of learning obedience to the Lord, a step bringing them closer to being "one with Him."[8]

March 18 became the most spiritually incandescent day in the school. The brethren came bathed and dressed in clean clothing and arrived before sunrise, as the Prophet had requested. He had promised them the privilege of a "day of revelation and vision." After a few hours of exhortations and business, Brother Joseph talked of faithfulness and of spiritual things, then requested that each brother kneel and pray silently, with uplifted hands. A short time of sacred prayer passed when, indeed, the Spirit of God opened eyes, and the men saw wondrous visions. They marveled. At the accustomed time, with the others, Orson partook of the sacrament and felt an extraordinary closeness with the Redeemer. While basking in this transcendent peace many participants "saw a heavenly vision of the Savior, and concourses of angels." Afterward the Prophet declared, "You are now prepared to be the apostles of Jesus Christ because you indeed know of his existence." The divine promise made before the school began—that the Lord would allow the members to behold his presence—had been fulfilled. The things that Orson experienced were so infinitely sacred that he would keep them in his heart as a cherished gift from his Maker.[9]

The School of the Prophets continued until mid April. The group had been blessed with the gift of tongues, with lively discussions and divine instruction, with the Word of Wisdom, and with the opening of the heavens. They had been prepared to testify and teach more boldly than ever before the profound truths of the everlasting gospel of Jesus Christ.

The light of the gospel burning in their hearts, Orson and the others received assignments for short missions. Orson accompanied Hyrum Smith to Elk Creek, Pennsylvania, about seventy miles away, just beyond the Ohio border. For several diligent weeks the two traveled and preached and taught and baptized. They returned to Kirtland in late May, enthusiastic about their success.[10]

Now twenty-eight years of age, Orson had thoughts of pursuing another kind of success, that of obtaining a bride. For a long period he had been saving money to prepare for the responsibility of a home. He resumed teaching grammar, as he had done for several months before his recent mission. He felt this a sufficiently secure vocation that he could support a wife. His cash in hand had grown to $275.00. In addition to this, a friend in Florence owed him about $150.00.

With Orson considering that he had enough money saved for marriage, the Prophet reminded him, early in June, that the Lord had commanded the Saints to build a temple, a "House of the Lord," in Kirtland, and that funds were scarce. The Lord had revealed his displeasure that construction had failed to begin. Joseph Smith suggested, pleasantly, that Orson donate all of his money to the Temple fund.

As much as Orson loved the Prophet, this request surprised him. "I wish to think about it two or three days first," Orson replied, "and to pray about it." To give all the money he had in the world seemed a heavy draft.

The Prophet's kind expression denoted sympathy with Orson's confused feelings. He questioned, "You want to obtain the mind of the Lord upon the subject?"

Orson answered eagerly that he did.

Again the Prophet spoke in tender tones, "I have already obtained it." He paused, giving Orson time to recollect that the Lord's requests often seem difficult. He continued, saying that if Orson wished to comply with the Lord's wishes, he could answer now.

Orson sensed urgency. He had no desire to displease the Lord. He shared a firm handshake with the Prophet as he said, "The money is ready." Joseph Smith manifested warm approval. Orson retrieved the $275 and paid it willingly, without reserve. He would start over on his "wedding stake."[11]

Joseph Smith, as President of the High Priesthood, had the previous March chosen counselors, Sidney Rigdon and Frederick G. Williams. June 6 the presidency requested Orson to be their clerk. Orson felt humbly honored. He would enjoy close association with the Prophet and with Sidney. He would be pleased to get better acquainted with Frederick, a quiet and kind man of forty-five who, for time to serve the Lord, gave up the practice of medicine when he joined the Church.[12]

Many Church members rallied to the Prophet Joseph's call to build the temple, and the cornerstone-laying ceremony proceeded July 23. This came just seven weeks after men hauled the first load of stone and began shoveling trenches for the foundation. Orson received the privilege of participating in the impressive ceremonies of laying the four cornerstones. He and other leaders—the Prophet Joseph Smith, Hyrum Smith, Joseph Smith, Sen., Newel K. Whitney, and Frederick G. Williams—hefted the first stone into place.

A few days later Orson departed to serve a second short mission in Elk Creek, Pennsylvania. His companion, Zebedee Coltrin, joined him July 30 in Thompson, nineteen miles along the road. "In Pennsylvania," Zebedee recorded in his diary, "the Lord blessed us much in healing the sick and tending to other business. We baptized there and ordained one elder . . . and the Lord poured his Spirit upon us in a wonderful manner. . . . We returned," stopping and preaching in various places on the way, "and the Lord gave us a good time."[13]

Encouraging feelings prevailed in Kirtland the summer of 1833 until Oliver Cowdery arrived in late August from Independence, Jackson County, Missouri, or Zion, with a report about frightful mob violence. His own slight figure, and the worry in his dark brown eyes, emphasized the precarious position of the Saints. Gravely, Oliver recounted that the Church printing press had been destroyed and that the Saints feared for their lives. Apparently some of them had not heeded the warning letter Orson helped pen in Kirtland months before.

Multiple factors had influenced the Missouri conflicts. The Saints, working together, prospered, and they grew in numbers as more arrived. The old settlers feared being outnumbered and outvoted. Ministers became concerned that their congregations, and thus incomes, would dwindle if people liked the new religion; they began tirading against the newcomers. Slave owners feared rebellion among their slaves if the Mormons, who discouraged slavery, gained influence. Some Mormons acted arrogantly, proclaiming that the Lord had given them the area, and other people had no right to be there.

In mid July, agitated authorities and citizens had drawn up a manifesto against the Saints and set up a meeting to discuss their apprehensions. The county clerk, a judge, constables, and additional prominent citizens signed the document. It listed several anxieties: that the Mormons were "daily increasing in numbers," that the Mormons "would corrupt our blacks" by encouraging them to desire freedom, and that the Mormons continually "declare openly that their God hath given them this county of land, and that sooner or later they must and will have possession of our lands for an inheritance." The manifesto emphasized that if the Mormons "refuse to leave us in peace, as they found us—we agree to use such means as may be sufficient to remove them."[14]

From the meeting, July 20, emerged between four and five hundred riled men moving with ill-boding deliberation. At the brick home of William W. Phelps, the mob burst in the door, tramped up the stairs, and heaved the Church printing press, type, books, and paper through the windows, spraying shattered glass in all directions. Outside grew a mangled heap that included copies of the Church newspaper and of the partly printed Book of Commandments. Then louder, with ramming, tugging, pounding, and throwing, they trashed the building and threw out the furniture. Stunned Saints fled and hid in bushes, corn fields, and groves of trees. The mob next rushed to Sidney Gilbert's store, started throwing things out, and threatened to tear it apart. They stopped when Sidney promised to pack up and close his doors. Their rage wild, the shouting and cursing horde found and captured Church members Edward Partridge and Charles Allen, smeared them with caustic tar, and covered them with feathers. Night brought an end to the rampage.

Three days later mob members, carrying weapons and a red flag, demanded that Church leaders renounce their religion and live as ordinary citizens, without belief in miracles and revelations. In this encounter Oliver Cowdery and the other elders of the Church felt led by the Spirit to enter into an immediate treaty with the mob to leave Jackson County, their Zion, before the end of the year. They hoped that this promise would prevent the shedding of blood. Afterward, when leaders explained this to the Saints, they agreed to the conditions. With this uneasy truce in place, Oliver began his hurried trip to Kirtland to confer with the Prophet Joseph and learn what the Saints in Missouri should do.

In Kirtland, Joseph Smith shed tears while listening to Oliver's account. What could he do from so far away? If he were to go to Zion, his presence would make matters worse![15] But someone must go, a man or men fearless, who communicated well, understood Church policy, and listened to the inspiration of the Spirit. The Prophet chose Orson Hyde and John Gould.

John Gould and Orson set out on foot, strapped to their backs their valises packed with bedding, a few clothes, and written instructions from Joseph Smith. During their westward trek of a thousand miles they covered about forty miles per hot and sultry summer day. They hiked country sparsely settled, most of it wild and unbroken. Swimming rivers, they pushed their valises before them on logs or rafts. They found Independence, Missouri, attractively situated. On the extreme western boundary of United States territory, its location displayed beautiful countryside with lush, rolling prairies, sparkling streams, and verdant forests. In this ideal setting, chosen by God for future greatness, Orson's heart ached when he saw the pile of rubble that had been the printing office and listened to details of the vile attacks of July 20.[16]

The words of counsel that Orson and John brought from the Prophet Joseph comforted the bewildered Saints in Independence. The Prophet urged them to live the commandments of God, obey local laws, and cooperate with civil authorities. They should take no offensive action, but could defend their lives and property if attacked again.

The Saints asked William W. Phelps and Orson to take a petition to the governor of Missouri, Daniel Dunklin. Dated September 28, this document outlined the damage already done, requested redress, and asked for future protection. In Jefferson City, a few days journey from Independence, Governor Dunklin showed courtesy but said he could make no commitments because the attorney general was away. He assured Orson and William that he wanted law and order in the state and would do anything he could to protect the Saints. Back in Independence, Orson and William reported what they considered encouraging results of their session with the governor.

The Prophet Joseph, in the meantime, felt concern about the Saints in far-away Missouri and about the welfare of his representatives. October 12 he inquired of the Lord about them. Revelation assured him that "Zion shall be redeemed, although she is chastened for a little season. Thy brethren, my servants Orson Hyde and John Gould, are in my hands; and inasmuch as they keep my commandments they shall be saved."[17]

Orson and other brethren engaged in prolonged prayer and discussion about the best course to pursue. As a warning to the mob, October 20, they publicly declared that they would "defend our lands and houses." Opposite to what they had hoped, this stirred the mob leaders to ride around "sending rumors." At first the mob received only minor support, but substantial numbers rallied to their cause ten days later, October 30, when they learned that the Saints had hired lawyers to defend in court the rights of the Mormon settlers.

The night of October 31 an armed mob of forty or fifty attacked a small Mormon settlement on the Big Blue River, near Independence. While women and children shrieked, screamed, and cowered, the mob severely damaged houses and whipped several men.

In Independence the next night, Orson and others watched helplessly and horrified while a clamoring mob hurled stones at the homes of the Saints, battered down doors, smashed windows, and destroyed furniture. Surrounded by the mob, Orson's group made no rebuttal when the mob glared, shook fists, and threatened to "wring your heads off from your shoulders!" Orson's feelings sickened when the riotous swarm split down the doors of Sidney Gilbert's closed-up store and also demolished his home while his terrified family fled. Daylight revealed streets littered with fabrics, handkerchiefs, and clothing from the store.

The wings of rumor beat furiously the next few days. Exaggerations merged with facts in the conflicting stories that swirled rampant from person to person.

Orson and John felt bound and fettered. Neither legally nor physically could they change matters. Yet they carried goods, comforted, and tried to encourage. After a few days, though, of helping friends flee Independence in bitter weather, they sensed impressions that they should return and report to the Prophet. November 6, sad about leaving the Saints in such turmoil, they boarded a steamer.

On the way, to leave a public record of what he had seen and heard, Orson wrote a letter to a newspaper in Boonville, a town scores of miles downstream from Independence. The editors of the *Boonville Herald* printed the letter under the caption "The Mormon War," explaining in an editorial comment, however, that they thought the report false. Orson's letter, from "On Board [the] Steamboat Charleston, November 8, 1833," began, "I am two days from Independence, the seat of war." He wrote about the mob at Big Blue, the beating "of the Mormonite men . . . with stones and clubs," the attack on the store and homes, and about another ravage at Big Blue when the Mormons, prepared, defended themselves.

He added that two days before he left, "the Mob collected again in the town of Independence, to the number of two or three hundred, well armed. They called it '*calling out the militia!*' probably for the purpose of lessening the magnitude of their crime in the eyes of [the] community." In Independence, he continued, "things were in a state of great confusion." (Mobs drove 1200 Saints from their homes. The bleak winter suffering grew beyond calculation.)

In Kirtland, November 25, Orson and John sadly reported to Joseph Smith. All agonized about the violence in Jackson County.[18]

Orson resumed his duties as clerk to the First Presidency and felt of their anguish for the far-away Saints in this trial of their faith. When asked why the "innocent are compelled to suffer for the iniquities of the guilty," Joseph Smith responded that even as the prophet he had the same question. "I cannot learn from any communication by the Spirit to me," he wrote to the Missouri Saints, December 10, "that Zion has forfeited her claim to a celestial crown, . . . except it may be some individuals, who have walked in disobedience. . . . But . . . one [revelation] says, that after much tribulation cometh the blessing. . . .

"[W]hen I inquire concerning this subject," the Prophet continued, "the voice of the Lord is: Be still, and know that I am God! all those who suffer for my name shall reign with me, and he that layeth down his life for my sake shall find it again."

Six days later, December 16, the Lord gave Joseph Smith answers to his questions: "[C]oncerning your brethren who have been afflicted, and persecuted, and cast out from the land of their inheritance . . . , they must needs be chastened and tried, even as Abraham, who was commanded to offer up his only son. For all those who will not endure chastening, but deny me, cannot be sanctified. . . .

"[T]hose who have been scattered by their enemies, . . ." the Lord added, "should continue to importune for redress, and redemption, by . . . those who are placed . . . in authority over you—According to the laws and constitution of the people." The Saints should appeal to constituted authorities, the revelation said, so that if the authorities failed to act in mercy toward the innocent they would "be left without excuse" at the judgment seat of God.[19]

During the next two months Kirtland had its own concerns. Local apostates caused general mischief and began seeking the lives of Joseph Smith and others. Thus Church leaders kept constant lookout for personal safety. Men laboring on the temple took turns guarding at night to prevent the work being vandalized. Among the Saints, poverty reigned. Debts hung over the Church, the most depressing being the mortgage on the temple site. Orson, as clerk, often knelt with the First Presidency, his heart touched by the intensity and devotion of their prayers to the Almighty.

February 17, 1834, the Prophet organized a "standing council for the church" to assist the Presidency, Orson being among the twelve high priests appointed by revelation to this "high council." In their February 20 meeting, the council selected several brethren to fulfill preaching missions, and also "voted that Elder Orson Hyde, accompanied by Elder Orson Pratt, go east to obtain donations for Zion, and means to redeem the farm on which the house of the Lord stands." Orson felt pleased that he could do something to help relieve the burdens of Joseph Smith.

Four days later, February 24, the Prophet received a revelation that added to the purposes of the present missions. The missionaries should recruit men to travel to Zion. In a meeting in his home, of the high council and assembled Saints, Joseph Smith told that the Lord had instructed him to go to Missouri, "to assist in redeeming it." When he asked the group for volunteers to go with him, faces showed bright interest, and uplifted hands, including Orson's, responded. The Lord had commanded: "[S]ay unto the strength of my house, my young men and the middle aged—Gather yourselves together unto the land of Zion. . . . Let no man be afraid to lay down his life for my sake. . . ."

"[S]ome thirty or forty [men] volunteered to go, who were present at the Council," Orson and his co-clerk, Oliver Cowdery, recorded. "[We] decided unanimously that [we should] go by land [as the safest route, rather than by river]. Joseph Smith, Jun., was nominated to be the commander-in-chief of the armies of Israel." They set their departure date from Kirtland as May 1, nine weeks hence.[20]

February 26, Orson Hyde and his energetic companion, Orson Pratt, departed to gather funds for Kirtland needs and recruit men to march to Zion. Joseph Smith and others left at the same time, to travel different routes eastward. Missionaries Hyde and Pratt—in familiar towns in northeastern Ohio, western Pennsylvania, and western New York—received less money than hoped. To their call for marchers, a few young brethren responded and promised to be in Kirtland by May 1.

In mid March the traveling groups met in pleasurable reunion at Avon, New York. Here, March 17, the Prophet Joseph conducted a conference, inspiring missionaries and local members to renewed energy in seeking men and funds. The assemblage decided to make a concerted effort to collect two thousand dollars, a huge sum, to use to deliver the Church in Kirtland from debt. Four local men were assigned to gather this by April 1. And "Elder Orson Hyde," the conference decided, "should tarry and preach in the regions round about, till the money should be obtained, and then carry it with him to Kirtland."

In spite of the four brethren diligently contacting Church members and friends, and Orson delivering eloquent and persuasive speeches, the fund grew slowly. March 31, discouraged at being far short of the goal, Orson wrote to the Prophet Joseph and asked how long they should try to get the entire two thousand dollars.

Orson and the others continued working while waiting for a reply. When it came, Orson unfolded the letter eagerly and read what Joseph Smith had written April 7: "We . . . were much grieved on learning that you were not likely to succeed according to our expectations. Myself, Brothers Newel [Whitney], Frederick [Williams] and Oliver [Cowdery], retired to the translating room . . . and unbosomed our feelings before God; and cannot but exercise faith yet that you, in the miraculous providences of God, will succeed in obtaining help." Grateful for their support, Orson read on, "The fact is, unless we can obtain help, I myself cannot go to Zion, and if I do not go, it will be impossible to get my brethren in Kirtland, any of them, to go. . . ." Orson's eyes opened wider as he read. His mission to obtain money held vast consequences.

"Now, Brother Orson," the letter continued, ". . . beseech [Church members], in the name of the Lord, . . . to lend us a helping hand; and if all this will not soften their hearts to administer to our necessity for Zion's sake, turn your back upon them, and return speedily to Kirtland; and the blood of Zion be upon their heads, even as upon the heads of her enemies. . . ."[21] Orson folded the letter slowly, new resolve kindled in his heart.

Echoing the authority of the Prophet Joseph's words, Orson preached. Money for the Church continued to come in only slowly.

Likewise, Orson received minimal sustenance for himself and often was refused meals at homes where he knocked. One day he walked a long distance with nothing to eat. Late at night someone finally allowed him a place to sleep. But he had grown very hungry.

Meditation brought sleep, and then he awakened to an extraordinary experience that rewarded him for his diligence. A profound peace encompassed him, and, as sudden light surrounded him, he beheld a glorious noble visitor. Marveling at the magnificent favor of receiving a Heavenly guest, Orson marveled more when the angel handed him food, as had happened to the ancient prophet Elijah. The food, a fruit Orson had never before seen, tasted delectable beyond his powers of description. As well as providing nourishment, the celestial messenger spoke comforting words and told Orson of future duties and privileges that would be his, among them that he would have the gift of prophecy and that his *"words should be fulfilled."* Of this sacred visit, Orson spoke only rarely in his lifetime, instead treasuring it as a personal strength and guide.[22]

Before April 27, Orson returned to Kirtland, sad to be bringing only $160.00. This and other donations to the Prophet totaled $347.65. More than a week before, however, even though the $2,000.00 had not yet been collected, Joseph Smith felt impressed that he definitely should lead men to Zion. Many of those who converged to start from Kirtland brought supplies and personal funds to help defray costs.[23]

Orson also learned that in a conference April 6, under the direction of the Prophet Joseph, a discussion had centered around Church members calling themselves "Latter-day Saints," to differentiate from Saints in earlier times. The resolution passed unanimously.[24]

CHAPTER 4

... to Zion ... a wife ... witnesses. ... *(1834–1835)*

Arise ye, and let us go up to Zion.
—Jeremiah 31:6
*Whoso findeth a wife findeth a good thing, and
obtaineth favour of the Lord.*
—Proverbs 18:22
*Ye are my witnesses, saith the Lord, and my servant whom
I have chosen: that ye may know and believe me, and understand
that I am ... God.*
—Isaiah 43:10

ZION'S Camp, a physical march with spiritual guidance, began with more than one hundred and thirty young and middle-aged men. They left Kirtland in early May, 1834, destination Jackson County, Missouri, a thousand miles west. Many said farewell to wives and children. Orson said farewell to pretty young Marinda Johnson. The marchers took wagons loaded with necessities for the persecuted Missouri Saints, as well as firearms and ammunition for themselves. Their course had been laid out and details distributed by the traveling elders so that recruits could join them on the trail.

As prearranged, Orson journeyed to Florence and found four brethren waiting for him, ready with rifles and the money they had gathered. Orson collected a debt owed to him, about $150.00, to donate to the camp as he had promised the Prophet he would. Milo Andrus, one of the Florence men, had a problem, however, and Orson's mischievous nature came to the rescue. Milo's father resented the Mormons and threatened twenty-year-old Milo that he would send the sheriff to return him to Florence. Orson knocked on the elder Andrus's door and inquired about conditions on a specific road out of Florence. Orson then sent Milo and a companion out of town by a different route. Sure enough, Milo's father and the sheriff followed the road Orson named and missed their subject.

When Orson and his small band joined the main group May 11, west of Mansfield, Ohio, Joseph Smith had already begun organizing the men into companies of ten or twelve. Each company divided camp duties: cook, tend fire, put up and take down tent, get water, run errands, tend wagon and horses, and act as commissary (purchase and take care of food). The brethren in Orson's company elected him their captain.[1]

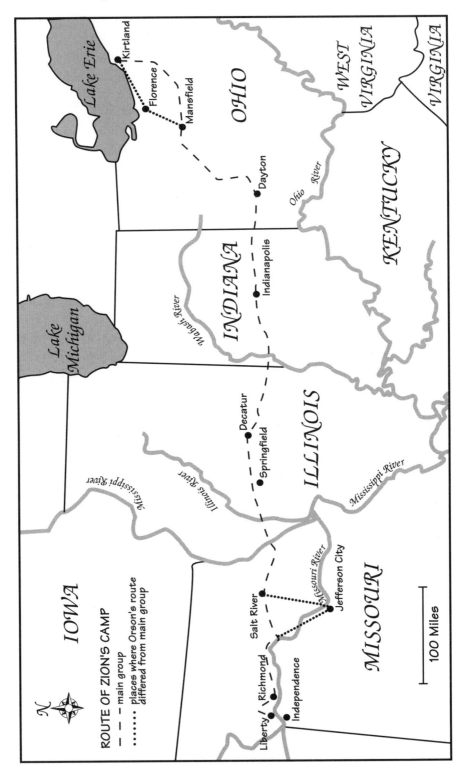

The routine of each day cultivated obedience and cooperation. In late afternoon the Prophet chose the spot for the day's flag-bearer to set up the flag, and the camp pitched a dozen tents in close formation. Men cooked and ate supper, the trumpet sounded, and from each tent the hum of prayers arose. Through the night armed men took turns standing guard duty. At four o'clock each morning trumpet notes sounded again. Men rolled from their blankets and again knelt in prayer.

On good days Orson and the others stepped along smartly, carrying their guns, their heads high. They whistled and sang, while wagons creaked and harnesses jangled. They were warmed by the sun, refreshed by light rains, and shaded by stretches of trees. They drank from clear wells and cool springs. Around their campfires they ate bread and Johnnycake and corn dodger (hand-molded cornbread fried with bacon or ham), some purchased and some camp-made. They relished fresh honey, sweet milk, tangy cheese, and fresh-killed venison. And they laughed with their Prophet. Many had not been as privileged as Orson to know the personal greatness of this man.

On discouraging days, hardships enhanced unity. In swamps the mire-covered men helped the horses move the wagons by pulling on ropes and pushing on wagon boxes. As they walked the men were overheated by blazing sun, drenched by torrents of rain, and unshaded on stretches of road with no trees. Blood soaked their stockings when feet rubbed raw. They drank brackish water and strained out "wigglers." They forced themselves, when food was bad, to swallow rancid butter and strong bacon. The Prophet worked as hard and got as muddy as anyone else. His quiet fortitude gave men strength. He refused to eat better food than others, though men wanted him to do so because of their respect for him.

"Our camp," Orson Pratt wrote later, "was often visited by spies from Jackson County who were seeking to know our numbers and to find our leaders." But observers seemed unable to accurately count the marchers. In reports, onlookers numbered them as at least 500, one time 600, and another time 1,000.

The marchers felt protected by the Spirit when their guided answers to questions helped them conceal their purpose and the identity of Joseph Smith. Dialogue with onlookers developed good-naturedly:

"Where are you from?"

"From every place but this, and we will soon be from this."

"Where are you going?"

"To the West."

"What for?"

"To see where we can get land cheapest and best."

"Who leads the camp?"

"Sometimes one, sometimes another."

"What names?"

"Captain Wallace, Major Bruce, Orson Hyde, James Allred. . . ."

The Prophet taught that God's interest in the march extended even to conversations. Some men complained about poor and scanty food, or lack of comforts, or seeming unfair treatment one to another. May 17 most of the horses turned sick. Joseph Smith said that the Lord allowed the problem, and if the brethren humbled themselves and became united the horses would recover. Only one horse died, owned by Sylvester Smith, a man unwilling to curb his complaints.[2]

Along the way the spies threatened that an armed enemy would destroy the marchers. These threats were usually general, but May 21 several brethren expressed anxiety to Joseph Smith when reports reached them that enemies planned to forcefully prevent the group from passing through Indianapolis, Indiana. The Prophet smiled, put up a hand, and said, "In the name of the Lord . . . we [will] pass through Indianapolis without the people knowing it." Near the city he asked numerous men to climb into the wagons and asked the teamsters to drive singly, rather than in a group. The walking men used different streets. As the day passed, the inhabitants of Indianapolis wondered "when that big company would come along."

Orson later commented: "Many times we lay down at night worn out and supperless, and apprehensive that our enemies might pounce upon us before morning; but the Lord was with us, and His angel went before us, and we passed through threatened dangers unscathed." Others also mentioned angels, stating that they had seen them with the camp.

In discussions around the campfires the Prophet taught, and the men became eager for these sessions. Sometimes Brother Joseph opened the things of heaven to them. Sometimes he talked humorously. Always Joseph Smith's love for them was apparent, an anchor for their actions. The men learned that whereas they thought of the here and now, the Prophet Joseph thought in eternal perspectives and gave them eternal glimpsings. Joseph Smith loved the earth and its creatures and yearned to have people obey God's laws so that God could bless their efforts toward peace. When rattlesnakes occupied a good campsite, and men prepared to kill them, the Prophet requested that the snakes be carried away. He asked the men to refrain from killing any animal or bird unless necessary for food. He said that "when men lose their vicious dispositions and cease to destroy the animal race, the lion and the lamb can dwell together."

One day, walking behind the Prophet, Orson saw brethren ahead watching a squirrel in a tree. Then he saw Joseph Smith pause and borrow a gun from one of the men. The Prophet lifted the gun to his shoulder and shot the squirrel. It fell to the ground. He handed the gun back and walked on. This all happened so fast that no one noticed if he had a twinkle in his eye. An idea hit Orson. The Prophet had seemingly violated one of the principles he had been teaching, but maybe he was testing the men. Orson stooped down, picked up the squirrel, and said, "We will cook this, that nothing may be lost." Joseph Smith overheard, stopped, and turned around. His next words verified Orson's thought. He commented warmly that he had shot the squirrel to see if his brothers would heed the precept he had so recently taught them about animals. The fact that they learned in spite of his poor example revealed that they had truly learned.[3]

After a month of travel, a few men still expressed complaints in spite of the Prophet's love, patience, pleadings, and reproofs. June 3 he called them together during the midday rest period, climbed onto a wagon wheel, and in a resolute voice announced that he would deliver a prophecy. Orson narrates that "the Prophet . . . uttered in substance the following language:— 'Brethren, . . . you have grieved the Holy Spirit. I have reproved you often . . . and you have not heeded the admonition; and now, therefore, so sure and certain as you behold yonder sun shining in the heavens, . . . just so sure and certain will the destroyer lay you waste, and your carcasses shall fall and perish like rotten sheep [sheep with the rot].'"

The men thought the scourge might come from enemies. The spies that had followed the camp these several weeks often changed clothes and horses to conceal their identity, but none of their threats had materialized. Now approaching the Mississippi River, they threatened more boldly that an armed force would stop Zion's Camp from leaving Illinois and crossing the river into Missouri. That night Joseph Smith ordered out a double picket guard and asked every man to remain dressed, with gun loaded, ready to fight.

The next day, June 4, the apprehensive group reached the river and found only one ferry boat to take them across the mile and a half of water. Rowing all across would require two days. Orson's company, while waiting their turn, decided to spend part of their wait praying. They walked into the forest. Surrounded by dense green trees they knelt, and one after the other they pled with the Lord that their lives would be spared from their enemies and that they would return to their homes and loved ones. A sweet peace enveloped them.[4]

While crossing the Mississippi no foe appeared, and two days of walking brought the group to the Salt River settlement of Saints (later Paris, Missouri), where the Prophet had previously arranged to meet his brother Hyrum. Hyrum had gone to Michigan for recruits and arrived at Salt River the day after Joseph Smith. With Hyrum's group and those who had joined along the way, Zion's Camp now consisted of just over 200 men, a few wives and children, and 25 baggage wagons.

The Prophet planned to remain at Salt River for several days to reorganize the men, repair wagons and arms, wash clothes, shoe horses, and undergo military exercises. He sent Parley P. Pratt and Orson Hyde south to Jefferson City to consult with Governor Dunklin. Was the governor "ready to fulfill the proposition which he had previously made to the brethren to

reinstate them on their lands in Jackson county?" Would he provide "a sufficient military force . . . to protect [the Jackson County Saints] in the possession of their homes?" And was he planning to "take some steps to punish the
persecutors [of the Saints]?"

Orson and dynamic Parley journeyed two days to reach Jefferson City.
Governor Dunklin remembered Elder Hyde's visit of a year before and said
that in spite of what he promised then, now he dare not follow his previous
plan to help the Saints. This would plunge Missouri into bloody civil war. He
suggested that the Saints keep peace by selling the lands from which they had
been driven. Orson and Parley knew the revelations from the Lord to the contrary and replied that the Saints could not do this. Because they refused to
consider selling, the governor advised the same as he had advised before,
recourse to the county courts. "I entertain . . . no doubt," said he, with finality, "but that these courts, that have full jurisdiction, will do you ample justice in the case."

"He knew better," Orson wrote of the incident. "He knew that . . . magistrates, constables, judges and sheriffs were engaged in the mob, and were
sworn to destroy us. He well knew that to refer us to these courts for justice,
was like referring us to a band of thieves to sue for the recovery of stolen
property." Though disappointed, Orson and Parley departed with dignity.
Orson summarized: "We were compelled to return with the same knowledge
and comfort that we had before: God with us and everybody else against us."
June 15 they overtook Zion's Camp in Chariton County. Brother Joseph listened soberly to their report.

Difficulties multiplied as Zion's Camp persevered the four days after
Orson and Parley's return. Threats from armed enemies increased. Water was
scarce and terrible. Few people consented to sell supplies to the camp. Orson
and the others ate small rations of corn meal that they made into thin mush.
One respite in this harsh period occurred when Joseph Smith's brother William killed a large deer that provided welcome soup. The fourth of these days,
June 18, Joseph Smith was sick; the men waded waist-deep through a muddy
slough, then slogged on; and that night, one mile east of Richmond in Ray
County, they camped on a prairie, exposed to their enemies. The Prophet
directed that they arise early the next morning and move on before breakfast.

The marchers and wagons passed through Richmond about daybreak,
before the townspeople awoke. The camp learned later that this thwarted an
intended mob ambush. After nine miles they stopped for a good breakfast.
From a settler who expressed sympathy for them, the commissary had bought
bacon and also milk to make corn dodger. Liberty, Clay County, headquarters
of the exiled Saints, lay only twenty-one miles away. The Prophet planned to
arrive there before nightfall.

The camp set out again after breakfast, eagerly anticipating arrival at
their destination, but complications beset them. One wagon broke down.

Another wagon lost wheels. The men fixed the problems, but by late afternoon they had covered only six slow miles.

They waded through six inches of water across the ford of the east branch of Fishing River and followed the road up a broad hill to a high ridge where stood a large old log meetinghouse. With the day almost gone, they could not reach Liberty and decided to stay in this favorable spot. The place had firewood, space to pitch tents, grass for the horses, and water at the river.

In surprise, men looked up when five horsemen disrupted the evening bustle by bounding into camp from the west. With offensive oaths and angry waves of their arms, they shouted that all of the marchers would be dead and sent to "hell before morning." Already, the clamoring visitors yelled, escape was impossible. To destroy the camp, over two hundred armed men had begun to surround it: sixty from Richmond, seventy coming east from Clay County, and another eighty from Jackson County.

The riders turned and disappeared down the westward road, their horses' tails flying. A young man, standing near Joseph Smith and eager to be of service, volunteered to fight right then. The Prophet smiled at this earnestness. "No," he replied, "the Lord will give us a bramble to keep off the dogs this night."[5]

In what had been a clear western sky, a low black cloud appeared and grew speedily. The atmosphere became threatening and windy. Orson and the others finished a hurried meal, then scurried and carried everything into wagons and tents. To be rolled up in a blanket, asleep in a snug tent, seemed the best place to wait out a rainstorm.

But the monstrous storm allowed no sleep. Lightning streaked and thunder boomed and the ground trembled. Wind blew in frenzied wails. Then water came as though poured over a gigantic waterfall in the sky. Tents crumpled or tipped, in spite of men's efforts to hold them upright. Lightning illuminated the old church. Men ran to it. Inside, drenched, they looked at each other wide-eyed, seeing by the eerie, incessant lightning. Claiming parts of benches, they lay down. They had kept their guns as dry as possible, loaded ready for an attack from the mob.[6]

Orson's inner commotion matched the storm. He had no fear of either man or beast. But lightning terrified him! The fierceness of it took his breath. The hugeness of its menacing claws, with their darting touches of destruction, churned the blood in his veins. Orson knew his terror was unreasonable, but dread remained.[7]

In spite of his physical turmoil as the storm raged, Orson experienced a spiritual peace. He and his companions, safe, observed a grand display of heavenly power, like Moses seeing the hurled Red Sea save the children of Israel (Exodus 14:28), and like Joshua watching a deluge of hailstones save his army (Joshua 10:11). The storm quieted suddenly. Flickers of far-away light and muffles of thunder mingled with patters of moisture falling from the eaves. A cool breeze wafted a gentle benediction.

In the morning the men found the river running high and swift. After spreading tents and clothes to dry in the sun, the men responded to Joseph Smith's request that they discharge all of their firearms. The noise of the myriad blasts resembled an extravagant Fourth of July celebration. Most of the guns fired, and the Prophet expressed pleasure that the men had succeeded in keeping them dry. He ordered the guns reloaded, ready for an emergency.

A scouting party that Joseph Smith sent westward, returned and reported that the branch of Fishing River on that side of the ridge also ran high, turbulent, muddy, and uncrossable. The marchers could not leave by the impassible road; neither could the mob use it to get to them. The brethren finally understood the reason for the hindrances of the day before. The Lord had arranged the delays in travel that he might surround his servants during the night with protecting walls of water.

The swift river torrents would soon recede, however, and Joseph Smith ordered a move northward a few miles to some secure place on the prairie where the camp could defend itself in case of enemy attack. Also, the horses needed fresh pasture, and the men needed sources of supplies. Walking northward, Orson and his companions grew astonished to see that a devastating hailstorm had skirted their camp. Around them the stones of ice had riddled leaves, cut down crops of corn, strewn branches of trees helter-skelter on the ground, and destroyed other trees. Again the brethren knew that the Lord had been kind to them.

Other men also knew that the Lord had protected Zion's Camp. The day after the move, three delegates from Ray County visited. One of them identified himself as Colonel Sconce, the leader of a mob who had planned to help annihilate the marchers. He wanted to meet the group, he said, whom "an Almighty power . . . protects." Colonel Sconce related that on Thursday evening he "started from Richmond, Ray county, with a company of armed men, having a fixed determination to destroy you." When his band approached the Fishing River ford, the pelted hail of the sudden thunderstorm beat holes in their hats. Their horses galloped away. Then rain soaked their ammunition, rendering their guns useless. Little Fishing River, he said, rose so rapidly they could not cross it had they still wanted to do so.

Colonel Sconce asked about the dark stories he had previously heard concerning the marchers' intentions. He wanted to know the truth. The Prophet Joseph arose and, without telling his name, told that the group had walked a thousand miles, armed only for self-defense. They brought clothes and other supplies to the suffering Jackson County members of their church who had been driven from homes and stripped of possessions. The marchers also hoped to arrange their friends' reinstatement to the lands from which they had been driven. The Ray County men, impressed, promised to try to stop the wild rumors about the Mormons.[8]

From friends, reports reached camp about the Jackson County contingent of the mob. The horsemen who had made threats Thursday afternoon had been part of the first forty men from Jackson County to ferry across the Missouri River, leaving many waiting their turns. The boat returned for another load, but a squall delayed it. Thus, only the forty had crossed to help "kill Joe Smith and his army" when the hail and wind and rain assaulted them. They sought shelter beneath wagons, inside hollow trees, and in an old shanty. Rain ruined their ammunition. After their terrible night they headed back for Independence. At home they learned that seven of their fellow mob members had drowned trying to follow and assist them.[9]

The next day, Sunday, June 22, the sheriff of Clay County visited Zion's Camp, and a meeting convened. The sheriff surveyed the group and said, "I have heard much concerning Joseph Smith, and I have been informed that he is in your camp; if he is here I would like to see him."

Orson and the others were surprised when the Prophet arose and replied, "I am the man." Friendly discussion followed, and the sheriff, like Colonel Sconce, showed relief to learn of the marchers' peaceable intentions. He asked for a written summary of what Joseph Smith told him. He would publish it in the newspaper, he said, with his own endorsement, to calm the fears of the populace. A scribe prepared the document. Joseph Smith, Orson Hyde, and four others signed it.

These developments perplexed the men in Zion's Camp. For a thousand miles they had followed the Prophet Joseph Smith—had endured heat, hunger, and fatigue with him in order to come and rescue their friends—and now it seemed that the Lord was doing all the rescuing. What was the purpose of the hardships of their march?

The same Sunday that the sheriff visited camp, the Lord gave answers to the Prophet, declaring that "it is expedient in me that mine elders should wait for a little season for the redemption of Zion—That they themselves may be prepared. . . . For behold, I do not require at their hands to fight the battles of Zion. . . . I . . . say unto the strength of my house, . . . I have heard their prayers, and will accept their offering; and it is expedient in me that they should be brought thus far for a trial of their faith."[10] Zion's Camp had provided education for these men, even though they thought that the Lord wished them to fight for Zion. By subjecting them to the "refiner's fire" the Almighty instructed about sacrifice, faith, obedience, and cooperation.

Monday, leaders of the camp met with the exiled brethren in Clay County and with civil officials. To prevent raising more fears among the local inhabitants about this large group of armed men, they decided to refrain from marching to Liberty as originally planned. The supplies they had brought, a godsend for the Saints, would be dispensed through local Church leaders. The marchers would disperse.

The trial of the faith of the men of Zion's Camp, however, required another test. About midnight Tuesday night, Orson awoke with a start. He heard cries and moans coming through the dark tent walls. Then he heard shouts of "Cholera!" He dressed quickly. The light of bobbing lanterns revealed men stricken suddenly and powerfully. Guards had collapsed, their guns dropped by their sides.

John S. Carter placed his hands on the head of an agonizing friend to give him a priesthood blessing. Before he could speak he fell to the ground himself. The Prophet Joseph also tried to heal by the laying on of hands. He, too, felt clutched "like the talons of a hawk" and fell helpless, in great pain. Soon he recovered enough to sit up. "If my work were done," he said to the brethren clustered round, "you would have to put me in the ground without a coffin. . . . When the great Jehovah decrees destruction upon any people, and makes known His determination, man must not attempt to stay His hand."

Fourteen camp members died. They died "like sheep with the rot," just as Joseph Smith had earlier predicted that they would. Later, recollecting the cholera scourge, Orson talked of the earlier murmurings in camp, the Prophet's reproofs, and the prophecy. "But did the Prophet . . . ," Orson added, "turn to be [the] enemy [of those stricken] because he had spoken hard things against them? No! His heart was melted with sympathy [when he looked at the suffering around him]— his bosom glowed with love, compassion, and kindness; and with a zeal and fidelity . . . [of] a devoted friend in the hour of peril, he personally ministered to the sick and dying, and aided in burying the dead. Every act of his, during that severe trial, gave additional assurances to the [members of the] camp that, with all their faults, he loved them still."

After several days the plague ended. A peculiarity about it surprised the survivors: the stricken seemed to be touched indiscriminately. Some who died had been faithful, and some who survived had been the most consistent complainers. The Lord's ways are above man's ways, as is told of some who perished in the time of the Savior in Luke 13:1-5.

July 3, Joseph Smith discharged the men of Zion's Camp. They received certificates declaring that they had completed the march to Zion, as the Lord had requested. Each man could decide his further course, whether to stay in Missouri or to return home.

Wilford Woodruff later summarized the expedition. "We gained an experience that we never could have gained in any other way," he said. "We had the privilege of beholding the face of the prophet, and we had the privilege of travelling a thousand miles with him, and seeing the workings of the Spirit of God with him, and the revelations of Jesus Christ unto him and the fulfilment of those revelations." And the Prophet Joseph Smith declared that the Zion's Camp participants "offered their lives, and . . . made as great a sacrifice as did Abraham."[11]

July 9, in a group of eighteen men, which included Joseph Smith, Orson started for home. Two wagons, one open and one covered, pulled by two horses each, carried their tent, valises, utensils, guns, food (when they could buy extra food), and the makings of their "table." To set up their table they stuck its four forked sticks into the ground, laid two cross-sticks upon them, then topped this with the end boards of a wagon. The group also had a buggy, pulled by one horse, and two extra horses. Men walked considerable distances when difficult roads caused stress for the animals. Men and horses suffered from lack of water and food and shelter, other times from rain and mud, and also from stretches traveled in intense heat. In some areas the men had to whip lethal green-headed flies off the horses. In one place an attack by a wild hog upset the table.

On the other hand, intermittently the travelers enjoyed good weather, received kindness, ate delicious food, and found adequate accommodations. About two-thirds of the way, the Prophet and three others embarked on the remainder of the journey by stage. Orson and his companions arrived in Kirtland August 4.[12]

From May to August, 1834, while absent from Kirtland as part of Zion's Camp, Orson missed vivacious Marinda Johnson. Tall and slender, with dark lustrous hair, olive complexion, and wide-set hazel eyes, she was ten years younger than he, had reached her nineteenth birthday June 28. Three years before, Orson had observed her lively spirit when he attended the conference at her parents' home in Hiram, Ohio. After her family moved to Kirtland more than a year ago, to the home with the wide front porch and commodious rooms, he became better acquainted. When in the Johnson home he relished good meals and good talk with the family, treasured his friendship with the sons near his age, Luke and Lyman, and especially enjoyed Marinda's sunny disposition and animated conversation. She fit well into the warm hum of domesticity, Orson noticed.[13]

The time came when Orson made specific visits to Marinda, and she accompanied him on walks and to local activities. This girl did magical things to him. Her intelligence refreshed him, her laughter charmed him, and her gentleness relaxed him. Her orderly thoughts and ways matched his own. With her, he could talk freely of everything. He wanted this comfort of sharing to last forever.

The funds that Orson had saved to support a wife had been given to the Church, and Orson felt peace in complying with the Lord's request that he do so, but his financial situation made him hesitant to consider marriage. Though Marinda wore tasteful clothes and lived comfortably, Orson decided that if he waited to marry until he saved more, he would wait too long. He hinted about the matter to her, and she communicated her mutual feeling of readiness. He proposed, and she accepted. They would marry, work, and get rich together.

During their long talks they had found similar original reactions to the Mormons. They had both considered the "golden Bible" a hoax and the thought of a modern-day prophet absurd. Marinda had first heard strange stories of these things while attending a girls' school with her sister Emily in a town neighboring Hiram. This occurred the same spring, 1831, that Orson preached against the book in the Florence area. At school, Marinda and Emily received a letter from home requesting them to return.

At home Marinda learned, in disgust, that they had been asked to come because of a meeting with Joseph Smith in their parents' home that evening. She felt contempt and disgrace that her parents would entertain this "ridiculous fake" and that she must be present. She walked into the meeting at the last moment in total rebellion. The Prophet raised his head and looked into her eyes.

In surprise, she sensed that he discerned her disdainful thoughts concerning him, but he smiled. Never before had she felt such shame. Anger melted "as snow before the sunshine." Conviction came to Marinda that Joseph Smith *was* what he claimed to be. Never, thereafter, did she doubt. That same spring, April 1831, she received baptism.[14]

The next fall the Prophet Joseph, his wife Emma, and their small children moved into the Johnson home. The Johnsons basked in this close association. When telling Orson about it, Marinda recalled many happy times. She also recalled sad times, especially the anguish of the terrible night when the mob dragged Joseph Smith outside, beat him, and smeared him with tar. Her admiration for the Prophet prompted Marinda to ask for a curl of his hair, clipped while kind hands cleaned off tar. When she told Orson about this, her slim fingers opened the locket she wore around her neck. Inside lay the precious wisp of light brown hair.[15] Orson understood Marinda's reverence for the Prophet.

Whenever anyone talked with Orson about Marinda, Orson thought more about her laugh and the touch of her hand than about the words spoken. This happened one day when Joseph Smith made an unusual statement, "God has given that woman to me. Do not marry her."[16] These words surprised Orson such that he failed to notice if Joseph Smith's eyes had the twinkle that so endeared him to the people when he said something outlandish. The Prophet did not persist. Perhaps this was one of his tests, like shooting the squirrel in the tree last summer. Maybe Joseph Smith was making sure Orson really loved Marinda.

Orson and Marinda said their wedding vows September 4, 1834. Marinda's brother Lyman received a bride the same day. Dressed in their best clothes, the two excited couples stood in turn before the Justice of the Peace, Sidney Rigdon.[17] New chapters had begun.

The year 1835 began favorably. As a man with a wife, Orson felt abiding comfort. As clerk to the Presidency, he treasured his association with the Prophet Joseph and the others, now including Oliver Cowdery who had been chosen an assistant president. As a worker at the Kirtland Temple, Orson's tired muscles prompted personal satisfaction in watching the edifice rise. As a high councilman, he listened to jealousies and complaints stirred up among the Saints by the adversary, and he rejoiced in the guidance of the Spirit to handle them. As a member of the new School of the Elders, similar to the earlier School of the Prophets, his mind expanded with new knowledge and thoughts. As a schoolteacher, he felt rewarded when his students grasped the concepts he taught.[18]

He attended a significant meeting February 14, 1835, in the new school room under the printing office, for members of Zion's Camp and friends. Joseph Smith began by opening his Bible and reading the fifteenth chapter of John. Here the beloved apostle, John, told of Jesus and his apostles in a room in Jerusalem eating a Passover supper, part of a Passover season that would be different from all other Passovers. The Messiah—the "lamb without blemish," the Firstborn of the Father—would give his life for mankind as the great and last sacrifice to which the teachings of Moses alluded. Knowing this, the Savior tried to prepare his twelve apostles for the days of trial ahead. "Greater love hath no man than this," Jesus said, "that a man lay down his life for his friends. Ye are my friends, if ye do whatsoever I command you." Joseph Smith related this to a vision shown him of the glorious mansions in Heaven of the Zion's Camp brethren who died of the cholera. Continuing, the Prophet emphasized Christ's statement, "Ye have not chosen me, but I have chosen you." Brother Joseph related this to the present by saying that God had a purpose in allowing the trials of Zion's Camp. Those who walked to Zion, willing to give their lives, would receive powerful callings in the service of the Lord.[19]

Today, the Lord had directed, twelve apostles should be chosen, in accordance with a revelation received in 1829. The men reserved for this calling had now received enough trials and experiences to prepare them. The 1829 revelation had designated that Oliver Cowdery and David Whitmer, witnesses of the Book of Mormon, do the choosing. Joseph Smith directed Martin Harris, a third witness, to join them. The Prophet asked the three to pray, which they did. Then the Presidency blessed them by the laying on of hands. Consultation, with obvious united inspiration, produced results. The first person named was Lyman E. Johnson, Marinda's brother. Lyman had been chosen by the Lord to be an apostle! The fourth name called was Orson Hyde. This was overwhelming!

Orson hardly fit his own picture of an apostle. He had shortcomings. The other eleven also had shortcomings. But, in the 1829 revelation the Lord had not declared that the Twelve be perfect, only that they desire, "with full purpose of heart," to serve him. Close friends Brigham Young and Heber C. Kimball, sturdy and dynamic, both possessed unfailing faith. David W. Patten, spiritual and diligent, was best known for the marvelous gift of healing with which he had been blessed. Brothers Lyman and Luke Johnson were true in their commitments. William E. M'Lellin, a zealous worker, had been a leader of the Saints living in Missouri. John F. Boynton had conscientiously served missions and was the only one of the group never to have been in Missouri. Orson Pratt, of keen intelligence and education, had often raised his voice as a resounding trump for the Lord. His brother Parley, equally diligent, had, like Orson Hyde, previously been a Campbellite preacher. William Smith, brother of the Prophet Joseph, at times had trouble controlling his temper, but he was a masterful speaker and a devoted worker. Thomas B. Marsh had lived in Missouri and been a strength to the Saints there.[20]

Time allowed for only three apostles to receive their ordinations in the February 14 meeting. The next day Orson Hyde and others received theirs. Through Oliver Cowdery the Holy Spirit reaffirmed the promises to Orson from previous blessings that he would teach the nations of the earth and go to both Jew and Gentile. He was also blessed that his faith would be made perfect, that angels would uphold him, and that all who heard his voice would know him to be a servant of God. Also Oliver said, "We know that he loves Thee, [O, Lord,] and may this Thy servant be able to walk through pestilence and not be harmed; the powers of darkness shall have no ascendancy over him." Oliver made two unusual promises: "he shall stand on the earth and bring souls till Christ comes," and "he shall be like one of the three Nephites." Did these words mean that Orson would not experience death, as had been promised the Book of Mormon's "three Nephites"? Or would his eventual ministry be to work from beyond the veil with peoples of earth to bring about the Lord's purposes?[21] Orson knew that all priesthood blessings were conditional upon the recipients remaining worthy of them.

The Prophet Joseph asked President Cowdery to explain to the Twelve their unique charge as apostles of the Lord Jesus Christ. In his careful way, Elder Cowdery talked at length. Summarized, some high points of his speech were:

> It is necessary that you receive a testimony from heaven for yourselves that you have seen the face of God and bear this testimony to the world. Your ordination is not complete till God has laid His hand upon you.
>
> You will have difficulties. Should you come short of your duty, great will be your condemnation; for the greater the calling the greater the

transgression. Let your ministry be first. It will require your whole souls; it will require courage. Yea, nations will oppose you—you will be considered the worst of men. When God pours out His Spirit, the enemy will rage; but this has been the case ever since the days of righteous Abel.

I warn you to cultivate great humility. Beware, lest your affections be captivated by worldly objects. Cast off your doubts, your sins, and all your unbelief. God does not love you better or more than others. You are as one; you are equal in bearing the keys of the Kingdom to all nations. Be prepared at all times to make a sacrifice of your lives, should God require them in the advancement and building up of His cause. Be always prayerful; be always watchful. You will need the mind of Enoch or Elijah; you must be prepared to walk by faith, however appalling the prospect to human view.

You are called of God. If you mind your calling, you shall always prosper, and nothing can prevent you from coming to God. He can give you wisdom, intelligence, power, and joy.

President Cowdery asked each new apostle to step forward to receive the oath and covenant of the apostleship. In his turn Orson humbly extended his hand to Oliver. Oliver clasped it, looked into Orson's eyes and asked, "Do you with full purpose of heart take part in this ministry, to proclaim the Gospel with all diligence, with these your brethren, according to the tenor and intent of the charge you have received?"

Orson answered a firm, "Yes."[22]

The Council of the Twelve met regularly, together and with Joseph Smith. They appointed Orson Hyde and William M'Lellin their clerks. As their first joint venture the Prophet counseled them to fulfill a mission to the eastern states. They worked out times and distances, and published their schedule of conferences in the March issue of the Church newspaper, the *Messenger and Advocate*. Saints in the various areas should prepare for their visit. March 28, the Prophet received further revelation from the Lord for them. They were "special witnesses of the name of Christ," and "form a quorum, equal in authority and power to the three presidents [of the Church]." The Lord reminded them to make their decisions with righteousness and patience and brotherly kindness.[23]

May 2, two days before the Twelve planned to leave, a general council of priesthood members assembled in Kirtland for instructions and fellowship. At the beginning of the meeting, Joseph Smith told the apostles, seated together, that even though they held equal privileges, for functional purposes they needed a system of seniority. The seniority, he said, would be by age. Orson and the others compared birthdays, stood up, and reseated themselves in order. Thomas Marsh, thought to be thirty-five and the oldest, thus became the president of the quorum. David Patten was near the same age.

Brigham Young and Heber C. Kimball were each thirty-three. Orson was next, at thirty. The other seven ranged in age from twenty-nine to twenty-three, the last four being twenty-three.[24] Future events would suggest that the Lord called the Twelve at young ages that they might be molded and taught.

May 4, at two o'clock in the morning, two wagons driven by friends carried the Twelve from Kirtland. Parting from families had been painful. Marinda's brave faith gave her the courage to say good-bye, even though she expected their first child. Orson hoped to return before the birth.

At Fairport, Ohio, the Twelve boarded a steamer and crossed Lake Erie to Buffalo, New York, then paired off, valises on their backs, and traveled different routes to preach between scheduled conferences. As on other missions, they received both railings and warmth. They taught Church members and solved misunderstandings and gathered donations for the temple in Kirtland. They also preached to public congregations. For several weeks they worked in western New York, an area familiar to Orson.

In June a letter arrived requesting Brigham Young, William Smith, and Orson Hyde to return briefly to Kirtland, where they would testify in a court case involving Joseph Smith. They complied, remained in Kirtland a short time, and then returned to the mission.

After rejoining the Twelve, Orson traveled in areas new and in areas familiar. New were northern New York, Kingston in Canada, and northeastern Vermont. Familiar were northeastern Massachusetts, New Hampshire, and Maine. The Prophet Joseph had instructed the Twelve to share their resources and keep careful records, which they did. Joseph Smith also said they could ask Church members to assist them, and throughout the mission they received generous hospitality. In turn, the apostles' preaching strengthened the faith and broadened the understanding of the Saints. The apostles also baptized many new members.[25]

In late August, in Maine, a letter arrived regarding William M'Lellin and Orson. Weeks before, in a letter that William wrote home to his wife, he mentioned Sidney Rigdon's school. His wife showed it to Church leaders. "You say that it will not be in your power to go to school this summer," William wrote in part. "I am glad that it is not, since Elder Hyde has returned and given me a description of the manner in which it is conducted; though we do not wish to cast any reflections." A Council—consisting of Joseph Smith, Oliver Cowdery, Sidney Rigdon, Hyrum Smith, and others—reviewed the letter and decided it insulted the presidency. They then composed their own letter.

"We hereby inform Elders M'Lellin and Hyde," their letter said, "that we withdraw our fellowship from them until they return and make satisfaction face to face." The letter continued that men, especially men of authority, should refrain from speaking to their families or anyone else in an evil manner of the leaders "which God has set in His Church. . . . We have evil insinuations enough in Kirtland to grapple with that are suggested by the father of lies, without having them from those who are sent out to put down insinuations. May God bless you to be more wise in the future."

This blow-up of a casual remark shocked Orson. Like most institutions, Sidney's school *could* use some improvements. But, when Orson pondered, and reminded himself again that he was a Church leader, he comprehended the poor taste of negative statements from him. In private he should have expressed his concerns to Sidney, or maybe to the Prophet. Of course, when Orson confided in William M'Lellin, he had no anticipation that his sentiments would be read publicly in Kirtland. In the future he must be more careful. The letter with reproof for Elders Hyde and M'Lellin had little effect on their mission, for they continued to function as clerks and to preach.

The Twelve arrived back in Kirtland September 26. The Prophet manifested pleasure to see all. For Orson and William to "make satisfaction face to face," Joseph Smith called a meeting the same day to discuss the school incident. At the Council, Orson and William expressed their regrets, admitting that they should have used more wisdom. The discussion resulted in them receiving friendly forgiveness and full fellowship.[26]

Another gladness, Orson's first day home, had come when he again saw the happy tilt of Marinda's chin as she greeted him, again heard her laugh, and again held her close. She showed him the soft clothing she had made for their awaited baby. Before long, the joyous day of birth came, and they called their baby boy Nathan, in honor of Orson's father.

Joy plunged to sadness when Nathan died shortly after his birth. Orson and Marinda felt a bewildered loss that their baby, so wanted, was gone. In subdued conversation they tried to understand why the Lord had required another sacrifice of them. Marinda put away the soft clothes, but tears still fell at unexpected moments.[27]

Orson became dismayed by another disappointment after the temple committee store received their fall and winter goods. He approached the store manager, Reynolds Cahoon, and asked for materials to make a warm cloak. Orson had no money, so he offered to pay the bill in the spring. Elder Cahoon countered that the money must be paid by January when his own bill came due. This response surprised Orson. Other people were trusted until spring for payments, and his own $275.00 donation of many months before had helped set up the store. Orson walked home without the materials, convinced of Elder Cahoon's unfairness. As days passed he tried to forget the matter. Maybe other factors existed that Elder Cahoon had chosen not to explain.

Unexpectedly, a few weeks later, Orson obtained money enough to buy a cloak. At the temple store, Elder Cahoon said he had sold all the materials for winter cloaks.[28]

Again Orson relegated to the back of his mind his resentful feelings, but they resurfaced November 5, at Joseph Smith's home, when he listened to the Prophet's scribe read a revelation of censure to the Twelve received two days before. Orson became so intent upon the words that he failed to notice the solicitude in Brother Joseph's manner that told eloquently of his awareness of the humbling experience of receiving the Lord's reprimand. "Behold they [the Twelve] are under condemnation," the revelation began, "because they have not been sufficiently humble in my sight, and in . . . that they have not dealt equally with each other in the division of the monies which came into their hands, nevertheless, some of them dealt equally, therefore they shall be rewarded." The part about the money surprised Orson, for he knew that he had withheld no funds from the Twelve for his own use. The Lord continued, repeating that "they must all humble themselves." The revelation then mentioned the former sin of Orson Hyde and William M'Lellin. This gave Orson defensive thoughts, and when the scribe finished, Orson expressed dissatisfaction with the revelation.

The Prophet patiently encouraged Orson to examine his heart. Brother Joseph's assuring manner helped Orson to understand that his vexation would help no one, least of all the Twelve. If all of the apostles felt as he did, unity would be impossible. Yes, he had erred. The Lord knew his thoughts. He accepted the revelation and would do better.

November 12, Joseph Smith met with the Twelve and declared pleasure with their renewed efforts at seeking spiritual strength and united courage. He would support them every way he could. He reminded them of Satan's viciousness and his ignoble designs to destroy the Church. To help the apostles more successfully combat the forces of darkness, the Prophet said, they needed the endowment of power that the Lord had promised to give them. They would receive this divine blessing in the temple, soon to be completed. While waiting for the bestowal of this hallowed gift they should be faithful, watchful, and prayerful.[29]

Orson's next dealing with the temple committee store encouraged him. His shirts were wearing out, in spite of Marinda's careful mending, and he called at the store for cloth for shirts. Again Orson had no cash, and Elder Cahoon agreed to wait until spring for payment. He cut the required amount of fabric and bundled it.

Orson's reassurance became short-lived. He now taught a school, and some of his adult male students labored on the temple. To pay their school tuition, they wanted part of the credit for their temple hours to be applied at the store toward Orson's bill. This seemed to Orson a way to benefit all concerned. He called at the store to see if arrangements could be worked out. He received a negative answer. Orson's frustrations returned. He remembered his $275.00 that had helped the temple committee store, and he also recalled that during his recent mission he gathered donations for the store and gathered nothing for himself. "But," he thought, "after all this, it may be right, and I will be still."

Orson was discovering more challenges of being an apostle. Great self-control was required to always remember to think before speaking, to always set a good example, and to always be humble and teachable. Also, the Twelve had no role-models. Joseph Smith was an apostle, true, but he stood bigger than life, a remarkable individual, and his duties differed from theirs. As well, the Twelve must earn livelihoods, which prevented them from being as constant a support to each other as while together on their recent mission.

Though Orson practiced silence, stories flared up his resentments again. William Smith, of the Twelve, the Prophet Joseph's brother, could go to the store, Orson heard, and get whatever he pleased, with no restraints. Rumor placed his debt at seven hundred dollars. Also, stories claimed that William was a silent partner in the concern, but not acknowledged as such or his creditors would make a haul upon the store. Orson remembered that on the recent mission of the Twelve, William had seemed as willing to share as the others. Now Orson wondered if William had been willing only because he had extra privileges at home.

Orson could remain quiet no longer. His emotions matched the gray cold December days. He was in debt, rather than prospering. He could get little credit at the temple store, and William Smith had unlimited credit. His and Marinda's baby had died. Also, he had been excited about learning the Hebrew language and pleased that Joseph Smith asked him to take charge of the project, but now even that lost its appeal. Why was so much discrimination aimed against him? He would go directly to the Prophet and find out. But, he had learned the sad results of mentioning his irritations without caution, and he knew that in a vocal recitation his annoyance might cloud his meaning. He would write his grievances.

December 15, Orson penned his letter. Joseph Smith could read it during lulls from the throng of other business. In detail Orson wrote of his disappointing dealings with the temple store and of what he had heard about William. Then he questioned, "I would now ask if each one of the Twelve has not an equal right to the same accommodations from that store, provided they are alike faithful? If not, with such a combination, mine honor be not thou united."

The recent distresses, Orson said, "have disqualified my mind for studying the Hebrew language, at present. . . . I . . . thought that I should . . . get out of debt; and to this end I proposed taking the school; but if I am not thought competent to take the charge of it, or worthy to be placed in that station, I must devise some other means to help myself, although . . . ordained to that office under your own hand, with a promise that it should not be taken from me.

"The conclusion of the whole matter is," Orson continued his reasoning, ". . . [i]f one [of the Twelve] has his support from the 'public crib,' let them all have it; but if one is pinched, I am willing to be, provided we are all alike. If . . . impartiality . . . can be observed by all, I think that I will not peep again. If I am damned, it will be for doing what I think is right."

He added wistfully, "There have been two applications made to me to go into business since I talked of taking the school, but [they are] in the world, and I had rather remain in Kirtland, if I can consistently." Orson walked to the Prophet's home that frigid afternoon and left the letter.

The next day Orson received an apologetic message from Brother Joseph that somehow, after he read the letter, he lost it. The following day Orson took another copy to the Smith home. The Prophet was ill, but he spoke kindly to Orson and invited him to tarry and read the pages aloud.

The Prophet had been saddened, he said, when he read Orson's letter. His concerns grew that Satan, with subtle devices, had tried to tempt and destroy Elder Hyde "by causing a division among the Twelve whom God has chosen." Brother Joseph's patience lifted Orson's spirits, renewing his knowledge of why the Saints loved Joseph Smith. He cared! The Prophet explained the situation of his brother William; some of the stories about him were false. Regarding the temple store, Joseph Smith agreed that Orson had been treated unfairly. The Prophet forgave him cheerfully for the ingratitude in the letter, and Orson regained the serene spiritual closeness of former days. The Prophet said that he would talk with Elder Cahoon and tell him "that we must sustain the Twelve . . . for the burden is . . . coming on them heavier and heavier."

Orson walked home with a light step. He would direct the Hebrew school.[30] How could he have been taken in by rumors? And why had he not been more understanding of the temple store's problems? Now past the difficulty of admitting his own arrogance, and again in tune with his Maker, he felt the uplift of true humility. When he had acknowledged his own faults, his soul had been washed clean by the distillation of sweet peace from higher realms. He thought that he would never again succumb to enticings from Satan.

By invitation, December 29, Orson and Marinda together attended a meeting in the home of Marinda's sister, Alice, and her husband, Oliver Olney. Joseph Smith, Senior—father of the Prophet and affectionately called "Father Smith"—presided. In his appointment as Patriarch to the Church he gave "patriarchal blessings" for the benefit of the Saints in their personal lives. Previously, Father Smith had given blessings to Orson and Marinda, and they felt privileged to be invited to hear words pronounced for others. The meeting proceeded, with a rich outpouring of the Spirit. Father Smith looked at Orson and Marinda. He smiled and reached out, saying he sensed inspiration to give blessings to them.

"Brother Hyde," the blessing for Orson began, "In the name of the Lord Jesus Christ I lay my hands on thy head the second time to bless thee. . . ." Strong words followed: "Thou hast a great work to do in the Earth and thou must be faithful and do thy duty or blood will be found in thy skirts." Magnificent continuing words restated promises already given, among them that "thou shalt travel from Land to Land . . . and be a mighty man in the Earth," that "no power of the enemy shall stay thy hand," and that "Thou shalt . . . bring many of thy fellowmen into the kingdom."

Next Marinda sat in the central chair. "The time will come," Father Smith intoned, "when thou shalt be left by thy husband—for he must go to foreign Lands and preach the Gospel—he will be great in the hands of the Lord, having a great work to do among the nations of the Earth. Thou wilt have afflictions and sorrow for thy husband—but [if] thou wilt give him up to his calling and trust in God thou shall be blest. In the absence of thy companion the Angels of heaven shall minister to thee—they will give thee instructions and comfort thy heart." Orson felt unbounded gratitude to the Lord hearing that Marinda would be watched over. "The Lord will give thee Children," Marinda's blessing continued, "and thou shalt be able to bring them up in the admonition and righteousness of the Lord—they shall run up and call thee 'Blessed.'" Knowing how much Marinda yearned to be a mother, Orson rejoiced at these words.[31]

CHAPTER 5

. . . *Elijah*. . . . *(1836)*

> *Behold, [saith the Lord of hosts,] I will send you Elijah the*
> *prophet before the coming of the great and dreadful day of the*
> *Lord: And he shall turn the heart of the fathers to the children, and*
> *the heart of the children to their fathers, lest I come and smite the*
> *earth with a curse.*
>
> —Malachi 4:3, 5-6

DURING the first three months of 1836, as the temple neared completion, eager anticipation filled Kirtland. The Prophet spoke often of the transcendent blessings awaiting the Saints.

In this period, while craftsmen finished temple details, Orson spent nearly every weekday in the building enthusiastically directing the Hebrew school. This was a part of the continuing education the Prophet recommended for Church leaders. The school began January 4 in the upper west room, with Joseph Smith teaching the sessions. Before this, for several weeks, he had studied Hebrew textbooks purchased in New York by Oliver Cowdery. School duties soon increased for Orson, and, January 21, he was released as clerk to the Presidency.

Mastering the Hebrew language became an intriguing adventure for the several dozen students. They read from right to left. They sounded and wrote the twenty-two alphabet characters into words with no vowels. They laughed at themselves for awkward mistakes. And they helped each other. After only two weeks they began reading in the Hebrew scriptures, grateful to the Lord for rapid progress. Studying scriptures in another language gave the text a freshness, a new perspective.[1]

In addition to this and other educational privileges for priesthood holders, the Prophet Joseph provided opportunities for spiritual enlightenment in small meetings of "anointing and blessing." This was preparation, he said, for more extensive edification to be received at the dedication of the temple to the Lord. In one of these meetings, the evening of January 22, in the same room where they had attended school that day, the Twelve were anointed and blessed. In their blessings they received many promises. The heavens opened to them. Angels ministered to them and mingled voices with theirs. The Twelve spoke in mighty power with the gift of tongues. Unceasing praises magnified thrilling inner serenity. The heavens seemed to burst with gladness as the angels communicated their joy that further powers held by the ancient prophets would soon be brought again to earth.[2]

At the beginning of the Hebrew course, William M'Lellin and Orson had traveled to the seminary at Hudson, Ohio, and hired Mr. Joshua Seixas as their instructor. His reputation as a Hebrew scholar was excellent. He arrived in Kirtland January 26. Working with the class, he soon expressed admiration with what they had learned in three weeks from their textbooks. Three and a half weeks into the professor's course he began extra instruction for ten advanced students, including Orson. The school met for twelve weeks. March 31, two days after the closing session, Orson penned a personal letter of appreciation to Professor Seixas and in it told of his gratitude for the "extra privileges which I have enjoyed."[3]

At the House of the Lord, skilled Saints accomplished the finishing, plastering, painting, and decorating. Tall and majestic, the temple measured fifty-nine feet by eighty feet, two stories and an attic high, built on the most elevated spot on the Kirtland plateau. Its bluish-white stucco walls glistened when the sun sparkled from tiny flecks of crushed china and glass. Its spire, one hundred and ten feet high, could be seen for miles, a monument of devotion and sacrifice.

The Saints had been sustained in their temple labors for the last three years by the knowledge that divine guidance directed their efforts. Men had often worked night and day, at times with little food. They diligently quarried, cut, hauled, and set stone in place; cut and hewed timber for supports and woodwork; carved and planed moldings and benches and pulpits; plastered walls; and painted interior surfaces. Women and girls spun, knit, and sewed to keep the men clothed and to make carpets and curtains for the House of the Lord.[4]

Temple dedication morning—Sunday, March 27—dawned an exhilarating spring day. By seven o'clock many Saints had assembled outside. They came on foot, on horseback, in wagons, and in carriages. Horses were tied to every post and rail in sight. The outer doors, on the east, opened at eight o'clock, and the crowd swarmed into the entry hall. Brothers Joseph, Sidney, and Oliver ushered at the inner doors, greeting each person and directing them to a section in the assembly room. The lofty ceiling, the clean lines, and the bright illumination from tall arched windows inspired a feeling of worshipful serenity. At the apostles' section in the upper west end, Orson opened the section gate, stepped up two steps, and sat down in his assigned seat in the row second from the top, directly to the right of the pulpits for the Melchizedek priesthood presidency.

The services began at nine o'clock. President Sidney Rigdon stood and stepped to the pulpit in front of his bench, and the whispers of nearly a thousand people quieted. He greeted the group. The choir, seated in elevated pews in the four corners of the room, raised their voices in joyous anthems, magnificent harmony that soared and reverberated. President Rigdon stood again. He spoke of the devoted toils and the extreme privations of those present who had labored on this noble structure, and tears came to many eyes. The Prophet Joseph, as part of conducting the sustaining of the officers of the Church, asked the Saints "to acknowledge the Twelve Apostles . . . as Prophets, Seers, Revelators, and special witnesses to all the nations of the earth, . . . and [to] uphold them by [your] prayers." The people assented by rising to their feet. Orson's heart swelled with humble gratitude.

At last came the hallowed time of dedication of a temple to God, an act that had not been accomplished for centuries. Standing at his center pulpit over and up from Orson, Joseph Smith offered the dedicatory prayer. He expressed gratitude to the Lord for help in building the holy house "that the Son of Man might have a place to manifest himself to his people." He requested the blessings of faith, knowledge, and diligence for the Saints. He asked for blessings upon all the nations of the earth, and especially for Jerusalem, that "from this hour [it] may begin to be redeemed," and that "the children of Judah may begin to return to the lands which thou didst give to Abraham, their father." He also pled for blessings for the scattered remnants of Israel. His final words pertained to people present: "And let these, thine anointed ones, be clothed with salvation, and thy saints shout aloud for joy. Amen, and Amen." Orson repeated with the congregation a firm "Amen."

The strains of a hymn of jubilation written for the dedication—"The Spirit of God like a fire is burning!"—rang out from the choir in resounding celebration. The Spirit of God truly was burning. The veil between the heavenly and mortal worlds became transparent, and mortals saw angels. Church leaders bore testimonies. Brethren distributed the sacrament of the Lord's Supper to the vast number present. After all this President Rigdon offered the benediction.

The proceedings of the day then received a "seal." Upon direction, the congregation arose and in unison pronounced, "Hosanna, Hosanna, Hosanna to God and the Lamb! Amen, Amen, and Amen!" The glad voices repeated this a second time, and then a third.

Profound silence followed the exuberance of the hosanna shout. The Saints' unity gave them reluctance to make any movement or sound that might mar their feelings of spiritual gratitude. Then Orson perceived movement in the row behind him. Apostle Brigham Young stood and spoke in tongues. Apostle David W. Patten gave the interpretation, after which he, too, spoke in tongues. Next, the time now after four o'clock, Joseph Smith stood, blessed the congregation in the name of the Lord, and the meeting adjourned.

Spiritual manifestations continued this Sunday evening in a priesthood meeting in the temple, attended by over three hundred brethren. Joseph Smith talked about the spirit of prophecy and encouraged the men to speak. Brother George A. Smith stood. As he began prophetic words, the rushing sound of a mighty wind filled the temple. The congregation arose simultaneously, inspired by invisible guidance. Many spoke in tongues and prophesied. Others saw magnificent visions. The Prophet announced that angels filled the temple. Outside, Orson learned afterward, astonished people in the neighborhood heard the unusual sound from within the temple and saw, resting upon the edifice, a brilliant light, a "pillar of fire." They came running to investigate.[5]

Wednesday the brethren met again, fasting, and the joy of heaven continued to spill over into mortal realms. The group enjoyed exhortations and prophecyings, also blessings pronounced with the laying on of hands. In the evening the Twelve broke the bread for the sacrament. Joseph Smith told the brethren that "the time we are required to tarry in Kirtland to be [more fully] endowed, will be fulfilled in a few days." The Prophet left the Twelve in charge of the meeting, and manifestations continued during this session of worshiping the Lord in His now dedicated house. Some brethren beheld the Savior, and others saw angels.[6]

The climax of this incredible week came the next Sunday afternoon, April 3. In the morning, inspirational sermons had uplifted a full assembly in the temple. In the afternoon the Twelve blessed the bread and wine of the Lord's Supper. The Prophet and his counselors served it. Then the pulpit curtains were unrolled from their rods near the ceiling. The lower edges rippled down, and the veils enclosed the pulpit of the presidency. Afterward the Prophet related the extraordinary events that transpired in the sanctuary within the veils. By the pulpit he and Oliver knelt, bowed their heads, and prayed. "After arising from prayer," Joseph Smith afterward recounted, "the following vision was opened to both of us. . . .

"We saw the Lord standing upon the breastwork of the pulpit, before us. . . . His eyes were as a flame of fire; the hair of his head was white like the pure snow; his countenance shone above the brightness of the sun; and his voice was as the sound of the rushing of great waters, even the voice of Jehovah." The Prophet related that the Lord Jehovah, Jesus Christ the Messiah, pronounced,

"'I have accepted this house. . . . Yea the hearts of thousands and tens of thousands shall greatly rejoice in consequence of the blessings which shall be poured out. . . .'"

The majestic and soul-stirring vision of the resurrected Christ closed, and the heavens opened a second time. "Moses appeared before us," Joseph Smith's account continues, "and committed unto us the keys of the gathering of Israel from the four parts of the earth, and the leading of the ten tribes from the land of the north."

Next, "Elias appeared, and committed the dispensation of the gospel of Abraham, saying that in us and our seed all generations after us should be blessed."

Then, Joseph Smith tells, "another great and glorious vision burst upon us; for Elijah the prophet, who was taken to heaven without tasting death, stood before us, and said:

"'Behold, the time has fully come, which was spoken of by the mouth of Malachi—testifying that he [Elijah] should be sent, before the great and dreadful day of the Lord come—To turn the hearts of the fathers to the children, and the children to the fathers, lest the whole earth be smitten with a curse—Therefore, the keys of this dispensation are committed into your hands; and by this ye may know that the great and dreadful day of the Lord is near, even at the doors.'"[7]

Elijah returned his priesthood keys to earth in the season when Jews throughout the world expected him, at the time of the Feast of the Passover. During the evening of April 1, 1836, devout Jews celebrated the Passover meal as had their ancestors for thousands of years, in as beautiful and festive a manner as each could. They expressed gratitude to the Lord for his help to Moses and their forefathers in Egypt. They reminded themselves of the bitterness of bondage, and they renewed their hope of eventual deliverance from the bondage of the pains of this earth by resurrection and immortality. They refreshed their faith that Elijah would herald the coming of the Messiah and that His coming would bring joy and peace to those who watch and prepare. They remembered Elijah by setting for him a chair, a plate, and a goblet of wine, and by opening the door that he might enter. April 3, during the period of the Passover festivities, the Prophet Elijah indeed returned to earth as the Lord had promised he would. Clothed in immortal glory, he returned to the Kirtland Temple.[8]

In the Kirtland Temple this sabbath the scope of the power endowed again upon mortals was grand beyond comprehension. The Lord Jehovah himself appeared in glory and accepted the Kirtland Temple as His house, a prelude to the bestowal of priesthood keys. Moses restored the keys for the children of Israel to be gathered "the second time," a gathering prophesied by ancient prophets.[9] Elias brought the keys relating to the Lord's promise to Abraham that "in [his] seed shall all the nations of the earth be blessed." In fargone times the birthright to carry Abraham's promise passed to Isaac, then to Isaac's son Jacob, or Israel, then to Jacob's son Joseph, and then to Joseph's son Ephraim. Hosea prophesied that Ephraim's descendants would "be wanderers among the nations," and thus mixed with other cultures and unidentifiable as a people. Zechariah prophesied that in the last days Ephraim "shall be like a mighty man, and . . . shall rejoice in the Lord." Through revelation, Joseph Smith had learned that descendants of Ephraim, as Gentiles, were joining the Church. They had the responsibility to take the blessing of "the gospel of Abraham," the gospel of obedience and sacrifice, to the world, and the Prophet now possessed the birthright priesthood keys to enact the processes that would eventually accomplish this.[10]

The keys brought by Elijah restored the power to bind all of Heavenly Father's righteous children, of the whole earth, in genealogical order, and further, to bind them in eternal covenant with the Father that they might become heirs to eternal blessings. Were this power not restored, it would be a waste of time for the Messiah, the Son, to come. He would need a covenant people on earth, connected by priesthood power with the covenant people in heaven, through whom he could prepare for the resurrection, foreseen by Ezekiel, and for the wondrous millennium during which the work of binding would continue. In Joseph Smith's later words, the "work of Elijah . . . [is to] seal the children to the fathers, and the fathers to the children." He added that with the keys Elijah brought, "we [must] redeem our dead, and connect ourselves [by priesthood authority] with our fathers which are in heaven, and seal up our dead to come forth in the first resurrection." The ordinances required for these "sealings" were to be done in temples.[11]

. . . *nations, and isles afar off.* . . . *(1836–1838)*

> *Hear the word of the Lord, O ye nations,*
> *and declare it in the isles afar off.*
> —Jeremiah 31:10

ORSON left Kirtland early in April of 1836, missionary work again his focus. He traveled south to Portage County, Ohio, and for three weeks sounded the warning voice and baptized a few people.[1] During early May, after his return, he remained at home with Marinda for several days, a precious interlude. Then he departed again, for a longer mission.

The familiar hills and hollows of western New York bloomed in spring finery, and Orson found more friendliness than during his last stay. After two rewarding months, he received an appeal for assistance from Parley P. Pratt in Canada. Parley was unable to fill all the requests he had for preaching and teaching. Orson felt good about complying, finished up his own business, and said good-bye to friends. In Buffalo, New York, July 26, he unexpectedly met Joseph Smith, Hyrum Smith, Sidney Rigdon, and Oliver Cowdery on their way east. The friends spent a glad few hours together.[2]

Orson continued on, going northward past Niagara Falls and across the west end of Lake Ontario to the prospering waterfront city of Toronto. Here he was welcomed by Parley and his wife Thankful. Parley had received permission for his wife to accompany him. Orson thought this a fine idea. Already Parley had organized several branches of the Church. Now two apostles, together and separately, in Toronto and in the villages and farms round about the forested flat countryside, proclaimed the restored gospel to eager listeners.

As always, antagonists raised their voices too. Parley and Orson could usually ignore them and let harangues run their course, but one loud and "learned" Presbyterian minister refused to be ignored. With bombastic disdain he insisted on a debate. At length, to keep peace, they consented. The date was set for a few weeks hence, the Bible the standard of truth, and the Mormons having the opening speech. Before the scheduled time, urgent business called Parley to Kirtland. Orson would meet the challenger alone.

At debate time, in a grove, with wagons arranged for pulpits opposite each other, exuberance prevailed as about "one acre of people assembled." Orson watched in humor as the priest arrived with almost "a mule load of books, pamphlets and newspapers."

After the opening prayer Orson presented, in his allotted half hour, the basic premise that the true Church of Christ must be patterned after Christ's organization in the New Testament, "composed of apostles, prophets, elders, teachers and members, who have been baptized (immersed) in the name of Jesus Christ, and who have received his spirit by the laying on of hands . . . [by] authorized servants." Members of Christ's Church would believe in "visions, angels, spirits, prophesyings, revelations, healings and miracles of every kind, as described in the New Testament." Orson said further that "any creed or religious body differing from this New Testament pattern could not be considered the Church of Christ."

The priest stood, head high, and spoke with vigor, but he avoided answering Orson's premise. Instead he introduced his papers as evidence of Mormon delusion.

Orson refused to consider the false accusations, evading being drawn into a second premise of debate until the priest had answered the first. The audience showed fascination with Elder Hyde's comparison of the Bible and modern religion.

Alternate rhetoric continued, a half hour each, until dinner time. Then the combatants enjoyed a two-hour interlude of good food with their respective friends.

After the recess, the debaters returned to their pulpits. From the wagon opposite Orson's, the firing grew less and less spirited. During his turns, Orson preached the gospel, based on New Testament texts. He felt invigorated, guided by the Spirit of God.

At last the priest jumped up, contempt on his face. He raised his fist to the sky and shouted, "Abominable! I have heard enough of such stuff."

"Gentlemen and ladies," Orson rejoined, closing the debate, "I should consider it highly dishonorable to continue to beat my antagonist after he had cried enough." The priest snatched up his books and papers in anger. Immediately following the debate, about forty people were baptized into the Church. Orson would be pleased to report success to Parley.

When Parley returned to Canada from his trip to Kirtland, he brought Marinda with him. Now the mission field became "home" for Orson.[3]

Orson felt that the printed word could be a powerful help to the work. He had previously penned an article titled "A Prophetic Warning." In Toronto in August he published this as a "broadside," a large sheet of paper printed on one side—the first missionary tract in the latter-day Church. In the tract Orson stated its purpose, that "every individual into whose hands it may fall . . . may know . . . of the fulfilment of the words of . . . the Prophets."

In the tract Orson detailed past apostasy from the gospel by both Jews and Gentiles and thus the need for a restoration. Referring to the many prophecies in the Old Testament promising that the children of Israel will be "gathered" in the last days, he wrote: "The Jews rejected the Messiah when he came to them" as a carpenter from Nazareth, "and the Gentiles received him." The Gentiles received him by listening to his apostles who walked the countryside and preached, also by being baptized and living the commandments the apostles taught. These same commandments, and the same authority to baptize, had now been restored to earth. The people who became part of the restored kingdom of God, the latter-day Saints, had a message for Jew and Gentile.

In the future, Orson's tract continued,

> when [the Messiah] comes the second time, the Gentiles will be entirely unprepared to enjoy his glory; but the Jews will be brought in[to the kingdom of God[4]] by virtue of the promise and covenant which God made with their fathers.

> [Orson's sketch explained the] cause of the Jews rejecting the Redeemer. . . . It was their previous departure from the law which God gave to them by Moses. The law was given them as a schoolmaster to bring them to Christ; and had they not made it void through the tradition of their Elders they would not have disowned their King. The Lord said to them, himself, "If you had believed Moses you would have believed me, for Moses wrote of me [see John 5:46]."

> [Of the Gentile apostasy Orson's treatise added,] The gospel was committed to the Gentiles [by Peter and the other early apostles after the Messiah's crucifixion] for the express purpose of preparing them for the second coming of Christ, as the law was given to the Jews to prepare them for his first coming. But [over the centuries] the Gentiles have made void the gospel through the tradition of their Elders.

Then, using the same reasoning that he used in the debate with the priest, Orson outlined the organization and spiritual gifts of Christ's Church in New Testament times and said that these had been rejected by the Gentiles. But, he went on to say, God again had authorized servants on earth to administer the gospel. Orson and others handed out many of the tracts.

By October the Canadian mission flourished, with organized Church branches in the capable hands of a strong group of priesthood holders. Parley, Thankful, Orson, and Marinda returned to Kirtland.[5]

In Kirtland, they found the appearance of prosperity on every hand: new homes and businesses finished, and others under construction. Cheerfulness abounded, and blessings from heaven seemed showered abundantly upon the Saints. The citizens envisioned a thriving metropolis around their magnificent temple. Renewed pleasure came to Orson as he again attended uplifting meetings with Church leaders and Saints.

As part of Kirtland's economic development, the Prophet Joseph promoted the founding of a bank, following the trend in Ohio of small new banks becoming common. With a bank of their own, Church members could readily pool their resources, those with more means helping those with less means. Then as the recipients prospered and repaid their loans, increasing numbers could be helped. November 2, a meeting convened to organize The Kirtland Safety Society Bank. Oliver Cowdery was asked to go the long distance to Philadelphia to purchase plates with which to print the bank notes. Orson Hyde was delegated to journey the 160 or so miles to Columbus, Ohio, with a petition to the Legislative Assembly for a state bank charter.[6]

Before leaving, Orson investigated ways that he might earn a living. He decided to enter into a business partnership with Jacob Bump and Edmond Bosley. Brother Bump already had a store, and Orson had storekeeping experience. December 5, 1836 the partners borrowed $850 from Eliphalet Boynton. For another $150, Boynton also worked for them and supplied goods. The partners were to recompense him by June. This gave them plenty of time, they thought, to develop a thriving business.[7]

In Columbus, soon after the Assembly convened December 5, Orson tried to get legislators to recommend a bank charter for Kirtland. He met disappointment. Seekers from other communities found the same reception. The political climate this year was unfavorable for new bank charters. A charter for Mormons met extreme coldness.

Orson, empty handed, and Oliver, with the plates made in Philadelphia, were both back in Kirtland by January 2, when Joseph Smith called a number of brethren to a meeting to revise decisions about the bank. They opted to organize a private joint-stock company, similar to others in the state. To use the plates already purchased, they decided on the name Kirtland Safety Anti-Banking Company. When printing notes, they would stamp on additions changing "BANK" to "Anti-BANKing Co." Joseph Smith and Sidney Rigdon were selected as the chief officers.

Publicly the Prophet cautioned, as he had emphasized before, that if the Saints made honest transactions, without selfishness, to assist others, the bank would thrive. He encouraged Church members to buy stock in the venture.

Early January, 1837, saw many bank notes printed and exchanged. Jacob Bump received the first notes and circulated them from his store. Orson delayed investing in the bank. He wanted to buy a home and property. He would wait to purchase bank shares until his financial footing improved.[8]

Within a few weeks of opening, the Kirtland Bank encountered deep trouble. Many factors contributed complications, among them that the society's assets consisted mostly of land, which could not be redeemed in cash. Enemies of the Church managed to obtain notes and demanded cash. Soon no cash remained. Subscribers suffered heavy discounts.

Nevertheless, bank problems failed to stem the tide of speculations and extravagances. Numerous Saints had become more excited about the riches of the earth than about the riches of the Spirit. The glory of the temple dedication had evolved into a feeling that the Lord was rewarding the people with material goods because they had been diligent. Land, bought on speculation, sold for ever-increasing prices. Stores carried a wide variety of goods, available on credit. Women walked proudly in new dresses, and men drove handsome new carriages, putting off paying for them. Businesses continued to fill their shelves to satisfy the desires of the townsfolk.

Two of the more extravagant new store dealers, members of the Twelve, were Lyman Johnson, Marinda's brother, and John Boynton. During missions in the eastern states in 1836, they borrowed thousands of dollars from faithful Saints and ordered an enormous supply of goods in New York City. They expected to pay back the borrowed money when the stock sold. Shipments arrived in Kirtland, and people purchased, planning to pay later.

The Prophet Joseph and others, alarmed by the spiraling fascination with worldly goods, preached against the increasing speculations in property and against buying beyond one's means. But many Church members had already contracted heavy debts and ignored the Prophet's counsel. Time would take care of their problems, they thought. Many who started commercial enterprises, or who purchased bank shares, lacked an understanding of business, which added complications. Joseph Smith, doing all in his power to help the Kirtland economy, borrowed from other institutions to try to keep the banking society solvent.[9]

Orson anticipated that his and his partners' business would do well, and he purchased property, as did Marinda. For a total of $3,900, January 25 and February 11, 1837, Orson bought two lots from Newel K. Whitney. Now he and Marinda could have a residence of their own, to which they would welcome a new baby in the spring. For $1,500, February 1 and March 20, Marinda purchased two additional nearby lots from her father. With more than two acres they had plenty of space for barns and gardens and orchards.[10]

At times Orson thought about the success of his published tract in Canada in introducing people to the Church. Other enterprises, also, could benefit from ease in circulating their message. Maybe the Bump, Bosley, Hyde business should be expanded to include printing. The growing population of Kirtland could probably support another press besides the one owned by the Church. When Orson mentioned this to Joseph Smith, though, the Prophet counseled him against the venture. But Orson did not dismiss the idea.[11]

By spring, financial problems had fractured the local Church members into two groups: those, getting fewer, who said that Joseph Smith was a Prophet no matter what, and those who claimed that the Lord was obviously not guiding their leader or else conditions would be better. Credit entanglements had become a nightmare, with people losing property. Like lined-up dominoes, that fall as each touches the next, when one person could not pay a creditor, then the person he owed could not pay his creditor either. Lyman Johnson and John Boynton lost heavily and grew angry. They had thought that nothing connected with the Church could develop serious problems.

People forgot that Joseph Smith had been warning them all along. They said that if he were truly a prophet he would never have started a bank or would have taken wiser steps to prevent difficulties. The mutterers included bank officer Warren Parrish who, it was learned later, took bank money regularly for his own use.

The turmoil became so serious by May that more people seemed *against* Joseph Smith than *for* him, even among the members of the Quorum of the Twelve residing locally. The Johnson brothers and John Boynton had publicly disavowed the Prophet. Parley P. Pratt became disgruntled with a property matter and said derogatory things; his brother Orson echoed his conclusions. Orson Hyde, too, developed questions. Conversations with his unhappy brothers-in-law, a lack of the prosperity he had anticipated, and all the other clamor, brought confused thoughts. Brigham Young and Heber C. Kimball were the only two apostles in Kirtland who remained steadfast for Joseph Smith.[12]

In addition to vexations within the Church, harassments from without increased. Most were loud harangues about the struggling Kirtland Bank, but some threatened violence.

Grandison Newell initiated a lawsuit that involved Orson Hyde. Grandison filed his complaint April 13, 1837 in Painesville, nine miles from Kirtland, charging Joseph Smith with attempted murder. Grandison Newell for years had been an avowed enemy of the Mormons, perhaps from jealousy, or maybe from concern about business competition. Since the time Orson, as a young man, had labored in Grandison's small iron foundry in Mentor, this man had grown wealthy and influential. Now he employed many men in both a large iron foundry and a huge chair factory. He ridiculed the Saints at every opportunity. Two years previous he led a mob of about fifty men who pelted Parley P. Pratt with eggs and drove him out of Mentor. Now Solomon W. Denton, a disgruntled young man recently excommunicated from the Church "for lack of faith, non-observance of duties and contempt," claimed that the Prophet two years before had asked him to assassinate Grandison Newell. Denton would testify to this.

News of Grandison's charge reminded Orson that he and others had discussed harassments with the Prophet in the bank a few months before, and the conversation had turned to Grandison Newell. As the discussion continued, Joseph Smith's customary forbearing manner changed to agitation. The way Orson heard, the Prophet indicated that if Grandison Newell again led an attacking mob, the Saints should defend themselves, adding that Newell deserved to "be put out of the way, or where the crows could not find him." Later Orson asked Joseph Smith to clarify his seeming threat. The Prophet regretted his outburst, he explained. With his usual kindness he added that he "had no intention to hurt Newell, but . . . I felt injured by him, and spoke rashly and inadvertently in the heat of passion."

By the time of Grandison's lawsuit, Orson had become confused by the turmoil around him and the rampant claims about Joseph Smith being a fallen prophet. Most of the brethren with whom he discussed the situation had also developed spiritual haziness, failing to allow the Prophet moments of human frailty. Not until later did Orson learn that he and many others misinterpreted Joseph Smith's worried look these days. The Saints were not following the Lord's counsel, and Brother Joseph was pained. Where would this lead the Church? He preached, he pleaded. Even stalwarts treated him with disdain.

Orson happened to meet Grandison Newell and mentioned the Prophet's words in the bank. A gleam came into Grandison's eyes, and he asked Orson if he would testify in court to what he had heard. Orson considered, and he said, "I [hope] truth might ever prevail with me." After more discussion, Orson thought of his own convictions and added, "I shall not swerve from truth and fairness, even should it go against Joseph Smith." Thus, Grandison Newell drew Orson into a sensational anti-Mormon lawsuit. Solomon Denton would also testify, as would Warren Parrish, who had been in the bank the day of Joseph Smith's agitation and who had recently opposed the Prophet publicly in other matters.

About Grandison filing his complaint, a local historian, James H. Kennedy, later wrote, "Giving form and substance to the grave rumors that had been for a long time afloat as to the dangers to be apprehended from the Mormon Church, this charge caused the wildest excitement. The hearing was awaited with the deepest interest." Grandison fanned the flames. In an open letter to Sidney Rigdon, published in the *Painesville Telegraph* May 26, he declared that Joseph Smith had tried "to procure my death" and gave details.

Spectators jammed the preliminary hearing, June 3, 1837, in the Painesville town-house, before Justice of the Peace Flint. The accused, Joseph Smith, sat in his assigned place, his demeanor one of compassion, of sorrow. Orson was the prosecution's first witness. From the witness chair he repeated the conversation in the bank, his discussion of it with the Prophet afterward, and his discussion of it with friends. Each person in the room listened intently.

"Does the witness think that Smith intended to take the life of Newell?" a lawyer next queried.

"I cannot say that I do;" Orson answered, "though I felt some alarm, spoke to others of it."

"How long have you been acquainted with Smith, and what is your opinion of his character as a man?"

"I have known him for some time and think him to be possessed of much kindness and humanity toward his fellow beings."

"Has there ever been any difficulty between yourself and Smith?"

"Yes, there has been at times about the printing business and concerning Newell."

Solomon W. Denton, the next witness, claimed that he had been asked by Joseph Smith to kill Grandison Newell. Other witnesses for the prosecution—Newel K. Whitney, Luke Johnson, and Reynolds Cahoon—testified also and agreed essentially with Orson.

The prosecution called up their last witness, Warren Parrish. The anticipative viewers expected to hear condemning testimony. However, his words, as reported, were, "Does not recollect distinctly, but thinks he has heard Newell's name mentioned at the Bank; was often there when Smith was present, but has no remembrance of hearing Smith utter any threats against Newell or others." Looks of dismay filled faces in the room. The lawyer for the defense cross-examined Warren Parrish, and he answered, "[I] am an officer in the church; have been acquainted with Smith for some time; think him to be of kind and charitable disposition; have often heard him exhort his people to do no violence."

After the examination of witnesses for the defense, Justice Flint, known to have little sympathy for the Mormons, referred the case to the next term of the Court of Common Pleas.[13]

Immediately after the hearing, Orson's reflections on the various testimonies caused him serious deliberation. When he testified he thought he was only being honest. However, he could have told the truth and not sounded so *against* Joseph Smith. But he felt *against* Joseph Smith. Why did he?

Orson's self-scrutiny led him to recognize his confusion. He began to see that by questioning the inspiration of the Prophet's actions, he followed the same pattern that had emerged in late 1835 when he became disgruntled with the temple store. Over the past many weeks, angry questioning feelings had become more frequent, while feelings of peace had diminished. He had gradually, he now realized, given more credence to men who disobeyed God's Prophet than to the Prophet himself. He had begun concentrating on Joseph Smith's human imperfections rather than on his spiritual integrity. But the process had seemed so natural he failed to notice it happening. He must do now the same as he had done when upset with the temple store situation, talk with his leader.[14]

The day after the hearing, Orson found Joseph Smith at Sidney Rigdon's imposing clapboard residence across the road from the temple. When Orson entered the home he saw the Prophet, Sidney, and Hyrum standing together, ready to place their hands upon the head of seated Heber C. Kimball and give him a blessing. Joseph Smith explained warmly that the Lord had called Heber to be the leader of a mission to England.

England! This stunned Orson. A mission to far-away England! Orson recognized suddenly that in his own activities, with the physical world tumbling all around, he had neglected the spiritual world. He had been doing little for the Lord except attending a few meetings in Kirtland. His heart melting in repentance, he pleaded, "Brethren, I acknowledge that I have sinned before my God and you, and I beg of you to forgive me."

The Presidency and Heber exulted at the change in Elder Hyde's attitude. Orson spontaneously continued, his thoughts hardly staying ahead of his words, "If you find me worthy, I desire to accompany Brother Kimball on his mission to England, or," he added quickly, "go on any other mission. I want to do whatever is the will of God."

The Prophet smiled kindly, giving no immediate answer to Orson, but indicating that Heber's blessing should proceed. The blessing was incredible. ". . . God will make you mighty in that nation in winning souls unto Him;" the Prophet said, "angels shall accompany you. . . ; you shall be mightily blessed. . . ." After the amen, Joseph Smith said Orson should also receive a blessing. The Lord's words to Orson rang similar to Heber's. Orson would go to England too![15]

The importance of the mission the Prophet explained. The severe dissensions in Kirtland had been prompted by the subtle schemes of Satan. To save the Church from destruction, the Lord had revealed that missionaries must now be sent to England. In this new field of labor they would find many people ready to learn and live the gospel, to bring fresh and sturdy strength to the Church.

In mere moments, Orson's life had changed direction. England! Across the ocean! As Heber's companion. Heber was four years older than Orson, tall, stately, and powerful. With piercing black eyes, balding head, and a quiet smile, merriment came easy to him, but in a way that enhanced his profound faith and steady courage.

Orson walked down the sloping road to his home. Just two weeks before, May 21, Marinda had presented him a daughter, Laura Marinda, who seemed to be healthy. When Orson thought of Nathan's small grave, Laura's preciousness increased. Orson wanted to see her first smile, bounce her on his knee when she grew bigger, share her laughter, and hear her first word. The thought struck him that maybe Marinda and Laura could accompany him.[16]

The Grandison Newell legal matter continued. In the Court of Common Pleas, June 9, the week after the preliminary hearing, Judge Humphrey dismissed the case on the grounds of insufficient evidence. Grandison Newell fumed. He vented his frustration in a letter to the editor of the *Painesville Telegraph*, published June 30, complaining that the judge "insinuated that my hatred, not my fear, induced the prosecution." He also complained that "the corroboration of Hyde was wholly disregarded, and his testimony laid aside as having no weight in the case." A week later the editor published his own editorial rebuttal and agreed with the judge.[17]

June 13, 1837, Orson, Heber, and two unseasoned missionaries started for England. Lacking funds, their trust in the Lord gave them the courage to begin this incredible undertaking. During the nine days of preparation, Orson and Marinda had accepted, sadly, the Prophet's advice that she remain at home. The other two missionaries were Willard Richards, a recent convert, devout, a doctor of medicine; and Joseph Fielding, recently arrived in Kirtland from Canada, of sincere faith. A native of England, eager to return and preach to his relatives, Brother Fielding had written to his brother James Fielding about the restored gospel; his sisters had also written.[18]

By carriage with friends, the four traveled to Fairport on Lake Erie and then took an overnight steamboat to Buffalo, where a Church member was to meet them with funds for the mission. No Church member met them. The four needed money and tarried all day, but in the evening they boarded a line boat on the Erie Canal and continued eastward. To stretch their meager means they ate the simplest of cold fare. At Rochester, Heber sent Orson on to New York City to meet brethren expected from Canada to join the mission. Willard planned to visit briefly en route with friends and relatives who owed him money. Orson traveled the fastest way possible, by packet boat. Packets ran by schedules rather than waiting at docks to fill up with passengers or cargo.[19]

In New York City, Orson saw people everywhere, all intent on their own purpose, be it selling flowers on a corner or hurrying by. And he saw innumerable buildings. Most rose three or four stories, bunched together between narrow streets. Myriad chimneys projected skyward. Occasional church towers and steeples rose taller. West on the Hudson River, east on the East River, and south on the Bay, Orson saw boats and ships of all sizes and shapes. He remembered excitedly his boyhood dreams of sailing the seas.

The only Latter-day Saint in New York City, young Elijah Fordham, arranged for Orson to board with his sister-in-law, Mrs. Fordham, for a dollar a day. When Joseph Fielding came he stayed at the same place. So did John Goodson, Isaac Russell, and John Snyder, converts that Orson knew in Canada. With people on the streets the missionaries talked about the gospel and distributed copies of Orson's pamphlet, *A Timely Warning*, revised from his *Prophetic Warning* and reprinted in Kirtland.[20]

Heber and Willard arrived June 22. Figuring every way possible, if the group spent their money for daily living while waiting for the next ship, they would have insufficient funds for passage. The next morning Brother Fielding received an unexpected donation. The missionaries elatedly purchased tickets, twenty dollars each, to Liverpool on board the *Garrick*, to sail June 30. They would bring their own provisions and sleep on a deck, second cabin, one accommodation higher than steerage.

To stretch their means the missionaries moved into a small room in an unfinished storehouse owned by Elijah Fordham's father, straw on the dirt floor underfoot. For five days they subsisted again on simple cold fare. They paid a penny a day rent to be lawful tenants and then also sawed, hammered, and raised the walls of a building for Mr. Fordham. On the Sabbath, amid their trunks, they fasted, held a sacrament meeting, and talked. Feelings of unity deepened, and a spiritual peace testified that the Lord approved of their efforts and would continue to bless them. Monday and Tuesday they handed out pamphlets. Wednesday they spent fifty dollars for provisions for the trip.

Thursday, June 29, the seven companions hefted barrels, boxes, and trunks, jostling with many other people hauling supplies and cargo aboard the *Garrick*. In case they were delayed—in a "calm," or blown off course, or crippled in a gale—they had purchased more provisions than the minimum for the expected thirty-day voyage. Their enormous mound contained a barrel of Indian meal [cornmeal] to make puddings, half a barrel of flour, one hundred pounds of crackers, forty pounds each of rice and sugar, two gallons of honey, one gallon of molasses, three hams, and cooking utensils. In addition to their food and personal trunks, they had trunks brought by Brother Goodson full of copies of the Book of Mormon and the Doctrine and Covenants to sell in England. (The Doctrine and Covenants—the compiled revelations that replaced the destroyed Book of Commandments—had been published in Kirtland in 1835.) In their assigned space the missionaries made room to roll up in their buffalo robes to sleep on the deck. The next day a boat towed the *Garrick* out a few miles, and she anchored.[21]

The *Garrick*, magnificent and new, was the largest packet ship sailing the ocean, and this, her third crossing of the Atlantic, would be exciting, a race against the *South America*. The owner of each ship had wagered ten thousand dollars that his vessel would reach Liverpool, England, first. Saturday morning, July 1, Orson watched in fascination as the ship's crew shouted and scurried, unfurling banks of huge sails. The race began.

For Orson, sea travel proved the grand adventure he had anticipated. Freedom from seasickness pleased him. He saw huge whales off the shore of Newfoundland. The swelling and subsiding ocean reminded him of the hills and valleys around Kirtland. And consistently, behind them, he saw the billowing sails of the *South America*.

Their third Sunday, Heber arranged with the captain for a religious service on the aft quarter deck and asked Orson to speak. More than two hundred persons assembled: officers, crew, and passengers from several nations. Orson prayed and then preached, feeling buoyed by quiet inspiration. He talked movingly about the resurrection being a gift of the Savior to all mankind. Later a representative of the cabin passengers found Elder Hyde and, with tears in his eyes, expressed the gratitude of all. This excessive praise made Orson uncomfortable, and he gently responded that God should have all the acclaim.

This same week the race across the ocean ended with grand flourish. From the lofty masthead on Tuesday, many days sooner than expected, the lookout sighted Ireland. In the Irish Channel on Wednesday the scenery in every direction captivated: surging water ahead, the green hills and rocky cliffs of Ireland and Wales to the sides, and the full sails of the *South America* in the distance. By some miracle would the *South America* pass the *Garrick*? The last stretch, up the River Mersey in dawn light, Thursday July 20, became a regal pageant. Exhilarated passengers, waving and cheering, thronged the decks, and a fair wind blew. Above him Orson saw the sails taut as drumheads, and around him he heard the crew loudly jubilant. The majestic *South America* plied only about ten ship-lengths astern. Eighteen days and eighteen hours after leaving New York, the *Garrick* won the race.

The *Garrick* anchored in the harbor, and a small boat came alongside. Orson, Heber, Willard, Brother Goodson, and other passengers climbed eagerly down the rope ladder into the bobbing shell. Orson felt enveloped with encouragement. He had sensed the same spiritual quickening when he first saw Liverpool in the distance. As the boat approached the pier, Orson, Heber, and Willard exchanged glances and stood up, muscles poised in readiness to leap ashore. Heber jumped, landing on the steps of the dock. Orson followed. Then Willard. The three stood together—in England. They watched Brother Goodson, his face resolute and his hand clutching a heavy purse of silver. He took no chances of losing the purse in the water, but sat until the sailors moored the little boat. Brothers Fielding, Snyder, and Russell came ashore on another boat.[22]

After managing unsteady decks, Orson felt strange standing on the firm dock. He looked around at the countless ships and boats, at the maze of boat basins, wharfs, and long multi-storied brick warehouses in this renowned seaport of Liverpool. Beyond, in the city with a population of around 190,000, he saw narrow angled streets, monstrous buildings, innumerable chimneys, tops of squared-off church towers, and a smoky steel-gray sky. Around him he heard curious throaty English spoken by the bustling people, and he interpreted little sense from their words. He had jumped into the unknown. Everything he saw and heard seemed foreign to him, but well anchored, moored, or established. Glancing at his companions, he saw mirrored in the faces of the Americans the same bewilderment he felt. They had come to a formidable wilderness to deliver a message that burned like fire in their hearts. This fire gave them courage to face challenges.

Together around Liverpool, the missionaries saw contrasts of extreme poverty and splendid wealth. The city had recently grown prosperous through worldwide commerce in shipping, and in many areas the group walked on spacious paved thoroughfares while admiring fine new brick mansions roofed with slate and stately public buildings graced with Grecian columns. They tried to avoid adjacent areas of old narrow streets with their look and smell of neglect and decay. In the demeanor of the people, however, they saw the greatest disparity. Women in dresses elegant and costly stepped down from coaches and with disdain ignored the pitiful visages of humanity who approached with bony hands outstretched, rags hanging from their bodies. Beggars, clamoring for survival, also approached the missionaries. Orson anguished that he had no pennies to give.[23]

In the afternoon, in a rented room, Orson wrote a letter to Marinda. Though July 20 was the true date, Orson's excitement about the trip taking only eighteen days and eighteen hours caused him to write July 18. He told of the relaxing voyage, of the festive arrival, and of the confidence felt by the missionaries. With poetic enthusiasm, his words flowed onto the paper, "Let me assure you, my dear wife, that the Lord God Omnipotent is with us, therefore fear not concerning us, but pray for us that we may ever keep humble at the feet of our master, that righteousness and truth may be our motto, grace our support and eternal glory our reward."

Visualizing Marinda, he smiled to himself and continued, "I want to see you and the little babe very much; I have seen you a number of times in dreams, but when I awoke it was not a reality. May the Lord bless you and all that pertains to you; and when the voyages of life shall be over, may he bring us into that port of everlasting rest where storms and tempests will assail us no more, and where separation will not be known. . . .

"We shall remain here for a few days," he also wrote, "until we can determine what course to pursue, and in what directions to travel."[24]

Friday their luggage cleared the Custom House, and Saturday morning Heber announced that inspiration had directed: "Go to Preston." Early in their afternoon journey the gray and grandeur of Liverpool gave way to green countryside. Through the coach windows Orson saw a world of miniatures: small fields enclosed with low hedges and snug villages filled with thatched-roof cottages. Picturesque village names graced tall signposts: Mughull, Ormskirk, Burscough, Much Hoole. After thirty northeast miles they came again to gray and grime, the large industrial borough of Preston.

The streets and the market place thronged with people wearing bright ribbons showing their political preferences. Queen Victoria had ascended to the throne just two days before, and today was election day for members of parliament. The coach made slow progress through what seemed like all 40,000 men, women, and children of Preston, and the missionaries stepped down into a carnival of color and sound and movement where bands played and banners waved. One missionary left to find lodgings. Orson and the others, unaccustomed to such election pageantry, stood on the sidewalk beside their trunks and watched the colorful, noisy scene. What would be the results of their missionary labors in this busy place?

Men carried a huge banner into the street and released its folds overhead, revealing the golden letters, "TRUTH WILL PREVAIL." Orson and his companions stared. "The hand of Providence hath unfurled this banner before your eyes," spiritual emotions blazed into their minds, "for your comfort and for the confirmation of your faith and hope, that your message shall take root in the hearts of the people and prevail."[25]

The group carried their baggage into rooms on Saint Wilford Street, and then Joseph Fielding hurried away to visit his brother, the Reverend James Fielding, here in Preston. Joseph returned jubilant. His brother was eager to converse with the missionaries.

At his home James Fielding welcomed the group. Forty-four years old, and self-assured, he was one of the thousands of "non-conformist" British clergymen who preached doctrines varying from those of the Church of England. In this crowded industrial time, with the wealth in the hands of a few, the Church of England catered to these few. The independent ministers taught the common people to endure their misery and their inferiority, and to hope for an eventual glorious existence in heaven. The more people a minister could attract to his church, the faster he personally prospered.

The Reverend James Fielding wanted to hear about the Church of Jesus Christ. He had already told his congregation about the concepts contained in his brother's and sisters' letters and had asked his followers to pray that missionaries would come to England and explain further. Until late that night he kept Orson and the others in animated conversation, and he invited them to attend Sabbath services in his own "Vauxhall Chapel" the next day.

In this modest but well-built two-storied brick chapel the missionaries listened to James Fielding. At the end of the meeting he announced with zest that an Elder from America would be the speaker in the afternoon. Eager expressions rippled among the people.

In the afternoon, members of the congregation brought numerous friends, and all paid rapt attention to Heber. In his sincere way he helped each person feel the reality of God's interest in everyone. Learning and living the precepts that the Savior himself had taught, required neither the ability to read and write, nor clerical robes, nor wealth. The basic teachings of the gospel included faith in the Lord Jesus Christ, repentance, authoritative baptism by immersion, the laying on of hands for the gift of the Holy Ghost, and obedience to the commandments of God. By following these principles, joy could be felt in this life no matter what one's circumstances. People need not wait to get to Heaven to be happy.

As the people comprehended that their speaker declared they had the same stature in the sight of God as did those with greater privileges, amazed looks registered on faces. Heber continued with a brief history of the restoration of the gospel. He pronounced that the authority to perform the works of God had been restored to earth by angels to a poor and uneducated young man, Joseph Smith. The lad had been confused about the teachings he heard from ministers, and he prayed for enlightenment. He received answers, learning that the peace and guidance of God are available to every person who asks with faith. When Heber sat down, Orson arose and bore a dynamic testimony of the truth of Heber's words. The congregation responded elatedly.

In the evening, to an even greater assemblage, John Goodson preached and Joseph Fielding bore testimony. Wednesday evening people again flocked to hear the preachers from America. Surrounding the missionaries after the meeting, they expressed gratitude that the Lord had sent the religious message that contained authority and visions. Several members of James Fielding's church confided that in recent months, while praying for the missionaries to come, they had envisioned Orson and Heber, identified as servants of God. They felt comforted, the people said, to be taught the things of heaven by men in ordinary clothes who talked of God clearly and who, like the Savior, expected no monetary pay for preaching.

James Fielding, on the other hand, had also become astounded, but in a different direction. Many members of his church, upon whom he depended for his comfortable livelihood, might leave him and follow these newcomers. After the Wednesday evening meeting he closed his ears and his chapel to the missionaries.

As a result, people invited the elders to preach in their homes, and by the following Saturday nine persons had requested baptism. Heber agreed to perform the ordinances the next day, Sunday, in the river.[26]

"Brother Kimball," Isaac Russell pled in a strangled voice, "I want you should get up and pray for me that I may be delivered from the evil spirits that are tormenting me." To these startling words, in the dimness before Sunday dawn, Orson and Heber awoke.

Heber, next to the wall, slipped off the foot of the bed and stood. Orson swung his feet around and sat on the edge of the bed. They placed their hands on the head of the suffering man, though Isaac, at other times, had claimed to be beset by evil spirits, and Heber considered him illusionary. But Heber prayed and asked the Lord to rebuke the evil. Before he finished his prayer, however, his voice wavered, and his mouth clamped shut. His whole body began to shake, then he reeled from loss of balance, toppled to the floor, and groaned. Orson—appalled—stared, as a solemn thought came: "The evil spirits are exceeding angry because we attempted to cast them out of Brother Russell, and they made a powerful attempt upon Elder Kimball as if to dispatch him at once." Orson immediately grabbed Heber's shoulder and lifted. But Heber remained senseless and fell back. By now Willard had followed Isaac into the room. Orson, Willard, and Isaac lifted Heber onto the bed. He lay apparently lifeless, and an ominous sensation pervaded the air.

"It seems that the devils," Orson agonized as perception came to his mind, "are determined to destroy us, and prevent the truth from being declared in England." Next, to his horror, Orson's vision unveiled, and he saw the throng of awful attackers. They rushed at him with knives, threats, imprecations, and hellish grins, Orson's astonishment extreme at their sinister appearance. These full-statured, bizarrely-clothed devils, men and women, possessed every form and feature of mortals, but some had hideous distortions in face and body. They seemed infuriated, their words and actions expressing confusion and misery. The sight sickened Orson, but he stood between Heber and the venomous host. Summoning spiritual power, he eventually forced these fiends of hell to begin to retreat from the area of the room. As the last savage imp departed, he turned around and said, as if to appease Elder Hyde's strenuous opposition to them, "I never said anything against you!"

Orson replied, "It matters not to me whether you have or have not; you are a liar from the beginning! In the name of Jesus Christ, depart!"

Orson, Willard, and Isaac turned their concerned attention to Heber, stretched out on the bed. They laid their hands on his head and, with priesthood authority, in the name of Jesus Christ, rebuked the influence of the evil spirits. Immediately Heber roused. Looking around, he began to get up.

In agonizing pain, drained of strength, Heber's body refused to stand, so he knelt, and he prayed. His energy beginning to return, he arose and sat on the bed with his companions, facing the room and fireplace. Before any significant discussion ensued, the veil withdrew from the eyes of all four missionaries, apparently that they would *all* know with surety the reality of the occupants of the realms of darkness. The space before them seemed to open up, and they watched the demoniac host advance toward them in legions, behind leaders, like armies surging to battle, the repulsive belligerents foaming and gnashing their teeth at the mortals. The evil horde pressed close—virulent and desperate, looks of vindictive malignity on their faces—within a few feet of the missionaries, making eye contact. In addition to human forms in this repulsive spectacle, Orson and the others saw snakes in both corners of the old fireplace, hissing, writhing, and crawling over each other, producing soulracking effects upon the observers.

The missionaries, abhorrent, watched this repugnant spectacle for one and a half hours. Willard timed it by his watch. Heber perspired profusely, his clothes becoming as soaked as if he had been in a river. His excessive pain diminished only slowly. After the experience he wrote: "I learned the power of the adversary, his enmity against the servants of God, and got some understanding of the invisible world."

Later, back in America, Heber asked the Prophet Joseph if a spiritual deficiency on his part had allowed the evil spirits to overcome him. Joseph Smith smiled. "No, Brother Heber," he said, "at that time you were nigh unto the Lord; there was only a veil between you and Him, but you could not see Him. When I heard of it, it gave me great joy, for I then knew that the work of God had taken root in that land. It was this that caused the devil to make a struggle to kill you."[27]

At nine o'clock as scheduled, the morning bright, the elders met their baptism candidates in the spacious park on the bank of the calm, wide River Ribble, which formed the south boundary of Preston. Among the thousands of people taking their Sunday stroll in the park, gossip spread about this strange event of public baptism by immersion. A huge crowd of curious spectators soon lined the Ribble's banks. Though still weak from the clash with the devils, Heber baptized the nine candidates. One of them, George D. Watt, won a foot race to be the first baptized.[28]

This same day an excited man, twenty-nine years old, found the missionaries. His dark eyes shining, he introduced himself as Alexander Neibaur, a Jew. "You have a book?" he asked eagerly. Handed a Book of Mormon, Neibaur opened it caressingly. He had seen this book, he declared, in visions and had been waiting for the message he knew it contained. He had accepted Christianity in Germany, then came to England as a surgeon and dentist. He settled in Preston and married an English girl. That morning, while his wife scrubbed and whitewashed their front steps, he overheard a neighbor tell her that new ministers from America claimed that angels had visited earth with important messages. He found these ministers as quickly as he could, and he knew that they had the truth when he saw the Book of Mormon. He asked for baptism.

Slowly Heber answered. He advised Dr. Neibaur to wait and learn more, a puzzling response because generally people received baptism upon first request. But, the tone of Heber's words denoted inspiration. For reasons known to the Lord, a delay must be accepted by this, the first Jew to request baptism into the fold of the Messiah in the latter days.

Dr. Neibaur's countenance fell, but he would follow counsel. The missionaries handed him a Book of Mormon. He accepted it gratefully and departed. In three days he returned. He had neither slept nor eaten, he said, but had read and pondered the wondrous book. Again he asked for baptism. Again he was advised to wait until he was prepared.

Incredulously he declared, "Gentlemen, I *am* prepared!" He recognized, however, these men to be apostles of God. Wait he would. In the meantime he would attend meetings and continue to study.

Alexander Neibaur kept his vow, for months, waiting for the apostles to approve his baptism. He did this in spite of persecution and derision, and persuasion from friends disappointed that such a brilliant man planned to throw away his future by joining the Mormons. Isaac Russell baptized him April 9, 1838, and he remained faithful his entire life.[29]

Meanwhile, after the Sunday baptisms, encouraging days continued. Monday the missionaries fasted and prayed, thanking the Lord for help and blessings. They asked for further guidance, and it came, that they should separate. In the next few days four of them traveled to distant areas. Joseph Fielding began to preach in villages around Preston. Heber and Orson remained in the city, and that week they baptized nineteen more people. The next Sunday morning, August 6, the two preached in the market place by the tall obelisk to a huge friendly crowd of wealthy and poor.

That afternoon, in the home of a Church member where Heber and Orson now lodged, regular Latter-day Saint Sabbath meetings began in Preston. The new Saints gave rapt attention to the unadorned proceedings: listened quietly to the opening prayer, observed the apostles kneel and pronounce the sacrament prayers, and in reverence felt their own sacred inner stirrings as they partook of the sacrament of the Lord's Supper. Next, Heber and Orson performed twenty-seven confirmations, in preparation for organizing the members into a branch of the Church.

To be confirmed—receive the gift of the Holy Ghost—members in turn sat with the apostles' hands resting gently on their heads and listened intently to inspired phrases. A powerful feeling of tranquility permeated the room. While Heber spoke, an amazing thing happened to Orson. In a vision he saw an angel recording the pronounced words. After the meeting Orson told Heber of his experience. The two rejoiced to be given a witness that the Lord accepted their works. In contrast to the infernal world they had seen the previous Sunday, Orson had glimpsed the heavenly realms and marveled at the privilege of receiving visual assurance that the Lord approved of the missionaries' efforts.[30]

"The whole town is on fire [about the gospel]; and through the strength of the Lord we are fanning the flames," wrote Orson to Brother Goodson, September 12. "The people begin to come in from the country to get Baptized. . . . Such an excitement was never in Preston before, I presume to say, upon a religious subject." Heber had left Orson in charge at headquarters, and a month had sped by in a mosaic of varied experiences cemented together with praying and fasting and heeding the Spirit. Orson coordinated communication for the Church in England. He answered missionaries' questions contained in letters. He worked with the Preston area members, broadening their gospel knowledge and teaching them their duties. He preached often, in nearby villages as well as in Preston, and was usually the only missionary in the city, though Joseph Fielding and Heber returned periodically.

He had scarcely time to eat or rest as public interest in the Church increased incredibly. He often preached to groups jammed into small homes with listeners at the doors and windows. Multitudes heard about the new religion from their friends, and other multitudes learned about it from reading Orson's *Timely Warning,* which he reprinted and distributed. Temperance halls in towns and villages were opened to the missionaries because they abstained from using alcoholic beverages.[31]

Though he devoted his energies to Church work, Orson thought of home, especially in September when a letter arrived from Marinda. "I never wanted to see you more than I do at this time . . . ," he answered her September 14, "yet I am glad you are where you are, and that I am where I am."

He was glad to be where he was, he explained, because "I labor in the vineyard night and day and the Lord labors with me.—There has been between one and two hundred baptized in this place since we came." He loved these converts, and he added, "They know how to do but little else than to spin and weave. . . . They are extremely poor, most of them not having a change of clothes decent [enough] to be baptized in, but they have open hearts and strong faith."

This poverty is what made Orson glad that Marinda was where she was, and he continued, "Whoever comes here for loaves and fishes will realize their expectations as much as our Kirtland <u>speculators</u>. If brother Joseph never advised correctly before, he <u>certainly</u> did when he advised the brethren to leave their women at home." Orson recounted the details of the missionaries' subsistence: "We all pay 2 English shillings per week for our lodging, which is nearly 50 cents, and then we buy our own provisions at the market and it is cooked for us.—The brethren [men who have joined the Church] will frequently divide the last loaf with us, and will do all in their power for us. If it had not been for [the sale of] brother Goodson's books, I know not how we should have lived."

The Lord watched over the missionaries, Orson added: "The priests talked of putting me in prison for preaching without a liscense from under this government. I made application to the Clerk of the <u>peace</u> for a liscense, but he informed that I could not obtain one until the court of quarter sessions which would be in October. I thought it would not answer for me to be idle until that time, therefore I continue preaching in houses, and in the streets, and on the public grounds, and in the market places, and am liable to be taken & thrust into prison any day when informed against: But the priests dare not really do this for fear of the people, for all men, almost, consider us to be prophets of God. Thus by the power and goodness of God we still continue to preach."

The missionaries' uplifting method of preaching astounded the people, Orson related: "We have not said a hard word against the priests since we came here, neither have we spoken against any sect, yet they say all manner of evil against us. The people have discovered this difference between us, and they are most agreeably surprised, and it gives us unbounded influence. We tell them that God has not sent us to judge and condemn another man's servant: But he has sent us to preach the kingdom of God."

Orson filled a "large paper," but he yearned to say more. He turned the paper sideways and, across what he had already penned, he composed a prayer:

I feel that I am far from home and no arm to lean upon but the arm of the Almighty. . . . O Lord . . . , [let thy servant] be sanctified, a vessel of honor to bear glad tidings to those who sit in darkness, and call upon poor wandering prodigals to return to their father's house. . . .

O Lord, remember the partner of all my joys and sorrows; and when she reads this epistle from her dear and affectionate husband, Bless, O bless her with the same love and joy that now inspire my bosom. Let her enjoy health of body and peace of mind. When she is sick, do thou heal her. When she is cast down, do thou raise her up. When she is sorrowful, do thou comfort her. When the tear of deep affection steals down her cheeks, do thou cheer her mind with the prospect of once more seeing the object of her earthly hopes and with open arms embracing her nearest and dearest friend.

And now O Lord, have thou respect unto the little babe which thou hast given us. Take it not from us, but let it remain as a source of comfort unto its parents. . . . Let the babe and her mother be faithfully preserved until thy servant shall return to his home.[32]

In the work, spiritual guidance continued remarkably. Frequently when together, Heber or Orson began to relate a vision or a dream or a thought only to learn that the other had experienced the same prompting. Joseph Fielding recorded in his diary, October 10, that "Bros. K. and H. seem to act in perfect unison and as led by the Spirit of God. I feel myself highly favored of the Lord in having so much of their Company. They both dreamed a few nights ago that they were in a strong Ship on full sail in a very narrow Channel, sometimes seemingly too narrow to admit the Ship; sometimes filled with Earth or Rocks and other old vessels; but they sailed on with great Strength in spite of all. This answers well to the State of the Church at this time. The Priests are all endeavoring to stop it, but it goes on the faster."

Priests often wanted to argue publicly with the apostles, but, Orson narrates, "We tell those who wish to contend with us that we have business of more importance."[33]

Two of the other missionaries, Brothers Goodson and Snyder, opposite to Orson and Heber, were baptizing few in their respective areas. Discouraged, they returned to Preston at about the same time in late September and requested release. They seemed unable, in the face of mockery and threats, to learn to rely on the Lord. Instead they lived in fear. For the good of the mission, Heber and Orson decided, they could go home. The two sailed for America October 5, and later both left the Church.[34]

Willard Richards, on the other hand, developed over-earnestness and over-endurance. In November he wrote to Orson, described his tattered clothing and scanty food, and asked how to survive physically. He had refused, he said, to accept the members' offers to raise money for him, but rather heeded the Lord's command to go without purse or scrip.

"[W]hen they offered to raise some money for you," Orson answered, "you ought to have encouraged them. . . . The fact is, Bro. Richards, if we always give way to this false delicacy [of refusing help], we may starve to death. 'The Labourer is worthy of his hire' [Luke 10:7]. It would be nothing contrary to the spirit of the Gospel to call upon the people for contributions whenever you want money or clothing. Altho God has commanded us to go without purse or scrip from our homes, yet he does not design that we should labor in his vineyard and faint for want."[35]

The frustrations of helping missionaries develop faith were offset for Orson by the joys of the Saints' meetings. In Preston the Latter-day Saint services had become renowned for the amazing preaching of the apostles and for the "best singing in town." In the Temperance Hall, which held 800 people, the congregation sat in ascending circular rows of seats, and the leaders sat on a raised stand. The musicians used the fifteen-foot center section that formerly had been a cock-pit. The lilting soprano of a flute, the warm alto of a clarinet, the mellow tenor of a bassoon, and the rich notes of a bass viol accompanied the singers. Throngs massed into the Mormon meetings such that people fainted from lack of fresh air and had to be carried outdoors. The Preston Saints became so numerous that Heber and Orson divided them into five branches. These new Church members grew in experience. They conducted meetings and shared the care of members' needs.

In mid October, Heber and Orson obtained their licenses to preach. In November the work slowed when the companions became severely ill "with a kind of influenza cold" that raged in the area. General weakness, sweating, and back pain from kidney problems left them with little strength. Heber performed a few baptisms, even though ill, but Orson was confined to his room most of the time for over two weeks.[36]

While ill, November 13, Orson received a letter from Marinda with the glad news that she and Laura were well and comfortable. With gratitude he read of her "fine lot of pickles" in their crocks and also the "corn, beans, and potatoes in plenty" that she had stored for winter.

Because paper and postage cost precious funds, Heber gave Orson space, November 16, to answer Marinda at the end of a letter he had written to his wife Vilate. Knowing that planting time would come before he arrived home, Orson suggested that she find someone else to help her "start a good early garden in the spring." Writing about his illness, he remembered his exhilaration on board ship and said that if he could be "constantly sailing the ocean" he would be in top form. Planning "to set sail for America about the first of April next (if the Lord will)," Orson commented that "right about the time little Laura Marinda is a year old you may expect her to see her 'Pa.'"[37]

Orson recovered and resumed his energetic schedule. Heber recovered too and again traveled about. "It is with difficulty," Orson tells of this period, "that I can get enough to pay my Lodging, etc., etc., at the close of each week. The Brethren who go into the country to preach return to this place as headquarters and remain, some longer and some shorter time, and it falls to me to foot the bill. . . . It requires no little <u>faith</u> to live in England by preaching the gospel, and I have learned that our old-fashioned Yankee 'Spunk' is the principal ingredient in this precious compound [of success]."

Living the gospel in England required faith of the members as well as of the missionaries. "Many members loose their jobs . . . ," Orson explains, "not because they neglect their work and duty, but in consequence of their religion. Not seldom we [the missionaries] give them the last shilling we have, so they can buy bread." Each time they did this an unexpected source provided their own necessities.

In February the apostles began making plans to leave for home in April. Orson wrote to Willard Richards and to Isaac Russell and asked them to return to Preston.

Heber, Joseph Fielding, and Orson, to leave everything in order, visited for several weeks among the branches around Preston. Diligently, with little sleep, they preached sermons, baptized people, organized branches, instructed members, and healed the sick. Willard returned to headquarters and accompanied them after March 7. Their hearts melted at the devotion of the Saints. Though hardly able themselves to subsist, members donated enough money to the missionaries, in minute amounts, to pay for passage home. Everywhere, tears of parting were accented by gratitude for glorious gospel truths.[38]

As a farewell in Preston the missionaries conducted an all-day conference, Sunday April 8, in the Temperance Hall. More than half of the fifteen hundred people[39] who had been baptized attended. Heber announced the Lord's guidance that Joseph Fielding remain to preside over the Saints in England and that Willard Richards remain as his first counselor. Many other brethren also received new responsibilities. In the evening Heber and Orson spoke nostalgically and gratefully and said that they expected to return to this beautiful land. Tears ran freely.

At nine o'clock the next morning, Heber, Orson, and Isaac left by coach for Liverpool. A large tearful crowd stood and waved until the coach lost them from view.[40]

The missionaries wondered what they would find at home. Letters had told that the Church bank in Kirtland failed, causing much bitterness. Apostasy increased. Persecution compelled the Prophet, with many others, to leave. They fled to Missouri. Marinda and Heber's Vilate waited amid troublous circumstances for their husbands to return.[41]

After a ten-day delay in Liverpool, the missionaries boarded the *Garrick*, the ship that brought them to England. This voyage, however, proved unlike the first. A violent storm battered and tossed the vessel for days, ripped rigging, and shattered superstructure. The excessive turbulence made Orson so desperately seasick that he changed his mind from thinking he would always like to sail the ocean on missions.

Heber, Orson, and Isaac arrived in New York City on Saturday, May 12. The next day they found Brother Elijah Fordham, who had helped them before. He told that a branch of the Church flourished in the city, with Elder Orson Pratt in charge. Seeing Elder Pratt again brought great joy. They all attended worship services with about eighty converts. Elder Hyde learned, with elation, that many of the converts became interested in the gospel after reading his *Timely Warning* that he and his companions had distributed the previous June.

The eager returnees continued their journey the next morning, and for nine days they traveled on steamboat, train, and barge. They entered Kirtland May 21, Laura's one-year birthday. Glad celebration abounded in the Hyde abode. "Pa" had come home.[42]

CHAPTER 7

. . . sorrow. . . . (1838–1839)

> *For mine iniquities are . . . as an heavy burden . . . because of my*
> *foolishness . . . , and my sorrow is continually before me. . . . I will declare*
> *mine iniquity. . . . Forsake me not, O Lord.*
>
> —Psalm 38:4, 5, 17, 18, 21

UPON Heber and Orson's May 1838 return from England to Kirtland, Ohio, Orson exulted in reunion with his wife Marinda and daughter Laura. A few friends also welcomed the returning apostles. Joseph Smith had been gone since January. Faithful Saints followed. Many, unable to sell their property, simply abandoned the results of their diligent labor. Far West, Missouri, had become, under the Lord's direction, the headquarters of the Church. Now, in Kirtland's streets, unrest and loneliness prevailed. Windows of empty homes stared forlornly on unkempt yards.

Marinda told Orson the sad details of steadily worsening conditions after he left for England. Dissenters banded together against Joseph Smith, his family, and his supporters and called themselves the "old standard." Some Church members sued the Prophet for debt, impoverishing him and his relatives. For Joseph Smith's safety, supporters stood guard at his home. Marinda's brothers Luke and Lyman, and many other Church leaders joined the dissenters. They said that Joseph Smith's promises of peace and prosperity would never be realized. Marinda's father sided with his sons.[1]

Orson and Heber felt promptings from the Lord to also head for Missouri, and they prepared to move their families. May 25, Orson sold his property back to Newel Whitney for $2,500, $1,400 less than he had paid for it. He felt fortunate to sell at all. Marinda's father allowed her to retain title to the two lots he had sold to her. He said that she and Orson would be back as soon as Orson recognized Joseph Smith's deceit. Several times Heber and Orson preached in the temple about the success of their recent mission and buoyed up the sinking spirits of some Saints who remained in Kirtland.[2]

During the hot sultry July journey to Missouri, Heber and Orson directed a company of about forty people in eight families. For days they jostled in wagons southeast to Wellsville, Ohio. Then they rode by riverboat for hundreds of miles descending the Ohio River southwest the length of Ohio, Indiana, and Illinois, and northward up the Mississippi River to Saint Louis, Missouri. The intense heat brought illness to Orson and most in the group.

While ascending the Missouri River west from Saint Louis, low water caused their boat to repeatedly run upon sandbars. Sometimes thirst forced the general passengers to drink water from the muddy river, even though the boat hands warned them that this would make them sick. Cabin passengers and crew had enough clean water for their needs.

The boat's officers showed contempt for the Mormons. When the boat stopped to "wood up," the Kirtland men hurried ashore with buckets to obtain good water. This gave the officers "fun" at Mormon expense. "The boat would often start before the brethren could get back," Heber's daughter Helen narrates, "but when they came running and shouting with their pails of water, the [officers] would [return] ashore and take them in and roar with laughter at their ludicrous appearance, more especially Brother Hyde who was very fleshy."

After many delays and much discomfort, they arrived at Richmond Landing, Missouri, forty-three miles south of Far West. They unloaded their goods and traveled eight miles to Richmond. Marinda's brother, Lyman E. Johnson, lived here, as did several other apostates who had parted ways with the apostates in Kirtland. Lyman welcomed the whole group. He even "ordered dinner at the hotel for all of his old friends," Heber's daughter Helen relates, "and treated us with every kindness." He invited the Hydes to remain in his home for a rest, and the Hydes accepted. They bid farewell to Heber and the others, who, by wagon, traveled to Far West, arriving July 25.

Orson's weakness and fevers grew worse, but after a few days in Richmond he yearned to depart. A friend provided a ride over the stretched-out Missouri countryside to Far West. This expanding city of the Saints contained wide streets and generous lots, grain fields, vegetable gardens, livestock, tents and wagons, frame homes and log homes.[3]

Embraces and handshakes welcomed Orson and Marinda. They felt overjoyed to again greet Joseph Smith. Orson had almost forgotten, being absent so long, the power of the courage and love that emanated from the Prophet. Brother Joseph expressed great pleasure that they had arrived and spoke glowingly about the successes of the British mission. Friends generously housed the Hyde family.

Orson learned of developments. The previous April the Lord had designated to the Prophet the full name by which the Church should be known: The Church of Jesus Christ of Latter-day Saints. The Saints were grateful for this clarification.

Also, Church leadership had changed as unrepentant leaders had been released and replaced. Removed from the First Presidency were Second Counselor Frederick G. Williams and Assistant President Oliver Cowdery. Hyrum Smith was now Joseph Smith's Second Counselor. Removed from the Council of the Twelve were William M'Lellin, Luke Johnson, John Boynton, and Lyman Johnson. Oliver Cowdery and Lyman Johnson had come to Far West, but became increasingly disgruntled. Sidney Rigdon had preached graphically, June 17, what became known as the "Salt Sermon," inviting the "salt that had lost its savour" to leave. Soon Oliver Cowdery, Lyman Johnson, David Whitmer, and John Whitmer (the latter two being official witnesses of the Book of Mormon) moved south to Richmond.

By revelation, July 8, the Lord had designated four new apostles: John Taylor, from Canada; John E. Page, absent on a mission; Wilford Woodruff, who had marched with Zion's Camp; and Willard Richards, the devout missionary still in England. The same revelation directed that "next spring" the entire Quorum of the Twelve should "depart to go over the great waters" to England. This pleased Orson.[4]

Right now, however, fevers, pain, and exhaustion overshadowed all else in Orson's world. But beyond his sphere, Missourians again felt concern about the gathering Saints, who now numbered ten thousand. Again public officials feared that Mormons would gain the majority of the votes in the state. The smug attitude of some Church members of their own superiority added fuel to the uneasiness.

Public anxiety had increased after the Saints' Independence Day celebration, July 4, where Sidney Rigdon delivered a fiery oration denouncing past persecutions and declaring a "war of extermination" against any mobs that might plague the Saints. The general tone of the day evolved into a "Declaration of Independence" from abuse, the Saints' resolve being to counter any injustices. Afterward the speech was published, and the local populace viewed it as an official threat from the Church. Public unrest about the Mormons increased, but when Orson and his family arrived in Far West, resentment had not yet been boldly manifest.

Then, August 6, concrete harassment erupted. A vicious mob attack prevented Saints from voting in the town of Gallatin, north of Far West. As weeks passed, other reports came of troops and mobs, uproar and confusion.[5]

Even with the confusion, Orson felt peaceful. He had been diligent during his British mission and now saw no urgency to jump into matters already being handled by others. Though he was only thirty-three years old, his severe illness brought thoughts of impending death. He had faith, however, that his recent labors had earned him a place in God's kingdom. "When I returned from England," he recounts, "my spirit was pure and my soul loved virtue. I was unconscious of guilt. When I lay sick at Far West I thought if I could depart [by death] I should be at rest."[6]

Rest was about all that Orson could do. August 31 he sat on a council that heard complaints, but this exhausted him. Try as he might, his physical weakness deprived him from becoming part of the inner workings of the Church. He felt detached, like an unneeded drone, disheartened at being a burden to those around him.

Mostly confined, Orson only heard the opinions of the people who came and visited him. In many ways this added to his detachment, as each visitor interpreted events according to his own experiences and attitudes.

The Prophet Joseph came by whenever possible, but demands regretfully left him little time for visits.[7] This contrasted with former times when Orson helped make policy. Now, while not even on the fringe of decision-making, subtle changes in Orson's feelings about the Prophet crept into his thoughts.

Thomas B. Marsh—president of the Twelve, pleasant company, "full of anecdotes and chit-chat"—also called at Orson's bedside. He deemed the stories concerning the dark plans of the mobs exaggerated, judged that the Saints had little to fear from the Missourians. Additionally, he was miffed at the Prophet. July 25, a few days before Orson arrived in Far West, Thomas's wife had been tried before Church tribunals for withholding cream strippings from a friend with whom she had agreed to share equally for making cheese. Thomas insisted on his wife's fidelity even when Joseph Smith chastised her. After this, Thomas began to withdraw himself from Church involvement.[8] He conveyed his feelings to Orson, surmising that Joseph Smith had become indecisive and out of harmony with the Saints. And Thomas paid attention to Orson, which meant a great deal to the sick apostle.

Sidney Rigdon also paid attention to Orson, and his opinions diverged from those of Thomas B. Marsh. His inflamed words predicted bloodshed. To prevent it, he declared, Church members had the imperative duty to obey Joseph Smith or any counselor in the presidency without question. And "if any will not," he said, drawing his hand across his neck, "they shall have their throats cut from ear to ear." Thus, according to Sidney, the presidency would use violence, if necessary. Though Sidney said these things, Orson's thoughts fleetingly questioned, "Can the spirit of God dwell in that man's heart?" Orson had never heard the Prophet Joseph or Hyrum Smith use the kind of language Sidney attributed to them.[9]

Orson's fevers caused an increase in his confusion. Was Joseph Smith becoming indecisive and unhelpful, as Thomas claimed, or becoming a tyrant, as Sidney indicated? Orson was too sick to analyze wisely, but he preferred Thomas's anecdotes to Sidney's fire.

Word reached Far West, October 15, that homes of Saints at Di-Ahman, several miles to the north, had been burned and plundered. Hurriedly the Prophet left with about one hundred brethren, armed for defense, Thomas B. Marsh among them. They functioned under county officers as part of the county militia.

In an unseasonable snowstorm three days later, compulsive Thomas returned, and he visited Orson. His anxiety a match for the cold, he said that at Di-Ahman, Joseph Smith had ordered retaliatory burning and plundering and that the orders had been carried out. Unfortunately, he failed to tell that he personally had not heard these orders, and Orson was too ill to sort fact from rumor or from overreacting emotion on Thomas's part. Alarm in every word, Thomas said that now the Missourians would give no leniency to the Saints here in Far West. Dreadful scenes, he pronounced, lay ahead.

On edge, Thomas told Orson that he had been suspicious that this would happen, and now he felt angry that he had let himself be duped into believing Joseph Smith. Oliver Cowdery, the Johnson brothers, and all the others were right, he said, that Joseph was a fallen prophet, a dictator with empty promises, a "Nero" with no concern for the lives of innocent men, women, and children. The grandiose hallucinations of Joseph Smith were again being shattered, just like in Kirtland. Ahead lay turmoil, ransacked communities, devastation.

Orson, his mind a stressed haze attached to a weak and tortured body, remembered the things Sidney had said about Church members obeying the presidency, and about bloodshed and battle. Horrified at what might happen to his beloved Marinda and Laura, Orson knew that his weakness prohibited any defense of them on his part. He expected to die soon anyway, and he must think of their safety. Anxiety dominated conversation as Thomas and Orson decided that to save their families they must pack up and leave immediately, the frightful weather notwithstanding.[10] Orson's dusky condition prevented the consideration that Thomas might be acting the coward.

Orson wrote a rushed letter explaining his and Thomas's departure and handed it to a trusted friend. Essentials were packed hurriedly and loaded into the wagon after dark. The canvas top would keep out some of the wet and cold. Into the wagon climbed Thomas, his wife Elizabeth, their several children large and small, Orson, and Marinda with bundled Laura. Thomas slapped the horses' backs with the reins and the wagon lurched out of town. In Far West, Thomas's sister and her husband, Lewis and Ann Abbott, would harvest his corn and potatoes, and care for his pigs and heifer.

The next many hours became a blur to Orson, cramped in the jarring wagon. The Marsh family showed consideration, and Orson felt gratitude to them, even though Thomas seemed agitated. He had led Orson to believe that he would settle three miles out of town, safe from the assaults of mobs that he thought would demolish Far West. However, with only brief stops, he traveled on to Clay County and then on to Richmond, Ray County.

The apostates in Richmond befriended Thomas and Orson, stating their willingness to render every assistance to escaping Mormons. Thomas asked David Whitmer and Oliver Cowdery, separately, if they still claimed to have seen angels during the restoration of the gospel. (David's testimony in every copy of the Book of Mormon stood as a witness that an angel had shown to him the gold plates; Oliver had experienced many heavenly manifestations in connection with Joseph Smith.) They both gave positive and emphatic replies. "In the days when Joseph received the Book of Mormon, and brought it forth," David stated, his face animated, "he was a good man and filled with the Holy Ghost." David's look saddened. "But he has now fallen." Oliver spoke similarly.[11]

When local non-Mormons learned the identity of Thomas, and of his concerns, they sent a committee to ask him to write a statement about the activities of the Mormons. As President of the Quorum of the Twelve Apostles, he decided to sound the warning voice and disclose to the public what he thought to be the insidious designs of Joseph Smith. He and Orson, October 24, six days after leaving Far West, talked with Henry Jacobs, Justice of the Peace for Ray County. Thomas stated that Joseph Smith, in dastardly and secretive design, planned conquest with the sword and had already begun. After writing embellished details about what he heard and saw at Gallatin and "Diahmon," Thomas added that "the prophet is to take this State, and . . . the United States, and ultimately the whole world . . . [and has said] that he should yet tread down his enemies, and walk over their dead bodies; and that if he was not let alone . . . he would make it one gore of blood from the Rocky Mountains to the Atlantic Ocean." Thomas signed his affidavit. Mr. Jacobs notarized it.

Orson's clothes hung limply from his emaciated frame as he watched, physically and mentally exhausted, spiritually numb. Mr. Jacobs turned to him and asked for his declaration. Orson hesitated, but then he wrote: "The most of the statements in the foregoing disclosure of Thomas B. March [sic], I know to be true, the remainder I believe to be true." This was a borderline honest statement. He believed that Thomas had heard the stories of unlawful acts, and he, too, had heard some of the assertions about Joseph Smith. Had better-informed sources than Thomas been Orson's, he would have known that Joseph Smith had not ordered burning and plundering at Di-Ahman, but that mob members, for the purpose of turning public outrage against the Mormons, had removed their belongings, burned their own houses, and then loudly blamed the flames on Joseph Smith and his friends. However, some overzealous Mormons had plundered.[12]

After Thomas signed the paper his anger became resolve. Rather than try to reclaim his goods in Far West, he would find a different place to settle. He wrote of his decision to his sister Ann and her husband the next day, October 25. "I determined this day to leave here for the Mississippi [River]," he wrote. "I have left the Mormons . . . [and] Joseph Smith Jr. for conscience sake, and that alone, for I have come to the full conclusion that he is a very wicked man." Thomas tiraded on regarding the wickedness of Joseph Smith and Sidney Rigdon, their "burning" and their "pillaging," and added:

"I fear that many innocent among you will have to suffer. O my sister my brother, be up and out of that place before it is too late." Thomas also said that he "intended to have left you the deed for the place you live on but forgot it, I will however convey it to you by mail." He continued that Lewis and Ann should use his stored harvest and his livestock.

Thomas finished his letter and then handed it to Orson, asking if he wanted to use the remaining blank space. "Bro. Marsh has kindly offered me a place to write a few lines in his letter," Orson penned, "and I cheerfully accept of it.

"I can say with him," Orson went on, "that I have left the Church called Latter Day Saints for conscience sake, fully believing that God is not with them, and is not the mover of their schemes and projects." Having no desire to disparage any person, he added, "I do not wish to enter into particulars here.

"There are many in Far West for whom I entertain the highest regard," Orson continued, hoping that Lewis and Ann Abbott would show his message to friends. "Their kindness I have seen, and their hospitality I have shared during my sickness, and the sickness of my family. Let them think of me as they will, I can assure them, that they will ever live in the memory of a grateful heart."

Concerned about his obligations, Orson asked a favor: "There are some few debts which I owe there, which I would have settled before I came away, could I have done it consistently. But I have left property enough to pay four times the amount which I owed. But if they [my creditors] should not get it in that way I will pay them if I live, and get any thing to do it with."

Worried about mobs, he admonished, "I do really hope that my friends will hasten and get out of Caldwell County as <u>soon</u> as <u>possible</u>. My calling is to warn men to flee from the wrath to come; I therefore in the fear of the Lord, warn all the honest in heart to flee out of Caldwell County as soon as possible."

Orson signed his name and then realized that friends might wonder where he and Marinda would reside. He added a postscript: "I shall probably go with Bro. Marsh and settle where he settles."

Orson also wrote a letter to Father Johnson in Kirtland and said that he, Marinda, and Laura had left Far West and were safe. Now that he had learned about the "wickedness" of Joseph Smith and others, he understood Father Johnson's warning in Kirtland.[13]

The same day that Thomas and Orson wrote letters to the Abbotts, October 25, 1838, news reached Richmond that Mormon armed forces had begun to rampage and "that Richmond [will] be sacked and burned by the Mormon banditti tonight." This news deepened Orson's conviction that Thomas had led him to take the correct course. People ran and shouted in the streets. Women and children fled in great alarm to stay with friends and relatives elsewhere. Some men prepared to repel the attack while others galloped their horses away at top speed to surrounding towns and counties with an anxious summons for reinforcements to gather in haste. On every hand could be heard cries of "The Mormons must be exterminated!" and "The

Mormons must leave the state!" Amid all this commotion, the Marsh and Hyde families remained in seclusion.

No attack materialized in the night, but the next day noise and uproar besieged Richmond. Brandishing guns and shouting, men poured into town, ready to fight the Mormons. The frenzied "troops" multiplied to two thousand. This riled throng set out for Far West, spurred on by the clamor and the clenched fists of the people staying behind. Boastful news spread that marauding Mormons in another part of the state had been stopped and killed. The truth of that story, Orson learned later, was that a company of Mormons had rallied to defend others when a mob attacked them at dawn, October 25. Dead lay three of the brethren, including David W. Patten of the Council of the Twelve.[14]

A few days after David Patten's death, a startling event involved Thomas and Orson. They were "sitting in a log cabin together in silent meditation," Orson tells, when suddenly Thomas sat upright as though reacting to a slap on the shoulder. Orson saw no other person, but he felt the hallowed presence of a being of spirit. Then he heard a man's voice implore, with deep anxiety and solicitude, "Thomas! Thomas! why have you so soon forgotten?"

Silence followed, and the color drained from Thomas's face. When he spoke, his voice low, he told Orson that David Patten—their fellow apostle who recently died a martyr's death—had visited them. Earlier, Thomas said, he and Elder Patten "had made a covenant to remain true and faithful until the end."

In spite of David's warning, Thomas remained unchanged. He and Orson concluded that they must leave Richmond. Their affidavit could result in dire personal consequences if the Mormons sought revenge. They said farewell to Marinda's relatives and to others. They mailed their letter to Thomas's sister in Far West, October 30, before departing.[15]

They traveled eastward about seventy-five miles and stopped in Howard County, Missouri, where they found shelter and anonymity. They had come far enough that the Mormons were not a burning issue. Howard County, settled for years, boasted timber, streams, mills, salt licks, and fertile hilly farms that produced, for down-river trade, much grain, hemp, and tobacco. Most of the folks had come from Kentucky and displayed kindness to strangers.[16]

Over the weeks, news of the Mormons came haphazardly and blown out of proportion. Orson and Thomas knew not what was truth. Repeated reports, however, indicated that their fears of devastation in Far West had materialized.

They would eventually learn that on October 27 their affidavit reached the Governor, Lilburn W. Boggs, who disliked the Latter-day Saints. This affidavit—signed by two of the highest officials in the Church—seemed sufficient evidence to Boggs that the festering Mormon sore should be excised from Missouri and Joseph Smith stopped in his aggressive acts. The governor, as commander-in-chief of the state's militia troops, called men to arms. In his order he repeated the cries of the mobs that the Mormons had reached "the attitude of open and avowed defiance of the laws" and "must be treated as enemies and <u>must be exterminated</u> or driven from the state."

Companies of "militia" grew in numbers and virulence, their leaders mostly previous mob members with designs against the Mormons. Like a devouring monster they clamored forth to fulfill the governor's extermination order. Several men in one Mormon settlement, Haun's Mill, were cruelly murdered. Arrest of Joseph Smith, Hyrum Smith, and Sidney Rigdon resulted in their being bound in chains. Imprisoning walls also restrained scores of other Saints. "Militiamen" devastated Far West, boasting of people killed, women ravished, homes burned, goods plundered.

November 9, guards shoved Joseph Smith and numerous other captives into an abandoned building in Richmond and kept them under guard, cramped together like animals. The next week, at a "trial," the reading of the Marsh-Hyde affidavit and other documents echoed harshly against them. Most of the men, however, were released November 24 and 28. The captors took the Prophet, Hyrum, Sidney, and three additional men to Clay County to Liberty jail. Officials locked Parley P. Pratt and four others in Richmond jail.[17]

In Howard County, Missouri, the winter of 1838-39, Orson attempted to shape a life without the Church. Marinda remained a caring figure of love. Orson found employment as a schoolteacher, an occupation he liked; and his health improved slowly. But he felt empty, and his changes in mood puzzled him. In moments of anger he wanted to scourge the Mormons. In moments of sadness he remembered the joys he had shared with them. Sometimes his perplexed mind reeled in such turmoil that he could neither work nor sleep. Frequently he found himself weeping without seeming cause, and he asked himself: "Why in God's name is it so? What have I done that I am left in this situation, or . . . suffered to fall into this dilemma?"

Orson's confusion[18] led to evaluation. When called to be apostles, he and the others had received warnings: "Beware. . . . Be always prayerful; be always watchful. . . . [T]he enemy will rage." Orson at length understood that he had failed to be sufficiently prayerful or watchful, but had let Satan encourage prideful thinking. His emptiness had come because he had listened to the wrong voices and drifted into thinking his own wisdom greater than that of the Lord's Prophet. The impact of this cold reality made his sickness of body as nothing compared with his sickness of soul. Why had he believed the words of Sidney Rigdon and others about offensive designs on Joseph Smith's part? Orson now knew that when he signed the affidavit, "I did not possess the light of the Holy Ghost."[19] Now, whether his voluntary removal from

Church fellowship would be permanent or temporary was up to him. Would he be rejected if he tried to go back?

The knife of excruciating torment turned within him at news of Far West with charred homes, butchered herds, and suffering friends. His heart split in two for the atrocities that the affidavit had obviously intensified.

Discerning that he had been in the grasp of Satan, the author of fear and anger and loss of hope, Orson prayed to the Lord as he had never prayed before. He felt overwhelmingly humble, devastatingly unworthy. In his agony the beginnings of hope glimmered. One answer to his prayers came as a vision. In it he received graphic instruction, he narrates, that "if I did not make immediate restitution to the Quorum of the Twelve, I would be cut off [from the Church and everlasting blessings] with all my posterity." More terrifying, the vision revealed, after death he would be cast among the Satanic host, a consequence of his denial, in essence, of his past immense spiritual enlightenment.[20]

For restitution Orson could bring back no homes nor lives, nor could he unwrite the affidavit. No matter how humiliating it would be to admit his guilt, he must ask forgiveness of the Prophet Joseph and of the Twelve. Orson had asked forgiveness before, but never in concerns so grave as his present crisis.

Early in February, Orson felt that he should wait no longer to begin his official entreaties to retain fellowship in the Church. Trusting in the Lord, he bundled his frail body for protection from the weather, carried a knapsack of necessities, and trudged the seventy-five westward miles to Richmond.

He managed the courage to visit the Richmond jail, where he conversed with Parley P. Pratt through the crevices in the thick walls. Yearning for the strength of Sampson, Orson wanted to pull down the timbers and free the prisoners. Parley was kind.

Orson planned to go next to the jail in Liberty and talk with the Prophet Joseph. He learned, however, that the jailers were refusing to admit anyone, because an attempt had been made a few days before, February 8, to rescue the prisoners.

A lonely figure in the winter landscape, Orson walked on toward Far West, thirty-five miles to the north, to seek forgiveness of Brigham and Heber, his senior apostles. Part of this stretch of his journey was recorded by Joseph Allen Stout: "I [Stout] was on my return [to Far West] . . . with a span of mares and wagon, . . . and on the wide prairie I saw a man walking behind me. I reined in the team to let him overtake me, and who should it be but ORSON HYDE, who had apostatized in the fuss." Brother Stout's distaste at seeing an apostate melted at the sorry sight of Orson, looking "much fatigued," his face thin. "I invited him to ride with me, which he was very thankful for."[21]

At Far West Orson cringed as he viewed burned skeletons of houses, strewn haystacks, and furniture broken to rubble. Many Saints had fled in the grim winter weather. Mob pressure had forced Brigham Young to depart February 14, a few days before Orson arrived. Hundreds of families had only tents for shelter.[22]

Orson sought Heber. The two had shared crusts of bread, relentless ridicule, stirring prayers, and spiritual manifestations. On many occasions Orson had been strengthened by this friend's compassion. At sight of Orson, Heber's eyes widened in surprise. Then his smile beckoned through his tears, and the two men embraced. At the touch of Heber's strong arms, Orson felt his penitence accepted.

In their time together Heber showed understanding as remorse poured forth, Orson unburdening the heartache of his smitten conscience. He admitted that he had brought upon himself "stain and blemish, . . . a day of affliction and darkness. I sinned against God and my brethren." Fear for the safety of Marinda and Laura had been his initial concern, he disclosed. After his long absence in England, thoughts were unbearable of having them, the only individuals on earth who cherished him as family, injured or snatched from him. Orson now recognized that his faith in the Lord's power to preserve and comfort had faltered. His lack of faith caused his light of spirituality to flicker. In the dimness he blasphemed his calling as an apostle and was dealt the displeasure of the Almighty. "I have eaten the fruits of disobedience and infidelity and drunk the bitter cup of charging God and his servant with folly; I know the fatal consequences."

The two friends talked about Orson's position as an apostle. Joseph Smith had written to Brigham and Heber, January 16, proposing that Brother Lyman Sherman replace Orson Hyde in the Council of the Twelve. Brother Sherman, at that time extremely ill, died January 27. Heber had taken this as a sign that "it was not the will of God for a man to take Brother Hyde's place."[23] Orson learned, also, that the Prophet had not ordered burning and plundering at Di-Ahman. This knowledge pleased Orson.

December 16, in a letter from Liberty jail, Joseph Smith had comforted the "scattered . . . persecuted . . . and afflicted" Saints in the Far West area and assured them that "Zion shall yet live though she seemeth to be dead," and that "the very God of peace shall be with you and make a way for your escape from the adversary of your souls." About specific apostates, including "Marsh & Hyde," the Prophet proclaimed that "in the name of the Lord Jesus Christ we deliver these characters unto the buffetings of satan."[24] No wonder December had been so dismal for Orson. He had been without any shielding of the Holy Ghost, directly inflicted with the dark intimidations of evil. He had been required to overcome this by his own exertions.

Orson asked Heber what he should do now.

"Give up your school," Heber replied, after thoughtful contemplation. "Remove your family and gather with the Church."

"But do you think the Brethren will forgive me?" Orson queried.

"Yes."

Orson felt great relief, and then he ventured, "Will you defend my case?"

Heber promised that he would. He also invited Orson to "come back and go with me to England." Orson resolved to try to be worthy of having that privilege.[25]

Orson also talked with other Saints in Far West. From them, too, he received encouragement.[26] Though the decision to come had been difficult, and the errand strenuous, he was grateful that he had made the effort.

Missouri and Illinois places significant to Orson 1838–1839.

Orson returned home and began preparations to move. He arranged to end his teaching obligation and accepted the offer of Marinda's brother-in-law, Oliver Olney, to send a team to pick up his family and their goods in April and take them to Iowa Territory. They would settle west of the Mississippi River, north from the main body of Saints settling in Quincy, Illinois, east of the Mississippi.

Arrangements in place, Orson penned an earnest letter, March 30, to Brigham Young, now president of the Quorum of the Twelve, in Quincy, Illinois, to express "the feelings and desires of my heart." He told of his bleak winter, of his longing for reunion with the Church, of his visit with Heber, and of the team coming for his family. "As to the terms upon which I can be received back into my place," he went on, "I shall not be particular: for to live in this way I cannot: and to join any other Society, I have no more disposition than to eat when I am full."

He also told of his immediate situation: "There is a fine chance for me in a wholesale Grocery here, can get good wages and am now in the owner's employ until the team comes. Had I better remain here any [length of] time in order [to earn money] to fit myself for a mission, or a campaign, or had I better leave as soon as the team comes for my family. . . ?"

Orson continued his letter by writing of the pain of repentance: "The chastening hand of the Lord has done for me that which nothing else would, I think. If the church will accept me as a minister, or a soldier, or a door-keeper, they can have me." He felt that the cleansing purges of the Lord had made him a new person, and he stated, "I have literally died and been raised from the dead since I was last at Far West. . . .

"Brigham, will you forgive me? Will the church forgive me? If so, God will forgive me.

"Please write me immediately on rec't of this and tell me all you think to be for my good. Direct to New Franklin, Howard County, Mo."

His heart overflowing with love for the Saints and with the sweet peace that true repentance brings, Orson continued, "Whatever the church may decide upon respecting my case, they may rest assured that the following are the real wishes of my heart,

I truly wish Mount Zion well
What e're becomes of me.

"With a fresh remembrance of former times, and former scenes," Orson concluded his letter, "with feelings of the tenderest kind toward you, and all with whom you are connected, I subscribe myself your younger brother in a distant land feeding swine." Orson mailed his letter April 3.[27]

Thomas Marsh remained inflexible. Many years passed before he came back to the Church, a changed man. In his public confession, he stated that he had eventually figured out that "my apostasy began" when "I became jealous of the Prophet, and then I . . . spent all my time in looking for the evil. . . . [The] Devil began to lead me . . . [in] anger, jealousy, and wrath. . . ; and the Spirit of the Lord being gone, . . . I was blinded. . . . I got mad, and I wanted everybody else to be mad."[28] Orson's months of observing Thomas's unhappy anger strengthened his own determination to accept instructions of his superiors in God's kingdom.

In Iowa, the Hydes soon settled across the river from Quincy. Here Orson could keep informed of developments in his behalf. He felt encouraged about his quest for fellowship when he learned, with gratitude, that at a conference, March 17, Brigham Young had withheld his name from consideration when several other apostates, including Thomas B. Marsh, had been officially excommunicated. This occurred before Orson wrote his letter to Brigham.

The joyous news came that Brothers Joseph, Hyrum, and Sidney, free from prison, arrived in Quincy on April 22. They held a general conference May 4, a time of happy reunion for the Saints from a wide area. In Illinois, ten thousand refugees from Missouri had been befriended with food and shelter and space by civil authorities and residents.

A happy event of the conference, for Orson, was the result of his name being presented. Heber recorded what transpired: "I [Heber] had previously informed brother Hyrum Smith of Orson Hyde's feelings of repentance and desire to return to [full fellowship in] the Church. Hyrum partook of the Spirit, and when Joseph presented the name of Orson Hyde . . . , Hyrum and I plead for him according to the Spirit that was in us; Joseph then remarked, 'If my brother Hyrum and Heber C. Kimball will defend Orson Hyde, I will withdraw my motion [to release him from his position].'"

The Saints voted that Orson "be allowed the privilege of appearing personally before the next general conference of the Church, to give an account of [his] conduct; and that in the meantime [he] be suspended from exercising the functions of [his] office."

This decision not to excommunicate him was most lenient, Orson knew, and later he wrote of it with gratitude, "I lost not my standing in the church, . . . yet not because I was worthy to retain it, but because God and his servants were merciful. Everlasting thanks to God, and . . . his servants . . . [for] encouragement and comfort in the hour of my greatest sorrow."[29]

Orson's health had improved, but he remained thin. Now physical labor, with its cleansing power, answered his need to sustain his family and to obtain means to gather with the Saints. "I bought me a good ax," he says, "and went to chopping cord wood and put up my 2 cords per day [two cords being a stack four feet high and eight feet square]."

He saved a portion of his earnings for a twofold purpose. First, he knew the impossibility of his personally making restitution for the heartache and losses that the affidavit had caused. As a token of his deep remorse, and to show sacrifice on his part (his strenuous labor and his donation), he applied the rules for forgiveness given to ancient Israel by retaining "some money and goods of the hard earnings of my own hands [to give to the Church] as a sin offering." Second, he felt that he should symbolically "prove . . . that conscience and principle and not want have induced [my] return."

In May, Saints began moving to the area of the small town of Commerce, on a bend of the Mississippi River about fifty miles north of Quincy. Here the Church acquired huge tracts of land from local residents. Some was improved, but generally it lay uncultivated and swampy. This became Church headquarters.[30]

An overwhelming requirement remained in Orson's quest for forgiveness of the Saints. He must speak with Joseph Smith. Apprehensive as to how the Prophet would receive him, Orson nevertheless made his way to Commerce to present his sin offering. Meeting former friends usually at first proved awkward, after his problems and long absence, and he felt extremely humble about meeting Joseph Smith. Blunders and inconsistencies on Orson's part had been forgiven by the Prophet many times already. Would he now—after the awful breach of trust he had committed—be received with a patient chastisement or an overflowing warmth? For the warmth Orson hardly dared hope. He felt unworthy of warmth.

Hesitantly Orson opened the Smith gate. He had barely stepped into the yard when a door opened. Brother Joseph came running to meet him, his arms out in welcome.

"O Brother Hyde, how glad I am to see you!" the Prophet exclaimed, as he wrapped his arms around Orson's neck. Both men "wept like children."

Their tears at length abated. Brother Joseph said that he came out of the door so quickly when Orson had hardly opened the gate because the Lord had told him of Orson's approach, and he had been watching out the window.[31] This generous forgiveness from the Prophet Joseph soothed balm to Orson's wounds.

In June, Orson gratefully received an invitation to a Council of the Twelve meeting in Montrose, Iowa, where Brigham Young lived. Montrose lay directly across the river from Commerce. Wilford Woodruff, one of the new apostles, wrote of the occasion in his journal: "June 25 I spent the day in Montrose with the Twelve, there being six of the quorum present. Orson Hyde was one of the number, and a more humble and penitent man I never saw. . . . Brother Hyde for several months past has had a deep sense of his high-handed wickedness, and the horrors of hell [have] rolled over his soul even to the wasting of his flesh; and he has now humbled himself in the dust, desiring to return to the Church."

The next day, in Commerce, members of the Twelve discussed Orson's situation with Sidney Rigdon and Hyrum Smith of the First Presidency. After the discussion, Orson received invitation to another meeting the following day. Wilford Woodruff recorded of this meeting: "June 27th I spent the day in Commerce in Council with the Presidency and Twelve. We had an interesting day. Joseph was president of the Council. Brother Orson Hyde was restored to the Church and the Quorum of the Twelve in full fellowship by a full vote of the Council, after making an humble confession and acknowledgment of his sins, &c."

In a July 2 meeting the Prophet Joseph instructed the Twelve about their mission to England, to which the Lord had previously called them. Orson would be unable to leave before the Saints voted on his status at the next general conference in October.

July 7, the Sabbath meetings in Commerce convened in the open air, as usual. Most of the Twelve delivered farewell addresses. Upon request, Orson also spoke to the large gathering as preparation for the Saints to accept him back among them. With vividly painful recollection of the ease of beginning to walk down wrong paths, he "alluded to his own late fall," the minutes of the meeting recount, "[and] exhorted all [of his listeners] to perseverance in the things of God." He "bore testimony to his knowledge of the truth, and the misery of falling from it." He declared his love and gratitude to the Saints for their kindness to him and "expressed himself one with his brethren."[32]

Orson returned to Iowa to wait until he could act officially in his apostleship. Much afterward, John Taylor of the Twelve compared Orson's time of trial with that of Peter and his denial of the Savior. "Peter went out and wept bitterly," Elder Taylor commented. "And so did Brother Hyde weep bitterly. He . . . told me [years later] that he would give his life over and over again, if it were possible, to wipe out the recollection of that act."[33]

. . . *toward Jerusalem*. . . . *(1839–1841)*

> *And the word of the Lord came unto me, saying,*
> *Son of man, set thy face toward Jerusalem.*
> —Ezekiel 21:1-2

ORSON'S joy abounded when in the first session of the fall general confer-ence—in Commerce, Illinois, October 5, 1839—the congregation voted that he now "stand in his former office." After a year under a shadow, he could again help promote the gospel of Jesus Christ! This past summer had been difficult. Orson had yearned to function with the Saints. Also, he and his family suf-fered the same devastating fevers and ague (chills) that plagued multitudes of other settlers on both sides of the Mississippi, in exhausting heat, as rains poured and swamps steamed.[1]

The apostles were among the stricken Saints, but in late summer, to ful-fill the mission in England assigned them by the Lord, seven of them left at different times amid severe hardships: Wilford Woodruff, John Taylor, Parley and Orson Pratt, Brigham Young, Heber C. Kimball, and George A. Smith. John E. Page had some excuse for being unable to yet leave. William Smith had been under a cloud the same as Orson Hyde, so he also tarried.[2] Willard Richards, in England, would be ordained when the other apostles arrived. A twelfth apostle remained to be chosen.

In spite of their ill health, Orson and Marinda wanted to move from Iowa Territory across the river to Commerce to renew a closeness with the Saints. October 29 a friend took them and their few belongings to the old two-story log home of Joseph Smith, in the south part of Commerce, to inquire where they might seek lodging. Earlier the same day, they learned, the Prophet and several companions had left for Washington to present before the United States Congress the petitions of the Saints asking redress for their property losses in Missouri. Brother Joseph's wife Emma looked weary, but her welcoming smile conveyed concern for them. She saw that they suffered from "ravaging disease" and that Marinda expected a baby. She invited them to remain with her, even though she was already caring for her severely ill children and a second needy family. The Hydes had not expected such kind-ness. In Commerce, all around the "flat" near the river, and scattered over the hillside sloping up to the east, families crowded into all kinds of shelters: tents, wagons, and cabins.[3]

During the next two weeks Orson's health improved rapidly, and November 14 he left for Philadelphia, eleven hundred miles away, to preach and to gather funds. Sidney Rigdon had written *An Appeal to the American People*, giving details of the Mormon persecutions, and he requested that Orson, while en route to Philadelphia, assist Brother George W. Robinson in getting it printed in Cincinnati, Ohio. Sidney wrote this booklet to convince sympathetic people to donate to the destitute Saints. Orson caught up with Brother Robinson in Springfield, Illinois. As the two traveled and preached, they appealed for money to pay for the printing.

Walking the prairie of western Indiana, in violent storms of wind, snow, rain, and hail, brought the ague upon Orson again and forced him to stay in the homes of Church members for a few weeks. Brother Robinson continued on to Cincinnati and engaged the printing. Orson preached as much as he could and received limited contributions.

"About the 6th of January [1840]," he narrates, "I started for Cincinnati to get the books and carry them on eastward to distribute them and raise all the funds I could for the church, but when I arrived there, the books were not done, and would not be short of about ten days. At this time my health became so poor through exposure, etc., that I abandoned the idea of going any farther east at that time; but concluded to leave the books and return directly home, and take some little time to recruit my health; and also, till the cold weather was past, and then try it again."[4]

Orson felt overjoyed to be home and to hold in his arms the tiny blanketed bundle that he described as a "little girl." Emily Matilda had been born December 13.

Orson's family stayed for a short time with Heber's wife, Vilate, in her fourteen-by-sixteen-foot log cabin up beyond the bluff of the hill. Vilate wrote a letter, February 2, 1840, to Heber in New York City. He was still gathering funds to cross the ocean. She gave Orson space at the end, and he told Heber about being "at your house on a 'sort' of a visit," and that he had arranged "to live at the Cosin place." Yearning to join his Quorum, he added, "It is my calculation to start for England immediately after the April conference this spring 'if the Lord will,' and I hope to have the pleasure of crossing the ocean . . . with yourself and some others of the 12. . . . [M]y anxiety to sound the gospel trump is very great."

In the small rented Cosin cabin, Orson and his family still suffered with the ague. Somehow Orson and Marinda managed to care for each other and their daughters, but Orson anguished at seeing his frail little Laura and Emily shiver and chill even when he held them close to him wrapped in blankets. He despaired for the lives of all in his household.[5]

One night in early March he and Marinda retired to bed as usual at about nine o'clock. Marinda fell into exhausted sleep, but Orson remained wakeful, contemplative. Did the Lord have an assignment for him? In the darkness, staring at the close log walls, he saw only deep shadows. Would he be physically able to complete an assignment?

Suddenly the darkness dispersed into bursting clouds of light, and Orson beheld scenery come into view. Transfixed, he watched a pageant of color and detail in a series of fascinating vistas of buildings and streets, diverse in character. Revelation told him that he viewed specific cities, among them London, Amsterdam, Constantinople, and Jerusalem.

Jerusalem! Eight years had passed since the Prophet Joseph pronounced that he would "in due time" go to Jerusalem. Now, while viewing the breathtaking incredible panorama, Orson heard the voice of the Spirit say, "Here are many of the children of Abraham whom I will gather to the land that I gave to their fathers; and here also is the field of your labors." Orson also heard: "Take ... proper credentials from my people, your brethren; and also from the Governor of your State, with the seal of authority thereon, and go ye forth to the cities which have been shown unto you." At last Orson was going to Jerusalem!

The time had come, the voice said, for the beginnings of the fulfillment of the prophecies about scattered Israel. Orson, with the authority bestowed upon him as an apostle and a prophet of the Lord Jesus Christ, should declare the words of Jeremiah unto Judah: "Blow ye the trumpet in the land: cry, gather together, and say, Assemble yourselves, and let us go into the defenced cities. Set the standard toward Zion: retire, stay not: for I will bring evil from the north, and a great destruction. The lion is come up from his thicket, and the destroyer of the Gentiles is on his way; he is gone forth from his place to make thy land desolate; and thy cities shall be laid waste, without an inhabitant [Jeremiah 4:5-6]."

And then Orson received authority from the Lord to fulfill the words of Isaiah: "Speak ye comfortably to Jerusalem, and cry unto her, that her warfare is accomplished, that her iniquity is pardoned: for she hath received of the Lord's hand double for all her sins" (Isaiah 40:2).[6] According to this decree the land was ready to be dedicated with priesthood authority for the "gathering." Apostolic priesthood power provides a significant role in the destinies of people and nations. The prophet Amos declared, "Surely the Lord God will do nothing, but he revealeth his secret unto his servants the prophets" (Amos 3:7). Joseph Smith had told the Twelve that their office held "the keys ... to unlock the door of the Kingdom of heaven unto all nations." For the Holy Land to receive her prophesied blessings an apostle must unlock the door, must give her the spiritual strength to overcome the adversary's grasp.[7]

About the journey, too, Orson received specific charge from the Lord: "Let your warning voice be heard among the gentiles as you pass; and call ye upon them in my name for aid, and for assistance. With you, it mattereth not whether it [the assistance] be little or much; but to me it belongeth, to show favor unto him who showeth favor unto you. Murmur not, therefore, neither be ye sorrowful, that the people are slow to hear your petition; but do as has been told you, and all things shall work together for your good, if you are humble and keep my commandments; for it must needs be that all men be left without excuse, that a righteous retribution may be awarded to all." The vision showed Orson the specific tasks that he should perform during this unprecedented mission, but he was told to keep many of the details to himself until their fulfillment in Jerusalem.

The phenomenal presentation closed, and the backdrop of Orson's world became again the night. With intermingled amazement, resolution, and humility, he felt overwhelmed. The thrilling revelation had lasted six hours. How astounding that Marinda, sleeping beside him, remained unstirred.

Dawn brought form to shadows, and Marinda awoke. Orson related to her, in wonderment, the extraordinary vision, and her hazel eyes grew wide. He continued to marvel, as did she, as he answered her questions. At length he asked, "Can you willingly let me go?" She and he had talked of this mission before, and her smile answered "yes." Her words answered "yes" also, but he knew, and she knew, that challenges lay ahead for both of them.[8]

To Joseph Smith—who had returned from Washington March 4, with no success in getting compensation for the Saints—Orson related details of the glorious things he had seen and heard. The Prophet reacted as exuberantly as had Orson. He asked Orson to tell his experience to the Saints in general conference.

Thus, April 6, 1840, in the grove on the bluff, Orson spoke to the Saints. He felt weak and looked like a skeleton, with his suit fitting loosely after his struggle with the ague, but spiritual energy strengthened him. He told the amazed congregation, seated on benches before him, of his resplendent vision. In far-away Jerusalem, as required of the Lord of an apostle, he would offer a prayer dedicating the land for the return of scattered Israel. The Prophet proposed the motion that "Elder Orson Hyde proceed on his mission to the Jews." The people, imaginations afire, voted assent.

The next speaker, Apostle John E. Page, continued the soul-stirring theme of the gathering of the Jews. Three afternoons later, during the last session of conference, the Prophet Joseph announced that after Elder Page talked with such interest about Elder Hyde's visit to the Holy Land, "I felt an impression that it would be well for Elder John E. Page to accompany Elder Hyde on his mission." The congregation ratified this proposal.[9]

Joseph Smith dictated to his clerk the letter of recommendation that the Lord had requested for Orson:

> . . . the constituted authorities of the Church of Jesus Christ of Latter Day Saints, . . . from the signs of the times, and from declarations contained in the oracles of God, . . . are forced to come to this conclusion [that the] Jewish nation have been scattered abroad among the

Gentiles for a long period; and in our estimation, the time of the commencement of their return to the Holy land has already arrived.

As this scattered and persecuted people are set among the Gentiles as a sign unto them of the second coming of the Messiah, . . . we have, by the counsel of the Holy Spirit, appointed Elder Orson Hyde, the bearer of these presents, a faithful and worthy minister of Jesus Christ, to be our agent and representative in foreign lands, to . . . converse with the priests, rulers and Elders of the Jews, . . . obtain . . . information [about the Jews] . . . , and communicate the same. . . .

As Mr. Hyde has willingly and cheerfully accepted the appointment to become our servant, and the servant of the public in distant and foreign countries for Christ's sake, we do confidently recommend him to all religious and Christian people, and to gentlemen and ladies making no profession, as a worthy member of society, possessing much zeal to promote the happiness of mankind, fully believing that they will be forward to render him all the pecuniary aid he needs to accomplish this laborious and hazardous mission for the general good of the human family. . . .

Orson agonized because he was leaving his own family ill and destitute in a small borrowed cabin. Rather than glass in the windows, greased paper admitted a little light and provided meager protection against cold. Marinda, recovering from the ague, assured her husband that she would stretch the cornmeal and the few other groceries as far as she could. When she felt better she could do knitting and sewing for others and probably even teach a few students. Three year old Laura already helped with little Emily. With the Lord's assistance she and the children would manage. With the Lord's assistance Orson too would manage. He was able to relinquish Marinda from their farewell embrace only because he knew he was leaving at the bidding of Almighty God.[10]

Feeling weary, older than his thirty-five years, Orson left Nauvoo (the chosen name of the expanded Commerce), the morning of April 15, with "not the first dollar, neither two coats nor a cane nor an umbrella."[11] By nightfall he arrived in Lima, thirty miles to the south. Elder Page joined him the next day, and the next a Church member gave them a ride twenty miles farther south to Quincy. For a zealous couple of weeks here, they held many meetings and received some ridicule, but they baptized twenty-three people and gained funds.

They also became better acquainted. Forty-one years old, John had been baptized in 1833, had lived in Kirtland, Ohio, and had served two rewarding missions in Canada. In the fall of 1838 he brought a company of converts from Canada to Far West, Missouri. He was chosen an apostle December 19, 1838, but the pleasure of his ordination had been offset by the mob-inflicted sufferings that caused the deaths of his wife and two children. With the remainder of his children he settled in Warsaw, about twenty miles south of Nauvoo.

Eager for harmony in their mission, Orson and John covenanted "that if we are insulted, or imposed upon we will stand by each other even unto death, that we will not separate unless to go a few miles to preach a sermon, and that all monies shall go into one purse." They calculated their expenses to and from Jerusalem at more than a thousand dollars apiece. Gleaning would be sparse in England, so they planned to raise their funds in America. This would probably require a year or two of traveling about.

"The Lord is truly with us, and enables us to speak with a power that finds way to the hearts of the people," Orson wrote April 28 to the Nauvoo brethren. He added that the "people have treated us kindly, and have been very attentive to hear the word."[12]

In Quincy they obtained the further credentials Orson's vision had instructed:

> QUINCY, Illinois, April 30th, 1840.
> Having been informed that the Rev's. Orson Hyde and John E. Page, elders in the church denominated Latter Day Saints, are about to depart on their mission to Europe—and having heard the former gentleman preach—and having been made acquainted to some extent with the characters of both, it affords me pleasure to say, that I was much pleased with the sermon delivered by Mr. Hyde; and the reputation of both gentlemen for talents and christian-like deportment, so far as I have been made acquainted, are unexceptionable; and as such, believe them to be entitled to the respect and kind treatment of all.
> (Signed.)   THOMAS CARLIN,
> Governor of Illinois.

From Columbus, Illinois, the next day, May 1, Orson and John wrote a letter to the Prophet Joseph and confided, "The mission upon which we are sent swells greater and greater. As there is a great work to be done in Germany, as manifested to us by the Spirit, the following plan has been suggested to us; viz., to write a set of lectures upon the faith and doctrine of our Church . . . ; and get the same translated into German, . . . publish it when we arrive in Germany, and scatter it through the German empire. Is this correct?

". . . we do not wish to step beyond our limits . . . ," the letter continued, "by taking liberties that are not ours. . . . The fact is, we did not begin to see the greatness of our mission before we left home." The two missionaries asked the Prophet to "write to us at Cincinnati."

They accepted the offer of a ride for three hundred eastward miles, with "the privilege to stop and preach by the way." This took six weeks, over the spring green prairies of Illinois, via Jacksonville and Springfield; and part of Indiana, via Pleasant Garden and Indianapolis. Along the way they often stayed with Church members. Elder Page reported this hospitality to the Nauvoo Saints and added, "Elder Hyde is truly a humble servant of the Lord, and a very agreeable companion in the ministry. Our hearts are one, our faith is one, and the strongholds of Satan quake before us."

Funds accumulated only slowly, however, and in mid June the missionaries decided to try preaching in separate towns. Indeed, during a week in the Indianapolis area they gained contributions faster. They traveled on east a hundred miles and before the end of June arrived in Dayton, Ohio. They preached here for only a few days, feeling "hurried to Cincinnati," fifty-two miles to the south. En route to Cincinnati they walked different roads and preached in towns along the way.[13] This ended the part of their original covenant that they would travel together.

In Franklin, Ohio, July 7, Orson reported to the Prophet Joseph what he had learned about the Jews: "The Jews are gathering;" he said, "and have issued orders, or a circular, and universal proclamation for their brethren, in all the world, to return to Palestine, for the land is ready for their reception. 'But there is none to guide her among all the sons whom she hath brought up. . . .' —See Isaiah 51:18. . . . As Jerusalem has no sons to take her by the hand and lead her among all the number whom she hath brought forth, Bro. Page and myself feel that we ought to hurry along and take her by the hand; for we are her sons but the Gentiles have brought us up.

"I am informed," Orson continued in his report, "that both England and Rusia, have extended protection to the Jews in Palestine; and proffer to aid them in their return." Paraphrasing Isaiah 49:23, Orson added, "Let Kings become nursing fathers, and Victoria a nursing mother; and I will say, roll on thy righteous cause, thou King of saints."

For centuries zealous Jews had tried to accomplish the movement of multitudes back to their homeland to fulfill the prophecies they knew so well. Efforts met only moderate success. The added power of dedication of the land by apostolic authority would diminish the strength of Satan to hinder the gathering.[14]

Orson arrived in Cincinnati before Elder Page and was pleased that the hoped-for letter from Joseph Smith waited. He broke the wax seal eagerly, unfolded the paper, and read thrilling words penned by the Prophet May 14:

> I am happy. . . that your mission swells "larger and larger". . . . Although it appears great at present, yet you have but just begun to realize the greatness, the extent and glory of the same. If there is anything calculated to . . . arouse [the Saints] to enterprise and exertion, surely it is the great and precious promises made by our heavenly Father to the children of Abraham; and those engaged in seeking the outcasts of Israel,

and the dispersed of Judah, cannot fail to enjoy the Spirit of the Lord and have the choicest blessings of Heaven rest upon them in copious effusions.

Brethren, you are in the pathway to eternal fame, and immortal glory; and inasmuch as you feel interested for the covenant people of the Lord, the God of their fathers shall bless you. Do not be discouraged on account of the greatness of the work; only be humble and faithful. . . .

In answer to your inquiries respecting . . . translation and publication . . . I entirely approve of the same. . . .

Orson remained in Cincinnati for six generally agreeable weeks, with only minor opposition. The Saints felt blessed to have "our beloved brother Orson Hyde," "a mighty man of God," among them, one member reported to Church leaders in Nauvoo. The same member added, "Bro. Hyde has a great many calls to converse with the people in different parts of the city which he attends with pleasure." Orson also felt pleased with the response of the public to Sidney Rigdon's book, *An Appeal to the American People*, that had been printed in January. The book proved to be a good fund-raising tool, and Orson invested in the reprinting of two thousand copies. This required a fair portion of the money that he and John had collected. The sale of books should quickly renew the funds and add more.

In order to reach people faster, in late August the missionaries decided to separate. Church members begged Elder Hyde to remain in the Cincinnati area, just as listeners to his powerful sermons had begged him to tarry in other parts of Ohio, but he felt compelled to hasten on. He would take books east to sell in Philadelphia. John would follow on the next available boat. At parting, Elder Page had many books and $23.31 in cash. Elder Hyde had many books and funds enough to pay his fare to Philadelphia. Elder Page "stood on the levee," Orson tells, "and witnessed my departure on the Steamer which was about to ascend the beautiful 'Ohio.' As I stood upon the deck, he waved his handkerchief from the shore in token of 'adieu.' I immediately went below in tears with the impression that he would not join me again during this mission."[15]

Orson's eight-hundred-mile journey took three weeks, by river steamer, stagecoaches, and more steamboats. In mid September, Philadelphia Church members welcomed him. Orson felt "at home" in Philadelphia, with its busy docks along the Delaware River, stately public buildings, numerous hotels, and the housewives who emerged each morning from hundreds of rows of homes and whitewashed their steps, reminding Orson of far-away Preston, England.

Philadelphia became the center of Orson's popular and successful activities that extended into New Jersey, across the Delaware River. He preached sermons, sold books, took derisions in stride, accepted donations, and baptized converts. The weeks passed without any communication from Elder Page. A conference Orson scheduled for October 17 and 18 convened an enthusiastic congregation. More weeks passed, and Orson continued to speak and baptize, unable to fill all the requests for his time.[16] Then the day came that he had to travel on to New York City to preside over a conference he had scheduled.

The conference in New York City, December 4, renewed acquaintances and energies, and Orson had a new base for his efforts. In January, 1841, he accepted invitations to preach in New Haven County, Connecticut, seventy-five miles northeast. This was the area of his boyhood, and he felt grateful that the Lord now allowed him to visit it.

In Oxford, Connecticut, Orson's heart warmed with nostalgia. In the center of the village the Episcopal Church, with its square tower, still dominated the scene. But the western farm district on and around Good Hill held the greatest interest. Here, in a modest home, his mother had heard his first cry and rejoiced that her seventh son seemed healthy. As he walked the old roads, he saw again, reposed in winter quiet, the hilly farms and the rock walls that he remembered.

Humphreysville (later Seymour) brought more memories. On a bend of Pearl Street, south of Bladen's Brook, his father rented a home and farm before Orson was six years old. Here he had spent carefree times with his brothers and sisters until their mother died when he was seven.[17]

In late January, back in New York City, Orson read the January 15 issue of Nauvoo's *Times and Seasons*. He was elated to learn that Nauvoo's population had increased to three thousand, that the city had been incorporated, and that construction had begun on a Temple of the Lord. Then, unexpectedly, he saw his own name:

> Elders Orson Hyde and John E. Page are informed, that the Lord is not well pleased with them in consequence of delaying their mission, (Elder John E. Page in particular,) and they are requested by the First Presidency to hasten their journey towards their destination.

Stunned, Orson stared at the paper in his hand. He thought he had been diligent, and he had baptized many. Obviously, though he had been diligent in preaching, he should be more diligent in traveling.

He lacked the full amount of money he had hoped to obtain before leaving America, but he concluded to trust in the Lord, as his vision had instructed, and as the words in front of him enjoined. Because *the Lord* wanted him to hasten on, the remaining funds would apparently be obtained somehow on the way. Orson replaced his threadbare clothes with new ones, purchased supplies for the ocean voyage, secured passage on the next available ship, and wrote a letter to Joseph Smith asking if he should wait in England for Elder Page.[18]

And where was Elder Page? He remained in Ohio. After he and Orson separated in Cincinnati, he later told, he "returned to Dayton, and Milton, and sold books, with the intention of following Elder Hyde as soon as practicable; but [I] stayed a day or two too long, and the river closed by the frost, from one to two weeks earlier than usual."

Not knowing even if Apostle Page still lived, Orson sensed ever stronger that his own destiny was to travel a third of the way around the world with his only abiding companion the Holy Spirit.[19]

Before leaving New York City, Orson received an extraordinary gift. A man from Philadelphia found him, handed him a purse, and said the gift had been sent by an anonymous stranger. The stranger had heard Elder Hyde preach and was "[i]mpressed by [his] intense earnestness . . . and his determination to fulfill the mission assigned to him in spite of lack of money." The donor made one request, that the Mormon apostle pray for him on the Mount of Olives. Orson opened the purse, and gold pieces glittered. In disbelief and overwhelming gratitude he picked up the coins one by one, counting. The purse contained $200, a fortune. This brought Orson's cash, after expenses so far, to $500. This would last far into his remaining journey.

As long as Orson lived he supposed that the gold came to him from a wealthy Philadelphia Jew. After Orson's death the truth became known to his family. The stranger, Joseph Ellison Beck, a thirty year old farmer of moderate means, lived in Freehold Township, New Jersey, across the river from Philadelphia. Orson's preaching touched his heart, and he donated his savings.[20]

February 13, 1841, on the ship *United States*, "We left the [New York] dock with the prayers and blessings of [a crowd of] Saints," Orson tells. George J. Adams of New York City accompanied him. As the shore receded from view, Orson reflected: "I have friends at home who would never let me want for the comforts of this life, if I would but remain with them. I have also, a good and kind-hearted wife, and two lovely little girls, whose last embraces will long be remembered. . . . My eldest [daughter], . . . three years of age, would frequently come to me, a few days before I left, and put her arms around my neck, and say, 'O my pa, don't go away and leave your little daughter, and little sister and Ma; but stay at home with us, for I will be a good girl.'"

Orson's pondering continued, that he would "not see them again for years, if ever." He might suffer "abuses, slanders, and perhaps violence . . . in distant nations." So what reason could he give to others for leaving his native land, he asked himself, and then he exulted: "The vision of the Lord, with floods of light and glory burst upon me; and the voice of the Most High bade me arise and go, trusting in him. . . . [K]nowing that the Lord has spoken to me, I am not only willing to go to Jerusalem, but to die there if necessary. Paul once said, 'behold I go bound in spirit to Jerusalem not knowing the things that befall me there' [Acts 20:22]; and so say I."

Strong winds caused high waves, but moved the ship along smartly, and passage to Liverpool took only eighteen days. Orson arrived March 3, in time to share a few weeks assisting others of the Twelve in their mission before their planned April departure for home. He found Elders John Taylor and Willard Richards residing in Liverpool, and the three experienced a jubilant reunion. Orson also enjoyed being with past local acquaintances and had the added pleasure of meeting new converts. After two days he and Brother Adams journeyed on to Preston. Again Orson's return among the Saints brought great rejoicing.

March saw Orson so busy speaking and traveling among villages, that he "hardly [had] time to eat or sleep." In late March, Heber C. Kimball arrived in Preston from London and shared Orson's speaking and visiting schedule. What a thrill Orson felt walking again with tall and confident Heber along familiar city streets.[21]

The last day of March, preparatory for April Conference, Orson, Heber, and Brother Adams traveled to Manchester, now Church headquarters in England and about thirty miles southeast of Preston. Manchester's many rivers, canals, and bridges wove among its gigantic mills, factories, and warehouses related to cotton manufacture. It was a huge city compared with Preston, was even a good deal larger than Liverpool. Visiting Parley P. Pratt and his wife Mary Ann brought more gladness to Orson. Parley had been assigned to an indefinite stay in England as Church printer and editor of the newly established *Millennial Star*.[22]

Other apostles arrived for Conference from various parts of England, and Orson's joy increased with each one he greeted. He had been separated from some of them for nearly four years. April 2, all nine of the Twelve in England had arrived in Manchester, and Brigham Young, president of the Quorum, conducted a Council meeting in the home of a Church member. Had Orson's arms been able to stretch to match his jubilation he would have embraced eight men at once, for "if we were angels sent down from heaven," he said, "we could hardly love one another more." Like in past times, Orson served as clerk, and his elation spilled over into the minutes: "To meet once more in council, after a long separation, and having passed through many sore and grievous trials, . . . caused our hearts to swell with gratitude to God for his providential care over us."

Brigham Young had developed into a truly inspiring leader. Everything about him—his full even features, his deep-set gray steady eyes, his look of wise honesty—affirmed that he gave his best efforts to the Lord's work and expected the best of everyone else. All of the Twelve had matured, had grown more sure of themselves.

The Twelve had molded the Church in England into a dynamic organization. Since their arrival a year earlier, 1840, they had been building upon the foundation that Heber and Orson left in 1838 and that had been kept alive by others. Brigham summarized later that "through the mercy of God we . . . established Churches in almost every noted town and city in the kingdom of Great Britain, baptized between seven and eight thousand, printed 5,000 Books of Mormon, 3,000 Hymn Books, 2,500 volumes of the *Millennial Star*, and 50,000 tracts, and emigrated to Zion 1,000 souls."[23]

The April 6 conference proved spiritually refreshing, and harmony prevailed again the next day in a Council meeting of the Twelve. Seven would be returning to the United States, Parley would remain in Manchester as Church leader and printer, and Orson would proceed to Jerusalem. Unitedly Orson's brethren laid their hands on his head and invoked the blessings of Heaven upon his undertaking.

Orson resumed his energetic pace, trying to respond to the many requests for his time. In Manchester April 17, no letter of instructions having arrived from the Prophet Joseph, Orson wrote to him that "if I hear nothing from you to the contrary, I shall if the Lord will, hasten on as fast as possible. . . . I do not feel at all disheartened at the prospect of going alone. I fully believe that the Lord will open my way before me." In many places Orson spoke about his mission and with gratitude received small coins, gladly sacrificed by people who had little for themselves, but desired to assist the Lord's work.[24] During all of his activities he baptized people who requested membership in the Church.

May 4, Orson left Manchester for London, 183 miles to the southeast. In the vast metropolis he tarried about a week and presided at the May 16 conference of the Saints. George Adams, who had crossed the ocean with Orson, also attended. Since the April conference he had been serving as a missionary in Bedford, fifty miles northwest of London. Orson accompanied Brother Adams on his return, intending to stay with him for two or three weeks to finish writing the book to publish in Germany. Orson felt that he should finish the book where Saints would give him bed and board. Once he started through strange lands he needed to travel as fast as possible so that his funds would last to cover expenses. In June Orson returned to London, the thick manuscript of his book finished and tucked into his baggage.[25]

In London he tried to fulfill the Lord's instruction that he "converse with the priests, rulers and Elders of the Jews." Orson composed "a very polite note . . . requesting the indulgence of a personal interview" with the "Rev. Dr. Solomon Hirschell, Pres't Rabbi of the Hebrew society in England." In reply he received regrets that the visit could not be granted because Dr. Hirschell had broken his leg in a serious accident.

Disappointed, Orson wrote again to the rabbi, expressed his sorrow about the accident, and explained that he had desired to discuss "those things pertaining to your nation, with which my mind is deeply affected." Prevented from presenting his thoughts in person, he now wrote them, commenting that "the writings of the Jewish prophets have won my affections; and the scattered and oppressed condition of that people, has enlisted the finest sympathies of my heart." Unable, "by any existing document or record, to identify [myself] with your nation," Orson said that he nevertheless felt a kinship and trusted that the rabbi would accept the words of the Lord to Hosea the prophet that in the last days "I [the Lord] will say to them which were not my people, Thou art my people" (Hosea 2:23).

Then, "to show that divine appointment is claimed as the main-spring that has sent me forth," Orson detailed the blessing wherein Joseph Smith pronounced the remarkable words, "In due time, thou shalt go to Jerusalem, the land of thy fathers, and be a watchman unto the house of Israel." Orson continued by relating his vision about visiting Jerusalem.

Orson's prophetic view of the glorious destiny of the Children of the Covenant gave his further words to the rabbi a ring of poetic majesty:

> When I look at the condition of your fathers in the days of David and Solomon, and contrast that with the present condition of their descendants, I am led to exclaim, "How are the mighty fallen!" Then they possessed a kingdom—a land flowing with milk and honey. . . . But now, no kingdom—no country. . . .
>
> . . . [T]he time has arrived when the day-star of your freedom already begins to dispel the dark and gloomy clouds which have separated you from the favor of your God. Ere long it will be said to you: "Arise, shine, for thy light has come, and the glory of the Lord has risen upon thee" [Isaiah 60:1]. . . .

"Now, therefore, O ye children of the covenant!" Orson lovingly pled with the whole house of Israel at the end of his letter,

> Repent of all your backslidings, and begin, as in days of old, to turn to the Lord your God. Arise! Arise! and go out from among the Gentiles; for destruction is coming from the north to lay their cities waste. Jerusalem is thy home. There the God of Abraham will deliver thee. (See Joel 2,32) There the bending heavens shall reveal thy long-looked-for Messiah in fleecy clouds of light and glory, to execute vengeance upon thine enemies; and lead thee and thy brethren of the ten tribes to sure conquest, and certain victory. Then shall thrones be cast down, and the kingdoms of this world become the kingdoms of our God. . . .[26]

A hundred years later the dire warning words of the Lord's prophet, Orson Hyde, would be fulfilled in what would become known as "the holocaust." Had the Jews, particularly in Germany, heeded the 1841 warning they would have fled the Gentile cities north of Jerusalem and averted appalling extermination.

June 15, almost ready to leave London and resume his journey to the Holy Land, Orson wrote letters home. To the Prophet Joseph he sent a copy of his letter to the rabbi. Among additional items, he summarized his observations in Great Britain:

> It is very hard times in England.–Thousands . . . have nothing to do, and are literally starving. Trade of all sorts is at the lowest ebb. Very cold and dry. No harvest, unless rain come soon.
>
> You will discover that the greater part of the English brethren, have always worked under masters; and they have not so much notion of planning and shifting for themselves, particularly in a strange country, as the Americans.–They want some one to be a kind of father to them, to give them plenty of work, and plenty to eat; and they will be content. They are a very industrious people whenever they can get employment; and by a little fatherly care, they will soon get way-wised to the country, and be enabled to shift for themselves.

Orson took his passport to the Court of Saint James in London. Here the United States consul approved it. Ready to depart, Orson bid farewell to the London Saints.[27]

"In good health and enjoying a comfortable measure of the Holy Spirit, on the 20th of June [1841], I left London for Rotterdam, in Holland . . . ," Orson tells. "The fine Steamer, Battavier, brought me safely over the billows of a tremendous[ly] rough sea in about 30 hours. Never did I suffer more from sea-sickness than during this short voyage; but it was soon over. . . . In ascending the waters of the Rhine . . . the numerous Wind-mills which I beheld in constant operation led me to think, almost, that all Europe came here for their grinding."

Rotterdam, "a fine town of about 80 thousand inhabitants," impressed Orson with its tree-lined clean streets, tall buildings, and numerous canals. Procuring lodging at a hotel, he discovered, gratefully, that "most of the business men here speak a little English—some speak it very well."

He had other grateful feelings too, when he saw the flag of the United States. "I never knew that I was, in reality, an American," he recounts, "until I walked out one fine morning . . . along the wharf, where many ships [from around the world] lay in the waters of the Rhine. Suddenly my eye caught a broad pendant floating in a gentle breeze over the stern of a fine ship . . . , the stripes and stars. . . . [M]y heart leaped into my mouth, a flood of tears burst from my eyes, and . . . my mouth, involuntarily, gave birth to these words, *'I am an American!'*"[28]

In Rotterdam Orson called on the leading Hebrew rabbi, Emanuel Joachim Löwenstam and received a kind reception. The rabbi—a compact man with a round face, large oval eyes, no visible neck, and a fringe of beard around his jaw—understood no English. Conversing through an interpreter became a new experience for Orson. Feeling apart from his own conversation, he asked Mr. Löwenstam his views. Did he expect "the Messiah to come directly from Heaven or . . . to be born of a woman on earth?"

The rabbi replied that he expected the Messiah "to be born of a woman, of the seed and lineage of David."

"At what period do you look for this event?" Orson questioned.

"We have been looking a long time, and are now living in constant expectation of his coming."

"Do you believe in the restitution of your nation to the land of your fathers, called the land of *promise*?"

"We hope it will be so," the rabbi responded. "We believe that many Jews will return to Jerusalem and rebuild the city—rear a Temple to the name of the Most High, and restore our ancient worship. Jerusalem shall be the capital of our nation—the centre of our union, and the Standard and Ensign of our national existence. But," he added, "we do not believe that all the Jews will go there, for the place is not large enough to contain them. They are now gathering there almost continually."

Orson told the rabbi that he had written an address to the Hebrews (the message he had already presented to the rabbi in London) explaining his mission and his understanding of their bright destiny. He was arranging for the publication of five hundred copies in the Dutch language and would deliver one to his host. Orson kept his word, but when he came, Mr. Löwenstam happened to be away.[29]

June 24, the American consul in Rotterdam checked Orson's passports and other papers. He wrote a certificate that the credentials appeared "in good order."

Leaving Rotterdam after a week, Orson rode a coach for seven hours about thirty miles to Amsterdam. Here he remained only one night and parts of two days. "I called on the President Rabbi here, but he was gone from home. I left at his house a large number of the addresses for himself and his people, and took coach for Arnheim on the Rhine [Germany, later part of Holland]."

"When I first landed in Germany," Orson tells, relative to finding himself where no one spoke English and the miracle that ensued, "I was dropped from the coach on the side walk; I could not tell them where I wanted to stop . . . [nor] tell anybody what I wanted. . . . I did not remain in that situation long until I found a way to get to an hotel, where I was soon forced, by . . . the cravings of my appetite, to make known my wants . . . in the language of the people among whom I was cast. . . . God is in all this; . . . He, by the power of his spirit, . . . gives power [to his servants] to utter the thoughts He wishes to communicate. . . . The Lord will always open our way if we are faithful."[30]

The same evening Orson boarded a boat and began crossing Germany. For three days he traveled low flat countryside up the Rhine to "Mazenty"

(Mainz). From Mainz he rode a train for seven hours to Frankfurt. From Frankfurt he traveled for thirty hours, covering two hundred miles, to Regensburg (also called Ratisbon), in Bavaria, Germany.

Orson intended to remain in Regensburg only long enough to secure steamboat passage to travel down the Danube River through several countries to Constantinople. But he met complications. He would enter Austria in about eighty miles. Because of his limited knowledge of the language, he had failed to learn that he should have had his passport checked by the Austrian Ambassador in Frankfurt. "I had to forward it," he tells, "to the Austrian Embassador of Munich [Germany] and procure his permission, signature, and seal, before I could enter the Austrian dominions. This detained me five days."

A delay in Europe could be disastrous if his money ran out. In the United States and England he could preach and ask for donations, but in Europe and Asia his lack of language skills prevented preaching. Setting off across Europe had been a true "leap of faith."

This delay at Regensburg, however, proved to be a blessing. Compelled to remain five days, he decided to stay longer and learn German scientifically. He felt frustrated in his cocoon of not understanding what he heard around him.

"I became acquainted with a lady here who speaks French and German to admiration," he narrates, "and she was very anxious to speak the English—she proposed giving me instruction in the German if I would instruct her in English. I accepted her proposal." In less than two weeks, on July 17, he wrote a letter to Joseph Smith telling of his progress, stating that he had been "engaged eight days in this task. I have read one book through and part of another, and [have] translated and written considerable. I can speak and write the German considerable already, and the lady tells me that I make astonishing progress. . . . The people will hardly believe but that I have spoken German before; but I tell them, neicht [nicht], not. [They had no understanding, as he did, of how much help he received from Heavenly sources.] The German is spoken in Prussia, Bavaria, and in all the States of Germany—Austria—the south of Russia, and in fine more or less all over Europe."

Orson had also been told another advantage of a delay in Germany: "It is very sickly in Constantinople, Syria and Alexandria, at present; I would rather, therefore, wait until cool weather before I go there."

Sitting and writing to loved ones far away gave Orson longings for their companionship. Letters received thus far comforted him, had been read and reread. Expressing thankfulness for letters, he wrote, "They soften the hard and rugged path in which Heaven has directed my course. They are buoyancy in depression,—joy in sorrow."

To Joseph Smith, words poured from Orson's pen, welling up from the inner desires of his heart: "Tho now far separated from you; and also from her who, with me, has suffered the chilling blasts of adversity, yet hope lingers in this bosom, brightened almost into certainty by . . . the gentle breeze of the spirit of God . . . [to] my anxious and enquiring heart, that . . . [I shall] embrace again the friends I love. . . .

"Were it consistent with the will of Deity," Orson continued, ". . . most gladly would I retreat from the oppressing heat of public life, . . . and bask in the affections of my own little family circle. But the will of God be done! . . . I yield, O Lord! I yield to thy righteous mandate! imploring help from thee in the hour of trial, and strength in the day of weakness. . . .

"Lord, bless my wife and children, and the hand that ministers good to them in the name of Jesus Christ. Amen. Adieu for the present."[31]

Though missing his loved ones, Orson savored seven weeks in Regensburg, a fairy tale city of medieval mansions. Orson lived in the commodious home of his tutor with every privilege of the household, including comfortable quarters, servants to drive the carriage, and a sense of belonging. The two daughters in the family, older than his own, brought extra delight into his life as they shared their city with him and mastered English words.

During his Regensburg weeks Orson learned German well and began learning French. He also wrote "a very lengthy communication to the Jews of Constantinople, and . . . procured its translation into French and German. . . . I made many friends," he adds, "and some of them are ready to forsake all for Christ's sake; although I found them all Catholics."

August 31 he left Regensburg aboard a steamer.[32] Ahead of him coursed a thousand miles and more of the Danube, the mighty river highway between Europe and Asia. His "family" in Regensburg would wait eagerly for his return. In gracious Vienna, Austria, the consul wrote him a letter of introduction to the "imperial consul [and the official's cousin] of Austria, at Galatz, near the mouth of the Danube."[33] Many miles beyond Vienna, Orson saw the splendid and ancient city of Buda, on the high west cliff side of the Danube, strong and protective of the city of Pest on the low east side (these later combined into one city, Budapest, Hungary). Then for days the boat passed broad plains and marshes and sandy stretches. Beograd, Serbia (later Belgrade, Yugoslavia), marked the beginning of the Balkan Peninsula. People spoke mostly the tongue-twisting throaty sounds of the Slavic dialects. Usually a few spoke something Orson understood, and to these he talked of the gospel. The Danube eventually again reached mountains, then serpentined through these summits and the spectacular long narrow gorge of the Iron Gate. As the river next crossed flat, marshy plains under a colossal dome sky, Orson saw numerous towns in Rumania on the left, and in Bulgaria on the right, and stopped in many of them. Orson had now seen more sizes and shapes and colors of water vessels, buildings, villages, and cities than he had known existed.

At last, amid marshes wide and deep, the boat docked in Galatz (or Galati), the port of the Danube Valley, and ninety marshy miles from the Black Sea. Orson took his papers to the Austrian consul, and the man delighted in seeing the letter from his cousin in Vienna. As they talked, both men felt so much at ease, Orson tells, that "I drank Champagne with the Austrian Consul who told me to make his house my home." The consul told Orson that so many Austrian Jews were moving to Syria and Palestine that his "government had established a general consulate at Beyrout [Beirut] for their protection."[34]

Continuing his steamer voyage, Orson traveled down one of the many mouths of the Danube to the Black Sea. Years later he talked of his journey thus far and said, "I am a witness that the gospel has been proclaimed all along the Danube." The boat plied south across the west end of the cloudy Black Sea waters and along the winding eighteen miles of the Bosporus Strait. The Bosporus fascinated Orson with its high hill sides, its villages and palaces and gardens, its fishermen, and its colorful sea birds.

Then he gazed upon Constantinople. The city appeared just as he had seen it in vision. Its coral tile roofs and domes and minarets crowded over its several hills. Cypress trees added refreshing green. And its slopes descended gently into the famous blue natural harbor, the Gold Horn, that curved inland for six miles. Orson found no reason to tarry. In the noisy and crowded open markets, along the twisted narrow cobblestone streets, and at the busy dock, the people were more foreign to him than any in his experience. Not only did the men's turbans and the women's veiled faces seem strange, but the words sounded as unintelligible as the squawking of the seagulls flying around the harbor. To fulfill his divine assignment Orson "sent a lengthy communication to the Jews in Constantinople, in the French language, but . . . reserved a copy of it in the German."[35]

The next three hundred miles took Orson southwest across the Sea of Marmara and through the Dardenelles Strait. Past the strait his course turned south-southeast on the Aegean Sea, winding among islands large and small, until the boat docked at ancient Smyrna (later Izmir, Turkey).[36] He was now in Biblical territory. The apostle Paul had sailed the many-isled Aagean nearly two millennia before, and Orson became the first apostle of the Lord Jesus Christ known to history to visit this area since then.

"When we left Smyrna for Beyrout," Orson's narrative continues, "we only took in stores for one week, thinking that would surely be sufficient, as the voyage is usually made in four days; but we were nineteen days on the passage. A number of days I eat snails gathered from the rocks, while our vessel was becalmed in the midst of several small and uninhabited islands, but the greatest difficulty was, I could not get enough of them. I was so weak and exhausted that I could not go on shore after the slight exertion of drawing on my boots." In this stretch of the journey he passed near the Isle of

Patmos, where John, the "Beloved" apostle, received the vision from Heaven that he recorded as the book of Revelation.

Crossing the eastern end of the clear blue Mediterranean, Orson arrived in "Beyrout" (Beirut, in Syria, later Lebanon) in mid October, six weeks after leaving Regensburg. From the boat, Beirut looked peaceful, with its backdrop of the towering snow-capped Mountains of Lebanon and with trees, flowers, and new buildings amid the ancient ones; but after going ashore Orson learned of conflicts.

"The country [Syria] is in a terrible state," Orson wrote following his brief sojourn. "While I was at Beyrout, a terrible battle was fought in Mount Lebanon, about six hours' walk from Beyrout, between the Drewzes and Catholics. It was said that about four hundred were killed on each side. An English officer, returning from St. Jean d'Acre to Beyrout, was taken by the Drewzes, and would have been killed had not the Pasha [ranking Turkish military officer] come to his rescue. He said that he found ten human bodies in the street on his way without heads. Thefts, murders, and robberies are taking place almost continually.[37]

"The American missionaries at Beyrout and Mount Lebanon," Orson continues, "have received official notice through Commodore Porter, our minister at Constantinople, from the Grand Sultan [ruler of Turkey], that hereafter they can have no redress by law for any violence, outrage, or cruelty, that may be practiced upon them by the people; and [the Grand Sultan] advises them to leave the country. This course is approved of by Commodore Porter. I read the correspondence between him and Mr. Chassan, our Consul at Beyrout.

"But all is going on in the providence of God," Orson declared. " Syria and Palestine must ferment and ferment, work and work, until they work into the hands of Abraham's children, to whom they rightly belong; and may the God of their fathers bless the hand that aids their cause."[38]

From Beirut Orson's boat sailed to the ancient port of Jaffa, the Biblical Joppa. He walked narrow streets to the consulate. The consul wrote him a letter of introduction to an American missionary in Jerusalem.

October 20, his second day in Jaffa, Orson wrote to Parley P. Pratt that he had made arrangements, "at a most enormous price," to travel the remaining thirty-four miles to his destination with a caravan armed for protection against highway robbers. Then, "just as I was about to start from the American Consul's . . . a company of English gentlemen rode in from Jerusalem with many servants all armed, and they were to return immediately. . . . I can go [with them] for little or nothing, comparatively speaking.

"I have only time to say a few words;" he continues, "but through the favor of heaven I am well and in good spirits . . . and have plenty to eat. I now have [no problems] but land pirates, in the shape of Arabs, to encounter. An Englishman seems like a brother, let his religion be what it may. . . .

"My journey has been long and tedious, and consequently expensive. If I get back to England with money enough to buy my dinner, I shall think myself well off. . . .

"The servants are now waiting for me, and I must gird on my arms and be off. . . .

"May the Lord bless you all in England and in America. And I pray that He will bless my wife, and my dear little children; God knows that I want to see them—yea, and all the Saints. . . . You will hear from me again at the first opportunity, if the Arabs don't kill me. There is no post here; letters are sent by private conveyance, through friends, etc. God bless you and the cause of Zion is my last prayer."[39]

CHAPTER 9

... *he shall come and pray.* ... *(1841–1842)*

> *[King Solomon, at the dedication of the temple he built in Jerusalem, prayed to the Lord:] Moreover concerning a stranger, that is not of thy people Israel, but cometh out of a far country for thy name's sake; (For they shall hear of thy great name, and of thy strong hand, and of thy stretched out arm;) when he shall come and pray toward this house; Hear thou in heaven thy dwelling place, and do according to all that the stranger calleth to thee for: that all people of the earth may know thy name, to fear thee, as do thy people Israel; and that they may know that this house, which I have builded, is called by thy name.*
>
> —I Kings 8:41-43

IN the distance, from the top of a rounded hill on the winding road from Jaffa, "my natural eyes, for the first time beheld Jerusalem," Orson wrote of Thursday, October 21, 1841. He forgot the overpowering heat and the dusty road and the barren countryside. True to his vision of nineteen months before, he saw far away the domes and towers and square buildings, the tall slim trees, and the enclosing wall of his destination. "As I gazed upon it and its environs, the mountains and hills by which it is surrounded," he tells, "and considered, that this is the stage upon which so many scenes of wonders have been acted, where prophets were stoned, and the Saviour of sinners slain, a storm of commingled emotions suddenly arose in my breast, the force of which was only spent in a profuse shower of tears."

Orson traversed more road with the caravan of Englishmen and saw the Holy City in increasing detail. By conversation and observation he learned that "Jerusalem at this time contains about twenty thousand inhabitants; about seven thousand are Jews, and the remainder mostly Turks and Arabs. It is enclosed by a strong wall from five to ten feet thick. On those sides which are most accessible, and consequently most exposed to an attack, the wall is thickest, and well mounted with cannon; it is from twelve to thirty feet in height. The city is situated on the south-eastern extremity of an inclined plane, with the valley of Kedron [Kidron] on the east, and the vallies of Hinnom and Gihon on the south and west, all converging to a point in the valley of Jehosaphat, south-east of the city."

Orson entered Jerusalem through the west gate, the Jaffa Gate, and saw narrow crowded streets. He saw homely brown camels and small donkeys. The people wore varied attire: Turks in turbans, blousy shirts, vests, and billowy knee-length trousers; Arabs in colorful robes; Jews in the more subdued styles of the countries from whence they came.

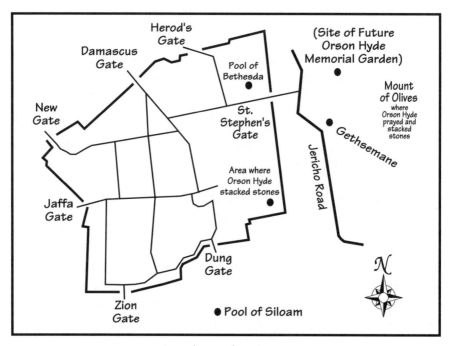

Jerusalem and environs.

Orson's English traveling companions, for whose protection he felt so grateful, directed him to the home of Mr. Whiting, the American missionary to whom he had the letter of introduction from the consul at Jaffa. Mr. George B. Whiting, his wife, and his four little girls had just moved into this home, but even in their disarray of unpacking and arranging they treated Orson with genuine friendship. Sitting and conversing with Americans gave Orson the feeling of reunion with loved kinfolk.[1] Mr. Whiting regretted that their unsettled situation prevented them inviting Orson to stay in their home, but he "very kindly went with me to the Latin Convent," Orson recounts, "which is a sort of hotel or home for strangers, and there engaged for me my board and lodging at a reasonable compensation, and said that he would keep a little watch to see that I was well taken care of."

In his room at the Latin Convent, Orson at last relaxed, thankful to the Lord for blessings. He had rested little since leaving Beirut and "felt worn down with fatigue and a want of sleep, as well as being almost overcome by the excessive heat."

After only an hour or two, a knock at the door interrupted his quiet. He arose still tired, opened the door, and was surprised that two more Americans introduced themselves. They were Mr. Charles S. Sherman and Mr. Charles Gager, missionaries like Mr. Whiting. Orson invited his callers to sit and again relished hearing and speaking his native tongue. The three conversed about America and also learned a little about each other. Mr. Gager, twenty-seven years old and unmarried, was originally from Connecticut, like Orson.[2] Orson told his callers that his own mission in Jerusalem would require but a few days, and they assured him that they would be pleased to assist.

Orson's tired body cried out urgent silent signals to him. He thanked the missionaries for their visit, told them of his extreme fatigue, and asked that they grant him time for needed rest. Then he would be grateful for the privilege of an interview with them and Mr. Whiting together. The men agreed on a time.

Orson slept and then awoke refreshed. Next, sitting with pen in hand, he translated into English the German copy of the lengthy communication he had written to the Jews. He had worked out that document carefully, and he felt that it could clearly present to these ministers in Jerusalem the purpose of his mission.

At the appointed time the group met in Mr. Whiting's home, and in the friendly surroundings Orson told his story. He read to them his document, and he expounded many details concerning the Church, its history, its ordinances, and its government.

His listeners, at first eager to hear, asked questions, but eventually they became more cautious and admitted that Orson's convictions "appeared incredibly strange" to them.

Orson sensed that they liked him personally, though his views discomforted them, and he requested that they grant him the favor of an introduction to some of the principle Jews in the city. Their reaction amused him. Each hesitated, cleared his throat, and made a number of "*hem*" sounds. "Commonly," Orson thought, "this means no more than to allay a little irritation, or tickling in the throat, . . . but from the peculiarity of their tone and cadence, I judge they wish to be a little metaphorical, and . . . mean the following:–'We have our scruples about complying with your request, lest it might detract from our influence and popularity!'"

Quickly the Americans decided among themselves that Mr. Johns, the English consul, might be the most proper man to grant Orson the desired favor. Mr. Whiting would have time to attend to the matter in a day or two.

Orson thanked Mr. Whiting for his kindness and said no more about introductions. In spite of their hesitation to comply with his request, Orson felt affection for the American missionaries, helpful and courteous strangers in a strange land. When saying farewells at the end of the visit, he expressed sincere gratitude to his hosts. When he later departed from Jerusalem he left his blessing upon these Americans.

"I concluded . . . that I would try to discharge my duty before God, without subjecting any one to the humble mortification of giving me an introduction . . . ," Orson's account goes on. "Summoning up, therefore, what little address I had, I procured a valet d' place or lackey, and proceeded to the house of Mr. Simons, a very respectable [German] Jew, who with some of his family had lately been converted and joined the English Church."

Orson greeted the Simons family in German and asked if they spoke English. They replied, "Yes," an agreeable sound to Orson's ears. They smiled and asked Orson in German if he spoke English.

"Ya, Mein Herr," he replied. He introduced himself and told them about his mission. They seemed interested.

Two ministers of the Church of England resided with the Simons family. Sickness confined one to his bed. The other, a German and a Jew by birth, came in and found Orson visiting comfortably. After introductions Orson "took the liberty to lay open to him some of our principles" and handed him a copy to read of the communication to the Jews.

The German minister, a man of obvious self-importance, read the pages and handed them back. He "said that my motives were undoubtedly very good," Orson recounts, "but he questioned the propriety of my undertaking from the fact that I claimed God had sent me. . . . He said that miracles, visions, and prophecy had ceased." The minister reacted so typically of ministers in general that when Orson later reported this incident he analyzed:

> If, indeed, I had gone to Jerusalem under the direction of some missionary board or society, and left God out of the question altogether, I should have been received as a celestial messenger. . . .
>
> The course which the popular clergy pursue . . . looks to me as though they would say: "O Lord, we will worship thee with all our hearts, serve thee with all our souls, and be very pious and holy. We will even gather Israel, convert the heathen, and bring in the millennium, if you will only let us alone that we may do it in our own way, and according to our own will. But if you speak from heaven to interfere with our plans, or cause any to see visions or dreams, or prophecy, whereby we are disturbed or interrupted in our worship, we will exert all our strength and skill to deny what you say, and charge it home upon the devil or some wild fanatic spirit, as being its author."
>
> That which was looked upon by the ancient saints as among the greatest favors and blessings, viz., revelation from God and communion with him by dreams and by visions, is now looked upon by the religious world as the height of presumption and folly. The ancient saints considered their condition most deplorable when Jehovah would not speak to

them; but the most orthodox religionists of this age deem it quite heterodox to even admit the probability that he ever will speak again. O my soul!

In the Simons home Orson and the arrogant Jewish German minister continued to talk, and they developed disagreements. Orson decided to meet the divergence directly. Smiling, he looked straight at the man and told him that he should repent and be baptized for the remission of his sins, that he might receive the gift of the Holy Ghost.

"What," said he, "*I* be baptized?"

"Yes, *you* be baptized." A smile continued to flicker on Orson's face.

"Why," said the flustered minister, "I have been baptized already!"

Seeing that the learned man felt threatened, Orson became more serious and said quickly, "You have probably been sprinkled, but that has no more to do with baptism than any other ordinance of man's device; and even if you had been immersed, you would not have bettered your condition, for your priesthood is without power."

Regarding the priesthood, and referring to the fact that the Church of England had broken away from the Catholic Church, Orson's words sped on, "If, indeed, the Catholic Church had power to give you [the Church of England] an ordination, and by that ordination confer the priesthood upon you, they certainly had power to nullify that act, and take the priesthood from you; and this power they exercised when you [the Church of England] dissented from their communion. . . . But, if the Catholic Church possessed not the priesthood, of course your claims to it are as groundless as the airy phantoms of heathen mythology. So, view the question on which side you may, there is no possible chance of admitting the validity of your claims to it [the priesthood]."

The minister refused to accept the reasoning of this upstart religionist from the west. When Orson wrote later of this encounter with a Jew who had been converted to "Christianity" he commented, "There is more hope of those Jews receiving the fullness of the gospel, whose minds have never been poisoned by the bane of modern sectarianism" than there is for those Jews who cling to their own tradition.[3]

Sunday morning, October 24, 1841, Orson Hyde arose from sleep in Jerusalem "a good while before day." A feeling of hallowed destiny filled his soul. This day he would accomplish the purpose for which, guided by the Spirit, he had traversed lands, rivers, and seas from one side of the world to the other. His authoritative acts as a prophet, seer, and revelator of Almighty God would increase the divine temperings relative to this Promised Land. After his pronouncement of an inspired apostolic blessing, spoken upon the ground to which it applied, the mantle of the Lord's protection and guidance would settle subtly upon it, and Satan would be unable to thwart Jehovah's plan. The scattered children of the Covenant would come home, and for them the countryside would become fruitful.[4]

Softly he closed his door at the Latin Convent. In the subdued light—carrying his small case with paper, pen, and ink—he walked along age-worn streets. The warm morning air and the near ancient buildings echoed sacred footsteps and utterances of earlier prophets and of the mortal Messiah. In the closeness, a few other early risers moved about, intent on their own errands. Inside the east wall of the city he waited but a brief time before the guards pushed open the portals of Saint Stephen's Gate beneath the solid square-built superstructure. Ahead, through the high and tunnel-like stone arch of the gate, he saw the Mount of Olives, colors and forms muted with diffuse morning light. Indistinctly he saw the Mount's few trees, its rocky places, and the outline of buildings on its crest.

Orson followed the road down the hill from the gate, headed southward on the Jericho Road, crossed the stone bridge over the wadi of the Brook Kidron, and walked on. Daylight brought focus to the scene. In the valley of the Kidron the hillsides to the east and to the west looked similar to other tan Palestine hills, with a few scrubby bushes, scarce hardy trees, rock out-croppings, huge washed-out gullies, and a small number of substantial fortress-like buildings rising out of juts of stone. The trees in this barren landscape curved southward, bent by prevailing winds. In contrast, the walls of Jerusalem, high to the west, looked strong and unyielding. A feeling of quiet anticipation pervaded the atmosphere, a feeling that all happenings here were but prologue for greater events to come.

Orson turned left onto a rock-strewn path and with reverent step entered a gate in the stone wall that enclosed the Garden of Gethsemane. Here grew ancient olive trees. From their gnarled trunks, branches sprouted out at unexpected angles. Orson touched a young smooth branch. His fingers bent the supple bough, and musingly he plucked it. In his meditation, dream-like except for the feel of the cool branch in his hand, he pondered a momentous scene enacted centuries before:

> Here the Son of the Virgin bore our sins and carried our sorrows—here the angels gazed and shuddered at the sight, waiting for the order to fly to his rescue; but no such order was given. The decree had passed in heaven, and could not be revoked, that he must suffer, that he must bleed, and that he must die. What bosom so cold, what feelings so languid, or what heart so unmoved that can withhold the humble tribute of a tear over this forlorn condition of the Man of sorrows?

Tears spent, Orson left the garden reluctantly and continued his walk up the Mount of Olives. He estimated that he had come "just about one English mile." He now stood on top of the mount hallowed to both past and future.

Here the resurrected Savior had risen to heaven. Here, according to the promises of ancient prophets, the Savior, the Messiah, would stand again in glory
at the last day.[5]

Paying little attention to the shrines, the churches, and the ancient cemetery, Orson gazed around. Eastward about fifteen miles in the distance he saw
the Dead Sea and the River Jordan. And the day was so clear that westward,
far beyond the Kidron Valley and Jerusalem in her noble setting amid the
Judean Hills, he saw the Mediterranean Sea. The panorama appeared precisely
as he had viewed it in vision a year and a half before. "I saw no one with me
in the vision," he recalled, "and although Elder Page was appointed to accompany me, yet I find myself here alone."

Rapt with admiration at the significance of the land before him, he
meditated, "Is it a reality that I am here gazing upon this scene of wonders?
or am I carried away in the fanciful reveries of a night vision?" The sunlight
that now warmed his back also shone upon Jerusalem, caressing it with soft
golden hues. "Is that city which I now look down upon really Jerusalem. . .
? Is that small enclosure in the valley of Kidron, where the boughs of those
lonely olive trees are waving their green foliage so gracefully in the soft and
gentle breeze, really the garden of Gethsemane. . . ?

"Oh, yes!" his heart responded to his queries, as the olive branch in his
hand caught his eye and he held it before him. "This branch . . . demon-
strates that all is real!"[6] The slender gray-green leaves quivered, and Orson
glimpsed the silver of their lighter sides.

Tranquil, ready to pray and write Spirit-inspired words, Orson found a
secluded place and sat. "In solemn silence," as he had seen in vision, he
smoothed out paper in front of him, dipped pen in inkwell, and began to
write, offering, on this sacred day, "to him who lives for ever and ever," this
prayer:

> O Thou! who art from everlasting to everlasting, eternally and
> unchangeably the same, even the God who rules in the heavens above,
> and controls the destinies of men on the earth, wilt Thou not conde-
> scend, through thine infinite goodness and royal favour, to listen to the
> prayer of thy servant which he this day offers up unto thee in the name
> of thy holy child Jesus, upon this land where the Sun of Righteousness
> sat in blood, and thine <u>Anointed One</u> expired.
>
> Be pleased, O Lord, to forgive all the follies, weaknesses, vanities, and
> sins of thy servant, and strengthen him to resist all future temptations.
> Give him prudence and discernment that he may avoid the evil, and a
> heart to choose the good; give him fortitude to bear up under trying and
> adverse circumstances, and grace to endure all things for thy name's
> sake, until the end shall come, when all the saints shall rest in peace.

Now, O Lord! thy servant has been obedient to the heavenly vision which thou gavest him in his native land; and under the shadow of thine outstretched arm, he has safely arrived in this place to dedicate and consecrate this land unto Thee, for the gathering together of Judah's scattered remnants, according to the predictions of the holy prophets—for the building up of Jerusalem again after it has been trodden down by the Gentiles so long, and for rearing a temple in honour of thy name. Everlasting thanks be ascribed unto thee, O Father! Lord of heaven and earth, that thou hast preserved thy servant from the dangers of the seas, and from the plague and pestilence which have caused the land to mourn. The violence of man has also been restrained, and thy providential care by night and by day has been exercised over thine unworthy servant. Accept, therefore, O Lord, the tribute of a grateful heart for all past favours, and be pleased to continue thy kindness and mercy towards a needy worm of the dust.

O thou, who didst covenant with Abraham, thy friend, and who didst renew that covenant with Isaac, and confirm the same with Jacob with an oath, that thou wouldst not only give them this land for an everlasting inheritance, but that thou wouldst also remember their seed for ever. Abraham, Isaac, and Jacob, have long since closed their eyes in death, and made the grave their mansion. Their children are scattered and dispersed abroad among the nations of the Gentiles like sheep that have no shepherd, and are still looking forward for the fulfilment of those promises which thou didst make concerning them; and even this land, which once poured forth nature's richest bounty, and flowed, as it were, with milk and honey, has, to a certain extent, been smitten with barrenness and sterility since it drank from murderous hands the blood of him who never sinned.

Grant, therefore, O Lord, in the name of thy well-beloved Son, Jesus Christ, to remove the barrenness and sterility of this land, and let springs of living water break forth to water its thirsty soil. Let the vine and the olive produce in their strength, and the fig tree bloom and flourish. Let the land become abundantly fruitful when possessed by its rightful heirs; let it again flow with plenty to feed the returning prodigals who come home with a spirit of grace and supplication; upon it let the clouds distil virtue and richness, and let the fields smile with plenty. Let the flocks and the herds greatly increase and multiply upon the mountains and the hills; and let thy great kindness conquer and subdue the unbelief of thy people. Do thou take from them their stony heart, and give them a heart of flesh; and may the Sun of thy favour dispel the cold mists of darkness which have beclouded their atmosphere. Incline them to gather in upon this land according to thy word. Let them come like clouds and like doves to their windows. Let the large ships of the nations bring them from the distant isles; and let kings become their nursing fathers, and queens with motherly fondness wipe the tear of sorrow from their eye.

Thou, O Lord, did once move upon the heart of Cyrus to shew favour unto Jerusalem and her children. Do thou now also be pleased to inspire the hearts of kings and the powers of the earth to look with a friendly eye towards this place, and with a desire to see thy righteous purposes executed in relation thereto. Let them know that it is thy good pleasure to restore the kingdom unto Israel—raise up Jerusalem as its capital, and constitute her people a distinct nation and government, with David thy servant, even a descendant from the loins of ancient David, to be their king.

Let that nation or that people who shall take an active part in behalf of Abraham's children, and in the raising up of Jerusalem, find favour in thy sight. Let not their enemies prevail against them, neither let pestilence or famine overcome them, but let the glory of Israel overshadow them, and the power of the highest protect them; while that nation or kingdom that will not serve thee in this glorious work must perish, according to thy word—"Yea, those nations shall be utterly wasted."

Though thy servant is now far from his home, and from the land bedewed with his earliest tear, yet he remembers, O Lord, his friends who are there, and family, whom for thy sake he has left. Though poverty and privation be our earthly lot, yet ah! do Thou richly endow us with an inheritance where moth and rust do not corrupt, and where thieves do not break through and steal.

The hands that have fed, clothed, or shown favour unto the family of thy servant in his absence, or that shall hereafter do so, let them not lose their reward, but let a special blessing rest upon them, and in thy kingdom let them have an inheritance when thou shalt come to be glorified in this society.

Do thou also look with favour upon all those through whose liberality I have been enabled to come to this land; and in the day when thou shalt reward all people according to their works, let these also not be past by or forgotten, but in time let them be in readiness to enjoy the glory of those mansions which Jesus has gone to prepare. Particularly do thou bless the stranger in Philadelphia, whom I never saw, but who sent me gold, with a request that I should pray for him in Jerusalem. Now, O Lord, let blessings come upon him from an unexpected quarter, and let his basket be filled, and his storehouse abound with plenty, and let not the good things of the earth be his only portion, but let him be found among those to whom it shall be said, "Thou hast been faithful over a few things, and I will make thee ruler over many."

O my father in heaven! I now ask thee in the name of Jesus to remember Zion, with all her stakes, and with all her assemblies. She has been grievously afflicted and smitten; she has mourned; she has wept; her enemies have triumphed, and have said—"Ah, where is thy God!" Her priests and prophets have groaned in chains and fetters within the gloomy walls of prisons, while many were slain, and now sleep in the arms of death. How long, O Lord, shall iniquity triumph, and sin go unpunished?

Do Thou arise in the majesty of thy strength, and make bare thine arm in behalf of thy people. Redress their wrongs, and turn their sorrow into joy. Pour the spirit of light and knowledge, grace and wisdom, into the hearts of her prophets, and clothe her priests with salvation. Let light and knowledge march forth through the empire of darkness, and may the honest in heart flow to their standard, and join in the march to go forth to meet the Bridegroom.

Let a peculiar blessing rest upon the presidency of thy Church, for at them are the arrows of the enemy directed. Be thou to them a sun and a shield, their strong tower and hiding place; and in the time of distress or danger be thou near to deliver. Also the quorum of the Twelve, do thou be pleased to stand by, for thou knowest the obstacles which we have to encounter, the temptations to which we are exposed, and the privations which we must suffer. Give us, therefore, strength according to our day, and help us to bear a faithful testimony of Jesus and his gospel, and to finish with fidelity and honour the work which thou hast given us to do, and then give us a place in thy glorious kingdom. And let this blessing rest upon every faithful officer and member in thy Church. And all the glory and honour will we ascribe unto God and the Lamb for ever and ever. AMEN.[7]

Enacting the plan shown him in heavenly vision, Orson gathered stones and arranged them in a careful pile on the top of the Mount of Olives. This, the tangible witness of his apostolic act of dedicating the land for the Lord's purposes, accorded with the ancient custom of witnessing holy events with stacked stones. Jacob and Joshua and others did the same.[8]

His momentous obligation fulfilled, and profound thoughts contemplated, Orson retraced his way to the Kidron Valley, walked a short distance southward on the Jericho Road, and then turned right to circle the city of Jerusalem. He passed "the tombs of the prophets" and came to the stone-lined recess of the Pool of Siloam, the edges worn smooth from millenniums of use. Here he looked far into Hezekiah's Tunnel beyond its rock arch. Also, he stepped into the pool "and freely washed."

He thought of claims he had heard that in the Savior's day baptism was done by sprinkling because of a scarcity of water in this arid land. "I found plenty of water [at the Pool of Siloam] for baptizing," Orson tells, "besides a surplus quantity sent off in a limpid stream as a grateful tribute to the thirsty plants of the gardens in the valley." Regarding baptism he thought too of the Pool of Bethesda, which he had seen during exploration inside the city. "The pool of Bethesda, which had five porchs," he narrates, "remains in the city, but in a dilapidated state, there being plenty of water to meet the demands of the city of a better quality and more convenient—this vast reservoir is consequently neglected. . . . [F]rom its vast dimensions, it would certainly contain water enough to immerse all Jerusalem in, in a day."

Orson continued his circuit of the city. On the northwest he passed the main entrance, the beautiful Damascus Gate. Intricate stonework scalloped the golden-hued towers above it.

"The customs and manners of the people of the east are so similar to what they were in the days of our Saviour," Orson's account goes on, "that almost everything which the traveler beholds is a standing illustration of some portion of scripture: for example, I saw two women grinding wheat at a little hand-mill, consisting of two small stones with a little rude tackling about it, the whole of which one man might take in his arms and carry almost any where at pleasure. One [woman] would turn the top stone until her strength was exhausted, and then the other would take her place, and so alternately keep the little grinder in operation. It appears that our Lord foresaw the perpetuity of this custom, even to the time of his second coming; for he said, 'Two women shall be grinding at the mill; one shall be taken and the other left' [Matthew 24:41]; and for aught I know, these two I saw were the identical ones. I also saw the people take a kind of coarse grass and mix it with some kind of earth or peat that had been wet and reduced to the consistency of common mortar, and then lay it out in flattened cakes to dry for fuel. I then, for the first time in my life, saw the propriety of our Saviour's allusion, 'If God so clothe the grass of the field, which to-day is, and to-morrow is cast into the oven, &c.' [Matthew 6:30]. . . . One may read of the customs of the east, but it is not like seeing them."

Orson returned to the city and "found my feet and legs completely coated with dust; for the whole face of the country was like an ash bed in consequence of the great length of the dry season. I then thought how very convenient it must have been for the ancient disciples to fulfil one injunction of the Saviour, 'shake off the dust of your feet' [Matthew 10:14]."

During Orson's walk around Jerusalem, he tells, "my spirit struggled within me in earnest prayer to the God of Abraham, Isaac, and Jacob, that he would not only revolutionize this country, but renovate and make it glorious." Months later Orson stated prophetically that "Jerusalem will rise up, . . . [b]ut not to benefit those who oppress or limit the rights of men because they are Jews." Referring to his personal involvement he also declared: "I am not a Jew, neither am I a son of a Jew; but I am a friend of the Jews."[9]

Orson returned back inside Jerusalem, and there, he narrates, he walked up "what was anciently called Mount Zion, where the temple stood." The mount contained no "more than one acre of ground," he estimated. "[A]s I stood upon it and contemplated what the prophets had said of Zion in the last days," he adds, ". . . I could [not] bring my mind to believe [that] . . . their words pointed to this place. . . . But on the land of Joseph, far in the west, where the spread eagle of America floats in the breeze and shadows the land; where those broad rivers and streams roll the waters of the western world to the fathomless abyss of the ocean; where those wide-spreading prairies . . . and extensive forests adorn the land with such an agreeable variety, shall Zion rear her stately temples and stretch forth the curtains of her habitation. The record of Mormon chimes in . . . beautifully with the [Bible] scriptures to establish this position."

On Mount Zion, as on the Mount of Olives, he piled up stones as a witness of the achievement of authoritative acts to retrieve the Holy Land from its centuries of spiritual slumber. Then, in compliance with the prediction of the Prophet Joseph Smith ten years before, he performed one more sacred obligation that rested upon him as an apostle of the Lord Jesus Christ. Holding a "rod of nature" (wood) in his hand, "a token against the rebels [power of Satan]" (Numbers 17:6–10), he stretched forth his arm, and asked God to answer the Mount of Olives prayer. He acted in the same capacity as had Aaron for Moses, as a spokesman for God's Prophet on earth.[10]

The Lord used some of Orson's experiences as opportunities for slender threads of recorded history to be woven into the fabric of his Jerusalem sojourn. These threads fulfilled the eternal law that "in the mouth of two or three witnesses shall every word be established."[11]

One witness, among the "many Jews" Orson visited in Jerusalem, was Mr. Mamreov. From the Jerusalem Turkish authorities he had obtained a charter to open "his home as a center where Christians, Jews, and Mohammedans might come and be friendly." Mr. Mamreov showed deep interest in Orson's mission, asking many questions about "a new American prophet and a golden Bible." In later years this kind host's daughter, Madame Lydia Mountford, became a world lecturer, and spoke glowingly of what her father had told her regarding his conversations with "the first 'Mormon' missionary who went to Jerusalem."[12]

William Hayward, a British seaman, also filled the Lord's purpose of becoming a witness to Orson's mission. Twenty-four years old, a big man with curly red hair, and a cook on a British ship, he spent leisure hours in Jerusalem during his vessel's layover in the Jaffa port. In Jerusalem he met Orson Hyde and listened to him tell of the rites he performed on the Mount of Olives. Orson's fluency and dynamic presentation fascinated him. He continued to listen when Orson expounded gospel principles. Eventually, back in his native England, he sought out the Latter-day Saint missionaries. Their further teachings strengthened his convictions, and he asked for baptism. All his life he remained faithful to the Church and felt that he had been especially privileged to be in the Holy Land at the same time as Apostle Hyde.[13]

Charles Gager, one of the three Americans Orson visited soon after his arrival in Jerusalem, by his untimely death became another recorded witness to Orson's mission. Before Orson left the city, Mr. Gager grew "very unwell with the jaundice" and desired to accompany Orson to where he could be treated by doctors who spoke his language. Unable to book passage directly to Alexandria, Egypt, with plans to send Mr. Gager on to England, Orson arranged for the two to travel first to Cairo.

Leaving Palestine, they sailed across the southeast corner of the Mediterranean, came to the flat and monotonous delta of the Nile River, and then ascended the broad waters of the eastern branch of the Nile for eight miles to Damietta, Egypt. At Damietta they and shipmates endured a "six days' quarantine" in the harbor.

During their passage of a hundred miles up the lake-like Nile to Cairo, Mr. Gager's condition worsened. Orson cared for him as well as circumstances allowed. November 15 the ship docked at Bulack, Cairo's port on the wide river, and Orson hired four men to take the missionary on a stretcher to the American consulate. Orson followed them, carrying his friend's baggage through the maze of streets in Cairo, a vast metropolis of flat-roofed, yellow limestone houses and hundreds of mosques. At the consulate Orson assisted in putting Mr. Gager upon a good bed, then employed for him a competent Arabian nurse and an English doctor. The physician examined him and told Orson that Mr. Gager suffered severely from typhus fever. The doctor doubted that he would recover. At about two o'clock in the afternoon Orson sadly left the consulate.

At the dock he booked passage to Alexandria and was told that he had time for sight-seeing. In geography books he had read about the awesome Sahara Desert, and he arranged to look personally upon it. He saw "the wide expanse and motion of sand filling the air as the drifting snows do." Wind filled "the air with sand so that it was with difficulty we could open our eyes, without endangering our sight." In the part of the desert viewed, "I saw neither plant nor flower of any kind . . . , nor even a shrub on which a camel could browse." Viewing this as an extreme example of selfishness, he thought, "You [the desert] will drink every drop of moisture and every drop of dew that distils from heaven, and in return you send forth no plant or flower, ungrateful soil!"

Back in the port of Bulack Orson boarded the boat for Alexandria, and just before "pushing off," he tells, "a letter came from the doctor, stating that poor Mr. Gager died in about two hours after I left him." Not until the following March, through government channels, did Charles Gager's family in

Connecticut receive word of his Cairo death and publish an obituary.[14] In England, in the January *Millennial Star*, Parley P. Pratt printed the account that Orson had written of the death. Charles Gager's demise thus became a historical witness of Orson's mission.

After 150 miles down the west branch of the Nile—like the east branch, slow-flowing, with flat delta landscape on either side—Orson stepped ashore in Alexandria. Tall Pompey's Pillar reminded travelers of the ancient magnificence of this huge city, the principal port of Egypt.

A shipmate, going directly from Alexandria to England, agreed to carry a letter for Orson and post it there. Hurriedly, November 22, Orson wrote to Parley, reporting that he enjoyed "good health." He wrote about some of his hardships, briefly outlined his visit to Jerusalem, enclosed a copy of the prayer he had written on the Mount of Olives, and told of the illness and death of Mr. Gager.

Of his immediate plans he said, "I am now about to go on board a fine ship for Tri[e]ste, and from thence I intend to proceed to Regensburgh, and there publish our faith in the German language. There are those who are ready and willing to assist me. . . . If I had money sufficient I should be almost tempted to take passage on board [the Oriental steamer] to England, but this I cannot do.

"On receipt of this," Orson added, "I wish you to write to me immediately, and direct [the letter] to Regensburgh, on the Danube, Beyern, or Bavaria. If you know anything of my family, tell me. . . ."

Orson's expectation of rapid travel met disappointment. His ship remained in the Alexandria harbor for six days until November 30, quarantined. Then, after a week of coursing over the waves of the blue Mediterranean with the ship's sails billowing majestically in the wind, the weather turned into a terrible sea storm "off the Island of Candia [Crete], about the 7th of December."

December 21, three weeks after leaving Alexandria, the ship sailed into the port of Trieste. Alpine heights dominated the east and north skyline, and the deep blue waters of the Adriatic Sea stretched to the west. Orson gazed longingly at the clustered homes on the gentle hill to the immediate east. He felt eager to set foot on firm ground and be on his way.

But again a quarantine had been imposed, of four weeks. Contemplating four more long weeks cramped aboard ship disheartened all aboard. This delay, however, provided Orson time to record his mission experiences while fresh in his mind.

With the vessel secured to the Trieste dock, Orson's world became steady enough for him to write a letter, and to Marinda he did, that day. "I feel glad, and more than glad," he said, "that I have seen Jerusalem. Face never answered more correctly to face in water, than Mt. Olivet did to the vision I had in Nauvoo.

"It is only about 250 miles from this," he wrote, telling her of his plans, "to Bavaria where I made a stop last summer; and as soon as I am released from this prison, it is my intention to go there and publish the principles of our faith in the German language, unless I shall be differently advised in the letters which I hope to receive. It is directly on my way to London. . . . First over the Alps to Munich, then to Ratisbon [Regensburg], from thence to Frankfort, on the Maine, and then to Mayenz and down the Rhine. . . . [From] Germany, I shall go to England, if the Lord will, and there spend a short time, and then return to you."[15]

January 1, 1842, Orson composed a lengthy letter to his "Dear Brethren of the Twelve." On this New Year's day of golden brightness he wrote for hours, giving details of what he saw, said, heard, and felt in the Holy Land. And he prophesied:

> It was by political power and influence that the Jewish nation was broken down, and her subjects dispersed abroad; and I will here hazard the opinion, that by political power and influence they will be gathered and built up; and further, that England is destined in the wisdom and economy of heaven to stretch forth the arm of political power, and advance in the front ranks of this glorious enterprise. The Lord once raised up a Cyrus to restore the Jews, but that was not evidence that he owned the religion of the Persians. This opinion I submit, however, to your superior wisdom to correct if you shall find it wrong.

"There are many Jews," Orson also wrote, "who care nothing about Jerusalem, and have no regard for God. Their money is the God they worship; yet there are many of the most pious and devout among them who look towards Jerusalem as the tender and affectionate mother looks upon the home where she left her lovely little babe."

Orson felt uncertainty about his letter reaching Nauvoo, so sent it to Parley P. Pratt in England with a long cover message. Orson asked Parley to "publish it by itself in pamphlet form, as soon as possible, and send a copy to each one of the Twelve, three to the Presidency of the Church, and one to my wife. . . . I wish you, also, to send five copies to my brother, Abijah Hyde, Oxford, Newhaven County, and State of Connecticut, that he may send one to each of my other brothers [Asahel and Ammi], and one also to each [of] my sisters [Sally and Laura], and [tell him] that I wish them and their families to consider themselves embraced within the circle of every good wish expressed in it."

Orson also asked Parley to distribute copies for sale, and with the proceeds to pay the printer, then to direct any profits "for the benefit of my wife and children." Expressing his yearnings to see his loved ones, Orson continued, "Perhaps I feel too anxious about my family, but where the heart has only few objects to share its sympathies, upon those few objects the sun of affection shines with warmer and more brilliant ray. My family is my earthly all; and of late my feelings concerning them are very peculiar. It is nearly a year since I have heard anything of them. . . .

"I hope . . . to get news from you and the church when I get [to Bavaria]," Orson added in a postscript to his message to Parley. "I hope also to hear something from my wife. I feel that a word from her would be more precious than gold; yet I am afraid to hear lest she may be in trouble, or some of her friends dead—a father or mother perhaps, or brother or sister. Yet I try to comfort myself with the thought that my long absence is the cause of all my bad feelings. The Lord knows, and I pray that he may bind up every aching heart. Fare-thee-well; thy brother in the Lord." Later Orson learned that his feelings were correct about Marinda losing a loved one. Her sister Alice, wife of Oliver Olney, died in July of 1841.[16]

January 17, 1842, the last day of his "confinement on ship board," Orson composed another letter, this one to the "Brethren and Sisters at Nauvoo." Thinking of the joys Marinda had brought to him, and wanting all husbands to appreciate their wives, especially if unkind words might have been spoken at frustrating times, he counseled, quoting the apostle Paul, "'Husbands,' whoever you are, 'love your wives, and be not bitter against them' [Colossians 3:19]. The delicacy of their sex, the vivid perceptibility of their mind[s], and the soft and engaging virtues of their heart[s], which weave themselves into the rugged recesses of man's masculine temperament and constitute him a fit member of society, render them entitled to the warmest affections of your heart, and to the generous protection of your arm."

Orson arrived in Regensburg before the end of January. He found letters from Marinda and from Joseph Smith, dated 14 November, and two letters from Parley. He felt so "thrice glad" that he "laughed and cried altogether." He was pleased to learn of Church progress in England and Nauvoo, and he rejoiced even more to receive Marinda's encouragement and love, to learn that she and the children fared adequately.

Orson had carried his January 1 and 17 letters with him to Germany. January 30 he added a note, bundled all of the pages together, and sent them off to Parley.

Elder Pratt printed three thousand copies of Orson's letters and in the *Millennial Star*, April 1842, advertized: "We have pleasure in announcing to the churches and the public that we have just published, price fourpence, the Letters received from Brother Orson Hyde, entitled 'A Voice from Jerusalem,' containing a sketch of his travels and ministry to the East, which we feel assured will be read with great interest by all." In the August issue of the *Millennial Star* Parley reminded his readers to buy the booklet "not only for its intrinsic value, but because the profits of it are to be appropriated for the benefit of Elder Hyde's family."[17]

Orson remained in Regensburg for seven relaxing months, grateful for the hospitality of the same well-to-do family with whom he stayed before. He continued his study of German and French in exchange for teaching further English to his hostess and her two daughters. He gave English lessons to other students too. His earnings slowly brought him enough to publish his book and to pay for his travel home.

Regarding his book, in his unbounded thankfulness for the Lord's watch-care over him, he felt an earnest obligation to translate his explanation of gospel truths into as beautiful a German as possible. He prayed and he studied and he worked. At length, with help from one of his students, he grew satisfied. In Regensburg he presented the manuscript "to the censor and the city commissioner, to get permission to publish. . . . I received the answer," he tells disappointingly, "that the requested permission could not be granted, since [the text] contained principles that were so different from those which had already been introduced to the people in the country, that they would cause excitement and unrest among the people. Should I try to publish and distribute the book, all copies would be confiscated and I (as I was told by a third person) would be fined or arrested.

"To be fined or to be arrested, for the cause of virtue and religion, does not alarm me." Orson continues. "However, to see my efforts and my money, which I intended to use for the benefit of my fellowmen, wasted, may give sufficient excuse for my efforts to try to sow the good seed in a more friendly soil."

Orson carried his manuscript to Frankfurt and at length found a printer who agreed to publish it. The book's title began *Ein Ruf aus der Wüste. . . .* Translated into English, the full title page says: *A Cry From The Wilderness. A Voice From The Dust Of The Earth. A brief sketch of the origin and the doctrines of the "Church of Jesus Christ of Latter Day Saints" in America, known to some as: "The Mormons," by Orson Hyde, a Priest of this Church. Frankfurt, 1842.* The book contained 115 pages.

Orson returned to Regensburg. August 10 he reported to Parley. His publication was "now in press," and he was "well and prospering."[18]

In his book Orson told a little of his own background and of his faith in God: "Although I left my home without a gulden, neither a coat nor a cane nor an umbrella, I have never lacked the necessities of life. I always had enough for myself and I had always something for the less fortunate. My trust in the Lord, who talked to me in the visions of the night and whose voice I heard in the forests of America at day, has not decreased in the least, for I believe that He will sustain me in every trial, and uphold me with the wings of his mercy, until I have finished my work."[19]

In the main part of his book Orson related the account of Joseph Smith and his visions, explained the origin and contents of the Book of Mormon, recounted the restoration of priesthood powers and the organization of the

Church, and detailed the beliefs and practices of the Church. He assured his readers that the Latter-day Saints based their beliefs on the same foundation as did all Christians: the Old and New Testaments. "No one has the right to add something to these Scriptures, or to take something away . . . ," he added. "See [Deuteronomy 4:2 and] Rev[elation] 22:18–19. But if the Lord should deem it wise to give a new revelation to mankind subsequently, . . . this would not be an addition, or the work of man, but the work of Him who had declared through the mouth of His Son, that all hidden things would come to light, and all secrets would be revealed. Therefore, those who know the scriptures already, have sufficient reasons to believe that they can expect more." On another page Orson wrote that "the cornerstone of our Church was hewn from a rock in a quarry, without having been subject to the polishing chisels of any of the religious sects; and hence it was capable of assuming the form the great builder wanted it to have."[20]

In words eloquent Orson stated his desire that "everybody . . . may know, that God has established His Kingdom, and lifted up His ensign. . . . His voice will be heard even to the ends of the earth. . . . Zion's banner is unfurled and invites the righteous . . . to rest in its shade. . . . And it is my constant prayer and my immutable faith, that Heaven may continue to reveal its word to us, until the knowledge and the glory of God will fill the whole earth, and wars will be unknown to the nations."[21]

Orson distributed many copies of his book and then prepared to leave Regensburg. He "pri[z]ed very highly" the friendships he had made.

He arrived in England in mid September, enjoyed warm reunions with old friends, spoke to captivated audiences about his mission, and applauded the great strides the Church had made in membership during his absence.[22]

Orson soon sailed for America, leaving Liverpool September 25, 1842 on the ship *Medford*. He presided over the 214 Saints aboard, bound for Nauvoo by way of New Orleans. Fair weather accompanied them. At the mouth of the Mississippi River, however, their good fortune changed. The *Medford* became stuck on a sandbar and remained for thirty hours. It finally arrived in New Orleans November 13. Though the Saints felt privileged to travel with Elder Orson Hyde, his zeal bothered some of the other passengers, and a Church member had overheard men plotting to take his life after the ship docked. The member informed Orson, who in turn talked with the Captain. The Captain allowed Orson to proceed ashore before others, thus preventing problems. Passengers from the *Sidney*, who had arrived two days earlier, joined company with the *Medford* passengers for the remainder of the journey. The emigrants stayed three days in New Orleans, then embarked on the large river steamer *Alexander Scott.*

The group traveled rapidly up the Mississippi River until beyond the mouth of the Ohio River. Here they ran aground. After three days stuck fast, and getting cleared again, they journeyed to within ninety miles of Saint Louis. Here the river flowed insufficient water to carry them farther.

At the beginning of this delay, Orson, intensely desirous to get home, appointed someone else the charge of the company and set out on his own. Nauvoo lay more than two hundred miles away, and he reached that cherished destination, "the city beautiful," December 7. He later learned that the vessel remained grounded for three weeks. The emigrants finally made their way to Saint Louis, but winter had set in, with the river frozen beyond. Circumstances forced the company to remain until April.[23]

Approaching Nauvoo, Orson tried to recognize old landmarks, but great changes gave it an unfamiliar appearance. His astonishment at the prosperity and rapid growth caused him to later exclaim, "[N]othing but the distinguished blessings of a bountiful providence upon the untiring hand of industry and perseverance could have adorned the vacant prairie with such a vast number of beautiful dwellings, and converted the forest into fields and beautiful gardens. . . . I felt something the same as I did while standing on Mount Olivet on the east of Jerusalem and viewing the surrounding country: said I to myself, 'Is this a dream, a vision, or a reality?' Circumstances demonstrated the reality of the scenery: so when I c[a]me to the residence of my wife and children, . . . shared with them the warm embrace,—then sat down with them all hanging about my neck,—I said, 'It is, in reality, Nauvoo.'"[24]

With Orson's and Marinda's loneliness of separation past, it seemed not quite so long, but Orson agonized when Marinda told him of her adversities. Especially difficult had been the previous year as cold winter approached. She lacked enough fuel to keep the drafty cabin warm, her food supply had dwindled, and her health had declined. She wondered if she would survive to see her husband again. She thought her heart would break when little Laura and Emily cried with discomfort.

The Prophet Joseph learned of her plight, and he sought the Lord's guidance in her behalf. In answer to this petition he received a revelation directing Ebenezer Robinson and his wife to care for her and family. Brother and Sister Robinson obeyed the Lord's command and took the Hydes into their home, even though they too suffered illness. Their love and care revived Marinda's spirits and her strength. Marinda handed Orson her copy of the treasured revelation. He read:

> December 2, 1841. Verily thus saith the Lord unto you my servant Joseph, that inasmuch as you have called upon me to know my will concerning my handmaid Nancy Marinda Hyde—behold it is my will that she should have a better place prepared for her, than that in which she now lives, in order that her life may be spared unto her; therefore go and say unto my servant, Ebenezer Robinson, and to my handmaid his wife—Let them open their doors and take her and her children into their

house and take care of them faithfully and kindly until my servant Orson Hyde returns from his mission, or until some other provision can be made for her welfare and safety. Let them do these things and spare not, and I the Lord will bless them and heal them if they do it not grudgingly, saith the Lord God; and she shall be a blessing unto them; and let my handmaid Nancy Marinda Hyde hearken to the counsel of my servant Joseph in all things whatsoever he shall teach unto her, and it shall be a blessing upon her and upon her children after her, unto her justification, saith the Lord.[25]

Gratitude filled Orson's being when he saw the date on the paper. The revelation had been received by the Prophet just weeks after Orson's prayer on the Mount of Olives. In that prayer he had requested that "a special blessing rest upon" the "hands that have fed, clothed, or shown favor unto the family of thy servant in his absence, or that shall hereafter do so."

PART TWO

(1843–1852)

And it shall come to pass in the last days, that the mountain of the Lord's house shall be established in the top of the mountains, and shall be exalted above the hills; and all nations shall flow unto it.

And many people shall go and say, Come ye, and let us go up to the mountain of the Lord, to the house of the God of Jacob; and he will teach us of his ways, and we will walk in his paths: for out of Zion shall go forth the law. . . .

—Isaiah 2:2-3

CHAPTER 10

... *Martha and Mary*. ... *(1843)*

> *Martha received him....*
> *And ... Mary ... also.*
> —Luke 10:38-39

THE cultured attributes of Mary Ann Price revealed a woman of intelligence, education, and self-confidence. Twenty-six years of age, petite, attractive, and quiet, she possessed the qualities of a cherished Latter-day Saint wife. Meager, however, were prospects of marriage for her and many other single women in Nauvoo early in 1843. They outnumbered the eligible men because more women than men joined the Church.[1]

Mary Ann, often called Mary, had arrived in Nauvoo from England in November 1841 and felt gratitude to the family who shared their home with her in exchange for help in the household. Her varied skills served her well in domestic tasks and in tutoring children. Her mother had trained her competently in homemaking arts. Also, Mary Ann had received a valuable education at Broad Oak Academy in Gloucestershire, England. She had been born June 5, 1816, in Lea, Herefordshire, to loving parents who lived comfortably. Regarding religion, her father thought that the denominations of his day lacked the "true priesthood," but he felt good about attending church and praying. He and his wife taught their children strict adherence to the standards of the Church of England. Her father's attitude led Mary Ann to read the Bible avidly, to reflect, and to study other religions. She reached the conclusion that "all the Christian denominations embrace some truths, but none of them are in accord with the Scriptures of the New Testament."[2] June 30, 1836, when twenty years of age, she married Thomas Price, who was her cousin. As the years passed, she sorrowed that no children came to them. She gained solace from a close association with her own family. Her father passed away in January 1840.[3]

Mary Ann became the first member of her family to join the Latter-day Saints. She narrates her conversion:

> In the year 1840 a man and his son were employed to paint and paper my home. . . . I had previously been informed that they had embraced some strange [religious] delusion: But knowing the man was sober, industrious . . . , and had been the leader of the [local Church of

England] choir for thirty years, I could not suppose that [the rumor] was true and waited, thinking that he would introduce the subject. In this I was disappointed. After two weeks . . . I ventured to ask him, he said: It was true that he had embraced the faith of the Latter day Saints and if I would allow him he would bring me some of their books. He first handed me the "Voice of Warning" [by Parley P. Pratt,], then other works touching the first principles of the Gospel of Jesus Christ. These [books], together with his own testimony, alarmed me for I found myself believing! What should I do? . . .

I could no longer resist the truth, for such it appeared to me, and [I] . . . requested to be baptized. I did not venture to consult with my [husband or] friends, thinking I was old enough to judge for myself; and, I must confess, fearing opposition from those I dearly loved. [In the fall of 1840 I was baptized.]

Soon after, I informed my sister [Emma] of what I had done. She was very much shocked! But after hearing [the gospel message, she] became convinced and followed my example.[4]

When Mary Ann's husband learned of the baptism, he disapproved. As months passed, Mary Ann tried to share the beauties of the gospel with him, but Thomas grew intensely adverse to her affiliation with the Mormons. Mary Ann agonized, and she prayed fervently. "Must I give up all—kindred, friends, society and the comforts of life?" she wondered. "This seemed to be the sacrifice required," she tells. At length she took specific anguish to the Lord: should she join the company of Saints scheduled to gather in Liverpool by September 21 and sail for the United States? She loved her husband, and she loved the gospel, but keeping both appeared impossible. Which should she forsake?

Increasingly she felt that the gospel must be her priority. She knew, though, her incapability to face the emotional trauma of telling Thomas. She developed a plan: she would leave at night while he slept. She secreted belongings to take with her. In the bedroom she emptied a sea chest in readiness. Every time she opened the lid, the loud squeak of its hinges grated her nerves. A thought struck her, and she prayed. She sought a further witness to her impressions. If the Lord truly wanted her to depart, she would open the chest while her husband lay asleep and the hinges would make no noise.

The decisive night arrived. Mary Ann lifted the lid. Silence. Mary Ann's heart pounded. She closed the lid. Again silence. She carried the chest out of the room.

Her "dear young sister (Emma), . . . [as] beautiful in person as in spirit," traveled with Mary Ann to Nauvoo. In this new country they intended to prepare for a happy future reunion with their mother, brothers, and sisters. All of them had joined the Church and hoped to sail.[5]

The crowded frontier conditions of expanding Nauvoo disappointed the young women. Established Saints provided board and room to newcomers as best they could, but inadequate accommodations and insufficient food caused health problems. Many deaths resulted, Emma's being among them in March of 1842. Mary Ann describes this as her "first great trial" in Zion. "Oh, the sadness of that hour!!"[6] Mary Ann yearned for the comfort of her family. She soothed the pain by serving those around her and by cherishing her association with the Saints. She remembered that the Lord had directed her to Nauvoo. However, she had no promise that life would be easy.

In early 1843 at Mary Ann's residence, an unexpected gentleman asked for her. Introduced as Elder Orson Hyde, the visitor bowed as he lifted his hat. Looking in wonderment at a *Church leader*, calling on her, she saw a smiling robust man of princely bearing in well-pressed clothes. She had been aware that he returned from his Jerusalem mission two months before.

Orson presented letters of introduction to Mary Ann and explained that he had crossed the ocean from England on the ship with her mother, brothers, and sisters. He expressed disappointment that the frozen river prevented their company from reaching Nauvoo this past season. He talked only briefly about her family and invited her to visit his wife. At that time he would tell Mary Ann more about the voyage and his conversations with her mother and the others. Mary Ann accepted the invitation.

Carefully, before the appointed time, she fussed with her hair and her attire. A carriage pulled up, and Elder Hyde knocked again at her door. Riding in the carriage, she and the apostle talked of general topics. And Elder Hyde told her that he had invited the Prophet Joseph to meet with them. Surprised and thrilled, Mary Ann was pleased that she looked her best.

In the Hyde home, Marinda greeted Mary Ann warmly. Mary Ann felt at ease. Joseph Smith arrived and shared friendly handshakes. Mary Ann experienced the same glow as always in his presence. She retained a precious memory of the first time she and her sister Emma met him. A present for the Prophet, sent with them by their brother in England, provided their first "introduction to that great man! We were struck, or rather, impressed with his noble bearing and gentle manners!!"

The Prophet, Elder Hyde, Marinda, and Mary Ann talked. The conversation moved to various subjects, and Mary Ann enjoyed being part of it. She especially delighted in hearing Elder Hyde's details about his trip from England with her family. She noted, as well, the obvious happiness of him and his wife in being reunited after nearly three years apart.[7]

The Prophet Joseph guided the conversation to marriage and said that the trial of separation from loved ones belonged to earth life only. In the glorious realms of Heaven, worthy husbands and wives could have the privilege of being together in an eternal covenant. The Lord had revealed this wondrous principle to the Prophet several years before, when he had prayed for understanding about another concept involving marriage.

He had inquired "to know and understand wherein . . . the Lord justified . . . Abraham, Isaac, and Jacob, [and] also Moses, David and Solomon, [and others] . . . [in] their having many wives and concubines." He received the answer that to those ancient servants "I, the Lord, commanded" the practice. Further, in the "last days," "the dispensation of the fulness of times," all principles from previous righteous dispensations, or periods of earth's history, would be restored.[8] This restoration included "plural marriage," a man marrying more than one wife. This principle must again be lived among the Saints. This the Lord himself pronounced to the startled Prophet Joseph.[9]

The reason for the restoration of plural marriage, the revelation continued, was "to prove you all, as I did Abraham, and that I might require an offering at your hand, by covenant and sacrifice." Lived in accord with divine edict, the Lord added, plural marriage could bring rewards during mortality as well as during immortality. Men and women "sealed" by true priesthood authority remain together in eternal bonds.[10]

While listening, Mary Ann's throat constricted, and she felt agonizing inner throbs. Her avid scripture studies had given her no problem with Biblical patriarchs practicing "plural marriage," but certainly this arrangement did *not* fit into modern times! She "resisted [the idea] with every argument I could command," she relates. "With my tradition, it was most repulsive to my feelings and rendered me very unhappy. . . . I could not reconcile it with the purity of the gospel of Christ."[11]

Despite her dissent, the Prophet remained calm. Years before, he had been through the mental anguish she now experienced, and he had come to recognize this reaction as appropriate. The Lord wanted his children on earth to spurn plural marriage except when He required compliance. The greatest eternal principles earn the greatest rewards but also the greatest punishments. People could not, without severe divine censure, themselves choose for men to have more than one wife at a time. The scriptures contain examples of this. Jehovah gave both David and Solomon many wives, but David lost his eternal exaltation because of his sins relative to Uriah and Uriah's wife. David took that which was not lawful. Solomon received condemnation for acquiring wives contrary to the Lord's rules.[12]

The Book of Mormon contained an opposite situation. Lehi, a prophet, taught monogamy. Some of his descendants, however, used the examples of David and Solomon to justify plurality of wives. Lehi's son Jacob denounced this, under inspired mandate, reminding the people that the Lord had censured both David and Solomon for their unrighteous acquisition of wives. Jacob delivered the Lord's words, "For if I will . . . raise up seed unto me I will command my people; otherwise they shall hearken unto these things [men having only one wife]."[13]

The Lord had decreed to Joseph Smith that, in righteousness, the Saints should live this law to hasten the purposes of the Kingdom of God. They would receive transcendent recompense for their obedience. Also, from human reasoning, more women than men seemed devoted to the gospel. Future exaltation in eternal worlds would require a means for the entrance of every worthy person to be sealed in the marriage covenant. Plural marriage provided this.[14]

Mary Ann's consuming thoughts caused her to pay little attention to the quiet demeanor of Elder Hyde and Marinda. The steady look in their eyes showed compassion and personal understanding for Mary Ann's feelings. Obviously they had been taught the principle of plural marriage and had accepted it. Mary Ann did not now contemplate what their struggles might have been when the Prophet Joseph taught them.

Joseph Smith completed his teachings about marriage, and the conversation moved to other topics. Departure time came. Elder Hyde and Mary Ann had ridden only a short distance toward her home when the apostle cleared his throat. With the background rhythm of horses' hoofbeats, his hands holding tightly to the reins, he asked Mary Ann what she thought of the Prophet's explanation of plural wives. He apparently assumed that she had been converted to the principle. Before she could answer, he turned his head and spoke directly to her, "Would you consent to enter my family?"

Shocked, Mary Ann's heart screamed against this unexpected intrusion into her privacy. Despite what the Prophet had said, she wanted no further mention of the subject. Quickly, fully meeting Elder Hyde's gaze, she replied, "I cannot think of it for [even] a moment!"[15]

Mary Ann reacted typically. Joseph Smith himself had lacked the courage to teach the revelation until "an angel of the Lord threatened to slay him if he did not reveal and establish this celestial principle."[16] The Prophet commanded Heber C. Kimball three times before he agreed to enter the practice. Then Heber became distraught over his compliance, until his wife received her own witness from the Lord of its correctness. Brigham Young later said that "at the time Joseph revealed the doctrine; I was not desirous of shrinking from any duty, nor of failing in the least to do as I was commanded, but it was the first time in my life that I had desired the grave, and I could hardly get over it for a long time."[17]

The hours of night, after her visit to the Hyde home, brought no sleep to Mary Ann, only doubts: "Oh, is it possible that I have left my home and family to come far out into the western part of America, believing that I was following a company of real servants and ministers of God's holy work, to now be confronted with such an abominable, soul-distressing principle or policy as the Prophet himself has declared to me?"

The next day her turmoil made eating impossible. She longed to talk about her reeling thoughts, but she felt it unthinkable to confide such a grave matter with anyone she knew in the city. Only one course seemed open to her: to seek her God. During the past many months, every time she opened her chest to the loud squeak of its hinges, she remembered that the Lord had revealed his will to her before. Maybe he would again. The Church was God's Church, and she believed Joseph Smith to be God's Prophet. She had to *know* if she believed correctly. Surely a true Prophet of God would not lead her into forbidden paths. She decided to find a secluded spot and pray.

This bleak wintry day Mary Ann walked past where the homes decreased in number. Leaving the road, she wandered among the barren trees. In the somber surroundings she knelt on the frozen ground and heaped the folds of her skirt around her legs. Fervently she prayed. For enlightenment she pled. Was this unbelievable doctrine really from God? With intense yearning she long entreated her Maker in every manner of imploring words she could phrase. Sighing after her "Amen," she arose.

No immediate answer settled in her mind or sounded in her ears. The landscape appeared the same as when she came—dreary and unresponsive. She started to retrace her steps. After walking only a short distance, she noticed a change in her feelings.

In wonder she looked around as warmth and comfort from "an unseen force and power" enveloped her. Joy filtered into every part of her body. Unexpectedly her voice burst forth in song. Beautiful and lilting words, unfamiliar, rang out; she was singing in tongues. Doubts melted away. "This new language of endowment is from my Father in Heaven, and in full answer to my soul's desire," she realized. With complete conviction, she knew that the Prophet Joseph had truly received the revelation he had explained. Regarding this sacred manifestation to her, in later years she said, "I had a testimony of the divine origin of the revelation on marriage and have never, from that time, doubted the purity and exalted teachings of the Prophet, Joseph Smith!"

Though she now *knew* that God sanctioned the plurality of wives for this time and place, she pondered much during the following weeks. She thought about the preparations her mind must make for living a new kind of life, and she made them. She sorted through her feelings about the husband she had abandoned in England. Did her running away free her to marry another? Here on the frontier, faraway spouses—pursuing their own lives with no desire for reunion—were considered a part of the past that needed no apologies. This, too, she accepted. She would go forward.

Eventually Mary Ann visited the Prophet and related to him her remarkable experience. She told him that she now felt "ready to accept the principle of plural marriage."

Joseph Smith smiled. He explained that inspiration had assured him of her worthiness and capability to embrace this holy principle. He added that only the leading men of the Church were at this stage expected to practice plural marriage. The Prophet had chosen Mary Ann as a suitable companion for Orson Hyde and his wife Marinda, but the decision was hers. Perhaps she would prefer Apostle Parley P. Pratt. He would soon be returning to live in Nauvoo after his long sojourn in England.[18]

"Thus it rested for a while," Mary Ann recounts, "and Mr. Hyde married another young lady." The woman who became Orson's second wife, Martha Rebecca Browett, like Mary Ann had come from England. She was twenty-four years of age, born June 5, 1817, in Tewkesbury, Gloucestershire. She, her mother, and two brothers joined the Church, and they came together to Nauvoo in 1841. "Neat, industrious, and tidy" Martha supported herself as a skilled seamstress.[19] The Prophet officiated at the wedding, sealing Martha to Orson "for time and for all eternity." Marinda gave her full consent and stood as one of the witnesses.[20]

"In the mean time," Mary Ann explains, "I was trying to learn the character of the leading men" in order to select an eternal companion. Her conviction strengthened that with spiritual help she could do things she previously thought impossible. "I soon learned, to my satisfaction, that Mr. Orson Hyde was a conscientious, upright and noble man." She also felt assured that Marinda would welcome her into the family.

In a quiet ceremony, July 20, 1843, Mary Ann Price became the bride of Orson Hyde. "[Marinda] received me into her house," Mary Ann tells, "as her husband's wife!—Sealed to him by Joseph, the Prophet, in her presence. . . . Mrs. Hyde had two sweet little girls and I soon learned to love them and their dear mother."

Marinda, age twenty-seven, was a year older than Mary Ann and two years older than Martha. All three had birthdays in June, Martha and Mary Ann the same day. Orson was thirty-eight. Outwardly Martha and Mary Ann lived in the Hyde home to help Marinda and the children. Their status as wives remained private, the same as that of other plural wives in Nauvoo. Precaution was necessary to prevent rebellion from within the Church and persecution from without. The future held the season for public announcement of the practice. If plural wives became pregnant they remained secluded, as most women did anyway during the latter months.[21]

Martha and Mary Ann learned, to their surprise, that Marinda had not been sealed to Orson. Instead Marinda had been sealed as an eternal, but not a mortal, wife to the Prophet Joseph Smith. Gaining an understanding of this situation required explanation:

Many times in the weeks following Orson's December 1842 return from Jerusalem, the Prophet Joseph had conversed with him. The Prophet listened avidly to details of the mission. He also instructed. For months he had been teaching the other resident apostles about marriage for eternity. God's kingdom is a kingdom of order, Joseph Smith taught, with specific precepts governing the priesthood sealings of husbands and wives. All are based on the principle that a woman can be sealed for eternity to only one man. The ancient Israelites understood that a widow belonged to her first husband. Her deceased husband's brother should marry her and "raise up seed to thy brother." Also, in the days of the Savior, the people understood that in Heaven, after death, a woman could be claimed by only one man.[22] The Lord taught the Prophet Joseph that the everlasting priesthood, the power to bind on earth and in heaven, allowed five kinds of priesthood sealings of husbands and wives:

First, a living woman could be sealed to a living man for time and for eternity. This might be done at the time of their original marriage or later in a separate ceremony.

Second, a living person could be sealed to a deceased person for eternity, with someone standing as the proxy for the deceased person. This would ordinarily involve living widows or widowers being sealed to their deceased spouses.

Third, a deceased man and a deceased woman could be sealed to each other for eternity, with two living people acting as proxies. This would most commonly be done for persons married to one another on earth, who die before receiving their priesthood sealing.[23]

Fourth, a living man and a living woman could be married for *time* (mortality) only. Generally this would involve widows previously sealed for time and eternity to their first husbands. These women could be married to later husbands for *time* only.[24]

Fifth, a living man and a living woman could be sealed for *eternity* only. They would not be husband and wife during their sojourn on earth, but would be after death. Seldom would this type of sealing be performed.[25]

With Orson, the Prophet talked gently about Orson's courtship of Marinda nine years before. Joseph Smith had then, in earnest, pronounced the warning words: "God has given that woman to me. Do not marry her." He had refrained from belaboring the statement, letting Orson think the words jestful. At that time the principles of plural marriage had already been revealed to him. Additionally the Lord had declared that Marinda, with others, belonged to Joseph Smith for eternity.[26] Hesitant to teach what he knew would be a devastatingly explosive doctrine, the Prophet made no further move to prevent Orson's civil marriage (for mortality only). Since then he had carried in his heart the burden of knowing that some day he must tell his friend of the Lord's decree.

Orson's bewildered thoughts cried out that he disbelieve the Prophet. But he knew better. Orson had considered the diligence and hardships of his Jerusalem mission a great sacrifice. Now he was asked to sacrifice more than his time, his talents, and his means to the work of the Lord. He was asked to accept the fact that his wife, his beloved Marinda, would belong to another in the next sphere of existence. Were his feelings akin to those of Abraham when commanded to sacrifice his son Isaac?[27] Would the mandate have been lifted had he not signed the affidavit against the Lord's Prophet in 1838?[28] Orson knew Marinda's worth. Her loyalty to the Lord's cause had never wavered, even when her father, brothers, sisters, and husband turned against it. Her devotion to God knew no bounds. Indeed she was a select daughter of the Most High. Marinda's sealing to Joseph Smith for eternity, not time, had been performed in April of 1842, many months before Orson's return.[29]

Orson struggled to accept the anguishing shock of learning that Marinda had already been sealed to the Prophet for the eternal hereafter. He agonized. He wept. He prayed. He knew the consequences of an apostle acting contrary to the Lord's wishes. He wanted never again to suffer that misery. Not only did he converse long hours privately with the Prophet Joseph, but he and Marinda together conversed with Joseph Smith.[30] Orson gained a new understanding of the part of the Lord's revelation for Marinda, in December 1841, that she should "hearken to the counsel of my servant Joseph in all things whatsoever he shall teach unto her, and it shall be a blessing upon her and upon her children after her, unto her justification, saith the Lord."

Orson's torment, his distress, he overcame. His questions, his laments, he resolved. The day arrived that he received the sublime prize of the sure witness of the Holy Ghost. He *knew* the correctness of Marinda being sealed to Joseph Smith. A consolation was that Marinda would share eternity with the finest man Orson knew, the man he loved most on earth. She could not possibly have done better. And in the meantime Orson would cherish her and would live the ancient law of Israel, that of "raising up seed to his [gospel] brother."

. . . *many things.* . . . *(1843–1844)*

> . . . *in . . . many things he ministered.*
> —2 Timothy 1:18

WHILE learning about and adjusting to plural marriage, Orson's other early 1843 endeavors varied widely:

With the Prophet Joseph, Orson attended meetings, read German, and engaged in long discussions. December 27, 1842, to January 10, 1843, Orson and others shared a wintry trip with Joseph Smith to Springfield, where the Prophet, even though falsely charged, must stand trial. The court dismissed the accusations. January 20, in Nauvoo, Joseph Smith, Hyrum Smith, and the Twelve met to discuss Orson Pratt, who had been excommunicated the summer before. Elder Pratt had believed false rumors about Joseph Smith and polygamy, but eventually he understood the truth and had faithfully demonstrated repentance. The group approved reinstating him in the Twelve. This, however, posed a dilemma. Amasa Lyman had been ordained an apostle the previous August to take Orson Pratt's place. Elder Pratt's return would give the Quorum too many members. The Prophet Joseph had contemplated taking Orson Hyde out of the Twelve to be a counselor in the First Presidency, giving Orson Pratt the calling to the Jews. After discussion, however, he chose to put Amasa Lyman in the Presidency and leave Orson Hyde holding "the keys to the Jews." Afterward the group walked to the icy river, where Joseph Smith rebaptized Orson Pratt. Back on the bank the Prophet reordained him an apostle. Joy abounded.[1]

The Prophet's compassion extended to Orson Hyde's family also, about their residence in a crowded, rented space. When Joseph Smith had advised Orson and Marinda to make room for another wife, their need for a new dwelling became urgent, and the Prophet authorized Orson to ask publicly for assistance. Orson's resultant letter, published February 1 in Nauvoo's *Times and Seasons*, stated his need. Contributions enabled him to purchase a lot, February 10, for $500. The same day, in preparation for additional wives, he deeded the land to Marinda, that she would have the security of her own property. The one-acre lot was on the northwest corner of Carlin (afterward Hyde) and Hotchkiss Streets, closer to the bluff than to the river.[2]

Meanwhile, Orson was elected to the Nauvoo City Council, February 6. Nauvoo contained about 12,000 people, and for them Orson entered into lively dialogue about items as diverse as licensing businesses, building bridges, and making rules about stray animals. He also helped consider solutions for serious concerns. How should the Council deal with the "grog shops, and card shops, and counterfeit shops"? These "shops" were liquor-drinking and gambling establishments, and secreted places where counterfeit coins were made. They had begun appearing in Nauvoo as the city attracted settlers of various convictions. What should civil officials do about threats of violence against the Saints from outsiders? Did the city have any jurisdiction to regulate members whose faith in the Church waned to the point that they circulated lies about Church leaders?[3]

In mid February Orson savored a three-day preaching jaunt with the Prophet Joseph and two other brethren, in two sleighs, to Shokoquon, Illinois. The second day, Elders Hyde and Orson Pratt's sleigh upset. Elder Hyde hurt his hand, and the horse ran away—minor setbacks. The Prophet and his companion caught the horse and brought it back.[4]

At home, after his late winter marriage to Martha, Orson's family adjusted to the plural wife arrangement. Because assignments kept him away much of the time, Marinda did most of the adjusting. Martha, sometimes carrying her resourcefulness to being "proud-spirited" and "technical," found her transitions difficult, but she tried to be congenial.

March 13, Orson departed for a speaking tour to Quincy, fifty miles to the south. He delivered ten lectures, baptized three persons, and returned home March 30. March 31, he and Marinda attended an evening turkey dinner party with the Prophet and others.

April 1, Orson departed again, with the Prophet, for a four-day carriage journey to and from Ramus, Illinois. Orson preached, April 2, and said, "It is our privilege to have the Father and Son dwelling in our hearts." During the noon meal the Prophet modified the statement, saying that the Father and Son are glorified beings, occupying their own spaces. Then Joseph Smith augmented the correction with marvelous truths, published later as Doctrine and Covenants 130:1-17. In the afternoon meeting the Prophet remedied Orson's earlier sermon. Afterward he taught Orson further; a few of his statements later became Doctrine and Covenants 130:18-23. In an evening meeting the Prophet explained many scriptures. He became so pleased with the response of those around him that he turned jestful. In closing his remarks he mirthfully alluded to Orson's extraneous preachings of the morning and asked Elder Hyde "to get up and fulfill his covenant to preach three-quarters of an hour, otherwise I shall give him a good whipping." Noting Brother Joseph's sportive tone, and grateful that his own error had inspired such heights, Orson reacted properly. He arose and stated, "Brothers and sisters, I feel as though all has been said that can be said. I can say nothing, but bless you."[5]

As well as treasuring experiences with Joseph Smith, Orson treasured the privilege of associating with most of his brethren of the Twelve. Absent on assignments were John E. Page and Lyman Wight (ordained in August 1842). Orson said that "notwithstanding the joy of a husband and father . . . in again being united with his family after such a long and hazardous vacation as mine to Jerusalem . . . , no love ever experienced was equal to the love I had for my brother apostles." The Twelve held meetings, and they savored shared dinners and parties with their wives.[6]

Nauvoo and environs.

The Twelve, and the Saints in general, were surprised in April when Sidney Rigdon attended general conference, his first in two years. Sidney—once a dynamic asset to the Lord's work, and officially still a counselor to Joseph Smith in the First Presidency—had been moody and uncooperative ever since his Missouri imprisonment, harassment, and loss of property. Within the past year, rumors indicated a turning against the Prophet Joseph. Joseph Smith had even declared to the Twelve his own resolve to "throw [Sidney] off, and carry him no longer." But lately Sidney seemed repentant and had begun again serving the Saints. Conference convened on the floor of the open unfinished temple, white limestone walls reaching from four to twelve feet high. After the presentation of Sidney's name for a sustaining vote, he spoke to the crowd and claimed poor health as the reason for disregarding his responsibilities. He sounded sincerely contrite. The Twelve took no replacement action, and the congregation, through pity (Orson felt), voted "almost unanimously" to retain him.[7]

April 19, Orson was unable to attend a meeting of the Twelve with Joseph Smith in his office, but afterward he learned that the Prophet declared that the apostles' next co-operative mission would be in the United States. Speaking words more significant than the group recognized, he had said, "The Twelve must travel to save their lives. I feel all the veins and strata necessary for the Twelve to move in to save their lives." Without dwelling upon this somber prediction, the Prophet said that most of the Twelve should soon travel varied routes east as far as Maine. They should preach on the way, gather money for the temple and other Church construction, and meet in Boston. Boston inhabitants would be pleased to have them in their midst. Twelve hundred residents had petitioned for Elders Heber C. Kimball and Orson Hyde to come and preach among them. Brother George J. Adams, with whom Orson had traveled to England on his way to Jerusalem, arranged the petition.[8]

June 1, Joseph Smith announced the Lord's desire about a major mission for Orson Hyde. Eventually he and George J. Adams should go "to Saint Petersburgh, in Russia; . . . to introduce the fulness of the glorious gospel of the Son of God, to the people of that vast empire." Later Joseph said that to this Russian mission "is attached some of the most important things concerning the advancement and building up of the kingdom of God in the last days, which cannot be explained at this time." Unforeseen events would prevent Orson or Brother Adams from serving this mission to Russia as mortals.

Meanwhile, construction on Orson's new home progressed. The cellar was dug, the foundation stone walls laid. The back-and-forth rasp of saws produced mounds of fresh-scented sawdust, and hammers rang on nails. Men "raised" the walls June 10.[9]

June 28 a Church announcement in the *Nauvoo Neighbor* told that the Fourth of July patriotic speeches would be delivered morning and afternoon by Orson Hyde and by George J. Adams. Also, "At the close of each address a collection will be taken for the especial purpose of assisting to complete Elder Hyde's house." On the Fourth of July nearly 13,000 people congregated in the grove near the unfinished temple. Elder Hyde addressed the crowd "in a very able and appropriate manner." Generous contributions came in after his speech, more than Orson needed. He proposed that part be used to assist Joseph Smith in the expenses of current persecution.[10]

For part of July, Orson and many other brethren served short missions throughout Illinois, preaching the gospel and providing correct information to the public about the recent illegal arrest of Joseph Smith. Orson traveled to Lee County, one hundred and fifty miles northeast of Nauvoo.[11]

Soon after Orson's return home he wed Mary Ann, July 20. The adjustments began again, and Mary Ann adapted more easily than had Martha. Orson and Marinda grew to love them both. Marinda had been marvelous in allowing Martha and Mary Ann time and space to find their niches in the family structure. In the process, bliss at times failed. Tears sometimes flowed. Tempers occasionally flared. But laughter rippled. Countenances glowed. And hearts warmed. The Hyde household became family. Mary Ann's family had arrived in Nauvoo April 12, and she had helped them get settled. Martha spent time with her own family too. In the Hyde home Laura and Emily delighted in the greater attention they received after "Aunt Martha" and "Aunt Mary Ann" (or "Aunt Mary") joined them.

Orson was pleased with the progress of his six year old daughter Laura. While he traveled in Europe and Asia, Marinda taught her to sew and to read. Orson gave her a Book of Mormon. Sitting close together, father and daughter shared precious hours with the book, father helping daughter with the complex words. Laura completed the volume. One time she read sections to the Prophet Joseph. This surprised and delighted him.[12]

The new Hyde home—a frame dwelling eighteen feet by twenty-four feet, facing east—seemed palatial to the family after its completion and their move into it. Its symmetry was pleasing: a porch across the front with four squared posts, a door in the center flanked with two windows, four small upstairs bedroom windows above the porch roof, and chimneys standing sentinel at both ends of the top roof. Inside, Marinda and Martha and Mary Ann worked together to make it "cheery and bright."[13]

Another matter in Nauvoo grew decreasingly cheery and bright—the actions of Sidney Rigdon. Since the sustaining vote he received in April conference, his actions had not improved. Orson attended a summer meeting where the Prophet Joseph chastised the Twelve severely for their backwardness in April conference. He said to them, "Why will you suffer the Church to put that old hypocrite upon my shoulders again, after I have thrown him down? But as you have neglected to help me put him down, you will have it to do yourselves when it will cost you more to do it than it would now."[14]

Parley P. Pratt, like Orson, finished building a new home, and he and Orson left Nauvoo, August 17, to join others of the Twelve already serving missions in the eastern states. Orson hoped to return home by November before the birth of Marinda's baby. The journey to Boston, by way of Chicago, took three weeks. A conference in Boston, September 9, 10, and 11, furnished a warm reunion for the eight apostles attending, among them John E. Page. Orson had last seen Elder Page three years before when they said farewells in Cincinnati. After the meetings the apostles dispersed through the eastern states. They sought funds and preached, filling a need to counteract newspaper articles that voiced alarm at the Mormon "threat" to the country. Homeward bound in Philadelphia, October 3, Orson savored oysters, a favorite dinner.[15]

Orson entered his own door in Nauvoo, pleased to see Marinda still "with child." Orson Washington Hyde was born November 9, his parents thrilled to have a son.

But this happiness proved brief. Marinda became severely ill, and, in addition, their baby lived only two weeks.[16] They buried him sorrowfully, as they had their first son.

Meetings of the Twelve resumed. In one of these councils Joseph Smith said, "[T]here is something going to happen; I don't know what it is, but the Lord bids me to hasten and give you your endowment before the temple is finished." For this sacred purpose Orson and others assembled December 2, 1843, at the invitation of the Prophet Joseph, in the room over the Prophet's brick store.[17]

The "endowment" teaches the eternal purpose of life on earth. Joseph Smith had first administered the ordinance to a few Church leaders the previous May. He explained afterward that he had instructed them "in the principles and order of the Priesthood, attending to washings, anointings, endowments and the communication of keys pertaining to the Aaronic Priesthood, and so on to the highest order of the Melchisedek Priesthood, setting forth . . . all those plans and principles by which any one is enabled to . . . come up and abide in the presence of the Eloheim [Gods] in the eternal worlds." The Prophet also explained that he had "instituted the ancient order of things [temple rites] for the first time in these last days. And the communications I made to this council were of things spiritual, and to be received only by the spiritual minded: and there was nothing made known to these men but what will be made known to all the Saints of the last days, so soon as they are prepared to receive, and a proper place is prepared to communicate them, even to the weakest of the Saints; therefore let the Saints be diligent in building the Temple."[18]

The Prophet continued administering priesthood endowments to selected leaders. After he had carefully instructed the apostles about every ordinance of the holy priesthood, he rejoiced, exclaiming, "Now if they kill me you have got all the keys, and all the ordinances, and you can confer them upon others. . . . [T]he hosts of Satan will not be able to tear down the kingdom as fast as you will be able to build it up." He added that ordinance work by proxy for the dead must wait until completion of the temple.[19]

Increased spiritual blessings in Nauvoo were offset by increased temporal problems. The Saints needed money. No government aid had resulted from the petitions that Joseph Smith took to Washington, D.C., four years before; and both local revenues and widespread pleas for support failed to meet needs. Additionally, the Saints wished to be better understood by their fellow United States citizens. Rumors of treacherous acts among local leaders, including misrepresentations about polygamy (still a private matter), were causing caustic reactions both in and out of Nauvoo. Also, armed guards patrolled along the river to prevent hostile Missourians from entering Nauvoo, kidnaping, and causing general disturbance.[20]

November 28, discussion among Church leaders had resulted in the writing of a memorial to again petition the federal government for assistance. The memorial contained a summary of the conflicts in Missouri, told of the threats that prevented Saints from returning to recover their holdings or sign deeds to sell them, and asked for "redress for grievances or [exertions to] shield us from harm in our efforts to regain our lost property."[21] Orson and others left Nauvoo early in December to visit various places and get signatures on copies of the memorial. During this short assignment he received a letter from the Church leaders asking him to also "get paper to print the Doctrine and Covenants, and get new type and metal for sterotyping the same." He returned, successful, in late December.

While returning, his concerns for the Saints deepened December 28 when he learned that in Lima, twenty-eight miles south of Nauvoo, a recent anti-Mormon meeting convened. The participants resolved that local Mormons must give up their guns or leave within thirteen days, and that Mormons would be prevented from raising another crop in that region.[22] These resolves afterward failed within their deadlines, but the feelings persisted.

In Nauvoo Orson learned that the City Council had passed the final draft of the memorial to Congress. Beyond outlining the Missouri persecutions, the expulsion, and that in "vain had we appealed to the constituted authorities of Missouri for protection and redress," it stated that "exiles or expelled 'Mormons' have lost in property and damages about two millions of dollars" and that the "State of Missouri continues her ravages, persecutions, and plunderings, by kidnapping said exiles from Illinois, and by other depredations." The petition asked for compensation and also that "the mayor of Nauvoo be . . . empowered . . . to call to his aid a sufficient number of United States forces, in connection with the Nauvoo Legion [Joseph Smith had been elected General of the Legion], to repel the invasion of mobs, keep the public peace, and protect the innocent from the unhallowed ravages of lawless banditti that escape justice on the western frontier." Orson Pratt would take the memorial to Washington, D.C. when the ice broke up and allowed river travel.[23]

By 1844 "Nauvoo the Beautiful" contained an estimated 15,000 inhabitants, and her renown brought an increase of both friends and foes. In a letter to the England Saints, dated January 20, Orson reported, "Brother Joseph Smith is daily thronged with visitors of every grade, from different parts of the United States. Some are being aroused to put down the work, because, they say, Joseph Smith is getting too much power. . . . [O]thers say that a man who possesses power and skill to obtain influence among an enlightened people must be worthy of it, and so it goes."[24]

With national elections scheduled for 1844, in November 1843 Joseph Smith had sent letters to prospective candidates for President of the United States asking their intended "course of action" regarding the Saints. Some sent no answers; others sent noncommittal answers. The resulting concern for the future of the Church led to a meeting January 29, where Joseph Smith and Hyrum Smith, the Quorum of the Twelve, and others, decided that Joseph Smith should become a Presidential candidate. The group formulated an energetic plan to publish the Prophet's views and to send out numerous men to speak in public, advocating the just causes for which Joseph Smith stood. This should effectively help the public to recognize the law-abiding nature of the Saints.[25]

Meanwhile, however, fanatical anti-Mormon activities continued. February 17 a group in Carthage, eighteen miles southeast of Nauvoo, held a convention to contrive a sure way to drive the Mormons from the state. The Prophet Joseph learned of the threat and in a meeting February 20 talked of possible troubles ahead. "Send out a delegation and investigate . . . California and Oregon, and hunt out a good location," he directed the Twelve, "where we can remove to after the temple is completed, and where we can build a city in a day, and have a government of our own, get up into the mountains, where the devil cannot dig us out, and live in a healthful climate, where we can live as old as we have a mind to." The Twelve appointed a committee to investigate the western territories.[26]

Concern accelerated steadily in Nauvoo, and Joseph Smith met with the Twelve and other leaders more often than in the past. In one glorious meeting, with about sixty men present, Orson included, the Prophet stood for three hours and expounded about the kingdom of God, his face glowing. He made a portentous prophecy. "My work is about done;" he said, "I am going to step aside awhile. I am going to rest from my labors; for I have borne the burthen [burden] and heat of the day. . . . And I roll the burthen off my shoulders on[to] the shoulders of the Twelve Apostles." While saying this he clasped the lapels of his coat and, as if to take it off, rolled his coat back upon his shoulders. Looking at the Twelve, to whom he had already given all of the priesthood keys entrusted to him by heavenly messengers, he said, "Now round up your shoulders and bear off this kingdom."

After the meeting, Orson and others discussed the Prophet's comments. "We did not consider . . . ," Orson narrates, "that he was going to die or be taken from us; but we considered that as he had been borne down with excessive labors. . . , he was going to retire to rest and regain his health, and we should act under his direction and bear the responsibility of the work." In meetings afterward, Joseph Smith said that he had rolled the responsibility of the Church onto the shoulders of the Quorum of the Twelve and that they would have the duty of leading the Saints.[27]

Orson spent part of March 1844 in Saint Louis. He preached, encouraged Church members, acquired paper for printing, and purchased iron, steel, nails, and other supplies needed for continued temple construction. By much exertion he raised money enough to pay for the supplies.

In Nauvoo, Joseph Smith's Presidential candidacy had been announced in the *Times and Seasons*. Fifteen hundred copies of his views on government had been printed. Hundreds of brethren would soon spread out over the country to promote the gospel and advocate Joseph Smith for President.[28]

The Prophet decided that another memorial should be presented to Congress and that Orson Hyde should take it and work with Orson Pratt, who had already left with the first memorial. Orson made hurried preparations to be gone from home for several months. Hoping to augment family income, he advertised for sale, in the *Nauvoo Neighbor,* copies of his German *Ein Ruf aus der Wuste [A Cry from the Wilderness]*. He also notified the City Council of his departure plans. Orson had already missed many meetings. After he left for his eastern assignment, the Council replaced him.

Joseph Smith's new memorial involved the vast territories of Oregon and Texas, west of the United States. These areas were drawing settlers, and the Prophet preached increasingly that the Saints should seek peace somewhere in the west. Orson received two copies of the new memorial, one addressed to Congress and one addressed to President John Tyler, asking for "the privilege of raising 100,000 men to extend protection to persons wishing to settle Oregon and other portions of the territory of the United States, and extend protection to the people in Texas." In this capacity Joseph Smith asked that he be made a "member of the army of these United States."

When the Prophet Joseph handed the documents to him, Orson asked about his personal responsibility. He wanted to do nothing to hurt Joseph Smith. The Prophet smiled confidently and said, "Go and do the best you can. Act like a king and get the very best things done for us that you can." He signed credentials for Orson, dated March 30, 1844, giving him authority "to transact such business as he may deem expedient and beneficial for the party whom he represents."[29]

Orson left Nauvoo April 4. April 23 he arrived in Washington, with its mammoth government buildings, stately and substantial, and its wide expanses of green spring lawn, attractive pools, and many kinds of trees. He found Elder Orson Pratt and learned with disappointment that the original memorial remained with the Senate judiciary committee.

In pleasant consultation the next day—with members of the House of Representatives from their home state, Illinois, and with the senior senator from Illinois, James Semple—Elders Pratt and Hyde learned that the House already had two bills before it about Oregon. Also, Congress had no constitutional authority to appoint Joseph Smith a member of the army of the United States with the power to raise troops, as the petition requested.

Considering his esteem for Joseph Smith, Orson wanted to prevent the Prophet's reputation "from being impeached by congress, by his asking a thing not constitutional." All the men in Washington with whom he had conversed said that the Mormon memorial would fail to pass anyhow, so,

Orson thought, "there can be nothing lost by erasing that part, and there might be something saved."

In the copy of the memorial for Congress, Orson erased the request about Joseph Smith being made a member of the army. Because the power to make such an appointment belonged alone to the President, Orson left the request in the copy for him. "If the altered document shall pass congress," he reasoned, "then I will take the one addressed to the executive and get his approval and signature without that alteration, and thus between the two powers get the entire memorial passed. . . . In case the bill should not pass in congress, I still have the same opportunity to apply to the President and get his approval, if possible."[30]

The next morning, April 25, Orson wrote to Joseph Smith. "A member of Congress is in no enviable situation;" he penned, "if he will boldly advocate true principles, he loses his influence and becomes unpopular; and whoever is committed [to true principles] and has lost his influence has no power to benefit his constituents, so that all go to figuring and playing around the great points."

Explaining briefly his own actions, Orson wrote, "Mr. Semple said that Mr. [Joseph] Smith could not constitutionally be constituted a member of the army by law; and this, if nothing else, would prevent its passage. I observed that I would in that case strike out that clause. Perhaps I took an unwarrantable responsibility upon myself; but where I get into a straight place I can do no better than act according to what appears most correct."

The same day that Orson composed his letter, Mr. Semple arranged for Elders Hyde and Pratt to view the White House that evening and be introduced to the President of the United States. The White House impressed Orson. President John Tyler also impressed Orson. Orson felt surprise to find him "a very plain, homespun, familiar, farmer-like man." President Tyler expressed regret about the troubles the Saints had endured in Missouri and inquired of their circumstances in Illinois. Orson told him of their labors in making a swampland productive and of their needs for equipment and commodities that they might continue to progress. The two Mormons spent a "very agreeable" hour in the White House and left still hopeful for good results from their efforts.[31]

Elders Pratt and Hyde decided that they should not simply wait for help, but should "tease [Congress] until we either provoke them or get them to do something for us." The following morning the two drafted a bill requesting two million dollars, as outlined in the earlier memorial. They petitioned that the money "be deposited in the hands of the City Council of Nauvoo, and by them dealt out to the sufferers in proportion to their loss." They handed the bill to the committee on the judiciary for the Senate, who still held the original memorial.

The same day, April 26, the two Orsons conversed at length with Stephen A. Douglas, former judge of the Illinois supreme court and now a Representative in Congress from Illinois. Judge Douglas showed them a book, containing a map of Oregon and the report of an exploration of the country lying between the Missouri river and the Rocky Mountains, by Lieutenant J. C. Fremont of the corps of Topographical Engineers. Orson, elated, expressed a wish that "Mr. Smith could see it." Judge Douglas agreed to mail a copy to Nauvoo. In the evening Orson wrote to Joseph Smith of this good fortune, saying that the "book is a most valuable document to any one contemplating a journey to Oregon."[32]

Orson stayed in Washington only a week, talking with members of Congress and attempting to reason with them. However, he considered his efforts futile. He gave the memorials to Mr. Semple of the Senate and Mr. Wentworth of the House of Representatives for presentation. Nothing now remained to be done but wait for results. He and Elder Pratt needed money to sustain themselves. Answers to their prayers disclosed that one of them should travel, preach, and seek donations. This became Elder Hyde's assignment. He would proceed to Philadelphia. They would correspond, and, if necessary, "the railroad cars" would bring Elder Hyde back "like the wind."[33]

In the Philadelphia area Orson preached, baptized, advocated Joseph Smith's candidacy for President, and accepted donations for sustenance. He read the newspapers and, in items about the Mormons, noted an increasing rumble against the Prophet. Also, in the *Times and Seasons* from Nauvoo, he read of increasing internal problems. Robert D. Foster, Wilson Law, and William Law, former influential Church leaders, had been cut off "for unchristianlike conduct." Orson sensed a foreboding. Being so far away, and wishing to know the truth, he prayed for accurate knowledge of events occurring in Nauvoo. In answer to his earnest pleadings, he gratefully received "many dreams and visions."

Orson's concern led him to warn the Saints in the eastern states to disregard derogatory stories about Joseph Smith. Orson wrote an article in Philadelphia May 30, and *The Prophet*, the Church's newspaper in New York City, published it June 8:

> God has never chosen Messrs. Laws, neither Dr. Foster nor any of their Satellites, to reform or save the Church. When the wolf enters the fold and begins to tear, rend and devour the sheep; know ye that the good Shepherd never sent him. These men are determined to rend and tear in pieces. . . . Joseph Smith is not a fallen prophet. Men might as well talk to me about a fallen sun, as to talk about [Joseph Smith being] a fallen prophet. . . .
>
> Joseph Smith will shine forth like the sun, and be loved by millions, when his present opposers will be compelled to come and worship at his

feet, and to know that God hath loved him. Although his enemies may kill him, (if God permit,) and the dark cloud of death obstruct his rays for a time; yet the spirit of life from the Almighty, will animate his sleeping ashes, and cause him to shine forth with an additional lustre.[34]

After five weeks away, Orson returned to Washington June 8 to meet with Elders Heber C. Kimball and Lyman Wight, who had brought letters and instructions from Nauvoo. One instruction directed Orson and the others to attend a national convention in Baltimore, Maryland, July 13, and present the name of Joseph Smith for President of the United States.

From a council of Church leaders in Nauvoo, Heber had brought a letter for Orson, answering his of April 25 and 26. Orson broke the seal of the letter and eagerly began to read. But as he read, his eagerness changed to dismay. The letter reprimanded him for altering the document given him by Joseph Smith.

Orson's momentary reaction of anger changed to chagrin. Had he really done wrong? The brethren in Nauvoo must have misunderstood his letter of April 25. He thought about what he had written regarding changing Joseph Smith's memorial. Yes, his brief explanation probably seemed superficial. He should have detailed more explicitly the reasons for his action.

The next day, June 9, contrite, Orson sat down to recount why he had erased some of the Prophet's words. He acknowledged "that the blow which has fallen upon me, has been inflicted by the hand of friendship . . . ," and begged his brethren to realize that "If I have committed an error there is one . . . consolation . . . , I have committed it with a heart unreservedly devoted to your best interest." In his letter Orson gave a full account of his meeting with Mr. Semple and explained his feelings about trying to solve the problem of requesting something unconstitutional. Orson had felt, he added, that from the Prophet he received "a shadow of authority" to make decisions "as I may deem expedient and beneficial for the party I represent. . . . Pursuant to that impression I went to work as industriously and prudently as possible. . . . I am sorry that I have committed the error, and if the council will forgive this offense, I will assure them that I shall never again, under any circumstances, be inclined to take a like responsibility. If I knew of anything more that I could say or do to give you satisfaction, I would most certainly do it."[35]

Heber C. Kimball and Lyman Wight had spent but a few days in Washington when, on the morning of June 11, Heber announced in disgust that they would leave and seek fields of labor more receptive. They planned to find Brigham Young and Wilford Woodruff, who had also come east from Nauvoo.

The petitions from the Saints had now been rejected by both houses of Congress, but Orson still needed to present the last memorial to President Tyler. He had learned that the busy President "devotes two hours each day to business calls, from 11 until 1 o'clock. Many from all parts of the Union call daily to see him. He, consequently, is able to devote but little time to each visitor." The same day that Heber and Lyman left Washington, Orson waited his turn outside the President's office and was then admitted. President Tyler greeted him as graciously as he had weeks before, inviting Orson to sit down. Orson explained the purpose of his coming and handed the memorial to the President.

President Tyler read the document attentively. Looking up, he remarked that the object was unquestionably a good one, regarding the settlement of Oregon. He explained that the government planned to establish "a line of forts . . . for the protection of all United States Citizens emigrating to that Territory." He patiently conversed, answered Orson's questions, and illustrated that he could not confer special privileges upon any citizen group.

Though disappointed, when Orson afterward reported the interview to the Church council in Nauvoo, he admitted that President Tyler "was very frank, open, and condescending." He detailed the conversation.

"Now, I will tell you how I feel about our government," Orson continued. "If you were to issue an order and direct it to me to go and demand the keys of the United States treasury, and remove the deposits and funds to Nauvoo, I should undertake it with just as much faith as I should to ask them to do anything else under God's heavens for the Latter Day Saints."

In the same June 11 letter Orson wrote of his own plans that "if God permit, I shall leave tomorrow morning for Long Island and Connecticut." After he had signed his name he paused, thinking of the deep anxiety about the Church that had developed in his mind during recent weeks. He added a postscript,

"A dark cloud hangs over the churches. We apprehend a storm at hand. I have been very busy in barring down the hatches. I fear, however, some will jump overboard, but we will do the best we can. Knowing who is at the helm [the Lord], and a skillful pilot, we shall be sure to make the port though the sea be boisterous."[36]

As Orson traveled northward, eventually reaching Boston, he preached among Church members, he listened to public sentiment, and he read the newspapers. His apprehensions deepened, and he wrote another article for *The Prophet*:

> To the Saints scattered abroad: Greeting.
> Whereas, The public journals are teeming with red hot lava from the craters of some disaffected ones in Nauvoo, I would caution all who feel an interest in the prosperity of Zion's cause, to enter into your closets and pray to Almighty God, that his spirit may lead you in the path of truth, and that you may be preserved from any and every rash or hasty movement. . . .

Do I believe the tales that are told concerning Nauvoo, and the conduct of Gen. Smith [The Prophet Joseph, General of the Nauvoo Legion]? I believe them not; I would, therefore, caution all the Saints to be slow to think evil of him, whom almost all men have sought in vain to destroy.

I have sailed enough on the high seas to know that in times of storm and tempest, our desired course, if we had it not before, cannot then well be obtained.—This requires a clear sky and a meridian sun; so also on the voyage of Life. . . .

Be admonished then by your friend and brother, to hold on your course until the storm subsides . . . ; then if you shall be dissatisfied, you will have a more proper time to obtain the course that will bring you to your desired haven.

. . . your brother in the new and everlasting covenant,

ORSON HYDE.[37]

Thursday afternoon, June 27, 1844, in public Faneuil Hall in Boston, an indefinable melancholy enshrouded Orson, Brigham Young, Wilford Woodruff, and others. Trying to study maps, they were unable to make simple decisions about where each should labor. Then other concerns gave Brigham and Wilford reason to leave. Orson and the remaining brethren attempted again to discuss plans, but the gloom deepened. At length, feeling no heart to look at maps, Orson walked to the farther end of the hall alone and paced the floor, searching his soul for a cause of this somberness while profuse uncontrollable tears ran down his face. Afterward Orson learned that perplexing sorrow and depression had almost overcome Brigham and Wilford too, as they sat in the railway depot.[38]

The brethren persevered in their duties, and the bleakness diminished. After five days Orson was assigned to work in the area of New York City and southwestern Connecticut. He soon departed from Boston. In New Haven, Connecticut, he shared a room with Elisha H. Davis, one of the missionaries sent out to preach the gospel and encourage the candidacy of Joseph Smith for President.

In New Haven, July 9, twelve days after his despondent Thursday, Orson heard the familiar droning call of a newsboy pealing out the headlines. The apostle halted abruptly when he discerned numbing words. Waving a newspaper high, a newsboy shouted,

"Joe Smith, the Mormon Prophet, has been killed!"

Stunned, Orson felt as though his breath had been knocked from him by a falling tree.

Disbelief came to his rescue. He had heard this kind of rumor before.

And yet—just now—the chilling words seemed to throb with finality. He purchased a paper. He read that Joseph Smith and his brother Hyrum had been imprisoned in Carthage jail, then were shot to death June 27, in the afternoon. The report, in disdainful sentences, implied that notorious criminals had been trapped and silenced.

Was the Prophet Joseph—beloved Brother Joseph—really dead, truly gone from earth? "No!" Orson's mind shouted. "Yes," murmured his heart, as he recalled his feelings of desolation on June 27. He mechanically returned to his place of lodging.

In the room that Orson shared with Elisha H. Davis he lay down upon a couch and spread the newspaper over his face, a barrier against annoying insects, against unwanted news, against even thinking. In the dimness he willed his distressed mind to become blank that he might retreat to the oblivion of sleep.

His next conscious sensation came through the haze of awakening. He felt hands pressed soothingly upon the paper over his face. Then his spiritual eyes perceived the Prophet Joseph and Hyrum standing near him, majestic and peaceful. Leaving his side, they walked across the room, passed through the doorway, and vanished. This sacred manifestation witnessed that these revered friends dwelt, alive, in another sphere. Their hands had rested upon him in comfort and blessing.

Orson removed the newspaper and saw Brother Davis writing at a nearby table. Orson jumped to his feet—startling his companion—and exclaimed, "Oh, Brother Davis, they have murdered the Prophet!"[39]

Orson felt, in this time of lamentation, a duty to console Church members. In New York City, the day after receiving the news of the assassinations, he spent hours reassuring. Many Saints asked in anguish, often with hands wiping tears from eyes, who would lead the Church. Orson affirmed to them that the apostles would receive the necessary inspiration to move ahead. He *knew* how thoroughly he and his brethren had been schooled in receiving divine direction. With absolute conviction he could say, "As long as God has a Church on the earth, He will govern it."

Thinking of how overwhelming the news of the martyrdom would be to Church members in England, he wrote to them, July 10, a brief letter of assurance. "[L]et all the Saints be humble and faithful," he penned, "and let the elders stand firm at the post of duty. . . . [E]re long some of us will come to your help. Let every thing go on just as if the prophet were alive. There may be an Elisha that has caught the mantle of Elijah. . . ."[40]

While Orson comforted Saints, the July 13 political convention in Baltimore began and ended. Orson's commission to attend and recommend a Prophet of God for President of the United States had been nullified by gunfire.

July 18, Orson arrived in Boston to consult with Brigham Young, President of the Twelve. Spiritual promptings had brought Heber C. Kimball, Wilford Woodruff, and Orson Pratt also. The five sat in council, and they knelt in prayers. Vividly they recalled the Prophet's words of a few months before when he rolled his coat back over his shoulders and said, "I roll the responsibility of this Church onto the shoulders of the Twelve." In sober earnest he had spoken. Orson and his companions felt an urgency to return to Nauvoo, but also inspiration to move cautiously, as newspaper articles indicated that in some areas their lives would be in jeopardy because of their past association with Joseph Smith.

Also, they discussed Church leadership. Though Amasa Lyman had been selected as a member of the Presidency back in January 1843, this action had never been brought before the Church for a sustaining vote. He had continued to function as an apostle. But what of Sidney Rigdon, the surviving third member of the First Presidency? During the year since the Twelve had helped retain him in his position he had attended few councils and done little for the Saints. Word had arrived in Boston that in mid June he took his family to Pittsburgh. In spite of his recent selfish living, the apostles felt it proper to invite him to meet with them at Church headquarters. He would probably decline. Orson, appointed to write the letter, requested that he join the Twelve "in Nauvoo as soon as consistent, to comfort the saints in the day of their extreme grief . . . ; and after we have rested and mourned for our martyred brethren, we shall sit down together and hold a council."

Another decision resulted from Orson having no funds for his homeward passage. He should deliver an address about the murders and afterward collect money. He and others posted notices with the time, place, and purpose of the speech. That evening, in a hall on Washington Street, he reminded the group that prophets of God have always been opposed and many of them killed. "It is a dark time now," he admitted, "but it will soon be light." Encouraging hope, he said, "In consequence of the death of the prophets, the [secular] editors . . . say the work . . . will stop, and die. But . . . I will prophesy that instead of the work dying it will be like the mustard stock that was ripe, that a man undertook to throw out of his garden and scattered seeds all over it, and next year it was nothing but mustard. It will be so by shedding the blood of the prophets. It will make ten saints where there is one now."[41]

Two days later, July 20, Orson Hyde and Orson Pratt left Boston together, traveled to New York City, labored with the Saints there for two days, and then started homeward. July 24 in Albany, New York, they found Brigham Young, Heber C. Kimball, Wilford Woodruff, and Lyman Wight. By railway the group rode during the night, the next day, and into the night of July 25, to Buffalo, at the east end of Lake Erie. They slept for a few hours in a hotel. In the morning they discovered other returning Latter-day Saint missionaries in the same hotel. The larger group continued on together, embarking on a steamer.

Orson had learned that Marinda left Nauvoo after the martyrdoms and returned to Kirtland to stay with her family until matters quieted. Orson would stop in Kirtland too. Part way across Lake Erie, at Fairport, twelve miles from his destination, Orson bid his companions good-bye and carried his baggage ashore.[42] In Kirtland, at the Johnson home, conversation bounced in a glad jumble at his arrival, with everyone talking.

In a quieter moment Marinda gave Orson details about the Prophet and Hyrum. She told of the tumult in Nauvoo just prior to the martyrdom. She expanded on Orson's inspired dreams and visions that this uprising differed from the previous one in Missouri. In Missouri, primarily outsiders agitated the problems. This time, apostates raised the anti-Mormon sentiment to storm pitch. On their own printing press the Higbees, the Laws, and Dr. Foster published sensational slander against the Prophet Joseph and the Church. As mayor of Nauvoo, Joseph Smith ordered the press destroyed. Men carried out the order. Commotion grew worse. Civil authorities issued a warrant for the Prophet's arrest. To prevent persecution to others, Joseph Smith submitted. He, Hyrum, John Taylor, Willard Richards, and others were taken to jail in Carthage. Two days later a mob stormed the jail. With musket rifle balls they killed the Prophet and Hyrum and seriously wounded John Taylor. When news of the deaths reached the city, the shock to the Saints brought uncontrollable lamentation. This grew into indescribable despair as the wagon, bringing the lifeless bodies home, rolled dolefully through the streets.[43]

Years later Orson summarized:

> Do you suppose that Joseph Smith was permitted to be killed because the Almighty had anything against him? No. But he [the Lord] wanted the ungodly that rejected [the Prophet's] testimony to fill up the cup of their iniquity; and hence they were permitted to take away his life, after he had accomplished the work he came to accomplish, and not before; they could not touch him before he had done the work he was sent to do—before he had laid the foundation of this kingdom. And when that was completed, he might be taken from the troubles of this world.[44]

The trials in Nauvoo seemed far away, though urgent, as Orson enjoyed his few days in Kirtland with Marinda and the girls, Marinda's brother Luke and his family, and Mother Johnson. Father Johnson had passed away. Orson wanted to stay longer, but his duties called him to join the Twelve. Marinda would remain in Kirtland for the time being.

CHAPTER 12

. . . foundation of apostles. . . . (1844–1846)

> *Now therefore ye . . . are built upon the*
> *foundation of the apostles and prophets, Jesus*
> *Christ himself being the chief corner stone.*
> —Ephesians 2:19–20

UPON his arrival in Nauvoo—Monday, August 12, 1844, a week and a half after he said good-bye to Marinda in Kirtland—Orson discovered a tenuous unity, though the absence of the Prophet and Hyrum hung on the air as an almost tangible vacuum. Another death also left a vacuum, that of the Prophet's brother Samuel, who had passed away as a result of mob-caused afflictions. At home Orson found Martha and Mary Ann functioning about as others, bewildered and sad, but going about daily tasks.[1] In the next few days they and others shared with Orson their experiences, and he later outlined what was told to him:

Sidney Rigdon received the letter sent by the apostles to him from Boston, and he started immediately for Illinois. Orson narrates,

> He arrived here on Saturday, the 3rd day of August. . . . Some two or three of the Twelve were here, but not a quorum. By these he was kindly . . . received. [His coming surprised the Saints, as they well knew] that Mr. Rigdon declared when he came out of Missouri that he would never follow any revelation again that did not tend to his comfort and interest, let it come from Joseph Smith, God Almighty, or anybody else; for he said that God was unjust in suffering him to be so ill-used as he was in that state.
>
> [The few of the Twelve in Nauvoo] requested . . . a private interview with [Sidney] the next morning [Sunday, August 4] . . . before public service should begin.

Sidney failed to attend their council. Then, at the public gathering, he hurried "to the stand to preach."[2] On the stand, portly Sidney had displayed pomp and energy.[3]

> [H]e testified that [he had received a revelation that the Prophet] Joseph . . . held the keys of the kingdom and would continue to hold them to all eternity, . . . [that] the kingdom must be built up unto him, and that

. . . a guardian [must be] appointed to build up the church unto Joseph Smith.

Sidney also said that the army of Israel must be raised to dethrone the kingdoms of the world.

The Prophet Joseph, Orson knew, had taught that the Church should be "built up to Jesus Christ, and . . . that there is no other name whereby we can be saved."[4] Apparently the day had come that Joseph Smith foresaw, when the Twelve must act decisively against this man whose earlier fervor had been such a strength to the Saints. Orson's account continues:

> Mr. Rigdon wished [a] meeting called on Tuesday to attend to the choosing of a guardian, as his domestic . . . concerns . . . require[d] his immediate return [to Pittsburgh]: But . . . [he was] persuaded . . . to postpone it until Thursday, so that word might be sent to all the branches in this [area]. . . .
>
> Tuesday night, August 6th, five more of the Twelve returned, among whom was the president of our quorum. . . .
>
> Thursday came, August 8th, and Mr. Rigdon appeared early . . . , and began to speak. He urged his claims [as a Church officer of long standing, with the right of guardianship] . . . , and [he] was just about to ask an expression of the people by vote; when lo! to his . . . mortification, the president of our quorum [Brigham Young] stepped upon the stand, . . . and with a word stayed all the proceedings of Mr. Rigdon. [President Young called another meeting for the afternoon].
>
> [In the afternoon meeting] [o]thers of the Twelve . . . assisted President Young in [presenting] the true principles on which the church was to act; which were so plain . . . that Mr. Rigdon, himself, refused . . . to have his name voted for, either as spokesman or [as] guardian to this church.
>
> [By Brigham Young] the question was then put . . . [to] the several quorums of [priesthood] officers . . . [who were] arranged in order: "All in favor of supporting the Twelve in their calling, signify it by the uplifted hand." The vote [of the quorums] was unanimous; not a hand being raised in the negative.[5]

Orson explains the purpose of this procedure of voting:

> There is a way by which all revelations purporting to be from God through any man can be tested. Brother Joseph gave us the plan. Says he, "When all the [presiding] quorums are assembled and organized in order, let the revelation be presented to the quorums. If it pass one, let it go to another, and if it pass that, to another, and so on until it has passed all the quorums; and if it pass the whole without running against a snag, you may know it is of God. But if it runs against a snag, then,"

says he, "it wants inquiring into. You must see to it. . . . Let no revelation go to the people until it has been tested here."[6]

The leadership of Brigham Young, as president of the Quorum of the Twelve, gave purpose to the Saints. They rallied under his guidance to work at finishing the temple and accomplishing other endeavors that the Prophet Joseph had started. Brigham Young was forty-three years old, a giant in faith, and well-tempered on the anvil of experience in leading people and in making decisions. Decisiveness added breadth to Brother Brigham's wide chest and sturdy sloping shoulders, causing him to seem taller than his medium height. His complexion was fair, his hair light brown and wavy, his forehead high, and his chin firm. Reflecting his mood, his gray-blue eyes twinkled with glee or melted with love or shouted with reproof. Believing that everyone should be a useful member of society, Brigham Young did all in his power to help people achieve success.

August 12, the morning of the day that Orson arrived home, the apostles had made major decisions. John Taylor would remain in charge of the printing office. Wilford Woodruff would travel to England to supervise the work there. Brigham Young, Heber C. Kimball, and Willard Richards, as a unit, would direct the Church in America.[7]

President Young asked the Twelve to assemble at his home August 15. They should fast before coming. The meeting proved reminiscent of the precious occasions of heavenly manifestations that Orson had been privileged to attend with the Prophet Joseph. The Council discussed many matters. They resolved to spread the gospel throughout the world and to fight wickedness. Orson relates that "we . . . counted the cost of the stand we have taken, and . . . firmly and unitedly, with prayer and with fasting . . . decreed in the name of Jesus Christ, that we will honor our calling, and faithfully carry out the measures of the prophet so far as we have power, relying on the arm of God for strength."[8]

The next Sunday, August 18, Orson attended Sabbath services with Martha and Mary Ann. Before the meeting, President Young said to the Twelve, "I want you to disperse among the congregation and feel the pulse of the people, while I go upon the stand and speak."

The services began with prayer and singing. Then President Young stood and began talking. While Orson watched, an astonishing thing happened. "As soon as President Young opened his mouth," Orson recounts, "I heard the voice of Joseph through him, and his words went through me like electricity. 'Am I mistaken?' said I, 'or is it really the voice of Joseph Smith?' It was as familiar to me as the voice of my wife, the voice of my child, or the voice of my father.

"This is my testimony," Orson adds, "not only the voice of Joseph did I distinctly and unmistakably hear, but I saw the very gestures of his person, the very features of his countenance, and even the *stature* of Joseph. The very size of his person appeared on the stand before us in the person of Brigham. And though it may be said that President Young is a complete *mimic*, and can mimic anybody, I would like to see the man who can mimic another *in stature* who was about *four or five inches higher than himself*. And it went through me with the thrill of conviction that Brigham was the man to lead this people.

"I know [partly through this manifestation] that he was the man selected of God to fill the position. Every one in the congregation—every one who was inspired by the Spirit of the Lord—felt it. They knew it. They realized it."

Mary Ann had the same experience as Orson. Wide-eyed, her gaze glued to the speaker, she whispered to Orson and Martha, "It is the voice of Joseph! It is Joseph Smith!"

Martha, on the other hand, looked perplexed, and answered Mary Ann, "I do not see him. Where is he?"[9]

Orson learned afterward that what he called a "manifestation of the power of the Almighty" had been experienced by Church members in the August 8 meeting, ten days before. Then, too, people had seen "the power of God resting on an individual."[10]

During the next two weeks Sidney Rigdon challenged Brigham Young's position as leader. His obvious desire for personal power had the opposite effect to his intent. It helped solidify the body of the Saints in unity under the Twelve. Orson had planned to leave August 27 for Kirtland, Ohio, to get Marinda and the girls, but the situation in Nauvoo prompted him to remain to support Brigham Young. Orson's narrative continues:

> After Mr. Rigdon was rejected by this people as a leader and guardian, he was no longer in such . . . haste to get back to Pittsburgh. . . . On Monday night . . . Sept[ember] 2nd, he began his secret career to divide the church. . . . He commenced privately to teach that it was not necessary to build the Temple—that it never would be built—that God had rejected us because of our iniquity. . . . He ordained men to great and unheard of offices in the church. . . . He also selected several . . . to fit out his great army. On Tuesday the bubble burst, and his secret was no longer his own. It reached the ears of the Twelve. . . .
>
> On Tuesday evening, the same day, President Young and myself visited him at his own house, and called him to an account for his proceedings. . . . The utter . . . consternation into which this man was thrown on finding that his scheme was exploded, I will not attempt to describe. . . . We labored much with him. . . . Late in the evening, our whole quorum visited him, together with Bishop [Newel K.] Whitney and several others. . . . He . . . treat[ed] our whole proceedings with contempt. . . .

The notice appeared in the "Neighbor" of Sept[ember] 4th, a Wednesday, that fellowship [of Church leaders] was withdrawn from Sidney Rigdon, and that on the next Sunday . . . his case would be presented before the church for their action. . . .[11]

Sunday, September 8, Orson marveled that over six thousand people came to the meeting. For five hours they listened, Orson being one of the speakers. When presented the motion "that Elder Sidney Rigdon be cut off from the church, and delivered over to the buffetings of satan until he repents," the congregation responded with an almost unanimous vote. Sidney's supporters, about ten people, voted against it. President Brigham Young pronounced an official excommunication and "delivered Sidney Rigdon over to the buffetings of Satan, in the name of the Lord, and all the people said, amen."[12]

September 10, Sidney Rigdon left Nauvoo to return to Pittsburgh, and Orson departed on the same boat, bound for Kirtland to get his family. Brigham Young asked him to warn the Saints of Sidney's underhanded intentions to tear down the Church. Orson should do everything possible to counteract the false rumors that Sidney would undoubtedly generate. A traveling Church member named Hollister would assist Orson.

The day after leaving Nauvoo, on the steamer en route to Saint Louis, Orson found Sidney and—as a friend and with remembrance of his own time of trial and the strengthening help of friends—tried to convey the love and compassion that he felt for Sidney and the hope of his return to the Church.

Sidney listened patiently, but with aloofness. In a condescending tone he replied, "My course is marked out before me, and I shall pursue it."

Upon arrival in Saint Louis, Orson discovered, to his surprise, that Elder Rigdon's excommunication was already known. That evening, Wednesday, Orson preached. Sidney declined to attend. Orson reported this to Brigham Young the next day. He wrote, also, that the Saints in Quincy and Saint Louis were, "all warm for the Twelve."

Elder Hollister had left Thursday morning on a "very swift boat" for Cincinnati and Pittsburgh. He carried letters from Elder Hyde, and would himself also warn Saints about Sidney. Sidney, the berths on the fast boat all taken when he inquired, would leave "on a very slow boat" that would go out Thursday evening or Friday morning.[13]

Orson preached again on Sunday, and Monday he discovered that Sidney had tried to thwart his efforts. That morning, a letter Sidney had left with the editor appeared in the *People's Organ* in Saint Louis. Sidney accused the Latter-day Saints, and particularly Orson Hyde, of trying to blackmail him. Orson promptly wrote his own letter to the editor, refuting Sidney's words. The editor published it also.

Orson left Saint Louis and continued up the Ohio River toward Cincinnati. En route, September 19, he penned another letter to the Saints in Pittsburgh to strengthen his previous warning about Sidney Rigdon.[14]

Orson eventually reached Kirtland, helped Marinda pack, and with her and the girls started homeward. Their traveling pleasure was marred somewhat by reading Sidney Rigdon's name in newspapers and scanning his slanderous words denouncing the Saints in Nauvoo.

Orson continued to counteract Sidney's barrage. In Cincinnati, on October 21, he wrote a letter for *The Prophet* in New York City. "I have just heard from Nauvoo," Orson declared. ". . . [T]he people there are now settling down in a strong and heavenly union. . . ." Orson added, about Sidney Rigdon: "He is going his whole length in lies and slander, . . . charging the Saints in Nauvoo with things that eye hath not seen, nor ear heard. . . . Let not the Saints in the East be insulted by such a tirade of abuse and slang."

Orson's mission of warning was about over by the time he and his family reached Saint Louis on their way home. Church members welcomed them. In a conference, November 10, Orson delivered two discourses. The people declared the conference "the best . . . ever enjoyed by the Saints in this place."[15]

In mid November, Orson, Marinda, Laura, and Emily walked off the steamboat at Nauvoo. Atop the hill, the beauty of the silver-white walls of the temple betokened peace.

Again in the teeming trade metropolis of Saint Louis—where he had been sent "to preach to the saints and strengthen and encourage them"—Orson read the 1845 New Year's Day issue of the *Times and Seasons* from Nauvoo. William W. Phelps' description of the temple told that the edifice was now "up as high as the caps of the pilasters, and it looks majestic." William wrote of its white limestone exterior, its attractive windows, and the font "in the basement story . . . for . . . baptism, . . . as was the case in Solomon's temple, and all temples that God commands to be built."

Brother Phelps also described the apostles. "They were known from before the foundation of the world. . . ," he said, "Their names are Brigham Young, the lion of the Lord; Heber C. Kimball, the herald of grace; Parley P. Pratt, the archer of paradise; Orson Hyde, the olive branch of Israel; Willard Richards, the keeper of the rolls; John Taylor, the champion of right; William Smith, the patriarchal Jacob staff; Wilford Woodruff, the banner of the gospel; George A. Smith, the entablature of truth; Orson Pratt, the gauge of philosophy; John E. Page, the sun dial; and Lyman Wight, the wild ram of the mountain. And they are good men; the best the Lord can find; they do the will of God, and the saints know it.[16]

Orson returned from Saint Louis to Nauvoo January 24, but he remained for only three weeks before Brigham Young sent him back, to raise money, buy supplies, and investigate stories of a Church member defrauding the Saints "under the authority of our private seal." Orson found the stories true and took action. He remained in Saint Louis for a month and raised what money he could, but he had to request some from Nauvoo. "The brethren here are mostly poor," Orson wrote when he asked for funds. "Those who have faith, have little or no cash, and those who have cash have little or no faith." He eventually purchased iron, steel, nails, oil, white lead (paint), and turpentine for the temple.[17]

Increasingly the Twelve felt an urgency to encourage far-away Saints to gather to Nauvoo and bring their means to help finish the temple. "Do you wish, dear brethren," Orson Pratt penned in an eloquent appeal," to see the house of our God built up, adorned, and prepared according to the commandment and pattern given? Do you wish to enter into its sacred courts and receive your washings and anointings, and the keys of knowledge and power? Do you desire the eternal seal of the priesthood placed upon your head by which your progenitors for ages past and your posterity for endless generations to come shall be secured to you in a covenant that is everlasting?" In April general conference the theme continued. Church leaders exhorted the raising of all food possible, to help sustain the people who would come to work on the temple. Church members needed the power of the anticipated temple endowment, they were reminded, as a protection against Satan.[18]

The Saints heeded the admonitions to plant ample crops, and good spring weather helped the crops grow. But problems from outside Nauvoo increased.

Back in January, after intense lobbying by anti-Mormons, the Illinois legislature had repealed the Nauvoo Charter. This left the city with no civil government. Church leaders often reminded the Saints that if they obeyed the commandments of the Lord they could live in peace without civil magistrates. Priesthood brethren watched the streets and highways in continual rounds, reporting any inconsistent behavior and all movements of strangers. When watchers reported suspicious men with military or civil authority approaching the city, the apostles made no public appearances. Brigham Young had no intention of any of them being arrested on trumped-up charges of wrongdoing. Dissident groups outside Nauvoo intercepted some letters and newspapers, both to and from the city.[19]

As long as the Saints could maintain Nauvoo as a refuge from the storms of persecution they could work on the temple that the Lord had commanded them to finish. Their temple venture must not fall short of the diligence required in offerings to the Lord. If they wished blessings from God they must obey His commands. For setting the capstone on the temple walls, Brigham Young scheduled a May 24 early morning ceremony but requested no public announcement. The Twelve continued cautious in their movements because of unwarranted writs for their arrest.

May 24, a cool beautiful Saturday morning, Orson climbed one of the two sets of corner stairs and joined many other Church leaders, the brass band, and a choir on the unfinished roof of the edifice, sixty feet in the air. The services began at six o'clock. The band played, and the choir sang. Then a profound silence reigned as all eyes looked to the top southeast corner of the temple walls where a worker, trowel in hand, spread mortar. Other men lifted the last huge hewn stone into place. President Brigham Young swung a large beetle (wooden hammer) and positioned the capstone precisely. At twenty-two minutes after six o'clock President Young raised an arm and pronounced the capstone set. From the band came the resounding strains of the "Capstone March," composed for the occasion. This music and the earlier band music brought people running to find out what was happening.

"The last stone is now laid upon the Temple," Brigham Young pronounced, his voice carrying well through the crisp morning, "and I pray the Almighty in the name of Jesus to defend us in this place and sustain us until the Temple is finished and we have all got our endowments." President Young raised his arm and led the congregation as they shouted three times in exuberant unison, "Hosanna, Hosanna, Hosanna, to God and the Lamb, Amen, Amen, and Amen." The temple walls, and the heavens too, seemed to reverberate with joy.

During the closing jubilant hymn Orson and the other apostles left unnoticed for "our places of retreat, out of the way of constables and officers who are prowling around the city from Carthage."[20]

The Saints' concerns of persecution contrasted with the peaceful appearance of their city. Gardens thrived. Flowers bloomed. The beauty of Nauvoo astounded newcomers. A sister who arrived the day before the capstone ceremony, wrote home to England two weeks later about "the splendid city," adding that "great things have been accomplished. . . . Though there have many [Saints] come in here that had nothing when they landed, yet they are getting along very well as to living, and very few families are so poor as not to have a cow, and it only costs one halfpenny each day to keep them well [tended].

"For this money," she went on, writing about the cows, "the shepherds drive them on to the large prairies each day, and bring them home at night. It is delightful to see them coming into the city at night, in droves of hundreds, each one with a small bell to the neck, tinkling as they pass along. As the droves enter the city, they immediately separate in every direction, each going to their own home; they look like the herds of ancient Israel."

Amazed at how fast trees had grown, the sister continued, "Though the city has been founded but a few years, yet many of the fruit trees in the gardens and orchards appear as though they would be bending under . . . fruit in the fall of the year."

She mentioned meetings also: "The congregations are exceedingly large on the Sabbath, it is pleasing to see what attention they pay to the teachings given, which are highly edifying and interesting." Another sister wrote to England that "we have the privilege of sitting under the teachings of the twelve, which is like apples of gold in pictures of silver."[21]

The Twelve felt extraordinary unity as they led and encouraged the Saints. Heber C. Kimball tells that the Twelve often "united in prayer . . . that our enemies should not have power to come in here, with vexatious writs, for his servants, . . . and they have not done it. Is not this a miracle? Yes; and we have asked for rain, and it has rained; and we have asked for God to heal the sick, and he has healed them without an exception: that is, he has healed them or they are mending in answer to our prayers. . . .

"[We] are of one heart and mind . . . ," Elder Kimball continues. "[Our] hearts are glad; [our] spirits are united; it revives [us] to meet with each other."[22]

June 8, the Twelve discussed the need for a shelter for the meetings of large congregations. Before the Prophet Joseph's death he had talked of using a tent, and he called it a tabernacle. The Twelve decided to follow this plan. Orson Pratt recorded that the canvas tabernacle would be built "in front of, and joining the Temple on the west. The form . . . will be that of an ellipse, its longer axis running north and south, parallel to the front of the Temple. Its height will be 75 feet in the centre; its sides sloping at an angle of 45 degrees. The area of its base will be sufficient to contain eight or ten thousand persons; its seats will gradually rise one above another in the form of an amphitheatre. This will be intended for preaching to the vast congregation; while the temple will be used for the meeting of councils and quorums, and the administrations of ordinances and blessings, and preaching to smaller congregations, &c."

In the June 8 meeting, knowing Orson Hyde's ability to raise funds, the Twelve assigned him to travel to the eastern states and buy canvas. He should also buy type to print the history of Joseph Smith. Again Orson prepared to leave home.[23]

Mary Ann requested a favor of him, that he would write a letter to her. Because she was known not as his wife, but as a "domestic," a helper in his home, this posed concerns. But she wanted more than to share what he wrote to Marinda. She wanted her *own* letter. They decided to use fictitious names. Mary Ann would be "Sylvia H. Thomas," and Orson would be "N. G. T."[24] The meaning of the initials was their own secret.

June 17 the Council of the Twelve gave Orson his credentials. The paper told that the tabernacle would require about 4,000 yards of canvas, and, with other fixtures, would "cost between one and two thousand dollars." Elder Orson Hyde had been "authorized to raise the necessary funds by loan, by contribution, or tithing." The credentials asked "the saints [to] be liberal in their donations." Orson folded the paper carefully.

Traveling for five weeks by steamboat, stagecoach, and rail, Orson gleaned funds during stops in Saint Louis and other points down the Mississippi River, up the Ohio River, and overland eastward. He also preached and baptized. In Philadelphia, July 27, he lectured. Then he spent a couple of weeks in the city and in Chester County, a few miles west. His compelling pleas met success.[25]

One day Church members offered him ice cream, a rare treat, and the young woman who served it reminded him of Mary Ann. Orson had written letters home, but he must fulfill his promise to his third wife. He found a quiet spot and began. How strange to call her Sylvia, but his mind saw his own gentle Mary Ann. His affection warmed his phrases:

My ever dear Sylvia,   Philadelphia August 6th. 1845.
     I now seat myself with pen, ink, and paper to write to one whose memory does and ever will remain a source of pleasing reflection to me, for thy patience and submission have won for thee that which otherwise could not have been thine own. The part of humility is a safe one. It conducts thee through the ever green valleys of a quiet and peaceful mind, beside the pure and limpid stream of excellence and moral worth, and as its current passes by thee, transmitting thy virtues to others, thou art slowly ascending to the bright summit from whence it gurgles, that in thy lofty habitation, thy pleasure may be completed in looking back upon thy journey and witnessing thousands comparatively happy under the influence of the example which thou hast set before them. If, indeed, a grievance should enter our hearts in the domestic circle, the victory gained by seemingly not to notice it is, nine times out of ten, worthy of a laurel more unfading than to strenuously resist every occurrence that truth or fancy may say is oppressive.
     In this letter is enclosed a ten dollar note. It is good. I took it from the bank myself. I send it to you for the sole purpose of administering to the wants of the poor and sick. It is now the sickly season of the year, and perhaps there are some poor sick ones in Nauvoo that have no means of getting medicine, or some little niceties that a sickly delicate person craves. You are to use your own judgment as to who is worthy and who not, and also what to get for them. So if you are able, go about, enquire and hunt up the wretched, the miserable and destitute, and wisely administer to their relief according to your ability, and he that is faithful over a few things shall be made ruler over many, and let the blessing of the poor and them that are ready to perish, come on thee. Let no one out of our house know this. God will know it and that will be sufficient.
     Pray for the success of my undertaking and for the Spirit and power of God to attend me. At present my prospects are cheering. I think I

shall accomplish that which I have undertaken and return to you by about the first of October.

I want you to continue to look to M. [Marinda] for counsel and listen to her advice. She will always counsel you for your good, for your comfort and salvation, and if you have her favor, you have mine. I have desired and still desire to see you, that I may impart to you some instruction with words of comfort and encouragement. My long silence may cause you to say like Israel, "The Lord hath forsaken me, my Lord hath forgotten me." But if my pen has been still my thoughts have not, and they are toward you for good, and also towards all our House. The Father who gave light, gave also air and water. These are all useful equally, the one with the other, and should all be regarded as the gifts of Heaven to happify man on the Earth. Still, light may become darkness, causing man to stumble; air may display thunder and lightning sending man to ruin with its red hot bolts, and water may drown him. When these elements abide in their calm, usual, and steady course, they all serve to keep man above the troubles and vexations of life, and cause him to pass onward in his orbit with a light and joyful heart. Here is a figure, let him that hath understanding apply it as a wise steward of the manifold grace of God; and be not overcome of evil, but overcome a jealous fear by a liberal and a cheerful submission to circumstances that you cannot control.

My kind love to your sister Emily. May the Lord bless her, and give her comfort, happiness and immortality in obeying the counsel of truth.

Give M. [Martha] a kind word for me. Comfort her all you can, and you shall be comforted. She means to act wisely, and do right, and so do all our family. We will do right and not wrong God being our helper.

I want you to attend strictly to those children and make them mind you while under your tuition, and it shall be better than money in your pocket. Those little ones are very near to me. They daily cling around my heart. Tell little Em that pa remembers the great red apple, and L. [Laura] will get something if she learns well and is good. Emily has been a little in the dark, but she shall arise and shine for her Lord hath said it. Let her not be over anxious about it, nor murmur in her heart because it is mentioned, but commit herself to the care of Him who has all power on Earth and in Heaven. Comfort her and stand by her, and you shall be blest, for I love her, & those who love her I can love, and those who love you & M. shall be blest.

And now what more shall I say? All goes well in the East. Oh! I have just had a great plate full of ice cream, and altho it was brought to me by a —— who helped me to eat it also, still I thought of you all the time, and only wished we could have such a treat in Nauvoo. She was a fair representative of yourself, and you could not blame me if I felt a little partial to her. I may some time show her to you. You will not be jealous, for she is to be married soon and going out to Nauvoo.

Now fare thee well, My girl. I am as
Ever Your N. G. T.

I have you requested to write me in my [previous] letter to E. which you will no doubt have done. An answer to this [present letter] would not probably reach me 'ere I return, so however much I may wish, I cannot ask you to write [again].[26]

Mary Ann treasured this letter her entire life.

From Philadelphia, August 12, Orson sent his energetic schedule to be published in the Church's newspaper, now called *The New-York Messenger*, in New York City. Orson Pratt had succeeded his brother Parley as editor. Elder Hyde planned an ambitious itinerary in spite of summer heat: New York City, August 17; Hempstead, Long Island, August 20; Boston, August 24; Salem, Massachusetts, August 25; Georgetown, Massachusetts, August 26; and Peterboro, New Hampshire, August 28. His article included an appeal that funds be ready for him when he arrived in each place.[27]

Orson's constant exertion in very hot weather injured his health, but he kept as fast a pace as possible. By August 24 he realized that his mission would take longer than planned and reported this to Bishop Newel K. Whitney in Nauvoo. "Will you see," he asked, "that my family are helped a little if necessary." After his scheduled engagements, Orson traveled back to New York City. He had raised about eleven hundred dollars and hoped to get still more. He continued on to Philadelphia and area, where indeed the funds grew.[28]

September 11, again in New York City, he purchased "105 pieces of Imperial Russia Duck of a firm and excellent quality, and shipped it for Pittsburgh by Bingham's line at $1.05 per hundred pounds," he reported to Brigham Young. "Each piece will run from 38. to 41 Yds. I have paid $10= a piece amounting in all to $1050.00. This am[oun]t I have paid in cash this morning. The expense of transportation will be about 50 or 60 Dollars more which I have on hand and ready to pay. I borrowed about $50 or 60 Dollars in St. Louis. This I intend to pay on my return. With this exception, I have obtained all on tithing, and that too, in small sums, and I do assure you that grass has not grown under my feet. I have laboured day and night - have baptized many into the Kingdom, some of whom have wealth to help build up Zion. The Lord has been with me, and enabled me to speak to my own astonishment. Thanks be to his name.

"I have now completed my mission in the East," Orson continued his letter, "and obtained that for which I was sent. But I have not got the first thing for myself—no not even a pair of gloves or suspenders since I left St.

Louis. I . . . intend to rest a little now for a week or two by preaching and baptizing, and raising some clothes for myself and a few articles for my family, and hurry on to Pittsburg to meet the canvas there, and bring it on the same boat with me to Nauvoo." Orson also told of purchasing the requested printing supplies and added, "I think I will stay long enough to visit a little—crack a bottle or two of Champaign, and rig myself out with a new suit of clothes."

Though Orson needed new clothes he had delayed buying them until he had accomplished his assigned mission. He tried to keep the Lord's errand ahead of his own and in this regard said to Brigham Young, "[I]f ever I am inclined to slide away by myself I hope the brethren will throw every stumbling block in my way possible to prevent me." At the end of his letter, yearning to see his family, Orson asked President Young, "Will you just take a peep into my house and tell them God bless them for me. I shall come soon if all is well."

The *New-York Messenger* of September 13 published a notice about Elder Hyde: ". . . On Sunday the 14th he will be in Boston, and on Tuesday evening, the 16th, he proposes lecturing in Lowell if the friends there will procure a house and give notice in the daily papers in that place. Elder O. Pratt proposes to accompany him."

The September 20 *Messenger* contained the following: "Elder Hyde [l]eft us on Friday evening last [September 19], for the west, with a cheerful heart, after having faithfully and expeditiously accomplished the object of his mission, in procuring a Tabernacle of covering to shelter the congregation of Israel from the burning rays of the sun. Peace go with him."

October 17, Orson's family welcomed him home.[29]

Orson marveled at what had happened in Nauvoo during his four months' absence. Bounteous harvest provided enough stored grain to feed the Saints for two years. Workers on the temple had installed the windows, and at eventide the panes reflected the gold of the setting sun. The finished tower added grandeur, guiding eyes heavenward above the west front of the edifice.[30]

But mob problems had grown also. In small Latter-day Saint settlements, enemies had killed Saints' cattle, destroyed grain fields, and burned forty-four buildings. Frightened families hurried to Nauvoo for protection. The governor of Illinois received false reports of depredations by Mormons and in late September sent four hundred state troops with officials to investigate. Brigham Young told the governor's delegation the facts, but with little hope of compassion. The time seemed at hand that the Prophet Joseph Smith had foreseen when the Saints must flee jealous rage for refuge in the Western wilderness. Discussion among somber Church leaders resulted in an official statement to the state delegation that the Mormons would leave as soon in the spring as grass on the prairies would support livestock. The visiting officials agreed that this promise would "allay the excitement at present existing in the public mind," with the hoped result that citizens would "restrain and withhold all further violence." The Saints would plant no winter wheat, Brigham assured the delegation, as proof of the decision to depart. After a few weeks three hundred of the troops departed. One hundred remained to keep peace.

October 5 through 8, general conference had convened in the unfinished temple. On makeshift seats placed on rough floors, the Saints listened to Church leaders encourage faithfulness and give detailed instructions about preparing to move.[31]

Nauvoo had been converted to a vast wagon manufactory with the clanging of hammers on iron and the rasping of saws on boards. Twenty-five companies had already been organized for travel. With one hundred families in each company and an average of five people per family, twelve thousand Saints were preparing to leave Nauvoo. The decision had been made to use the tabernacle canvas for tents and wagon covers. Again, in the wisdom of the Lord, Orson's efforts served the Saints in an unexpected way.[32]

During the next several weeks neighborhood chatter varied in content and tone:

"Did you hear about the sad incident in the Morley Settlement yesterday [October 18]? Two houses and three stables were burned by armed mobbers!"

"How many peaches did you dry and pack for our journey? And how are you coming with your dried apples and dried pumpkin?"

"The women at our home have kept our loom humming night and day weaving the carpet for the temple."

"Messengers reported today [October 27] the irritating news that troops are on their way again, to arrive tomorrow. The Twelve are in hiding."

"The workmen in our Hundred are building fine wagons. Men are learning new skills from the carpenters, blacksmiths, and mechanics."

"How terrible! Kind Brother Durfee, in the south part of the county, was decoyed out of his home by a strawstack fire [November 15], then shot and killed."

"The plasterers finished the attic story of the temple [November 22], where we will receive our endowments."

"Is your family's thousand pounds of flour for the journey all back from the mill?"

"The painters finished painting the attic of the temple [November 26]."

"We are discouraged, too, that our property is unsold. The enemies' tactics to hinder sales are succeeding, and they will just take over our homes and our fields after we are gone. We could get ready to leave much easier if we had money from selling our property."

"I heard that yesterday [November 30] the attic story of the temple was dedicated to the Lord in prayer by our leaders."

"We are progressing well with our assignment of sewing robes and garments for use in the temple. The curtains are about ready too. The Twelve are working long hours in the building making partitions and arranging curtains, furniture, and pictures just right."

"I saw Brother Phelps [December 4] carrying potted cedar trees into the temple to place in the 'Garden Room.'"

"We can hardly walk around in our home because of the big pieces of canvas spread all over that we are sewing into tents and wagon covers."

"Officials of the Catholic Church are here in Nauvoo [December 9] talking with our leaders about buying our property and leasing our temple."

"At last! Endowments have begun! This afternoon [December 10] I saw the Twelve and their wives and other leaders entering the arched front doors."[33]

Orson and Marinda attended this first endowment session. Marinda felt ungraceful with her baby due in less than two months, and she set a leisure pace ascending one of the zigzag stairways on either side of the wide entrance hall. The upper rooms were beautiful. The cleanliness and order of everything inspired a hush. The sunlight streaming in the skylights of the large center hall inspired a loftiness.[34]

The procedures this first day were primarily training. By Joseph Smith, most of the Church leaders had received, and been taught to administer, the rites of the endowment. The endowment required a few hours. During the first segment, sisters administered the washing and anointing to women, promising them a shield of protection by the Lord, according to their faithfulness. Brethren administered the same to men. Progressive group instruction followed, the brethren seated on one side and the sisters on the other, all in clean white robes. Each group walked quietly from room to room between presentations, hearing the sacred word of the Lord about the purposes of earth life and receiving the necessary knowledge to enable them to regain the presence of their Father in Heaven. The Prophet had required the Twelve to memorize every word of the ceremonies exactly as the Lord revealed them. Orson's phenomenal memory was a great asset.[35]

As weeks passed, the Twelve asked many faithful brethren and sisters to help officiate, and increasing numbers of people attended temple sessions. Martha and Mary Ann received the endowment December 17. President Young had planned to close the temple on Saturdays, that the clothing could be washed, but the great eagerness of Saints to receive the endowment influenced temple workers to wash the clothes at night and hang them by the stovepipes in the various rooms to dry. The endowment sessions usually ended long after sunset. The Twelve, particularly Brigham Young, often then slept in the temple. The officiators ate in the temple, too, of the abundant provisions brought by grateful Saints. Any extra food was given to the needy in the city.[36]

Being in the temple kept Brother Brigham out of sight of the occasional officers seeking his arrest. A United States marshal, with a few troops, spent a week in Nauvoo the latter part of December, but his searching found no apostles.

The marshal left December 30, and this respite in the threat of arrests prompted a celebration. Also, one thousand endowments had been given. To the lively strains of fiddle and flute, the Saints danced in the unfinished part of the temple.[37]

January 11, 1846, being a Sunday, no endowments would be performed, and the Twelve used this opportunity of privacy for meeting with the few Church members already "sealed" in plural marriages. The marriages that priesthood authority had sealed "for time and eternity" at home, would be repeated at the altar and a permanent temple record made. The altar—sides sheathed in white linen, scarlet damask cushions on top and covering the low platform around the four sides—had been recently finished, in the southeast upper temple room, and dedicated to the Lord. In the dressing rooms Orson, Marinda, Martha, and Mary Ann changed to white temple clothing and white temple robes. Brigham Young stood at the end of the altar as Orson and Marinda knelt on either side, right hands clasped over the top cushion. When Brigham Young pronounced the priesthood words that resealed their marriage before God, the sealing covenant "for time" pertained to Orson and Marinda, but Marinda was already sealed to the Prophet Joseph Smith for eternity. Orson knelt twice more at the altar with Martha and with Mary Ann in turn. Serenity prevailed.[38]

In Nauvoo diligence continued: work on the temple, study of books and maps about the western regions of the continent, and wagon construction. Orson purchased one sturdy wagon from his friend, James H. Rollins, with whom years before he had shared the attic sleeping space of the old Whitney store in Kirtland. Gold paid for the cost, seventy-five dollars. The Hyde family traveling provisions were also in order.[39]

As prepared as possible to move, Orson turned his attention to the unfair stories being circulated in newspapers throughout the United States against the Latter-day Saints. January 14 he wrote a letter to the people of America and sent it to the *New-York Daily Tribune*. The *Tribune* published it February 5. "Should we settle down in the Western wilderness where there is no established Government," Orson wrote in regard to support of civil officers and law, "we should have to govern ourselves, or go ungoverned until some Government should take us in. Should we settle where there is an organized Government, we intend to support that Government. We are Americans by birth, . . . and if we can have equal advantages with other citizens, we want no other worldly Government. We consider it the best Government of any nation in existence, if its laws can be administered impartially."

In an effort to counteract reports that the Latter-day Saints planned to foment uprisings among the Indians, Orson went on, "Some of the last instructions given us by our martyred Prophet concerning the Indians, were, that we teach them to be at peace among themselves, and also to be at peace with the 'white man'—to cultivate the earth, and to become civilized and industrious. We consider it for our good and also for theirs to abide his instructions."

Orson wrote of the persecutions against the Saints and then declared, "We design to go and settle in some distant valley. . . . None need fear that we shall ever take part against America . . . ; and should our services be required, we should not like to back out from the service of our Country."

Orson ended his letter with hope: "[O]ur prayer is, that truth may be exalted, mercy flourish, and justice be established throughout the earth."

In Nauvoo, however, justice seemed far distant. New rumors brought the alarming report that enemies of the Church planned to intercept the Saints, stop them from traveling westward, and annihilate them. January 18, still mid winter, uneasy Church leaders held a meeting with the captains of the emi-grating companies "to ascertain the number ready and willing to start should necessity compel our instant removal." Every captain in the meeting reported his company ready. A committee of trustees was chosen to remain in Nauvoo to sell Church property and aid families to emigrate before mobs made exo-dus impossible. If the Twelve departed first, pressures should decrease, giving the remaining Saints "a better opportunity to dispose of their property, settle up their business, and prepare their wagons and teams for a removal in the spring."[40]

At this apprehensive period the lusty cries of Marinda's newborn son filled the Hyde home January 23.[41] Orson and Marinda named him Frank Henry. How would a tiny baby fare in frigid weather in a canvas-covered wagon?

February 2, during an intense meeting, the Twelve, the Nauvoo trustees, and a few others "agreed that it was imperatively necessary to start as soon as possible." Brigham Young counseled: "[P]rocure boats and hold them in readiness to convey our wagons and teams over the river, and let everything for the journey be in readiness, that when a family is called to go, everything necessary may be put into the wagon within four hours, at least, for if we are here many days, our way will be hedged up. Our enemies have resolved to intercept us whenever we start. I should like to push on as far as possible before they are aware of our movements."

Thus their enemies prevented the Saints from waiting for grass to grow on the prairies. As refugees they must haul hay and grain for their animals and plan to buy feed from settlements along the way. This meant that they needed to take many more vehicles than planned. Some families, loaning their teams and wagons to others, would remain in Nauvoo. The teams and wagons would eventually be sent back to their owners so that they could follow.

February 4 the first group, with wagons and animals, ferried across the river.

February 7 the last ordinances were administered in the temple. Before this, in preparation for departure, many items of furniture and decoration had been removed.

February 8, a reflective Sunday, the Council of the Twelve met in the attic of the Lord's House, the southeast corner room. Kneeling around the white and scarlet altar, they asked the protection of the Most High upon the building, requested blessings upon their move west, and petitioned humbly that the Lord would accept the labors of his servants in the Nauvoo area. They pled with the Lord for the privilege of someday finishing the temple, that they might officially dedicate the entire structure to him.[42]

The same day, to the Sabbath meeting in the grove near the temple, people came dressed warmly against the strong wind. Orson and others of the Twelve gave their farewell addresses, exhorting the Saints to faithfulness and patience.

Families continued to ferry over the river. Except when floating ice made crossing too dangerous, the mile-wide Mississippi carried a continual stream of wagons and teams.

February 10 the Quorum of the Twelve appointed Joseph Young—senior president of the First Council of Seventy, and brother of Brigham Young—to remain in Nauvoo and preside over the Church during the exodus.[43]

February 15 Brigham Young and other leaders ferried their families and goods across the river to Iowa. Orson's own tightly packed trunks, sacks, and barrels had been secured in his wagons against rolling and jostling. His oxen were well fed. His furniture and other non-essentials would be left behind. But Marinda lay ill. To help in any way that he could, Orson rode his horse onto the ferry, crossed the river, and joined the Saints in the Sugar Creek camp.[44] He would return and remain in Nauvoo until his family could travel.

At Sugar Creek, new arrivals milled around, found camping spots, and cleared away the deep snow to pitch tents, all adding noisy clamor to the grand hodge-podge of animals, wagons, and humanity: red-cold noses, the cries of women giving birth to babies in makeshift shelters, fathers and sons chopping wood together, and children running and playing in the snow and the nearby forest. In this new adventure even the grown people turned child-like, asking Brigham Young questions on every side. President Young delegated and organized and chastised and instructed and assured. At sunset the hubbub slowed. In the frigid air the campfires blazed comfortingly. Saints sang, laughed, compared little and large domestic catastrophes, and prayed.[45]

In some ways Orson found returning to Nauvoo difficult. Hearts leaned westward now. The clanging and packing continued on, with hundreds of families still preparing to depart, but an emptiness prevailed. Smoke curled from fewer chimneys by day. Candles glowed from fewer windows by night. Nauvoo's chapter as a spiritual center had ended.

Though Joseph Young had been designated to preside in Nauvoo after the Twelve left, as long as Orson remained he was the leading Church authority. The two worked together to keep the wagons moving. In a few days the extreme cold became a blessing. The Mississippi River froze over, and heavy wagons by the scores rolled easily across. But many frightened people also crossed, unprepared with enough supplies for a journey. This would pose problems for Brigham Young, Orson and Joseph knew, but efforts failed to stop them.

Seven members of the Twelve already accompanied President Young, with Orson Hyde planning soon to join them. The other four apostles were elsewhere. Wilford Woodruff had started home from England. Lyman Wight had gone off toward Texas with a group of Saints scouting for a place to settle. William Smith had refused to acknowledge Brigham Young as his leader and had been excommunicated in October. John E. Page had returned to Nauvoo some months previously and assisted the Twelve. However, when plans dictated leaving the area and its comforts, he rebelled and was disfellowshipped February 9. He remained around, preaching for the apostate cause.[46]

February 28 Orson wrote to President Young: ". . . My wife is a little better. . . . There are many strangers in town buying furniture, stoves &c." Three days before this, hoping that they would soon be on their way, Orson and Marinda had signed their home over to an attorney to sell. Martha witnessed the bond, signing as usual, "Martha Browett."[47]

The "Camp of Israel" moved out from Sugar Creek on March first, under the leadership of Brigham Young. The caravan contained almost four hundred wagons. Besides provisions for people and animals they were well supplied with artillery.

The Hyde family in Nauvoo received a pleasant surprise early in March when Marinda's brother Luke visited. Luke Johnson had remained in Kirtland, Ohio since his departure from the Church eight years before. His feelings about the Saints had now changed. He had heard of the planned exodus from Nauvoo, he said, and wanted to reunite himself with the Church and help all he could.

In Nauvoo the next Sunday, March 8, an astounding number of Saints, thousands, gathered for Sabbath meeting. Orson introduced Luke Johnson, one of the original Quorum of the Twelve. The Saints in Nauvoo had heard of him, but most had never seen this tall strong man with the resolute face, long chin, high forehead, and dark hair. Orson asked him to speak. Luke addressed the congregation reverently.

Orson added that long conversations had convinced him of Luke's worthiness to return, and he recommended a vote for rebaptism. A vibrant field of hands gave hearty acceptance. At five o'clock that afternoon, in the river, Orson baptized Luke and three other people. A huge crowd attended. Luke planned to return to Kirtland to get his family.

Orson felt that the day's proceedings significantly weakened the position of Nauvoo's apostates, and he reported to Brigham Young that "the confession of Luke and baptism nailed the flag to the mast head of the Mormon ship."

Orson continued with a prophecy regarding an esteemed former Church leader, Oliver Cowdery, who had left the Saints in 1838. "Oliver will come next," was Orson's prediction.[48]

March 10, Nauvoo residents welcomed a courier from Church headquarters at a camp fifty-five miles to the west. Among many letters was a surprising directive from Brigham Young and others of the Twelve to Orson Hyde. His quorum directed him "to stay at Nauvoo and dedicate the Temple, if the Twelve [do] not return." What an overwhelming development! Orson yearned for his temporary position as the leading authority in Nauvoo to end. Marinda's health had improved; she could sit up the greater part of each day and before long should be strong enough to travel. The Hydes had planned to depart soon.

Joseph Young also received instructions and shared them with Orson. "Nauvoo . . . is no place for the saints," Brigham Young had written to his brother Joseph, "and the spirit whispers to me that the brethren had better get away as fast as they can. We pray for you continually. . . . [T]he dark clouds of sorrow are gathering fast over that place. . . . If we do not come back, Brother Orson Hyde, yourself and others had better go into the Temple, when the lower part is done, if you are there, and pray and offer up your supplication to the Most High, and [officially] leave the house in the hands of the Lord."[49]

Orson's recent few weeks in charge of Nauvoo had been a new experience for him. He prayerfully thought about needs. The first consideration was the temple. Truman Angell, a persevering man, would competently oversee its finishing. Second was the emigration. Joseph Young energetically kept the companies working together with hope of leaving Nauvoo before the outside mob threats of massacre became reality. At present the state troops appointed by the governor held off the mobs. Third was the sale of property. The trustees, though having less success than desired, continued diligent. The fourth concern was the apostates. No one was doing anything about them.

How should Orson react to these dissenters? With increasing noisome speeches they tried to convince Saints that Brigham Young was uninspired, that Church members should remain in Nauvoo. After all, the Lord had directed the founding of this city. Apostate James J. Strang made the loudest fuss, claiming that the Prophet had appointed him to become president of the Church. John E. Page's self-pitying voice aided him, as did others.[50]

Saturday, March 14, four days after Orson received the unsettling letter asking him to remain in Nauvoo, the Lord enlightened him about dealing with the apostates. Orson had arisen early. In the cool quiet he pondered, and he prayed. At length he received divine direction and recorded words that came into his mind as rapidly as he could dip his pen into the inkwell and guide it across the paper. He wrote:

> In my meditations, this morning, the Spirit of the Lord came upon me, and I was moved to write: and being grieved in my spirit on account of false pretences by evil designing persons to gain power, and lead away the flock of God; It whispered [to] me and said:
>
> Evil men, ambitious of power, must needs arise among you, and they shall be led by their own self-will and not by me. Yet they are instruments in my hands, and are permitted to try my people, and to collect from among them those who are not the elect, and such as are unworthy of eternal life. Grieve not after them, neither mourn nor be alarmed. My people know my voice and also the voice of my spirit, and a stranger they will not follow; therefore such as follow strangers are not my people. Behold James J. Strang hath cursed my people by his own spirit and not by mine. Never at any time have I appointed that wicked man to lead my people, neither by my own voice, nor by the voice of my servant Joseph Smith, neither by the voice of mine angel: but he hath sought to deceive and Satan helpeth him; but before of old was he one that was ordained to gather the tares of the field, and mine angels have chosen him to do it because he was a wicked man, even as Judas was chosen to betray his Lord. But his spirit and ambition shall soon fail him, and then shall he be called to judgment and receive that portion which is his mete, and his treacherous followers, who have forsaken the counsel of their brethren and turned from the covenants of their God, and have cast asunder the tenderest ties, must drink from a bitter cup.
>
> Let no man who putteth his trust in me be troubled about his rights. The worthy shall have their rights and no power can prevent it, for I will give them the hearts of my people, and their voice is my voice, even as my voice is the voice of my father; and what they bind on earth I will bind in heaven. But the unworthy have no rights except these, repentance or condemnation. If they act upon the former, behold they are justified, but if not, they must suffer the consequences of the latter.
>
> By this you may know the unworthy among my people: for whomsoever they reject, the same are rejected of me. And woe to such as shall follow him who hath been rejected by my people. If my people sin I will

correct and chasten them because I love them, yet I will not reject them, neither give my kingdom to other people, for behold the end draweth nigh, and judgment will I pour out upon your oppressors and upon those who accuse you to hide their own iniquity and their shame, and to get power for unholy purposes and not for the building up of my kingdom. Let such beware lest they fall by the hand of the *destroyer,* whose arrows are plague and pestilence, before their designs are accomplished.

Let my saints gather up with all consistent speed and remove westward, except such as are counselled to tarry and must needs remain to settle their business according to the counsel of my servant Joseph Smith, in the day that he was with you in the flesh, and also according to the counsel of my servants, the Twelve whom I have chosen, and who have abode in me.

Let there be no more disputes or contentions among you about doctrine or principle, neither who shall be greatest, but hearken to those things which I have spoken unto you, and which have before been given and you shall rest in my kingdom, and have glory and honour for ever and ever—Yea! Saith the Spirit, and the Spirit is truth, and the truth abideth for ever: Amen.[51]

Exhilaration filled Orson's being as instructions from Heavenly spheres flowed to paper. Reconfirmed was his knowledge that the Almighty continued to pilot the course of His people. The gallant ship of the gospel would emerge from all barrages with mast intact and sails full.

Desiring to have copies of the precious words of the Lord for Sabbath meeting the next day, Orson printed the revelation on the Church press, still operable. In the Sunday meeting the congregation listened raptly as Orson told of his recent concerns and shared his gratitude at receiving the Lord's direction. Reverently he read the revelation, and brethren distributed copies.

Orson channeled his worries away from the apostates, and, as increased foreboding enveloped Nauvoo, tried to figure ways to reduce the clamor of the many apprehensive Saints alarmed because they lacked means to procure wagons, teams, and food for travel. Orson had no ready answers when men and women begged for assistance that he was unable to give. Though weary of "the cries of the poor every hour, and almost every minute, and at every corner of the streets," he tried to be patient and understanding. By the next Sunday his prayers for guidance had a partial answer.

"It is the will of God," he told the congregation, "that every man who has money, after fitting himself out for the journey, should leave the balance of his means to fit out others." The following Friday, March 27, he reported to Brigham Young, "We are doing the best we can. I find that as poor a hand as I am, it would have been rather hard for them to [have] got along without me. The Lord has given me just power enough to hang on in the storm and keep my head above the water."

Orson told President Young of the frustrations he felt because of the complaints of the poor and then explained another concern. "Men," he wrote, "who have let their teams go in the first company, expecting them to be sent back, are almost crazy about them. They teaze me and the trustees for teams, when as yet the first team has not been received by them. And it is not possible to answer the orders at present."

But amid the varied anxieties Orson reported positive occurrences: "There are some buyers here just now, but they appear to be fearful, lest they have to share the same fate of the mormons. Yet there are some sales effected by individuals." Also, "In the midst of strife and confusion, many are being baptized."

Though he had hoped to include the temple dedication as part of April conference, Orson wrote that the "temple will not be finished to dedicate on the 6th of April. It will take nearly to the first of May: say about the 20th of April.

"Tell me," Orson requested of President Young, "where the first settlement will be made if you can, and at what place property and people shall land at on the Missouri river most commodious to that place, provided they wish to go by water. . . . I have told the poor to cross the river into Iowa, and travel west as far as they could till they find jobs, or a good chance to put in a crop. If they could go 20–30–50–100 or 200 miles do so, but keep on or within call of the 'old mormon trail.' Is this right? . . . In fine, am I doing right or wrong? I think I am doing right, but if you think I am not, I will tack ship and stand on another course at the wind."

Of his own discouragement Orson wrote, "The trustees and all the rest of the brethren who cannot get away now want me to stay with them just so long as possible. They say they cannot get along at all without me. It is no desirable job to stay where hell boils over every breeze that blows, yet I will do as you say. . . . The people look to me as a father, and feel that they shall be without defence when I go. To hear their complaints of poverty and inability to help themselves away, and petitions for help, is enough to make one crazy."

Feeling lonesome for his companions of the Twelve, Orson concluded, "I should be glad if some of you could be here at Conference [April 6]. I think you might come back in safety. . . . My love to all the Council and Camp."[52]

In Nauvoo, Orson urged the Saints to leave as fast as possible. "Don't wait for the Companies," he instructed, "but go whenever you get ready." This worried the trustees, particularly Almon W. Babbitt. At the upcoming conference Brother Babbitt wanted Elder Hyde to advise the Saints to stay in Nauvoo for the trustees' protection against mobs until they could settle up the business. Orson answered, "I cannot do it. Your safety is in your weakness, not in strength or numbers. . . . A large number remaining would be very likely to provoke an attack by enemies." Orson had positive knowledge, from beyond the veil, that he counseled according to the wishes of Heaven. An angel of the Lord had appeared to him in a night vision. The glorious being stood near him and said: "This people can not stay here."[53]

While exerting every influence to push the Nauvoo Saints on their way, Orson thought also of the Church members in England. Feeling that they needed some official guidance to counteract any apostate pressure that might reach them, he sent a copy of the revelation that he had received March 14, directing that it be published in the *Millennial Star*. He added an assuring letter, dated April 5. About the apostates he commented: "These followers of Mr. Strang tell the most horrid lies. . . . When they are here, in our city, they will say that many hundreds have joined them in some other parts, and when they go to some other parts, they will say that many thousands have fallen in with Mr. Strang in Nauvoo, when the plain fact is, that I do not know of ten persons in Nauvoo that have joined Mr. Strang."

Orson refrained from voicing his apprehensions and wrote of the good happenings, among these that "many [converts] are coming to Nauvoo and being baptized daily. The Saints are selling out and removing west; hundreds of families are coming here from other States, and fitting out for a campaign in the wilderness. It is a great work." He encouraged the Saints in England: "Be faithful, dear friends, over a few things, and God will make you rulers over many."

April general conference typified the diversities of recent weeks. Rain caused adjournment of sessions. Good preaching filled other sessions. Orson received a blank letter containing a bullet, obviously from some enemy as a threat of violence. And Orson baptized twenty people.[54]

None of the Twelve from the western train had managed to return for conference, but a week later Orson's spirits soared when Wilford Woodruff arrived from England. What a comfort to have another member of his quorum with whom to discuss matters.

The last two weeks of April, a period of hectic urgency, Orson describes as "tangled" days of "great distress." April 16, news arrived that the Governor of Illinois planned to remove state troops May 1. Orson pushed harder to get as many people as possible away by then, because "mobocracy is likely to be the law." In the face of such a threat men and women toiled longer hours to get wagons ready. Soon teams crossed the river both day and night. The sacrifices and hardships made Orson's heart ache. Fortunately the governor changed his order about the troops, and they remained, but Orson kept his gun loaded. The same as in other families, someone of his household always remained awake during each night on guard shift, watching for trouble.[55]

Some of Orson's consternation diminished upon the arrival of a letter from Brigham Young, dated April 21, with answers about settlements and return of teams. A settlement would be made mid-way across Iowa in the vicinity of Grand River and another on the far side of Iowa near the Missouri River. Fields would be cleared, plowed, and planted for the benefit of Saints coming after the first companies. As soon as borrowed teams helped accomplish the heavy work in the first settlement they would be returned to Nauvoo. Though the people who had loaned the teams would not receive them as soon as desired, Orson had an answer to their pleadings.[56]

Through this time of turmoil the work on the temple continued until the hammering of the last nail and the application of the last swath of paint. The temple was beautiful. "Since the dispersion of Jewry, probably, history affords us no parallel to the attachment of the Mormons for this edifice," wrote an observer and admirer of the Saints. "Its erection had been enjoined upon them as a most sacred duty. . . . [T]hough their enemies drove on them ruthlessly they succeeded . . . completed even the gilding of the angel and trumpet on the summit of its lofty spire."

The temple was finished April 30, and that very evening Orson conducted a private dedication. Joseph Young, Orson Hyde, Wilford Woodruff, and about twenty other elders of Israel attended, clothed in white temple robes. Orson gave to Joseph Young the privilege of offering the prayer. Brother Young prayed that no mob would disturb them during the meeting, and he dedicated "the Temple and all that pertain[s] thereto to the Lord, as an offering to Him as an evidence of the willingness of His people, to fulfill his commandments, and build His Holy house, even at the risk of their lives." Also, among other things, he asked the Lord to "direct the brethren of the camp of Israel, open the way before them and lead them to a place of his own appointment for the gathering of all the Saints."

The group in the temple experienced a hallowed manifestation. "While the earth was wrapped in the mantle of darkness," Orson recounts, "and while we were engaged in prayer, asking our Father to accept the building, the glory of the Lord shone throughout the room in matchless splendor like unto the rays of the sun, emanating from every side." After the prayer the brethren pronounced the "Amen" with resounding emphasis. Next they raised their voices "in the united Shout of Hosanna to God and the Lamb," and the power of the utterances of a few men seemed strengthened by the exultant intonations of angels.[57]

The public dedication of the temple was accomplished the next day, Friday, May 1. In this edifying meeting Orson offered the dedicatory prayer.

The following Sunday, May 3, Orson was one of the speakers in the Sabbath services in the House of the Lord. He tried to convey to the people the glorious principle that, in peopling this earth, God's unchanging purpose was to train his children to return to him, to become like him. Orson said,

[I]n this House [w]e have been anointing and ordaining kings and priests unto God. . . . When a man has received this gospel, anointing, and endowments, let him go to the dust, but he will arise and take his place on his throne. . . .

There are different stations in the next world, and men will be dealt with according to the deeds done in the body. . . . A man that does his duty and obtains the priesthood and honors it will have his reward, his exaltation, thrones, and dominions. . . . I have seen this by vision. . . . The Lord owns all the thrones and will give us some. . . . Worlds and dominions are continually being formed, which adds to the glory of God.

Following Elder Hyde's speech, Elder Woodruff spoke at length also. He pronounced that the "Saints . . . [are] now received as a church with our dead. This is glory enough for building the Temple."

At a later time Brigham Young explained more about the Lord's command to finish the Nauvoo Temple. "Everything at Nauvoo went with a rush," he said. "We had to build the Temple with the trowel in one hand and the sword in the other, and mobs were upon us all the while, and many crying out, 'Oh! the Temple can't be built.' I told them it should be built. This Church should not fall; and the Lord said if we did not build it we should be rejected as a Church with our dead. Why did He say it? Because the Saints were becoming slothful and covetous, and would spend their means upon fine houses for themselves before they would put it into a House of the Lord."[58]

With the temple dedicated to the Lord, the satisfaction of accomplishment elated Orson, but his wisdom continued taxed to the limits as he concentrated his energies on the cares of departing.

And his heart went out to Brother Brigham directing the multitudes of Saints on the prairies of Iowa. Grim reports of hardship had come back to Nauvoo, tribulations almost unreal to Orson, not personally involved. The emigrants had endured "howling tempest[s], . . . clattering rain[s], . . . violent hail storms, . . . drifting snow, and . . . chilling winds." Traversing vast stretches of deep mud, or camping in wretched wet and cold, the Saints had struggled unbelievably as together they repaired and rescued their wagons broken and mired, shared their soggy supplies, tended their sick, and buried their dead.[59] Here in Nauvoo where people had the shelter of homes, mobs threatened their destruction. On the prairies people had freedom from mobs, but violent weather exacted privation and misery.

In Nauvoo zealous activity continued. Saints removed the last furnishings from the temple. Men, women, and children scurried to and from wagons at many homes and then left, increasing the numbers of forlorn abandoned buildings. But in every corner of Nauvoo flowers bloomed. Their sweet perfume and their cheering hues of red and pink and orange and yellow and lavender gave promise to the Saints of better days elsewhere. Diligent work had made Nauvoo a garden spot and could do the same in other places.

Like the bright flowers, a refreshing letter arrived for Orson and Wilford from their fellow quorum members in the Saints' new "Garden Grove" settlement almost midway across Iowa. This rare letter was rich with the flavor of a personal meeting in which these men who loved each other more than brothers projected their energetic and jovial natures. The composing of the letter–dated April 30, the last day of April–commenced at ten o'clock at night. It began, "Beloved Brethren," and the first sentence set a jocular mood: "After enjoying a very interesting chit chit in council this evening we feel disposed to chat awhile with you, lest we do not get the privilege again this month." This month indeed! Two hours after they started the letter the month ended. This unusual letter helped Orson to recapture the feeling of being in the midst of his quorum, of sharing conviviality.

Orson felt both sad and glad as he read. He was pleased to learn of the Garden Grove settlement and its beautiful setting. He was saddened to read that the Saints slept in leaky tents and that they stretched meager food. He winced a little at the letter's good-natured, but sarcastic, comments on the complaints he had written to Brigham Young about conditions in Nauvoo. He felt embraced as he received a scolding with tongue-in-cheek phrases: "[W]e wish you to fit yourselves out with a year and a half's provisions as speedily as possible & come on unless bro Hyde has become so attached to his new responsibility that he does not like to leave it. In that case he is at liberty to tarry awhile longer." Orson could envision Brigham Young's serious face, but also the mirth in his gray eyes.

The letter rubbed banteringly at Orson's complaining. "We truly feel to rejoice," it said, "that bro Hyde has had the opportunity & disposition for the first time to shoulder a little of the burden that has hung on our shoulders so long. He has manifested by his letters that his cares were great & his burden heavy, but they have been no greater or heavier than has rested on us for years, & it does us good to see Judah's Lion arise in his might & shake himself, & roar with thundering voice against the wolves & other beasts of prey that surround the fold of Ephraim. Go on, dear bro. Thunder away. [T]he longer the yoke is worn the lighter it grows." Even with this rubbing, Orson sensed that the "too much" commenting about his complaints said to him that his friends understood.

The rejuvenating letter went on about business matters and disposition of funds if the Nauvoo Temple could be sold. "[P]erhaps the best method to accomplish [talking together about decisions]," the letter continued good-naturedly, "would be for you [Orson and Wilford] to mount your nags or mules & come & sit in council with us [in Iowa], and return, all of which would consume 7 or 8 days. [A]nd the visit will do us all good if you will be as glad to see us as we will you."[60]

. . . labours, journeyings. . . . (1846–1848)

> *. . . labours more abundant, . . .*
> *journeyings often. . . .*
> —2 Corinthians 11:23, 26

IN mid May 1846 the Hyde family crossed the Mississippi River from Illinois into Iowa in a company of about fifty wagons. Forty-one years of age, Orson had added a few pounds to his already ample frame. Marinda and the children—Laura age eight, Emily six, and Frank three months—enjoyed health, as did Martha. Mary Ann, expecting a baby, exulted that motherhood at last would be hers. Her health was good also, so travel seemed no great concern. Her family had planned to accompany them, but her brother, William Price, and brother-in-law, Richard Bentley, were counseled to stay in Nauvoo to help defend the city if the need arose. Mother Price and Mary Ann's younger brother and sister remained too.[1]

An 1846 traveler described Iowa as a "great land sea" with "bald prairies," "hard rolled hills," and "scattered water courses." Where prairies ended, forests grew thick. Orson's company crossed these prairies and hills in four challenging weeks. Mary Ann narrates that the three hundred mile trek, "journeying with my husband and family from Nauvoo to Council Bluffs . . . fast travelling through storms of rain," left her "very much fatigued." They rested only briefly at "Garden Grove" and "Mount Pisgah," where the Saints had built log cabins and planted crops, on thousands of acres of land, for future Church emigrants.

When Orson's company came to the plain of the Missouri River below the jutting Council Bluffs, June 17, reunions with friends were jubilant. Brigham Young and the main company had been here only three days. Workers were building a ferry to cross the river, but getting everyone and everything across would be a massive undertaking, a major hindrance in the western trek. A favorite diversion, for old and young these summer days, was picking delicious wild strawberries.[2]

Church leaders needed to arrange to remain temporarily here on Indian lands. The Pottawattamie Indians owned the land east of the Missouri River; the Omaha and Otoe nations owned the land west. Orson's second day at the Bluffs, June 18, he and other Council members rejoiced when visited, Orson Pratt tells, "by the great chief" of the "Pottowattomie Indians" who "was an educated man and spoke English fluently." Attired in Indian apparel of vivid colors, he greeted the white "chiefs" with courtly aplomb. "He said we were welcome among them," Orson Pratt continues, "and kindly offered us the use of timber that grew upon their lands for fuel, or any other needful purpose."

Two days later, June 20, at the invitation of the United States Indian Agent, Major Mitchell, Church leaders (including Orson) and their wives, and the Church band, attended a party at the Agency. The ride to Trading Point (also called Trader's Point and Point-aux-Poules) took the group south from the Mormon ferry site and around a wide bend in the Missouri River. Guests included Saints, the villagers connected with the Indian post and with fur-trading, and the grandly adorned Indians. The band played. Dinner was served. The band played again. A soloist sang a few songs. Many guests danced. The Saints felt welcomed.

Because families were crowded near the river and gaining density on the hillsides and bluffs, Orson and some who came with him, including the Browning family, scouted for their own spot to park their wagons, pitch their tents, and pasture their animals. The men explored the lush ridges, coves, and timbered areas and found an ideal glen with plenty of trees. It was "a large hollow," James A. Browning describes, "hard by springs of excellent water." Located six miles east of Trading Point, up a long valley and over a few humpy hills, the secluded vale became first known as "Hyde's Camp" and then "Hyde Park."[3]

The Saints had been at Council Bluffs less than three weeks when they received a staggering request from the United States government for five hundred men. An army officer, Captain James Allen, arrived July 1 from Fort Leavenworth, the United States Army's frontier post one hundred and seventy miles to the south. He asked for a battalion of Mormon volunteers to march more than sixteen hundred miles and assist the United States in the recently-declared war with Mexico. The men would "be mustered . . . into the service of the U.S., and from that day will commence to receive the pay, rations, and other allowances given to other infantry volunteers." In a meeting with Captain Allen the Twelve asked many questions, and then they held meetings by themselves.

What an astonishing development! Brigham Young had sent Jesse Little to seek help from the government for the Mormon refugees. But, while the Saints suffered because of being expelled from their homes, with no government protection, men would be reluctant to leave their loved ones in this wilderness. Though the proposal asked further hardships of everyone, blessings would result. The Lord had apparently inspired the President of the United States to provide this means to help the Saints. Just months before, Orson had written: "[I]t is our faith that God will do all things right; and should our services be required, we should not like to back out from the service of our Country."

After much discussion, the Twelve held a decision meeting. In his turn Orson declared, "If I could be spared and it was the mind of the Council that I should go I embrace it immediately. It gives us a chance of clearing our name from the stigma that has been cast upon it by our enemies." The Council accepted the call, knowing that they must preach mightily to convince the distressed Saints to respond. The Camp of Israel would be unable to move on westward this year.

Several of the Twelve had moved their families across the Missouri, and Orson felt that he should too. Accordingly the Hydes settled in the new main camp at Butterfly Bluff west of the river. Orson's wives did most of the packing and unpacking, as duties kept him busy.[4]

While the Twelve vigorously circulated instructions about the Mormon battalion and recruited volunteers, groups of Saints with their wagons and herds rumbled constantly into the Council Bluffs area. Col. Thomas L. Kane arrived July 11 from Fort Leavenworth. He had earlier gained a personal interest in the Mormons and been influential in procuring the battalion request, but he was also curious. He had heard wild and colorful tales about the Mormon exiles and wanted to learn the truth. His impressions:

> [O]n the road . . . my horse my only travelling companion, . . . [I became] wearied to death of the staring silence of the prairie, before I came upon the objects of my search.
>
> They were collected a little distance above the Pottawatamie Agency. The hills of the "High Prairie" crowding in upon the river at this point, and overhanging it, appear of an unusual and commanding elevation. They are called the Council Bluffs. . . . To the south of them, a rich alluvial flat of considerable width follows down the Missouri. . . . Across the river . . . the hills recur again. . . .
>
> [The lowlands on both sides of the river] were crowded with covered carts and wagons; and each one of the Council Bluff hills . . . was crowned with its own great camp, gay with bright white canvas, and alive with the busy stir of swarming occupants. In the clear blue morning air, the smoke streamed up from more than a thousand cooking fires. Countless roads and by-paths checkered all manner of geometric figures on the hill sides. Herd boys were dozing upon the slopes; sheep and horses, cows and oxen, were feeding around them, and other herds [grazed] in the luxuriant meadow of the then swollen river. From a single point I counted four thousand head of cattle in view at one time. As I approached the camps, it seemed to me the children there were to prove still more numerous. Along a little creek I had to cross were [many] women . . . washing and rinsing all manner of white muslins, red flannels, and parti-coloured calicoes, and hanging them to bleach upon a [great] area of grass and bushes. . . .

[As days passed] [t]here was something joyous for me in my free ram-
bles about this vast body of pilgrims. . . . Not only in the main camps
was all stir and life, but in every direction, it seemed to me I could follow "Mormon Roads," and find them beaten hard and even dusty by the
tread and wear of the cattle and vehicles of emigrants laboring over
them. . . . [A]t night, if I encamped at the places where the timber and
running water were found together, I was almost sure to be within call
of some camp or other, or at least within sight of its watch-fires. Wherever I was compelled to tarry, I was certain to find shelter and hospitality, scant, indeed, but never stinted, and always honest and kind. . . . I
can scarcely describe the gratification I felt in associating again with
persons . . . of refined and cleanly habits and decent language.[5]

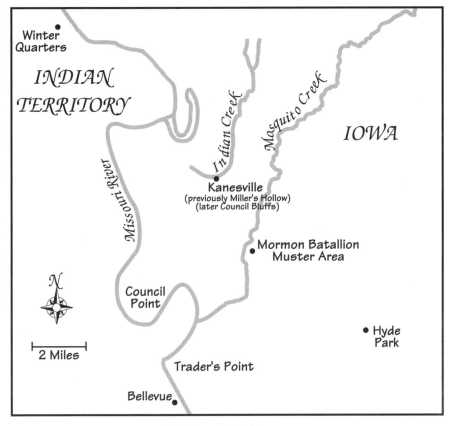

The Council Bluffs area.

When Colonel Kane arrived, enlistment details had been decided. Brigham Young, others of the Twelve, and additional riders on July 12 visited
camps on both sides of the river and also visited approaching companies to

announce a meeting the next afternoon in Elder Taylor's camp near Mosquito Creek. Here, in a forested area on the river plain, a large bowery had been built of poles and covered with brush as a shelter for meetings.

At the Battalion enlistment, July 13, with an American flag hoisted to the lofty top of the "Liberty Pole," a tree mast, members of the Twelve spoke, among them Orson Hyde. Orson also helped record enlistments for the lines of brethren volunteering.

The compliance amazed Colonel Kane, as did the announcement of a farewell ball in the bowery, later in the day. At the party he was further astonished by the "merry dancing . . . of the Mormon Israel," and that the Council of the Twelve attended,

> with their wives and children. . . . Their leading off the dancing in a great double cotillion, was the signal bade the festivity commence. To the canto of debonnair violins, the cheer of horns, the jingle of sleigh bells, and the jovial snoring of the tambourine, [the Saints] did dance! . . . [The crowd] follow[ed] the fiddle . . . [in] French Fours, Copenhagen jigs, Virginia reels, and the like. . . . Light hearts, lithe figures, and light feet, had it their own way from an early hour till after the sun had dipped behind the sharp sky-line of the Omaha hills. . . .
>
> [S]ome splendid Indians, . . . in cardinal scarlet blankets and feathered leggings . . . [made] foreground figures for the dancing rings . . . staring their inability to comprehend the wonderful performances. . . .
>
> Silence was . . . called, and a well cultivated mezzo-soprano voice, belonging to a young lady with fair face and dark eyes, gave with quartette accompaniment a little song.

The maiden, Susan Devine, at this farewell party sang the hauntingly lovely strains of "The maid of Judah." The original poetry of the pensive melody tells of weeping because Zion has been wasted by enemies and declares that the "city of our God" will ever be revered no matter what the heartaches ahead. The words had been changed, however, to reflect that the Saints had brought Zion with them and that "Again shall the children of Judah sing."

"There was danger of some expression of feeling when the song was over," Colonel Kane adds, "for it had begun to draw tears! but breaking the quiet . . . , an Elder [Brigham Young]" gave the benediction, asking "the blessing of Heaven on all."[6]

July 16, three mornings after the dance, the soldiers marched away. One of them was Daniel Browett, Martha's brother. Orson describes that the battalion's loved ones "look[ed] through affections purest tears upon the departure of their friends under the solemn strains of martial music, 'To the Girl I left behind me.'" Ever after that day, thoughts of the call and departure of the Mormon battalion awed Orson. "Did we refuse? Or did the Government have to call the second time?" he later reflected. "No! Five hundred of our best men volunteered at our country's call to go to Santa Fe and from thence to California, —went, leaving the lame, the halt and the blind, with mothers, wives and children in tents and in wagons unprotected in an Indian country with little else than wild roots and herbs to eat," and "the yell of the savage and the howl of the wolf . . . [to] comfort . . . them."[7]

With the battalion on its way, the Twelve met in Orson Pratt's tent on the flats and turned their attention to their own quorum. John E. Page was discussed, again, and officially excommunicated. Previous discussion and prayer had determined that Ezra T. Benson should take his place. Brother Benson, thirty-five years old, industrious, and faithful, had been summoned from the settlement of Mount Pisgah. In the meeting he was ordained an apostle.

In a meeting the previous day, July 15, the Twelve had considered problems in England. "[B]y dreams and by visions—by word and by letter," Orson details, "did we know in the American wilderness, that all was not going right in [England]." The Council decided that Elders Orson Hyde, John Taylor, and Parley P. Pratt should go and investigate.[8]

After much discussion and prayer, the Hyde family decided to move back across the river to Hyde Park, even though Church leaders had invited the wives of Elders Hyde, Taylor, and Pratt to remain with them. Here on the west side of the Missouri, many decisions were still being made about temporary settlements for thousands of people and for livestock "without number," and Orson wanted his family secure.

Also, concerns focused around Mary Ann. Her baby was due in about two months, and her brave smile failed to conceal her continued misery after the fatigues of crossing Iowa from Nauvoo. Anxiety about her family added to her unease; she hoped they would arrive soon. Marinda's brother, Luke Johnson, should be coming too. Comfortingly, Martha's mother had come with Martha.[9]

July 25, Orson disposed of several items. This summer he would need no carriage and horses, no extra oxen to plow fields, and less food for his family than was on hand. He sold his carriage. Newel K. Whitney, short of needed items, gratefully accepted "two yoke of oxen, ten barrels of flour, and a bushel and a half of beans." Orson's two horses, which had been lost, and then returned by Indians, he turned over, with other things, to Brigham Young. For some of the articles he received $271.00 credit on the Church books.[10]

The same day the family moved out of their camp. At the river they waited their turn on the ferry. Over several miles of road their remaining oxen toiled to Hyde Park, where cabins were going up. During the next few days Orson assisted as much as possible.

Before Orson departed, the glad moment came when shouts of welcome greeted Mary Ann's brother-in-law Richard Bentley, her brother William Price, her mother, and other family members, as their wagons rolled into the hollow. Even with the dust and the rumpled clothes from the tiring journey, William remained obviously a genteel Englishman, handsome and quiet. And Richard, his intelligent eyes deep-set under his thick shaggy brows, still emanated executive stability. They reported that times in Nauvoo had been apprehensive, but had not reached armed assault. Orson hired Richard and William "to make rails to fence forty acres of land and also to put up the fence." Corn, wheat, potatoes, and other crops had been planted, and must mature. Orson wanted no stock to get into the fields and ruin them. Assured, also, that everyone would be housed as soon as possible, Orson said his farewells. He intended to be back from England in time to move out with the Saints in the spring, "with the first that go."[11]

July 31, Elders Taylor, Pratt, and Hyde left Council Bluffs aboard a scow, or open flat-bottomed boat with wide square ends. During daylight for a few days they floated down the Missouri River, in slow places pulling oars to add speed. Nights they tied up and slept on shore. August 4, they reached Fort Leavenworth.

In Fort Leavenworth they beheld a grand sight, the pageantry of the one hundred tents of the Mormon Battalion. In glad reunion the brethren welcomed the apostles at their campfires. Orson reported to Brigham Young three days later, that "the boys . . . are well treated and in fine spirits." Consistently Orson referred to groups of Church brethren as "the boys," whatever their ages. Orson's letter went on, "The boys have been liberal to us to contribute for our mission," to the amount of several hundred dollars. Advance pay enabled the battalion recruits to do this.

Part of this pay prompted Orson's letter. "We send to your care the sum of Five Thousand Eight Hundred and thirty Five Dollars," Orson explained, "mostly for the friends and families of our Soldiers. . . . Our men have received $42.00 Each in advance, it being for one year's clothing at the rate of 3.50 pr. month. This was unexpected." Orson added the comment that "Providence seemed to have ordered our course this way"—members of the Twelve being on hand when the soldiers received the funds. "We have laboured here day and night to get this matter arranged to send the money to the bluffs. . . . We have saved many hundred dollars that would otherwise have been spent to no good—or for nick nacks."

When Orson and his companions had received the funds they discussed how to transport the amount back to Council Bluffs? Spiritual promptings sent Parley carrying it on horseback and the other two hurrying eastward. As soon as possible Parley would catch up.[12]

By September 2, John and Orson arrived in New York. They "felt the Spirit moving us forward, so much so," Elder Taylor writes, that though "Elder Pratt [was] in Boston, we thought it expedient, rather than wait two or three days for him, to proceed immediately to Liverpool." Parley arrived before their ship sailed, but lacked funds for fare.

Inspired with foreknowledge, Orson said, "We shall have a rough passage, and barely escape shipwreck by the skin of our teeth." His prediction came true. "We sailed from New York," he details, "on the 8th day of Sept on board the Packet Ship, 'Patrick Henry.' . . . Our passage in the Cabin was $75.00—We had a tremendous rough passage. . . . [O]n Saturday the 19 of Sept. A hurricane raged in all its fury for about 12 hours. Our bulwarks on the main and quarter decks were dashed in, every rag of canvass carried away— Maintop gallant mast carried away under bare poles— Ship nearly unmanageable - in the troughs of the sea - buried frequently in a world of waters. We thought of family, home, and of God. . . . But thanks be to Heaven, the winds abated and the storm hushed in silence, and we arrived [in Liverpool] on the morning of the 3rd [of October]."[13]

The apostles' assignment was to regulate the "Joint Stock Company." Organized by the men presiding over the Church in England, Reuben Hedlock and Thomas Ward, the company collected money from the Saints with the object of paying passage to America, a laudable objective at the outset. But things had gone awry, the leaders apparently unable to resist the temptation of available funds.

After Elders Hyde and Taylor stepped ashore in Liverpool, they found Church members and learned, they reported to Brigham Young, "that money was daily coming in to the Joint Stock Co. and that it was received by a set of men who ate and drank it up and squandered it away. . . . The poor Saints were laying up their pennies, their sixpences, their shillings &c. and remitting it to the Joint Stock Company, thinking that they were paying their passages to America thereby—depriving themselves of many comforts and necessaries. . . . [We] ascertained that of the £1500= paid in to the Company nearly every pound had been squandered and lent to irresponsible favorites - and that the expenses of the Company were running on at the rate of £300 annual salaries to its officers - £100 annual rent besides stationary, clerks &c. &c. and at the same time not any business done at all, and not one penny made. The officers had given no bonds or security, but could dispose of the funds as they thought proper, and no one responsible."

The day that they arrived the Elders published a circular and had it distributed among the Saints. It announced their arrival, advised the Saints "to patronize the Joint Stock Company *no more for the present*," and scheduled a Conference in Manchester for October 17. "We met Ward and his associates on the same afternoon [October 3], and heard their stories," Orson reports. "They were much confused at our sudden appearance there. . . ."

The apostles felt a heavy responsibility to protect the innocent Saints and to help them understand that Hedlock and Ward had failed in their stewardships. Their irresponsibility did not represent the ideals of the Church or the wishes of the Lord. In no possible way could the struggling Church leaders in the wilderness by the Missouri River assume obligation for the deplorable actions. Elders Hyde and Taylor held meetings and visited privately with individuals. Parley P. Pratt—having been given funds by a kind Latter-day Saint in New York City—arrived October 14 and assisted his brethren.

In Conference in Manchester, October 17, Orson announced the annihilation of the Joint Stock Company. For the present the apostles would direct the English Saints.[14]

Before October passed, sad family news arrived. Mary Ann had been "prematurely confined." Her baby, a tiny girl whom she named Urania, was born August 15. "[O]n [August] 27 my little one," she recounts, "was taken from my embraces to the other side." Orson grieved. How could he comfort Mary Ann? Beyond the main Mormon encampment, knowledge of her being his wife was a sacred trust. He had to remind himself that God knew best. During a quiet time he wrote a poem. His wives' names all began with M, and to "M" he addressed his words. Marinda and Martha would understand that though written to all of them, at this time he had particular concern for Mary Ann:

> Oh, M! thou aggrieved one, whose love is so pure,
> Whose heart, like a fountain, that flows always sure;
> Thy mind with much care has oft'times been opprest,
> And thou, like thy Master, hast no place to rest.
>
> A stranger and pilgrim on earth, doom'd to roam
> With men of the forest to seek for a home;
> In far distant wild-woods where nought can be heard,
> But yells from the savage and screams from the bird.
>
> . . . .
>
> To the wife of my bosom these lines are address'd,
> I left her encamp'd in a vale of the West,
> By the shores of Missouri's dark waters so rough,
> Near the old Indian village pronounc'd Council Bluff.
>
> Though the ocean's proud billows between us now rise,
> Yet Hope's brightest visions appear to mine eyes,
> That time's rapid flight through God's mercy and grace,
> May bring me in safety to her warm embrace.[15]

As "President of the American deputation," Orson's duties included encouraging the Saints in good works, instructing them in correct principles, and inspiring them to gain spiritual strength from their trials. He and his companions decided that he could best do this with his pen. He would serve as the temporary editor of the Church's newspaper, the *Millennial Star*, while Elders Taylor and Pratt and other newly-arrived missionaries traveled among the members. Orson began his editorship duties immediately. Then, with things running smoothly, he managed a preaching trip to familiar Preston, where a missionary recorded his arrival: "Every soul was glad . . . ; and although it was some years . . . since they had seen him, he was fresh in their minds, and they flocked around him like chickens about their mother."[16]

For the three months Orson served as editor of the *Millennial Star*, October 1846 to January 1847, his editorials covered a wide variety of subjects. Among these he recommended that "shareholders [in the Joint Stock Company] will have to lose the amounts which they have paid, unless those shareholders who have not as yet paid anything, shall feel disposed, from a sense of justice, humanity, *equal rights*, and equal burdens, to come nobly forward voluntarily, and contribute . . . to the aid of others who have suffered in this enterprize." He also wrote of amusing changes to his name caused by the habit of the English to drop or add the sound of *h* to words. As in other articles he referred to himself with the editorial "us," "we," etc.: "*Persons procuring post-office orders to send to us are requested to be particular in giving our name [to the Post Masters] correctly. Some orders have come payable to 'Horse and Hide'—some to 'Horson Ide.'*"[17]

In three months the Saints in England responded sufficiently to the tireless efforts of the apostles and other American missionaries that "the church [rose] from a worse than lukewarm state, to a lively zeal." Even most of the officers of the Joint Stock Company repented and tried to rectify the hardships they had caused. At a farewell party for the apostles, held January 14 at the large Music Hall in Liverpool, joy in the gospel echoed in "instruction. . . , spicy remarks . . . , and . . . spirited song." Parley P. Pratt and John Taylor sailed January 19. Orson would remain for a few weeks more.[18]

Orson completed the business in the office and turned the *Millennial Star* over to Orson Spencer. Elder Spencer would also be in charge of the Church in England. A man of integrity and tried experience, he had formerly served as mayor of Nauvoo. Assisting him would be trusted Franklin D. Richards. The Church was in good hands. Next, Orson Hyde traveled, according to previous plan. First he journeyed north from Liverpool to Edinburgh, Scotland. He held meetings, instructed, and ordained. Back again and south of Liverpool in Cheshire he did the same. Everywhere, he preached electrifying speeches, conversed with the Saints, and evaluated progress. His zealous exertions in behalf of the Saints brought their gratitude. One member wrote a poem expressing the feelings of many, calling Orson "the BRANCH *of peace.*"[19]

Orson sailed for home February 24 on the ship *Empire*. "The wind was fair and strong for seven or eight days, and we fondly indulged the hope that we should make the passage in about 16 or 18 days," he afterward recounted. But a storm arose, and furious winds ruined sails. "It then took about a week to mend and patch . . . [and to rig] the spare ones on board." After forty-one days the *Empire* docked in New York harbor the evening of April 6. Five weeks later, May 12, Orson embraced his wives and children in Hyde Park, Iowa. He found them "all in good health and in good condition; and for this blessing I feel very thankful to my Father in heaven."[20]

Orson learned that Brigham Young and others of the Twelve had headed west in April in a vanguard wagon company of mostly men. Using their maps and guidebooks, they would scout the way to the Rocky Mountains. Many in this company planned to return in the fall to take their families west the next spring. From England, Elders Pratt and Taylor had arrived at the Missouri River camps in mid April. They consulted with President Young before his departure, and were now directing hundreds of families of a second group outfitting to cross the plains. This second huge company had food supplies for a year and a half, anticipating no opportunity this year to plant and harvest. Before Brigham Young left, the Twelve decided that Orson Hyde should remain at the Missouri River and direct matters.

Orson's colossal assignment was to oversee the thousands of Saints in both Winter Quarters, on the west side of the river, and in Iowa Territory (Council Bluffs), on the east side. He was to be particularly mindful of the families left by both the Mormon Battalion and the pioneer company. To help him, two High Councils (twelve brethren each) had been organized, one on each side of the river. In the broader aspect—because of impossible communication with Brigham Young—he was also the highest Church authority available to members anywhere east from the Missouri River.[21]

The previous fall the Saints had established their "Winter Quarters" on an elevated plateau west of the Missouri River, several miles north of their first ferry. Here they built an orderly city of straight streets with approximately 700 dwellings. With near timber scarce, Orson marveled at how many men had hauled logs from deep ravines north and south and also from across the river. Most roofs were straw and dirt spread over poles, and they tended to leak under heavy rains. Orson sympathized with the families who had built their snug winter homes entirely of turf and willows and straw; spring storms, thaws, and warm sunshine had begun disintegrating these.[22]

Many graves in the cemetery attested to the hardships of the past season. Orson heard about the illness and the meager food. But the future looked bright.

"There are large fields of corn," Orson wrote May 30, "put in on both sides of the river—hundreds and thousands of acres. . . . It is almost incredible the amount of labour done." Food would be needed by the families already here and by many Saints continually arriving, those who had stopped for the winter along the Missouri River and on the Iowa prairies. The previous fall the last destitute and ill Saints had been heartlessly driven from Nauvoo and were headed west.[23]

Orson's family, in Hyde Park east of the Missouri River, lived as comfortably as other sojourners. In the sheltered hollow, with its excellent spring water and abundant trees, Richard Bentley and William Price had constructed a double log cabin of hewed logs. Prices and Bentleys lived in one end of the cabin and Hydes in the other, each family's room "some ten or twelve feet square." A few other families had built cabins nearby.[24]

During the last half of May and early June, while many Saints prepared to leave with Elders Pratt and Taylor, Orson's minor administrative duties afforded him the rare opportunity of working in his fields. The physical labor rejuvenated him. Rain helped the melons and vegetables and grain to sprout into sturdy plants, promising bounteous harvest.

His prayers contained pleadings for guidance as a leader in this wilderness, with no civil government or law-enforcement officers. Always a few Church members lacked commitment to the general good. Also, unruly persons fleeing from justice in the United States stopped in this frontier region. Rumors and eyewitness accounts of unlawful acts trickled to Orson. "On my return from England," he recounts, "I found that . . . *orthodox* Saints or Mormons . . . had imbibed the spirit of bogus making [manufacturing counterfeit money] and stealing." This saddened him, that a few people felt their hardships earned for them the right to any ease or comfort that presented itself. This minority saw nothing wrong in passing counterfeit money or in aiding unprincipled characters who stole and butchered neighbors' cattle for sale of the meat. How should Orson deal with these problems?

By spiritual whisperings, as he entreated and meditated, Orson learned the course required of him. In the positive aspect he should encourage the Saints to tend their crops, conduct schools, and live the Lord's commandments. In the negative, he should call down the powers of Heaven, as had the prophet Elijah anciently, to quell the increasing problems.

The Apostleship indeed possessed the power to bless or to curse. Joseph Smith had emphasized this to Orson years ago: "When you speak in the name of the Lord, it will prove true; but you must not curse the people—rather bless them." Now, however, Orson should exercise both powers to preserve the Saints from wickedness and temptation. Joseph Smith on occasion, in his love for his fellowmen, had been required to do the same.[25]

Orson announced his zealous plan privately in Winter Quarters June 3, prior to the departure of Elders Pratt and Taylor. The three attended a meeting of the small band of Church police, or guards. Here Orson pressed for the group's cooperation in his course. Both Parley P. Pratt and John Taylor endorsed his request. By mid June, Elders Pratt and Taylor, and more than 1,500 other Saints, bid farewell to friends in the Missouri River settlements.

Orson had decided to maintain a home on the west side of the river for the summer. He and part of his family moved into the dwelling in Winter Quarters vacated by Bishop Edward Hunter.

June 20, 1847, in Sabbath meeting in Winter Quarters, Orson began his public campaign to increase law and harmony among the remaining Saints. With ringing words he denounced sinful deeds. He asked transgressors and all who knew of transgressors to report offenses to him. In sweeping terms he declared that repented irresponsible acts of the past would be forgiven immediately in order that reformation could begin. He pronounced that unrepented misdeeds would result in prompt vexations. The spellbound congregation responded with animated expressions of support, but also a few averted eyes. Afterward several people talked with him in private. The refining movement had begun.[26]

However, before the day ended, a problem more serious than stealing confronted Orson. Devastating news arrived that a young man, returning with his family on business toward Winter Quarters from the west, had been killed by Indians. Also killed were four or five men sent by the United States Indian agent on official matters. Believed to be among them was Agent Mitchell's son.

Orson spent a busy Monday investigating. He found the Omaha Indian Chief, who promised to deliver up the offenders. Orson returned to the east side of the river and consulted with the Indian agent there, Major Mitchell. Major Mitchell was at the time also acting for the absent agent of the west side of the river. Orson and the Major agreed to raise troops, for a show of strength when they met with the Omahas. Orson would recruit Mormons. Major Mitchell would recruit Catholics, half breeds, and Frenchmen.

The next morning Orson composed a rousing letter to the High Council at Winter Quarters, updating them on developments and summoning aid. He asked for fifty mounted and armed men and for provisions. He and Major Mitchell would bring troops from east of the river, and all would meet on Thursday at the old Indian agency at Bellevue. "We want men enough to awe [the Indians] without fighting," Orson wrote.

On Thursday, Orson's fervor deflated to humiliation. The expedition had been canceled, leaving him insufficient time to notify the Winter Quarters men. Major Mitchell had taken no steps to muster troops after ascertaining that his son was not among the murdered whites. Neither had he been prompt in informing Orson. Besides, he said, he lacked sound authority to chase Indians on the west side of the river.

Reluctantly Orson released his own troops, but, feeling that Major Mitchell should taste some disgrace too, Orson induced the agent to ferry across the river with him for the rendezvous with the Winter Quarters men at Bellevue. As expected, a small vanguard from Winter Quarters waited. Obedient to Elder Hyde's counsel, these scouts reported, Hosea Stout was on the plateau up beyond the hillside ready for battle. With him were fifty-three men on horses and two baggage wagons of food and ammunition. In this excursion of folly Orson let Major Mitchell do the talking.[27]

The Indian problem unresolved but quiet, Orson turned his attention again to the reformation.

During June and July, to implement the Lord's reformation plan, Orson conducted many meetings on both sides of the Missouri River. In the meetings, Saints responded well to his graphic explanations of cursings and blessings. Orson reminded his listeners that the Almighty yearned to prosper them. He said, "If you will observe my words [as an Apostle of the Lord Jesus Christ] and do them, you will be blessed with seasonal showers and good crops."

Orson enjoyed the early summer of 1847. He rejoiced with the thriving Saints, preached often, worked in his fields (about thirty cultivated acres and a garden of "an acre and a half"), delighted in his family, relished appetizing meals, and gained weight.[28]

Orson needed to consult and counsel in Saint Louis, and late July seemed a good time to make the trip. Settlements functioning smoothly, the busiest harvest days a few weeks away, and family well (except toddler Frank uncomfortable with teething), Orson said his goodbyes the early morning of July 27.

In one of the Missouri River towns where the steamboat stopped, Orson received an astonishing surprise. He met five returning brethren from the Mormon Battalion and listened eagerly to their report. They were part of about 150 people who, because of poor health, had been discharged from the Battalion in three separate groups and sent to Pueblo (in what later became Colorado). From Pueblo they traveled north to Fort Laramie (in what later became Wyoming). Brigham Young and the pioneers had passed Fort Laramie about a week previously. Except for the five who traveled east more than 500 miles, now talking with Elder Hyde, the others journeyed west to catch up with Brigham Young.

Orson arrived in Saint Louis on August 4, completed his business, returned home, and resumed the routine that included working in his fields. Lacking machinery, he, Richard Bentley, and William Price threshed their "wheat with oxen by having them tread it out on a floor made on the ground, and . . . winnowed it with the wind."[29]

His local leadership duties resumed also. October 3 he conducted a conference on the east side of the river in Miller's Hollow on Indian Creek near the bluffs, about seven miles northwest of Hyde Park. He reminded the Saints to be generous in paying their tithing from their abundance "for [the benefit of] the poor." As well as helping the poor, paying tithing helped curb greed.

Cautioning about greed, Orson said that each family should resist the temptation to acquire more land than would meet their needs. "The Lord cursed the ground for man's sake, when [Adam] transgressed," he said, "and I think that the rich man who has the most land in his possession has the greatest curse."

Orson reminded his listeners that at "the conference in the summer I told you that if you would observe my words and do them you would be blessed with seasonable showers and good crops. This has been truly verified and . . . the Lord . . . has blessed you."[30]

As Orson anticipated the return of many of the Twelve from the mountains, gratitude abounded that, with the help of the Lord, order and peace prevailed among the Saints at the Missouri River. The Lord's method of discipline had worked. October 31, ecstatic Saints greeted the returning pioneers.

Soon Orson crossed the river and visited his brethren in Winter Quarters. Heaven's watchcare had given people and animals health during their long journey, and had preserved them during buffalo stampedes, grizzly bear frights, and Indian attacks. In the Valley of the Great Salt Lake, a thousand miles to the west, streams had been dammed up and the water used to irrigate crops in newly plowed arid soil. City streets had been laid out and twenty-seven log dwellings constructed before the returnees left.[31]

In Winter Quarters on November 8, 9, and 10, Orson enjoyed three days of meetings with his quorum, and after his return to Hyde Park he yearned to be with them more. Personal concerns, however—an ill wife, preparations for winter, and his hired man about to leave—occupied every minute. He contented himself to wait until early December to join with them in scheduled meetings on the east side of the river in Miller's Hollow.

The evening of December 2 a few traveling friends, including William Appleby, arrived at Orson's home after "facing a piercing northern blast, accompanied at intervals with snow." They stayed overnight. Brother Appleby wrote that he found Orson and "family well, and indeed a brother and friend. . . . I spent a happy time at Br. Hydes, every thing around him to eat and drink to make him and his family comfortable, A family that is certainly calculated to make him happy. He informs me that he raised 60 Bushels of potatoes from one half Bushel of Seed, and turnips so large that two of them would not go into a half Bushel measure."[32]

In their November meetings the Council of the Twelve had considered many pressing matters. How should they meet the needs of the Saints in the far parts of the United States and in the British Isles? What should they do about the insistence of Indian agents that the Saints abandon Omaha Indian lands, including Winter Quarters, on the west side of the Missouri? What plans should they make to retain the homes and farms and communities of the Saints on the east side of the river, in Iowa? Had the time come for the organization of a new First Presidency of the Church in order that the Twelve might be more free to travel about among the Saints?

The scheduled conference began on Friday, December 3, "in a large double block house" in Miller's Hollow. The first day's two sessions progressed well. On Saturday, however, the second day, the remainder of the conference was postponed. Frigid weather prevented an outside meeting, and, in Brigham Young's words, "the Saints congregated in such large numbers that we found it impracticable to continue . . . , so that we adjourned for three weeks to build a house capable of holding the Saints." In spite of extremely cold weather, two hundred brethren volunteered to raise a large structure.[33]

With the Sunday conference sessions canceled, and the members of the Twelve already on the east side of the river, they decided to hold a Sabbath council meeting at Orson Hyde's home. Orson rode from Miller's Hollow the several miles to Hyde Park and helped prepare. The Hyde ceiling leaked, so the meeting would convene in the Bentley side of the cabin.

Sunday, December 5, 1847, the eight men arrived in Hyde Park, breath of men and horses forming clouds in the frosty air. Elder George A. Smith brought his wife Bathsheba. "[A] good feast," relished as a midday meal, and pleasant afternoon conversation, added to the bonds of closeness. At dusk, five o'clock, the meeting began. The fire received Orson's regular attention, warmth emanating from the blazing wood in front of the large backlog in the fireplace. The nearness of the cabin walls enhanced the feelings of unity in the small room.

Brigham Young, president of the Quorum of the Twelve, disclosed that the need for a Presidency of the Church "lies with weight upon my mind," adding, "I have been stirred up to do this by the Spirit of the Lord." He asked the other apostles to tell their feelings upon the subject. In turn, Heber C. Kimball, Orson Hyde, Orson Pratt, Willard Richards, Wilford Woodruff, George A. Smith, Amasa Lyman, and Ezra T. Benson manifested sincere opinions. They conversed more, and they prayed, a sublime outpouring of the Holy Spirit assuring the nine companions of Heaven's acceptance of their efforts.

Absorbed with the enveloping peace in the room, Orson looked upward in sudden astonishment when he heard a rich encompassing voice. The sound originated somewhere beyond and above the circle of brethren. Quickened to the center of his soul, Orson knew the source: "The voice of God came from on high, and spake to the Council." The words were brief, the message direct: "Let my servant Brigham step forth and receive the full power of the presiding Priesthood in my Church and kingdom."

"Every latent feeling was aroused, and every heart melted . . . ," Orson recounts. "This was the voice of the Almighty unto us. . . . We knew and realized that we had the testimony of God. . . . [We] did hear and feel the voice from heaven, and we were filled with the power of God."

Orson was still comprehending that the Twelve had just been directed to appoint Brigham Young President of the Church, when a knock at the door startled him. He arose, opened the door, and stared out into the darkness at an unusual sight. "Men, women, and children," he tells, "came running together where we were, and asked us what was the matter." Puzzled at the excited neighbors' words, other men joined Orson at the door and listened to explanations:

"Our houses shook, and the ground trembled, and we do not know but that there was an earthquake." The Council members, Orson adds, had "felt no shaking of the earth or of the house, but were filled with exceeding power and goodness of God."

"There is nothing the matter," Orson and others told the anxious group at the door. "Do not be alarmed." One of the Twelve smiled and added, "The Lord was only whispering to us a little. The voice of God has reached the earth. He is probably not very far off." Mouths opened in astonishment. The peaceful demeanor of the apostles subdued the questioners, and all began to leave, wonder on their faces. Orson closed the door.

Back in the room, quiet meditation prevailed in the spiritual and physical warmth as each man cherished his own private thoughts. Then Orson felt impressed to speak. He said,

"I move that Brigham Young be the President of The Church of Jesus Christ of Latter-day Saints and that he nominate his two counselors, and they three form the First Presidency." The other apostles nodded agreement. One seconded the motion, and it carried unanimously. Brigham Young chose Heber C. Kimball as his first counselor and Willard Richards as his second. These two brethren had already been acting as his assistants.

Conversation explored new avenues. The momentous decisions of this day would be presented to the people in conference in a few weeks, after completion of the new log meeting house. Some of the Twelve could now be assigned to travel.

Sweet had been the five hours, but long had been the sit. Just after ten o'clock the nine men stepped outside into the winter night, walked a little among the few cabins, and breathed crisp air. Invigorated, they filed into Orson's home, where the women had set out an evening repast. Wilford Woodruff called it "a feast of pie and strawberry wine." Later George A. Smith related to his wife Bathsheba the details of the "great manifestation of the Holy Spirit . . . poured out upon those" in the meeting, and she afterward recounted her own experience: "I slept in the cabin that night and the sweet influence of the Holy Spirit which had been enjoyed in the Council, still remained."

Ever after this occasion, Orson's heart swelled with thankfulness at thoughts of the reorganization of the First Presidency of the Church "happening in my own little retired and sequestered hamlet, bearing my own name."[34]

In Orson's home the next day, December 6, the nine apostles conversed upon many subjects. Orson received the assignment, to "go to the East to procure means to help the Saints."[35] This should begin as soon as possible. Departing a few days afterward, he knew he would miss the delayed conference three weeks later.

From December 24 through 27 the scheduled meetings convened in Miller's Hollow in the mammoth new cottonwood "Log Tabernacle" that smelled of freshly cut wood. The capacious interior, forty feet wide and sixty feet long, dwarfed any person who stepped inside.[36] Each day of the conference more Saints attended, until on the concluding day, December 27, 1847, about one thousand people crowded into the building. Orson learned later about the extraordinary sessions. Afterward he recounted that on the last memorable day "the propriety of choosing a man to preside over the Church was investigated. . . . Brigham Young was chosen to fill that place without a dissenting voice, the people not knowing that there had been any revelation touching the matter. They . . . seconded the voice of the Lord from on high. . . . Yes, the voice of God was the voice of the people." An attendee adds, "The Spirit of the Lord at this time rested upon the congregation in a powerful manner, insomuch that the Saints' hearts were filled with joy unspeakable; every power of their mind[s] and nerve of their bod[ies] . . . awakened." Also, a "breathless silence" enveloped the vast congregation as spiritual vibrancy touched each person. The voting was done by "Solemn Assembly," each priesthood quorum in turn, and then the remaining Saints.

Saints in other parts of the world sustained the action in their conferences as they received the news.[37] Again the Lord had a First Presidency in his Church and one man on earth as his spokesman. Orson Hyde was next in seniority after Brigham Young and Heber C. Kimball. Because these two now held positions in the First Presidency, Orson became the president of the Quorum of the Twelve Apostles. New members would be added eventually to bring the number again to twelve.

Meanwhile, Orson had journeyed eastward to gather funds for the Saints. He left his Kanesville home December 9, and arrived in Saint Louis "in 12 days from the Bluffs," he wrote. "But, Oh! to ride on horseback on the prairies, facing a cold wind always, for 450 miles, I will not comment upon it, neither how badly I was chaffed from the calf of the leg to the highest seat of honor upon the saddle." In the same hurried December 28 letter, to Brigham Young, Orson added that his diligent efforts had so far raised $500.00.

Church leaders had decided already that Orson would again be left in charge of the Missouri River camps when Brigham Young and all possible others departed for the West in the spring. When President Young announced this, he said of "Brother Hyde" that "no man has done better. He is a splendid man." One of Orson's duties would be to publish a newspaper, because the Church needed a written voice. In preparation for this, in Saint Louis, Orson arranged for "a press and type for the Bluffs, to be sent up by the first boat, with paper, Ink &c. and men to carry it on," he reported. In addition he had purchased "sash, doors and glass for the [printing] House or office." In President Young's letter Orson enclosed a letter for Marinda with the request to "Please send" it across the river to her.[38]

In January, Orson arrived in Philadelphia. Here Col. Thomas L. Kane, the army officer who had been impressed favorably with the vagabond Saints the year before, extended to him every hospitality. Orson delivered a letter written to the Colonel by the Twelve, asking if he would use his influence to soften hearts and open purses to assist the Saints. He would. Orson gathered funds only briefly in Philadelphia. Marinda was expecting a baby in late February, and, though he yearned to be with her, Orson had anticipated arriving home a month after that. However, his diligent appeals for funds succeeded so well that he started home before the end of January.

In February 1848, for eleven winter days, Orson pressed his tired horse toward Hyde Park from Saint Louis. Both he and his horse developed saddle sores. The sores grew raw, almost unbearable. Overnight rests in homes of scattered Saints were too few and too short. To keep his spirits up Orson tried to think lightly of his discomforts. He would soon be home after an absence of two months. His worn appearance gave no hint of the hundreds of dollars gathered from Saints and friends and packed carefully into his knapsack.

He arrived home February 14, before Marinda's confinement. The next day he wrote a hasty note to Brigham Young. Luke Johnson, Marinda's brother, delivered it across the river. In the letter Orson explained not coming himself because of "my horse and myself being badly galled, and a party [Marinda's baby] hourly expected at our house." February 18, Brigham Young and Heber C. Kimball visited the Hyde home and received the means Orson had obtained. Anxious days passed. The birth signs had been a false alarm. After an impatient two weeks, Marinda gave birth to Alonzo Eugene on February 28.[39]

Orson's duties as a leader resumed. At every opportunity he encouraged diligence in raising crops and livestock, and in preserving native fruits, berries, and nuts. He wished "to have the poor so situated that they can all be producing and by the blessing of God, we may be able to fill this country with good things, that the thousands who may flock here, may have enough to eat while resting for a season on their way to the valley." Each resident family evaluated personal situations. "Do we have enough wagons, oxen, and provisions to transport us across a thousand miles of plains and mountains and then sustain ourselves after we get there?" was the challenging question, "or should we stay here and plow and plant and cultivate and harvest?"

Along with counseling about going or staying, national matters became part of Orson's responsibility, 1848 being an election year. March 27, Church leaders met in the Log Tabernacle with about sixty selected Church brethren and heard the pleas of a delegate from the Whig party of Iowa. He spoke graphically about the persecutions of the Saints in both Missouri and Illinois, depredations allowed while Democrats held office. He pledged Whig compassion and help in return for votes. The votes would help oust the Democrats and elect General Zachary Taylor as President of the United States.

Brigham Young summarized the feelings of the brethren: "[The Whigs] have readily admitted that we were an industrious, innocent, persecuted people; and although to us it looked rather suspicious, that the Whigs of Iowa should at this peculiar juncture become deeply interest[ed] in our welfare, . . . our . . . unparalleled suffering . . . ; still the caucus concluded to reply to the communications of the Whigs." Orson became chairman of the committee to draft the reply. They adopted a long document written by Willard Richards. In essence it agreed "that if the Whigs of Iowa would . . . use all their powers to suppress mobocracy, insurrection, rebellion and violence in whatever form . . . then the saints would pledge themselves to unite their votes with the Whigs of Iowa at the elections of the current year."[40]

However, this pledge must not be made public, even among the Saints, until election time drew near. Orson would have to expedite the particulars, as President Young and the others would be far away. To prevent public furor, the timing must be judicious. Orson must plan carefully.

General conference began April 6, 1848, in Miller's Hollow. The prominent theme was "going west" and helping others to go west. Another significant event of the Conference occurred the third day: "On motion of Orson Hyde, the place hitherto known as Miller's Hollow was named Kanesville, in honor of Col. Tho[ma]s L. Kane, who [has] ever been a true friend to the saints."

Miller's Hollow, now Kanesville, which had been procured from the Pottawattamie Indians, would soon become the headquarters of the Church east of the Rocky Mountains, with Orson Hyde as the leading authority. Winter Quarters, on Omaha Indian lands, must be vacated, the settlers either wagoning west or ferrying their goods to the east side of the river. The Indian agents insisted that the Winter Quarters log cabins remain.[41]

While numerous Saints prepared to move their families either far westward or near eastward, Orson moved Marinda and the children, also Martha and her mother, northward to Kanesville from Hyde Park.[42] Kanesville was the most convenient location from which to direct the Church. Mary Ann remained in Hyde Park with her brothers William and Charles. Charles had married in the fall of 1847.[43]

Orson and Marinda's home was on the sloping base of the golden bluff forming the north side of the narrow section of the hollow. The Tabernacle, backed by the same bluff, stood a short walk to the northeast. At the bottom of the slope flowed Indian Creek, "a little meandering stream easily spanned by a few planks resting upon logs reaching from bank to bank." Log dwellings and tents were scattered in random arrangement on each side of the brook, most of them on the south, and most dwellings enclosed by their own rail fence. This left no defined streets as such, just haphazard spaces between the fenced properties. Westward the flat plain stretched three miles to the river, with luxuriant grass, flowers, and occasional small lakes. The far bluffs on the other side of the Missouri seemed backed only by limitless sky. Mostly grass covered the bluffs sheltering Kanesville. The few shrubs and trees had survived the past practice of the Indians to set fire annually to the hillsides.[44]

From Kanesville radiated several roads. One, on the river plain, led south to Council Point and Trading Point. A second road, clearly visible from the Hyde cabin, wound southeastward up a glen and branched out to numerous cloistered hamlets of Saints in the hills and hollows above the bluffs. Northward, up the long valley of Indian Creek, a road led to the ferry across the river to Winter Quarters and to several additional roads to various settlements of Saints. Another road ascended from Kanesville eastward up a glen to settlements in that direction.

In Kanesville, Orson began accumulating logs for a printing office. His earlier printing press arrangements had failed to materialize, making another trip east necessary. He wished to go soon in order to start his newspaper. But many Saints needed guidance, so before he could leave home "the emigration for the Valley must be off."

Also, before he left home, Orson followed his admonition to others, "to cultivate the soil extensively—to sow all the wheat they could." He planted twenty acres of wheat, far more than his family would need. This alarmed some brethren; they thought he "was going to apostatize."[45]

May 24, he visited Winter Quarters. At the ferry landing he waited his turn and then squeezed himself and his horse onto the crowded barge. These days the ferry always carried capacity loads of people and goods moving east or west. In Winter Quarters the changed appearance of the town was astonishing. Numerous cabins and dugouts stood abandoned. A constant caravan of wagons and animals and families climbed the road on the nearby steep hill and disappeared over its crest. The parade, Orson learned, had been perpetual for nearly two weeks. Brigham Young was almost ready to get under way. Orson Pratt had left for England. Wilford Woodruff was preparing to move east of the river temporarily until ready to depart on a mission to the eastern states.

Nine days later, June 2, Orson and a group again rode into Winter Quarters and observed only about 150 wagons still being readied for travel. Brigham Young had been gone a week. Orson rode up the western hill with

Wilford Woodruff and a few others, headed for farewells with the departing Saints in their organizing camp.

From the high bluff east of the Elkhorn River the sight of 400 wagons of the organizing camp, far below and widespread on the extensive plain, was beautiful. Herders tended vast herds of livestock. And westward, miles beyond the "Horn," the lush and spacious flats of the Platte River merged into the western horizon. Someday Orson too would follow that wide life-giving river toward the mountain haven of the Saints.

Orson and his companions arrived in camp at about four o'clock in the afternoon. They had seen no wagons during their thirty up and down and winding miles from Winter Quarters. They learned that 200 wagons had already started the westward trek. He and those with him met with Brigham Young for last-minute counseling, and they remained overnight.

The next morning the western sky threatened rain, but Orson's group stayed until ten o'clock, reluctant to turn their horses back eastward. Returning, they had been on the road from the Elkhorn about an hour when a horrendous storm overtook them, thunder and lightning, gale winds, pelting rain. Men and horses had no shelter, so ducked their heads and suffered. The storm moved on. Orson and his companions dried before they rode down into Winter Quarters.

The storm had changed Winter Quarters: wagon covers torn to shreds, debris everywhere. For months obviously blessed by the Lord, it now seemed no longer a refuge for anyone. Before the end of June, more wagons of Saints followed the trail west from both sides of the Missouri.[46]

Two members of the Twelve, George A. Smith and Ezra T. Benson—both mild mannered—had been assigned to stay and assist Orson with the Saints who remained. The immediate territory over which the three presided covered extensive farms and settlements on rich soil about thirty miles north, east, and south from Kanesville, containing about 15,000 Saints. The area had timber enough if used wisely. The Pottawattamie Indians had been removed by the government, but a few other Indians remained.[47]

With the emigration for the mountains underway, Orson delegated local matters to his counselors and prepared his covered wagon for his planned journey east. "I left my home in Pottawatamie county on the 24th of June," he reports. "My object in going abroad was to obtain a printing press, fixtures, &c. I expected to raise the necessary funds by donations, sub-scriptions [to my forthcoming newspaper], . . . &c." His printing office was built. Also he needed to raise funds to pay the debts that the First Presidency left for him to meet.[48]

Another purpose of the trip was to take Mary Ann to Saint Louis where she would reside for a while with her sister, Lavinia, recently married to John Hodges. One reason for Mary Ann leaving was Martha's jealousy. Living in her own home with her mother, and known as Martha Browett, Martha felt left out of Hyde family happenings. She became offended if not told details about other private family conversations and activities, felt slighted when no slight was meant. Numerous Church members knew her marital status, but plural wives were not to be "public" here and now. Because polygamous relationships would feed rumors that might foster persecution, Brigham Young had requested most men with more than one wife to go to the Valley. People "of the world" were increasing locally: the Gentile merchants setting up shop, the seasonal traders, and other travelers. Still, Martha wanted to be seen with Orson in public, desired to have people observe her husband's graciousness with her, his high regard for her. Orson tried to compensate in private for what was unwise in public, but she felt neglected. Having Mary Ann in Saint Louis would stop any of Martha's fretting that Orson might spend more time with Mary Ann than with her and she not know.

Letting Mary Ann leave was a difficult decision, though, tearing Orson between his duty to the Church and his duty to his wives. He hoped that the time would soon come again, like in cloistered Hyde Park, when his whole family could enjoy togetherness, laughing, sorrowing, helping one another, and working side by side.

June 26, two fast Iowa prairie days from home, Orson's small group caught up with Wilford Woodruff, leisurely traveling with his wife, children, and several brethren to his assigned eastern states mission. Some nights the company camped in groves of trees by springs or streams. They also stayed in the settlements of Mount Pisgah and Garden Grove, where Orson and Wilford preached. A few evenings they gratefully found Church members who allowed them to stop on their property. July 5, almost across Iowa, they arrived at a member's farmstead in mid day and arranged to camp. That night divine warnings saved Wilford's carriage and occupants from being demolished in a severe storm.[49]

Two days later, near Nauvoo, Wilford and Orson parted for a few days. Orson traveled upriver to Burlington, Iowa, "to see a small branch of our church there and to send a young man from thence to England" to obtain promised funds for the Church. In Burlington, Orson adds, he "was introduced . . . to several principal men in the place; and talked politics and religion, Mormonism and anti-Mormonism while with them. . . . They wished to know of me what my political sentiments were. I freely and honestly told them that I was in favor of the election of Genl. Taylor."

Intermixed with the talk of elections, Orson mentioned "my wishes to obtain a press, and they said they were willing to aid me. . . . They asked me if it would be opposed to my feeling to lend them my influence in the election of General Taylor. I told them, 'Not at all.' I intended to give the old general what little influence I had any how. They gave me letters of introduction to some Whig members in Congress at Washington City. And they were good letters . . . honorable and gentle."

From Burlington, July 8, Orson wrote to Elder George A. Smith in Pottawattamie County. Orson was convinced, he said, verifying what Church leaders had decided months before, "that it will be for our interests and for the interests of the country to vote the whig ticket generally." Orson cautioned Elder Smith to "say nothing about this except to a few leading men among us until about the time of the Election; then make your rally." Orson addressed a letter to the Saints the same day, to be read to them nearer the election.

Orson returned the thirty-five miles to Nauvoo and reunion with Wilford. They started down the Mississippi on Tuesday and arrived in Saint Louis the middle of Wednesday night. Orson remained in Saint Louis for a few days. He visited old friends, preached to the Saints on Sunday, July 16, and lingered in Mary Ann's company.

Hurrying on, he was in Cincinnati July 22. Though uncomfortable in weather extremely warm and rainy, he investigated printing presses and found what he wanted.[50]

Orson arrived in Washington before the end of July, and success followed. "I borrowed, by the aid of the letters that I took, eight hundred dollars in gold," he narrates, ". . . and gave my paper on demand for the same." He would use this money for his press and fixtures.

Though successful, for many miserable days "a southern fever" simmered as hot in his body as the overpowering sultry summer weather. Recovering, he traveled on to Philadelphia. Here he had a relapse. He drank "rivers of composition and other Thompsonian fixings," and at length, the latter part of August, regained his health.[51]

As well as health complications, Orson encountered apostate difficulties stirred up by Lyman Wight, still officially one of the Twelve. Lyman had helped lead a group of Church members to Texas, for scouting purposes he said at the outset. After finding a promising location he began a communal settlement. Church leaders had been charitable and hoped he would return to the fold. But his attitude turned bitter. Recently he published an outrageous sixteen-page pamphlet against the way Brigham Young and the others managed the Church. He invited Church members to join him in what he said would become a Utopia.

To help Saints ignore Lyman's invitation and to refute Lyman's accusations, Orson published an answering circular. Remembering the devastating results in England when local Church leaders had set up a system of gathering "common stock" seemingly for the good of the body of the Saints, Orson saw troubles ahead for Lyman's communal venture and sounded the voice of warning:

> Why does brother Wight teach and enforce a doctrine that Joseph Smith never did, nor never would, sanction? Namely: a community of

goods, or property thrown in together as common stock. Though this doctrine has sometimes been practiced by good men, . . . the original purpose and design of God was to make men accountable for their stewardship, and therefore, "to one he gave five talents, to another two, and to another one; and to every man according to his *several ability*" [Matthew 25:15]. The whole course and order of nature—the constitutional organization of man—the voice of the martyred prophet of the last days, and the eternal purpose of God, all stand opposed to brother Wight's "common stock" principles; and no people can prosper that enforce this as a law among themselves.

Eventually Lyman Wight was excommunicated, and he never sought reinstatement.[52]

During Orson's homeward journey he relished overhearing conversations on deck and dock about the Mormons, but his amusement turned to dismay when he read in the newspapers that *he* had caused a political uproar. He was glad to be traveling unobtrusively, as he and other elders often did. To be "Esquire Hyde, a gentleman from Connecticut," or some other indefinite person, saved much jeering. Church leaders had learned to travel quietly in this time of persecution to the Saints.[53] The two letters that Orson wrote to Kanesville from Burlington—recommending that the Saints vote the Whig ticket—had been opened illegally and the contents published. In a furor, newspapers heralded that Orson Hyde, a Mormon apostle, had corrupted the ballot box by accepting a bribe of $1000 for the votes of the Saints.

Orson purchased his press and type in Cincinnati and planned a short stay with Mary Ann in Saint Louis before departing in time to arrive in Kanesville before general conference on October 6,[54] but trying to counteract the political noise about himself caused delays. To newspapers he wrote letters stating that he had not been bribed. Rather, Whigs in Burlington had given him letters of recommendation, he explained, to assist him in borrowing money, $800, to buy a press. From Saint Louis he made a trip upriver to Nauvoo to investigate the opening of his earlier letters. He discovered that a jealous Church member had unsealed them, added embellishments, and revealed their contents.

Orson's Burlington letters began many complications for the 1848 election in Iowa. A "lost" Kanesville poll book resulted in Mormon votes not being counted. Later, in February of 1850, the poll book was "found." Heated discussions followed. Though Zachary Taylor had received the national presidential vote, the Mormon vote in Iowa would have sent a Whig to Congress rather than the Democrat who was seated. Uproar resulted. Politicians, farmers, and editors all over Iowa formed opinions. Bitter accusations between Whigs and Democrats finally resulted in a mid 1850 investigation. In this, Orson and numerous others testified before federal officials. Speculations and arguments about the episode were discussed and journalized for years. In 1914 the dispute was considered "the most famous contested congressional election case in the history of Iowa and one of the most famous in the history of the nation."[55]

Meanwhile, in Saint Louis, while investigating and answering the charges about his corrupting the election, Orson also had the option of keeping busy answering pamphlets of several apostates. These publications contained "revelations" and prophesied doom for the "Brighamites." Orson ignored them, as their preposterous claims assured their demise. Orson had answered the one by Lyman Wight because Lyman was one of the Twelve.

While countering problems, Mary Ann's presence buoyed Orson, and he bid her farewell reluctantly. "[I]n fine health and spirits" he arrived home October 15.[56]

Kanesville was growing. More hewn-log dwellings had been built during Orson's absence. His own "to be" printing office stood as a central sturdy structure on the southwest corner of what had evolved into intersecting main roads, Hyde Street and Main Street. Hyde Street began at Orson's home, crossed Indian Creek, and continued southeast up the glen. Main Street began on the river side of town, roughly paralleled Indian Creek here at the bluffs, and continued with the creek northward. On Main Street, signs identified several stores. Kanesville now even boasted tavern accommodations—food and lodging for travelers—at the Union Hotel, a large double log house up the glen on Hyde Street. A sizeable building in progress would be a school.[57]

Now, also, "Pottawattamie County" claimed civil officials, but this diminished Orson's duties only slightly. He still consulted day and night about personal and public problems and decisions.

Orson exulted when men arrived from the Valley bringing news that things were going well for the Saints in the Rocky Mountains. Wagons, and earlier-borrowed teams of Kanesville area Saints, arrived back from the Valley too, gladdening many families.[58]

A general conference convened the last weekend in October "as a kind of finish to" the sessions during Orson's absence earlier in the month. Before it closed on Sunday afternoon, October 29, a stirringly memorable event occurred. While speaking to the huge congregation in the Tabernacle that afternoon Orson noticed, across the room, a stranger walk in quietly through one of the front doors. The stranger seemed familiar. Sudden recognition stopped Orson in mid thought. He hurried down from the pulpit, and the two men "threw their arms around each other for joy." The familiar stranger was Oliver Cowdery. Orson led Oliver to the stand and introduced him, trim and refined, with large brown eyes. For almost eleven years he had been out of the Church through disaffection.

Oliver Cowdery accepted Elder Hyde's invitation to address the congregation, and his eloquent words projected love as he recalled his close association with the Prophet Joseph. Glorious visits of holy angels to Joseph Smith and Oliver Cowdery became a reality to this new set of Church members as Oliver declared "in the same manner as he used to do" that the visions and revelations were accurately reported.

Oliver voiced his surprise "to see such a sea of strange faces." The Church had grown astoundingly. Thousands more resided in the West. He now realized, Oliver told, that "if you want to follow the right path, then keep the main channel of the stream. Where the body of the Church goes, there is the authority." He declared that "this people have the true and holy priesthood; for the angel said unto Joseph Smith, Junior, in my hearing, that this priesthood shall remain on the earth unto the end."

In Kanesville, Monday evening, Oliver visited George A. Smith and Orson. He said that he hoped to remain with the Saints and had brought his wife and daughter with him from Wisconsin. The three men talked long. Oliver said that he had "not come for place or office." Elders Hyde and Smith felt that he had truly repented, and they invited him to attend the High Priest Quorum meeting the first Sunday in November. Orson asked him to remain the winter and assist in the printing office. Oliver accepted the invitations.

Sunday morning, November 5, in the Tabernacle, with the High Council seated in their place, Orson conducted the High Priests' monthly gathering. After regular business, and upon invitation, Oliver Cowdery arose and spoke about his feelings, of his years away from the Church, that he had "sustained an honorable character before the world" during his absence, and that he wished to return. Much discussion followed, many questions and answers. For years Oliver had felt that he retained all the authority that had been his in the early Church period and that he should be permitted to use that authority. He told the brethren that only recently had he learned "of the Revelation which says that the keys and power conferred upon me, were taken from me, and placed upon the head of Hyrum Smith. And it was that Revelation which changed my views on this subject." That revelation had been received by Joseph Smith on January 19, 1841, in Nauvoo, and no reason existed for Oliver to have known about it. He resided far away. But the present tone of his voice evidenced that the experiences he had shared with Joseph Smith had been too sublime for Oliver to take lightly a revelation given to the Prophet by the Lord.

When all questions seemed satisfactorily answered, and a motion for Oliver Cowdery's rebaptism had been moved and seconded, Orson asked for a vote that "Brother Oliver be received by baptism and that all old things be forgotten." This vote carried unanimously. A week later Orson performed the baptism.

Orson valued Oliver's help in setting up his press, and he enjoyed Oliver's speeches and conversations. Oliver planned to join the Saints in the Rocky Mountains. The next summer, with inadequate means, he thought he would go for sure the following year. Then, during an extended visit at the Missouri home of his brother-in-law, David Whitmer, he became ill and passed away, March 3, 1850, a year and a half after his rebaptism.[59]

Regarding this same November that Oliver Cowdery joined with the Saints, Orson learned later of a sad occurrence in Nauvoo. A mob torched the Nauvoo Temple. Only the stone walls remained.[60]

On a glad November note, "[A] company of the Mormon [Battalion] soldiers . . . just returned [to Kanesville] from California, . . . [where] a number of them were employed in digging a [mill]race for Captain Sutter and found a gold mine. . . . The brethren went to digging, and brought with them to the Bluffs a quantity of pure virgin gold." December 9, the returned soldiers and their families "were feasted at the tabernacle on a general collection of good things." Afterward they danced.

The Mormon soldiers had not been required to fight battles, thus none lost their lives in duty. But after their California discharge, Daniel Browett, Martha's brother, and two others were killed by gold diggers in the California mountains. This news brought mourning to their families in Kanesville.

December 30, George A. Smith and Ezra T. Benson penned a report of the year. Among other things they wrote:

"Elder Hyde has got his printing establishment all ready, and is only waiting for his foreman to come from St. Louis, who is daily expected. . . .

"There are about fifty branches [of the Church] organised, all doing well, as a general thing. . . .

"Elder Hyde is here at home presiding and is a terror to evil-doers, and a comfort and support to the Saints. Before him sinners in Zion tremble and the Saints rejoice, and he enjoys himself first-rate, and we . . . are doing all we can to strengthen his hands, and forward the work of the Lord."[61]

CHAPTER 14

. . . *gold*. . . . *(1848–1850)*

> . . . *much more precious than . . . gold.*
> —1 Peter 1:7

THE closing days of 1848 found snow drifted high on the prairies beyond Kanesville, piled deep in the timbered areas, and packed slippery on Kanesville roadways. Hills provided fabulous sledding for laughing children. Frozen lakes on the river flats developed grand "hieroglyphics" carved by skating young folks. And smoke rose comfortingly from chimneys. But Orson knew that outward appearances of calm misled. People in many cabins subsisted on scant rations. To the needy, food was increasingly more wanted than gold.

"We had many poor among us before Winter Quarters was evacuated," Orson explains, "and having contributed much in teams & wagons, &c. &c. to help off the emigration last spring, the people here suffered many inconveniences by it. Add to this the fact that about one Hundred families from Winter Quarters, most of them very poor and destitute, were thrown upon our hands." Also, with less animal power than desirable, harvesting the vast fields of corn and potatoes had been slow. Then, beginning the first week of November, mercilessly harsh snowfall prevented further crop gathering. Orson took his concerns to the Lord. What should he do?

Enlightenment was given him, and he shared it at the Sabbath meeting in the Tabernacle on December 31. He told of his concerns and of the answer, delivering the word of the Lord. "[T]omorrow morning, before the sun rises upon the birth of a new year," he declared, "you should come and deliver into the tabernacle, for the benefit of the poor, a goodly portion of your flour, corn-meal, beef, mutton, pork, chickens, cheese, butter, eggs, bread, pies, cakes, potatoes and vegetables." Broadening his requests, Orson asked the merchants of Kanesville "to liberally contribute of your calicoes and dry goods, as well as your tea, coffee and sugar."

He expanded the topic and pronounced the Lord's blessing. "In the name of the God of Israel," Orson's voice resounded, "whosoever has these things delivered before the sun dawns on the year 1849, shall be blessed beyond measure. And it will return upon your heads four-fold in what you set your hands to do, and you shall prosper exceedingly." Inner stirrings told Orson that the prophecy would be fulfilled, no matter how unlikely it seemed.

At dawn the next day a throng brought abundant contributions over trails of snow and ice. Many came five or six miles. The merchants brought generous amounts too. At the Tabernacle, Orson distributed the vast goods to those in need. The recipients rejoiced in this seeming "year of jubilee."[1]

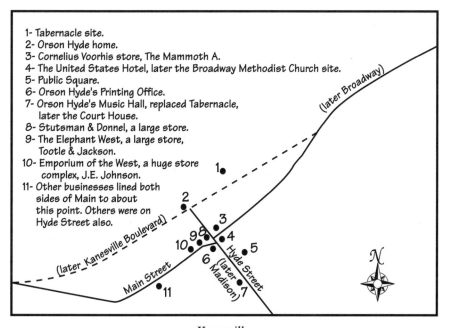

1- Tabernacle site.
2- Orson Hyde home.
3- Cornelius Voorhis store, The Mammoth A.
4- The United States Hotel, later the Broadway Methodist Church site.
5- Public Square.
6- Orson Hyde's Printing Office.
7- Orson Hyde's Music Hall, replaced Tabernacle, later the Court House.
8- Stutsman & Donnel, a large store.
9- The Elephant West, a large store, Tootle & Jackson.
10- Emporium of the West, a huge store complex, J.E. Johnson.
11- Other businesses lined both sides of Main to about this point. Others were on Hyde Street also.

Kanesville.

Kanesville merchants already anticipated that 1849 would be a jubilee year for them because of magnetic reports of fabulous gold fortunes to be had in California. Crowds of emigrants were expected here on the frontier wanting outfits for crossing the plains. In the fall the merchants had received large supplies of goods before ice closed the river.[2]

The first issue of Orson's newspaper, THE FRONTIER GUARDIAN, came off the press February 7. Being able to send published messages to the scattered Saints would alleviate a little of the frustration Orson felt in his snowy isolation. A few months before, in Saint Louis, he had hired a printer, John Gooch, but ill health in the Gooch family delayed his arrival in Kanesville until mid winter.

In his first editorial Orson expressed his thoughts about newspapers: "The press is a powerful engine, for good or for evil." Using the traditional "we" pronouns, Orson stated that in deciding the "matter that flows from our pen" his "most ardent wish, and sincere prayer [is] that the words we employ, and thoughts we record may be the dictation of that Spirit that is destined to bless the world. . . . Should we fail to realize this, in consequence of any momentary excitement or vexation, we hope to find forgiveness with both

God and man." He stated that the "principles of our religion will always have a conspicuous place in our columns," and he would "spare no pains or labor to keep up a healthy moral atmosphere." He hoped, as well, that anything published "for improvement in science and learning" would be helpful to the "education of our youth." Regarding "political questions," he announced that "it is not our present design to interfere to any great extent." He also recommended, because the "season of emigration will soon open, and outfitting for the mountains and 'gold regions' will soon commence," that businessmen advertise their commodities and services "to induce new comers to postpone their purchases till they arrive at the Bluffs." This would bring money to Kanesville and thus assist Saints to obtain outfits to emigrate to the Salt Lake Valley.[3]

The four pages of the first issue of the *Guardian*—size 16½ x 23 inches, one sheet of paper folded in half—indeed contained variety. It included edification from both a doctrinal article by Orson Pratt and an epistle from Brigham Young, laughter in witty stories splashed with romance and plays on words, pathos in poetry, and amusement in a stranger's description of Kanesville. As guardian of the well-being of the people, Orson mentioned the heavy winter snows and advised inhabitants living on the river lowlands and along streams to expect spring flooding and be prepared to move to higher ground. In another article he admonished Church members to seek more spiritually valuable things than gold.

To gain revenue for his newspaper, Orson obtained advertisements. Hiram Clark described his Union Hotel. Dustin Amy was prepared to do all kinds of tinsmithing. Lawyer Merritt's office was in the Union Hotel. Doctors Williams and Johnson offered their professional services. The tailor, Mr. Chadwick, would do "Cutting . . . at the shortest notice." Blacksmith Carter would make anything in his line. And Orson announced his own print shop, equipped and ready to do all types of printing "under the supervision of a skillful workman." Of the several stores in town, two—"Smith & Tootle" and "Needham & Ferguson"—had placed advertisements, listing a variety of goods. For payment they would accept cash, gold dust, dry hides, beeswax, and furs.

The second issue of the every-other-week *Guardian*, February 21, 1849, again contained items for both the local populace and for far away readers planning a journey to the gold fields. Farmers should plant wheat, oats, flax, barley, and corn. From the barley, with "the hops which grow spontaneously in large quantities through this section, a most excellent, wholesome, and cheap beer can be made." Gold diggers were assured "that every article needed in the Gold Mines, from a crow-bar to a sieve, from a barrel or sack of flour to the broad-side of a baconed porker, can all be had here at equally as low rates as can be purchased on the Mississippi."

As the weather had continued severe, Orson reminded the Saints that their tithing of food and clothing would help the less fortunate. Further, in helping others, they should tithe their time as well as their goods. That "the needy . . . may not lack fire-wood," George A. Smith admonished, "we advise that every tenth day during the cold season, the brethren all turn out with their teams, and those who have no team, take their axes to cut and prepare the wood."

Orson had needs too, and he wrote about himself as "a Preacher in this town on whom many of the citizens of this county and of other parts frequently call for advice, counsel, and instruction upon various questions." Orson added that the "Preacher is not a rich man, and . . . his house is so thronged with comers and goers, that it seriously interrupts the arrangements of his domestic or family affairs; and, moreover, the business of some is of such a nature that they require to see him alone by himself. In this case, he is obliged to go out of doors, or send his family out, which is very uncomfortable at almost any time; but more particularly so in this extreme cold weather." To build an office "that he may have a place to give counsel in," and that would "cost about one hundred dollars," Orson urged contributions of "labor, lumber, nails, glass, sash, 18 inch shingles, corn, flour, pork, and even money." For payment of subscriptions to his newspaper, Orson announced that he would take commodities such as flour, corn, hard wood rails, and shingles.[4]

With two issues of the *Guardian* distributed, Orson found time to write to Mary Ann, still with her sister Lavinia Hodges in Saint Louis. Besides fond thoughts of her, other things prompted him to write. She had sent gifts to Kanesville with the merchant Brother Needham. The merchant Mr. Voorhis, planning a trip to Saint Louis, offered to deliver a letter to her.

Orson's letter started out chatty, with news of the family (from Marinda to three year old Frank) and news of Mary Ann's brothers and sister: William (who had recently visited Kanesville from Hyde Park), Charles and his wife Elsa, also Elizabeth and her husband Richard Bentley (who had moved into Kanesville). As the letter progressed, Orson's yearnings for Mary Ann's presence increased. Then a sanctified feeling enveloped him, and with priesthood authority he pronounced upon her the most precious of blessings. On the outside of the letter he wrote, "Mrs. Mary Ann Price, Saint Louis, Mo."

Dear Sister Mary,   Kanesville Feb'y 27. 1849.
        Mr. Voorhis is soon to leave for Saint Louis, and I improve the present moments in writing to you. We are all well at present except Sister Martha. Her health is not very good. Frank and all the children were much pleased with the presents you sent them by bro. Needham. Your letters by him came safely; but the one you speak of that was sent by mail, we have not re'd. The can of Oysters came safely, and all our family being fresh water folks, I was allowed to enjoy them alone; particularly after I told them that they had been cooked before

they were dressed. My compliments to Mr. Hodges for this rarity from the Sea.

I have sent you the first and second Nos. of the 'Guardian,' and trust that you will have examined the pages before you get this; and as they contain most of the news, I shall omit a repetition of it in this.

Our county has become organized, and the law of the Gentiles is again in force over us. But as we intend to live above the law, it cannot harm us. If we fulfil all its requirements, we shall be free. Last evening, I married Capt. Geo. D. W. Robinson to Miss Jane Sutch. They go soon to Saint Louis. W$^{\underline{m}}$ was here yesterday. He was going to Mill. He was well with the exception of a bad cold. Bro. Bently was here also yesterday. He was well. Charles has cut his foot, but not badly, I believe. Elsa & Elizabeth are as well as could be expected. If Elsa's name were Mary the 41$^{\underline{st}}$ verse of the first Chap. of Saint Luke might apply to them very well.

William does not get married yet, and has not been out to one of our parties. Yesterday was the first time he has appeared in Kanesville this winter. The pretty girls have spared no pains to show off to the best advantage at the dances, and they succeeded well. But William's eye caught not a glimpse. Yet I think he intends to do something in the line of getting married before long.

I could have wished you were here to enjoy our holy-day recreations. We, perhaps, did not have so many luxuries as some other places afford; but we had good company, good music, good feelings, good girls and good boys: But we did not have them all. We had good cakes, beer, pies, cheese, chickins, & Pigs; besides many other good things too numerous to mention.

You may, possibly, be looking for, or desiring a word of counsel from me. I shall probably be at Saint Louis before you come up. It is my feelings, at present, that you had better remain in Saint Louis for the season: More particulars I will tell you when I see you. In the meantime, write me the 1$^{\underline{st}}$ opportunity you have by private conveyance after you get this, and let me know how you will be situated there, and what you would rather do.

There are a great many going to the Valley, or at least, intend to go. The Gold Fever rages some among us. All upper Missouri intend going to the "Gold Region."

I often think of you, and ask myself how you get along. I shall see you this Spring if the Lord will, and then I will tell you more than I can write.

Remember me kindly to Lovinia and to Mr. Hodges. I wish them prosperity and peace. Life is short at best, and I trust they will both obtain an inheritance in the Kingdom of our God.

For the present, I must say; Mary, Good by.- May God, our heavenly father bless thee– May his angel protect thee– May the visions of thy mind be instructing, and may the thoughts of thy heart cheer thee. The blessing of a friend is thine, and this letter is the bearer of it to thee. Thou shalt have Eternal life in the Name of the Lord, and he shall give thee the witness of this truth when thine eye passes over these lines.

Marinda sends her kind love to you and to Lovinia. Laura & Emily also. Frank says, "I will write poor Mary a letter. I will send her my love," he says. Martha will write herself.

As ever, I am still

Yours most affectionately
Orson Hyde.[5]

In the fulfillment of his myriad trusts, Orson's devotion to the Saints gave him the constant challenge of properly leading the people, solving local problems, and still finding time to write and choose items for publication that would uplift, inform, entertain, and instruct. His editorial comments in the *Guardian* of March 7 about the lack of mail for two weeks, and thus lack of news, both informed and entertained: "The regular mail, or rather, irregular mail, could not be depended upon [in the winter] in consequence of the deep snow; and for some reason, unaccountable to us, the mail is very irregular, even when the roads are good. . . . We don't know but that we may be so 'hard up,' that we shall be obliged to fill up [the newspaper] with 'Jew David's, Hebrew Plaster,' or some other medicine that possesses virtue enough to make a young man out of an old one, and have enough left to make a little dog."

In this third issue of the *Guardian* Orson gave instruction in an article he titled "Did You Curse the Whisky Seller?":

> From a certain speech that we delivered the other day . . . , some have drawn the inference that we cursed the whisky seller; . . . we now reduce to writing what we did say. . . .
>
> Some tell us that they have no means of going to the Valley only as they sell whisky to get the means to go. Such are in a fair way to get to the Valley, but not to the Valley of the Great Salt Lake; . . . they are in the broad road that leads to the valley and shadow of death.
>
> Others justify themselves by saying: "If we do not sell it, somebody else will, and we might as well have the profit of it as others.". . . If others will bathe their hands in human blood for silver or gold, it is no reason why you should. . . .
>
> Some will say that there is but little liquor sold in this country, in comparison to what there is in many other places. . . . Vice of any kind does not sink to its lowest depths at the first plunge. There must be a beginning to effect anything, good or bad. . . .

We did say that the gain of whisky sold here in opposition to the feelings and wishes of the great majority of the community, should be cursed. We did not say that the person should be cursed who sold the liquor, but we said his gain should be cursed. . . . We said further, that there were those who sold whisky, and Mormons too (but not Saints), that would turn a deaf ear to the cry of the widow and orphan. . . . A pint of whisky, we said, would probably constitute the extent, the grandeur and the glory of the kingdom over which such would reign in the eternal world, with a little pile of fire and brimstone under their throne.

Orson tried to prevent a flood of whiskey among the Saints, but he had no power to stop the spring floods of water resulting from the deep winter snow. In March the snow melted, causing a tremendous rise in streams. Many families by creeks vacated their habitations. The raging water carried off bridges and for several weeks rendered the roads impassable. All of the mills ceased grinding because of the high water, but none received serious damage.[6]

Early 1849 newspapers and mails revealed mounting excitement about the gold fields of California, and the fascination of gold sent even Orson's imagination into extravagant fantasies. Chuckling one morning, he related his dream of the night. Diligently digging in the California mountains, his shovel thudded on a solid mass. Great effort and prying turned out a pure gold lump weighing two hundred and fifty pounds, and left four more in the hole still larger! Philosophizing about his dream he remarked, "[H]ere on the frontier, so near California, we can't help having some golden dreams of enormous size."

Ever since the Mormon Battalion soldiers returned to Kanesville the previous fall with gold, Orson felt a mounting challenge to keep the shining lure in proper perspective for anyone who would listen. Gazing into a pouch of gold did something to a person. The luster of the particles of gold dust, and the sheen of undulated nuggets, caused unintentional soaring reactions in heart and head. The heartbeat quickened, and the mind saw visions of mansions and carriages and fine clothes. This was "gold fever."

In a March 21 editorial Orson extolled the value of local agriculture over metallic riches, stating that "this region is well adapted to agriculture, and is very productive and healthy. . . . [I]t will afford from fifty to seventy-five bushels of corn to the acre—from twenty to thirty bushels of wheat—potatoes and turnips, any quantity to the acre you please. . . . While thousands and tens of thousands are going to dig in California mines for gold, let us go to and fill the frontier region with provisions of every kind—supply the emigrants and gold diggers, and have plenty of means to buy their gold when they come back. We say to our friends then, if you cannot go to the Valley this year; come as far as this place, and dig for corn and potatoes.

"The question has been asked," Orson said in a speech in conference on April 7, "'Will we cut off from the Church those who go to the gold "diggins" without counsel?' I say, 'No, we will not cut them off. There is no law transgressed thereby for which we should cut them off; but they may stand a chance to get their heads cut off at the mines.'"[7]

From downriver the season's first boat arrived and docked at Council Point on April 15. Loaded with merchandise for Kanesville stores, the *Mustang* also brought a few passengers on their way to the gold regions. A mid April report from Saint Joseph, about one hundred miles downstream, had encouraging aspects regarding the "Gold Seekers." It declared that "in and camped in the immediate neighborhood of St. Joseph, upon both sides of the river, [are] more than one thousand men, the greater part of whom are fully supplied with oxen, mules, wagons, and complete outfits for a journey across the plains, as soon as the grass is sufficiently grown to support their teams. Not a boat arrives at our wharf but brings more or less of these adventurers. . . . More hardy, enterprising and intelligent companies of men cannot be raised than these; young and active, looking into the future and towards the 'land of promise' with high hopes and through a golden medium."

Orson received information that between 600 and 1000 wagons were on their way overland toward Kanesville, headed westward. Anticipating the needs of the travelers, and deciding that he, like his neighbors, might as well have goods to sell to them, Orson placed a notice in his April 18 newspaper that in exchange for the *Guardian* he would accept "[c]orn, potatoes, corn-meal, flour, beans, beef, pork or bacon, butter[,] eggs, chickens, pigs, mutton, lumber, oak or walnut wood, gold and silver coin or dust . . . *if brought soon.*"

During the last two weeks of April, hundreds of wagons began arriving from Iowa, Michigan, Wisconsin, Indiana, Illinois, Ohio, and other places. Their owners found spots to camp near the streams on the flats, and Orson visited among them. The campers respected him as the leader of the Mormons, among whom they must remain until grass grew on the plains. Though now travel-worn, the equipage of the adventurers received Orson's admiration: expensive wagons, superior animals, fancy camp stoves. The aroma of bubbling kettles of stew and fresh biscuits in Dutch ovens attested to excellent cooks. Orson surprisingly found no drunkenness among the men. True to the previous report from Saint Joseph, this season's gold seekers seemed "generally fine looking men; hale and hardy," Orson observed, "well raised apparently, and above the medium of society in general."[8]

To help these travelers feel a little closer to the homes they had left behind, and to benefit himself, Orson devised the plan to "publish any man's name in any future number of the Guardian, and mail a copy of it to his friends in any part of the world that he may direct us, for one dime, if he will leave us his name and the address of his friends." The May 2 issue of the

Guardian contained 128 names. Following issues contained legions more, in addition to the usual items, religious and secular.

Camping spots in and around and beyond Kanesville and Council Point during the first two weeks of May became incredibly crowded and widespread. Days in Kanesville became more hectic. Men by the dozens thronged off the river boats at Council Point, their purses bulging with money to buy outfits. Wagons and wagons and more wagons rolled into Kanesville, needing a space to camp, their owners eager to buy last-chance supplies before their two-thousand-mile journey across plains and mountains and deserts. Often, because of the mass of animals and covered wagons in the streets, Orson had difficulty walking from his home to the printing office. The deluge jammed stores with men who had long lists of needs. Store clerks became exhausted. And outside, each traveler wanted to pull his wagon up directly to the store's door. A loaded wagon had a tight squeeze to move away through the clog of waiting animals and vehicles. Besides items procured in the stores, the gold seekers bought much from the area farmers, huge amounts to take with them, and corn to keep their animals alive now. The Public Square, up from the *Guardian* office, and east of Hyde Street, became a busy market place.[9]

Prices of commodities in mid May fulfilled Orson's earlier prophecy that blessings "will return upon your heads four-fold in what you set your hands to do, and you shall prosper exceedingly." In his own case, he received seven dollars per hundred pounds for flour, ground from the wheat of his twenty acres, after sharing generously with the poor. Resident Robert Campbell adds:

> [E]very kind of business was animated. The blacksmiths and wagon makers were kept constantly busy, shoeing horses and repairing wagons. Many were also engaged in making trades. The emigrants were under the necessity of exchanging their battered wagons for a stronger kind, and to replace their jaded animals with others in better order.
>
> Many of their old wagons had to be sold at nominal prices. Much of their overcharged freight had to be left and sold for what it would fetch.
>
> Frequently one, and occasionally two auctioneers might be seen knocking off useful articles at one time, some of them new, and sold at half the usual cost. Many of the Saints were thus enabled to fit themselves out for the journey across the plains.

Another development also helped fulfill Orson's prophecy: some gold seekers changing their minds about journeying farther westward. These recognized, after their ride of hundreds of miles to Kanesville, more hardships in this adventure than previously anticipated. Rather than continue, they sold for low prices their tired animals, their wagons that needed repairs, and everything else. For travelers undecided about whether or not to go on, Orson offered advise: "If [you] back out at all, now is [your] time, before [you] get out on the plains where [you] cannot get back without a guard which may be difficult to procure in that region. You must then 'hang together' or be scalped separate."[10]

At last, the third week in May, grass had grown, and the mass of gold adventurers resumed their westward trek, hundreds of their names preserved by Orson in the *Frontier Guardian*. The ferries ran unceasingly and by the end of May had transported these legions of California-bound wagons and men over the river. Meanwhile, the Saints made final preparations for their own emigration. The gold seekers had indeed been a blessing to them.

The intricate ways in which the Lord managed to bless mankind caused Orson to continually marvel. Until the influx of gold adventurers, he thought that the Lord had led the Saints to the Valley of the Great Salt Lake to enjoy sanctified seclusion. His recent ponderings promoted another view. To Brigham Young he penned his thoughts about this on May 20:

> There are hundreds and thousands and tens of thousands of men going through to the Gold Mines, and many thousands are intending to go by Salt Lake, and to winter there. They are mainly going with friendly feelings, and there will be a great field for preaching to them. . . . It is another imposibility for us to get by ourselves. God seems to be determined that we shall have the world around us and in our midst for they are his scourge, and he will use them when he will, and they are also dependent on us for life and salvation, therefore, the Lord will have them among us and in our midst, go where we will. The vast amount of cattle, horses and mules that will rush into the valley, will eat up every green thing for scores of miles around you. These men will want to trade in many things. I hardly know how to advise you to meet this great number of men and animals, if it were my place to advise you: But as it is not my place to do it, I know not how. But I pray God my heavenly father that you may have wisdom given you from heaven in the very hour you need it, to direct and guide you in all these things.[11]

Before 1849 the few other wagon trains on the plains had posed no anxiety for the emigrating Saints. This year, gold-diggers thronged the road "like musketoes," and local brethren feared starting because all grass might be eaten before them. Sharing this alarm, Orson announced that the Saints would tarry until June. Then they should be ready to roll.[12]

People, wagons, and herds departed the first week in June, but delays beset the last company. Orson felt concern about "the danger of [them] being caught in the snows of the mountains." Also, this group's leaving saddened him; with it would go George A. Smith and Ezra T. Benson, his counselors, his strength. Brigham Young had called them to the Valley.[13]

Orson had other concerns also. One case that he reported to Brigham Young involved William Hickman, now on his way to the Valley:

Last year we lost about forty or fifty horses and mules, stolen by Indians, and this spring we lost Twenty by them. . . . We warned our people not to feed them [Indians] or harbor them on this side [of the river] at all, but if they wished to give them any thing to send it over on their side. A small band of Pawnees were harbored at Carterville and fed by some whose sympathies for them were strong enough to make our counsel of non effect.

A company of Gold diggers passed by there and brought tidings into Kanesville that 25 Indians were . . . skulking in the brush. I at once concluded they were after more horses and requested some of our boys to go over and drive them away. We told them to make them go, and if they resisted, to send them where they pleased, or leave them by the way. They went over and routed them, and some say that William Hickman shot one of the Indians, and some people who were so full of sympathy and religion that they could violate our counsel in harboring Indians, have made a good deal of fuss about it.

The deed was a rash and hasty one under the circumstances, considering . . . squaws and children . . . were there. Yet there has hardly been an Indian on this side since, not another horse stolen. . . . Bro. Hickman was cut off from the Church here on account of it. It was wisdom and proper to do so. . . .

We do not want the Indians harmed, but neither do we want our whole frontier stripped of horses, and those who have prevented the Indians from doing it, we take pleasure in commending them to mercy, notwithstanding the action of the Council here. . . . [I]f you deal with him as you think the nature of the case requires, and then restore him [to Church membership], you will do, in my opinion, a good deed.[14]

At a conference held July 22, the Saints approved the High Council as Orson's counselors, but he still felt overwhelmed by his responsibilities. Besides providing for his large family—Marinda and the children, Martha and her mother, and Mary Ann in Saint Louis—and donating for every charitable purpose, Orson's other duties abounded. He wrote numerous letters of counsel to the Saints abroad in Europe and in America, because at this time such was impossible for the far away First Presidency. He selected and sent out elders, for the same reason as writing letters, then wrote advice and direction to them while they were away. He tried to be at the river to meet all Church emigrants who arrived on boats from parts of the United States and from England. He found homes and provisions for the arriving Saints left husbandless and fatherless by cholera on the way, cholera being rampant downriver this season. He attended all principal council meetings. He preached every Sabbath day and on other occasions. He granted hospitality to many comers and goers, his home always open and his table ready to share; and giving individual instruction in every intricate matter. He retired to bed late and arose early; about the only time he had for his personal business was while others slept. Some situations required him to chastise soundly. Others he handled with extreme gentleness. And always his welcome greeting remained hearty, a smile on his face, no matter his cares or how tired he felt.[15]

Orson made his living partly from his land, worked by others for a share of the produce. The *Frontier Guardian*, now self-supporting, also brought a little profit. To increase circulation he used many means. On sample copies he included notes such as:

> The Guardian is sent you from a brother's hand, that has created and brought it into being, without tithing the Church in any way for it. God has blessed my labors in connection with it heretofore, and with it, I send my blessing to you. If you like it, pray for me; and if you don't like it, pray for me more abundantly, for I need all the aid possible, both from heaven and from earth.
>
> Your Bro. in Christ,
Orson Hyde[16]

Orson gained great satisfaction writing for the *Guardian*. Two items that he tried to keep lighthearted, August 8, while giving instructions, related to the irksome problem of too many dogs in Kanesville and the continuing vexation of bogus coin makers:

Dog Killers—Attend!

By the law of the State, any person has the right to kill a dog that is found worrying a domestic animal in the streets. If about forty 'leven of the canine race were killed off in our little town, we should hear less squalling among the swinish free commoners of the street. The quiet peaceable cow, returning from the prairie at evening ready to impart a flowing pail of milk to her mistress, can hardly pass along the street without being tormented by every cur and whiffet that can yelp. Dog killers, be at your posts; and if dogs cannot be kept under reasonable restraint, let them atone for their cruelty by the half score.

A Stew.

The counterfeiters in Pottawatamie are stewing over a hot fire, it would seem from the fact that some of them are charging us with being accessory to the running away of a negro slave to the Salt Lake. . . .

Would you not look well to attempt to get that *"villainous Hyde"* arrested on a charge of this kind in order to punish him for breaking into your money making arrangements? . . . [S]ome of your fraternity went to Springfield and swore against us to get us punished for the crime of saying that any man that would make bogus money ought to be compelled to drink it melted. . . .

Well gentlemen, cook up the stew to suit your own appetites. But remember, if you boil the devil you must drink his broth. . . .

An August 8 news item stated that "citizens and friends" intend to "get up a good Choir of vocalists to be accompanied with instruments of various kinds." Orson encouraged this and had "sent for all the necessary music." In the same notice he announced that he "would like to build a hall for the musicians and for other purposes at an expense of about $500 if some of our good friends abroad or at home could feel to donate this amount." If the means failed to come in by donation, Orson planned to construct the building himself.

Orson had decided to build the Music Hall because of complications with the Tabernacle. When constructed in December of 1847, it stood on frozen solid earth, a rigid base for the log walls and puncheon floor (hewed split logs laid on the ground). Approaching two years of use, the floor had become unstable because of runoff water from the bluff behind the structure and from a pond nearby. In High Council meeting July 22, repairs were discussed, but no work resulted. In High Council meeting August 26, the group considered taking the structure down and rebuilding it on a spot without seepage. Study proved this impractical. Repairing the Tabernacle, also, after a few months of effort, seemed unwise. Eventually the edifice was torn down, its logs used for other purposes.[17]

At a big school celebration in early September, near the Tabernacle, around two hundred students from two schools in Kanesville and one in Council Point presented an excellent program showing their accomplishments. Orson commented, "[M]oney can never be more profitably spent than when paid to good teachers for the education of the youth."[18]

During the summer and fall of 1849, Kanesville merchants expended much money and effort to prepare for the next emigration season. Some stores changed hands or partnerships, and new stores materialized.[19] The most imposing new premises belonged to Joseph E. Johnson, a Church member. "J.E."—tall, lean, energetic, and flamboyant—arrived in Kanesville the summer of 1849 and changed things. He built what he described good-naturedly as "the first house in Pottawattamie County," actually the first *frame* building among hewn-log structures. His imposing mercantile complex arose on the other side of Main Street from the *Guardian* office, and he grandiosely named it "The Emporium of the West." Previously the stores had straightforward names like "Miller and Co." and "Voorhis & Co."[20] The other merchants began putting up colorful titles and figures on the signs over their doors.

"J.E." also added flair to the advertising columns of the *Guardian*, a change from the conventional polite listing of goods. His first ad, dated September 19, began in bold letters, "MORE GOLD DISCOVERED! TREMENDOUS EXCITEMENT! A NEW VARIETY STORE." He described clothing and cloth, school and home items, paints, saddles, medicines, "and a thousand articles too numerous to mention," with such words as "fashionable" or "splendid" or "amusing." He opened, "in the same Row" of buildings, a "BAKERY AND CONFECTIONARY STORE" where could "be obtained all varieties of Bread and Crackers for family or emigrant uses. Wedding, Fancy and Plain Cakes, Tarts, Jumbles, Pickles, Preserves, Jellies, Fruits, Nuts, Raisins, Syrups, Sweet meats, Candies in every variety; Cigars, Tobacco, choice Wines and Liquors, (By bottle or Case,) Cider, Ale, Mead, Cheese, Herring and Refreshments generally." Commercial Kanesville had entered a new era.

In mid September, with matters satisfactory in Kanesville, Orson traveled east to Keokuk, Iowa, and down the Mississippi River to Saint Louis to bring Mary Ann home. She might have remained longer, but her sister Lavinia, with whom she had lived, passed away in the spring. While in Saint Louis, Orson met with the Saints, instructed, and tried to strengthen where needed. He and Mary Ann rode a steamboat up the Missouri River and arrived home October 13.[21] Mary Ann was pleased that she would be home to welcome new babies into the family, Marinda's, expected this winter, and Martha's first child, due in several months.

Orson's resources for the *Guardian* would soon be scarce. River traffic was about to cease until spring, thus no mail or newspapers would arrive by boat. And probably little overland mail from the east would come during winter weather. Only one avenue seemed open to Orson for messages. "[W]e may be blocked in here, and compelled to look to Heaven alone for information," he explained to his readers. "However highly we regard that source we sometimes want information which that department does not care to be troubled with giving." By mid November only one mail had arrived in two months, except pieces brought by individuals. To fill the columns of his newspaper, Orson reprinted earlier speeches and writings of his own and of Joseph Smith's and of others.[22]

The evening of December 11, wagons and men arrived from the Valley. "President Orson Hyde and all the Saints," recounted one of the travelers, "received us with great joy." "Our arrival was hailed with . . . rejoicing and cheering . . . ," another traveler added, "and the blacksmiths brought out their anvils and used them instead of cannon, which made the hills and dales roar again, to spread the welcome news."

Elder John Taylor led the group, on his way to France as a missionary. Other members of the Twelve accompanied him, three of the four new apostles ordained in the Valley the previous February. They headed to missions also: Lorenzo Snow in Italy, Erastus Snow in Denmark, and Franklin D. Richards in England. Charles C. Rich, the fourth new apostle, was serving a mission in California. Orson relished the companionship of members of his Quorum, was elated to welcome the new brethren personally. Additional news pleased him too: the companies traveling to the Valley the past summer had nearly all arrived before Elder Taylor's group left, though the last ones met hardships from snows in the mountains.[23]

With pleasure Orson received a letter from the First Presidency, dated October 16. As Orson read the letter his enthusiasm grew, learning of a plan revealed to help the poor. "The Lord has been devising, or rather making manifest ways and means to facilitate the gathering of his Saints in these last days," the First Presidency wrote, "in helping to roll on the glorious work of gathering Israel."

The plan, called the "Perpetual Emigrating Fund," had been started, the letter said, with means donated in the Valley, already $6000. As an economy procedure, the poor would build their own wagons of wood, without any iron parts. The Fund would purchase supplies, as well as young oxen and cows. The best teamsters possible should be procured, experienced men, "gentle, kind and attentive to their teams." In the Valley the cattle and teams would be sold and the money returned to the Fund. The assisted people should work and pay back the amount that had been spent to complete their outfits. Outfits should be basic, with no luxuries of extra food, clothing, wagons, etc., the Presidency advised, because the "poor can live without the luxuries of life, on the road, and in the valley as well as in Pottawatamie and other places." These measures, in addition to continued donations from other Saints, would enable the Fund to help ever more emigrants.

Bishop Edward Hunter, the agent appointed to carry out the plan, had come to Kanesville with John Taylor's company. Orson happily anticipated working with Edward Hunter, whom he had baptized in Pennsylvania in October 1840, while on his way to Jerusalem. Much of the $6000 in the Fund was gold bullion. Orson advised Brother Hunter to take it and sell it to the United States Mint in Philadelphia. Brother Hunter would then return to Kanesville and prepare a company to emigrate in the spring.[24]

While in Kanesville for a few weeks, John Taylor wrote a report for the *Guardian* and said of the group's sojourn in "your beautiful little village on the frontier. . . . We feel to tender to [you] our warmest thanks for [your] kindness, hospitality and benevolence. We here meet a kindred spirit, and find that the presiding genius of this place [Orson Hyde] drinks from the same fountain, breathes the same air and revels in the same intelligence as do the master spirits of the Great Salt Lake Valley."

During the visit of the brethren from the West, December 20 festivities celebrated the completion of Orson's Music Hall. In the December 22 High Council meeting, Orson invited the High Council to hold their meetings in the building, and they accepted.

A day of celebration for the Hydes was December 28, when Marinda gave birth to a baby girl. They named this new daughter Adelia Annette and called her Delia.

With Marinda's baby here safe and well, Martha grew more eager than before for the arrival of her own baby in the spring. But her emotional problems intensified. She became increasingly upset about being an expectant mother with no noticeable husband. Things would be better, Orson kept telling her, when they moved to the Valley.[25]

Orson's closing *Guardian* editorial for the year 1849 reflected his thoughts. He reminded himself and his readers that

> . . . as a community, [we] have great reason to rejoice, and be thankful to HIM whose Providential care has been over us by day and by night. . . .
>
> As disciples and followers of the HIGH AND HOLY ONE, let each examine faithfully and carefully his or her conduct for the last year. Say to yourselves: Have I done to my neighbor as I would like my neighbor to do unto me? . . . Have I cherished the spirit of the gospel which is, *"good will to man?"* Have I written in sand the injuries and wrongs that I may have suffered from others, so that a few drops of repenting tears may obliterate them? Have I written on plates of steel the acts of kindness and generosity shown to me, and are they so deeply engraved that no storm of adversity can obscure their lines?

Orson's concerns about people's conduct extended to a problem he seemed unable to eliminate, the local consumption of liquor. Because the Church accepted the use of wine for the sacrament of the Lord's Supper, and in cases of illness as a mild sedative and a means of soothing apprehension, Orson felt that the Church needed some control of the sale of alcoholic beverages. He had proposed, the previous August, "that the High Council appoint a man to keep ardent spirits, and sell as his judgements shall dictate." The High Council then appointed one of their members, Aaron Johnson, "to manage the Liquor Business." Now Brother Johnson planned to emigrate. To maintain a controlled location where the Saints could purchase their wine for the sacrament and for illness, Orson published a notice in February: "A very good article of Malaga or Sweet Wine, for sickness and for communion, may be had at this office."[26]

In Orson's leadership role, prophetic insights had become as natural a part of his life as breathing. He shared enlightenment from the Spirit in diverse subjects in his newspaper. Two of these:

January 9, 1850:

> If those boys, who are planning to steal chickens for their party, will come to us for chickens, we will buy all they want, and make them a present of them. Don't steal them. . . .

March 20, 1850:   **KANESVILLE MARKET.**

In our last, we quoted corn at 35 to 40 cents per bushel, but our corn buyers complain, . . . as they were selling corn at that time for 25 cents per bushel and sacks returned. It is more than likely that we were mistaken: yet the spirit of prophecy was upon us, and we wrote according to its dictates; but the error lay in our not searching what manner of time the spirit of prophecy in us did signify when it testified beforehand that corn would be worth 35 to 40 cents per bushel. We thought it meant the time then present; but upon strict enquiry and examination we have become satisfied that the true time referred to will be about the 10th of April next.

Orson's careless mid March heed to celestial promptings resulted partly from his routine being disrupted by the Congressional investigation for the voting hassle of two years previous. J. F. Kinney, Judge of the Supreme Court of Iowa, headed the investigation delegation. Daniel F. Miller, the Whig candidate, and representatives of William Thompson, the Democrat candidate, accompanied Judge Kinney. Mr. Miller claimed to have won the election by the count of the Mormon votes, and he accused Mr. Thompson's supporters of "misplacing" the Kanesville poll books in order for Thompson to be declared the winner. The group arrived in Kanesville on March 13, 1850, and interrogations lasted several days. Orson gave testimony in two sessions, cooperating with officials of both sides of the issue. Judge Kinney seemed impressed by Orson's straightforward testimony and also by what he observed of the way Orson directed the lives of ten thousand people.

Orson received a gratifying surprise when Judge Kinney "admitted Mr. Orson Hyde, Editor of the Guardian, as an Attorney and Counsellor at law, to practice in the several courts of Iowa." Daniel F. Miller, the Whig candidate, humorously said to Orson,

"Elder Hyde, I intend to report you to the Council at the Salt Lake; for the Scriptures say: 'Woe unto you lawyers!'"

"I thought I would join the profession," Orson replied in a serious tone, "knowing it to be under divine censure, and raise it, if possible, to an elevation above the woe, and contribute to its numbers that we might be strong and respectable enough to plead successfully our own cause."

As weeks passed, Orson continued prophesying. In the April 3 *Guardian* he announced:

A valuable set of harness . . . was stolen . . . , belonging to Col. Lockwood Smith. He [Smith] is satisfied that no resident of this county took it, but believes it to have been taken by an emigrant whose displeasure he had particularly incurred. We would be most horribly mortified if any citizen of this county should be guilty of any such meanness and crime.

If the said harness is safely returned to its owner forth-with, or placed where he will find it, . . . well and good; but if not, let him who stole it . . . prove the strength of a Mormon prophecy: "he shall become blind, and a child shall lead him." . . . We say to the thief, return the harness to its owner! We are not trifling with you!

The harness was returned.[27]

April conference had been planned to last three days, but from many of the Branches no representatives came. Unseasonable cold had prevented roads from drying out, leaving travel "extremely bad." Distant Saints usually looked forward to a pleasant time of reunion and came with their teams and covered wagons, their bread and dinner and bedding, and camped in yards and fields of friends residing in and near Kanesville, but present conditions repressed this. The second day, April 7, Orson adjourned the conference until the next "pleasant sabbath."[28]

The cool spring weather caused problems for waiting gold-seekers. Arriving earlier this year than last, and in greater numbers, they filled the spaces around Kanesville with compact tent villages, most of them centered with a pole from which the United States flag floated majestically. Herdsmen tended vast numbers of livestock. Chilly weather delayed grass growth, and the gold-seekers had to buy corn for their animals. In mid March corn cost twenty-five cents per bushel. By April 3 it cost fifty cents per bushel and by mid April one dollar, even more than Elder Hyde had earlier prophesied. Corn was getting scarce.

This year, different from 1849, Orson noticed more "unprincipled men among the emigrants." A few stole corn or chickens, even a horse. Orson published a warning: "Let the thief go and perish in the mines if he will not reform, and let the sufferers bear with patience their loss and disappointment, knowing that the thief shall not be released from his prison until he has paid the utmost farthing. Justice will not relinquish his demands upon the offender though he leave the world: neither will the sufferer go unrequited, though he die before it happen. . . . Remember this!"

Even with problems, gold-diggers again helped Kanesville. The ten large stores and several small shops, also the area farmers, sold services, goods, and produce rapidly. Orson again increased *Guardian* sales by talking with men in the emigrant camps and publishing their names to send to friends and relatives.[29]

Another April event with mixed blessings and problems was the birth of Martha's baby, a girl. Martha and Orson named her Adella Marie. Though Martha ecstatically held in her arms a child of her own, she still coveted public appearances with Orson.[30] Orson knew, sadly, that he spent too little time placating her, but his duties demanded almost more energy than he possessed.

Orson also had apprehensions concerning the Church, and about these he wrote to the Presidency, April 25. "The doctrine is established in Washington," he said, "that all the leading Mormons at Salt Lake City are hostile against the Government of the United States, and are sworn to overthrow the Government when they have a chance." Lying apostates strengthened these prejudices, Orson added, and the lies received reinforcement from "reports which emigrants have sent back concerning your enmity to the Government, and the precious morsels concerning polygamy." Orson enclosed clippings as examples of items that "have soured the minds of the General Government." Orson also told of his frustrations about the long distance from him to the Presidency: "When I have read some things, I have felt as though I could wish to Straddle a lightning wire, and fly to the Valley and tell you."

The next day, April 26, having questions, Orson wrote a second letter. With Church tithing, which he had been ordered to send to Brigham Young, but which was his only extra money, should he pay the freight on goods President Young had ordered from England or let the goods be sold to pay the freight? When would he see the return of the cattle and wagons borrowed to aid the presidency in removing to the Valley and to haul public property there? The owners constantly asked about this. What about persons distressed from cholera, sickness, and poverty that Orson had no means to assist?

April 27, as men would soon carry mail to the Valley, Orson composed another letter to Brigham Young. In a letter sent the previous October, President Young had invited Orson to come to the Valley this spring. "I thank you for this invitation," Orson now responded, "and few things could give me greater pleasure than a trip of this kind this coming summer: But to leave this office and the Church . . . in the hands of any other man that I know of in this country, would certainly be hazarding more than I can feel myself safe to do. . . . Every thing is precarious with us here. Indeed, Cutlerism [led by Alpheus Cutler who had apostatized], in Five Hundred forms, would rage like wild fire through this country if the strong arm of power were not upon it all the time. I do assure you, Prest. Young, that it requires the utmost care, diligence and watching over this people to keep their Ey[e]s toward the Salt Lake Valley. . . .

"I want to do right," he added, "and to act honorably towards all men, and if you think that I need chastisement, I trust that I am not above receiving it, neither so wise and headstrong that I will not profit by it."[31]

For months, in speeches and articles, Orson urged local residents to plow and plant, that crops could be raised to sustain the poor the next winter and that farms would be attractive to newcomers who might wish to purchase. In the April 17 *Guardian* he declared that "he who developes the riches of the soil of Pottawatamie County . . . shall never come to want. . . . Fear not the clouds nor the cold weather, but plant and sow in faith. . . ." Orson reminded his readers May 1 that "the ground . . . [is] very dry, . . . in excellent order for plowing. . . . If you have no team, spade up your ground."[32]

Farmers planted, but they understandably showed discouragement. April had been exceedingly cold and windy. The ground dried. The wind and the constant emigrant movement stirred up continual dust until the earth seemed a moving cloud of haze, with men and animals choking. The goggle trade in Kanesville did an unprecedented business.

In May the weather continued dry and cold, with no rain or grass. "From ten to fifteen thousand California Emigrants have been quartered here from a month to six weeks, with . . . horses, mules, oxen and cows," Orson reported May 10, "and the consequences are, that our hay and grain, of every kind, . . . have been . . . consumed." The California emigrants must soon proceed west or return east. A few companies had already gone west, but word of hardships and of returning wagons trickled into Kanesville.

Echoing the despair of gold-diggers and populace, Orson wrote for the May 15 *Guardian* about an earlier prophecy. "Mr. Joseph Smith, when alive," Orson began, "said that none need fear a general famine while they could see the rain-bow in the clouds. That was a sure indication of seed time and harvest; but, continued he, when the bow disappears, or when it is not seen, look for famine and distress. Who has seen the bow in 1850? We have not." In spite of the seeming hopelessness of the situation, intimations of the Spirit encouraged Orson, and he counseled now as he had counseled for months: "[L]et no farmer slacken his hand in putting in seed."

The arrival of a company of Saints with Orson Pratt from Liverpool, England, cheered Kanesville residents in early May. Wilford Woodruff and a company from Boston, Massachusetts, were expected soon. The arrivals helped prompt Orson to publish May 15 that the adjourned conference sessions would be held the following Sunday. Orson welcomed Wilford Woodruff on May 16.[33]

Sunday morning, May 19, began fine and cool, the sun shining. The roads into Kanesville contained caravans of wagons, buggies, and carriages. At an early hour a large congregation gathered in the cove southeast of the printing office. For conference, Gentile merchants and numerous emigrants joined the Saints. Choir singing and band music augmented the pleasure Orson felt having two other members of the Twelve seated with him on the stand. George Coulson, of the High Council reported on Indian affairs, specifically "the shooting of those Pawnees last spring [by William Hickman]." He told that "President O. Hyde had had an interview with the chiefs of that tribe, and on their agreeing that all difficulties were settled, and that they should not molest our emigrants or the Californians as they pass through their lands he [Hyde] paid or caused to be paid the sum of fifty dollars." Brother Coulson asked the congregation to sustain this action and donate to

Church funds. Assigned brethren walked among the people, "and forty-eight dollars was received."

But the weather evoked the most remarkable occurrence of the conference, and developments began in the morning session. Before discussing weather, Orson conducted business with lengthy explanations and asking the congregation to vote on various items. Eventually he reviewed conditions and needs of the poor Saints collected in Pottawattamie County. He also talked of his frustration with being unable to rid Kanesville of "grog-shops" and public drunkenness. After portraying this bleak picture, Orson raised his voice in a tone of hope. "The priesthood and Saints hold the keys of blessings in their own hands," he declared. He then talked of the drought, saying that "we have . . . had but one shower of rain this year or since last fall, and we have not seen the bow in the heavens at all this season. The earth is parched up and dry.

"If you want rain," Orson continued, "open your doors and receive the poor, and you will have the blessings. The first thing to do to obtain rain is for each person who can, take a poor family and become a benefactor and temporal Savior to them at this time." He looked around and asked in emphatic tones, "Will you do it?"

"Yes! Yes!" the congregation responded.

To emphasize and solidify the positive responses to his questions, Orson asked for personal commitments, "You brethren who are willing to take in the poor and succor them, manifest it by raising your hands."

A multitude of hands went up all across the Conference ground.

"You who wish that the sin, curse, and evil that arises in this place from the grog-shops should rest upon the heads of those who keep such doggeries, and you who will take your stand firmly against those grog-shops, drunkenness and all vices, manifest it."

The congregation responded immediately, again, with raised hands and a resounding "Amen!"

Next Orson asked the assemblage another question, "Have I ever prophesied and it failed to come to pass?"

Again a reverberating answer, "No!"

"Then," Orson pronounced, "I prophesy in the name of Jehovah that we will have rain and our crops will be saved."

A hush enveloped the crowd.

"In the name of Him who sitteth in the heavens and judgeth all hearts," Orson went on in his well-known profound eloquence, "if it is your firm purpose to keep and live up to your covenants, I can promise you that . . . the king of day shall warm . . . the earth with his genial rays; that the clouds shall gather over you, and shower their blessings on the dry and thirsty land, and the earth assume its grand attire of living green; that the Saints shall be blessed with a plentiful harvest to sustain man and beast. And," Orson's words continued as his arm swept toward the emigrants on the edges of the group, "these my friends, shall be able to prosecute their journey, to reap the golden harvest that may await them."

Orson turned, asked Orson Pratt to pray, and sat down. Elder Pratt arose and stepped to the pulpit. Sincerely, in direct terms, he asked the Lord for rain, for ratification of the words just spoken. The morning conference session proceeded. As a special festivity at the end, a young couple walked to the stand and President Hyde joined them in marriage before the delighted gathering. Wilford Woodruff uttered the closing prayer.

The afternoon meeting began at about two o'clock. The sky was clear, the atmosphere cold and hazy. Elders Pratt and Woodruff addressed the congregation, reporting the past months' events in their lives. Then others spoke. Orson presented a few closing comments. Now the elements had changed. A warm breeze had arisen. Clouds had formed. Before the services ended, scattered large raindrops began falling. After the closing prayer people hurriedly began to disperse.

"The effect of this marvelous interposition of the Lord upon the emigrants present," resident Robert Campbell tells, "was such that they could not leave the ground without some demonstration on their part. Some of them, pulling off their hats, shouted, 'Hurrah, for Elder Hyde!'" A gold-digger ran up to Orson and pulled out a purse. Orson was astonished to be handed five dollars.

People climbed into covered wagons and carriages. Others ran for shelter. Before long the rain pounded down in torrents. One loaded vehicle, hurrying toward home, stopped, and the driver asked a walking man if he would like to step up and ride. The man responded,

"No, thank you; I have paid five dollars for this, and mean to take the benefit of it." He continued walking leisurely along toward camp through the drenching rain.

After the downpour, a bright clear rainbow arched the sky.[34]

During the next weeks, jubilation reigned in Kanesville. After the miraculous soaking May 19 rain, the weather turned warm. Farmers thrilled with the rapidity of the growth of their crops. Grass on the prairies grew luxuriant, and gold-diggers crossed the river as fast as the ferries could carry them. According to information that Orson obtained, the 1850 California emigration on the frontier was greater through Kanesville than any other place, "about 4,500 [wagons], averaging 3 men to the wagon, making 13,500 men, and about 22,000 head of horses, mules, oxen and cows."

Now the Saints' emigration must get underway. Back in January Orson had published that "we do not intend that any companies shall leave here for the Valley later than the 15th day of June—positively. The great snow storm that our last trains were caught in on the mountains last fall is a sufficient admonition to start our last trains one month earlier than the last ones started last year." Unable to meet the deadline, by June 8 only about half the Saints' wagons, 350, had ferried the river. Still preparing were Edward Hunter's Perpetual Emigrating Fund company and Wilford Woodruff's company. Totals this year would be about 700 wagons, 4,000 sheep, and 5,000 cattle, horses, and mules.

For Orson to encourage emigration required great faith, because when those with means, wagons, and animals departed, mostly the destitute tarried. Orson asked Wilford Woodruff to consult about this with Brigham Young in the Valley. If the present system continued, in a few years the Mormon community in Pottawattamie County would disintegrate. After this spring's emigration, not more than one yoke of oxen would remain for each seven families. How would the fields be plowed or planted? Orson asked Wilford to emphasize strongly to Brigham Young that the Church must adopt more strict instructions about people bringing poor Saints to Kanesville and leaving them for Elder Hyde to tend while their benefactors continued on to the mountains. Orson recommended that the poor tarry in the eastern states or in Saint Louis where available jobs could help them earn means to buy outfits.[35]

In June, Orson received—by what he called "Horn Telegraph," meaning ox team—another invitation from Brigham Young: "Beloved brother. . . . We anticipate a visit from you, with a portion of your family this summer." Orson craved consultation with Brigham Young. Previously he had dismissed all thoughts of traveling to the mountains this year, but the recent letter worked on his mind. It seemed to be an order. Could he do it? Taking any part of his family would be impossible, but maybe two or three other men would go with him, with horses, speedily. Orson yearned to travel westward, and enough companies were already on the plains that his small group would never be far from larger ones should they require assistance.

Orson would need to borrow the money to outfit himself. How would his family fare if he were absent? How would the *Guardian* fare? His family expenses, counting guests, amounted to eight hundred dollars a year. Wages for his hired help—his clerk, the foreman printer, and the printer's assistants—required twenty-five dollars every Saturday night, thirteen hundred dollars a year. *Guardian* subscriptions covered the printer's wages, but Orson's profits remained small. A little more money came from publishing names of gold-seekers, selling books, selling music, and selling school supplies. His most recent project, selling Hymn Books and copies of the Book of Mormon and Doctrine and Covenants, all of which he had ordered from England, had just begun and as yet helped little.[36] Though his financial situation had improved, with him not at home would profits from ventures diminish?

Orson discussed his thoughts with his wives and with a few friends, and he decided to ride the two thousand miles, to the Valley and back. Accompanying him would be Henry W. Miller, J.E. Johnson, and Joseph Kelley, all enterprising men. Henry and J.E. were merchants and had the equipment and goods necessary for the trip. They would help Orson with his needs, and he could pay them back later.

In the June 26 *Guardian*, Orson announced: "We hope to be off for the Valley before another issue. . . . We hope to return by the 1st of October." "The High Council will direct the affairs of the Church in our absence. . . . B[rother]s Mackintosh and Gooch will conduct the Guardian."

Orson's apprehensions, however, about leaving his stewardship of directing the Saints, almost overcame him. During his absence how would the faithful manage, and how would the rebellious behave? In the same June 26 *Guardian* Orson published numerous instructions, almost to the point of being finicky. He asked for new subscribers for his newspaper, for overdue payments, and for advance payments. He encouraged "vigorous efforts . . . to establish schools in every neighborhood." He reminded voters, in a long article about politics, to cast their votes on election day in August. He recommended that owners be sought for stray animals and denounced the practice of hiding animals and then asking a reward for their recovery. He promoted Sabbath attendance at the "house of worship." To farmers he gave many explicit directions, among them when to cut hay, plow ground, and plant wheat.

To everyone, for their well-being, Orson offered affectionate advice: "Be constant in prayer. . . . Refrain from vice, and intemperance. Profane not the holy name by which we are called: do good unto one another: Be kind, forgiving, and generous."[37]

. . . *deserts and mountains.* . . . *(1850)*

> . . . *in deserts, and in mountains.* . . .
> —Hebrews 11:38

BY the morning of July 4, 1850, Orson had lingered over goodbyes and embraces with Marinda and the children as well as with Martha and the baby. He was ready to head west. To the Kanesville Fourth of July celebration he wore his traveling clothes and his "Rough and Ready" hat. He had savored the firing of guns at daybreak and now enjoyed the gathering of about 5,000 people, the banners, the speeches, a grand procession, band music, prayer, reading of the Declaration of Independence, orator of the day, and a sumptuous dinner. To climax the festivities, the procession formed again and accompanied him, astride his horse, "a few miles as a mark of respect." A brief address by Elder Hyde "drew tears from the eyes of the stoutest heart," a resident recorded. "[I]t was like parting with a mother, a brother or a sister. He then bade his devoted friends and brethren farewell."[1]

Orson rode his horse, called by him his pony, to Bullock's Grove, old Hyde Park. Here he spent the evening with Mary Ann and others. In the morning he rode down the hollow to Browning's settlement, where Henry Miller and Joseph Kelley awaited him with horses and two wagons. A fine "double harness, brass mounted," presented to Orson by two Gentile friends, bedecked one of the teams.[2] After more farewells the three men departed and ferried over the river. They were truly on their way to the Rocky Mountains.

When the Saints in those mountains had applied for territorial government, they chose to name their area Deseret. From details given him, Orson had earlier described Deseret as a

> little interior world . . . in the Valley of the Great Salt Lake, embracing what is called the "Great Basin" of North America. . . . The lofty mountains mantled with perpetual snows—the sandy deserts—and the sage plains by which it is surrounded, present barriers too formidable, during the greater part of the year, to be successfully encountered. . . .
>
> The name selected for that country is borrowed from the Book of Mormon, where a description is given of the voyage of the Ancient Jaredites from the tower of Babel to the American continent, more than four thousand years ago. It is said that they brought with them seeds [of]

all kinds, and also "DESERET" which, by interpretation, is the honey bee. The bee and the hive being emblems of skill and industry, the citizens there [in the Valley], wishing ever to exhibit those qualifications, have chosen the above name.

The Government rejected the name Deseret, however, Orson had editorialized recently (April 17, 1850), "because it is a Mormon name. . . . Well, be it so. We . . . [believe] that whatever is, that we cannot, by honorable means, prevent, is right, and will turn for our good."

This same year the United States Government chose the name Utah for the Great Basin territory. Apparently without realizing the profundity of their decision, Congress partially fulfilled Old Testament prophecies made by Isaiah and Micah, that "it shall come to pass in the last days, that the mountain of the Lord's house shall be established in the top of the mountains." Congress chose the name because of "the Shoshonean Ute Indians who inhabited the region. The name of the Ute is derived from the Indian word *Eutaw* or *Yuta*, meaning 'dwellers in the tops of the mountains.'" Thus Isaiah and Micah could have prophesied that the mountain of the Lord's house would be established in "Utah," and they would have been accurate.[3]

Orson's group camped five miles beyond the Missouri River. Before nightfall the fourth companion, Joseph E. Johnson, or "J.E.," joined them. The company included Orson the acknowledged leader, Henry Miller rough and rugged, Joseph Kelley steady and reliable, and J.E. as enthusiastic for adventure as for writing flamboyant advertisements about his store. Around their campfire the men refrained from mentioning the families they would miss. Instead they discussed details of their bold undertaking to cross the plains twice with so late a start.[4]

July 9, four days after leaving home, they had traveled nearly two hundred miles. They had passed three companies of Saints and come to another company at the Great Platte River. They found the river shallow and two or three miles wide, with many islands and with timber. They had broken an axletree in the sandy ground, fixed it, and eaten such treats as shortcake, stewed apples, and a pie. J.E. was a good cook. July 10 they sighted antelope and a wolf. They had passed many graves of people who had died of cholera. Grass and water were plentiful, and mosquitoes were far more than plentiful, a terrible scourge.[5]

The mosquitoes grew worse. July 12 J.E. wrote about their previous night: "The wind died away in the evening, & the misquitoes came on like a hungry set of wolves & sounding like a hundred swarms of bees. We could not escape. Bros. Miller and Kelley were obliged to take the horses back two miles to another encampment, leaving Bro. Hyde and myself to do the best we could. The foe came on thicker & thicker until we had no possible means of defending ourselves. We could not wrap up so as to get rid of them, nor run so fast but [they] would be in our faces – Started as soon as day dawned, and about 10 O clock got away from them. Took breakfast. We are all nearly sick today. . . . Passed Fort Kearney at noon. . . . [At] 2 O clock . . . halted on the bank of the river. No wood & plenty miskitoes. Sleepy all day as I did not sleep a wink all night. Came up a severe wind and took away the muskitoes & almost took our waggons. Elder Hyde had a touch of the cholera last night when we were alone." Two days and many miles later the mosquitoes disappeared, and Orson's health was fine.[6]

Varied experiences continued. July 15 they saw a few herds of buffalo. They chased, but killed none for meat. To make their fire they used buffalo chips, dry buffalo dung the size of large plates. The blaze and heat were good, but the ashes too many. The next day they saw thousands of buffalo, the hills covered, an incredible sight. They still killed none, but they overtook Brother Foot's company of Saints and were served buffalo meat. They found it delicious, sweeter than beef. July 18 they had a terrible time crossing a branch of the Platte. Quicksand kept miring the horses. The men stowed their clothes in a wagon, to keep them dry, and doubled the teams. They spent an hour leading the horses taking one wagon across the two miles of swift current, deep to the men's chests. Then they led the teams back and got the other wagon. All were exhausted.[7]

July 19 they slept longer than usual and that night kept going until ten o'clock, when they reached the encamped Evans Company. The camp members who were still awake rejoiced to have an apostle among them. The next morning, July 20, an incident involved Elder Hyde's priesthood power without him even knowing. The Edward and Nancy Hall family had a four year old daughter Sarah who was unable to stand because of a dislocated hip from an accident two years before. Nancy Hall, a woman of sincere faith, decided that Apostle Hyde's arrival provided an opportunity for the hip to be healed. Morning chores complete, she said to Sarah, "I'm going to get a good man and ask him to bless you so God will make you well." But Nancy could not catch Orson's already departing group. Her faith, however, gave her a sense of elation that he had been near, and she returned toward the family wagon. To her intense surprise and joy, little Sarah ran to meet her exulting, "I can walk, Mamma, I can walk!"[8]

Adventures continued. July 20 Orson and group came to Brother Blair's company. With Brother Blair they left two horses that had "failed." July 22 they reached Scott's Bluff, a landmark of the plains. Its appearance was like "some vast & very ancient ruin of forts, towers, pyramids &c., towering up to an immense height." That day and the next they acquired three horses from companies they passed. This country of timberless prairies had a lonely feel. July 24 J.E. wrote: "Oh let me die a hundred deaths at home in the bosom of my friends rather than lay my bones upon these barren plains & the wild wind & wolves to sing the funeral requiem.

"I am getting so tanned up & with such a hairy face," J.E. continued, "that there is some [friends in the emigrant trains] don't know me, . . . and the others [Miller, Kelley, and Hyde] are if possible more altered than myself. . . . We still have about half of [our] eggs . . . , all the honey, nearly all the preserves, & some cheese, plenty of herring, some raisins, dried apples, pickles, 1 ham, 1 sack crackers, some codfish, plenty of flour, sugar, buckwheat flour, rice, coffee, tea, &c. . . . Came to the Fort Laram[i]e 4 O clock. Visited the store."[9]

The country had become hilly, with tall mountains in the distance. And again they saw timber. Nights were getting colder. July 29 they had come 750 miles from Kanesville and had 390 remaining, according to their guidebook.[10]

July 30, while two of his companions looked for lost horses, Orson started a letter to his acting editor, telling of conditions and happenings and giving advice. Orson added to the letter for several days, until he gave it to someone in a company traveling east who would carry it to Kanesville:

Upper Crossing of the Platte, July 30th, 1850. . . . We crossed the Platte yesterday, ferried over wagons and swam our horses. . . . We came on about nine miles through sand and encamped—turned out our animals and drove them about half a mile from the road to find grass, and in the night they wandered off. Bros. Miller and Kelley are after them. . . . Indeed, they have just fired a gun to let us know they are coming. All is right, we have only been hindered about three hours. This will learn us a lesson—no more to trust our horses to run at large during the night.

[F]rom Laramie . . . to the upper crossing of the Platte [is] a distance of one hundred and twenty miles. The road is mostly over rocks, sharp gravel and flint. This is severe on cattle's feet. They all ought to be shod, oxen, cows, and young cattle . . . [to prevent] their getting lame and having to be left on the road, a prey to wolves. . . .

Grass is very scarce, . . . eaten out root and branch, and in many cases the animals have even eaten out the wild sage.

Our health is good, but the mountain air is too strong for me, yet I think that I shall soon become accustomed to it. . . . Bros. Miller and Kelley have just come in with all the animals safe and sound. They wandered back about seven miles. The word now is, "pack up and hitch up," so I must stop writing. . . .

August 1st, at Independence Rock on the Sweet Water—all well. We have just passed through the Valley and Shadow of Death,—a country of about fifty miles in extent where the waters are deeply impregnated with Nitre, Saleratus, Sulphur, &c., &c. There is little or no grass at all through this region, but [it] is mostly a sandy desert. The carcasses of horses and cattle lying along the road side are very numerous, having perished through fatigue, hunger, and through drinking poisonous waters.

. . . We are now beginning to overtake the California and Oregon emigration. They have suffered much in the loss of teams and animals: And oh! the sacrifice of wagons, clothing, fire arms, beds, bedding, Buffalo skins, trunks, chests, harnesses, and in the loss of life. The road to gold is strewed with destruction. . . .

We have not progressed quite so rapidly as we anticipated when we left home. The trains of emigrants have held to our skirts as we passed them, and we have stopped and given the most of them a lecture or discourse. They have been greatly afflicted, and feel themselves chastened of the Lord. They are humble and child-like generally—familiar and generous. We felt it our duty to give them all a word of comfort so far as we had an opportunity.

There are about five hundred new graves on the route south of the Platte, and but three deaths are reported at Laramie as having occurred on the north side. We intend to return on the north side of the Platte and faithfully examine every foot of the entire distance on both routes . . . making observations which we think will be of essential service to the emigrating public another year.

It is Monday, Aug. 5th, if we have not lost our reckoning—one month and one day out. We are now on the Sweet Water, about thirty miles east of the South Pass. If wood were as plentiful as tools, wagon tires and iron in general on the road, we could have our hot dodger, coffee and fried or broiled bacon whenever we pleased. We have broken an axletree to our wagon today and have been engaged in putting in another. This is all done and we are in full rig again, ready to start in the morning for the South Pass. There is no grass through this country only on the margin of the creeks and streams. I portioned out our last horse feed to-day; but fortunately we have borrowed two sacks of flour of some Californians to be repaid in the Valley. This will help us through. We have left three horses on the way that had given out. They are in the hands of our emigrants, and we have eight very good ones along with us.

The Sweet Water is a beautiful stream. Its waters are clear, its banks low, its current rapid, and [it] glides over a bottom of sand, gravel, and granite rock. It reminds me of the days of my childhood when I ranged up and down some of the limpid streams and rivulets of New England, hunting bird's nests among the low pines and cedars. We can see many nice fish, but have not the requisite means of capturing them. They will not bite at the hook, but might be easily taken in a net or seine. These latter we have not. . . .

BIG SANDY, Aug. 8 1850, Thursday 1/4 before 10 A.M.

We have been here about two hours and a half and expect to remain here about two hours longer to give our animals a little chance for grass. They have had very little for the last three days, and here we have found an unfrequented corner where our animals get full bite. The eight or ten hundred wagons of emigrants and merchants trains behind us have but a sorry prospect. . . .

Sand and sage,—sage and sand—dead horses, mules, cows and oxen, with snow capped Mountains on your right and left, are about the variety which the eye meets in passing through this section. I would give a more flattering account of this region if I could conscientiously. . . . If Mr. [Asa] Whitney [merchant and railroad promoter[11]] had traveled these plains as we have, I think his rail-road speculation would materially diminish in his own estimation. I would not thank Congress for a grant of all the land that I have seen between Laramie and this place. . . .

We expect to get into the Valley by the 15th . . . , and hope to . . . return . . . to . . . Kanesville by the 25th of October next, if God will.[12]

By August 11, snow covered the mountain heights in every direction. August 12 the travelers arrived at Fort Bridger and tarried a few hours. Between South Pass and Fort Bridger the main California–Oregon trail led off to the northwest. August 13, on rough roads to the Bear River, merchants Kinkaid and Livingston caught up with them. Orson accompanied the merchants until the next day, when he rejoined his own group. They crossed the ford of the Weber River with a shower of rain. Then came the steepest part of the trail, rocky roads over monstrous mountains.[13]

Eager anticipation reigned August 15 while guiding horses down the bumpy road in the last close-walled canyon of the mountains. In the late afternoon the scenery opened up. Spirits soared as the men gazed in wonder upon a vast valley. West of it the waters of the Great Salt Lake glistened. Mountains all around towered to the skies. Streams ran across it. A spectacular view![14]

However, the general appearance of the sweeping valley told that the Saints faced great challenges in coaxing crops from an arid desert. The low parched vegetation of late summer stretched for miles, dry except for the green along the occasional stream of water.

The men pressed their tired horses forward. After a few dry miles they approached the settlement of the Saints. At first the city had looked like a collection of mud huts, but a nearer view revealed a beautiful sight, a huge garden laid out in regular squares, set off with remarkably wide streets. An acre and a half of vegetables surrounded most homes. The cottages, one story dwellings, were built of "unburnt bricks," sun-dried, called adobes (pronounced a-dō'-bees), their white bluish hue a pleasing color. The eves on many homes extended two feet wide to protect the walls from downpours.[15] Inhabitants who saw Orson and his companions coming, met and welcomed them with gladness.

"We had a joyful and happy meeting with our friends and brethren in the Valley . . . ," Orson reports. "Governor [Brigham] Young said that he hardly knew whether to laugh, cry, shout, sing, dance or preach; and finally said: 'Brethren, my house [one of his several homes built of logs on what later became First Avenue] and heart are open, and the free spirit reigns; do just as you please.' So in his large dining room, we preached, we sung, we told our stories, we rejoiced and gave thanks to God for his Providential care over us all. Tears of joy flowed freely from many eyes; and no more strange than true, we had music and dancing on the occasion. All this on the night of our first arrival in the City of the Great Salt Lake."[16]

During his 1850 visit in the mountains Orson wrote, "If any people on earth ever had cause to praise their God for suffering them to be driven to . . . a rich, healthy and productive land . . . it is the Latter-Day Saints." He had seen no other location like this. The clear atmosphere allowed views for great distances. Looking west, across miles of sparsely vegetated plain, the barren shore of the briny lake appeared nearer than it was. Far-away mountain islands formed the backdrop of the huge body of water. Near eastward the colossal bulwarks of the Wasatch Mountains loomed heavenward, solid and timeless. The mountains stood magnificent, always awesome, always the same, and yet always changing, not only with the seasons, but as a day progressed. In the early morning their rocks and vegetation might look subdued, in grays and browns and greens. In the evening a rosy hue might be reflected upon the crags and smooth-looking places, when beyond the lake the sun set in flaming oranges and pinks and reds. Majestic mountains to the south and north added their own sublimity to the scene.

Streams from the eastward mountains, and from the Jordan River flowing into the valley from the south, provided irrigating water for land plowed by the settlers. Dams diverted water from the streams into ditches, thence onto gardens or onto fields—a fascinating process. With watchcare and digging, shovels in hand, diligent farmers guided the water to run where needed. Vineyards and orchards would soon dot the landscape; already nurserymen nurtured seedling grapes, cherries, plums, apples, pears, and peaches.

The Valley boasted varied types of structures—log, frame, rock, and adobe brick. Though adobes formed most homes, and though firewood and logs had to be hauled eight to twenty miles from the canyons, some log homes had been built. Recently frame lumber became available for construction, with seven sawmills operating or almost ready to operate. Public buildings included the "Council House," of red sandstone, and several fine stores. Six grist mills and a large nearly-finished merchant flouring mill would be kept busy with the extensive wheat harvest. Wide streets allowed a wagon with oxen to turn around. Farms lay beyond the city.

Already around fifteen thousand Saints resided in this mountain refuge, and thousands more would be added with this year's soon-to-arrive wagon trains. Because of a lack of homes, some of these settlers, Orson learned, would "have to live in tents or wagons the coming winter." Towns were scattered for two hundred miles south to north. The accomplishments of three years amazed Orson.[17]

On the temple block his first Sabbath, Orson was asked to speak in both morning and afternoon services in the Bowery (sixty feet by one hundred feet). His morning address imparted poetic exhilaration as he shared with the people his satisfying feelings about Brigham Young. "A star may shine with comparative glory," he said, "but when the sun arises the star is obscured. When your humble servant [Orson] has been in midnight darkness around him, he may have emitted a glimmering light, but now being in the presence of the sun [President Young] that glimmering mostly disappears."

His afternoon words reminded the congregation of promises made by the Lord to the children of Israel after their exodus to their promised land (see especially Exodus 23:25). "The Valley and its products speak for themselves," Orson declared. "I am verily persuaded that this is the abode of God's people, as he has made his bulwarks. And the promise is: your bread shall be given you and your water shall be sure and your habitations are surrounded by a munition of rocks. You have the salt in yourselves and the savory influence is here. This section is more free from disease than ever men have been before. . . . The very key of prosperity is in your hands, for God will help those who help themselves."[18]

The Saints in the Valley enjoyed unexpected comforts. They had traded necessary provisions to California emigrants in exchange for furniture and other commodities. By the time wagon trains from the east reached the Salt Lake Valley, the travelers understood well that crossing hundreds more miles of desert to California required necessities, not luxuries.

A highlight of Orson's sojourn occurred August 27, as a guest at a lavish dinner party in honor of Capt. Howard Stansbury and Lieutenant Gunnison, of the Corps of the United States Topographical Engineers. They had just completed surveying the area of the Great Salt Lake and would soon return to Washington, D.C. The feast, hosted by Heber C. Kimball in his home, Orson described as "a most excellent and sumptuous dinner." His account continues: "In justice to the occasion, I must say that I did not believe that such a dinner could be prepared in . . . the mountains. Various kinds of meats served up in the most approved manner, and the finest kind of vegetables,—bread as white as snow,—and what gave it a richer flavor, it was from wheat grown in the Valley, manufactured in their own mills, and knead[ed], moulded and baked by Sister Kimball, herself. Then the puddings, the pies and the cakes, the butter and the cheese, the sweet meats, and the very white table linen, and the neatness and elegance of the whole service. . . . In place of champagne, we had the richest kind of melons when the cloth was removed."[19]

August 28, the day after the gala dinner, Orson eagerly joined Brigham Young, Heber C. Kimball, several of the Quorum of the Twelve, and others, along with the Band, for an official four-day trip to plan the city of Ogden, forty miles north. As the wagons wheeled along, sentineled by the lofty mountains to the east, the Great Salt Lake shimmered to the west, usually several miles from the road and beyond the relatively flat plain. The caravan received welcomes as it rolled into several new settlements, located where streams flowed across the plain from the mountains, settlements with new farms and fences and ditches, with flocks and herds, with young trees that would eventually be havens of shade. The industry and productivity thrilled Orson, as did handshakes with friends.

In the Ogden area the settlers resided along creeks and two rivers, also in and around two forts built as protection from the Indians. Brigham Young felt that an orderly central city should emerge. The officials gave speeches and helped local leaders plan the layout of streets. The band played. Orson rejoiced to again see prosperity: abundant wheat and other grains, watermelons, potatoes, and various vegetables.

Two weeks after the refreshing visit to Ogden, an unfortunate development caused consternation among Church leaders. An Ogden settler, angered by an Indian, killed him. Careful and diligent efforts resolved the problem peaceably, but the incident heightened Orson's awareness of the precarious position of the Saints. Not only must every pound of food be bought with the labor of irrigation, but the settlers must meet the challenge of living among the Indians with patience and respect.[20]

Upon his return from Ogden to Great Salt Lake City on August 31, Orson learned of the arrival the day before of the first company of Saints organized this season back in Kanesville. Captained by Milo Andrus, Orson's close friend from Ohio days, this company of fifty wagons left the Missouri River on June 3. Their trip arduous, a member's report cheered Orson. "Elder Hyde had told us the day we were organized," the report states, "that if we would be faithful and keep the name of our God sacred, we should be blessed with health and our lives would be preserved. We endeavored to do our duty to the best of our ability and the promises of God were fulfilled toward us; there was one death and one birth, so we were just as many when we landed in the Valley."

In addition to other rigors, the Saints felt the need for education. In this Orson received official responsibility. September 5, he was "duly sworn and initiated into the office of Regent of the University of the State of Deseret" (later the University of Utah). The General Assembly, or territorial legislature of Deseret, had organized the university the previous winter and appointed Orson a regent. Still mostly a dream, a university site of 560 acres had been surveyed east of Salt Lake City. Now classes convened in several small schools in the city. "A parent school for the education of teachers" would open in a few weeks, "as soon as a room is prepared for the purpose." This room, like the schools, would be in a private home. In his new position, Orson received the invitation "to deliver a Lecture to the Regency, on Education, on Saturday next, at 2 P.M. in presence of the Conference."[21]

General conference, in the Bowery, was held a month early, in September rather than October, so that Orson and others could attend and then start east. Saturday morning, the second day, President Brigham Young talked about Orson and his counselors in Iowa excommunicating some men. "I wish it distinctly understood," declared the President, "that there is not an apostle of Jesus Christ who now lives, or ever did live, or ever will live, but that man's word is law and gospel to the people if he magnifies his calling. The Apostles did right in this case; . . . and if this Conference think the same, signify it by the uplifted hand." The congregation ratified the action.

As a portion of the Saturday afternoon conference session, Orson delivered his education lecture. "Every person is under a responsibility to impart the intelligence that he enjoys, unto others," he said in part. "The child that is born into this world, is like a blank sheet of paper, susceptible of any impression. . . . Great honor has been conferred on parents to mould and fashion that mind, which is put into the tabernacle by the Almighty himself, that they [the children] may be qualified to fill the stations they are destined to fill. . . ." Orson went on, talking of the desirability of people becoming proficient in language to help them progress, and emphasizing the wisdom of hiring good teachers. For a few years this speech would be virtually Orson's only act as a University Regent.

During the conference the Perpetual Emigrating Fund was a central topic, and to it Church members subscribed several thousand dollars. In a later meeting Orson was appointed as one of the traveling agents for the fund.[22]

Orson planned to leave for Kanesville a few days after conference, but Apostle Amasa Lyman, expected momentarily from California, would likely bring a fair sum of money for the Perpetual Emigrating Fund. Orson decided to wait for this.

September 11, he and a few other Church leaders bantered about their personal weights. This resulted in the decision to settle the matter. The scale registered 241 pounds when Willard Richards, the heaviest of the group, stood on it. Next in weight was George A. Smith, at 222. Orson was third, at 211. Brigham Young, next, weighed 182. Almost the same, at 180, was Newel K. Whitney.

Just twelve days after this, September 23, shock flew through the community when Newel K. Whitney died suddenly of pleurisy at the age of fifty-five. His health had been good. He had been functioning diligently in his office as Presiding Bishop of the Church. Newel's passing stirred many memories for Orson; they had known each other since boyhood in Kirtland, Ohio. Orson felt honored to be asked to speak at the funeral the next day.

Orson, the first speaker, set an affectionate tone for the funeral. "Little did I anticipate," he began, "when I came to this Valley and associated freely with our brother who is departed, that I should be called upon to contribute this service. But God's ways are not as our ways. . . ." Orson told the family that their father and husband had gone beyond the grave to prepare a place for them. "If we could see with the eye of faith," he instructed, "we could see this our brother more tender for those who are now left behind. . . . How many dangers are warded off? How many blessings come? . . . [He is] anxious . . . to avail himself of every power in [your] behalf. . . .

"He may be . . . wanted there to fill an important station. . . . How few of the heads of the Church have been called away! . . . And we may expect to be benefited, although we cannot converse or sing with them, on earth."[23]

While in the Valley, Orson's rewarding experiences abounded, but sitting "in counsel and in conference oft with the officers of the church" he prized the most. His thankfulness knew no bounds at discussing his concerns in depth, not just writing his own side of situations. His main concerns were his dilemma about not being allowed to use tithing money when severe needs arose among the Pottawattamie Saints, and his burden of the debts that the Presidency had left in commercial establishments in the States. These subjects had been addressed, he learned, while he traversed the plains westward. President Young had written to him about them July 28.

"You seem to misunderstand our wishes in relation to tithing," Brigham Young explained in the letter. "We did not wish you to gather tithing from the poor Saints . . . and send it here. The grain and other produce raised by the farmers in Potawotamie should be used to feed the poor, the widow, the orphan, the infirm, and the needy. . . . When with you in directing you to gather tithing and send it here we refer[red] to such persons as may come into the Church and such as have never paid their tithing from other places."

Regarding Orson's past writings to the Presidency about debts, Brigham Young chided him a little. The President wanted a paper showing exactly what was owed and to whom; "but from all" of Orson's letters about it, President Young continued, "we have [not] yet learned . . . the situation of the books." When he had exact figures Brigham Young would appoint an agent to take care of the matter. Orson need worry about it no longer.[24]

Another quandary that Orson examined with Brother Brigham was Martha's complaining. The two men discussed possible solutions, but for Orson to display polygamy in Iowa was not the answer. The time was not yet right for the Church to announce publicly the sanctioning of plural marriage among its members. Both men hoped that the situation with Martha would improve.

While waiting to return home, thrilled with the progress around him, Orson was eager to finish his work back in Kanesville and bring his family to the mountains. Exultingly he wrote a letter to the Saints and handed it to the editor of the *Deseret News* for inclusion in this Church-sponsored newspaper that had begun publication a few months before:

> The "Son of Peace" reigns in this Valley; and as the time of my departure for the States draws near, I cannot leave without saying to the citizens of this fairy land: my peace I leave with you. I have shared the hospitality of my friends here, and have felt the warmth and enthusiasm of their greetings and salutations. . . . Oh industry! what has thou done? . . . [W]ith the blessings of our Father in heaven, thou hast made the wilderness and the solitary place glad for Thee, and the desert to rejoice and blossom as the rose. The waving harvest—the numerous stacks of wheat, barley, and oats—the ripening corn—the thrifty vines, producing the richest melons in the world—the cooling breezes—from the snow clad peaks—the crystal streams gushing from the mountain base and flowing through every garden, field and dewey-bed, clearly say, in language easy to be understood by the pure in heart who dwell here;— "This is the place for us."[25]

Apostle Amasa Lyman finally arrived from California on September 29. He brought less money than hoped, so the Perpetual Emigrating Fund was not swelled materially. But what the Fund had would help many poor Saints get to the Valley. The same day that Elder Lyman came, George A. Smith and Ezra T. Benson wrote to the Saints in England. "Brother Hyde," they commented, "has enjoyed himself in the Valley like a man in his father's house, and feels now as though he were leaving home, though in a hurry to get home."

Some of the final words Brigham Young said to Orson before his departure answered Orson's concern about his late traveling start and encouraged him in meeting the challenges in Iowa: "You will return in safety, and will have seven times the power you had before."[26]

For the journey Orson and his companions were glad to be joined by another company, led by John Brown. The combined group contained seven wagons, thirty-two animals, and sixteen men. Their late start, October 1, caused them concern for possible difficulties from early snowstorms and frigid cold. They felt greater security with the resources of sixteen men rather than just four. The arduousness of the journey would be lightened by the effervescence of J.E. Johnson. During the return he wrote his diary in rhyme, with occasional changes in meter. In their first few days of travel they enjoyed meeting the last companies of Saints who had earlier left Kanesville. They passed Fort Bridger October 6. A day or so later:

> We ate our dinners all so nice, then drove ten miles to Sandy,
> Which made 28 miles drive today, & killed a goose so handy.
> Then I stood guard & like to froze & boiled the goose so tough.
> We ate three meals out of one half, then we had goose enough.

Still on the Rocky Mountain plateau:

> In the morning how dreary. The horses were weary,
> All shivering with cold, frost, [and] wet.
> Our teams we soon rounded, & the antelope bounded,
> But not one for our suppers could get.

Before reaching Fort Laramie, October 21, "there was one horse died tho to save him we tried." One day they killed two buffalo:

> Which kept us busy most all day
> To get the meat & stow away. [They made jerky, "by slicing and
>   drying in the sun."]

November 5 they arrived at Fort Kearney, and six of the company departed southeast for Fort Leavenworth. John Brown and others remained with the Kanesville group, traveling the north side of the Platte, as Orson had planned on the way west.

> But oh the cold. Such freezing nights.
> And oh the frost how sharp it bites.
> Such sleepless nights, unpleasant dreams.
> In morn the ice floats down the streams.
> Four wagons now compose our train,
> Fifteen horses & half score men.

Orson and the others reached the Loup Fork River on November 9. Quicksand and deep water prevented their crossing. Hoping to find a place to ford upriver, they traveled north. They encountered difficult swamps, sand, small streams, and scarce food for the animals.

> And here the Pawnee Indians, too,
> Came round—a begging, staring crew.
> At night they'd sleep with us in camp
> And beg our grub, tho now grown scant. ["Appearing all the while
>   very friendly, they stole all the small articles they could con-
>   ceal, which they could not beg."]

After two days, in desperation, the travelers retraced their trail to the Platte. Soon they found a way to cross to the south side.

"[F]rom here down," John Brown wrote, "we had a severe time, having to follow the Platte to get feed for our animals, such as rushes, cottonwood bark or bows [boughs]. We had no road and frequently traveled in dry grass 8 ft. high on the bottoms." Also they cut roads and traveled miles to head unfordable streams. At Salt Creek they found the water running broad and high into the ice-splotched Platte.

> A raft we had to make, oh dear.
> And cold enough to freeze a bear.

With ropes, many times across wide Salt Creek, they pulled their raft full of goods one way and back empty. They consumed "near all day" getting wagons, horses, mules, goods, and men over. Two more difficult travel days brought them to the Missouri River at Platteville. Though ice ran in this river too, making crossing precarious, the Platteville ferry carried them safely.[27] Orson and his companions, eager to get home that very night, immediately set out in one wagon to traverse the eighteen or so miles north to Kanesville.

"On Monday evening, 18th inst.," a report in the *Frontier Guardian* narrated, ". . . we espied this covered wagon at a distance, and remarked 'there' was a wagon from the plains, when all of a sudden our friends made way to see, and soon came in possession of the desired information, viz: that President Hyde was at home. Mr. Joseph E. Johnson was caught about to enter his gate . . . , and Henry W. Miller, 'the Old Pioneer,' was *'on the track'* trying to get home as soon as he could. . . . [A] short time afterwards, cannons roared, guns fired, and our town, which was but a few minutes before in perfect silence, teemed with men, women, and children, to welcome our long looked for, and much respected friends and brethren."[28]

In the Hyde log cabin, warm and snug, tender reunion ensued: caresses, laughter, tears, exulting, and snatches of the telling of four and a half months' happenings. Orson was happy to be home. His family was happy to have him home.

CHAPTER 16

. . . *gain and loss*. . . . *(1850-1852)*

> . . . *things were gain to me,* . . . *and* . . .
> *I have suffered* . . . *loss.* . . .
> —Philippians 3:7-8

AFTER the initial pleasures of arriving home in Kanesville, November 18, 1850, Orson's gladness dimmed with reports of family illness and death. His households had suffered considerable sickness during his absence to the west, with their general health still "indifferent." All had survived, though, except Martha's baby, who died in July, only three months old. With her precious child gone, Martha's health declined.[1] Orson sorrowed deeply to have lost Adella Marie and to witness Martha's lack of vigor and extreme heartache. Efforts to cheer her brought little success. What could he do to help Martha?

But he was home, and he had seen the Valley. Knowing what the wagon trains faced when they left Kanesville, he could better fulfill his callings here at the Missouri River.

Two hours before daybreak the next morning, the "roaring of cannon and the noise of musketry" startlingly awakened the community. This signal, preannounced, heralded to residents that today Kanesville would celebrate the return of Elder Hyde and the others. By noon three or four thousand people assembled and organized a colorful procession. In order were the brass band playing favorite tunes, mounted escorts, community leaders, the "[l]adies of Kanesville, dressed in white with a beautiful [welcoming] banner," other banners, and other citizens. The procession moved slowly to the homes of the honored guests and conveyed them in handsome carriages—Orson rode in one "drawn by four beautiful grey steeds"—back to the public square for speeches, more music, more cannonading, and loud cheers. Orson, though uncomfortable with all the fuss for him, enjoyed the festivities.

The following Sunday, November 24, pleasant and clear weather blessed a conference held in the Grove, with "3 to 4000 persons" present. As the beginning speaker, Orson expressed gratitude for the safe return of his company. He praised God for the principles of the gospel. He thanked the people for their prayers during his absence and thanked Heaven that the prayers had been answered. He said that "all is right and good in the Valley." He talked of the Perpetual Emigrating Fund and reported that to it $20,000 had been subscribed. He and Brother Brown brought $5,000 with them, and they could draw up to $2,000 more, as needed. The balance would be retained in the Salt Lake Valley to prepare farms for the poor. He also announced the welcome development that the "tithing of Pottawatamie is to be kept for the poor of Pottawatamie." Brothers Henry W. Miller, Joseph Kelley, John Brown, and others also addressed the congregation. Good feelings prevailed.[2]

Though pleased to be home, Orson's visit to the Valley increased his yearnings to live there permanently. He planned to visit again the following summer, 1851, but in the meantime he must somehow provide for his family. Because he had raised no crops, he appealed in his newspaper to those "who may be a little in arrears for the Guardian . . . [to] bring us in corn, flour, potatoes, butter, cheese, beef, tallow, and some good hay. . . . Or, . . . give us a little cash which 'answers all things.' We have some borrowed money to pay, and we must pay it." In the next *Guardian* he further requested "some first rate hard wood for stoves" because "our ink is cold and stiff."

To augment his income, Orson began a "Storage, Forwarding, and Commission Business," publishing his initial advertisement in the first *Guardian* after his return, November 27, 1850. He had "already made partial arrangements" to receive "heavy stocks of goods" and forward them "to . . . Salt Lake in the Spring." He later advertised for freight haulers. He would pay them "ten dollars per hundred pounds, or two hundred dollars per ton . . . half cash and half goods in the month of March next at this place, or half cash then, and half goods after the first boats arrive in the Spring, when people can have a better selection than in March." He added: "None need apply except men of known integrity—who are careful, trusty and upright in all their transactions, who can control competent teams and safe wagons."[3]

Added to the challenge of earning a livelihood, he tried to comfort Martha, but she continued downcast. Her thoughts were resentful, her mothering arms empty, and her baby's tiny grave cold in the cemetery on the hill behind Orson's home. She insisted still that she loved Orson; but if he loved her, she complained as previously, he would show the community that she was his wife, would walk by her side. She threatened to make a public scene about being his wife—a neglected wife.

Orson thought of reorganizing the Church in Kanesville and appointing another man to preside. He could leave the country, go beyond Martha's reach. But his utmost priorities were obedience to his calling, and sacrifice for it, however stressful his personal situation. His present stewardship from the Almighty impelled him to remain right where he was. Even so, he also knew the unlikelihood of Martha being dissuaded in her threats.

Considering the distressing situation from every angle, the best solution Orson devised was to release Martha from her vows with him and allow her to marry someone else. She needed a husband—immediately—with whom she could be seen publicly as a wife, and from whom, privately and consistently, she could share attention and time. Mentally canvassing the local men, his mind rested on Thomas McKenzie. Thomas was steady, a conscientious leader among the Kanesville Saints. His wife had died in August, leaving him with their ten year old daughter Maria. At thirty-six years of age, Thomas was five years senior to Martha.

Orson approached Brother McKenzie and explained Martha's intense desire for a husband she could accompany and with whom she could share a home. Thomas wanted a wife, a mother for his daughter. He agreed to take Martha as a bride. Martha also agreed with this answer to her complaints.

Marriage arrangements proceeded. Orson gave Martha a civil divorce, but the cancellation of their eternal sealing would have to be done by Brigham Young. Martha seemed content, and engrossed herself in making her public wedding day memorable. As had become traditional in Kanesville, she carried cake and wine to the printer as respects for her published wedding announcement. The printer reported in the *Guardian*:

> MARRIED, In this town, by the Editor, on Monday evening last [December 9, 1850], Mr. THOMAS McKENZIE, to Miss MARTHA BROWITT, both of this place.
> > The Printers say the cake was nice,
> > And wine both red and flowing,
> > So may their hopes exceed all price,
> > With pure affection glowing.[4]

With his heartstrings stretched by Martha's laments, and his inner feelings tender toward the good things about her and the pleasant memories, Orson penned thoughts about women. The result appeared in the same *Guardian* issue as Martha's wedding announcement:

"Woman's Rights Convention."

Our opinion is sought upon the above subject from a reliable and respectable source. We are sorry that we have not wisdom and experience enough to enter into this subject with a zeal and an understanding that would do honor to the cause, and maintain inviolate the rights of the fair. But such as we have, we give unto thee.

It is the right of every woman to get married if she can, and to raise up just as fine children as any body else—to sweep the house and keep it clean—to captivate the heart of her husband, and thus prevent him from going astray:—It is her right to make, wash and iron his shirt—to give tone and character to the infant mind—to obey her husband in every thing that is right, besides in some things that may not be exactly right in order to keep peace in the family. She is a lovely creature. God bless her! She was our mother, our sister, and is our wife and daughter. She bears pain, sorrow and adversity with fortitude. She is forgetful of injuries—she exposes many faults and hides more. On the whole, the

balance of power is in her favor; and if the right of dominion and control is what she seeks, where is the monarch who is not her subject. Oh,
Woman! "thy right there is none to dispute,"—The last word is thine,
and the last good wish reserved in the heart of man belongs to thee.
Thou art all in all.

Would Martha read these words, and would she understand that Orson
desired sincerely that she be happy?

Orson wanted everyone to be happy. To help bring this about by keeping peace in the community, he continued using priesthood authority to deal
with undesirable activities. To people such as "a man killing an ox on Sunday
and hurrying a sale of the beef on Monday [because the beef was stolen],"
and "a lady that is guilty of shop-lifting," Orson published: "We will not tri-
fle with men or women in these matters. . . . If they will not [change their
ways] . . . , let them be troubled by fiends of darkness by night, and by the
destroyer by day, until they are wasted, and their names vanish and disappear
like smoke, and all Israel say, 'AMEN!'"

The upcoming term of the "Kanesville Academy" also interested Orson.
In mid December he urged parents to enroll their children and to pay the
teacher, that expenses of "tuition, fuel, house rent, and making fires" would
be met. His own older children, Laura and Emily, ages thirteen and ten,
would attend the school.[5]

Now living in the Hyde home to assist Marinda was Charlotte Quindlin
Johnson (Johnson being the name of her former husband). Born in 1802 in
New Jersey, a Church member, and a seamstress, Charlotte liked children.[6]
Marinda especially appreciated Charlotte's help with young Frank and Alonzo
and baby Delia.

Orson missed Delia's first birthday December 28, 1850, his duties requiring travel. He journeyed to Saint Louis to "spend two or three weeks, teaching
the Church, and purchasing . . . stock for the office, &c." He left home
December 21 and traveled the river road. Three days later, while waiting for
a stagecoach midway across Missouri at Glasgow, he reported Kanesville conditions and developments to Brigham Young and counselors. Ending in a
light mood, he wrote,

> In consequence of the Jews and Gentiles establishing so many grog-
> shops in Kanesville, we have prohibited dancing and recommended
> prayer this winter. So I cannot dance at all. Will not some of my breth-
> ren of the Council ask some pretty lady in my name to dance with him
> out there where there is no whiskey, so that my dancing may not get
> behind the times? This, you know, is very necessary.
>
> Now my sheet is full and heart too, and the stage will be soon with-
> out me, so I must bid you good night and be off—
>
> God bless you all, and also yours.

In Saint Louis Orson looked for a young man to help in the *Guardian* office. He found Richard Bee, a Church member recently arrived from Scotland who planned to travel on to the Bluffs in the spring. Orson asked him to write a composition, which he did, and the result so pleased Orson that he engaged Richard Bee "there and then . . . as an apprentice," to begin when he arrived in Kanesville.

Orson's business completed, he returned home from Saint Louis, and continued his duties. In early February, 1851, he and the High Council decided dances could resume the first of March, on the condition "that the members have paid their labour Tithing and free will offering, towards . . . improving for the poor."[7]

A February fire consumed a store and grocery on Main Street. The exertions of many citizens arrested the progress of the blaze, saving the entire north side of the street. "This should be a warning to every citizen to be careful about fire," Orson recommended. ". . . Had it not been a calm and still time, it would have been impossible to save the town in consequence of the great quantities of hay stored in the place."

The evening of February 15, within two weeks of Orson's earlier cautions about fire, a blaze started on the roof of his own three-room dwelling house. A little girl in the street saw it and immediately gave the alarm. "[C]itizens, en masse, turned out instanter." Some climbed a ladder to the roof, and quickly dashed on water, putting out the blaze. In the *Guardian*, Orson thanked his neighbors profoundly for "kindness and prompt and efficient action. But for them, in fifteen minutes more, we should have been reduced to worse than beggary."

Another fire incident involved a visitor, Sarah Allen. "I [stayed in the Hyde home] . . . assisting Sister Hyde for a few days," Sarah narrates. "One evening after I had retired she came into the room with a candle in her hand. Before leaving she accidentally set fire to a piece of cloth that reached to the curtains around the bed where I was sleeping. I awoke very suddenly and found my bed curtains all in flames. I instantly sprang from the bed, snatched the child that was sleeping with me and gave the alarm. My hands were burned but not seriously. . . . I felt to thank God for sparing our lives."[8]

In an April conference session April 6, Orson felt inspired to say to the large congregation that the Lord had rewarded their kindness to one another, and their fairness to the non-Latter-day Saint people among them, by giving them peace. "Some say," he continued, "that I am as kind to the Gentiles, as to the Jews or those in the Church. . . . [S]o long as a man conducts himself aright, whither he is in the Church, or out of the Church, he will be protected in his rights as long as I am your presiding officer."

Orson also mentioned his automatic judgeship. "Since I have been your presiding officer," he said, "it has fallen to my lot to serve you in the capacity of Judge, not only in matters of Church, but of State also . . . ; there being hitherto, no constitutional judiciary in the land. But, as the Legislature . . . [has ruled that] a District Judge is about to be elected; it becomes highly proper for me to tender to you the resignation of this part of my office."[9]

In early May, 1851, Kanesville bustled with Saints preparing to cross the plains, but other emigration activity was far less than in previous years. Few people had arrived by land or by river. Lack of purchasers for goods and produce prevented many Saints from preparing. However, "Just as despair began to hover about our farmers and merchants," Orson reported May 16, ". . . the tide broke in upon us; and although the rush is not so great and overwhelming as it was last year,—yet a fair business is being done. . . .

"The emigration this year is of a different character from what it was last," Orson continued. "They are not mere adventurers—to try their luck for a season and then return: but have their families along generally, showing that they go to the west to find permanent homes.

"If 'Uncle Sam' should gain some Territory in the Moon," Orson added, "we believe that the yankees would contrive some plan to emigrate to it, and hold it by actual possession."

The late California and Oregon emigration delayed the Saints' travel readiness, but most departed by mid June. Orson had warned that "Emigrants should keep a strong guard on the Plains against Indian depredations. We hear they are very bad." With the Saints on their way, Orson could finish his own preparations.

Activities of June's last two weeks kept him busier than seemed possible. He arranged for home and business to function during his absence. He sold his "Music Hall," more commonly now called "Hyde's Hall," to the County Commissioners; it would house County offices. Also, Judge P. E. Brocchus arrived on his way west to be one of the Associate Judges of the Supreme Court of Utah Territory. He and Orson decided to travel together.

In the midst of these activities, Orson dealt with Indians. Because he had heard that the Omahas "design[ed] evil against the emigrants," he invited the Omaha Chiefs to Kanesville. They came, bringing an interpreter. The Council included Indians, Orson, Judge Brocchus, a few hundred onlookers, and "the cannon or howitzer from Fort Leavenworth" that Judge Brocchus was taking to Utah. A loud demonstration by the cannon "spoke with an eloquence and power that made the Chiefs rather quail." Also, the Judge "spoke handsomely to them." The Chiefs "promised to restrain their young men from committing any depredations upon the emigrants so far as they could." And Orson promised, in return for good behavior, "to make them some presents after the emigration was over."

June 25, Orson attended a party, a farewell for him and a complimentary honor to Judge Brocchus. Guests enjoyed a sumptuous dinner in the upper room of the former "Hyde's Hall" and spirited dancing on the main floor. A special treat among the refreshments was ice water.[10]

At last, June 28, Orson departed from Kanesville, his riding horse Jim accompanying him, his wagon amply stocked. His family was doing well, Charlotte helping Marinda with the children, and Mary Ann remaining with her brother William at Hyde Park, now called Bullock's Grove. In the *Guardian* office young Richard Bee was an excellent apprentice. The editor of the *Saint Louis Daily Union* had published a jovial article June 21:

> We admire the theological tactics of Elder Orson Hyde. He is evidently a skilful athlete, and has studied in the most approved schools of the day. He would have the saints judge for themselves in all conflicting and rival claims to their confidence, . . . but woe to them if they form any other judgment than one favorable to him. He is a sensible man, and is undoubtedly the true prophet. . . . We are decidedly in favor of the apostolicity and mission of Brother Hyde. Hath he not seen a vision, and besides is he not an editor? . . . Never before the light of the nineteenth century dawned upon the world, had an editor a place among the prophets. We are anxious for the apotheosis of at least one of our fraternity, for we are aware that the great majority of us stand but a very poor chance. We therefore declare decidedly and emphatically for Brother Hyde; and are ready to maintain his cause with all the logic and eloquence at our command.[11]

On the plains, the most harrowing day of Orson's journey was July 11 in the sand hills "near one branch of the Loupe Fork," Orson wrote, "[where] we were assailed by a party of about three hundred Pawnee Indians, and robbed of between seven and ten hundred dollars. There were only seven of us, and about three hundred of them. I lost about eighty dollars worth of blankets, gun, clothing, camp furniture, and provisions, besides my Jim horse; but he fought himself clear from them and I redeemed him by paying forty dollars. [Judge Brocchus lost an expensive grey horse.] . . . Capt. Smith's three fifties [companies of fifty wagons each] were not robbed . . . , as they had passed before the Indians had taken their position on the route. I fear the remaining companies will suffer much by their depredations. I am now satisfied that there was a concerted plan between the Omahas and Pawnees, to rob and plunder the trains; but the Omahas stand back by reason of our talk with the chiefs, and leave the Pawnees to act alone. The Pawnees told us that they expected the Omahas up [here] and asked us if we had seen them." Orson added a philosophical note to his account: "We have been mercifully relieved of much of our loading[,] to our own serious inconvenience, but to the great relief of our teams."

Orson and his group arrived in Great Salt Lake City on August 17 after a "rough and tedious passage," they told a *Deseret News* reporter. They depicted the Indian incident as "the Indians . . . swapp[ing] shirts with [us], neglecting to present their blankets in return."

Discussions about the Indians prompted the First Presidency to publish: "During the great amount of emigration . . . , the Indians have received some insults and abuses which they are sure to resent, and the Saints and others who may have occasion to pass through these tribes . . . , will do well to be prepared to act on the defensive."[12]

Orson again felt keen satisfaction in the Valley. He visited with friends, attended many meetings, gave several speeches, spent hours in discussions with other Church leaders, was guest of honor at a party September 5, and attended general conference held again in September rather than October. One conference meeting brought him somber memories, being the funeral of Lewis Abbott, the widower brother-in-law of Thomas B. Marsh. Lewis and his wife Ann, thirteen years ago, had handled the property of Thomas and Orson after the two withdrew from Far West with their families. The Abbotts had continued faithful. Thomas B. Marsh remained in Missouri in seclusion. At the funeral Orson offered the benediction.[13]

As before, the Valley agriculture impressed Orson. He marveled at "[r]ipe peaches two and a half years from the stone, . . . the richest and fairest peaches that I most ever saw." Grape vines too, and apple and pear trees, flourished. This season's melons were superb.

Orson departed for home September 23, in company with two dozen other men, elated that among them were his former counselor, Ezra T. Benson, and one of the Presidents of the Seventy, Jedediah Grant. They accompanied him to "superintend the emigration the coming season[,] . . . to push the Saints to the Valley." Orson, also, had been directed to move his family to the Valley.[14]

The travelers thought they used sufficient caution against Indian attacks, but they changed their minds the night of October 20. Camped at the upper crossing of the South Platte, the night "severe," "extremely cold and dark," the noise of animals being driven away awakened the sleeping men. The guard could probably have been more alert, but the darkness and the stealth of the thieves, Cheyenne Indians, made detection difficult until too late. Orson lost four excellent mules, the two spans he used to pull his wagon. From another man the Indians took two fine animals, a mule and a bay mare.

The next day Orson and others visited the Indian camp, about five miles distant, in search of the stolen animals, but were unsuccessful. "If ever a poor fellow felt miserably independent," Orson comments about the episode, "I did. . . . No animals to feed, guard, or drive. My wagon and baggage on the bank;—grub, frying pan, and Coffee pot snug aboard, and not an animal to move the portable kitchen. Through the kindness of a friend more fortunate than I, I obtained the use of animals to haul me home."[15]

At Fort Kearney, Orson learned that Captain Wharton, Commandant at the fort, had used his troops and his cannon to recover property stolen by the Pawnee Indians from Elder Hyde's and other companies in the sand hills while westward bound. The property included, Orson narrates, "some fifteen or twenty horses and mules. Also a quantity of blankets, knives, and other articles. . . . Our blankets were recovered, but so dirty . . . that . . . the Captain gave them to his interpreter. I [received] none of my property taken by the Pawnees. The Judge's valuable grey horse was recovered, but in a very reduced condition—hardly worth bringing home."[16]

As the days passed after Orson's group left Fort Kearney, they increasingly saw bands of Indians traveling northward to the buffalo region, and the Indians indulged in a novel sport. They lit fire to the prairie grass and then watched the spectacular show of sweeping walls of flame curving away from them, with huge billows of smoke rising in the sky. The year before, when Orson rode home late in the season, the ground had been burned over. This was apparently an annual diversion of the Indians. Because the traveling season had essentially passed, this seemed harmless to the whites too.

Before this period, while returning across the plains, "we were very cautious . . . about allowing the fire to get out from our camps," Orson later told, but "about one hundred miles east of Fort Kearney, . . . [fire] was burning . . . all around us; and I made this remark, 'If the Indians are burning the grass in their own country, they cannot object to our burning it.'" The whites then kindled the same dynamic pageantry: embers from a campfire stick starting grass on fire, the crackle of new flames, bigger flames, then the roaring of tall blazes vigorously advancing in scope.

Though accustomed to being lambasted for many of his actions, Orson had no thought that burning prairie grass at the end of the emigrating season would cause an uproar. But it did. His accuser, who had traveled with him, said Orson destroyed vegetation so that there would be none for the animals of specific men. The complainant was disgruntled with Church leaders. Orson published an explanation. "I did set the grass on fire for a little boyish sport, in several places:" Orson concluded his narration, "But was it to injure . . . any one . . . ? God forbid! That is no trait of my character,—neither was it ever, from the days of my childhood . . . ; but from a lad I have ever had a strong propensity for innocent sport; and to break the monotony of the cold and dreary scenery over the Plains, I occasionally fired the grass for the sole pleasure and sport of seeing it burn—the Indians having set the example. I do not say that I did right; and I do not know that I did harm to any one: I know that no harm was intended."[17]

Orson arrived home in early November. "Here I am at the table as usual, driving ahead the quill," he summarized in the *Guardian*. "The Indians have relieved me of more than five hundred dollars on our trip, [but] I had a very good journey home. Came to the Missouri River in thirty-nine and a half days from the Valley."[18]

The finality that in a few months he would travel west to remain, now touched Orson's every action. He would miss the bluffs and the prairies, the rolling brown waters of the Missouri River, and traveling familiar roads, knowing the residents of each log home. He would miss the bustle of Main Street, Hyde Street, and the *Frontier Guardian* office, associating with his neighbors the merchants.

In a "Special Conference" November 8 and 9, a letter from Brigham Young and his counselors was read, appealing "To all the Saints in Pottawatamie" to come to the Valley with wagons and teams and food, or with handcarts if necessary, but "*Arise and Come home.*" The conference "closed with the best of feeling; and every face seemed looking westward." Orson was grateful to have Ezra T. Benson and Jedediah Grant to oversee the details of the Saints' emigration.[19]

In the November 14 *Guardian*, the first after his return, Orson's many paragraphs touched a broad range of subjects. Regarding personal needs, he called for "Corn and good prairie hay . . . and . . . Cash," for a "good New Milch or winter's cow," and for "a lad about fourteen years of age who can make himself generally useful among stock and about a house." For Church members Orson included news from the Valley and admonitions to prepare to move. To the general public, both here at home and in far places, he detailed "Things to be Remembered in Crossing the Plains," and that in Pottawattamie County the "valuable claims and improvements . . . owned and occupied by the Mormon population are for sale."

Orson looked at his own financial challenges with optimism. He had diverse properties that he could sell: his farm, his newspaper office, the printing press, and his home. His trip this past summer had cost a thousand dollars, and to move his family would also be costly, but his faith in the Lord's help gave him the calm assurance that "I ever will have enough, though I should not have a dollar beforehand in the world." Regarding a livelihood in the Valley, while there the decision had been made that he would edit another newspaper to be called "The Mountain Standard."[20] This pleased him.

To augment his income now, Orson continued to advertise his Storage and Forwarding business, and he reminded people owing him for newspapers and job printing that he would like to be paid. However, as he said in a time past, "If this is not attended to, the delinquent may rest assured of one thing;—We will not sue him if he never pays us."[21]

Again Orson was busy. He participated in all the principal councils and in all meetings of public interest, and he preached almost every Sabbath.

With this and all else, he became increasingly thankful that others had charge of the emigration.

He was also grateful that others had charge of overseeing the construction of fifty wagons to haul machinery to the Valley for making sugar. A Church member arrived in Kanesville in early November with the iron for the fifty wagons. John Taylor was purchasing the sugar-making machinery in England, and it should arrive at Kanesville in the spring, ready to be loaded and hauled westward.[22]

A local development was the petition of the townspeople for legal status for Kanesville. The county was being surveyed. The Saints, merely squatters, had marked property lines with posts and blazed trees. Now official boundaries were being set.[23]

Orson prepared the last 1851 *Guardian* issue reflectively. He would likely be its editor for only a few issues more, as he had been approached by a prospective purchaser. He realized that he would miss controlling a public press with its power to make easy announcements and its broad scope in trying to guide people's actions aright. He thanked his patrons for their support.

Orson's *Guardian* writings for the next several weeks continued with a pensive undertone, which included political concerns. During the summer, government officers, among them Judge Brocchus who had traveled west with Orson, had caused a stir in Utah Territory, denounced the Mormons, and returned east. Their written and spoken falsehoods caused escalating anti-Mormon furor: Governor Young must be replaced; the United States Government must send an armed force. Newspapers around the country repeated the falsehoods clarioned by the returned officers, and Orson countered with articles of his own, pleased that in the Lord's wisdom the *Guardian* had a wide circulation and thus helped stem the abuse. Also he mailed clippings of *Guardian* articles to national leaders.

Despite serious thoughts and actions, Orson penned lighthearted words. "On Sunday and Monday mornings last," he stated in January, "the Thermometer stood at eighteen degrees below Zero. It is well, perhaps, that the instruments are made no longer; if they were, there is no telling how cold it might become."[24]

Ideally, the Saints could have prepared peacefully and left Kanesville with few outside complications. This, however, was not to be. Peace was threatened by rumors circulated from downriver in Missouri. Orson thought the tales were started by underhanded men seeking to drive the Mormons out and then take over abandoned farms. Persecution, the fiery darts of Satan, from far and near and all sides, Orson knew, became swifter and thicker and closer to the mark whenever a movement promised to strengthen the Lord's stronghold on earth.

Distant animosity formed only part of the problem. Surprising hindrances illustrated the adversary's powerful local efforts to prompt the personal disgrace of Orson Hyde, the "President and Counsellor among the Saints east of the Rocky Mountains." A foment erupted in Kanesville, stirred by a Methodist clergyman, the Reverend William Simpson, who had been in town since the fall of 1850, over a year. Zealously he had preached mocking and scornful sermons to save the Mormons from their benighted ways and thus add them to his Methodist flock. Cooperation with the local populace, however, seemed beyond his interest. The inappropriateness of his tactics he failed to recognize, even when a number of Methodists, both in Pottawattamie and neighboring Mills Counties, joined the Mormons.[25]

Orson continued to refrain from direct editorial comment about the situation, but made indirect statements, hoping that the minister would tone down his battering of Orson and the Mormons.

The local populace considered Mr. Simpson's antics spice to daily living, but when reports from Missouri became more inflammatory against the Mormons, and when Kanesville citizens were mistreated while traveling through Coonsville, a few miles south of Kanesville, the local "Gentiles" called two meetings. In the gatherings, December 25, 1851, and January 7, resolutions were discussed and adopted as follows:

> *Whereas*, a false report has gone abroad, to wit: that there has been considerable difficulty and contention in this town and vicinity, . . . between the Mormons and those not belonging to their Church.
>
> Therefore, we, the so called *Gentile* portion of this community, do assert that the above reports are false, and that there is no truth in them, and that there has not, nor is there likely to be any disturbance in this County, between the Mormons and those differing from them in belief.
>
> We would further represent, that the Mormons of this County, (as a community,) are a peaceful, industrious, and law abiding people; and that we are, and have been, living in peace and harmony; and we hope that no persons, either at home or FROM ABROAD, will seek to disturb our amicable relations.
>
> And we would farther represent, that we are not Mormons, nor in any wise connected with the Mormon Church, or their people. . . .[26]

The statements of the Gentile meeting brought out in Mr. Simpson the opposite reaction to goodwill. His sermons became more jeering. Orson, unwilling to resist fanning the flame, on January 23 published his own thoughts after hearing a sermon by Mr. Simpson about the nature of God. In part, Orson wrote:

> If God is without form or image, after what model or pattern was man created? . . . If the Father is without form, image or likeness, what did the martyred Stephen see in his last moments? He declared that he

saw the heavens opened, and the son of man standing on the right hand of God.

If God has no form, how could Stephen tell whether the Son stood on the right or left hand of the Father? Or whether the Father was there at all? . . .

We respect the man [who gave the sermon], though in error, for he is created in the likeness and image of the true God; but his errors we do not respect. . . .[27]

Orson continued getting ready to move. As part of his preparation, before turning his office over to its new owner, in newspaper appeals he encouraged townsfolk to come and buy olive oil, dried apples, sugar, tea, coffee, school books, slate and lead pencils, writing paper, "Books of Mormon," Doctrine and Covenants, Hymn Books, Mormon guides across the plains, and back numbers of the *Guardian*.[28]

One item that Orson had refrained from selling in his office was tobacco. He had kept his vow of tobacco abstinence ever since the Prophet Joseph Smith received the revelation that tobacco was "not good for man,"[29] but an inner craving for the substance occasionally came. Having it near him would only increase his yearnings. He had enough other concerns to fill his time and thoughts.

The last weeks in February he moved out of his office and left everything in order for Jacob Dawson of Fremont County, Iowa, to take over. In the $2000 negotiation, Mr. Dawson's friend, A. C. Ford, assisted him financially. Orson felt comfortable selling to Mr. Dawson, who had high ideals and promise of being a fine editor. An Attorney and Counselor at Law, formerly a member of the Pittsburgh Bar, he had been connected with the office of the *Pittsburgh Gazette*.

Writing about the sale, Orson thought that he gave the new editor a good bargain. "My press, type and furniture cost me upwards of $1000," Orson told, and the "greater part of the type [is] nearly new. The buildings cost me $1000 more." Also he had "between thirteen and fourteen hundred subscribers," and his "advertising and job work" was "thrown in as the good will of the concern."

Orson's last issue as editor came off the press February 20, 1852 (Volume 4, Number 2). In his "Valedictory" he said, "[F]riend Dawson [is] fully installed in office, seated upon the tripod, and wielding the goose-quill Scepter . . . [in] the Sanctum." Orson bequeathed upon the new editor "our mantle and best wishes." Continuing, Orson prophesied: "We claim no particular merit as an Editor, yet humble as our exertions have been, we have recorded some sayings and chronicled some events that will be more fully appreciated at a future day."[30]

Jacob Dawson published the *Frontier Guardian* with no break in issues, but he made changes. He published it weekly rather than every two weeks and gave it a new name, *The Frontier Guardian and Iowa Sentinel.*

Other changes as well were coming to the newspaper scene in Kanesville. Almon W. Babbitt, a Latter-day Saint, sent notice that when he returned from the Eastern states he would bring a press with him and publish a second newspaper, *The Western Bugle.*

The transfer of his editorship duties gave Orson more time to strengthen the efforts of Ezra T. Benson in getting the Saints on their way. Elder Benson had been untiringly diligent. In the fall he had ridden night and day among all the Mormon settlements in western Iowa and organized forty companies, one in each Branch of the Church. During the winter he had encouraged and instructed them in their preparations.

Now, with spring approaching, meetings about emigrating companies convened in the Tabernacle in the Big Pigeon Branch on March 6 and 7. "The spirit of God was with us," Elder Benson wrote in a letter to Brigham Young about the meetings, adding that the "reports from the saints throughout the country were satisfactory beyond my most sanguine expectations."

"Brother Hyde was with us," the letter goes on, "and his remarks given in his characteristic good style and dictated by the Holy Spirit warmed up the heart[s] of the saints and seemed to inspire their souls with increased energy. He advised the brethren not to dispose of their claims for trifles, for every good claim would sell for a good price in cash or its equivalent in desirable property before the 25th of April."

Continuing his letter, Elder Benson rejoiced in the expectation of "a heavy emigration of our people. From the best information I can gather, there will not be less than five or six thousand souls from this county and about ten thousand in all." Seven hundred Saints were already on their way from England. "The Lord is surely extending his hand to assist in the gathering of his people." In addition to Saints, Elder Benson reported that the "emigration for California and Oregon will . . . [probably] exceed that of 1850."

When Ezra T. Benson reported the emigration meetings to President Young he also mentioned other observations he had made since arriving in Pottawattamie County, items pertaining to the activities of Orson Hyde. Word had trickled to the Valley that Elder Hyde was usurping more authority than he should, and Elder Benson refuted this:

> . . . I take great pleasure in saying to you that in visiting the different Branches of the Church in this district, I have not learned that he [Elder Hyde] had attempted to build himself up or cause any division or separate influence from the main body of the church. To my knowledge . . . his moral course and character are unexceptionable. He has fought manfully through the "Guardian" since his return. He has handsomely

whipped out every slink that has dared to yelp against us or any of the authorities in the Valley. He has forced the enemy boldly without yielding an inch of ground. Our situation has been critical indeed, and we were forced to walk as though we were treading on eggs. The report of the returning [government] officers raised a storm that for a while threatened to burst with fury upon our heads, but the Lord has helped us; the storm has been stayed, the threatening clouds have been dispersed and the rainbow of peace and tranquility is extended over our heads. I think we shall now be allowed to enjoy a calm long enough to get away from our enemies.[31]

Calm came only in snatches. March 6, the first day of the Big Pigeon meetings, the *Savannah Sentinel*—a Missouri newspaper that had already tiraded against Orson Hyde and the Saints—published a sermon against the Mormons called the "Frog Sermon." The paper circulated in Kanesville. Rather than crediting the text to a specific minister, the newspaper said that it "was delivered we understand, at Kanesville during the last winter, by a divine of the Methodist Church." The Reverend William Simpson had delivered it.

Orson had been told of the sermon soon after delivery and thought to send it to oblivion by ignoring it. But here it was in print. Was it published because Orson no longer had at his immediate command the weapon of the press to counteract it? Whatever the reason, Orson felt that he must now act.

In his Frog Sermon, Mr. Simpson compared the Mormons to the frogs described in the Bible, book of Revelation 16:12-16, the frogs that "come out of the mouth of the dragon, and out of the mouth of the beast, and out of the mouth of the false prophet." A few of the many accusations that Mr. Simpson made were:

> ... The Mormons teach that they are to exterminate all existing governments and churches—are to cut off all who oppose them, and they are to have supreme dominion over the whole earth. . . .
>
> They are like frogs in that they are continually immersing in every mill race, brook or pool, yet notwithstanding their repeated dippings, like the frogs, they remain slippery, slimy and unclean. . . .
>
> They are like frogs in the respect that when frogs become numerous they are a great pest to a country. Their croaking is annoying—and so the croaking Mormon is an annoyance to the Christian Church.—Like the frogs in Egypt, the Mormons are a dreadful plague in these last days.[32]

Determined to thwart Satan's efforts to influence people to disgrace the Lord's flock, Orson read the entire discourse in a Sunday meeting March 14. To every accusation he replied. Then, the same as he had done in many other vexing situations where the laws of man had no sway, he used the power that inspiration whispered to him to use, the sanction that he could have left unbidden if persuasive articles and pointed arguments had produced a leavening effect upon Mr. Simpson. In measured words Orson pronounced, "It is a false and wicked production. Its author shall not prosper in anything until he confesses and acknowledges that he did wrong, and was wicked and abusive in publishing the Frog Sermon."

The next Tuesday Orson received word that Mr. Simpson was "somewhat anxious to know the purport of [the] curse." William Simpson obviously knew the reputation of Elder Hyde's pronouncements.

Orson, hoping to finish the Frog Sermon episode, spread out paper and wrote. He detailed to Mr. Simpson the wording of the curse. Explaining that he had not cursed his addressee personally, he said, "I know not that you are its author—I never said that you were. Indeed, should hope that you were not." Orson suspected, from listening to Mr. Simpson in the past, that the minister had received outside assistance, that another composed the sermon. Orson wrote on, expounded somewhat on immersion, and ended with, "If a Mormon, or any one else, on Mormon credit, interrupts you or your property on account of any remarks that I have made, the same curse shall be visited upon that individual that I said should attend the author of the Frog Sermon, if he did not confess his wrong."

This began a published exchange—in the *Savannah Sentinel* and in Kanesville's new *Western Bugle*, printed on the second floor of J. E. Johnson's Emporium Buildings. It continued until April 28. In his last letter, answering Mr. Simpson's statements of Mormon claims regarding western Iowa, Orson said, "I have never taught, neither can you prove it, that this land all belonged to the Mormons and that you, Gentiles, were all to be cut off, either by God himself or by Mormon agency. . . . I have taught, sir, that the wicked who reject the truth, Jew or Gentile, will, in due time, destroy one another, or be destroyed by the hand of Providence. 'Nation will rise against nation, and kingdom against kingdom; and when Christ shall come to make an end of sin and bring in everlasting righteousness,' you will be cut off if you are not like him, and I also. The true Israel of God alone will stand in that day, and the land will be theirs—all theirs."[33]

Mr. Simpson's attacks diminished, but men in Fremont County, Iowa, downriver bordering Missouri, were rumbling against Elder Hyde on another subject, the county judgeship. During the weeks of the Frog Sermon bantering, rumors circulated that with the sale of his press Orson had also "sold" the Sixth District Judgeship. He was accused of accepting money, gold coin, to secretly influence the High Council to get a Whig judge elected by a solid Mormon vote. One reason for this claim, apparently, was that A. C. Ford, who had backed Jacob Dawson in his purchase of the *Frontier Guardian*, was an announced Whig candidate for the Judgeship. A few unprincipled Democrats in Fremont County held an "Anti-Mormon Meeting" in mid February and drew up inflammatory resolutions about "the unscrupulous villainy of Hyde and his council." Several newspapers published these. The group caused uproar by writing false letters to newspapers about Orson, the Mormons, and the Whigs, and they altered reports of meetings.[34]

Orson responded with a published affidavit, also with letters and articles, that he had accepted no bribes, had endorsed no one for Judge, had told no one how to vote, and had used no political influence with the High Council. The High Council published an affidavit stating the same. The leading Gentile men in Kanesville supported Orson and the Council. Editor Dawson in the *Guardian and Sentinel*, March 11, wrote explanations and added: "If we are not mistaken in deciphering signs and movements, the law of libel and slander will be duly enforced in this case. Mr. Hyde is regarded here as an honorable man, and his word will be taken for any amount of money, or any statement that he may make, (except about some of his religious notions) as quick as that of any other man in the country. He has many friends here who are not pleased at the slanderous charges made against him."

But accusations continued to appear in various newspapers.

Finally, in May, Orson gave up being courteous and indeed sued for slander. His suit was "against all the leaders of the Anti-mormon Meeting, & more particularly against the committee that drafted and reported the resolutions charging him with selling the Judgeship or the vote that would control the same." He stated his damages to be $10,000.[35]

A published account, by a correspondent, of the results, states that

the suit entered by Orson Hyde, in the Fremont district court, for slander and libel, against some of the citizens of that county, in the matter of his being charged, through the public prints, with selling the Judgeship for gold, is having rather a curious effect.

Evidently some of the defendants, or their friends, sought by means of a forged letter to frighten Mr. Hyde, and to Bluff him off. But being unsuccessful in this operation, they next threaten[ed], I hear, to kill Mr. H., if he shall go there to prosecute them. Prosecution was entered, upon which four or five of the party left immediately, and are said to have crossed the Missouri river. . . .

Since the filing of the papers, some of the defendants that did not run, I learn, have made two or three unsuccessful attempts to get up an indignation meeting, to ride A. C. Ford, Esq., on a wooden horse for being the attorney on the part of the prosecution, to ride the honorable sheriff for serving the papers, and Mr. Hyde for commencing suit. . . .

I have often heard Mr. Hyde say that he did not want their money. He wanted them to restore to him his reputation and character, which they had robbed him of without any cause or provocation on his part.[36]
. . .

Defamation of Orson Hyde in this matter broiled on until late in May. It subsided after the Governor of Iowa, a Democrat, prevented an election and appointed a Democrat as the Judge. The new Judge dismissed Orson's suit for slander by sustaining a filed demurrer "alleging that to charge a man with selling his printing press, and using his influence to have a man elected to an office, [is] not defamatory nor libelous."

Through it all, Orson kept his sense of humor. When approached for unwarranted help in a legal endeavor of public import, he announced:

> One thing amuses me much. In times of political strife and excitement, there are strong objections made against my using any influence in election matters; but when some persons have a real or imaginary claim against some of our people, I am appealed to because I have influence, it is said, to enforce collection without resort to law; and the claimant is saved the expense of an Attorney.
>
> All I have to say in the case is this: that I am willing to do what is reasonable in society; but to run and bark for any one, because he wants to save dimes in his own pocket, and thus cheat the profession, I cannot do it, particularly when my influence is considered so dangerous in political matters.[37]

A surprising political event was the news in May that the President of the United States, Millard Fillmore, had nominated Orson Hyde to the office of Associate Judge of the Supreme Court of the Territory of Utah. The appointment still needed the approval of Congress. Editors commented. "We congratulate friend Hyde . . . ," wrote Jacob Dawson. "We know Elder Hyde personally, and know him to be well qualified to fill that, or any other office in the Territory. He is an Attorney at Law, and a man of sound Judgement, and great discretion,—a gentleman in every respect, and a GOOD WHIG." Another editor, of the opposite political persuasion from Jacob Dawson and Orson, wrote that Elder Hyde would "look very graceful with the 'Judicial ermine' around his ample shoulders."[38]

In May, California and Oregon emigrants again swarmed Kanesville. Two steamers that arrived with supplies stayed a week and served as ferry boats carrying teams and wagons across the river. Families coming to Pottawattamie County bought farms. Though in early March Orson had predicted that farms would sell by April 25, the Saints were not upset that he had missed by a few weeks.[39]

At Bullock's Grove, old Hyde Park, Henry Plumer, short and heavy set, seemed pleased with the farms he had purchased from Orson and the others. Orson was grateful that someone industrious and enterprising had bought the acres. The two men had become fairly well acquainted since Henry's arrival the year before with his bride.[40]

Many Saints were on schedule with their preparations, also were plowing and planting to leave farms in good shape. Though sales had increased, some families still awaited buyers. A newspaper announcement May 19, by Elders Hyde and Benson, exhorted everyone who had not sold, and who were unable to buy wagons and teams, to prepare to go "in wheelbarrows and hand-carts." The first Mormon company would soon depart.[41]

Amid all the scurry, Elder John Taylor arrived from his labors in far away Europe. As planned, he had arranged for the machinery to manufacture sugar in Utah. It weighed forty tons. The duty on the massive crated apparatus, paid at New Orleans, was over £800. Wagons waited in Kanesville for the machinery.

Accomplishing another arrangement, in the May 26 newspaper Orson Hyde and Ezra T. Benson announced that "Joseph E. Johnson, Esq., of Kanesville, is appointed general Claim and Property Agent, for . . . disposing of such claims and other property as our friends cannot dispose of before they go west."[42] Energetic J.E. would remain in Kanesville another season or so to operate his Emporium Store.

May 27 Orson reported to Valley brethren regarding the "contests and battles in the war that arose by reason of the reports and letters of the runaway officers." He rejoiced that "under the blessing and providence of God, we were enabled to calm the troubled elements . . . [in] Washington. . . . The probability is that Gov. Young will not be removed. . . . I do not believe that any troop or force will be sent to the valley; at least, there is no appearance of it now. . . .

"In consequence of the press of business, together with some disappointment," Orson stated about his own plans, "it will be late before I can get off. Probably shall bring up the rear of this emigration. I shall not bring a press with me. . . . I expect to bring paper, ink, &c." Orson used twenty days of June for a Saint Louis trip, for supplies and arrangements.[43]

The latter part of June, Orson received news that the United States Senate rejected his nomination as a Utah Supreme Court Justice.[44] This was no surprise.

At home, only last-minute preparations remained. Elder Benson exulted in a July 1 letter to Brigham Young that six thousand local Saints had already started, "well rigged out." More would soon leave. "There are no hand carts nor wheelbarrow trains," he reported. "Before we could get one started, they would turn into wagons and teams. Miracles have been wrought here in getting off the saints, and this to my astonishment; and may the Lord ever be praised for his goodness."

The Fourth of July found Orson still in Kanesville, with his wagons packed. Though traditionally festive, this year "we had no very imposing celebration," the newspaper reported, many citizens "on their western way," others "preparing to start," and the remainder "pressed with a variety of business avocations. However, Orson Hyde delivered to the citizens his fare-well address, upon the public square, followed by John Taylor and others, and in the evening, some indulged in 'tripping the light fantastic toe.'" Also, eve-ning "fire-works of different kinds" illuminated the town; sky-rockets "shot far up into the sombre curtains of night" left "their long trails of fiery parti-cles behind. . . . The boys, too, the rising generation, had real sport with their fire-crackers and . . . general merry-making."

The next morning Orson's wagons carried his family out of Kanesville.[45] Another departing Saint had already reminisced in a letter to the town:

Some few years ago, a few oppressed and persecuted people came through this hollow then occupied by the Pottawatamies. The tall rank grass, the bounding deer, and the herds of elk were undisturbed, save by the hunting parties of the Indian tribe. No one thought of making a location here in "Whiskey Hollow," as then known. But winter quarters on the Omahaw lands, was the chief rallying point of the Mormon com-munity, till the main body left for Salt Lake; then the remnant and the merchants came over to this place, and friends Stutsman and Voorhis received their first stock of goods marked "Miller Hollow." Shortly up goes the Log Tabernacle in the midst of winter, an evidence of Mormon industry and zeal, and I wish it still remained as such. Then the town was governed by Mormon rule. No liquor shops, no gambling places, but peace and tranquility graced our resting place. Presently our friend Hyde started his paper, the benefits of which we hardly appreciated. His subscription list was large and extensive, a terror to the Back Woods Bogus Maker, and a praise to the well doer.—Since those primitive days, how changed the scene. Merchants flocked in, built up houses of trade—farms opened on every side—roads were made, and bridges built, and the town of Kanesville widely known. And where is the [secret] to all this? It is in Mormon industry. . . . They made the town; they built halls; they brought music and dancing with proper restrictions in their train; they brought civilization here. . . . Much enjoyment—much pleasure has been realized here, and both Mormons and friends have felt themselves at home. And now on the eve of our departure for a distant country, I must say farewell to it, the Bluffs; the quiet resting place of our dead. The hills and dales of Kanesville, are, and ever will be, dear to me and in time to come, my mind will flit to your snugly situated town with pleasure. Long may it live—long may it prosper. . . . [A]nd to many friends, to the place, and all its joys and comforts, I reluctantly say fare-well. . . . Sustain your town, gentlemen, one and all; and you, fair ladies, keep the gents to their duties, and thus mutually working, you mutually thrive. . . .

Another description delineates that

> Kanesville . . . is a fine, flourishing town, and contains about 300 houses; 16 mercantile establishments; 2 drug stores; 2 printing offices; 5 hotels; 4 groceries; 2 jewelers shops; 1 harness maker; 8 wagon shops; 2 tin-smiths; 2 livery stables; 2 cabinet shops; 5 boot and shoe makers; 2 daguerrean rooms; 5 practical physicians; 9 attornies at law; 1 gun-smith; 1 cooper; several ministers of different denominations; 3 barber shops; 4 bakeries; 1 mill; 7 blacksmith shops; and about 1200 to 1500 inhabitants.[46]

Though much had changed here at the Bluffs from when Orson came, the profusion of prairie strawberries remained the same, "large, nice, red, richly blushing, mellow and choice flavored . . . worth their weight in—*sugar and cream!*" The majestic Missouri river remained the same too, but on its "willow girt margin . . . vast herds of cattle are grazing and sporting in the shadow of the never quiet branches of green cottonwood."

In time to come, resident W. H. Robinson would recollect fondly, "I came to Council Bluffs in 1850. It was then Kanesville, and I was one of the three non-Mormons here. I was a merchant and was very glad to get the trade of the Mormons, and I found them to be as prompt as anyone else in paying their debts. Orson Hyde was their leader, and I will always say he was one of the best friends I ever had. He lived just across the street there and we were quite neighborly."[47]

In time to come, also, a local historian would write of the Mormon sojourn near the Missouri river. He also paid tribute to Orson Hyde: "Hyde . . . was the biggest man in western Iowa; . . . and even the Gentiles . . . acknowledged his sway." Of Orson's departure this historian chronicled:

> Orson Hyde led the last company of the Saints from the town. Perhaps it would be more accurate to say that he followed it, for old Gentile inhabitants of Council Bluffs used to tell how the editor of the Frontier Guardian . . . nailed up his loghouse near the abandoned log tabernacle and drove slowly down the wide curving business street of the village, waving his farewells to the half-regretful Gentiles.
>
> Finally his carriage was lost to view on the bottom trail to the Missouri that hurried a chocolate flood past the yellow bluffs, as restless and sinuous and melancholy as it had been on another . . . morning when the Saints first saw it six years before.[48]

Marinda Nancy Johnson Hyde,
Orson's first wife. (Courtesy of
Virginia Woolley Quealy.)

Newell K. Whitney Store, Kirtland, Ohio. Photographed by Orson Hyde's
son Joseph in 1920. (Courtesy of Virginia Woolley Quealy.)

A view of Jerusalem from the Mount of Olives in 1839, two years before Orson Hyde's visit. Sketched in 1839 by David Roberts.

Orson's portable desk, made of mahogany wood with brass fittings and leather writing surface. Undoubtedly he took a similar one to Jerusalem. (Copyright by Intellectual Reserve, Inc. Courtesy of Museum of Church History and Art. Used by Permission.)

Mary Ann Price Hyde,
Orson's third wife. (Courtesy
of LDS Church Historical
Department.)

The Orson Hyde family's home in Nauvoo, Illinois. Probably the back wing
was constructed after the Hydes left. (Courtesy of LDS Church Historical
Department.)

Joseph Smith with Church Leaders in Nauvoo, Illinois, ca. 1844. Joseph Smith is standing; seated from left to right are Hyrum Smith, Willard Richards, Orson Pratt, Parley P. Pratt, Orson Hyde, Heber C. Kimball, and Brigham Young. Painted by William W. Major. In the painting Orson Hyde's hair is auburn, the natural course for many redheads. This is the earliest known likeness of him. (Copyright by Intellectual Reserve, Inc. Courtesy of Museum of Church History and Art. Used by Permission.)

Orson Hyde's home, Kanesville, Iowa. Sketched by George Simons. (Courtesy of the Council Bluffs Public Library, Council Bluffs, Iowa.)

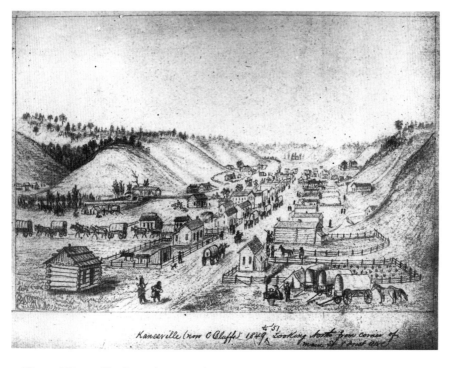

View of Kanesville from the west, the Missouri River side. Note Orson Hyde's home at the foot of a bluff, center of picture. Sketched by George Simons. (Courtesy of the Council Bluffs Public Library, Council Bluffs, Iowa.)

Entering Kanesville from the southeast on Hyde Street (later Madison). Note the Hyde home at the foot of a bluff (in from the left of the photograph about one-third of the photograph width). (A sketch by Frederick Piercy in his *Route from Liverpool to Great Salt Lake Valley*, 1855.)

Council Bluffs (formerly Kanesville) in 1858 from the northeast. Note Orson Hyde's home to the right of center. Sketched by George Simons. (Courtesy of the Council Bluffs Public Library, Council Bluffs, Iowa.)

BY ORSON HYDE.

KANESVILLE, IOWA, FRIDAY MORNING, FEBRUARY 7, 1851.

VOLUME III.---NUMBER 1.

The title from Orson Hyde's newspaper, published Kanesville, Iowa,
February 7, 1849–February 20, 1852.
(Courtesy of LDS Church Historical Department.)

Orson Hyde, probably done in a "daguerrean" shop in Kanesville, 1851 or 1852. (Courtesy of Utah State University Special Collection and Archives.)

Orson Hyde, engraving, 1853.
(Courtesy of Virginia Woolley
Quealy.)

Orson Hyde home, Salt Lake City, directly north of center of Temple
Block. (Courtesy of Virginia Woolley Quealy.)

Great Salt Lake City, Utah Territory, 1855. (A sketch by Frederick Piercy in his *Route from Liverpool to Great Salt Lake Valley*.)

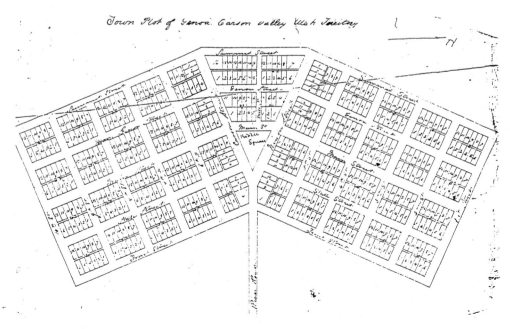

Plot of Genoa, by Orson Hyde, 1855. (Courtesy of Nevada, Department of Conservation and Natural Resources, Division of State Parks.)

Great Salt Lake City. Sunday
afternoon (Dec. 28th 1856

My Dear Mary: this afternoon I arrive at our home from meeting to write to you. I arrived at our home in this City on the evening of the 9th instant, and learned that the California mail left at 9 o'clock on the morning of the same day. I much regretted that I could not have arrived in time to let you know by that mail, that we all arrived safely, through cold weather. From stormy, sage brush and close drives greatly obstructed our way and hindered our progress. For about 200 miles on the last end of the journey, the snow was from one to three feet deep. From about half way, we left our wagon and a [?]. We found this much easier for our animals—but more inconvenient for ourselves, especially as we were finely deprived of a sleeping

Yours affectionately

Part of letter from Orson Hyde to wife Mary Ann, December 28, 1856. (Courtesy of Virginia Woolley Quealy.)

Ann Eliza Vickers Hyde,
Orson's fifth wife. (Courtesy
of Virginia Woolley Quealy.)

Julia Thomene Reinert Hyde,
Orson's sixth wife. (Courtesy
of Virginia Woolley Quealy.)

Elisabeth Josephine Gallier Hyde, Orson's seventh wife. (Courtesy of Adrian Hyde Hess.)

Log home of the Orson Hyde family in Springtown (later Spring City). (Courtesy of Virginia Woolley Quealy.)

Sophia Margaret Lyon Hyde,
when older, Orson's eighth wife.
(Courtesy of Morgan Hyde White).

Rock home of the Orson Hyde family in Spring City. (Courtesy of
Virginia Woolley Quealy.)

Orson Hyde, when older. (Courtesy of Virginia Woolley Quealy.)

. . . *went our way.* . . . *(1852)*

> *And when we had accomplished*
> *those days, we departed and went our*
> *way. . . , with wives and children.*
> —The Acts 21:5

IN their three wagons, July 5, 1852, Orson, his family, and his teamsters jostled along the road to the Missouri River ferry as part of a long line of wagons. They tried to disregard reflective thoughts of leaving their Kanesville home, and were about as successful as in disregarding the ninety-two degree fine weather. Orson had already crossed the plains four times, rapidly with horses. This trip, through the reactions of others, he would experience anew the vastness of the country and the foreverness of emigrant living.

The first night, enjoyment became scarce as the company bedded down the first time in their tents and wagons. A horrendous storm—deafening thunder, piercing lightning, and torrents of rain—lashed them. The quality of wagon covers and tents received definite testing.

Two evenings later all units had ferried over the Missouri and camped at old "Winter Quarters," ready to traverse together the trail north of the Platte River. This company, the Twentieth, was the last to leave Pottawattamie County in 1852. It contained five "Tens," divisions of ten or so wagons each. The Captain was Henry Miller, the "Old Pioneer," all lankiness and sinew, jovially and diligently rugged, with whom in 1850 Orson had first crossed the plains. Captain Miller organized the company and gave instructions. At eight o'clock the next morning, July 8, the "weather wet," the group started. They numbered 63 men, 58 women, 108 children, 63 wagons, 27 horses, and 390 cattle.

Of the total, Orson's outfit consisted of three men (Orson and two teamsters), two women, five children, three wagons, two horses, and seventeen cattle, assigned to the "first Ten."[1] Orson, forty-seven years old, was healthy, heavy, and energetic. Marinda, midway through a pregnancy, felt grateful for the help of Charlotte Johnson, the "domestic" who had been living in their home. Frank was six years old, Alonzo four, and toddler Delia only two and a half. The older daughters, Laura fifteen and Emily twelve, anticipated pleasant association with other young people.

In the Miller Company, Mary Ann, listed as "Miss Price," accompanied her brother William in the third Ten. The families of their brother Charles and their sister Elizabeth, the Richard Bentleys, traveled in the same Ten. William was the captain. William and Mary Ann had two wagons, four horses, and twenty-eight cattle. William drove his own wagon. To drive her wagon Mary Ann had hired William Mason—twenty-one years old, from England like herself. Her teamster's parents were also in this third Ten.[2]

Orson's teamsters, reliable Matthias Cowley and Richard Bee, had worked in the printing office. When the *Frontier Guardian* changed hands, Orson asked them to continue in his employ to help his family move. Matthias Cowley, twenty-two years old and of cheerful disposition, had been with Orson more than three years. Richard Bee, the seventeen year old Scottish lad, had spent a year in the *Guardian* office.

Richard had recently learned teamster skills. Long whip in hand, he must walk beside his oxen, crack the whip in the right places, and shout the right command words. Orson fitted up three wagons, two pulled by oxen and a lighter one pulled by horses. "I was assigned one of the oxteams," Richard recounts, "consisting of three yokes of oxen. I spent a week breaking in my team, or rather breaking myself in, as it was a new business to me. . . . [T]he team . . . [was] only half 'broken,' and I had a circus. . . . My actions were awkward, my expressions not so gentlemanly. . . . [I]t was a considerable time before I and my [six] oxen could understand each other. When . . . leaving Kanesville, I fell in behind a team and teamster that were expert at the business, and my oxen knew enough to follow a wagon."[3]

They left Winter Quarters, and days passed. The group members rode and walked in showers and in sunshine. They traversed hilly country and flat country. They crossed streams wide and narrow, on bridges or by fording. Each afternoon or evening they stopped their wagons in a circle corral. "Our corral was formed . . . ," one emigrant explains, "by the first wagon . . . stop[ping] at a designated place. The next wagon was turned a little to the right and moved forward till the front wheel of one was just opposite the hind wheel of the first and so on till all were disposed of, leaving room in front or rear, whichever was most convenient, for the stock to pass in or out. A few men stationed at these openings could keep all the cattle in very easily and we could better defend ourselves against Indians or other enemies." Good health prevailed. Orson, "full of life and vigor," rode around and showed personal interest in the welfare of everyone.

A week on the trail brought the company to the "crossing" of the Loup Fork River, the wide and deep quicksand-bottomed tributary of the Platte that had been impossible for Orson and his companions to cross on their return two years before. During emigration season an old friend from Kanesville operated a huge ferry boat on it, a rope ferry propelled by the river current. The ferry carried three large wagons on a load.[4]

As Richard Bee gazed across this river he had no inkling of the adventure the flowing expanse would afford him. "[W]e made preparations for ferrying the wagons," his account tells, "as the stream was so swollen we could not ford. The [loose] cattle we had to swim, and volunteers were called for to guide the herd across. . . . I offered myself . . . , not knowing any thing about the treacherous quicksands in the bed of the river. I was stationed below to keep the herd inclined towards the opposite bank, as they would be inclined to land on the side they went in. . . . [Driven by the boys on ponies whose duty it was to urge the loose cattle along,] [t]he herd presently reached me. I began to shout to turn the swaying herd. I realized I had been sinking, but did not know the cause. I . . . could not move. I was too proud or independent to cry for help, although hundreds of men, women and children were on the bank within saving reach. I was now surrounded by the cattle, but as fast as a post, immovable.

"As a drowning man would grasp at a straw," Richard continues, "I took hold of an ox's tail and hung on for dear life. He presently pulled me from my predicament, and I clung hard and fast till he landed me safely on the opposite shore. Then I thanked the Lord for my preservation from such an untimely death. . . . After all the company and effects were across, we proceeded on our journey as light and merry as a happy and jovial crowd could make it."[5]

Traversing the sand hills and bluffs beyond the Loup required several days, and Orson recalled vividly that here, the previous summer, Indians took his provisions and supplies. This year the emigrants had heard of no problems with Indians.

By now camp routine had become natural. "Every thing was orderly and systematic . . . ," Orson's daughter Laura explains. "We traveled twenty miles a day [or less], stopping an hour for a cold lunch and to rest the animals. Our hot meal was prepared when we stopped for the night. When the halt was called the oxen were unyoked, the fires lighted, and preparations for supper began. Supper over, the bugle sounded, calling the company to prayers, after which dancing, singing, and chatting were indulged in till nine-thirty or ten o'clock when again the bugle sounding signaled all to retire. Every family brought with them what books they could, and by lending and borrowing formed a circulating library which helped to pass away the time which otherwise would have hung heavy on our hands."[6]

Filling water kegs was a regular chore. On the trail the kegs became warm in the sun, and folks preferred drinking from cold refreshing streams. However, they were grateful for warm water when streams were distant.

July 23, with Fort Kearney seen across the river, an interesting man overtook the company. Headed for California, he had started from the Missouri River with a dog and loaded cart. His cart already discarded, he now had his dog and a gun. Orson offered to buy his dog. The traveler consented. He also accepted a meal. The next day a man in the fifth Ten volunteered to take the "Dog Cart Californian" as far as Salt Lake City.

At the beginning of the prairie section of their journey—facing a few hundred miles of a vast undulating sea of grass, more sandy roads, and the Platte River still to their left—they topped a dividing ridge. Here "an almost indescribable scene was presented to our view," Richard Bee relates. "An innumerable herd of buffalo was spread out before us, extending, according to approximate guesses—looking through telescopes, &c.—[over] an area of about 100 square miles. The prairie was literally black with them. Old frontiersmen who were along with our company estimated . . . about 1,000,000 head, migrating from their winter to their summer range. . . . [Though concerned about] stampeding among our own cattle, . . . we kept traveling, and as we approached, the vast herd seemed to sway to the right of us, all moving in concert with the leaders. . . . [W]hen night came we formed our camp. . . . A hunt was proposed and several parties started out. . . ."

Orson smiled at the excited optimism of the first-time buffalo hunters. He knew well that buffalo ran, as one traveler described, "as swift as horses, and although the old animals are the ugliest racers of any brutes, they get over the ground very fast, and an inexperienced rider is soon left to admire their beauty 'in the distance.'" In this and subsequent hunts, the bullets of a few marksmen successfully pierced thick buffalo skins. Men butchered felled animals, and the campers savored delicious buffalo steaks and stews. Extra meat was dried for future meals.[7]

Distant buffalo—large herds and small groups—became a common sight, but the travelers encountered near herds infrequently. Richard Bee writes of one apprehensive afternoon that "we had camped early . . . , to give our cattle and horses a chance of good pasture, as the grass and vegetation was luxurious. . . . Oftentimes feed along the line of travel was rather scant. We had not been long in camp when a moving black mass of something hove in sight. Our men were called out to collect the cattle together and drive them some distance from the camp to prevent a stampede, as a herd of buffalo, which the mass proved to be, were steering for the river to drink, and our camp lay directly in their course. At such times nothing could turn them. On they came, as it were with the velocity of the wind, and with a pandemonium of noises. . . . Some of our men . . . prepared for the onslaught by getting their guns in readiness. The herd at last reached us, ran directly through the camp to the river, crossed the river and kept on their course. However some of the herd was stopped by the rifles of our men, and seven of the beasts were brought low, some falling right by the wagons. There were no other casualties, and we remained in camp all the next day cutting up and drying the meat."

Except for occasional buffalo excitement, the prairie presented little change in scenery from day to day, and periodic evening dances provided a gala treat. On the night of July 30, Matthias Cowley had guard duty while a lively dance progressed. As his rounds, and calling out the hours of the night, brought him near the dancers, he shouted in cadence:

> Nine o'clock in advance; all is right;
> [A]nd oh, how I wish I could dance with you tonight![8]

The lighthearted occurrences helped the travelers to accept more readily the somber things, such as new graves along the trail, dug by companies ahead of them. Cholera caused most of those deaths, and the Miller Company suffered some cholera too. An attack seized Orson's son Frank, but he recovered. Less fortunate was Mary Ann's teamster, young William Mason. The excruciating throes of the disease—severe diarrhea, intense vomiting, and sharp cramps—wrung his life from him August 8. Lamentably, when William became ill that morning, a Sunday, he told no one. For extra rest, the company halted at two o'clock, and Orson addressed the congregation in worship services, having no idea that William Mason lay apart from the group suffering. When eventually found, William responded to no medication. Death came at eight o'clock in the evening. Sorrowful, William's parents and Mary Ann felt the attack unwarranted. Repeatedly cautioned to refrain from drinking stagnant water, William had refused to listen.

After her teamster's passing, Mary Ann drove her own wagon. Up to now three women had been driving wagons, lighter ones, with horse teams. After today four women were teamsters.[9]

August 9 the company camped opposite Chimney Rock, an imposing mountain jutting up from the plain on the other side of the Platte, its slender top pointing to the sky. The prairies would soon end. Before passing landmark Chimney Rock, the scenery north of the trail on their own side of the river had already become more interesting, with bluffs shaped like castles and fortresses.

Another change: the travelers now saw more Indians, but the natives were friendly. However, one episode caused great consternation. Laura and several friends stopped to gather flowers while the wagons lumbered on. Indians appeared suddenly and began talking with the surprised flower pickers. Pretty Laura, with her sunny manner, attracted the visitors, and they wanted to buy her. The boys thought the bargaining a joke and asked how much they would pay. The Indians offered two horses. The boys agreed to sell Laura the following morning. The natives departed, and the young folks scrambled to catch up with the wagon train, dismissing the incident as trivial.

Disbelief registered on several faces the next morning when Indians arrived in camp, two horses in tow, and demanded Laura. Shocked, Orson and other men arbitrated decisively to prevent the Indians from snatching her. Peace was made with gifts of sugar and flour. After the disappointed

Indians took their presents and horses away, the young folks received the lecture of their lives. No more did they bargain with Indians.[10]

The Miller Company traveled faster than some companies of Saints who left Kanesville before them, and during the first two weeks of August they approached, mingled with, and passed several groups. Seeing former neighbors brought pleasant snatches of conversation. A few complications arose, however, with companies in close proximity. The morning of August 14 the Miller Company cattle guards discovered that their stock had mixed with the cattle of the Seventeenth Company, camped one and a half miles west of them, and of the Fifteenth Company, camped one mile east of them. Men and boys worked strenuously "disentangling" the animals into the proper herds.

This day the travelers viewed, across the river, another significant landmark, the outpost trading establishment Fort John, often called Fort Laramie, located near where the Laramie River flowed into the Platte. The emigrants saw only from a distance what their *Emigrants' Guide* described as "about twelve houses, enclosed by a wall eleven feet high. The wall and houses are built of *adobes*, or Spanish brick." The fort marked halfway to the Valley. Winter Quarters was 522 miles east, and Great Salt Lake City 509 miles west.

The next day an anxious experience occurred when—after several miles of hard work for the teams, jolting over rough bluffs beyond the fort—the company forded to the south of the Platte in "water up to our axeltrees." Laura and Emily rode in Richard's wagon. Richard recounts that the wide river had a "rocky bottom, [and] a swift raging current. The teamsters generally had to walk, driving their teams across the ford. I was following [another wagon] with my team and as they were good to keep close up to the wagon ahead of them, I . . . [decided] to ride and drive instead of having to wade the river. . . . [At the] swiftest part of the current . . . some sheep came floating down and got tangled up with my cattle. . . . My leaders turned around to the right with their heads toward the wagon, and nearly upset it, so that I was obliged to jump out on the off side of the team. . . . [I] labored the leaders [with my whip] over their heads till their chains slackened and the wagon got righted, after scaring the two daughters of Elder Hyde who were riding in my wagon and also Brother and Sister Hyde who were in the next wagon following. I . . . [should have] obey[ed] counsel."[11]

Beyond Fort Laramie came transitions. Level sandy roads became rocky up-and-down roads, the beginning of traversing hills and mountains. For fuel on the plains the travelers had used buffalo chips, with their excessive smoke. During the remainder of the journey fuel would usually be timber or sagebrush. Sagebrush would be the main vegetation over the upcoming five hundred miles, different from the grassy world of recent weeks. Sage ranged from six inches high to ten feet high, depending on its location. A transition from staying on one side of the river was that in the week following the sighting of Fort Laramie and fording the Platte, the company forded the river twice more, back to the north side and then to the south side again.[12]

As August days passed, Henry Miller and Orson felt increasingly pressed for time. Summer would soon be over. They had previously crossed the mountains in the fall and wished no repeat of their experiences with cold and snow. They made plans to hasten travel.

Monday, August 23, they sent out scouts to find a good place to stop for a few days to rest and pasture the weary teams, to mend wagons, and to catch up on camp chores. Everything needed to be in good shape for the upcoming rougher roads that would be even harder on wagons and teams than the many past labors through sand. The company needed time to do thoroughly the things before done only in odd moments. The scouts found the ideal place, with plenty of wood and grass, two miles beyond Deer Creek. Wagons rolled and then camped.

One reason for stopping in this area was a known nearby bank of stone coal. Men could use this for fires for necessary blacksmithing, such as mending chains, shoeing oxen and horses, also cutting and welding iron wagon tires to fit snugly on their wooden felloes. For weeks the dry atmosphere had continually caused wooden wagon wheels to shrink, allowing iron tires to roll off. Watching a large iron rim roll away from one's wagon was disconcerting. Each time, though, someone retrieved it. A regular chore ever since coming to the prairies had been the temporary measure of "setting tires." This entailed "tacking thin pieces of wood to the felloes, then heating the tire with whatever fuel was available and setting it, . . . not always preserv[ing] the roundness of the wheels."

The fetched coal proved unsatisfactory. Then young men cut wood, dug a pit, piled it high with the timber pieces, covered them with dirt, and burned them slowly to make charcoal for smithing. This brought memories to Orson of the summer in Kirtland, Ohio, when as a young man he earned his living making charcoal. The wood supply near camp also provided means to mend wagons and yokes.

During the stopover the hunters procured buffalo, and many hands prepared it for drying. Other kinds of fresh meat had been eaten on the journey, including antelope and sage hens, but buffalo remained the most common.

Of a personal nature, also, much was done. Clothes were mended and washed. Dust was swept and shaken out of corners. Baths were taken. Many smells mingled—campfire smoke, drying meat, hot metal, clothes drying on bushes in the sun, bubbling stew, and baking bread.[13]

While camped and accomplishing good things, a frightening event jarred peace when Orson's youngest daughter suffered a serious accident. Marinda and Charlotte had two hams boiling in a large caldron on a hot fire, and the children played nearby. Suddenly a piercing cry rent the air. Little Delia had fallen backwards into the caldron. Richard Bee happened to be close. He ran to the pot, plunged his hands into the bubbling broth, and, heedless of the threat to himself, lifted soaked and steaming Delia, her dress dripping. "The child's body was frightfully scalded," Richard tells. "[H]er life was despaired of, but by careful nursing, and the ministrations of the priesthood, claiming God's blessing," she survived. Orson voiced unbounded gratitude to the Lord that with only seven people on earth to whom he was endeared as family, this precious one could remain with him. Richard's hands recovered.

Fine weather and three dances blessed the encampment. Monday evening hosted the first dance. At the second dance, Tuesday evening, violin strains, or "fiddlin'," enervated young and old in merry capering until eleven o'clock, three or four sets adorning the green at a time.

Just before the third dance, Thursday evening, a meeting convened. Captain Miller declared that they had done better than many groups, but ahead the way would be rougher, and feed for the animals would be scarcer. Also, waiting for each other to make repairs would require precious time. He proposed that the company travel in Tens rather than the entire company together. This would help them go faster and more comfortably. Smaller herds of animals could utilize small patches of feed that would not be enough for the whole herd in one place. The group voted unanimously to follow their leader's counsel. Orson admonished the people "to be just as obedient to the Captain of Ten as you have been to the Captain of Fifty. If you do this you shall arrive safely in the Valley."

Dancing in the firelight lasted until two o'clock in the morning, four or five sets at a time stepping to lilting music. This was the farewell ball before the groups separated.[14]

August 27 witnessed tender scenes. Men segregated the cattle, and in turn the Tens rolled out of camp. Friendships grown strong over the past several weeks were severed. Orson's heartstrings, as well, stretched. Mary Ann, in William's Ten, would travel more slowly than the advance group. Though Orson and Mary Ann had spent little time alone together these weeks, they had seen each other every day. How soon would they again enjoy this privilege?

In Orson's family on the trail, concern surrounded Delia. Though in pain in a jostling wagon, her body red and tender, each day brought a little improvement.

The scenery changed too. On a ferry the wagons for the last time crossed the Platte, the life-giving river that stretched from the mountains to the Missouri. From here to the Sweetwater River, sixty or so miles, lay desolate country with only rare creeks and few good springs. The company avoided several "unfit" alkali swamps and springs. They stopped at the dry lake designated in their *Guide* as a good place to gather saleratus (baking soda). Over a broad area the white crystals lay in a bed about a foot deep. The travelers scooped up many pounds to "rise . . . bread with, and . . . to wash with."

Sight of the Sweetwater River, wide and clear, prompted cheering words. Along the Sweetwater the travelers investigated famous Independence Rock, which resembled a huge sleeping tortoise on the edge of the sagebrush plain. Many emigrants' names had been painted on its sides. The *Guide* said that it measured "about six hundred yards long, and a hundred and twenty wide, composed of hard Granite." A few miles farther the wagons passed the cleft of Devil's Gate where the Sweetwater sluiced in a chasm between rocks four hundred feet high. Those people who walked over to see it closer came away impressed. The way continued winding, following the Sweetwater, with gradual ascents and some descents over arid plains. One day, snow-capped peaks—the Wind River Mountains—appeared in the distance to the right ahead. Each day they grew loftier. When these magnificent mountains finally towered north of the wagon train, more massive than most people in the company had imagined anything could be, the last Sweetwater ford was crossed. The next major traverse would be South Pass.

On high South Pass, after miles of long gentle rises and dips, the people exulted to see a stream running the same direction they headed. They had reached the Pacific side of the Rocky Mountains, had crossed the Continental Divide, the backbone of North America. Four times they forded Black's Fork. Weather became colder. Feed became scarcer. Near Fort Bridger, Orson's group found a good camp ground. And they had begun consistently meeting people from Salt Lake Valley, with provisions, coming to meet their emigrating friends.[15]

Saturday, September 18, the company descended Echo Canyon, where, in narrow places between high canyon walls, the travelers looked up at rust-red perpendicular cliffs and felt like they were crawling beneath the bows of colossal ships. The children delighted in scrambling up into the narrow gullies between "ships," facing the mountain walls, and shouting "Hello." The walls answered back. Another pleasant experience occurred in Echo Canyon in the evening when they came into a camp being set up by a company of missionaries going east. In the group were John Brown, with whom Orson had crossed the plains eastward in 1850, and Elder Orson Pratt. The two groups camped together and spent Sunday in preaching and reunion and resting.

Beyond Echo Canyon the advanced division of the Miller Company forded the Weber River and then began the toil over high mountains that appeared unconquerable. Wagons and teams and herds and people followed the trail up and around and up some more, many times, and then down and around and down some more, many times. They arrived in the Valley on September 22. Friends and relatives, having learned of their approach, greeted them on the main street. Teamsters gave the "halt" command to horses and oxen.[16]

PART THREE

(1852–1878)

> *. . . saith the Lord, . . . Therefore my people shall know my name; therefore they shall know in that day that I am he that doth speak: behold, it is I.*
>
> *How beautiful upon the mountains are the feet of him that bringeth good tidings, that publisheth peace; that bringeth good tidings of good, that publisheth salvation; that saith unto Zion, Thy God reigneth! Thy watchmen shall lift up the voice; with the voice together shall they sing: for they shall see eye to eye, when the Lord shall bring again Zion.*
>
> —Isaiah 52:5-8

. . . *build*. . . . *(1852–1855)*

> *Thou art called to labor in my vineyard, and to build up my church, and to bring forth Zion, that it may rejoice upon the hills and flourish.*
>
> —Doctrine and Covenants 39:13

WHEN Orson and his family, with their three wagons of worldly goods, pulled into Great Salt Lake City on September 22, 1852, friends had a place for them to stay until Orson built a home. Marinda joyfully renewed past acquaintances. The children soon ran about with new playmates. Orson felt elated that again he could associate closely with his brethren of the First Presidency and the Quorum of the Twelve.

Because Orson had been unable to bring a printing press with him, he had no newspaper to edit. The *Deseret News* hired Matthias Cowley, Orson's printer's assistant turned teamster, but they had no positions for Orson or his other assistant, Richard Bee. Orson had enough means to support his family at present, but before long he would need new resources for a livelihood. He and Richard accomplished a difficult wood-gathering expedition into the mountains the day after their Valley arrival. Richard eventually found employment elsewhere.[1]

A report in the *Deseret News*, when Orson read it, gave him insights into the Pottawattamie County, Iowa, problems of the previous season. Brigham Young had preached about these, and the newspaper published his sermon. He said that "every mobbing difficulty will add glory upon the heads of the humble, faithful and contrite in heart; it serves to prove [them] and give them experience, . . . preparatory for the saints to enter into their rest, and for the wicked to receive their punishment. . . . I thank the Lord Almighty, that he turned the key . . . last fall, and caused a tremendous commotion among the political elements. . . ; this gathered a great many more saints than if it had been fair weather all the time. This clashing . . . stirred up the people in Pottawattamie, and then they wanted to go to the mountains."[2]

Orson observed marvelous progress in Great Salt Lake City. In addition to the red sandstone Council House, in use for almost two years, a Social Hall neared completion. Large, built of adobes, it had two floors. A Tabernacle now stood on the southwest corner of the Temple block, the outside plastered and whitewashed, the inside floored. Because congregations gathered more numerous than the 2,000 to 3,000 it held, a brush-covered bowery had been added to the north for summer use. This accommodated 8,000. Around the Temple Block a sandstone and adobe wall was being built. The city had also grown by many new dwellings, but settlers had to traverse ever more miles to procure timber for construction and fuel. Because of the problem, this season's immigrants, rolling into the city regularly, received encouragement to settle beyond the Great Salt Lake Valley, particularly to the south.[3]

Mary Ann and her brother William, in the Price division of the Henry Miller Company, arrived September 30 and agreed to obey the counsel to continue on south. Two days later they set out for Provo, a few days' drive. Again Mary Ann and Orson said good-byes, but this farewell was temporary. Orson would soon build a home with a place for Mary Ann. Now she could reside with the Hyde family as a known wife, for the Church had publicly acknowledged the practice of plural marriage. Under the direction of Brigham Young, in a conference in August, Orson Pratt had announced the principle and discoursed about it.

At present, the Hyde family item of prime interest was the baby soon to be born to Marinda. The event occurred November 10, and the new son received the name Heber John. As had been the case for more than two years, Charlotte rendered kind assistance to Marinda.

Orson and Marinda discussed Charlotte. She and Marinda cooperated well. Should she be invited to be a wife rather than a domestic servant? Orson approached Brigham Young about taking the step, and President Young approved. Charlotte accepted Orson's proposal and became his wife November 21, 1852, for time and eternity.[4]

Plans for the Hyde home were being drawn by Truman O. Angell, with whom Orson had worked so closely in 1846 to finish the Nauvoo Temple. Orson's assigned double homelot, two and a half acres, faced the middle of the north side of the Temple Block. The home's upstairs windows would overlook the Temple grounds. Once begun, construction progressed rapidly.[5]

Orson preached regularly. One Sunday he talked about the future, the Second Coming of the Savior, and mentioned his own confusion about some Bible statements. It says that the Lord will come "as a thief in the night," also that "every eye shall see him," that he will "come in the clouds of heaven." Orson wondered if this represented translation mistakes. Brigham Young spoke after Orson and explained that these seemingly contradictory verses declare that the Lord will appear more than once. The Savior, President Young said, "will suddenly appear to his saints, in the temple, and at another time he will come in the clouds of heaven." He elaborated about these two appearances.[6] Orson felt grateful to be here with the Brethren where he could quickly have questions answered.

November 27 Orson was elected to the Utah Territory Legislative Council. He and Parley P. Pratt represented Salt Lake County. December 13, in the red sandstone Council House, the season's sessions began, and they continued for five weeks, until January 21.

An elating pause from legislative matters occurred the evening of December 22, in the Council Chamber, when eleven of the Quorum of the Twelve met: Orson Hyde, Parley P. Pratt, Wilford Woodruff, John Taylor, George A. Smith, Amasa M. Lyman, Ezra T. Benson, Charles C. Rich, Lorenzo Snow, Erastus Snow, and Franklin D. Richards. Orson Pratt was serving in Washington, D.C. Having this many of the Twelve together had rarely happened. "We met with the heart of one man," Orson said afterward, "in our faith towards each other, the Presidency, and the glorious work in which we are engaged." They planned to continue these meetings weekly. The group enjoyed a festive New Year's Day 1853 when they visited the homes of the First Presidency and the Patriarch of the Church. Two spirited bands followed them in their rounds and played outside each residence.[7]

Orson's public positions increased: January 14, 1853, reconfirmed as a Regent of the University of Deseret; January 17, made associate director of the Provo Canal and Irrigation Company; and January 21, made associate director of the Provo Manufacturing Company. In the Provo positions he acted as an adviser, with associate director George A. Smith doing most of the on-site encouraging and overseeing. Orson remained a member of the United States Bar, and February 7, as prosecuting attorney for Utah, argued a court case.[8]

In Utah Territory, civil proceedings and church proceedings often intermingled, but the groundbreaking ceremony for the Temple on the Temple Block, February 14, was definitely a church event. Saints gathered, warmly dressed. Bands played. From a carriage, with Orson and others of the Twelve around it, Brigham Young preached. Heber C. Kimball, hands uplifted toward heaven, offered the dedicatory prayer. Counselors Kimball and Richards of the First Presidency each swung the pick to help loosen a square of frozen ground. Orson Hyde swung also, followed by others of the Twelve. President Young shoveled out this first piece of turf, then "declared the ground broken for the Temple, [and] blessed the people in the name of the Lord." After this, many loosened and shoveled a little earth.

Every working day during the following weeks, diligent labor transpired at the Temple site. Shovelful by shovelful, men dug, lifted, and hauled soil. Church leaders, including the Twelve, worked as exhaustingly as everyone else. A goal had been set to lay the Temple cornerstones the first day of April conference. The effort succeeded.

April 6, a warm sunshiny day, the ceremonies included a dedicatory prayer at each corner of the Temple, after selected brethren set the stones in place. At the fourth corner, the northeast one, Orson delivered the last cornerstone-laying dedicatory prayer. He thanked the Almighty for causing "the wilderness and desert to rejoice," and he asked for blessings and protection in rearing the Temple. "Hasten thou the period, O Lord," Orson's eloquent petitions continued, "when this thine House, in the midst of the mountains, shall receive the Top-stone with the shouts of gladness, and be completed, and nations flow unto it—when people shall say, 'Come ye, and let us go up to the mountain of the Lord, to the house of the God of Jacob; and he will teach us of his ways, and we will walk in his paths: for out of Zion shall go forth the law,' making manifest . . . every true principle . . . that will remove the vail of the covering that has been cast over all people; and the Gentiles shall come to the light of Zion, and kings to the brightness of her rising. Roll on the hour, Eternal Parent, when the intelligence and knowledge obtained by thy servants, on this consecrated spot, shall prove a beacon light to the nations who are floating on the sea of time in a dark, cloudy day."[9]

The cornerstone ceremonies began a five-day general conference. The last day Brigham Young talked about manufacturing sugar. "The erecting [of] a suitable building, and preparing the machinery for operation," he said, "is in the hands of Elder Orson Hyde. . . . It forms a part of our public works."

Sugar-making had originally been planned as an independent enterprise, to be located in Provo, and construction began on a building for it. Wagons carrying the mammoth crates of machinery, and the large copper boilers weighing hundreds of pounds each, straggled into the Salt Lake Valley the previous fall. Most of them lumbered on to Provo.

Some of the machinery, however, stayed in the City. To experiment with sugar-making, men attached the hydraulic press to the water works of the public machine shop, formerly the blacksmith shop, on a corner of the Temple Block. Sugar beets had been planted in the spring in anticipation of the machinery coming. February 10, workers had dumped the first beets into the washer. February 12, the hydraulic press made its first squeeze, with about four bushels of beets. February 18, the first molasses ran out a spout. The syrup was dark, but hopes ran high for future success. Orson published a letter extolling sugar and other products that might be forthcoming.

The intricacies of February's small experiment illustrated the Provo location for sugar manufacture to be inconvenient. This project loomed as a more monumental undertaking than foreseen. Already much private and Church money had been invested to purchase the machinery and get it to Utah, and further debts mounted rapidly. Church leaders decided that for success the Church must take over the supervision, the debts, and the construction. The venture needed to be close to headquarters. Sugar manufacture thus had come under the control of the Quorum of the Twelve, with Brigham Young announcing, in March, Orson Hyde as the general manager.[10] Elder Hyde was better prepared for the job than some of the other Church leaders, having long ago, in Kirtland, worked in and then superintended, huge carding machines run by water power.

In March, Orson had traveled to Provo, spent a few days, and arranged for the balance of the sugar machinery to be brought to a site a few miles southeast of Great Salt Lake City, on "Big Kanyon Creek." The area eventually became known as Sugarhouse. April 11, the day following general conference meetings, in spite of uncomfortable wind, dust, and a little rain, Orson, Brigham Young, architect Truman Angell, and surveyor Jesse Fox rode to Big Canyon Creek and studied the terrain. They made decisions and drove stakes into the ground to mark the dam and the raceway. For two more weeks Truman Angell studied the books that came with the machinery and drew preliminary plans. April 21, men drove stakes to mark where earth should be removed for the tailrace, the wheelhouse, and the main building. Brother Angell thought the site ideal for the sugar works.[11]

Orson moved temporarily to the location to oversee. By April 20 he had started arranging for workers. April 25, Truman Angell came and instructed. The first Tuesday evening in May, Orson preached at Big Cottonwood, an area nearby, and raised men and teams enough to move dirt during the remainder of the week. He planned to begin to haul rock to the site the following Monday. If he could procure lime for mortar, workers could start laying rock the next Tuesday.

At the sugar works during the summer, numerous chores and projects needed manpower and supplies. These often materialized slowly and after much effort on Orson's part. Progress, consequently, suffered continued setbacks and delays. Orson gradually turned the superintending of the work over to others.[12]

Rewards and concerns fluctuated in Orson's personal world also. He felt contentment the summer of 1853 with his entire family, including Mary Ann, at last under one roof, working together, laughing together, praying together, and adapting to each other. Marinda and Mary Ann, good friends, found pleasure living side by side again. Charlotte, however, found adjusting to being a plural wife more difficult than she had expected.

The family garden showed promise of good vegetables and melons. This hope was diminished June 18 when a flood caused by heavy rain carried off part of the patch.

The Hyde home and yard still needed much finishing and furnishing, which partly required financial means. When a merchant friend offered ploughs to Orson for resale, Orson accepted. He advertised them in the newspaper, May 28, and again July 10. He would "exchange the fine lot of Ploughs . . . for good wall rock, pine lumber, wheat, oats, barley, hay and cheese, (if well cured) cash, cows, oxen, mules, sheep or goats."

Another undertaking, getting his year's supply of firewood, required excursions into the mountain canyons. Though a strenuous activity, the results brought satisfaction returning home driving oxen pulling heavy loads of logs. One time a mishap caused a delay at the mouth of Parley's Canyon while Orson readjusted his load. A recently arrived English brother stopped. After introductions the man looked surprised and said incredulously, "I never thought I would see an Apostle hauling wood with a yoke of oxen."[13] Orson chuckled.

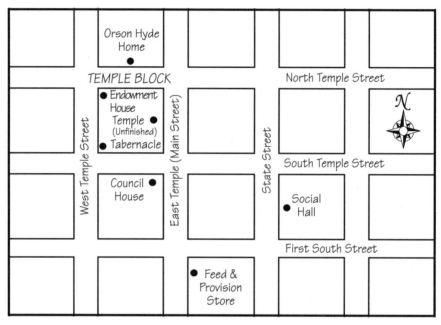

Salt Lake City

Orson's public service generally brought him satisfaction, but in his limited practice of law he encountered problems, even embarrassment. While defending cases professionally, to obtain cash, he sometimes became over-animated. This happened particularly when he pounded verbally upon those whom he felt guilty because of their own foolishness. Fiery vocalization came naturally to him, augmented by his years in Kanesville, where he had been "the law" and circumstances demanded strong words. Only in a half joking manner, Brigham Young publicly chastised the "chief apostle" for these agitated performances.

The conspicuous rebuke from President Young hit Orson hard. But reasoning brought discernment. The berating had nothing to do with Brother Brigham questioning Orson's loyalty. Brigham Young had demonstrated in the past, and continued to indicate, unquestioned trust that with complete fidelity Elder Hyde would fulfill his duties. The refiner's fire of suffering had taught Orson obedience. The President manifested confidence that because of Orson's inner strength he would hold up under pressure, whereas other men's resolve might crumple. Tongue lashings from Brigham Young would bring no rebellion from Orson Hyde. And the public reproof might inspire others to gain the determination and the unity of direction essential to the building up of the Kingdom of God here in the wilderness.

July 23, by letter, Orson apologized to Brigham Young for his public gracelessness and admitted that the scolding had helped him to crystalize his "own convictions of duty, propriety and decorum." Henceforth he would try "to maintain that self respect which the priesthood so reasonably and justly requires of those who are honored with being its bearers." He asked pardon. Because of the episode, he wrote, he had "concluded to decline taking any more Law cases to prosecute or defend, except at the request or suggestion of my presiding officers in the Church." His law work as a public servant would continue, it turned out, for in August he was again elected to serve on the Utah Territory Legislative Council.

During late summer and the autumn the annual droves of immigrants arrived, and one friend from Pottawattamie County brought to Orson the remainder of the money owed for the *Frontier Guardian* Office. The amount was $1,153.92, a definite boon to the Hydes.[14]

As October general conference neared, Church leaders discussed, and decided to sponsor, a settlement in the eastern portion of Utah Territory. The site lay one hundred miles east of Great Salt Lake City in the high country south of Fort Bridger. The main purpose of the outpost would be to improve relations with the Indians. Beginnings of a colony in the area in 1852 had been abandoned after Brigham Young received word that unhappy nearby Indians planned an attack. Now prospects had improved. Orson would be in charge of this challenging "Green River Mission" in the mountain wilderness.

In an afternoon October conference session, Brigham Young announced the names of apostles and others who would be in charge of gathering fifty families each to strengthen a number of settlements. Similarly, "Elder Orson Hyde [is] appointed to raise a company, to make a permanent settlement at Green river." The conference sanctioned these actions.

In the following morning session, October 8, the congregation listened with rapt attention as men received calls to serve missions. Orson read the list of the thirty-nine individuals thus far selected for the Green River settlement. James Brown, among them, recorded the purpose of the mission:

> Elder Orson Hyde is chosen to lead the company to somewhere in the region of the Green River, select a place, and there build an outpost from which to operate as peacemakers among the Indians, to preach civilization to them, to try and teach them how to cultivate the soil, to instruct them in the arts and sciences if possible, and by this means prevent trouble for our frontier settlements and emigrant companies. We are to identify our interests with theirs, even to marrying among them, if we will be permitted to take the young daughters of the chief and leading men, and have them dressed like civilized people, and educated.

It is thought that by forming this kind of an alliance we can have more power to do them good, and keep peace among the adjacent tribes as also with our own people.

It is known that there are wicked and cruel white men among the Indians, working up the spirit of robbery and murder among the savage tribes, and against the Mormon people. Our missionary call is to take our lives in our hands, as true patriots, and head off, and operate as far as possible against the wicked plots of white men who are trying to carry their plans to success through the Indians, and possibly set the savages on the war path, that the government might send troops out, and thus make a better market for the schemers' herds of cattle and horses.[15]

Because winter would soon preside over mountain areas, Orson instructed the first group of Green River men to be ready to travel by October 18. These men—young, healthy, and enterprising—would take no families with them. Each was to provide what he could of the necessities for the settlement. Orson asked for twenty wagons, basically a wagon for each two men, with oxen to pull it, as well as "one milch [milk] cow and a beef creature" for each two men. Supplies for each person included three hundred pounds of flour, seventy-five pounds of seed wheat, a half bushel of oats, a peck of barley, and forty pounds "of the seed ends of potatoes, nicely done up to be secure against frost." Also needed were seed corn, a variety of garden seeds, fruit seeds, arms and ammunition for defense and for securing game, and all kinds of tools and implements for farming and for mechanical operations.

Orson and the men received assistance in gathering the items. Families and friends helped. Congregations of Saints, called wards, helped. Merchants helped. The men met October 18, and they still needed many things. During the next two weeks they and Orson recruited, an activity at which Orson was well practiced.

In the Council House the evening of November 1, they met again. Everything had been gathered and the wagons carefully packed. Thirty-nine men reported themselves ready to start the next morning. In the meeting, three of the Twelve—Orson Hyde, Parley P. Pratt, and Ezra T. Benson—appointed officers for the Green River company. Elijah B. Ward, who had learned Indian languages, would act as "Pilot, and Shoshone, Utah and Flat Head [Indian tribes] Interpreter." His Shoshone wife would accompany him. The apostles blessed and instructed the men. The next day Orson waved farewell as this initial group started out in the early afternoon. In addition to their twenty loaded wagons and their ninety-three cattle, they had eight horses and mules.

"When this company was fairly under way," Orson tells, "I set right about raising another company of volunteers to follow the first; and in less than two weeks time I had fifty-three young, hardy men, well fitted out with large supplies of everything necessary—26 wagons, and from 2 to 5 yoke of oxen to the wagon; besides some 50 head of beef cattle and nearly as many milch cows;—mechanics of all sorts and kinds necessary;—tools and implements in abundance; besides clothing, blankets, leather, nails, &c., &c." The men included Orson's brother-in-law, William Price, still unmarried, who had moved from Provo to Great Salt Lake City the previous spring. This group, like the earlier one, held a meeting, November 14, where apostles blessed and instructed them. While organizing the second group, Orson received news that the first had arrived at Fort Bridger on November 12, "having had very good weather, good luck, and good health."

Orson planned to overtake the second group before they reached their destination.[16] At the outpost he would help to get everything in order and then return home. But complications delayed him two weeks in starting. Then, even on a sturdy mount, he encountered a difficult ride in the cold, over steep and snowy and rough mountain roads. "[C]loudy but pleasant" weather welcomed him at his destination, "Fort Supply," at about four o'clock the afternoon of December 9. The name of the settlement indicated the hope of its future role as a site where crops might be raised and stock maintained to supply weary emigrants with food and animals and other goods for the last mountainous section of their trek into the Valley. If this could be done, wagon companies from the east could start across the plains with lighter loads.

Orson approved of the location of Fort Supply, thirteen miles south of Fort Bridger. A broad plain contained abundant grassland and vast space for crops. The hills to the west supported ample trees for timber and fuel. Situated between two streams (Willow Creek, running down from the western hills, and Smith's Fork of the Green River), the outpost had plentiful water. North of the settlement the two streams joined. Fort Supply seemed an apt name. Bounteous products should be forthcoming.

The industriousness of the men impressed Orson. They had cut a great amount of timber, hauled it to the site, and constructed a blockhouse, cabins, and a fort wall. The blockhouse, a well-designed structure, had four identical wings, or rooms, that joined at the corners, forming a center room. This middle room contained two stories, the lower for storage, the upper the guardhouse. From here the countryside in all directions could be observed. All outside walls had portholes. The fort measured about twenty rods square, its picket walls built of logs sixteen feet long and a foot in diameter at the large ends. The large ends had been buried, touching each other, in a trench dug four feet into the ground. The skyward ends had been axed to points. Extra poles had been fitted and fastened snugly into the upper gaps. In one wall a wide gate allowed the herders to drive the stock in each night for safety from mountainmen (the few who were in some ways untrustworthy) and Indians.

Compact cabins, facing inward, began to line two of the outside walls of the enclosure.

The men reported to Orson that while coming over the mountains, wolves attacked and injured some of their livestock. During these few weeks in Green River country, men and animals had suffered from cold weather. Mountainmen had visited the compound recently and seemed envious. This, and rumors of Indian discontent, caused the company to maintain a regular guard rotation, with captains for every ten men, firearms in perfect order, and their "powder dry." Besides guard duty, and spending energy hauling timber out of the hills for fencing and construction, they sent out scouts regularly to explore the country. They held meetings, as well, and had classes in Indian languages.

To encourage the settlers in their laborious tasks, Orson held a meeting "at early candle light" in the blockhouse the evening of his arrival. He spoke inspiringly to the several dozen men. The next day, in weather still pleasant, he walked around and conversed. The men's work and defenses pleased him. He applauded their choice of location.

To assist in their assignment to befriend the Indians, Orson wrote a letter to "Washakeete" (Washakie), the area Shoshone chief, by reputation an honorable leader. Orson appointed five brethren to deliver the letter. Orson's friendly message used Indian phrases. He first reviewed what had transpired:

> Respected and esteemed friend, I have often heard of you, but never had the pleasure of seeing you or of making your acquaintance, both of which I desire and hope the time will not be long until I see you and make your acquaintance.
>
> A little more than one year ago, our people began to make a settlement on Green River, but learning that you and your people did not like us to form a settlement there, we left the place. . . . Since that time we have heard . . . that you were willing that our people should make a settlement on your lands on or near Green River. Therefore our Great Chief in the Great Salt Lake Valley, <u>Brigham Young</u>, has sent me with a number of men to make a settlement on your lands. We have located on Smith's Fork. . . . I am now with them, but shall leave them in two more sleeps to go to the Great Salt Lake Valley. I shall remain there until spring, and when the snow melts and the grass grows, I shall come back . . . , and hope to remain with them.

Orson continued by appealing to Washakie for understanding and for a harmonious relationship:

> I have heard that some white men have told you that we were a bad people, but in answer to this I would say to you, come and see. Our young men are learning to speak your language. They want to be united

with your people, and a number of our men want to marry wives from your people, and live with them, and live in your country. Our hearts are good towards your people, and we want to be friends. . . .

We would like some families of your people to come and live in our little settlement, so that we may talk with them and learn your language. I send you this letter by Bro. Barney Ward, who has a Shoshone wife, and some of our young men go with him to see you. I send you some tobacco and some shirts also, and my best wishes, and hope to see you myself when snow melts and grass grows. Then I want you to go with me Salt Lake Valley and see our Great Chief Brigham Young and have a talk with him, if you can when grass grows. . . .

I send you many good wishes and hope the Good Spirit above will be kind and good to the Shoshone nation and to their Great Chief and also to the Mormons and their Great Chief.

Will you send me word by Barney Ward and the young men what you think and how you feel, and they will write the same and send to me and to our Great Chief in Great Salt Lake Valley.

I am your Friend,

Orson Hyde

Orson conducted a meeting again the second night, Saturday. In a cheerful address he instructed the men and blessed them with all the blessings they could wish for. These would come, he pronounced, if the men proved faithful and obedient to their superiors.

On Sunday morning Orson stowed letters the men asked him to carry and left for Great Salt Lake City. The ride home, mostly downhill, took only three days. He had requested that a home be built for his family to occupy in the spring.[17]

However, Orson knew that moving to an isolated wilderness settlement would be difficult for Marinda. She was enjoying her comfortable home. She and the children had many friends. Also, she had just endured a heart-stretching period. She and Orson had buried their baby Heber John. This son died November 11,[18] the day after his first birthday and between the times that Orson had seen companies off to Green River. Also, Marinda was expecting another child. Spring would take care of itself.

Upon his return from Fort Supply in mid December 1853, Orson resumed his energetic schedule, both in public capacities and at home.

As a Regent of the University of Deseret, he helped promote education in all parts of Utah Territory. The University itself had no buildings and only a meager staff. Officers gave counsel and instruction to teachers and prospective teachers.

Orson's daughter Laura, like many other people, conducted a small school. Her own formal education had been of few years, but her parents taught her well. The time had been when Orson assigned her a specific amount of history or literature to read during the day. In the evening he discussed the topics with her. Books charmed Laura as they did her father, and this pleased him. Laura's students—her own younger brothers and sisters and the children of near neighbors—met with her in a room in the basement of the Hyde home. She proved an able teacher, and the youngsters gained a good foundation for their further education.

In January 1854, Orson was appointed Chancellor of the University of Deseret, the executive officer over the Board of Regents, with a term of one year. In this capacity he directed most of his energies toward an assignment from Brigham Young that the regents develop a reformed method of spelling. Because of confusing inconsistencies in English spelling, President Young felt that a part of "perfecting the saints" should be to generate alphabetical symbols that always represented the same sound. The regents worked diligently at this, and fashioned the phonetic "Deseret Alphabet." After several years, however, use of the alphabet proved impractical, and it was abandoned.

Regarding civic duties, in October 1853 Orson had resigned his seat on the Legislative Council. In January 1854 he received appointment on a committee to draft resolutions encouraging the United States Government to patronize the construction of a railroad from the Missouri River to the Pacific Ocean.[19]

As winter intensified, Orson often wondered how the brethren at Fort Supply fared. On a cold, snowy, windy Saturday night in mid January he partially learned. A man from the outpost made it to Orson's door to summon help for nine companions stranded near Big Mountain. The weather had been good at the fort when they set out with teams and several wagons to procure flour for the men and seed grain for spring planting. However, a snowstorm overtook them. By Friday evening the snow lay five feet deep, with more falling. Pulling the wagons became impossible for the oxen. The men tromped snow for hours that the animals might proceed, but this too became impossible. The men unyoked the exhausted oxen to browse for food, and the weary men slept. At daylight the cattle had departed. After following tracks for over a mile, the men became too fatigued, wading through deep snow, to continue. They then sent one of their number on horseback to seek help from Elder Hyde.

Even with slight attendance in Sunday meeting the next morning, January 15, Orson asked for three men and the use of thirteen horses to rescue the snowbound group. The stranded wagons could wait until spring. Sufficient men agreed to go, and the meeting was dismissed. Rescue proved successful.

On other occasions word reached Orson that a few men left Fort Supply as deserters, discouraged by the bitter cold, monotonous food, and confined conditions, but most stayed.[20]

For personal responsibilities Orson needed cash, and he needed building materials. He made arrangements to buy Valley flour and sell it from his home. He published an advertisement to this effect February 16. The ad also stated that he would buy pine flooring and one-inch pine boards. He still had ploughs for sale too.

Also, to earn money, he accepted a few court cases. But, like the year before, this brought censure. More than once, as testimony proceeded in court, Orson became excited and vocalized beyond the bounds of discretion. Though members of his quorum considered this behavior less than ideal, they retained patience with this quirk of his personality, and Orson continued to enjoy close association with them and the First Presidency.

March 11, sadness struck the Church at the death of compassionate Willard Richards, second counselor to Brigham Young. The general conference in April sustained Jedediah M. Grant as the new counselor. He also received ordination as an apostle.[21]

March 14, Orson wrote in the autograph book of his neighbor, Martha S. Heywood:

> What shall I say to Sister Martha S. Heywood?
>   I will say to her,
>
> Love your husband, love him <u>dearly,</u>
> Love his children, one and all;
> Make his home a cheerful dwelling,
> Sweeter than the church or ball.
>
> Light his house with smiles of gladness;
> Drive from ev'ry heart it's grief;
> Let not cares engender sadness
> When your hand can bring relief.
>
> Act your part with true devotion
> While you stay with mortals here
> Then arise with true emotions
> "To a more exalted sphere."[22]

As spring approached, Church leaders issued calls to additional brethren to serve at Fort Supply. March 29, Orson wrote instructions to these new recruits, and the *Deseret News* published his notice the next day. The men should bring potatoes and flour, all they could procure, as most of the supplies taken out in the fall had frozen. April 6 they would meet "and proceed to the Big Mountain, and bring in the wagons left there last fall." As soon as these wagons could be loaded the group would depart. Men indeed retrieved the wagons from Big Mountain. Goods received final loading. And the company of twenty-five—including Orson, Judge William Appleby, and several other men appointed as county officers—left Great Salt Lake City on May 1 for Green River.

During the first part of the trip the company found fine grass and roads. In the high mountains, however, things changed. Deep snow hindered. At swollen streams mud bogged the wagons. Repair of broken wagon parts caused delays. And one man died unexpectedly. After seven days the group reached their destination, the late afternoon of Sunday, May 7.

Still locked in winter, Fort Supply seemed bleak and isolated. The men, though, had worked hard. Plowed fields surrounded the fort, as did a secure stockade. Even with rain and hail pelting down, and the temperature ten degrees below freezing, the arrivals received jubilant greetings. The wagons of provisions and bundles of letters brought a profuse response of glad welcome. The men had lived for weeks on bread alone.

The hardships of the community in their winter cocoon had been severe, with the cold, the solitude, scant rations, and few families. Snow had been overwhelming, some drifted to the tops of their cabins. In spite of the men's care and diligence, many oxen had starved or frozen or been killed by wolves. In their isolation the men had done their best to keep their spirits up: held meetings regularly, listened to lectures and readings on various subjects, organized a debating society, and studied the Shoshone Indian language. They also entertained themselves by playing some dice and cards. And, though they had meager rations, they took in several families of starving Indians.

They had already planted some grain and vegetables, but these showed no signs of sprouting and growth. How could a settlement survive here? On this, the seventh of May, the temperature at this mountain altitude remained too cold for crops to grow.

Orson tried, in conversations and in meetings, to lift spirits and encourage. He commended "the boys" for diligence and kindness, but mentioned the improperness of playing dice and cards. To receive more blessings they should "shun the very appearance of evil."[23]

Judge Appleby organized the county by officially appointing the various officers. Court would be set up, not here at remote Fort Supply, but at a more central outpost near a ferry on the Green River.

Orson organized a delegation to the Indians. Cold and storms had prevented the December delegation from delivering his letter to Chief Washakie. Orson told the delegation: "[B]e wise as serpents and harmless as doves, . . . be cautious and do all the good that you can to the red men. . . . God will bless you." Orson also gave the men priesthood blessings. In his blessing to the leader, James S. Brown, he said, "Angels shall go before you, the visions of the Lord shall be open to your view, and no weapon that is raised against you shall prosper. You shall go forth in the power and demonstration of the Lord God, and be mighty in gathering Israel."

In another meeting Orson exhorted the men again to take Indian women for wives, and he spoke glowingly of the good this would do the Indians. After the meeting one man spoke to another of his honest reaction. "It may be all right," he said, "but my impressions are that President Hyde, as an apostle, should set the example, then say, 'Come on, boys,' instead of saying, 'Go on.' When he takes a squaw to wife perhaps I will."

Though Orson admired the great exertions of these Fort Supply brethren, his efforts to gain personal enthusiasm for living here met failure. Moving Marinda and the children to this wilderness, even to the adequate log cabin that had been built for them, seemed more than he could consider at this time. As yet, this was no place for families. In his mind Orson had been mulling the idea of building a store in the Salt Lake Valley with which to earn a living. Prospects at Fort Supply strengthened this consideration.

He had come to Green River County with indefinite plans for his length of stay. Now he had accomplished everything that appeared needful. Wednesday he and three companions began their return.[24] Back in Great Salt Lake City, he reported to Brigham Young and received no insistence that he reside at the settlement, alone or with his family.

June of 1854 continued busy for Orson. In addition to regular duties he worked in his garden of one-and-a-half acres: hoed, pulled weeds, and irrigated. He also spent time building his "Provision and Feed Store" and smokehouse on East Temple Street (later Main) between First and Second South Streets. His lot—on the east side, the second lot from the north corner—had a twenty-four-and-a-half foot frontage. Orson anticipated being operative by the time the California immigrants paused in the Valley to trade. He preached regularly in Sabbath meetings held at ten o'clock and two o'clock in the Tabernacle on the Temple Block. The afternoon services were sacrament meetings. When Orson spoke in these he followed the established procedure and usually blessed either the bread or the water, or both, in the middle of his sermon and then continued preaching while other brethren passed the sacrament to the congregation.[25]

During the Fourth of July celebration in the Tabernacle, Orson delivered a stirring and inspired address. He loved his country and its history. In his heart his testimony of Heaven's role in this history burned as he spoke. His animated movements matched his dynamic voice:

> We are met, fellow-citizens, to celebrate one of the most important events that ever embellished the pages of political history— . . . the bold, manly, and daring act of our fathers in the Declaration of the Independence. . . . They had . . . hearts of iron and nerves of steel to defend it by force of arms against the fearful odds arrayed against them. . . .

Remember Lexington, and Bunker Hill, and lastly Yorktown, with all the intermediate scenes . . . of the American Revolution! Remember the immortal Washington, chosen to lead our infant armies through the perils and hardships of an unequal contest, to the climax of victory and the pinnacle of fame! . . .

In those early and perilous times, our men were few, and our resources limited. . . . [Y]et our arms were successful; and it may not be amiss to ask here, by whose power victory so often perched on our banner? It was by the agency of that same angel of God that appeared unto Joseph Smith, and revealed to him the history of the early inhabitants of this country. . . . This same angel [Moroni] presides over the destinies of America, and feels a lively interest in all our doings. He was in the camp of Washington; and, by an invisible hand, led on our fathers to conquest and victory; and all this to open and prepare the way for the Church and kingdom of God to be established on the western hemisphere, for the redemption of Israel and the salvation of the world.

This same angel was with Columbus, and gave him deep impressions, by dreams and by visions, respecting this New World. . . . [T]he angel of God helped him—was with him on the stormy deep, calmed the troubled elements, and guided his frail vessel to the desired haven. Under the guardianship of this same angel . . . have the United States grown, increased, and flourished. . . .

The peculiar respect that high Heaven has for this country, on account of the promises made to the fathers, and on account of its being the land where the mustard seed of truth was planted and destined to grow in the last days, accounts for all this good fortune to our beloved America. . . .

One positive decree of Jehovah, respecting this land, is, that no king shall ever be raised up here, and that whosoever seeketh to raise up a king upon this land shall perish. . . .

God and our country, now and for ever, one and inseparable![26]

Orson received periodic news from Fort Supply. May 30 a severe freeze killed all the vines, corn, potatoes, and wheat. The potatoes grew again. Men replanted the wheat. Peas grew well, as did turnips. Men procured plenty of fish, elk, antelope, deer, and bear.

In early June the Fort Supply missionaries to the Indians had returned to the fort, and some came on to the Salt Lake Valley. One of these, James S. Brown, reported that Elder Hyde's earlier blessing on his head had indeed been answered. Though often in peril, he and his companions had been guided and preserved. Chief Washakie, the Shoshone leader, welcomed them into his camp in the magnificent Wind River Mountains. The handsome bearing and intelligence of Chief Washakie impressed the visitors. Brother

Brown later described him as "a bold, noble, hospitable, and honorable man. As an orator, I think he surpassed any man I ever met."

Chief Washakie convened a council of his Indians and the missionaries. In this meeting the "only objection that was raised to our proposition," James S. Brown recounts, "was when we suggested that some of us might want to take some of the young Indian women for wives. One old wise [Indian] counselor said, 'No, for we have not got daughters enough for our own men, and we cannot afford to give our daughters to the white man, but we are willing to give him an Indian girl for a white girl. I cannot see why a white man wants an Indian girl. They are dirty, ugly, stubborn and cross, and it is a strange idea for white men to want such wives. But I can see why an Indian wants a white woman.' . . . Chief Washakie, however, said the white men might look around, and if any one of us found a girl that would go with him, it would be all right, but the Indians must have the same privilege among the white men. With this the council ended."

In July Orson's brother-in-law, William Price, among men released from Fort Supply, arrived back in the Valley. Orson needed help in his store and asked William to be his partner. William accepted willingly.[27]

The "Flour, Feed, and Provision Store" kept both Orson and William busy. It did a brisk trade, as did the other stores already established, also the seven new businesses on East Temple Street, and the six additional new stores in various sections of the city. The California immigration brought enough business for all. Some of the merchants sold goods freighted into the Valley earlier in the season. Orson and William carried local produce, which sold as fast as purchased from farmers. In September, to replenish for arriving Saints, the two advertised that they would pay cash for oats, barley, butter, cheese, eggs, bran, and shorts (a by-product of wheat milling). A note added that the store also had a few ploughs for sale. These were left over from Orson's previous venture.

Orson's spirits soared at having good income. He at last began to feel secure about supporting his growing family. Not only were his children increasing in stature, but numbers increased with a new baby in the Hyde home. Marinda gave birth to Mary Lavinia July 10, 1854.

Another person also received a Hyde welcome—Orson's nephew Aurelius Miner, the son of Orson's sister Sally. He arrived September 1, and Orson soon discovered him to be a brilliant young man, age twenty-two, a graduate from law school. He had traveled to Utah specifically to meet the uncle that caused such interesting conversations in his family while he grew up in Connecticut. He made the journey across the plains and mountains with Judge J. F. Kinney, the new Chief Justice of the Supreme Court of Utah. The judge spoke highly of Orson Hyde, remembering him and other Saints from 1850, back in Kanesville, Iowa, when the judge investigated the election that involved lost poll books.[28]

In a speech in the Tabernacle, September 24, Orson admonished the Saints to live the commandments of God, seeking to become like Him. "We are created in His image and likeness," Orson expounded, "and I think He has been moving on the same track we are in, and we shall acquire the same experience if we listen to His revelations. . . . [H]e has felt about the same as we do. The other day when brother Hyde was mixing mortar, a person came along and said, 'Brother Hyde, is it possible that I see you mixing mortar?' 'Yes,' I replied, 'and when I stand up yonder, and see you poor fellows mixing mortar, I can sympathise with you.' I should hate to enlist under a General, and follow him to the field of battle if he had never been there; I should want him to have a little experience, and then I could follow him with some degree of confidence."

In a general conference session two weeks later, October 6, Orson mentioned another personal item, this one relating to scriptures. "I have once memorized the Bible," he said, "and when any one quoted one verse, I could quote the next. I have memorized it in English, German, and Hebrew, still I do not profess to be very familiar with it now, yet the sentiments and spirit of it are in my heart, and will be as long as I live, and still remain when I am gone to another sphere."[29]

Conference accomplished, Brigham Young took Orson and others with him to areas of former Indian disturbances south of Salt Lake City, planning October 10 to October 18 for the trip. President Young wished to counsel the citizens and to talk with the Indians who had caused the problems and now seemed friendly. Mary Ann accompanied Orson, which pleased him.

The group traveled south for four days, always surrounded by mountain bastions, some rising near at hand and others appearing less grand across miles of sagebrush vistas. The wagons ascended out of Salt Lake Valley through the "Jordan Narrows," a shallow canyon along the Jordan River, and rolled into Utah Valley, where the fresh waters of large Utah Lake glistened to the west. Here magnificent Mount Timpanogos dominated the east. The town of Provo, in this huge valley, was as far south as Orson had previously been in the Territory. At Salt Creek (later Nephi) stately Mount Nebo and her chain of lofty peaks towered to the east. After traversing the winding road southeast up Salt Creek Canyon, the caravan descended into long Sanpete Valley, high mountains guarding it east and west. In Sanpete Valley Orson and the others arrived at the stone and adobe Manti fort at dusk on Saturday, October 14. They had traveled 140 miles, as far south as they planned to go.

They had passed through the location where the previous year, as described by Orson, "several most excellent men [were] shot down by the hostile savage from his ambush. Much suffering has been occasioned by the Indian war. Many of our crops went to waste last year, by reason of it, which . . . occasioned rather a scanty supply of food. . . . [S]ome of our settlements lost almost every head of stock they had, by the Indians . . . , and have been compelled to cultivate their lands with few horses and oxen. . . . This year we have had peace with the red men [and plentiful harvest]."

In meetings in Manti and in Fort Ephraim, Brigham Young, Orson, and others commended and encouraged the settlers. At Fort Ephraim they also had a friendly visit with Indian Chief Arapeen.

During the caravan's return, at Salt Creek they conferred with camped federal officers. Judge J. F. Kinney, the new Chief Justice of the Supreme Court of Utah—whom Orson remembered admiringly from Kanesville times—was conducting a regular session of court in the Salt Creek school house. The court had the protection of about seventy-five soldiers commanded by Colonel Steptoe, who was wintering troops and horses in Utah before traveling on to California.

On the remainder of their journey home, the company met groups of Saints traveling southward to settle, and they consulted with Squash, another Indian chief. Afterward President Young talked about the Indians, saying, "[A]s we [the saints] have been twenty-four years in severe drill to learn what we know, we should be very lenient to the natives who have to start from a position so far below the vantage ground we had at the beginning." After all, though generally difficult to perceive, the Indians were Israelites, with great promises from the Lord recorded in the Book of Mormon. Church members should be patient with them and help them realize their potential.

The trip had been good, with pleasant weather, excellent company, uplifting meetings, and worthwhile conversations.[30]

Back at home in Salt Lake City, Orson resumed a satisfying routine. Each working day he walked the block and a half to his store. At home he enjoyed his family. He continued to preach in the Tabernacle and in various wards. He met with different groups of brethren in his leadership capacities. In Brigham Young's office he treasured leisurely visits and serious visits, feeling strengthened in the constant watchcare required to build up God's kingdom on earth.

Orson also wrote items for the newspaper. October 26 appeared his article about Colonel Steptoe and the other United States Army officers and men sojourning in the midst of the Saints. Orson commended the officers for their gentlemanly conduct and instructed the Saints to treat these visitors with respect. November 9 Orson called for more workers to help finish construction on the new bowery near the Tabernacle. November 23 he and the other two men on the Board of Examination for Teacher's Certificates announced that they were conducting examinations and giving certificates.

The newspaper also printed a December 23 report about a visit by Orson to Grantsville, a settlement west of Salt Lake City. "Since Elder O. Hyde was here preaching," the report states, "there seems to be a new impetus to every thing. Our fort wall which has laid dormant, is now under rapid progress, especially that portion of it which is to be made of pounded earth; and rock and adobies are being daily placed upon the ground for the remaining portion, and several rods of foundation are already laid with rock. The brethren are all united, and a good spirit prevails; every one manifesting, by their works, a disposition to obey counsel."[31]

Two family weddings occurred. Orson's partner and brother-in-law, dignified and refined William Price, thirty-six years old, at last became a husband in November. And Orson's daughter, Emily, age fifteen, became the bride, December 25, of George Ogden Chase.

In mid January 1855 Orson received an incredible request. Brigham Young asked him to preside over proceedings hundreds of miles to the west in Carson Valley, bordering the Sierra Nevada Mountains of California, the extreme western portion of Utah Territory.[32] This would end Orson's supervision of Fort Supply.

CHAPTER 19

... *westward*. ... *(1855)*

> *And from this place ye shall go forth into the regions westward; and inasmuch as ye shall find them that will receive you ye shall build up my church. . . .*
>
> —Doctrine and Covenants 42:8

JANUARY 17, 1855, Orson had been ill, mostly confined to his bed for four days, when he received a written message from Brigham Young. "Having for sometime contemplated organizing Carson County [the western boundary of Utah Territory]," President Young said, "whenever my mind should settle upon a suitable person to go and reside there two or three years, . . . it suggested itself to my mind to make the proposition to you. Would you be willing to take that mission, and if so would you like to receive the appointment of Judge of Probate from the present Legislative Assembly? . . . I should be pleased to know your feelings in relation to these propositions previous to making any move in the matter or suggestions to anyone else."

This request staggered Orson's mind. But he had said to the President recently that he was ready for anything that might be required of him. And, as he had written this very day about making decisions: "If the narrow principle [of] fear that something may go wrong . . . be allowed to prevail . . . , it will require yet several thousand years for the laws of God's Kingdom to extend over the Earth."[1]

Carson Valley lay eight hundred miles distant on the California Trail. There John and Enoch Reese, Church members, operated a trading post called "Mormon Station." The Reese brothers had informed Brigham Young that the valley was filling up with settlers. And the settlers disagreed about whether they lived in California or Utah. Most likely the valley belonged to Utah Territory. If so, Utah should provide direction and county officers.

A duration of "two or three years" Brigham Young had requested of Orson—not as a settler with his family, because of the unknown living conditions. Forcing from his mind thoughts of leaving family and comforts, Orson sent an affirmative answer to President Young. Orson would go, trusting in the Lord for guidance.

The next day Governor Brigham Young nominated Orson Hyde to fill the position of Probate Judge of Carson County, as part of the beginnings of organization. The Legislature approved this action. Orson would depart in the spring, when grass grew for the animals. In the meantime he would take care of scheduled commitments.

Monday evening, January 22, Orson gave the opening lecture of the Grammar School he would conduct "for thirty evenings, from six 'till nine o'clock." (The income would be welcome.) He titled the lecture "Science of the English Language." In part he said:

> . . . The value of an object is often (and not improperly) estimated by the amount of labour and toil required to obtain it. The precious metals are not often found in the streets or highways; but . . . deeply imbedded in the . . . earth. If you will have them, you must dig for them. They will cost you much time and labour. . . . Scientific knowledge [also] . . . is only found by those who seek it with all their heart[s].
> . . .
>
> The Presidency of this Church are the lovers of learning. . . . They do not want you to trust to it, however, as to God; but through it they want you to be able to present those truths that Heaven reveals, in [an] interesting and engaging light. . . . Lay hold, then, upon education! . . .
>
> Grammar, well understood, enables us to express our thoughts fully and clearly; and also in a manner that will defy the ingenuity of man to give our words any other meaning than that which we ourselves intended them to convey. . . .
>
> Remember, my friends, that you live in a progressive age—an age in which the inspiration of the Almighty is resting upon the world to disclose the principles of science, and bring them into requisition to fulfil his purposes, and they know it not! . . . Secure learning and virtue, and you will be great. Love God and honour him, and you will be happy.[2]

For two months, as Orson conducted three evening lectures to thirty students each week, other activities also involved him. He enjoyed an occasional dancing or supper party. January 29 he was admitted to plead at the bar of the Supreme Court of Utah. Regularly he preached. Also, he continued overseeing the finishing of the Temple Block bowery.[3]

Amid this public activity, a sorrowful occurrence beset the Hyde family. January 29, Orson and Marinda's six month old daughter, Mary Lavinia, died. Of Orson's eleven children born so far, only five remained. In spite of aching hearts, and a feeling of emptiness, life must go on. Death was part of life, no matter how hard to bear.

A bright event in Orson's life occurred February 6. He baptized his nephew, Aurelius Miner. Aurelius had decided to remain with the Saints.[4]

After Orson's school ended he received a letter of gratitude that had been written March 30. His students thanked him for his zeal and untiring patience, for the harmony and good feelings in the sessions, and also stated,

". . . your example has taught us that grammar, which is generally looked upon as dry and uninteresting, may be rendered both amusing and engaging. . . . And now, dear brother Hyde, as you are about to take your departure from this city, and settle down in a distant part of the Territory to fill an important station, we pray for Heaven's choicest blessings to rest upon you and yours, that you may be prospered in all things, and that you may be to many, what you have been to us—a blessing."

During the winter, and now on into spring, wintering soldiers caused problems. Though the officers continued gentlemanly, as Orson had noted in the newspaper the previous October, some soldiers tried to court Mormon girls and convince them of the foolishness of Church teachings. To counter these efforts, Church leaders preached boldly in the Tabernacle against "Gentile" influence, and they also published emphatic discourses in the newspaper.[5]

In one article Orson tried to educate the soldiers by painting a word picture of the glorious truths that had been given to the Latter-day Saints about the destiny of man and the destiny of the earth, "the greater portion of which [knowledge]," he wrote, "[has been] received by revelation from heaven in these days." Regarding the earth, he said that when

> it shall have filled the measure of its creation in its present sphere or orbit . . . it will leave its present track, and eternally roll in bright sunshine of everlasting day. . . . To prepare it for this glory . . . it was baptized in the days of Noah, for the remission of sins. It now awaits another baptism by fire and by the Holy Ghost. Then it will be prepared for another sphere, and its righteous inhabitants become sufficiently numerous to warrant its admission into the glorious union of worlds or states celestial, where God himself is President. . . .
>
> Ye children of nature! ye disciples and followers of the God of this world! Can you give us a better or more glorious view of things? . . . Judge not the servants of God to be your enemies because they tell you the truth. God would be angry with them if they did not; and in a coming day, you would curse them yourselves. . . .

With spring advancing, Orson's travel preparations and other activities intensified. Brigham Young had changed the length of stay from years to months, expecting that Orson could organize the county during the summer and return in the fall. Men were enlisted to accompany him. Also, Orson tried to contract with enough farmers to sell their produce to his store that its profit might take care of his family; this was precarious, as grasshoppers were devastating crops. As well, appointment came to Orson to help direct the Deseret Theological Institute, organized for the education of the people much as his grammar school had been. And he preached often. May 5, 1855, he participated in the dedication of the newly finished Endowment House on the northwest corner of the Temple Block. Again, after the long interval since being driven from Nauvoo, the Saints could receive endowments. This building would be used until completion of the Temple.[6]

During all of this constructive activity Orson felt apprehension about how settlers in the western part of Utah Territory would react to directions from a Mormon? He hoped that relations would be as congenial as they had been in Kanesville, Iowa. His concerns about dealing with Gentiles intensified after an alarming incident with the soldiers wintering in Salt Lake Valley. A Captain Ingalls abducted two young Mormon girls. This raised the ire of the public, and Captain Ingalls was brought to trial. But he was acquitted, being released in time to set out for California on April 29 with his fellow troops under Colonel Steptoe.

Orson talked of the Captain Ingalls episode in a Tabernacle address on May 6, using the soldier's name. "I say the curse of God be upon every such scoundrel!" Elder Hyde pronounced. A resounding "Amen" echoed from the congregation.

Orson experienced delays, but, almost ready to leave, he bid friends good-bye in a May 13 Tabernacle sermon. Bolstering his personal anxieties, he said, "If a person is never tried or tempted how can [he or she] gain the reward of overcoming?"[7]

Orson would miss his family, but they would function well without him. Charlotte had departed, a mutual decision.[8] Plural marriage, it turned out, had not suited her. Marinda and Mary Ann, on the other hand, were entirely congenial and cooperated well with the children. Laura was almost eighteen years of age, a young woman. Frank, ten, and Alonzo, seven, were fine companions. Delia, five, was a delight. "Aunt" Mary Ann lavished love on all of them; no more babies had come to her.

May 15, Orson and those who would travel with him brought their wagons and carriages together for organization and last minute preparations. The group included George P. Stiles, U.S. Justice for the third Judicial District; Joseph L. Heywood, U.S. Marshal[9]; and thirty-five other men hired as guards. Mary Ann's brother-in-law, Richard Bentley, was among the guards.[10]

The next morning, in the midst of the bustle of getting off, a messenger handed to Orson a letter from Brigham Young. The President and other Church leaders had left the previous week to visit the southern settlements. Brigham Young had written the letter May 7, before his departure, but through oversight, the person responsible for it had neglected to deliver it to Orson until now.

Orson opened the letter and read hurriedly that President Young wanted him not only to be in charge of Carson County, but to oversee the Church newspaper planned to be published in California. George Q. Cannon, assigned as publisher, with others had left the Salt Lake Valley several days before. Brigham Young wanted Orson to manage and control the finances. This request disconcerted Orson. He wished that he could have discussed the matter. For now, he would concentrate on getting to his destination. After arrival he could figure out how to handle his duties. Orson folded the letter and tucked it away.

An hour later, as loved ones waved hands and handkerchiefs, the company lumbered north. Lumps in throats and heartpangs of homesickness became swallowed up in the involvements of travel. To get around Great Salt Lake, the group drove north for about eighty miles. They ferried over the wide marshy Bear River, then made final organization plans. Trail experiences of the last several days helped them realize their needs and their strengths.[11]

Westward beyond the lush Bear River Valley the country became more arid, with low grasses and sagebrush and a few other bushes. Using his maps and travel guides, Orson spent hours riding ahead to seek out the periodic streams and springs by which they could camp comfortably and where good grass grew for the animals.

At Goose Creek, Orson's group proceeded on the California Trail, which came south from the Snake River. They sometimes passed gold-seeking companies, groups who had wintered in the Salt Lake Valley, or north on the Snake River, to get a spring start. They continued from one valley to the next over low passes. The scenery, as they traveled twenty to thirty miles each day, now consisted of far away snow-capped peaks, sage-covered mountains all around, and narrow or wide sage plains. The main occupants of the area seemed to be hordes of grasshoppers, an obnoxious annoyance. The sides of the trail lay littered with the casualties of earlier years: abandoned wagons and goods, animal bones and skins, and hastily marked graves.

Camp members' actions pleased Orson. He heard no profanity. All participated together in prayer times. They maintained good spirits and good health. Judge Stiles and Marshal Heywood also impressed Orson. They attended pre-dawn roll call, performed their share of camp duty, and stood regular guard hours the same as others. Cooperation was necessary, Orson wrote in a letter, "in this [Indian] country where we have to sleep with one eye open, one foot out of bed, a rifle in one hand and a revolver in the other." Several nights the Indians tried to capture the camp animals. The diligence of the guards prevented such disaster. Many nights Orson, at all hours, received summons away from his warm bedroll to direct action. He felt special gratitude for Spiritual guidance.

At length the majestic Ruby and Humboldt Mountains towered in the southwest. Extensive meadows and marshes indicated that the travelers had arrived at "the Wells," the beginning springs of the Humboldt River. Being the only river running west through the forthcoming mountains and plains, the brackish Humboldt determined the course of the California Trail.

The next day, after about five miles, the group arrived at a fork in the road. One track crossed over to the north side of the swampy undesirable stream, and the other track headed down the south side. Orson had been advised that the best road lay north of the Humboldt, but that saleratus (alkali) permeated everything: the grass, the water, and the dust, appearing all along almost as if a light snow had fallen. Because of this, and because Colonel Steptoe and his troops were now only eight miles ahead on the north road, Orson chose the south road.[12]

When Orson's group halted the evening of June 2, Colonel Steptoe and his troops were camped beyond the river. This posed questions that Orson, Judge Stiles, and Marshal Heywood discussed. The Colonel might have negative feelings about Orson's previous words in Salt Lake Valley against one of his men, Captain Ingalls. If the Utah company passed by the troops and made no call, the Humboldt being crossable here, Colonel Steptoe could say that they felt fear or shame. Orson and his companions decided it best to be sociable and pave the way for good feelings between the groups.

The Judge, the Marshal, and Orson waded their horses across the river and respectfully greeted the guard. The guard returned the respect and allowed them to pass to the Colonel's tent. When Orson dismounted, he left his pistols in the holsters on his horse.

Colonel Steptoe seemed genuinely pleased that they came. His kindliness reinforced the good feelings Orson already had for him. During amicable conversation, a disturbance at the tent door caught everyone's attention. Captain Ingalls and several other soldiers entered.

Captain Ingalls demanded that, relating to himself, Orson repeat his public words in Salt Lake City. The Colonel reproved Ingalls for touching the subject. Captain Ingalls apologized to the Colonel, but insisted that Orson report what he had said. So Orson told the Captain emphatically that he disapproved of him abducting the two minor girls.

Instantly Orson's face stung from a slap from Captain Ingalls, and he was looking into the Captain's drawn revolver. Orson's pistols hung outside on his horse.

Immediately guards ushered Ingalls out of the Colonel's tent, and the Colonel apologized, obviously distressed. He promised his guests that his officer would be dealt with according to his offense. As the three returned to their own camp, Orson felt that in spite of the tumult, their visit had been a wise choice, that their conversation with the Colonel had been beneficial in helping him to understand Orson's group and their assignments.

The next day Orson received word from Ingalls to expect a confrontation in Carson Valley. Orson resolved to keep his pistols close at hand when Steptoe's company arrived.[13]

Continuing westward, Orson and his men became ever more grateful that they had prepared well for their journey and that they traveled early in the season, with enough feed for the animals along the dusty trail in these dry valleys of stunted sagebrush, sparse grasses, and tenacious greasewood. They also rejoiced to find a few sweet springs and fresh streams. The bitter and cloudy alkali water in the Humboldt was barely tolerable.

The company continued from one valley to the next, surrounded always, all around, near or far, by gentle ranges of mountains. The wending way of the Humboldt was viewed from high places as a serpentine ribbon of two rows of scrubby willows across each plain. For days the men saw no tree anywhere, in valley or on hill. Mountain range after mountain range stood sage-shrouded. The prevailing muted soft color, a green-brown-gray, changed subtly to pinks, silvers, lavenders, or blues according to sky conditions and the time of day. But the travelers paid little attention to whatever beauty this desolate land offered. Like every traveler here before them, they concentrated on surviving, hurrying, that for as few days as necessary they would be forced to accept the dubious hospitality of the Humboldt.

They realized the truth of the tales they had heard not only of arid deserts, but of steep mountain passes, making this a trek to try the best of men. Sometimes, when the river occupied the entire narrow canyon between one plain and the next, the group had to go over and down "monstrous" hills to come back to the river. The wagons came down, Orson describes, with "[a]ll four wheels locked and men behind with larietts to hold back and keep the wagons from ending over upon the teams. Still we got along well and without accident."[14]

For roughly two hundred sun-searing miles, they followed the river west and somewhat northwest. Then the river changed course to the southwest. Guidebooks indicated that the company had two hundred additional miles to go. After two hot dusty days in this new direction they saw the noble snow-capped Sierra Nevada Mountains in the distant west. And they came to the welcome "Great Meadows," marking the near end of the Humboldt. Here the spread-out moisture sustained hundreds of acres of meadow and marshes, excellent sustenance for the animals. The stock guards, however, carefully evaded boggy areas.

After this respite the taskmaster Humboldt had one last harsh toll to exact from its followers: enduring the Humboldt Sink. Sloughs that Orson's group had passed previously were nothing compared to the decolored morass they now skirted. They passed miles of alkali flats, some wide and smooth, with tough plants edging them. In other areas small mounds, with hardy plants atop, dotted the sink. Open water, in patches large and small, looked like dirty milk and smelled of salt and sulphur—the same reek as rotten eggs. The sink also displayed green marshes, brown marshes, quicksand, and soggy earth.

Topping "The Ridge," the long low hill that marked the end of the Humboldt, another vast desolation stretched before Orson and his men. This was the most dreaded section of the journey, the notorious "Forty Mile Desert." Near The Ridge the company found the seepage spring that provided water, though distasteful. The guidebooks declared the water usable, and the men filled every container they had.

As the group proceeded across the menacing forty miles they saw no palatable water and no grass. They labored through increasingly deep sand. And they saw piles of the goods of mortals strewn along the arduous way. Much-mended wagons had fallen apart. Tattered and dirty clothes and numerous other items had been discarded to lighten the loads of faltering beasts. Bones bleached in the sun. Weakened gold-seekers' cattle lay dying or had recently died, causing sickening sights and an overpowering stench of the carcasses. How would later companies fare? Orson's group's animals did surprisingly well, none collapsing in this desert. Only two horses had been lost previously: sickness claimed one, and the accidental discharge of a gun took the other.[15]

Then the company came to Ragtown on the Carson River (seven miles west of what later became Fallon, Nevada). Ragtown boasted people and tents and trading posts and natural pastures and water—wonderful water, fresh and clear and cool.

Eighty more miles of hills and valleys up the Carson River trail—verdant with vegetation—brought Orson and his men, June 17, to Reeses' Ranch, "Mormon Station." To the west, the ramparts of the Sierra Nevada Mountains rose immediately, towering, and covered with trees. The trees were primarily tall, elegant, long-needled ponderosa pines. Carpeting the ground beneath these lay dropped needles strewn with big plump pine cones. To the east, flourishing grassland sloped away across the spacious valley. The settlement lay high enough up the incline to be safe from spring floods. From the pine-graced mountains an ample rivulet of cold water, wide though shallow, tumbled over granite rocks and sand.[16] On the stream stood Reeses' mill, described by observers as "a very fine large, three story grist mill, to which is attached the most complete saw mill we ever saw in motion, with a circular saw six feet in diameter. We witnessed it saw twice through a ten foot log, making a complete change of the mill, and sawing 28 feet of lumber in one minute and fifty seconds."

Mormon Station had grown to a thriving community of squat log cabins and newer frame dwellings, clustered on the slope around the mill and trading post. In these domiciles lived the men who worked for the Reeses. The place had become a busy way station, surrounded by clumps of emigrants' tents and covered wagons. The imposing log main building rose two stories high, fifty feet by thirty feet. The ground level of the structure held kitchen, dining room, and store; the upstairs contained two large sleeping rooms. The attached corral enclosed an acre of ground with a stockade fence (posts set two feet into the ground touching each other and standing upright ten feet in the air).

Reeses' many acres of fields and pastures spread east far beyond the buildings. The cultivated fields, enclosed with pole fences, displayed an abundance of wheat, barley, corn, fruit trees, watermelons, potatoes, turnips, peas, and other vegetables that travelers might want. Many oxen and mules and horses, some tired and some strong, grazed in the grass pastures. Fat ones had recently been traded away for the thin ones. These in turn would be fattened and then traded. The pastures also nourished cows, pigs, and chickens.

The Reeses' business thrived. In the store—in addition to flour, fresh garden produce, beef, pork, milk, cream, butter, and eggs—stood shelves and stacks of a wide variety of goods wagoned or packed from Salt Lake City or from California. In the blacksmith shop, clanging noises bespoke emigrants pleased to have new shoes nailed onto the hoofs of horses and oxen and for repairs made to wagons. Though travelers applauded all of this, they complained about the high prices. The rates were necessary, however, because of the costs of hauling goods, of losses, and of hired help.

Other ranchers' cabins and fences also dotted the valley. They, too, traded with emigrants, but on a less grand scale than the Reeses. Many bought flour and lumber here at Mormon Station.[17]

Orson's group found a good location and set up a compound of tents and wagons.[18] For a couple of days Orson conferred with John Reese and with other men to learn the attitudes of the people in this desirable valley. Then, June 19, Orson reported to Brigham Young. He told of the fatiguing trip, extolled that Reeses had "a most splendid mill and ranch," and acclaimed that "This is a beautiful valley. . . . There are also many valleys in this vicinity rich and fertile sufficient to make a State or an Empire. This is also a regular head quarters for the Indians of various tribes over whom Col. Reese has obtained a good & an extensive influence, and the way seems to be opening just right." In fact, Orson added, no Indians had beset his group the latter part of their journey. The ones they had seen seemed friendly.

Orson also explained to Brigham Young details of the boundary problem. The United States Congress had ruled that the California-Utah boundary followed 120 degrees longitude as far south as 39 degrees latitude, which was somewhere in or near Carson Valley. Then it angled southeast in a specified direction. If the longitude lay far enough east, or the angle far enough north, Carson Valley belonged to California. Orson continued:

> The people generally in this valley are anxious for an organization of some kind. They are much divided in their views and feelings. Some are willing to come under Utah, others claim that they live in California, while some want a distinct Territorial Government, embracing the valleys and country half way to Salt Lake. This Country has been neglected quite long enough if Utah wishes to hold it. . . .
>
> Governor Bigler [of California] is one of the road commissioners and has been looked for over here for the last ten days: but he has not come, and rumor now says that he is not coming at present. The settlement of

the boundary line between Utah and Cal. is now the only bar to an organization under the laws of Utah. If an organization be gone into before the line is established, exceptions will not only be taken to the jurisdiction of Courts; but the officer serving process will be resisted and probably shot down, whereas if the line were established it would silence all these difficulties. A regular border war may be got up if care and wisdom be not observed. I now, more than ever, see the necessity of bro. [Orson] Pratt's coming here with the [surveying] instruments to establish this line [as he had done in the Salt Lake Valley]; and unless it is done, any amount of costs may be saddled upon this section and be subjected to a thousand embarrassments not necessary here to name. It is a country whose importance is daily increasing. California is not going to take any measures to establish this line in my opinion, with the view of keeping the line in doubt that she may stand the better chance to get the country by hook or by crook. . . . The government at Washington will undoubtedly pay the expenses of the Survey. . . .

. . . We shall proceed with our organization if the Lord will; yet we shall try to stave off any and all writs and processes that may lead to a rupture before the line is established. The County Seat will not be located until we know that it is in Utah, as the place where the citizens can be best accommodated is said to be in California by some, but it is undoubtedly in Utah. I would say again, by all means, let Bro. Pratt come immediately unless the Lord direct otherwise.

Already Orson felt a keen ambition to retain Carson Valley for a home for Saints. "I would say, Secure, Secure for growing and increasing Utah," he praised. "As an Individual, I care not five cents about the line or country; but as an agent for a great people, I say that I want it secured. The timber, the water, the grass, the fish, the remarkably healthful climate and rich soil are elements of vital importance to the increasing strength, and glory of Zion. Its mineral wealth, though of minor consideration, is hardly exceeded by any portion of Cal. if they can manage to get water to it, which they are now endeavoring to do."

In only two days Orson had gained an overwhelming sense of responsibility. "With the views and feelings of the people here," he confided in his explanations to Brigham Young, "the work assigned me in this county is not the work of a week or month. It will require patience and perseverance to do anything to account."[19]

The next week proved busy. Orson rode around the valley and talked with people. He sent a group of his men on a scouting expedition. He circumvented any confrontation with Captain Ingalls when Colonel Steptoe and his troops sojourned in the Carson Valley before continuing their march. He evaluated. He prayed.

He at length concluded that to find direction for his concerns he must journey over the mountains to California and talk with Governor Bigler. Besides consultation with the governor, he needed to look into the progress of the Church printing enterprise that President Young had asked him to manage.

Orson beheld astonishing scenery while traveling the 280 miles from Mormon Station to San Francisco. Beginning June 25, he and his companions spent three days covering the first 80 miles: from Carson Valley, up to Daggett's Pass, down into Lake Bigler Valley (later Tahoe), up to Johnson's Pass, and down to Placerville. Orson had never imagined that mountains could rise so straight up, rock walls, reaching so high. The mules he and Judge Stiles and Marshal Heywood rode had no trouble on the zigzag narrow rock ledge trails, but the dizzying heights disquieted the men. In many places a slip of a mule's foot would mean a plummet to death. Everything here had been created in superlatives. Lake Bigler [Tahoe], high in the mountains between the two precipitous summits, was spectacularly beautiful—serene, azure, and colossal. Even the pines grew to heroic size. After the second summit and beyond the plateau, a rough and rapid descent brought the men to Placerville.[20]

Placerville, also called Hangtown, lay in gold country. Orson had never thought he would be in gold country, amidst miles of hills and valleys and streams from which men came and boarded the stagecoach to carry bags of gleaming nuggets and dust to the mint in San Francisco. Hotels and drinking establishments crowded both sides of the narrow dusty road through the town, but the community had its churches too: even a new Jewish synagogue, and had its steady element: the farmers and butchers and blacksmiths who earned a regular income filling the needs of the miners. Orson and his companions found a livery stable and arranged care for their mules. The men would proceed by the busy stage.

Jolting through hilly country for 50 more miles to Sacramento, they saw diggings, dams, flumes, and shanties of mining. They saw hotels along the way and many miners with picks and pans and pouches. Sacramento—in an extensive valley of fields and herds, at the confluence of the Sacramento and American Rivers—was a thriving city, the center of the gold country, the capitol of California.

The June 28 scorching temperatures in Sacramento seemed insufferable. Orson decided to hurry on. Bidding his companions farewell, he boarded a steamboat. The next day, 150 miles downriver, he reached "delightfully cool" San Francisco.[21]

The long intimidating journey from Mormon Station added to Orson's concerns about the diverse instructions in his letter from Brigham Young, handed to him just as he left Salt Lake City. Overseeing the Carson area, and managing financial matters of an ambitious Church printing venture in San

Francisco, would require his presence on both sides of the incredible Sierra Nevadas. President Young's letter gave other detailed advise as well. One item was: "I counsel you not to write or publish any thing that will require an apology from you." Brigham Young also cautioned Orson to refrain from criticizing any subject too adversely or hastily, to "mingle as little as possible with the politics of the day," to support civil authorities, and to avoid lawsuits "as much as possible." Orson should be a true friend to the Indians, and should "collect Tithing and forward" it to Salt Lake City.

The President's messages were usually to the point and often terse. Parts of this one, however, were tender, from friend to friend. Brigham Young suggested a purpose of the letter being to "carry with you, and occasionally look upon while far away. Peradventure, it will bring to your mind, in all its freshness and beauty, scenes which we have frequently had the pleasure of enjoying during a few short years of peace and prosperity. . . .

"Go and prosper," Brigham Young warmly concluded, "and may the Lord bless and preserve you in all time to come, and in eternity is the prayer of your friend and Brother."

Orson stepped onto a dock in San Francisco and looked around. Then he walked. He saw an unbelievable city built on hills, with roads up and down and sideways, street lamps along them. He saw numerous banking houses and trade centers and homes. The magnificent San Francisco Bay stretched away from the east side of the hills, and the sweep of the Pacific Ocean stretched from the west, with ships and boats galore, ranging from small skiffs to huge ocean-going vessels.[22]

Orson found George Q. Cannon and other brethren, who greeted him with gladness. With them he discussed his assignments on both sides of the Sierra Nevadas. All voiced concern for the magnitude of his challenges.

July 3, in San Francisco, Orson wrote a letter to Brigham Young to explain his dilemma and try to get directions. "By the laws of Utah," he reminded the President, "the Probate Courts are 'always open.'" He described his recent travels and added: "Say it will require two weeks to perform the trip back and forth. Meals over the mountains $1.00 each. It will cost me $50= cash for expenses each trip besides the cost of a mule to ride over the mountains and paying his charges until I return which may be from 5 to 10 dollars. . . ."

Orson sincerely felt, he wrote, that "I can attend to the paper in California, or to the affairs of Carson Valley. I have no choice which, but to run back and forth to attend to both, will consume much of my time in traveling and cost me more money for expenses than I now see where is coming from. Money is as scarce here or more difficult to be obtained than in Salt Lake City. . . . [B]esides in the winter, or say 7 months in the year I should not want to attempt to cross the Sierra Nevada Mountains. Some men may do it. I should not like to.

"I expect to go to Carson in a few days and organize—to attend to the mission and to prepare for a settlement," Orson continued. "I am ready to resign my judgship if you think best. . . . I shall act in Carson as far as I can till I hear from you."

Orson had told his San Francisco brethren of a dream in which he received a surprising suggestion as part of the solution to his turbulence. This facet of the solution was to use tobacco. The dream had brought memories of the pleasure tobacco had been to him many years ago. Could this dream be a true message, as many of his dreams were? His brethren expressed encouraging opinions. "My friends here," he now told Brigham Young, "advise me to use tobacco, Bro. Heywood especially. He thinks that I have given full proof of abstinence lo! these many years. He thinks that you can release me from my covenant of abstinence, according to my dream which was that you and Br. Kimball did so. I think that it would be a great relief to me. Nevertheless I will do as you shall think best."

During his several days in San Francisco, Orson tried unsuccessfully to recover debts owed to the Church by specific members. They had mortgaged their property to unwise limits, and Orson doubted that the Church would recover its investment. Joseph Heywood and Judge Stiles remained in California when Orson began his journey home.[23]

In Sacramento, on his return, Orson attempted to get action on establishing the boundary line between California and Utah. He walked with positive strides through the pillared portico into the brick capitol building, but had a disappointing conversation with Governor Bigler and Mr. Marlette, the Surveyor General. The two officials were cordial. They even promised to attend to the matter, but in tones doubtful and faltering. Obviously they wanted the line to remain unsettled until they could petition the United States Congress for all of the country on both sides of the Sierra Nevadas.

Back at Mormon Station at his tent compound, Orson discovered that things had changed little. The "boys" were employed in harvesting and whatever additional jobs they could procure. With the high cost of food and other goods they had to be diligent to get enough means to provide for themselves. The scouts that Orson had sent fifty miles east to the Walker River Valley were back from their expedition. They had found only "a barren sandy & rocky region." Orson would next send scouts twenty miles north to "Washaw Valley" and farther north to Truckee Valley. Orson requested this exploring in case the Saints were unable to procure enough land in Carson Valley for a settlement.

If the boundary survey proved Carson Valley to be in Utah, Orson wanted a Mormon settlement here. However, such might be impossible. "The best portions of it are all taken up by claimants whose modest inclinations towards the public domain," Orson tells, "have led them to grasp nearly all the land that joins them." The ranches contained 320 acres each, generally well fenced, with substantial barns and dwelling houses. "This may be all right," Orson adds, referring to the widespread homes, "yet it will preclude the possibility of a dense population, such as the valley is capable of sustaining, and which is so necessary for schools, [and] meetings." Orson estimated the population "to be about four hundred inhabitants, scattered along the river from 80 to 100 miles, and sparsely through some neighboring valleys."[24]

Orson had talked with enough of the settlers to learn that most of them preferred being part of California, rather than Utah, because of the nearness for trade and communication. Yet these same citizens would not resist being part of Utah. Even though he had to dismiss one meeting because of a drunk man's harassments, Orson had quieted fears that he would try to make Mormons of everyone or impose Mormon restrictions. He convinced them that he had come to organize the civil and constitutional laws of the land. But until the determination of the boundary line he could do little. He reported this to Brigham Young on July 15. "Remember me in your prayer circle," he concluded his letter, "and be assured that I will try to do all in my power to roll on the work of God."[25]

Feeling it imperative that he do more than sit and wait for the governor to act, Orson asked Christopher Merkley to choose two other competent men from among their group, travel over the mountains, and volunteer to assist the Surveyor General. Orson would follow in a week or so to encourage things. Brother Merkley selected Seth Dustin and George Hancock. The three set out the latter part of July.

Orson followed early in August, and when he arrived in Sacramento he was elated to find "the boys" and the deputy surveyor, George H. Goddard, adjusting instruments. They had the surveying equipment set up on the flat roof of a four-story building. For the few days while the adjustments were completed, Orson preached, and he visited with Church members in the area.

The morning of August 15 the surveying group left Sacramento and traveled to Placerville, where they began their observations. Here a government surveyor joined them. He would work on his assignment of mapping the country.[26]

In Placerville, Orson had a little time to spare, and because Carson County would soon need a district attorney to help Judge Stiles hold district court, Orson looked for an attorney. He met and liked L. A. Norton, young and enterprising. They chatted, and Orson felt good about the man's attitude regarding law, order, and fairness. Orson asked Mr. Norton if he would come to Carson and act as district attorney for the court.

Mr. Norton apparently liked the twinkle in his visitor's eye and the adventurous approach Orson made to challenges. He consented. Rather than waiting, and traveling by himself, he would accompany Orson and the survey group to Carson, even though the survey would make for a slow trip. During the days of their trek up the mountains they became better acquainted.

Norton was thirty-six years of age and obviously thought of Orson as "old." At fifty years, Orson was portly, robust, obviously in command of every situation, and yet concerned for everyone around him and willing to listen to suggestions. "The old man and myself," Norton commented about surveying together, "took observations by the north star. . . . I say *we* took observations; well, he took the observations and I looked on. We lay by the same camp-fire and slept under the same blankets, and Mormon elder as he was, I learned to love the old man."

Orson narrates about the survey that he had agreed to "furnish three competent men or efficient ones, and two animals. . . . This being complied with on my part, and more, by my giving up my own animal to pack, and taking it on foot through the mountains, the expedition was undertaken. [The men] brought the chronometers, thermometers, and Barometers by hand on foot from Sacramento City to measure time, temperature of the atmosphere, and height of mountains and depression of vallies. Astronomical observations began at Placerville. . . .

"From Placerville," Orson continues, "we proceeded along the old Carson route, taking observations every night [with the stars] and triangulations every day carefully, . . . from peak to peak. [This way we established] the relative positions of all the neighboring peaks."

Next they moved down into Bigler Lake Valley. From this camp, surveyor Goddard describes, they ascertained that "the initial point formed by the crossing of the 120th meridian, and the 39th parallel, falls in Lake Bigler."[27]

"Why could not Congress have acknowledged," Orson expounded regarding the angle, "the natural boundary which nature's God has ordained, . . . the principal range of the Sierra Nevada mountains, instead of the 120th degree of west longitude, where the [39th] parallel of north latitude intersects it. Mercy! this angle drops right into Bigler lake, and a salmon might swallow it, or might not. From this angle the line shoots off in a tangent to the south-east."

They camped at the lake "for ten days and nights or more," Orson goes on, and "took a series of observations and triangulations, bearings &c. Afterwards made other halts in the mountains. Our men were detained in those mountains so much longer than they anticipated that they became somewhat dissatisfied. They discovered that the country was being mapped, and many bearings taken with the view of aiding the Survey of the road. They considered this, extra service, and not forwarding the establishment of the line particularly: But as both [the] maps and the road across the mountains would prove highly convenient and useful to the public generally, . . . I encouraged them to continue to the last, which they have manfully done, remaining in the mountains many a chilly day and frosty night. It was a cold and stormy berth . . . [for my] men . . . carrying chain, packing instruments and doing every thing necessary."

The group trudged on to Mormon Station, where the surveyors would analyze their data. Orson described himself, after "climbing and scrambling about in the Sierra Nevada mountains, more or less, to find the line between the two counties," by saying that "I look about as much like a grizzly as like a white man—fat, ragged, and saucy."[28]

Attorney Norton, though now at ease with "Judge Hyde" and the few of his men on the survey team, had never dwelt among Mormons and felt apprehension about what awaited him at Orson's camp. He wrote of his first day, amid the "tents, covered wagons, and shanties," that "I soon found myself surrounded with Mormons, and my blankets, saddle-bags, overcoat, and traps generally were stripped from my horse and thrown down in a large tent which, from the appearance of things, seemed to be the tent of Hyde; and all seemed ready to perform the duties of body-guard generally to Hyde. They rushed around and soon had a substantial meal prepared, to which the elder and myself did ample justice.

"After dinner," Norton narrates, "I went back to the big tent (which, by the way, was subdivided), and commenced looking for my baggage, as I wanted a cigar from my saddle-bags. But imagine my surprise and chagrin, for on examination there was not a vestige of my plunder where I had left it, or in sight. I did not know what to do. I did not feel like coming out and getting into a row with the Mormons the first thing on my arrival, and Hyde had gone out among his people to attend to some of his many duties. Well, I was perplexed, but concluded on the whole to forego my cigar and await the return of Hyde. On his return I rather shamefacedly told the elder that my things had all disappeared and I could not imagine what had become of them. I noticed a broad grin overspread the old man's face, when he remarked that we would go and see if we could find them. On entering the tent he addressed one of the lackeys and asked him what was done with the gentleman's things. He immediately led the way to a small room partitioned off with canvas. Upon one side of the room was a long pole on two crotches set in the ground, and there, neatly brushed, hung all my clothes, saddle-bags, and fixtures; and I soon discovered that I was not a subject to be robbed by the Mormons, but rather to be treated as a favored guest."

This August night Norton's adventures accelerated. "The weather was warm," he recounts, "and the old elder, or rather the probate judge of Carson County, and myself stowed ourselves away in the tent, rolled in our blankets for the night. We had not lain long before we had a realizing sense that there were about as many fleas as there were grains of sand under us, and that we were surrounded and covered with them to that extent that we were compelled to beat a hasty retreat and seek other quarters. There was a small haystack near by, of which we took possession. We shook our clothing and blankets and again turned in; but it was no go. The old judge could not stand the assault as well as I could; he had a buffalo robe, and he finally got up, divested himself of every stitch of clothing, and rolled himself in his robe, the flesh side next to his body, and then curled down on the hay and was soon asleep. But as for myself, I had no alternative but to surrender at discretion and submit to the torture until morning. How the Mormons stood it I do not know."

Norton proved enterprising. The next day he studied his surroundings and did something about the fleas. "Now there was a beautiful cold mountain stream flowing through the place," he tells, "running and sparkling over its sandy bed, and a large bowlder had parted the stream a short distance above our quarters, and left a little island of sand about ten feet wide and twenty feet long, with a nice flow of water each side of it. I told the judge that I thought we might yet get the best of the fleas; that we could put a couple of armfuls of hay in the stream long enough to get the fleas out of it, then take it out onto the little islet, spread it out in the sun and let it dry; then soak our blankets for an hour, wring them out and let them dry; then put some poles and brush on the sand and put our hay onto that, and thus fortify against the fleas.

"The idea struck the old judge favorably," Norton's account continues, "and before night his slaves had carried the whole thing out to perfection, and it proved a success. And before the week had elapsed there were at least a dozen little islands with similar sleeping arrangements in the stream, made by throwing in rocks above and sand below."[29]

While Orson's "boys" conquered fleas, and also worked at the jobs they had found, the surveyors remained in the valley computing data. And court convened.

District Court sessions lasted September 3 through 6, with Orson clerking. Judge Stiles and Attorney Norton performed their duties well, but about the only business transacted was the naturalizations of foreigners. Richard Bentley received his naturalization. The few accomplishments, however, Orson narrates, "convince[d] the people that his honor, Judge Stiles, is an able and efficient judicial officer. The ease and dignity with which he presided, the lucid manner in which he explained every doubtful and contested point, caused all prejudice to yield and melt away into the most profound respect and anxious desire on the part of the people for the county organization to be gone into at once."[30]

When Orson had returned to Mormon Station with the survey team, he expected to find instructions from Brigham Young, but none waited. His former directives said nothing about returning home following district court. Norton would leave, and the "boys" would start for Salt Lake Valley with Judge Stiles and Marshal Heywood. Orson yearned to accompany them, but what of Carson County? With the unsettled conditions because of the boundary line, and with his position as probate judge, he felt he would be shirking his duty if he departed. Also, he still needed to organize and carry out the election of county officers. Orson had been functioning at maximum energy, but winter approached. He would have few cases in probate court. Beyond court he would have no people to lead, no farm to work, no school to teach, no newspaper to edit, no meeting house to preach in, no store to tend, and no family with whom to share warm winter fires. He missed Marinda and Mary Ann and the children. Thoughts of lonely months stretched ahead of him. Brigham Young would undoubtedly be sending families in the spring to settle. Maybe he would send one or both of Orson's wives.

September 4, with Judge Stiles' court still in session, Orson wrote a letter to the Church Presidency. The preliminary boundary decisions had brought "a great change here in the feelings of the people for the better," he reported. ". . . I should think that it would be well for some man of a little strength and forecast to be in this western part of the Territory to keep an eye upon things here. Yet I have no wish to stay if I am needed more in any other place."

Then Orson penned the request he had mulled over, prompted by thoughts of the winter. "But if I do stay I want a wife with me," he said. He suggested either "Marinda or Mary Ann" or that President Young could send "some one else." He mentioned a woman who had formerly expressed to Brigham Young a desire to be Orson's wife. "I declined that proposal or wish of hers," Orson reminded, "on account of a fear that she looked upon almost every thing on the dark side of the picture which would tend to weigh down ones spirits instead of lifting him up. But in this I may be mistaken."

In this same letter Orson related the cheerless feelings he had about the coming months and yet his resolve about his assignment: "I wish ever to be at the service of the church," he wrote, "and am determined to engage in nothing except that which I am sure is right and that will meet with your approbation. . . . [T]his has been the darkest and least desirable mission, and the most dull and discouraging prospects that ever presented themselves to me; But I have been determined and still am to hold on and to do all in my power to accomplish a good work here."

After District Court concluded, L. A. Norton said his farewells, and later he wrote his impressions of what he had observed in Carson County. "Elder Orson Hyde was sent out [from Great Salt Lake City] as the leading spirit of the enterprise," he said, "and . . . they could not have sent a better man for the position. . . . Orson Hyde and myself [became] fast friends. I found that the old man possessed a fine intellect, and a kind and genial disposition, all backed up by a liberal education. He had a versatile mind, and was possessed of great energy of character. . . . In fact I . . . heard him preach ofttimes; his text was always from the Bible, and was always of that instructive character that would interest intelligent hearers. And during all the time I was with him I never heard him preach one of their doctrinal sermons."[31]

The surveyors finished their work too. Carson Valley belonged to Utah! According to initial calculations Mormon Station lay 4,337 feet above sea level, the east summit over Daggett's Pass attained 6,825 feet, Bigler Lake reposed at 5,961 feet, the west summit over Johnson's Pass reached 6,743 feet, and Placerville measured 1,755 feet. "I wish to return thanks," Mr. Goddard expressed officially, "to Judge Hyde, of Utah Territory, for his efficient assistance in carrying out the objects of the expedition; to Col. Reese, of the Mormon Station; to Mr. Mott, Mr. Thorington, and their families, for their courteous and liberal hospitality; and to the inhabitants of Carson Valley generally for the promptitude with which any requirements I made upon them were immediately met and responded to; I owe thanks to the liberal proprietors of the San Francisco and the Placerville lines of telegraph, for placing their wires at our disposal for comparing the chronometer both at Sacramento and at Placerville; and to Mr. Herrick, of San Francisco, who kindly lent me a very excellent Borda circle [small astronomical instrument that measures angles], which has been of much service during the expedition." With the survey satisfactorily completed, the assistants from among Orson's men left to carry the instruments back over the mountains.

September 10, after packing their goods and dismantling their community of tents, Judge Stiles, Marshal Heywood, and the guard began their return to the Great Salt Lake Valley.[32]

September 20, successful county elections transpired. On the ballot Orson had placed a choice of locations for the County Seat. The voters affirmed his own choice, Mormon Station, and Orson changed its name to "'Genoa,' after the birth place of Columbus, him who discovered this glorious Land." Soon Orson surveyed the streets of Genoa, using basic instruments and the skills he had learned in the mountains. This gave him the distinction of naming the first town and laying out the first streets in what would later become the state of Nevada. Also, he took on other surveying jobs.[33]

September 30 he reported proceedings of the mountain survey and of the election to "Governor" Brigham Young. Two days later, October 2, he wrote to "President" Brigham Young, alluded again to the fact that he had no directive to leave, and expressed again his desires for a wife. He closed his letter pensively, wondering why he had still received no instructions:

> I cannot sit down in your Councils every week and tell all my thoughts, neither can I run in every day and talk and chat awhile as I used to do, and trust I shall again; therefore I trouble you with rather lengthy communications. You will pardon me I hope. . . . I have not rec'd a line from head quarters since I left, except through the news. Should be very glad to get a line now and then. But I put the most charitable or favorable construction upon it. If you thought I was going far astray, I am sure you would write me and correct me. So I shall go

ahead on my present course until you or the Lord direct otherwise. God bless you all forever Amen.

Orson continued surveying, and he also administered occasional court actions. Utah law empowered probate judges to try criminal cases as well as to rule in estate matters. September 10 he heard and ruled in a property jurisdiction conflict. October 3 a lawsuit was entered with him in a case "of Debt & Damages." October 27 he helped make a decision about water rights. October 28 he performed a marriage.[34]

October 28 became a jubilant day for him personally when a newsy letter arrived from Brigham Young. Written two months before, August 31, it answered Orson's of July 15. Even though assuming that Orson was probably on his way home, President Young included a few instructions, primarily about the debt in Sacramento. "If you are still there when this reaches you," Brigham Young wrote, "please to attend it and get that debt secured if not paid; do not let that slip through on any pretence of [the debtor Church member] going to do large things."

Orson answered Brigham Young the next day, October 29, from Genoa, promising to do what he could about the debt. He also reported: "My health and spirits are good. All is Well here at present so far as I can see, or at least as well as one could reasonably expect. The people here cannot be led and governed like they were Mormons or <u>Saints</u>. There are many mormons here, but I fear not Saints. Some very good folks not withstanding, even among the gentiles who would join the church if those who are called Mormons would honor their profession. I think some will join any how. I preach every Sabbath, and am engaged with the County Surveyor in running out claims. The Recorder has left and appointed me deputy recorder. I am pretty busy at present 'Judging the People,' Surveying, recording, preaching, building &c. &c. Not idle a bit."[35]

October 31, Orson received a marvelous surprise when the common occurrence of a wagon arriving from the desert developed into the uncommon occurrence of his wife Mary Ann stepping out of it. Brigham Young had been most expeditious. He had learned, October 5, from the returned Carson group, that Orson would remain the winter and wanted a wife. President Young purchased a team and arranged for James Townsend to take Mary Ann to Carson County. They started their journey October 10.

Brigham Young sent a letter with Brother Townsend that answered some of Orson's questions. Orson need have no concern for the newspaper in California, as George Q. Cannon would manage all details. Regarding another of Orson's requests, "Just use as much tobacco as will make you happy," Brigham Young wrote. "I trust you may find your health improved by it. So far as I am concerned I freely absolve you from all reproach by so doing." (In an earlier letter that failed to reach Orson, dated September 29 in reply to

Orson's of July 3, Brigham Young had written, "Concerning tobacco, make yourself <u>comfortable</u> by chewing and smoking all you wish until you come home, and then we will talk it over.") As well as answers, the October 9 letter from President Young included instructions that Orson "organize a military command, probably a battalion of infantry and a company of cavalry," also "organize a branch of the church in Carson County with a presidency of stake, high Council, &c."[36]

November 2, Judge Orson Hyde acted in his first criminal case. A black slave named Thacker was brought before him "for using language of a highly threatening character." Thacker was accused of saying that "he had spite enough in his heart against A. J. Wyckoff to kill him," and that "he could cut the heart out of Mrs. Jacob Rose and toast it on the coals." To protect the man from the wrath of an immediate public execution, Judge Hyde ordered his arrest. Then Orson determined that indeed Thacker had spoken the claimed sentiments, yet no crime had been committed. Orson fined Thacker fifty dollars for the costs of the suit and advised him, "for his own safety," to proceed on over the Sierra Nevadas to California and his master. "A man," Orson summed up the case, "may have malice enough at heart to kill another, and judgment and discretion to prevent him from committing the deed; he may have the ability to cut a lady's heart out and roast it upon the coals, and at the same time he may have good sense enough not to do it."

On other occasions Orson's log-walled "court room" saw additional heated scenes. One public controversial matter roused the feelings of the settlers, ranchers, and prospectors to great excitement. Fearing that Judge Hyde would rule in favor of a Mormon involved, they made threats openly that if he did so he would never live to get out of the courtroom. He prepared thoroughly. While delivering his carefully worded decision, he read it from his manuscript, his left hand handling the papers. His right hand, beneath the table, held a loaded six-shooter, cocked and ready for action. As he read he frequently heard the click, click of men cocking their pistols in the room crowded to the door. However, no firing occurred. The spectators accepted his decision.[37]

Orson's acts of fairness impressed his Genoa neighbors, and these settlers, in turn, generally treated him and Mary Ann kindly. Having Mary Ann to share his frustrations and joys brought great comfort to Orson, and he thanked Brigham Young in a letter November 17. Christopher Merkley would deliver the letter; he had returned to Genoa from taking instruments back to California and was ready to proceed on to Salt Lake City.

To President Young Orson also wrote of personal concerns, that from "letters and by verbal reports, I learn that my family live pretty short; and that the income of the store hardly supplies them with necessaries. If you feel like it, I wish you would speak a word about my taxes there, and have the payment put off till I can make some little arrangments or get something myself to pay them. I am doing considerable work here in surveying &c., but get not much but potatoes, barley, flour and labor in return."[38]

As days grew colder, Orson surveyed less, resulting in spare time, and the request that Brigham Young had made regarding the debt in California weighed on his mind. At this time of year the mountains stood as a seemingly invincible barrier, but Orson pondered. He decided to try to collect the funds due.

In December he and a young man named Willis started up the snow-covered Sierra Nevadas on mounts. They planned for Willis to accompany Orson over both summits and about twenty-five miles beyond, then return. This he did, and Orson proceeded on toward Placerville with his food and bedding behind his animal's saddle. Travel, however, became so difficult in the deep snow that after about three miles alone Orson returned too. He considered alternatives.

Back at home he remained a few days, made a pair of long, sturdy snow-shoes, again said good-bye to Mary Ann, and again started out with Willis. The animals made it up the first summit and down into Bigler Lake Valley, but the snow depth had increased since their previous effort, and part way up the second summit they could wade no farther. Orson and Willis tied the animals to a tree, secured Orson's gear to their own backs, and footed it to the top, where the snow now lay three and four feet deep. Beyond the summit Orson could carry a heavier pack than he could up the steep ascent.

He thanked Willis heartily and tied on his snowshoes. Willis departed to take the animals home, and Orson's swinging gait carried him among the tall pines on the high plateau country before the descent toward Placerville. Then snow began falling rapidly. In the fresh white powder Orson found that dragging his snowshoes required more exertion than he had anticipated. Travel became increasingly laborious in the relentless blizzard.

At about two o'clock in the afternoon Orson grew concerned that night might overtake him in the plight of being unable to strike a fire. Wood and logs lay buried under four feet of snow, and the fury of the storm had intensified to seemingly hurricane force, snow coming so fast that he could see less than twenty yards. He scooped bare a spot to build his fire, then many times climbed out of the snow nest to bring wood. He trudged, his snowshoes trailing, from tree to tree breaking off dead limbs and carrying them to his fire site. To add to his consternation, after he struck a blaze, several times the snow almost put the fire out. Also he had to clear blown snow from his nest. Another complication came when the fire melted the snow around it. Everything of Orson's became wet and frigid—his clothes, his blankets, and his food.

When darkness enshrouded his dismal domain, and the wolves howled, his fire required so much attention that Orson found no time for wrapping up in his wet blankets to lie down and sleep. Anyway, he felt sure that if he were to sleep he would freeze and then be devoured by the wolves. Snow and water prevented him from even sitting, and fatigue prevented him from standing. Half bent over, he spent the long night nursing his fire.

When daybreak at length came, the storm raged less furiously, but the air felt colder, and Orson resolved to start for home. After dragging his snowshoes for a few hours, the mid morning dim sun allowed him to see beyond the forested plateau to the mountain outlines. He looked in stunned surprise. He was headed not toward home, but toward Placerville. Because he had come so far, he decided to keep on in a westerly direction.

The snow grew increasingly deeper. When Orson at times stepped upon the top of a young pine tree almost sticking its tip above the snow, his snowshoes turned and capsized him. Then he struggled in a sea of snow, suspended head down and feet up with snowshoes tied to them, like a man in deep water with a bladder tied to each foot. His situation had become unbearable.

The sensible move seemed to be to turn again and take the back track, which he did. Numbly he walked and staggered, the biting cold growing more intense.

At about eight o'clock at night he arrived back at his fire site. To the doleful accompaniment of howling wolves in the dark forest, Orson poked among the coals, put on more wood, and kindled a blaze. The fire warmed him a little and dried him a little, but his urgent need was for rest. Beside the fire, on the hot ashes and the cold ground, he spread one blanket double, lay on it, and over himself spread two other blankets. As the prolonged night passed he alternately burnt and froze, and his feet felt less and less a part of him. Frostbite had apparently begun. And home lay many miles away. Orson perceived his mind slipping, and, knowing that a freezing person gradually loses awareness and sleeps peacefully into death, he supposed that he had almost accomplished his earthly mission.

Foreseeing complete exhaustion and the harsh reality that traveling would soon be impossible, he concluded that while still coherent he should mark his place of decease. With effort he picked up his snowshoes and labored through the snow to a pine tree. His fumbling fingers tied the long webbed frames in the branches. A traveler in the spring would spot them hanging here and thus discover the location of his demise. This last melancholy act performed, he struggled plaintively to his fire, stirred it again and added wood, rearranged his blankets, and lay down to die.

Orson's thoughts matched the stiffness of his body. Slipping into unconsciousness would be a welcome relief from the cold. Sleep, only sleep, seemed desirable. But, listening to the somber laments of the timber wolves, a part of his mind resisted. [39]

CHAPTER 20

. . . *Israel among the Gentiles.* . . . *(1855–1856)*

> . . . *remnants of Israel . . . among the Gentiles.*
> —Doctrine and Covenants 113:10

IN his snow-surrounded nest on the plateau west of the "second summit" of the Sierra Nevada Mountains, Orson expected death during the bleak night of December 22–23, 1855. Numbness of mind and limb increased, though he tried to combat sleep in his alternately warm and frigid berth near his ebbing fire.

Toward dawn a new sensation enveloped him—comfort—when, incredulously, he felt the gentle touch of hands upon his head. Afterward he was unsure whether his mortal eyes had opened or his spiritual eyes only visualized, but the hands belonged to his mother. Lovingly, concerned, she bent over him. And she spoke to him, who had last seen her when he was seven years old. Her imploring words, "Get up, my boy! Go on, go on!" quickened his heart and mind.

By extreme exertion of will Orson arose. Slowly, stiffly, he bound his pack and retrieved his snowshoes. At sunrise he made a sun course and began walking, if his movements could be described thus. Energized by the profound impact of his mother's urging, his legs lifted and dragged his feet. Forcing himself to keep moving, he rolled down hills whenever the incline allowed this method of travel. Periodically he ate from his diminishing food supply, careful to consume only half rations or less. At night he kept moving, trance-like, his feet and lower legs much swollen and hard as marbles. Could he really ascend the steep summit beyond the lake?

Somehow he conquered this "first summit." For the two days of his hard tracking in the glaring sun he kept to his course, the lingering reverie of his mother's solicitude impelling him on. The second evening, after rolling down much of the last snowy mountain, he lodged in a clump of willows and heard dogs bark. He had landed near Dr. Charles Daggett's residence a few miles south of Genoa. The barking dogs alerted Dr. Daggett to investigate, and he found Orson, exhausted.

Rather than bringing Judge Hyde into his warm home, Dr. Daggett took him to the nearby frozen-over stream. A hole was soon chopped in the ice, Orson's boots (his only pair) cut off his feet, and his stockings removed. He sat on the ice, his black board-like swollen legs and feet dangling in the running water to thaw them out. When they finally felt soft to the touch, Orson received assistance into the house. Dr. Daggett rubbed the thawed limbs with turpentine and then packed them in fluffy raw cotton. The next morning, Christmas Day, a buggy ride delivered Orson to Mary Ann.[1]

Mary Ann was exultant, astounded. Each recent day had added to her apprehension that her husband lay dead in the mountains. Willis nor the animals had returned to report or indicate that Orson proceeded west on the journey. Mary Ann feared that all had perished. Now Orson and she concluded lamentably that Willis and the animals truly became casualties of the howling mountain storm. The months ahead revealed no trace of him.

Agonizing days followed. Orson's painful feet developed huge red blisters, slowly turned from black to pink, and then dead tissue sloughed off. Orson felt deep gratitude for Mary Ann's loving care. With tenderness she followed Doctor Daggett's instructions. Immobility disconcerted Orson, but reports came to him of happenings among the settlers.

Developments transpired that disappointed. A group of inhabitants circulated a petition to send to the national government asking to be attached to California, and it gained many signatures. This motivated Orson to draw up another petition remonstrating the first one and including helpful information for the Utah Territory Representative in Washington, D.C. Orson sent his petition around the valleys and obtained a respectable minority of signers. But this prompted still another citizen petition for Washington. This one, Orson describes, "was got up for the ladies of the valley to sign stating that I was here with one of my spiritual wives, and they and their daughters did not wish to be connected to a government where such institutions were forced upon them." Only a few women signed it, and Orson decided the situation inappropriate for him to protest further.

"[W]e kept calm . . . ," he reported to Brigham Young, "and I think they are ashamed. In reality we are respected, but some affect to despise. We try to take a wise and prudent course, and I think we shall get along well until we leave. Mr. Motts, Cossers, W. B. Thorrington and Doct. Daggett are very kind to us, and also others. . . . Col. Reese and his lady have been very kind to us. The Col. has truly acted the part of a brother."

January 6, Orson received a cheering letter from Brigham Young, dated October 30, congratulating him on the success of "the organization of Carson County, the establishment of the boundary line &c." President Young also stated his "wish that you would mention a suitable man for the office you hold to fill that place when you return, which you are at liberty to do the ensuing season." This pleased Orson! And he was also pleased to learn from the letter that the subject of payment to the men who conducted the survey "will be laid before the ensuing Legislative Assembly for their consideration."

Orson answered January 13, 1856, two weeks and five days after his arrival home with frozen feet. He detailed his mountain disaster and went on:

"One foot now well, the other doing well, but looks as much like any thing else as a foot. Doct. says he thinks I will only lose my little toe on right foot. I feel first rate have only lost about 50 pounds of flesh with the freeze and pain. Tobacco is a good relief and amusement to me." In the same letter he expressed his gratitude for Mary Ann, and he recommended Dr. Charles D. Daggett for Probate Judge.[2]

Orson wrote again to Brigham Young, January 25: "Frozen feet cause the hand to tremble, so you must excuse. I believe the heart is steady and unquivering. . . . An Indian is doctoring my feet. He says no walk—no smoke—no drink fire-water, but sit still and do as he says, and in somi mannah (10 days) feet be heap goodie. I long for the spring to come that I may return to the city and council of the saints."

With the January 25 letter Orson included his resignation as "Probate Judge of Carson County Utah Territory . . . to take effect so soon as I am officially notified that this resignation is accepted and the vacancy caused by this resignation filled, so that the County may not be left without an acting Judicial officer of this class."

Days passed slowly as Orson maneuvered on crutches, his feet either wrapped or wearing Indian moccasins. "[T]hawed feet," he commented two months after his mountain ordeal, "are far more severe and tedious than frozen ones." Occasional letters were a welcome respite during his convalescence. Especially was he pleased, as in past seasons, when one came from Marinda. From his family he learned that on December 12 he became a grandfather at the birth of Emily's first child. He also received word that the January Legislature renewed his appointments as Probate Judge and as a Regent of the University of Deseret.[3]

Winter still held the weather scepter when Orson received a letter from Brigham Young telling that he was indeed sending settlers, to arrive in early summer, and among them would be an appointed replacement for Orson as Probate Judge. The tone of the letter indicated that President Young expected Orson to oversee settlement of the company. This, along with not being replaced in his legal duties as soon as he had hoped, convinced Orson that, in spite of his personal desires to leave, he should stay in Carson until fall. This he reported to President Young.

Orson considered possible settlement sites for the immigrants. He thought previously that new arrivals should buy out the established farms in Carson Valley, but he had changed his mind. If Saints attempted to buy out the inhabitants in a rush, prices would rise so high that purchase of farms would leave newcomers no means left to sustain themselves. Another option: the coming brethren could settle on unclaimed land north of Carson, where lay many splendid valleys, with plentiful timber, water, and grass. However, recent reports of extensive discoveries of gold in some of those valleys impelled Orson to consider that in a short time the area would be overrun with gold diggers, leaving no place for the Mormons. Orson must act decisively, and fast. He must explore the valleys north for one or two hundred miles, though he knew not how, with the condition of his feet. The trip would take about four weeks.

In addition, thinking of many needed homes and of the big trees on the mountain slopes, Orson decided a saw mill would be necessary in a new settlement. "We want a good saw mill instanter," he explained to Brigham Young in a letter March 22. "Six and Seven feet logs in diameter do not so readily roll up into log cabins. We want to saw them up." After his exploring trip Orson would send Brother Townsend over to California to arrange for sawmill irons.

Another factor in Orson's decisions was that the County Surveyor resigned. Orson intended to get himself appointed by the County Court as the new surveyor and then survey for the coming settlers as soon as he could walk without crutches.[4]

Orson calculated to discourage gold rushers by publishing that Mormons would begin settlements in valleys east of the Sierra Nevadas. He hoped that many Saints would come from California as well as from the Rocky Mountains and become a majority. Early in March he had written a letter to Brother Cannon in San Francisco to be printed in the new *Western Standard*. In the letter he appealed for Saints in California to move to Carson County. In a postscript he added, "It is supposed the mountains will be passable on the Johnson cut-off by way of Luther's pass, for pack animals, by the latter part of April; and on the old Carson route, for teams, about one month later."

March 23, the day before leaving on his northern expedition, he wrote another letter for publication in California in the *Western Standard*. Because he had no money for purchasing equipment, he appealed for funds and included an authorizing statement for James Townsend, who would soon travel to California to collect finances for "irons and fixtures for a good saw mill. . . ."[5]

Two local non-Mormons accompanied Orson on his exploring journey toward Oregon Territory. After about sixteen miles they rode their animals up the steep incline beyond Eagle Valley (the valley second north of Genoa's location), and they looked out over "Wassau" Valley (later spelled "Washoe"), lush with bunch grass. Another person enchanted by the scene describes it:

> Towards the setting sun loomed the Sierra, a procession of uprising heavily-timbered ridges broken by deep gorges, the central one scarred by landslides. From the foothills long piney fingers reached out eastward across the fertile fields and tule lands towards Washoe Lake, whose waters reflected the bright blue of the sky. Large detached groves of evergreens lay like parks here and there about the meadows. To the east,

climbing out of the sparkling waters of the lake, rose [a] range of grey naked hills. . . . Twelve miles long and seven wide Washoe Valley, enfolding Washoe Lake, was completely encircled by hills and mountains like a precious stone in a pendant. . . . Birds, wild animals and nomadic bands of Washoes [Indians] claimed this picturesque jewel of a valley as home.[6]

Orson liked this location and now had the same good feelings about it as when he surveyed in it several months before for a speculating settler.

In Wassau Valley, Orson's group rode along the western mountains. Beyond half of the basin's twelve-mile length, they arrived at the Hodgis property Orson had surveyed the previous fall, a choice piece on the north side of an ample stream. Piled in one area of the unoccupied ranch Orson saw "a quantity of cedar rails and timber cut for rails in the can'on next of said Ranch." Of particular interest to him were the "one hundred good and substantial Cedar fence post[s]" that he had paid for in the early part of December 1855. He and Hodgis had contracted that Hodgis would haul these posts to Genoa, but they still lay here. Mr. Hodgis had left the area, even though already elected County Constable. Orson decided that after the present excursion he must do something about this situation.

Fifteen miles beyond Wassau, Trucky Valley (later spelled Truckee, where the city of Reno would grow) favorably impressed the group, and they continued on. They traveled north 150 miles, primarily along the base of the Sierra Nevadas, but afterward they figured a total trip of 500 miles because they "rambled over and among the mountains," some of them extremely high. Orson, his crippled feet wrapped, felt grateful for transport on his steady mule. At campsites where the terrain allowed he used his crutches. At other times, and when he wanted to inspect the ground closely, he crawled around on hands and knees. He acted jovial about his handicap, and his congenial companions readily performed the chores difficult for him.

Gold fever raged in the northern region of the exploring trip, and Orson thought this area lay in California. Also, even though the group found land of excellent quality in the northern location, with vast stands of timber, the mountains were low. Consequently, winter deposits of snow would afford only a limited supply of summer water. After a thorough exploration, Orson considered the northern region less suitable for agriculture than Wassau and Trucky valleys. As well, these two lay nearer Carson Valley where supplies could be had. During the weeks of travel the three men endured cold nights and several storms, but Orson's feet improved.

Orson's travels had convinced him that Wassau Valley should be the central place for the coming pioneers. He and Mary Ann had heard previously that Richard Bentley would be among them. Orson figured to take up a large enough ranch in Wassau for Richard that Mary Ann could have a share and live close to her sister, Richard's wife. Then, even though Orson would return to Salt Lake City, he could eventually come back to this appealing area, and he would have a place.[7]

April 20, in the evening, Orson received an unexpected opportunity to send a letter eastward the next day, so he stayed up and wrote to Brigham Young. Normally, in their frugal manner of living, he and Mary Ann used only the fireplace blaze or embers for illumination after dark, but tonight he burned their last candle. He told about his recent trip and that in "some of the finest country and richest valleys I ever saw" he had "taken up many claims of land and water for the brethren. . . ." On a personal note he added: "I have only been keeping ship here, and holding on till I knew what was to be done. I am ready at any moment to let go and leave, or to hold on yet longer. I have not been rich enough to buy a pair of pants or boots since I left Salt Lake—have bought one hat only. Yet I am rich . . . so far as earthly comforts are concerned. When I went up north I wrapped up my feet in rags and moccasins. Wore no boots for two reasons. First, I had none to wear. Secondly, my feet are still so swelled that I could not wear them If I had them. But boots will come so soon as I can wear them. I could wear one boot now, but not two. I feel to care but little what I eat or wear, if I can only do my duty and enjoy the favor of God and that of my brethren. . . .

"I have inspired the farmers here," in regard to the anticipated needs of the coming settlers, he narrated, "to put in large crops of wheat, Barley &c. It is now up, but does not look very well on account of cool dry weather. They are preparing to put in large crops of potatoes, and other vegetables. Their beets and onions are mostly sowed and planted. . . . Provisions are scarce and dear here. Little or no flour for sale—we'll have to pack it over as soon as animals can cross the mountains. Plenty of good fish and rabits here—ducks & geese, some deer and antelope. The brethren can live here, however, if they can dig and work."

A week later, April 27, Orson felt prompted to write again to Brigham Young. He had received letters telling of destitute circumstances in many families in the Rocky Mountains, of food rationing, and that his own family struggled. He related to this, because he and Mary Ann, as well, had "not flour enough to last till harvest." He grieved that Saints endured hunger, and he had already sent a letter to William Price with "instructions about the disposition to make of what provisions we may have on hand [in our store]." Now, in this letter to President Young, he added his hope and prayer that "some effectual door may be opened for your aid and sustenance in due time. What ever my share in the provision store may be after my own familie's wants are duly considered in the absence of father and husband, is at the service of those poor and worthy Saints and strangers that [are] new comers, who naturally have none to look after them, who are helpless and none to provide for them. I want Martha [Orson's former wife, whose marriage with

Thomas McKenzie had failed] and her mother considered if there is anything."

About his health, he reported fast improvement, that he could "now walk about a mile without crutches before tiring out." He also expressed gratitude for the Lord's watchcare: "In my last, I told you that I was writing by our last candle. Since then a quantity of tallow with wicking has been brought in to be manufactured into candles at the halves [on shares]. So you can see that we have light again. Almost every needful thing seems to come along in a similar way! The Lord be thanked!"[8]

To help increase his blessings—specifically to try to recover his logs from Wassau Valley—Orson filed a suit in the Carson County Probate Court on April 30 against H. M. Hodgis. The same day the County entered suit against Hodgis for money he owed the County and for other items. Being "an absconded debtor," Mr. Hodgis' property in Wassau Valley was attached. A few weeks afterward his "Ranch No. 2" was sold to pay the debts.

Meanwhile, a hundred families of Saints would head westward from the Salt Lake Valley. Orson must be ready for them. He "prayed to God day and night for wisdom and knowledge." Along with his prayers, he planned. Though he sensed the approval of Heaven in his efforts, he felt isolated, a world apart from Church headquarters. He endeavored to act according to the direction he felt and according to what he believed Brigham Young's wishes would be if he knew all circumstances.

"This morning," he said in a letter to Brigham Young, May 11, "the last scab fell from my foot. I can go about now quite briskly." He also reported Mary Ann unwell. "I trust, however, that with the approaching warm weather, her health will recover."[9]

May 12, 1856, as Orson had expected, the Carson County Court appointed him to fill the vacant office of County Surveyor, and he readied his plans for Wassau Valley. He anticipated ranches for the Saints containing one-half to one Section each (640 acres in a Section), with condition to subdivide when necessary. He also planned the square blocks and wide straight streets of a central village near the west mountains and south of the large sparkling stream of mountain water that was the south boundary of the Hodgis ranch, already sold. May 19, Orson surveyed the 320 acres of "Ranch No. 3," or "the Cherry ranch." The north part of this would be the town, containing five-acre home lots for each family. This tract extended one mile east from the mountains and one-half mile south from the stream.

Northwest from the townsite, across the stream and in the canyon, stood a cabin that Orson had purchased for his residence. On the half-mile-square plot (160 acres), containing canyon and mountainside, he had an excellent location for his proposed mill. Brother Townsend was now in California ordering a set of mill irons, tools, and fixtures.[10]

Orson and Mary Ann moved from Genoa to the canyon cabin. In the shade of lofty ponderosa pines (with bushy long needles in tufts), Mary Ann soon tidied the dwelling and stowed their few belongings. Her health indeed improved with invigorating spring air. She enjoyed walks under the pines, the ground cushiony underfoot with sand and pine needles, large pine-cones, and small stones. Orson and Mary Ann liked this location, with a beautiful view to the east of Wassau Lake and the hills beyond.

In late June, Orson welcomed the wagon trains of settlers, with their herds, arriving from the Rocky Mountains. Some of the dozens of men brought families; some planned to prepare for their families to come later. Orson and Mary Ann felt special gladness to behold and embrace Mary Ann's sister Elizabeth and husband Richard Bentley, with their children, also her brother William Price. William had left his wife and baby at home. Missionaries arrived also, en route to the Sandwich Islands (Hawaii) and Australia. One of these, John Hyde (no relation to Orson), reported conditions in "Wash-ho Valley" June 30, telling of the "heavy emigration to this point; Elder Hyde has his hands full. He is building a saw-mill [with hired local assistants] . . . ; the plain is dotted with wagons and covered with cattle; this, another north of this [Steamboat Springs] and Truckee valleys are taken up by the brethren. . . . Several [well-improved and extensive] rancheros have been bought out [in Carson, Eagle, and Jack valleys], and the Mormon doctrine of go-a-head is the order of the day.

"The course pursued by Elder Hyde during his twelve month's stay here," the report continued, "has been marked with great wisdom; and now his counsel is, to the brethren here, to labour hard, settle up, mind their own business, to be slow of speech, and to live their religion; to fear God and work righteousness."

These hectic days demanded of Orson a myriad decisions about settlement and continual directions to the ten men employed on his mill. July 1 he sent other men and teams and conveyances to California to get the irons and the saws that Brother Townsend had ordered earlier. During daylight Orson and Mary Ann labored on the mill, driving construction ahead with all possible speed in order to produce lumber before winter. This left only nights for Orson to ride among the settlements and assess progress.[11]

Living in their tents and wagons, the brethren built their cabin walls of hewed logs, but would wait for lumber to add roofs, floors, doors, and windows. Also they herded livestock, cut hay, made fences, raised stables, and constructed corrals. They and their wives planted gardens and also the poplar saplings and rose cuttings brought tenderly to beautify their new homes. A few families became disgruntled at the exhausting toil to start settlements, packed up, and traveled on to California. Other men temporarily left, journeying to California with butter, cheese, eggs, and cash to trade for flour, groceries, and other articles to pack back over the mountains for winter consumption. Two of the sojourning missionaries, to earn money for their missions, helped Orson survey property. Also Orson still served as probate judge, because no replacement appointee came with the immigrants.[12]

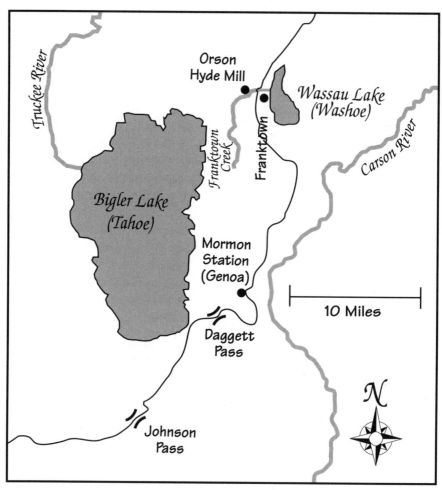

Genoa and Wassau (Washoe) Valley area.

Meanwhile, another problem had beset Orson after the coming of the wagon trains: a domineering federal judge, William W. Drummond. He arrived with the settlers to hold court, and his haughty demeanor distressed Orson. Also, Drummond possessed no legal authority to hold court. As judge of the Second Federal Judicial District of Utah, he had crossed the desert to act in a part of the Third District, with permission of sorts as a trade with Judge Stiles, but with no legal appointment. Orson had no means to restrain his actions, no recourse short of lynching. He felt helpless. "I presume," Orson remarked to a friend, "that all the legality of his Court arose from an oyster supper and a bottle of brandy." Later Orson learned that on just such an occasion the plan had indeed been concocted.

Orson experienced further resentment when Drummond demanded that he act as clerk of the court. Orson declined, but Drummond said that if he refused, another man would be appointed and Orson fined. On second thought, Orson agreed to serve. Perhaps he could guide proceedings a little.

As days in the barn-held court passed, Orson became increasingly appalled that Drummond's decidedly anti-Mormon attitude colored everything he did. He seemed intent on destroying the good feelings for law that Judge Stiles had accomplished in Carson County the previous fall. Utah law gave criminal jurisdiction to probate courts, but Drummond repealed this power in Carson County and ruled that if the probate judge participated in settling any criminal disputes he could be immediately shot. A man convicted of larceny was allowed to escape. Collected fines that rightfully belonged in the Utah Territorial treasury were ordered into the United States treasury. Drummond accepted the bribe of a horse from a non-Mormon, and he ruled against a Mormon in a case that seemed by Orson clear-cut in the other direction. Drummond disregarded many acts of the Utah Legislature and disrupted local taxation rules. In Orson's opinion, "for a cause that is as plain and true as two and two are four, he will call it five if he take a notion, especially if it is going to operate against Mormon interests." Court dragged out turmoil for most of July. Orson felt increasingly exasperated and helpless. And for many hours out of court—though his mill and the settlers needed him—he wrote court minutes and transcripts of minutes.

In addition to Orson's disheartenment about the judge, he was saddened when two of the sojourning Mormon missionaries sided with Drummond. Orson told one of them that his "logic amounts to nothing more nor less than that you cut off your head to get your scalp to make your self a pair of mocassins."

Drummond's actions prompted Orson to reflect upon his own feelings about law. "I can never consent," he concluded, "to make right and justice bend to the law, but the law must bend to justice. Law is but the opinions of men. Justice is an eternal principle that must endure forever and the test to which we must all submit sooner or later; but an unbiased Judge can generally administer Justice without much infringment of the Laws."

Though discouraged, Orson cooperated with the judge, and no blatant conflicts arose between them. When court ended, Judge Drummond left for California.[13]

July 30 Orson reported to Brigham Young, sending the letter with several brethren returning to Salt Lake City. As well as telling about Drummond's court, Orson told that many settlers had grown dissatisfied. These "think they want their bread and butter all spread for them, and because it is not some murmur and want to go back to Salt Lake. We can raise all we need here in a little time. It is great for grass, water, and timber right at our doors. We can get a load of wood every day in the year and every hour in the day, and I think they will get over their homesickness by & by."[14]

Orson's debt for his mill mounted, both for materials and for wages. Money received for public services here in western Utah proved insufficient for such a mammoth undertaking. He borrowed a large sum from Gideon Wood, one of the brethren who had come to settle. Orson and Gideon had been friends for many years; Orson had baptized him in Florence, Ohio, during his first mission.[15] Orson confided, in the letter to Brigham Young, that he needed two thousand dollars. "I should very much like to have my store sold," he added, "and I authorize you to sell it if you have a chance. It cost me about $3,500 Smoke house and all. It was built for cash, and at low prices as you are aware. . . . I want all I can get for it of course. But I would take Three Thousand cash down for it if I had the chance, provided I could do no better. In that case I want two Thousand sent here and one Thousand for my family there. . . . I know you have a thousand cares, but perhaps you can speak a word for me about it, without much trouble."

Orson yearned for communication from Salt Lake City. "I have received no letters of late from you or from any one else," he lamented in his July 30 letter to Brigham Young. Lack of communication with his superiors and his family tore Orson apart. He continually vacillated between the wish to return and the duty he felt to the Carson Mission. If he could receive specific instructions from President Young about staying or returning, this would reduce his insecure feelings. He wanted to see his mill in operation and see thriving communities of diligent Saints here, but he also wanted to see and know more about his family in Salt Lake City. He sometimes wondered if he was really doing any good in Carson. Other times he felt extremely needed and rewarded.

In early August a wonderfully welcome letter arrived from Brigham Young, dated May 29, two months before. This helped alleviate Orson's feelings of isolation, but the letter contained no specific instructions about him staying or returning. President Young did suggest, however, that if Indians posed problems, "it would be well for the brethren to build a fort to live in, and take care of their stock."

When Orson answered the President's letter he stated that the local Indians were "all peaceable and friendly. There are about 20 of them constantly around me now that I am obliged to feed more or less. I apprehend no disturbance with them. The Hostile Indians are 2 or 3 hundred miles distant from us."

August 4 a "very spirited" election, with 128 voters, resulted in both Mormons and old settlers receiving office. This satisfied Orson; he felt that all of the men elected would try to serve the best interests of the citizenry.[16]

Mill developments also encouraged. In early August, teams arrived with the "eighteen and twenty hundred" pounds of mill irons. The drivers reported arduous labor, a "thousand difficulties," on the precipitous road from Placerville over the mountains. The teamsters calculated that they "made three or four thousand dollars worth of improvement on the road." The mill machinery, ordered from eastern dealers, had been shipped around Cape Horn to San Francisco, then up the river to Sacramento. At Sacramento men loaded the gear onto the conveyances from Carson, under the supervision of William Price, and transported it on to Placerville. Here "the heavier parts were suspended between the wheels of a 'two-wheeled' cart, drawn by a string of oxen and sometimes mules. . . . The lighter parts, belting, fixtures and accessories were carried over the mountains by pack train, horses and mules." Orson reported to Brigham Young again August 18, and about his mill he wrote: "Dam built, Race dug, timber for wheel and mill frame all out and on the ground and much of it worked. Saw and Irons all here on the spot and men enough now at work."

The progress on the mill gave Orson hope that he would be able to see it in operation and then return to Salt Lake City before winter. Drummond's destruction of the probate court's power, except in cases where someone died or went crazy, left Orson's judgeship duties minimal. Anxiety about a trip eastward, however, resulted from reports that the Indians on the upper Humboldt had been stirred up and were committing many depredations.

Along with his personal unrest, thoughts of the Saints in Salt Lake City brought unsettled feelings to Orson, a sense that these far-away friends were experiencing, or would soon experience, troublous times. He wrote to his family that "there [is] a day of trial near at hand, and . . . it [will] be general throughout the Church." He reasoned that government foment against polygamy might be the cause of it. "Thank God, they can only kill the body!" Orson expressed.[17]

The Mormon settlers' homes, fields, and herds, their anticipated bountiful harvest of potatoes and onions, and their progressing mill, caused the "old settlers" to feel threatened by increasing Mormon power. In August they began holding meetings with the theme of thwarting the influence of these people from Utah's headquarters.

Wanting his mill to be secure, should he receive short-notice instructions from Brigham Young to leave, Orson signed the title of it over to his brother-in-law, William Price. The same day, September 2, Orson also signed the Cherry Ranch over to Mary Ann's brother-in-law Richard Bentley.

Orson and his neighbors decided that their little town near the sawmill needed a better name than the general "Wassau Valley." The first white baby had been born in the settlement August 14: Frank Bentley, son of Richard and Elizabeth. In honor of this first child, the village became Franktown.

From "Franktown," September 12, Orson wrote to Brigham Young. "My mill is up," he described, "and the workmen are putting in the gearing and Irons." He praised its workmanship. He estimated the mill's worth at eight to ten thousand dollars. Expressing his contradictory feelings about returning or remaining, with mill construction taking longer than planned, he said, "If I stay to complete my mill, I can hardly return this fall. I feel very anxious to go home, and also anxious to complete the mill for my sake and others. If I had means others might complete it. But to create means, requires personal attention."[18]

September 28 a Church conference convened in Genoa in the commodious home that Brother Simon Baker had purchased. Here Orson organized the Church, appointing various officers, as Brigham Young had long ago instructed him to do. Orson had delayed purposely. Earlier, many settlers were over the mountains, trading and packing provisions, while those remaining cut hay, built homes, constructed barns and sheds and other outbuildings, and made corrals. Also, before choosing officers, Orson had wanted "to allow the brethren time to . . . prove themselves a little in this new country."

Another of Brigham Young's instructions, organizing the military, Orson had put off for some of the same reasons as for delaying Church organization, but he felt keenly aware that President Young might be displeased about his procrastination. "You may think that I have not done right," he wrote to the President September 28, "and you may think correctly too, for not using a stronger influence to have the military organized and the laws carried out. . . . Our people have been in their tents and wagons and with their hands full . . . ; and I have thought that an attempt to organize the militia . . . would cause an excitement that would greatly check our preparations for winter."

Orson disappointingly had received no letters in the recent mail from Salt Lake City. He expressed hope, in his September 28 letter to Brigham Young, "that my delay in carrying out laws &c. will not induce you to omit writing to me. I have written every chance and about every mail: and also to my family. May God Almighty bless you all forever & ever . . . is my daily prayer for you all."[19]

In early September, Judge Drummond neglected to arrive for the court he had appointed. This cheered Orson, but the judge sent word that he would hold court the first week in October. Orson's conclusion, that Drummond was afraid to come, seemed verified when he also failed to arrive in October. Later Orson learned that Drummond distributed false reports of the July sessions, showing the Mormons in a decidedly negative aspect.

Even without Judge Drummond, civil conditions grew more tense in Carson County. The second week in October a conflict between Mormons and old settlers, over a piece of property, led to opposing sides arming themselves and almost shooting at each other, but the excitement subsided. However, a portion of "the old citizens," Orson wrote hastily to Brigham Young on October 16, "have become highly mobocratic. They are going to regulate all matters. They are going to Lynch the assessor and collector till he pays back any taxes that he may have collected. All costs that have been paid in any law case must be refunded. No man that is a Mormon can live who has more than one wife. Every thing must be regulated; and to this end they are said to be enlisting the Indians. They already have from six to ten, and they say they intend to bring 300. This is the talk.

"We intend to do our duty," Orson continued, "and meet what ever exigence that may arise. . . . They say that they intend to run our mill when it is done. . . . It is a noble mill and almost ready to run. It looks rich, with the Irons upon it. There is now no chance for us but victory or death; and in the name of the Lord, we are resolved to stand our ground and do our best. We will trust in him."

Not knowing if any of his letters were getting through to Salt Lake City, two days later Orson again wrote his apprehensions to Brigham Young. "We wish to dwell in peace; but if we must fight, we shall try to do our best, and if we are used up, we can never be used up younger. . . .

"I marvel greatly that I hear nothing from the City from any source," Orson went on, ". . . I am led to think that our letters are intercepted. I hardly know what to think about it. . . . We have many good and valuable men here who are worthy—God bless them and you also forever & ever, and me too is my earnest and sincere prayer." After ending the letter, Orson added a postscript: "Should we get worsted we feel willing to become a sacrifice (if God will) that a more righteous Judgment come upon the ungodly. But we do not intend to be used up if we can avoid it."[20]

In spite of expecting attack any moment, no attack came. Work on the mill continued, as did the regular chores of daily living.

In a letter to Brigham Young, October 22, Orson asked for more settlers, as he had already done several times. Civil agitation had diminished, and though Orson was anxious, and ever alert, he felt that the Saints would not be immediately annihilated. "We will hold on till Spring, or try our best, at least," he said. The letter would travel with several brethren who had decided to return to the Salt Lake Valley rather than endure the rigors of Carson County for the winter.

Amid local consternations, the celebrated day arrived of the mill being finished. It "is a good one," Orson expressed, "and I believe it is built by faith." A "splendid mill," is the way another person described it. The imposing structure had been built of mammoth logs; and the water cascading over the wheel at the end of the millrace turned the gearing at rapid speeds. With "savage" noise the saws, both upright saws and circular saws, tore into trees and transformed them into lumber at the rate of "six thousand feet in twenty-four hours."

Orson Hyde and William Price, now partners in the mill enterprise, had discussed how to charge for milling. With trees plentiful, the brethren could easily bring their own timber to be cut on shares. This would leave Orson and William with no cash, just stacks of lumber and no customers to buy it. They decided they must hire trees cut and then charge for sawed boards, even though this resulted in the hardship for some of the brethren of paying "from 25 to 50 dollars per thousand feet of lumber." Maybe in the future, when the mill debt was paid, and as the populace diversified, other arrangements could be made.[21]

The welcome mill products allowed the settlers to secure their homes against winter's onslaughts. Orson and Mary Ann could now relax a little, with more time to enjoy the remaining crisp autumn days.

November 3, 1856,[22] Orson's plans changed abruptly after a letter arrived from Brigham Young. Dated September 1, it stated that the President had received Orson's letters written through July 2, but no opportunity had arisen to send a reply. Accompanying the letter was a blank appointment for a new Judge of Probate, signed, ready for Orson to fill in the name and date. Regarding this, President Young said, "As to returning, act your judgement and wishes in relation thereto. The papers now forwarded to you will enable you to leave whenever you wish, and you can retain them if you chose untill you do." Orson *wished* to leave immediately, but the turmoil in his heart about the strife between Mormons and old settlers caused monumental doubts about the wisdom of departing.

Farther on in the letter Orson's eyes riveted upon this sentence: "Bro William Price is at liberty to return to spend the winter, and requested to do so." This was an order! And it had been written two months ago! Should William really set out for Salt Lake City with winter so close? Also, Indians on the Humboldt had recently robbed, killed, and butchered a group of travelers. Orson read on. While writing, Brigham Young had received Orson's of July 30 and learned of the havoc Judge Drummond had made of law in Carson County. His comments were less than complimentary for the judge.

Then President Young's last sentence jumped off the page, it seemed, sending Orson's emotions reeling: "Do not let the God of this world [represented by materialism] have too great an influence over you, but let the Spiritual influences of the Almighty guide you as well."

Memories flooded Orson's mind, memories of the times that his actions had caused necessary chastisements from his beloved friend, the Prophet Joseph Smith. During Orson's dismal days in exile in Missouri, he had pledged to himself that he would never again go against the prophet of the Lord. Had he done so now? Had he been too caught up in temporal matters to know the will of God?

William, Orson concluded, should indeed return to the Salt Lake Valley, immediately, even though late in the season and with dangers abounding. The

Prophet had summoned. And Orson would go with William. They would leave tomorrow with other brethren already prepared to depart. The remainder of the day was hectic. Mary Ann packed food and bedding. She also packed a special candle, whose light would remind Orson of her devotion. Orson notified the other men that he and William would accompany them. And, not knowing if the group's lives would be spared, Orson wrote a letter to Brigham Young to go by the California mail:

> Your letter of Sept. 2nd [1st] came to hand about one hour ago; and in reply, I hasten to say, that from the blank appointment for Probate Judge, and from the Spirit and tone of your letter I consider that your wishes are for me to return: . . . the caution you gave me can do me no harm, and perhaps much good; at any rate I intend to profit by every word of caution given me. Through much labor and anxiety our mill is sawing lumber. . . . We have paid out every thing to build it, and are some in debt. Yet we leave it in the hands of the brethren here to help themselves, pay or no pay, and William and I start tomorrow if God will for Salt Lake City.
>
> . . . in the name of the Lord we venture at about 9 o clock tomorrow morning in our working dresses as they are all we have. . . . But I trust we shall see you and rejoice together before this letter reaches you. . . .
>
> . . . My kind love to all the Council, and with best wishes for the Twelve and All Zion, I subscribe myself as ever, Your Brother in the everlasting covenant. May Heavens choicest blessings rest upon you all forever.
>
> Finished Nov. 4.

Orson and Mary Ann felt a need to commune with their Maker in special prayer before Orson departed from Franktown, Wassau Valley. To be by themselves, with no knock at their cabin door to interrupt their worship, they walked to a secluded place in the pines. Here they prayed.[23]

. . . *edifying and chastisement*. . . . *(1856–1860)*

> *I am the Lord your God, even the God of your fathers, the God of Abraham and of Isaac and of Jacob. I am he who led the children of Israel out of the land of Egypt; and my arm is stretched out in the last days, to save my people Israel.*
>
> *Cease to contend one with another; cease to speak evil one of another. . . ; and let your words tend to edifying one another. . . . My people must be tried in all things, that they may be prepared to receive the glory that I have for them. . . ; and he that will not bear chastisement is not worthy of my kingdom. . . .*
>
> *Now, therefore, hearken, O ye people of my church. . . . Be diligent in keeping all my commandments. . . .*
>
> —Doctrine and Covenants 136:21-24, 31, 41, 42

ORSON'S and Mary Ann's prayers were answered. The company reached the Salt Lake Valley safely. But the journey had been tedious. Orson and the other nine men (one with a wife and two children) had started November 5, 1856, from Franktown. For several days and a hundred miles, the wagons jostled north to the Truckee River, east down this watercourse, and northeast across the desert to the brackish Humboldt River. At one point friends overtook the group, bringing extra flour from Mary Ann. Up the Humboldt, Orson and the others traversed two hundred and fifty exhausting hill and valley miles. When the Ruby Mountains towered in front of them, they left the main river because of the reports of recent Indian depredations farther along on the California Trail. They traveled up the south fork of the Humboldt, rounded the southern portion of the Ruby Mountains and traversed north again in Ruby Valley. Friendly Indians helped them. No extraordinary hardships beset them. More than two hundred roundabout miles after leaving the main Humboldt, the company arrived in the area of Pilot Peak on the western edge of the Great Salt Lake Desert. Snow began to fall. Great Salt Lake City still lay two hundred miles away by the shortest route, close around the north tip of the lake.

Snow fell, Orson tells, "from one to three feet deep." To an Indian, in exchange for guide services, William Price gave his bright red flannel shirt. When about fifty miles from their destination, Orson adds, "we left our wagons and packed. We found this much easier for our animals, but more inconvenient for ourselves, especially as we were thereby deprived of a sleeping room, and were consequently obliged to make our bed in the snow." In one area the travelers picked red berries still hanging on bushes. These augmented their dwindling food supply. At times the group procured water by melting snow. Orson was told later that when William arrived home his wife hardly recognized her thin and haggard husband.[1]

At around five o'clock in the afternoon, December 9—twilight of a short winter day—Orson stepped across his own threshold. Exclamations of surprise and joy greeted him. Immediately, all effort was for his comfort, and he basked in the attention of his family. Family included wife Marinda—age forty-one, as regal as ever—and three young children—sons Frank and Alonzo, almost eleven and nine years, and daughter Delia, almost seven. Also in the city resided two married daughters, their husbands, and one grandchild. Granddaughter Emily—called "Em," because her mother was Emily—reached her first birthday three days after Orson arrived home. Daughter Laura had married the previous May to her cousin, Aurelius Miner. By letter Orson had learned of the marriage. He was fond of Aurelius, son of his sister Sally, but felt concern about the cousinship.[2]

In discussing news from beyond the family circle, Marinda told Orson that since September the Church had been astir with reformation, a spiritual awakening. The next few days, as Orson visited with fellow Church leaders, he learned more about the movement. For many months previous to September, a growing concern had welled up in Brigham Young's mind that "all is not well in Zion." His counselors felt the same impulses, that the leaders must use strong words to rouse the Saints from apathy and the "worldly" notions and behavior gaining influence among them.[3]

For nine industrious years the Saints had been here in the Rocky Mountains—the longest period the Church had known without being driven from homes. The challenge faced the First Presidency of inspiring the Saints to rise above the need of persecution to whet triumph to their faith. Rather they needed to do what they should because they desired to be Christlike. Though persistent in bringing wilderness to productivity, settlers had failed to adopt a pattern of spiritual diligence. Lack of attendance at meetings had become the rule with many, possibly because of the frontier demands of irrigating, chasing obstinate cattle, and being prevented by weather conditions, but also because of haphazard commitment. Selfishness manifested itself by people claiming more land than they needed. Pride in clothes, carriages, and homes magnified as comforts increased. Violations of the marriage covenant were being reported.[4]

December 1, 1856, Brigham Young's dynamic second counselor, Jedediah M. Grant, had passed away, "worn out in preaching reform." This gave President Young and his remaining counselor, Heber C. Kimball, increased responsibility. The burdens weakened the health of both.

Orson soon discovered that the First Presidency was flinging the "arrows of God" at all Church groups, the Quorum of the Twelve included. Chastisement, in fact, had already been aimed at Orson Hyde. In mid October, as reformation heat increased, Orson's letter of July 30 had arrived, telling about Drummond's court and that Orson had acted as clerk. Distressed, Brigham Young reacted. He was appalled by Drummond's illegal actions, disappointed that Orson had stooped to act as clerk in such sorry proceedings. Impulsively, President Young declared Orson "no more fit to stand at the Head of the Quorum of the Twelve than a dog!" Only later did Brigham learn that Orson at first refused Drummond's demands, then afterward clerked to save himself a fine that he would have been unable to pay. Hope also, of perhaps making the situation better by guiding the proceedings a little, prompted Orson to comply. Brigham Young additionally stated Orson to be "a stink in [my] nostrils,"[5] maybe because he was thinking about Orson's use of tobacco.

Brigham Young's style of leadership was well known. It fit the vastness of the Territory and the enormity of the problems of grasshoppers, adverse climate, scarcity of water, Indian depredations, people of varied backgrounds, and numerous other vexations. If reprimand was needed, reprimand he gave, whether to a fellow apostle or to a lazy farmer. Perhaps he was more strict with the apostle than with the farmer. The apostles knew him well and understood his methods. The farmer might need gentle treatment.

Historians, as well as Church members, noted President Young's unique ways. H. H. Bancroft observed that the "secret of this man's power . . . was . . . [that] he was a sincere man. . . . He possessed great administrative ability; he was far-seeing, with a keen insight into human nature." His "presence [was] imposing, . . . of one born to be master of himself and many others."

Richard F. Burton, another historian, was impressed that, as a masterful disciplinarian, Brigham Young used words, rather than violence, to accomplish progress. "[W]here occasion requires," Burton wrote, "he can use all the weapons of ridicule to direful effect, and 'speak a bit of his mind' in a style which no one forgets. He often reproves his erring followers in purposely violent language, making the terrors of a scolding the punishment in lieu of hanging for a stolen horse or cow."[6]

Upon Orson's Salt Lake City arrival, "through snow and storm for more than a month, . . . completely chilled and exhausted," he recounts, he stepped unprepared into the flurry of reformation. Telling of this, he continues, "My heart was then just as good as it ever was before . . . ; but being worn down by fatigue, cold and exhaustion, I could not be animated with that zeal, all at once, that I saw in some others. On this account I felt oppressed, and as though some of my brethren could not exercise compassion or make any charitable allowance for the condition I was unavoidably in. I felt grieved in my soul and cried earnestly to God in secret over my condition." Answer came in a dream, indicating that after a difficult swim in muddy waters, the waters would clear and he would feel peace. This comforted.

Orson became the fourth member of the Twelve in the area. Wilford Woodruff had resided in the City for a long time, helping compile and record Church history. Lorenzo Snow, assigned to preside in the Brigham City area, sixty miles north, was in the City for the term of the Legislature. Franklin D. Richards had returned from Europe less than three months previously. Orson soon regained his former dynamic energies and, with the other apostles, preached often.[7]

Heber C. Kimball, in a dynamic Tabernacle sermon December 21, not only admonished the people with stirring phrases to wake up to their duties and fulfill their great potential, he asked Orson Hyde, President of the Quorum of the Twelve, to lead out. He added that "leading this people is at times a harder work than drawing a large tree, top foremost." In the afternoon meeting Wilford Woodruff also asked Orson to lead out and continue the reformation.

Leading here in Salt Lake City was a matter different from Orson's previous experiences of being a leader to Saints in Kanesville, in Fort Supply, and in Carson County. In those places Orson held obvious local Church authority. Here Brigham Young held not only general authority, but also local authority. He was the one to whom people brought their problems, the one who decided even minor policy and course. The duties of the Twelve here seemed vague and indefinite.[8] Orson must figure out how to truly magnify his calling as President of the Twelve.

Sunday, December 28, when Orson had been home for nearly three busy weeks, he made time to write a letter to Mary Ann. He did this by staying home from the afternoon Tabernacle meeting. "Our prayers, in the pines, were heard and answered;" he penned, "and now let your heart rejoice and be glad. God has not forsaken us." Orson added that "I found all well at home and all right, even as I could wish, expect or desire, for which I feel very thankful."

In his letter he expressed gratitude to Mary Ann for her help and support, and he pronounced blessings upon her:

> . . . I arrived at our home in this City on the Evening of the 9th Instant, and found that the California mail left at 9 o'clock in the morning of the same day. I much regretted that I could not have arrived in time to let you know, by that mail, that we all arrived safely, though cold weather, snow storms, sage brush and deep snows greatly obstructed our way and hindered our progress. . . . The extra quantity of flour you thoughtfully forwarded to us was truly a God Send. But for that we should have suffered, and been compelled to subsist on horse or mule beef. It supplied a place equally as important as did the "Candle." God

Almighty bless you forever and ever for your thoughtfulness and care for my safety and welfare. Your lot shall be among Apostles and prophets of the Lord throughout all eternity, worlds without end Amen; and by them had in Eternal honor!

. . . I am truly thankful that you have been counted worthy to be rejected from and by the society of the world because of your faith and the position you occupy in relation to myself. Only continue a little longer and you shall see the time when those who affect to despise you, shall esteem it an honor to render you the most abject and menial service: But of this, boast not: but be patient, humble and prayerful; and though it be not in this life, it shall nevertheless be fulfilled. Blessed is the person who treats you kindly and shows you favor, not particularly for your sake, but for their own. The Lord hath shown me many things since I saw you–things that will make your heart glad. You have been faithful, kind, and affectionate. No woman could do better. Your lamp shall never go out, for your life is hid with Christ in God. Be thou therefore faithful and pray for your husband both day and night that he may have the Holy Ghost in strength and in mighty power. I could only wish that you were with us. But for the present, it cannot be. Remain faithful and devoted to your God and his cause–to your Lord [husband] and his interests and your reward will be sure.

Orson also told Mary Ann of the emigration and the reformation:

. . . The Emigration from the States did not all get in until about 10 days ago. About 100 Tons of flour have been taken out of this City to supply their wants while in the snow, also some two or three hundred teams sent out to aid them in. They started altogether too late to cross the plains– Some companies left the Missouri River as late as the 5th of Sept. with hand carts. This was a grievous error, occasioned by misunderstanding and mismanagement. The feet and hands of many were frozen and some perished altogether. But a host of them are come.

. . . I preach almost every night. There is a great reformation going on here, and great need of its continuance. Dead branches are being removed, Iniquity is coming to light, and the Devil is raging. But we are bound, by the help of God, to roll on the work, and awaken the people if thunders and lightnings equal to those of Mount Sinai or nearly so, will do it. The Sacrament is in mercy denied the people because of transgression, and repentance is being preached, with voices, such as you never heard. . . . There is no dodging. The hypocrite, the adulterer, and the transgressor are exposed and laid as bare as a picked chicken. . . . It is a warm time here and no mistake. It is good to the pure, but scorching to the ungodly. Preach repentance and reformation to those whose circle you move in; and by precept and example, encourage the good and reprove the bad.

Telling of general conditions, Orson wrote:

The winter has, thus far, been pretty cold, and about one foot of snow in the City and most excellent sleighing, which is being well improved. The weather has not been so cold as it was in Carson last year about Christmas time; yet the snow does not melt. There are no parties this winter; but fasting, praying, preaching and exhorting to repentance and reformation are the chief recreations of the season. . . . Provisions are tolerably plentiful. Potatoes are scarce and worth $1.00 per Bushel. Flour is worth from four to five Dollars a hundred, hay $15.00 per Ton.

Regarding Church leaders and also the political scene, Orson told Mary Ann:

Bro. J. M. Grant died on the evening of the first Inst. The Presidency are but just middling in health; and the responsibility now mostly rests upon myself, Bro Woodruff, Lorenzo Snow, and F. D. Richards who are all the Quorum of the Twelve now in this Territory. At a Special Election I was elected to fill the vacancy in the Legislature occasioned by the Death of J. M. Grant and am now acting as a member of that body.

Family news also became part of the letter:

. . . Charles and Elsa [Mary Ann's brother and wife] are well. They sent us up some very nice dried service & Elder berries the other day, and Bishop Bigler . . . from Salt Creek, says they are getting along very well & that Charles is a good boy and on hand. William [Mary Ann's brother who accompanied Orson home] and [wife] Martha are well. I was there yesterday. . . .

Our entire family have none but the kindest feelings towards you, and you may reckon me with the balance. George & Emily [Orson's daughter and husband] are well. They are here every two or three days. Aurelius and Laura [daughter and husband] are here, and Laura is very much improved and improving. About May she may have a party [her baby]. She would very much like it if you could attend! Such parties are not prohibited by the reformation. Marinda admires your taste in the selection of a dress. It pleases her. She sends her kind love to you and wishes that you were here. The boys [sons Frank and Alonzo] send their love to you and also Delia [daughter] with many thanks for the presents. They all wish you were here, and I too. Em [Emily's one year old daughter] would also say "<u>goodie goodie</u>" if you were here.

By way of instruction, Orson requested of Mary Ann:

Tell the boys to do the best they can for themselves and for me. I love the boys. God bless them in prosperity or adversity. It is all in a life time. But the pure in heart may rejoice always. My best love to all the saints, especially our mill hands and their families. God bless the pure in heart and life among you forever.

Orson closed with: "Write every chance. You will probably come home in Spring—More anon. Your affectionate husband O Hyde."[9]

December 29, the day after Orson wrote to Mary Ann, he was in Brigham Young's office and participated in a somber discussion with President Young, Heber C. Kimball, Wilford Woodruff, and Lorenzo Snow about the reformation. Brother Brigham appeared weary, despondent about the magnitude of trying to enkindle the people to regenerate holiness. His and Heber's reduced health hindered their efforts. The apostles, too, felt their exertions inadequate in rousing the Saints to greater obedience. What should be done? Elder Woodruff offered to surrender his apostleship so that someone more qualified could take his place. Elders Snow and Hyde made the same offer. Brigham Young waved these suggestions aside, with warmth in his manner. However, he did warn Orson to magnify his calling. For Orson's own sake, he should be careful to keep personal interests secondary to the building up of the kingdom of God.[10]

Orson, well aware of his inherent headstrong nature, determined again to try more diligently to lead out and inspire. He must apply his energies—as he had often been reminded lately—to his calling as an apostle of the Lord Jesus Christ. At this moment, though, Orson wondered how he could have led the Twelve from the great distance across the desert at Carson. He had been away a year and a half, and he still felt removed from the mainstream of the Church. Brigham Young, on the other hand, seemed to know about every man, woman, and child in the Territory.

Even when being chastened, Orson had no doubts of Brigham Young's love and concern, nor the love and concern of the other Church leaders who exhorted him to greater constancy. He knew that by their counsel, given in compassion and helpfulness, they tried to strengthen him. They made these efforts *because* they loved him. Orson, too, at times had to rebuke people he loved. And, as the greatest example, the Lord chastises whom he loves.[11]

A facet of the reformation was rebaptism. Saints could recommit themselves to the Lord, after true repentance, by being rebaptized. A new baptismal font had been constructed near the Endowment House on Temple Square. The First Presidency and other leaders had received the ordinance here beginning October 2. December 30, men filled the font, using buckets, with water from nearby City Creek. That evening Orson and fifty-four other brethren received rebaptism and reconfirmation.[12]

A few days later, January 4, 1857, Brigham Young called a new second counselor in the First Presidency, tall Daniel H. Wells. Brother Wells had already endeared himself to the Saints with kindness to the poor and with untiring efforts in military and legislative service.[13]

As weeks sped on, Orson advised Church members, acted on the Legislative committees to which he had been appointed, enjoyed his family, and preached frequently. In his sermons he reminded that peace begins at private firesides, he encouraged home manufacture, and he expanded the theme that a man who honors his priesthood will live the laws of the land as a matter of course. He urged frequent prayer, feeding the needy, and carefully storing grain.

Orson also completed the final sale arrangements of his store. The previous September, William C. Staines had made long-distance negotiations to buy it for $4000. In Wassau Valley, Orson wrote the deed of sale, and it had now been recorded in the Salt Lake County Land Records. Even with some income from the sale, Hyde finances continued tight. Marinda helped by taking in washing.[14]

Early in February, 1857, after the Legislature recessed, Orson traveled south on a strenuous preaching mission. He saw much growth of population and improved land in Utah Valley and in Sanpete Valley since his similar trip in 1855.[15]

Along with the other activities, Orson courted. The Hyde home was large and Orson's family small. He had fewer wives than most of the Church leaders. Orson courted Ann Eliza Vickers, who lived with her grandparents, Moses and Almira Daley, in Bountiful, just north of Salt Lake City. Long ago, while teaching school in Florence, Ohio, Orson had boarded with the Daleys. Afterward they became faithful Church members. Ann Eliza, born January 26, 1841, in Big Neck Prairie, Madison County, Illinois, had been left motherless at age two and been reared by her grandparents. Now sixteen, marriageable age in the pioneer environment, she was a petite five-feet-four-inches tall, and she was pretty, also kind and soft-spoken. She had a diamond-shaped face, large brown eyes, and lustrous brown hair. Her grandmother had trained her well in the intricacies of housekeeping, cooking, sewing, and gardening. The Daleys, and Marinda too, agreed with Orson that Ann Eliza would fit well in the Hyde family. Orson thought that Mary Ann would approve also.

Orson found opportunities to become better acquainted with Miss Vickers. He felt gentle respect for her, and his manner conveyed the message. When he at length proposed marriage, he assured her that she should make a sincere decision. He would regard her with friendliness even if she chose to decline his offer.

Though Ann Eliza's romantic dreams, at age sixteen, were not of marrying a man fifty-two years of age, she had friends who seemed happy married to older men. She sensed serenity while talking with Elder Orson Hyde. For years she had known him casually. She admired his polished look and manner. Though not dashingly slim, he was energetic, and delightful company. She was flattered that he found her attractive, and she felt comfortable with him. She accepted the proposal.

Heber C. Kimball performed the marriage of Orson and Ann Eliza, March 12, 1857, in the Endowment House. Orson looked into Ann Eliza's beautiful brown eyes as they knelt and he clasped her trusting hand over the altar. He knew that he would love her and could cherish her "for time and for all eternity."

Theirs proved a happy marriage. Ever after, Ann Eliza regarded it "a great honor to be the wife of an Apostle, . . . a good kind stalwart man."[16] Ann Eliza's personal sparkle and skills added a new dimension to the Hyde household. Adjustments were necessary, by all, but this had been expected.

A signal of edification and chastisement marked the April 1857 general conference. The second day, thousands listening, Brigham Young reminded the Saints of the reformation by reprimanding several Church leaders—Orson Hyde and Franklin D. Richards of the Twelve severely. Elder Hyde had been too worldly in Carson, and Elder Richards had allowed many of last year's immigrants to cross the plains too late in the season. Orson subdued the natural tendency to resentment by determining to be contrite rather than angry. This, he knew, from many times through the process, would bring peace.

This public reproof was no indication that Orson's Church standing had come under a cloud. He spoke in several of the conference sessions and conducted one of them. Brigham Young's complaints about Elder Hyde in no way diminished the love he showed for Orson the man—the congenial, eloquent, and persevering man.[17]

The Sunday after conference, in a Tabernacle meeting, Orson alluded to the chastisements to help people understand the inspiration of Brigham Young's actions. Brother Brigham's ambition, as God's representative on earth, was for all Church members to eventually gain a glorious life in eternal realms with their exalted Father. The Saints should feel love and gratitude for their President's anxiety. Orson declared that persons unwilling to accept counsel from the prophet were on their way to apostasy.[18]

President Young had planned a month-long trip to settlements north after conference, and he chose Orson among those to accompany him. "Governor Young," a newspaper account states, "Presidents Heber C. Kimball and Daniel H. Wells and Elders Orson Hyde and Franklin D. Richards with several others left this city on Friday, the 24th of April, to visit the settlement on Salmon river, to rest their minds, to invigorate their bodies, and to examine the intermediate country." The company comprised 54 wagons and carriages, 163 horses and mules, and 142 people, a sizable caravan. They ferried across the Bear River in two light boats they brought with them. They shared camp duties and good conversation. They traveled smooth roads and long rough roads. They saw farmland and mountains and deserts. They preached in scattered settlements. At their destination, Fort Limhi, 379 miles from Salt Lake City, they ate red salmon and met with Saints and Indians.

Afterward, reflecting upon the results of the journey, Brigham Young chuckled and said, ". . . we started from here to rest the mind and weary the body; and so far as the body is concerned, I believe all parties will agree with me in saying that we have done that most effectually." He also related, however, that during the trip his mind truly became rested. His body was reviving. In the same sermon, May 31, President Young expressed gratitude for the diligence and peace of the Saints during his absence. The next week, June 7, in another discourse, he declared the reformation a success and warned the Saints to continue diligence.[19]

June 14, Orson preached, reminding the Saints to keep up their guard. He expounded upon a request made by Brigham Young that they store, rather than sell, their wheat after the coming harvest, which promised to be abundant. This would be a great trial, Orson predicted, to store wheat rather than spend income from it for "clothing, boots, shoes, &c., (to say nothing of the silks, ribbons, laces, and other gewgaws,) to answer our desires." He explained: "There is hardly ever a commandment given to any person or persons before whom a temptation is not placed to decoy them, if possible, from an obedience to that commandment. . . . It is for us to abide in the counsel of God, and never turn aside nor cast a longing look upon the riches and comforts of this life, when we have to violate a holy precept to gain them."[20]

When Orson read his newspaper of July 1 he was shocked to learn that word had come across the plains that Parley P. Pratt "was shot" and died in Arkansas May 13. Parley had been a good friend.[21]

Orson and Marinda, in attempting to conform their mortal actions and attitudes to the spirit of the gospel, talked of Marinda's sealing, for eternity, to the Prophet Joseph Smith. As far as they knew, this had not been recorded. Talk led to action. Orson discussed the matter with Brigham Young, and the President agreed that measures should be taken. July 31, 1857, a "very warm" day, Orson and Marinda walked thoughtfully across the road from their home to the Endowment House. Inside they quietly greeted friends. Then they dressed in their white temple clothing. Kneeling at the altar, hands clasped across it, the two looked into each others' eyes with love. Orson acted as proxy for Joseph Smith. President Young, as he had done in 1842 in Nauvoo, pronounced again the sacred priesthood phrases that sealed Marinda to be the wife of Joseph Smith after this life closed. A clerk entered the details into the ordinance book.[22] This changed nothing at home, but Orson felt the serenity of knowing that he had fulfilled an obligation to his beloved friends, Marinda and Joseph.

August 17 became a special day in the Hyde home—Mary Ann arrived from the Carson mission. She had traveled with a large group of returning settlers. The excitement manifested by Orson, Marinda, Mary Ann, and the children enveloped young wife Ann Eliza too. As time passed, Mary Ann and Ann Eliza became close friends.

Mary Ann reported that the Saints in Carson fared well. They and the Gentiles had become generally friendly, with prospects of continued cooperation.[23] These developments pleased Orson. However, he was disappointed that the men who had contracted with him to operate his sawmill and pay him his due, had sent no funds with the returning company.

Orson's personal anxieties dropped to a minor role in the summer of 1857, when news arrived of a serious threat to the entire Church. The President of the United States had dispatched an army of 2,500 soldiers to march west to quell the "rebellious Mormons." Congress had been stirred up by false reports of Judge Drummond and others.

In pondering the situation, Orson concluded that the Church reformation had been a factor in the Government actions:

> [O]ur reformation was . . . first attended with the desire only of correcting some irregularities among us and of awakening the Saints to righteousness. . . . Our efforts were attended with results highly satisfactory to the upright and the good. We were led on by this spirit of reformation to expose and rebuke the evils of those among us who did not belong to the Latter-day Saints. This kind of preaching made them angry. . . . Their pens were then set in operation against us, and many false accusations were sent to the States by them. . . . [Some officials] had recourse to flight; and then told the awful and pitiful tale in the States, that they barely escaped with their lifes,—a fine cover for their unrighteous deeds . . . ; and they left no stone unturned to excite the Government to send troops. . . .
>
> . . . [B]y-and-by the word of assurance and comfort [from the Lord] came to us through our Prophet and Seer—the fearless Brigham . . . —"Sanctify yourselves before me; put iniquity far from you; assert your rights, and stand up to them; and behold, and lo! I will fight your battles, and the children of Zion shall be victorious; and the name of your God shall be magnified in the eyes of your enemies. Trust in me; be valiant and fear not, and the kingdom is yours." I may not repeat the word of the Lord through his servant verbatim, but give it according to memory. I am not, however, far wrong.

Reports in late July confirmed the westward movement of troops, and Church leaders acted swiftly and decisively. Orders to the militia units around the Territory called them to readiness for defense. A few men were assigned to travel and cautiously ascertain the size and movements of the approaching army. These scouts should also assist Mormon immigrants. Messengers departed to direct the Saints in Carson and other far-away settlements to sell or abandon their improvements and come to the mountains. Another messenger left to carry instructions to apostles and missionaries in the eastern states and in England to return home. This messenger also carried a protest to the President of the United States. At Brigham Young's request, workers hauled enormous amounts of dirt and buried the foundation of the temple, smoothing the ground.[24]

A memorable diversion from trying to prevent war occurred in a Tabernacle meeting September 6. Thomas B. Marsh, formerly a member of the Quorum of the Twelve, had arrived in headquarters to ask forgiveness after eighteen trying years away from fellowship with the Saints. Brigham Young permitted him to address the Sunday congregation. Thomas's wasted appearance dismayed Orson; he had aged significantly since Orson left him secluded in Missouri in 1839. But Orson thrilled that Thomas had finally repented.[25]

Unlike the gladness of a Church member returning, a September tragedy—the Mountain Meadows massacre—mortified the Saints. September 10, Orson tells, "I happened to be in President Young's office . . . when the messenger from Cedar City, not far removed from the Mountain Meadows, arrived." The messenger, James Haslam, had been sent nearly three hundred miles, in all haste, to seek Brigham Young's advice about "depredations and outlawry" of a company of California-bound emigrants. President Young gave him a meal and a written reply, to be delivered as fast as possible. The reply instructed the Saints to let the emigrants pass with no interference. Haslam hurried, but arrived too late. Most of the company had been murdered, and apparently by white men costumed as Indians. Years of investigations resulted from this sorest of blemishes in the history of the Church.[26]

Meanwhile, preparations continued for defense against the approaching army. September 14, Governor Brigham Young met with many leaders, Orson among them, and discussed options. This resulted in Governor Young the next day proclaiming martial law in the Territory. Soon 1,250 militiamen marched into the eastern mountains to fortify the trail. They also had orders to hinder the army but not attack. The men burned grass. They stampeded the animals in supply trains. They burned Fort Bridger (which the Church had previously purchased) and Fort Supply (formerly under Orson's jurisdiction), that the army could not use them or their assets.

In a discourse, October 4, Orson spoke to the Saints of continued faith and diligence:

> It appears that the Lord will open the way wherever he requires his Saints to go, however dark and hedged up it may seem. Yet, when the time comes for us to take one step, the way will open; and it is not

likely that we can see the final issue or the result of our journey at first. If we could see the end, there would be no trial of our faith; but all the time we must walk by faith, and not by sight. . . .

[I]t will be given to the faithful and pure before the Lord [to] . . . see how to take one step and where to place one foot; and if they cannot see where to put the second, they must wait till they *can* see where to put it. . . .

We shall be led into straitened places—into tried places; and now it is for us to prepare ourselves, to fortify our hearts, to fortify our spirits, that we never murmur against God nor against the Moses that he has given us.

Orson pointed out in another sermon that the army's main hindrance was having no prophet to lead them, "a man inspired of the Lord—one who can say, 'Thus saith the Lord.'"

October 25, Brigham Young reminded the Saints that the Lord guided events. "Sing hallelujah; for the Lord is here. He dictates, guides, and directs." President Young told of his "joy and comfort in seeing this people trying to live up to the spirit of . . . the Gospel," and he added his concern: "I am more afraid of covetousness in our Elders than I am of the hordes of hell."[27]

Early in November the company of several hundred Saints from Carson arrived. Orson felt overjoyed at the safe return of these friends. They had been prospering, but heeded the call of the Prophet. They abandoned fields, unharvested crops, fences, barns, homes, and beautification plantings, prompting a later Nevada historian to praise them for their willing sacrifice. Another observer added: "Oh, the Mormon roses and the Mormon poplars! Wherever the Mormons went they planted; wherever they have been, there roses bloom."[28]

In a sermon of comfort, November 15, Orson stated:

> . . . It never could have been said, "The mountain of the Lord's house shall be established in the tops of the mountains [Isaiah 2:2]," if we had remained in the valley of the Mississippi. . . .
>
> I believe, when the Almighty conceives a work to do, he will carry it through in some way or shape. Behold, we are here, a little people collected together in the mountains, and are short of the munitions of war. . . . And then look at the terrible odds . . . arrayed against us. See their thousands of well-trained troops and the millions of money at their command . . . , and they are schooled in all the tactics of modern warfare, except ours. . . .
>
> Just so sure as we as a people are pure and undefiled before God our heavenly Father, there is no power that can prevail against us. . . . [W]hen we contemplate that God is for us, and that all the holy angels in heaven are enlisted in our behalf, and we have purity, and sincerity,

and truth in our hearts, these are bulwarks which they cannot scale. God grant that we may be shielded with this kind of armour![29]

Hindrances forced the United States Army to winter in the mountains, and this development gave the Saints a season of optimism, even lightheartedness. During one Tabernacle meeting, President Young, in a festive mood, surprised Orson by stopping him in the middle of a discourse. Orson's family ever after referred to this incident as the "squash sermon." Orson, being his energetic self, had been punctuating his statements with dramatic arm movements and had moved around, turning to the right and to the left, and to the brethren seated behind him; to address everyone directly. President Young interrupted him and challenged him to maintain his attention toward the center of the Tabernacle. Then, to everyone's amusement, Brigham Young picked up a squash, carried it to the middle of the building, and told Orson to focus his attention on the squash. Orson sustained the gala mood by continuing, a smile on his face. "If Brother Brigham wants me to, I'll speak to a squash."[30]

Orson attended to matters of health too. One of his toes—frozen two winters before—bothered him. He consulted Dr. Washington F. Anderson, who removed the offending toe.[31]

During the winter of 1857-1858 Orson again served in the Legislature, remained a Regent of the University of Deseret, and preached regularly. Parts of his sermon of January 3, 1858—about governing the tongue and about the United States Constitution—would later become well known in Church annals. He began this discourse by talking of governing his own manner of speaking:

> Brethren and sisters, it has fallen to my lot this morning to speak unto you a short time as I may be led by the Spirit of the Lord our God. It is very natural for me, when I arise to address a congregation, to speak pretty energetically and pretty loudly also. . . . When I have spoken too loudly, I have done injustice to myself and probably to the congregation. I shall endeavour, the Lord being my helper, to modulate my voice. . . . At the same time, I do not want my mind so trammelled as brother Parley P. Pratt's once was, when dancing was first introduced into Nauvoo among the Saints. I observed brother Parley standing in the figure, and he was making no motion particularly, only up and down. Says I, "Brother Parley, why don't you move forward?" Says he, "When I think which way I am going, I forget the step; and when I think of the step, I forget which way to go."
>
> I desire that I may watch myself, that while I may be thinking what to say, I may not allow my voice to range unchecked or uncontrolled; and while I may seek to govern my voice, I hope not to be forgetful of matter for your edification.

Orson then talked about a different facet of governing, relating to others and self: "The principle of government among the Saints is . . . important, . . . the government of the tongue also. . . . And if we can govern the tongue, we may be considered qualified to rule; for the tongue, though a small member, sets on fire the course of nature, and is too often set on fire of hell.

"It is the tongue," he continued, "that causes the evils that exist in the world; it is the tongue that sets nations at war; it is the tongue that causes broils in the domestic circle; it is the tongue that causes the fire of animosity and ill-will to burn in our midst. If we can succeed in governing the tongue according to the mind and will of God, we have got peace in our families, peace in our neighbourhoods, peace in our community, and, what is more than all, we have peace with our God. . . . If we can govern the tongue, we are prepared then to enter upon the government of other matters; but I think we shall have plenty to do, at least for the present, to govern our tongues."

Farther on in the sermon Orson talked about the national government and the Constitution:

> It is said that brother Joseph in his lifetime declared that the Elders of this Church should step forth at a particular time when the Constitution should be in danger, and rescue it, and save it. This may be so; but I do not recollect that he said exactly so. I believe he said something like this—that the time would come when the Constitution and the country would be in danger of an overthrow; and, said he, If the Constitution be saved at all, it will be by the Elders of this Church. I believe this is about the language, as nearly as I can recollect it.
>
> The question is whether it will be saved at all, or not. I do not know that it matters to us whether it is or not: the Lord will provide for and take care of his people, if we do every duty, and fear and honour him, and keep his commandments. . . .
>
> [T]he Constitution of the United States . . . was framed by the inspiration of the Almighty, we readily grant. It has . . . been a partial shield to the Church in its infancy. . . . Now, look at the disgraceful roguery practised under that Constitution. . . . [It] serves but little purpose other than a cloak for political gamblers, merchants, and hucksters . . . ; for the wickedness of the people is determined to sweep it out of the way. Although it was framed by [God's] . . . power and goodness, yet with as much cheerfulness will it be overthrown as it was ever . . . framed. . . .
>
> What Constitution shall we be governed by, when unprincipled men have destroyed the Constitution of our Union? I will tell you what we shall have: while we walk in the favour of God, we shall have a Constitution. The Constitution written in the Bible? No. In the Book of Doctrine and Covenants, or Book of Mormon? No. What kind shall we have, then? The Constitution that God will give us.[32]

In early March, attempted negotiations with the army leaders failed. Colonel Albert Sidney Johnston, the commanding officer, declared that when snow melted and grass for the animals grew the army would continue west to regulate conditions in Utah.

March 18, Brigham Young summoned militia officers and Church leaders, including Orson Hyde, to a "Council of War." Bold speeches cemented resolve. The group accepted President Young's plan: abandon the city and burn it if necessary, the inhabitants moving to the south, "instead of fighting the U. S. Army, that is now on our borders." The city in ashes seemed better than the killing of "one good Elder."

The plan was preached and implemented in the many settlements in the Great Salt Lake Valley. Saints packed supplies and began moving south, after preparing their homes and other buildings to be torched if the army made any move to occupy or plunder. Rather than allowing the army to gain benefit from the labors of the Saints, Salt Lake City would remain intact only if the army marched through without any break in ranks and camped many miles beyond.[33] One of the buildings that might go up in flames was the new City Hall; Orson Hyde had offered its dedicatory prayer April 5.

April 13, Alfred Cumming, the federally appointed governor of Utah Territory, arrived without an army escort. He had traveled with the army, and was surprised to be courteously received in Salt Lake City. Observing people leaving their homes, he protested. However, Brigham Young, as President of the Church, stood firm. After two weeks of investigations, Governor Cumming understood the falseness of the charges against the people of Utah. He then dispatched messengers to Washington, D.C., reporting this, and he also requested the army to remain where it was.[34]

Meanwhile, the Saints continued moving south, wagons loaded with their most-needed belongings. They would camp out in wagons and tents or stay with friends or relatives until permanent decisions occurred. The move proved difficult for everyone, including Orson's family. Marinda carried a tiny baby, Zina Virginia, born April 23. Ann Eliza became a mother, May 13, at the Hyde's temporary abode in Springville, south of Provo. She and Orson named her first child, a son, Charles Albert.[35] Marinda and Ann Eliza both felt grateful for gentle Mary Ann's assistance.

The fugitive Saints, President Young with them, learned that on Saturday, June 26, the army indeed marched through Great Salt Lake City. The city remained deserted, an observer tells, "the houses unoccupied, the windows boarded up, and a few male inhabitants left to guard the houses [ready to set them afire] and tend the gardens keeping within doors and affecting to take no notice of what was going on. On the other hand, the army was equally nonchalant. . . .

"The army merely passed through the city [in ten hours]," the account continues, "and crossing the river Jordan by a bridge, encamped five miles off in a dusty pasture. No soldier was allowed to recross this bridge without written permission [from his superior officer]. The army marched on Tuesday to a point twenty miles southward."

Riders on swift horses kept Brigham Young continually informed of events, and Wednesday the President announced in Provo that "All who wish to return to their homes in Great Salt Lake City are at liberty to do so." He and several others departed at six o'clock that evening to lead the return. They arrived home at three o'clock in the morning.

Jubilation reigned in Provo the following Sabbath, the Fourth of July, Independence Day. Rousing music began sounding at four o'clock in the morning from the Provo brass band, and men raised a flag on the Liberty Pole. Enthusiastic speeches, later, in the bowery, rang forth from Orson Hyde and John Taylor. Through busy streets, all that day, teams pulled wagons filled with household goods and exultant men, women, and children, headed north. Promises had been kept by the Lord—no war raged.

Afterward Orson uttered prophetic words:

> This Kingdom has been for the last thirty years like an ebb tide—it has been receding from "its enemies"; but at the time the saints left Provo and returned to their homes, the tide began to flow; and within thirty years more there will be such a flood tide as has never been seen. This people will never more have to flee from their enemies, and the Kingdom of God will overcome all its enemies. Yet we must not boast of our own strength, but give the Lord the honor and glory and allow him to manage the ship.[36]

After the Saints returned to their homes in July 1858, a normalcy resumed, but *normal* now became different from *normal* before. The Saints' isolation had ended. The army constructed Camp Floyd about forty-five miles southwest of Salt Lake City. This presence brought a market for goods, but also brought an increase of crime. Problems arose mainly from some of the numerous camp followers, over whom the United States officers had no jurisdiction. Brigham Young kept the Church at a low profile. He requested no resumption of general Sabbath meetings on the Temple Block; the Tabernacle had been partly dismantled before the move south, and it stayed that way. Orson met regularly with other members of the Twelve. He preached infrequently, also traveled, earned a living, and cared for his family. Some travel took him to Provo, where he aided in providing better storage and security for wheat and flour in the Provo Tithing Yard.[37]

Orson's property, though not extensive, provided for his family's basic needs. In 1858 he received two listings in the Tax Assessment Rolls of Salt Lake County. In one list his "cattle" numbered one, and in the other schedule three. In one, his "swine" numbered one, and in the other two. Both valued his cattle at thirty dollars each and his swine at five dollars each. Both rolls gave him one vehicle. The two lists recorded his real estate worth as $6,600 and $5,000 respectively. Also, a newspaper article said that Orson's orchard produced good apples, with a "sprightly and pleasant . . . flavor."[38]

As a member of the directors' board of the Deseret Agricultural and Manufacturing Society, Orson helped with the Third Annual State Fair in early October. Citizens brought a great variety of goods: from cows to wheat, from beets to watermelons, from embroidery and essays to ropes, violins, and weaving. Orson functioned as a judge in the department of "Butter, Cheese, Hams, Bread, Sugar, Molasses, Vinegar, &c., &c."[39]

For convenience, the fair had been scheduled to be held the same week as October general conference. To the meetings this time, however, because the Tabernacle had received just partial repairs, only Church *leaders* from around the Territory received invitations. At this "Elders' Conference" Orson and other leaders stressed that the local officers should help the Saints to live righteously and to be diligent in raising crops. The "big move" had disrupted spring and summer farm operations, and many people resumed routine with difficulty. Fields and orchards had been blessed with providential rain during the summer, thus many crops grew without irrigation, but farmers had slacked at numerous farm chores. Orson Pratt, speaking of why the Lord had allowed the army to bring problems to the area, summarized "that it [is] necessary for the iniquitous to be in our midst in order for the purification of the saints." The conference reconvened November 13, and the theme of diligence continued. Orson Hyde preached that "We must bear testimony, by our works, that we are not drones in the hive. . . . If we don't take care of ourselves, nobody will take care of us."[40]

Between the two sections of conference, Orson Hyde and John Taylor were assigned to investigate a problem. From October 29 to November 2, they traveled north sixteen miles to Farmington, then thirty-four miles more to Willow Creek (later Willard), held meetings, and returned. In both places they considered complaints against local Church officials. In Willow Creek some Church members rebelled at their decision. When Brigham Young heard of this, he upheld the apostles' actions and said that "when any of the Twelve are abroad and at a distance from the First Presidency, they are virtually the First Presidency."[41]

Orson's ongoing Church responsibilities continued to be augmented by serving on various committees in the Legislature and by University assignments. As a University Regent he helped decide what school books to purchase for the Territory, and he helped procure slates (from the quarry near Provo) for school use.[42]

Beginning December 14, at the Social Hall, Orson taught a fifteen-week grammar course. The course included two three-hour evening sessions each week. As the classes continued, Orson watched satisfying improvements in his students.

In January 1859, public admonitions again sounded in Sabbath meetings from the pulpit in the Tabernacle. The building had undergone extensive remodeling.[43]

In early 1859 Orson pondered about what the Twelve should be accomplishing; he felt confined, "cooped up." Brigham Young directed Church activities, which progressed relatively smoothly, and the duties of the Twelve seemed perhaps trivial, primarily to exist from day to day, take care of their families, assist in various community duties, and again preach regularly. At times in the past, Orson and others had served in capacities where entire communities depended upon them for temporal guidance as well as spiritual inspiration. Were the Twelve now truly satisfying the trust of their calling? Were they sufficiently zealous in trying to preserve the Saints from the threatening shafts of the adversary?

Orson and other quorum members decided to fast and meet and pray and converse each day for several days, seeking enlightenment from Heaven. The meetings began February 21, in their own "Prayer Closet" in the Historian's Office. For pleasant hours the first day they prayed, they sang hymns, and they conversed. They agreed that the harmony they knew the Saints could attain seemed thwarted on every hand. They felt stymied as to what they should do. Orson even admitted to feeling listless, though he thought that perhaps part of the reason was his abstinence, right now, from food and tobacco. Ezra T. Benson voiced the opinion that the Twelve should not use tobacco. But Orson enjoyed it, and, back in his distressing Carson Mission days, Brigham Young gave him permission that remained unrescinded.

The second day the quorum reached a consensus. They should first fulfill whatever missions the Lord inspired President Young to give them, second be industrious and provide for their families, and third trust in God. The third morning Orson prayed powerfully and then prophesied that the "cooped up" period for the Twelve would end. The third afternoon, upon earlier invitation, the First Presidency joined with them and gave strengthening counsel. Essentially the counsel confirmed what the Twelve had already decided. They should continue to be more concerned for others than for themselves.[44]

The three introspective days caused Orson to scrutinize his own course. In the area of finance his family needed an increase. He had talked with Brigham Young, months before, about starting a dairy in a canyon, with a trading spot for immigrants. The President had discouraged the canyon setting. Now, February 27, 1859, four days after the deliberative meetings of the Twelve, Orson wrote to President Young about his persistent thoughts to make "a strike at a farm and dairy." He added, "I have no choice what I do, but I want to do something to grease my bread, and to get my bread without begging it if I can."[45]

Another situation that needed improvement seemed beyond Orson's control: his nagging concern about Martha, who was unhappy here in Salt Lake City. Years ago she had been basically content in his family. He had loved her and felt certain that she had loved him. But since their divorce in 1850 in Iowa, her marriage to Thomas McKenzie, and her subsequent second divorce,[46] Martha had become increasingly disgruntled. Recently she publicly aired old grievances against Orson, accusing him of mistreatment.

Her untrue insinuations upset Orson. Feeling unfairly attacked, he could not ignore her actions. But what reaction should he show? Compassion, fairness, and sincerity must prevail. His own home atmosphere was pleasant, his wives and children congenial. Martha, on the other hand, cared for her aging mother and had no children. Though her expert seamstress skills occupied her, perhaps she wished to return to the Hyde household. However, did Orson possess the charity to invite her? He searched his soul, and he sought divine guidance. After a time, conclusions developed. Yes, he could honestly offer a new proposal, but expectations must be clearly stated. Orson composed a letter to her February 28, 1859. He came directly to the point:

> Sister Martha,
>
> Impelled by a sense of duty to my God, I feel to say this much to you, that if you desire it, you can be received and acknowledged by me as a wife on the following conditions.
>
> The former troubles and difficulties of which you complain, must not be named to me, nor to any of my present family; nor yet, to any other person in or out of my house, by way of murmuring or complaint; neither your marriage with Br. McKenzie. I must be at full liberty to make any distinction in my family that I think proper—may speak or say any thing that I please to any one of them, at any time, without being held responsible to tell and explain it to another, unless I choose to do so:—In short, my will must be the law of my family.

Martha had been vicious in her recent verbal attacks, and Orson felt forced to firmness:

> Had you complied with the counsel of Br. Young, and seen me personally, the results of your latest efforts might possibly have been different, especially if I had been convinced that there was no wish or desire to investigate, revive, or introduce former scenes.

Though Orson preferred to forget past problems, Martha had aired them vehemently, with false overtones. Orson decided to put on paper the reasons for his actions at the time of their divorce:

> Martha, I do not wish to accuse or vex you unnecessarily, neither to advert to any by-gone scenes because forgiveness and charity are not in

my heart [because they *are* in my heart]. But a proper explanation requires me to say, that, in Pottowottomie Co. Iowa, you sought to force and compel me to acknowledge you publicly as my wife. You said that if you were my wife, you wanted to be acknowledged such, and to go in company with me, the same as Marinda; and that nothing short of this would satisfy you. You even threatened to expose me if I would not submit to your terms. I told you frankly and emphatically that I should not do it—that I would re-organize the church there—appoint a man to preside in my place, and leave the country, and go beyond the reach of all the evil that you could stir up. This requirement of me, at that time, was impracticable, unsafe, and you knew it as well as I. It was prompted by a vain and wicked pride. I thought that while I provided liberally for your comfort, you ought to have remained silent and contented while I was earning a little money to secure and provide for us a home in the valley, and if you really loved me as you professed, I think you would have done it. Your hasty and inconsiderate steps, at that time, drove me to advise your marriage with McKenzie that your great desire and ambition to be acknowledged as a wife, might be gratified. This requirement to acknowledge you as my wife while there, I then considered, and now consider, far outweighed, in criminality, by an hundred fold, all the causes of complaint that you ever had while connected with my family. But this I can forgive,– Nay, I have forgiven it, and wish never to name it more.

Looking at what he had written, Orson reasoned that he should soften his words, and yet impart the thoughts of his heart. Martha had once been dear to him.

Martha, allow me to speak plainly still further, yet kindly. You are a neat, industrious, and tidy woman: yet jealous, proud-spirited, technical, and exacting as a wife; and my advice to you is, that if you shall conclude to answer this letter at all, be not in haste to do it. Take time to pray, reflect, and consider; and remember, also, that the most shrewd, smart, and cutting reply, in your own estimation, may not redound to your greatest good. Still, if you write, I wish you to express your real feelings and sentiments: but take time sufficient to allow your mind to be fully settled, and settled right.

Again, he perceived, he should stress his sincerity:

After all that has transpired, I feel to make you the proposal before named, free from flattery, deceit or hypocrisy. I can never make one more adapted to your feelings or views in truth. I shall probably never make another, and a sense of duty to my God only, has induced me to make this: Yet it is in your power, by patience and a perseverance in well-doing, to gain the confidence and affection that you once shared. This is plain and undisguised; and admits of no technicalities. Be your conclusions what they may, in the plainness and honesty of my heart are the facts penned; and they are such as I feel willing to meet any where, now or hereafter.

Remembering their tiny baby, Adella Marie, whom Martha had laid broken-heartedly in a grave, he added,

> I will say further, that I cannot look, with indifference, upon any woman who, through my agency, has endured the afflictions of a mother.
>
> Truly,
>
> G. S. L. City Feb'y.28th 1859   Your Bro. in the Gospel
>   Orson Hyde[47]

Martha retained her distance.

Orson's course changed little. His grammar class continued until the end of March. He abandoned plans for a farm and dairy. Meanwhile, in keeping with the long ago designation given him as "The Olive Branch of Israel," he persevered in his sermons to foster harmony and thus peace. "If we resist the devil, he will flee from us," he preached May 15, "and on the same parity of reasoning, if we resist the good Spirit, it will flee from us also; the practices of many of the Saints indicate that they say to the Spirit of the Lord, 'Go thy way for this time, and at a more convenient season I will call for thee.' . . . Turn unto the Lord. . . . Be pure and upright. . . . Use the blessings of the Almighty wisely."[48]

The local peace remained tenuous, disrupted by the animosity of federally appointed officials and others. The night of August 31, Orson learned that he had personally become a victim. Startled by a knock at his door, he responded. By lamplight he saw a weary young man outside, his exhausted horse nearby, sides heaving, nostrils blowing. Urgency filled the man's greeting. Hurriedly Orson invited him in and listened to his report. Danger threatened Elder Hyde. The concerned messenger had ridden a hundred miles from Nephi, south of Salt Lake City, to inform him that Judge Eckles, after adjourning court, heard affidavits. One of these resulted in a warrant for Orson's arrest. The audacious charge was that Elder Hyde, two years before, had recommended the killing of the Parrish family in Springville, just south of Provo. Incredulous, Orson listened. Not only had the defamatory judge issued an arrest warrant, but he also requested a posse from the army at Camp Floyd to capture Elder Hyde.

Orson's mind raced in a jumble. After the messenger left he hardly knew what to do first. He began to pack a few things, and he sent a neighbor to ask Wilford Woodruff to come. Wilford arrived, and Orson rehearsed the situation. He must disappear and wanted the Presidency and Twelve to know that he would depart immediately, before the posse arrived. He would find a friend to conceal him, and then perhaps he would travel around until the excitement subsided.[49]

But why was he accused of instigating murder? William Parrish, who had become disgruntled with the Church and apostatized, prepared to take his family from Springville to California. But a group of ambushed masked men cruelly shot and knifed him, his son, and a neighbor, killing all three. The assailants remained unidentified. The only personal connection Orson now recalled was that a few weeks prior to the atrocious slaying, he had been in Springville as part of his mission south through Utah and Sanpete Valleys. No other apostle had been with him, thus he had no official witness of his actions and counsel.[50]

For more than three weeks Orson maintained a vagabond course. At first he hid, but no posse tracked him, so he merely stayed away from Salt Lake City, traveling privately, "visiting the branches abroad," and preaching to the people nearly every day. Judge Eckles' court remained adjourned, from lack of funds, facilities, and personnel.[51]

Orson returned home in late September, grateful to resume routine. Routine included frequent discussions with President Young, meetings with the Twelve, other meetings, and fall work in his orchard and garden. His new grape vines, planted in the spring, looked promising. October 2, Orson spoke morning and afternoon in the Tabernacle, the first time in many weeks. The following Thursday, the first day of general conference, he spoke in the evening session.[52]

For seventeen days in November, Ezra T. Benson and Orson traveled, "pursuant to instructions received from the Presidency of the Church, . . . to Cache valley, seventy five miles north, to organize the [young] settlements." Though they experienced "rain, snow, hail and sleet, fog and wind," the people were kind. The apostles held many meetings, gave names to several villages, organized and instructed officers, blessed the sick, and "blessed the people in the name of the Lord." On their way home they attended rewarding meetings in Brigham City and in Ogden.[53]

Less than a month later, December 23, Elders Hyde and Benson set out together again, this time over the snow to settlements south. By sleigh, in nine days they traveled as far south as planned, 150 miles to Fillmore. For a few days, in several meetings, they "taught the people the principles of life and salvation, . . . much to the edification and satisfaction of those who were in attendance." Then horses, sleigh, and men traversed over to the east side of the San Pitch Mountains into Sanpete Valley and visited settlements. In one community they noted that personal selfishness was preventing public progress. Elder Hyde remarked about this that "public interest is like a ship in a storm, which is only saved by every man working at the pumps. . . . [I]f the entire crew merely seek to secure their own personal property, and make no effort to secure the ship, she will in all probability be lost, and with her will go down the crew with all they possess, their selfishness included; hence it is a misfortune to be rich if our riches make us selfish." While continuing homeward from Sanpete Valley they preaching regularly. Their families welcomed them January 20, 1860. Orson felt "unwell" and grateful to be home.[54]

Rest brought recovery, and Orson's active pace continued. February 12 he spoke in the Tabernacle of a problem in the Church related to cooperation. "Many persons who have joined the Latter-day Saints have run well for a season;" he said, "but, understanding not that the Gospel is a progressive work with those who honour it, they have turned away from the faith—charged the Saints with inconsistency, but yet claim to believe in what they call 'ancient Mormonism.' The garment that is made for a child just born must be worn by a man when thirty years of age, is the doctrine of those stereotyped 'Mormons.' The Church is now nearly thirty years old. . . . When we become stereotyped in our feelings, there is an end to corrections, enlargements, and improvements. . . . The early commandments of God to his Church and the manner in which we were led at that time will not fit our case in all respects now."

In mid February, Brigham Young invited Orson to help ordain Orson's brother-in-law, William Price, a Bishop to oversee Goshen Ward, seventy-five miles south of Salt Lake City and west of Utah Lake. The President also asked Orson to accompany Bishop Price to his new assignment. In Goshen they were received kindly. Orson remained three days.[55]

This winter the First Presidency and the Twelve were involved together with sensitive matters involving Orson Pratt and doctrinal items that he had written. Elder Pratt resisted correction. In the course of meetings and discussions the subject came up of former speculative notions that Orson Hyde had preached, and quit preaching, about the resurrection. In one meeting Elder Hyde tried to encourage harmony by turning to Orson Pratt and saying quietly, "My opinion is not worth as much to me as my fellowship in this Church." Eventually Elder Pratt admitted blunder, and harmony prevailed.[56]

Orson Hyde's privilege and pleasure of almost daily contact with the cherished First Presidency and members of his quorum would soon end. After three and a half years in the city, President Young had asked him to move and direct matters in the Sanpete area, where he and Elder Benson had recently held many meetings. As Orson had earlier foretold, he and other apostles were being sent out into the field.

Brigham Young's request to Orson Hyde to move to Sanpete, "with a part of his family," had been issued March 2; the "part" could prepare for other family members to follow. One reason for now sending members of the Twelve to various sections of the Territory was that the United States Army was leaving Camp Floyd. Matters in the Salt Lake Valley no longer required the strength of the Twelve. "I want the Twelve," Brigham Young instructed, "to meet together in the City about once in two or three months, not longer than three months. I want them to preach in this Territory, and let other elders preach abroad. The Twelve are getting old now; let others do the preaching abroad." (Orson was fifty-four years of age and Brigham Young fifty-eight.)

With departure pending, members of the Hyde household reached decisions. "Sanpete County . . . was a new country and sparsedly settled," Mary Ann tells, "and [Marinda] preferred remaining in the City with her children. So it was agreed upon that I should go to Sanpete. . . . It was long before I could feel reconciled to be separated from the other part of the family, for I was sincerely attached to them." The children of Marinda's who would remain with her in their comfortable home were twelve year old Alonzo, ten year old Delia, and two year old Zina. Her son Frank, age fourteen, would go to Sanpete to help develop a farm for the family. Wife Ann Eliza, her two year old Charles, and new baby George Lyman, born March 16, would remain also.[57]

... *increase.* ... *(1860–1869)*

> *For of him unto whom much is given much is required; . . . For Zion must increase in beauty, and in holiness; her borders must be enlarged; her stakes must be strengthened; . . . [e]very man seeking the interest of his neighbor, and doing all things with an eye single to the glory of God.*
>
> —Doctrine and Covenants 82:3, 14, 19

IN two borrowed wagons, Orson, his wife Mary Ann, and his son Frank departed from their home in Salt Lake City, June 12, 1860. They headed south the one hundred and forty miles to settle in Manti, in Sanpete Valley. Leaving Marinda and Ann Eliza alone with five children had been difficult. To fourteen year old Frank the move represented *adventure.* Sheep—a buck and two ewes, packed snugly in beyond the farming tools in the back of one wagon—often bleated and shifted their weight.[1]

After emerging from Salt Creek Canyon into the northwestern portion of Sanpete Valley, Orson paid particular attention to general conditions, and he talked with people where he and Frank stopped the wagons. He found the settlers "overwhelmed with work, fencing, building, irrigating, &c." Crops, primarily wheat in this valley, were maturing slowly, owing to late frosts and dry cold weather. Little rain had fallen here this spring. Much grain had been sown, more than six thousand acres, but it had needed irrigation.

High mountain ramparts surrounded the sixty-mile-long and thirty-mile-wide Sanpete Valley, an encirclement that provided greater security to Indians than to settlers. The natives living in those mountains, close to the multiplying farms, easily came periodically and drove off cattle or with their arrows killed white men, and then rode swiftly back to safety. Because of grim experiences with Indian threats during the eleven years since the Saints began arriving, a log or stone fort (or started fort) centered each of the nine valley settlements. Only two towns had been continuously occupied: Manti since 1849 and Fort Ephraim since 1854. The 1852 and 1853 pioneers of Springtown and Mount Pleasant, attacked in mid 1853, moved to Manti. In 1859 they returned to their original plots. About this same time families settled Moroni, Gunnison, Wales, Fountain Green, and North Bend (later Fairview). The Indians had become generally peaceable. Most homes were small and plain, built of adobe brick. Manti, the largest settlement, lay in the southern part of the valley.[2]

The jostling trip consumed four days, and the Hydes, fortunately, found their planned Manti habitation adequate. The little stone dwelling had been built at the request of Brigham Young as part of a community project. Former occupants had left it much abused, but village men were plastering and partially repairing. While Orson began his public duties, Mary Ann and Frank organized their belongings. Through the kindness of townsfolk, a place was found to graze the Hyde sheep.

By observations and conversations, Orson perceived that the people in general applauded Brigham Young for sending an apostle into their midst. They had felt a need in their isolated area for focused local guidance. Orson's initial evaluations revealed two major concerns: what to do regarding the demands of belligerent Indians, and what decisions to make about constructing a road from the north end of the valley through Spanish Fork Canyon. A road there would reduce the traveling distance to Salt Lake City by fifteen miles. June 17, in a letter to President Young, Orson explained his perceptions and asked what his priorities should be. Brigham Young answered by return mail, declaring no hurry about the road.[3]

Relating to Orson's personal life, his former wife Charlotte lived in Mount Pleasant, but this caused little concern. In 1858, during the Saints' "move south," she came from Salt Lake City to Fort Ephraim in Sanpete Valley. After a year she joined the group resettling Mount Pleasant and remained. At present she earned her living as a seamstress. Later, teaching small school children, she would become affectionately known as "Aunty Hyde."[4]

Orson began a rigorous traveling schedule to speak in the Saints' meetings. And he tried to preach words applicable to situations at hand. A talk in Mount Pleasant, July 1, surprised some of his listeners. After pleading with them to think of each other and to help each other, he urged them—especially the males, the priesthood holders—to think more seriously of their personal deportment. "I can walk the streets of almost any of our settlements," he said, "and hear boys and men say, 'I'll be damned if I'll do it.' This makes me feel ashamed before the Lord, makes me blush for them. Men take their cattle or teams to the kanyons, and, when out of patience with them, curse and damn them, then turn right around and fellowship them [care for them], thus virtually taking their [the animals'] curse upon themselves. Will I fellowship an animal or person after cursing them? Nay! When I pronounce a curse on any thing I wish to withdraw my hand immediately, to sever the link that united us."

Orson traveled to Salt Lake City in July to return the borrowed wagons and get his cattle. After "preaching [his] way along through the settlements," he arrived in the city July 20. He stayed a few days and then started south on horseback, driving his cattle: "I arrived at North Bend on Sat[urday July 29] about noon. I came from Springville up Spanish Fork. . . . The Spanish Fork Kanyon road is very rocky, and needs much labor to make it a safe good road. . . . [H]ad good luck in driving my cattle, but [I] almost killed my horse, and he almost killed me. Shall ride horseback not much more."[5]

This unpleasant horseback ride home, plus the Sanpete traveling Orson had done, convinced him that weight and age gave him need of "a span of horses or mules and a lightish wagon, harness &c." The local Saints responded kindly to his requests for rides, obliging whenever possible, but sometimes he had difficulty getting where he wanted to go.

His limited income, however, prevented him from purchasing more than necessities. He had built a barn for Marinda in Salt Lake City before leaving, which depleted funds. Rent from his store provided his main cash income. Orson thought he had sold his store back in 1856, but the purchaser, William C. Staines, had been unable to make full payments. Pending further decisions, Brother Staines and Orson arranged for Orson to temporarily rent it to others, collect the rent himself, and pay the taxes.[6] He received some income by selling unimproved lots in Salt Lake City that had originally been laid out to him as security.[7]

After a few months Orson and Mary Ann decided to move to Springtown, more central than Manti in the valley. Also, Manti's water supply was becoming inadequate, and Springtown, as its name implies, had many "beautiful springs." From Springtown's main north and south thoroughfare, looking down the gently sloped street to the west where the Hyde homelot occupied one corner (later designated as the southwest corner of 100 West and 200 South Streets), a reminiscent scene was viewed—a miniature "Mount of Olives." On this hill to the west, sparse cedars grew. From a distance they passed for olive trees. Even the Springtown earth, underfoot, had the same golden hue as that of Jerusalem.

On the east end of the Hyde half block, Orson received help with logs carefully hewed, fitted, and mortared to create a comfortable one-and-a-half-story dwelling, facing east. Before laying the logs up, many shovelfuls of dirt were removed for a cellar under the house. The running spring in this rock-walled cellar would keep the air cool, providing a good place to store food. Orson eventually procured three-fourths of the block across the street north and also fields northwest of town.[8]

For October general conference time, Orson returned to Salt Lake City and enjoyed Marinda, Ann Eliza, his children, and Church leaders. After he returned to Manti, Wilford Woodruff noticed that the Hyde vineyard needed pruning, and he pruned it. He then recorded that Orson had "lost his crop two years in consequence of not understanding pruning his vines. He has cut out the new bearing wood & left the old standing. I have cut out the old wood & left sufficient of the new wood . . . for next years crop."[9]

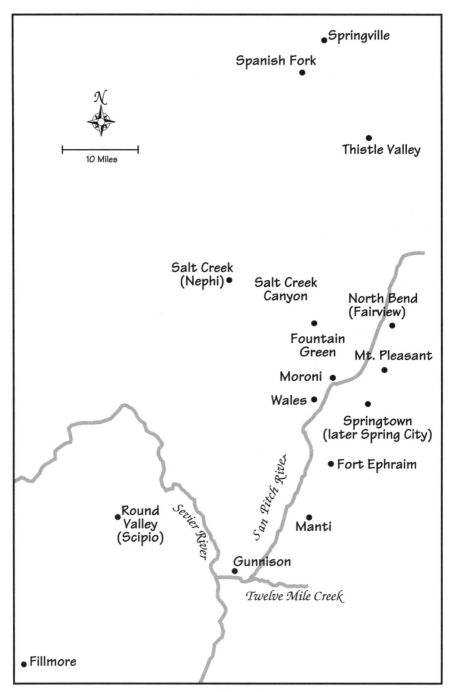

Sanpete Valley and area.

In Sanpete, Elder Hyde continued to regularly visit each settlement and help solve the concerns that surfaced. Little misunderstandings he could usually fix with a kind word and some objective reasoning. He and the bishops worked out larger problems together. His presence provided a focal person for mediations and direction. Problems arose as diverse as divorce, cattle thievery, and irregularities at the Manti tithing office. In November 1860, Orson and the bishops unitedly took a stand against unscrupulous merchants coming into the valley, buying at low prices, and selling at high prices. A private problem developed too: Orson had lacked time to harvest enough winter feed for his animals. Brigham Young authorized him to use "from the Springtown Tithing Office four tons of hay." One area of Orson's duties that showed promise involved Sanpete's Indians. Orson had shown them respect, and the natives reciprocated with respect. The threat of attack seemed past.[10]

Early in December Orson received instructions from President Young to visit Fillmore–southwest of Sanpete Valley, a round-about trip of eighty miles each way–and settle problems of intolerance, stealing, and shady practices of Church officials with the management of stray cattle. When the message arrived, Orson was already "crowding [his] house [in Springtown] forward with all possible haste." He sent a letter to the bishop of Fillmore telling of his expected visit in about three weeks, and he applied greater diligence to construction. He felt special gratitude to his friend Peter Graves, of Fort Ephraim, who shingled the house in "weather quite inclement." The Hyde family moved from Manti.

Orson started for Fillmore December 30, reluctantly leaving Mary Ann and Frank "in a half finished house." Along the way, Church members assisted him with rides and meals. In Fillmore, conversations and meetings solved the problems, even produced "gladness and rejoicing." Orson arrived back in Springtown the evening of January 11, 1861, grateful to be home. In "severely cold and stormy" conditions Mary Ann and Frank had managed to care for the animals outside, and for themselves in their house not as snug as desired. The work of frigid chores and keeping fires brought concern to Orson for the part of his family in Salt Lake City. When he reported his Fillmore trip to Brigham Young he added a marginal note: "I wish you would send some man down to my house, and see if they need wood or any thing. I will make it right when I come."[11]

Orson's efforts, his first six months in Sanpete, had brought marked improvements. "We feel grateful to our Heavenly Father for sending Brother Hyde to this county," settler William Black reported to Brigham Young in February 1861, "for he has done a good and glorious work here. When he came we were all in turmoil and confusion, neither life nor property was safe, and since he came he has been a blessing to the upright and faithful Brethren and Sisters, but a terror to evil doers. . . . God bless him. . . . Brother Hyde has been very kind to us, and has strove to comfort and encourage us all in his power."

Orson's exacting nature, and his deep realization of the blessings of obedience, at times rendered him seemingly harsh with others' inept behavior. But the First Presidency understood his methods. Daniel H. Wells, Counselor to Brigham Young, May 5 wrote to a Sanpete bishop: "As to Brother Hyde, let me give you a word of counsel, do nothing, say nothing, and, so far as possible, feel nothing in opposition to whatever course he may pursue, for if ever he seemed to feel the spirit of his calling he does now. He is moreover a good man, and holds the authority of the Holy Priesthood."[12]

The same month, Orson consulted with Brigham Young about a touchy situation involving several brethren improperly using community funds and probably commodities. President Young decided to call the offending men to serve missions, away from the local temptations. Orson delivered the appointments and reported back to the President: "[I] told them that you said that you did not know that I had done any thing <u>particularly</u> <u>wrong</u>, but thought I had been pretty hard on the boys, —that you told me to be kind to them now, —take them by the hand and help them, which instructions I was disposed to carry out." The brethren accepted their mission calls, and, in a community meeting, their neighbors approved this solution.

Orson's Church duties took precedence over his home chores and farming, but in these he continued efficient. Son Frank helped marvelously. Sandwiched between other duties, March 14, 1861, Orson "planted out some currants, strawberrys, Pie Plant [rhubarb] &c." He found time two days later for "laying up garden fence, setting posts &c. Worked till dark."[13]

He managed to get to Salt Lake City for April general conference. In the first session he had a dismaying experience. At the suggestion of others of the Twelve—all thinking the time was past to begin and Brigham Young not yet arrived—Orson began the services. The President afterward chastised him for this. The second day of Conference so many people attended that only half of them fit inside the Tabernacle. During the morning session Orson Hyde and John Taylor preached "to the 'outsiders,' . . . some of whom were standing, others sitting, either on blocks of marble [granite] prepared for the foundation of the Temple, or temporary seats arranged for the occasion."[14]

Back in Sanpete Orson's routine resumed, and weather grew warmer. To minimize travel, Orson often stayed overnight in various settlements, but, in times of summer heat, he reported to Brigham Young, June 22, "I preach every Sunday, and during the days of bedbugs, I continue to scud home at night to rest." In the same letter he told that at home, "I am fencing, building some out hous &c. and am doing my best to make things a little more comfortable around me." Duty kept Orson busy the remainder of the summer, part of the time laboring diligently with his son Frank "making corralls and garden fence."

No matter how efficient he was, though, Orson's exertions for the Saints left him insufficient time and energy to provide family requirements. And yet, it occurred to him, perhaps the Saints in general had no idea of his needs, because wherever he went he carried a smile and a cheerful word. But he must remedy his economic situation. Publicly, the fall of 1861, he explained his situation and asked for donations of money and goods. The Saints rallied. Again Brigham Young allowed him the use of tithing hay, partly because of Orson's duty to feed the teams and animals of many callers. The next spring (1862), fortunately, Orson considered his own hay sufficient, "as most of my stock has run on the range, and done very well."[15]

The winter of 1861–1862 Orson began attending the Territorial Legislature as the Council delegate from Sanpete County. The sessions convened in December and January, when men were the least busy with farm work.[16]

In the City, Orson preached and visited and spent reflective hours. In speeches and articles he sometimes used as a theme the national news of division among the eastern states that had led to Civil War early in 1861. In the Rocky Mountain haven of the Saints, the storms of war now reverberated in conversations and writings soon after they happened, as the telegraph lines from the east had been completed to Salt Lake City in October 1861.[17]

January 1, 1862, Orson wrote a notable letter in which he rehearsed an 1858 prophecy of his about the Civil War and added to it:

> Some four years since, in a discourse delivered in the Tabernacle in this city, I made the following statement:—"So sure as the storms of the mountains burst and hurl their fury upon the 'Twin Peaks' of the Wahsatch Range, just so sure is the storm of Jehovah's wrath about to burst upon the nation and people of the United States." This statement found its way into many of the Eastern journals, and drew forth some ludicrous editorials as to what "the Prophet Orson" had said. Call me by whatever name they will, I intend to tell the truth; and Time, that faithful revealer of all things, will test the merits or demerits of my sayings. You have scarcely yet read the preface of your national troubles. Many nations will be drawn into the American maelstrom that now whirls through our land; and after many days, when the demon of war shall have exhausted his strength and madness upon American soil, . . . he will remove his headquarters to the banks of the Rhine. . . .

Fulfillment of this prophecy came in 1866, with armed conflict between Prussia, Austria, and Italy.[18]

Thoughts of unrest reminded Orson of his gratitude for family peace. In Salt Lake City he enjoyed Marinda and Ann Eliza and the children, but he missed Mary Ann. In a short letter that he penned to "My Dear Mary," January 8, 1862, he mentioned, among other items, some sewing that Ann Eliza had finished. He also said, "I send you the Deseret News and minutes of yesterdays [Legislative] proceedings. . . . We are all well, and things are going right, or if wrong I do not know it. I want to see you very much, or at least hear from you. . . ."[19]

The peace in Orson's domestic circle contrasted with the pain he felt regarding his loved ones' needs, both here and in Sanpete. He prayed and he pondered about possible ways to gain more assets to help them.

In January, Orson thought repeatedly of far westward Carson and Washoe Valleys. The previous year the new Nevada Territory encompassed this area. In Washoe remained the sawmill and other improvements that Orson and his brother-in-law William Price had left in 1856. Orson and William were still owed a large sum for their property. Mary Ann's brother-in-law, Richard Bentley, had abandoned his property too, as had many other Saints called home in 1857. Perhaps Orson could obtain means from Washoe by writing a forceful letter. His thoughts about it led to strong spiritual encouragement. He discussed his feelings with Brigham Young, who gave him liberty to write whatever he liked.[20]

January 27, 1862, Orson composed his letter "TO THE PEOPLE OF CARSON AND WASHOE VALLEYS." Because his hands had developed a slight tremor, he asked a clerk to pen the final draft. Afterward known as the "Orson Hyde Curse," this letter and subsequent events memorialized Orson's name in Nevada history. Orson's letter described that his and William Price's

> valuable saw-mill . . . and . . . several land claims, . . . then [1856] worth $10,000, was rented to Jacob Rose for a limited term, at a stipulated price. On this rent he advanced one span of small, indifferent mules, an old worn-out harness, two yokes of oxen, and an old wagon. This is all that we have ever received for the use of our property in that valley, though we have sent bills for goods or merchandise. . . .
>
> We have been patient, and have not murmured. We have made little or no effort to sell our property there, because we considered that those who had it thought they were doing God and themselves a service by wronging the Mormons; and for me, I felt backward to do anything in the premises until the Lord should tell me what to do. . . . That time has now come. . . .
>
> That mill and those land claims were worth $10,000 when we left them; the use of that property, or its increased value since, is $10,000 more, making our present demand $20,000.
>
> Now if the above sum be sent to me in Great Salt Lake City, in cash, you shall have a clean receipt therefor, in the shape of honorable quit claim deeds to all the property that Orson Hyde, William Price and Richard Bentley owned in Washoe Valley. The mill, I understand, is now in the hands of R. D. Sides, and has been for a long time. But if you

shall think best to repudiate our demand or any part of it, all right. We shall not make it up again in this world in any shape of any of you; but the said R. D. Sides and Jacob Rose shall be living and dying advertisements of God's displeasure, in their persons, in their families, and in their substances; and this demand of ours, remaining uncanceled, shall be to the people of Carson and Washoe Valleys as was the ark of God among the Philistines. (See 1st Sam. fifth chapter.) You shall be visited of the Lord of Hosts with thunder and with earthquakes and with floods, with pestilence and with famine until your names are not known amongst men, for you have rejected the authority of God. . . . You have chuckled and gloried in taking the property of the Mormons, and withholding from them the benefits thereof. You have despised rule and authority, and put God and man at defiance.

Orson added that he expected reaction to his letter to be "taunts, jeers, and scurrilous indignation." But, he reminded, he would have taken no action about his Washoe property "had not the visions of the Almighty stirred up my mind."

A few weeks after sending the letter to a friend in Carson County, Orson received reply that it had been published, as requested. Orson acknowledged the reply March 11. Before this, March 1, he had sent a copy to Brigham Young, "so that if you should have a little time to laugh or scold, the reading of it may inspire you to do either."

Time passed, and the curse became largely forgotten.

Then, in 1880, eighteen years after Apostle Hyde pronounced the vexations, "a dam broke and the consequent flood wiped out the very site of the old mill town below it [Franktown] and ruined Sides' farm," subsequently wrote a Nevada historian; "in 1882, another flood swept away the adjoining town of Ophir; and a later one carried off the only remaining evidence of the Mormon settlements—the old Mormon meeting house, which floated farther than any other building, and was left in ruins on the shores of Washoe Lake." Jacob Rose and R. D. Sides, as Orson predicted, became part of history's oblivion.

When the floods raged, Orson's colorful career in Carson Valley had already been made legendary by Mark Twain in "The Great Landslide Case," chapter 34 of *Roughing It* (1872). Whereas Orson's 1862 letter named thunder, earthquakes, floods, pestilence, and famine, Twain made the curse a colossal landslide and changed the victim's name from Sides to Hyde. Twain obviously patterned the eloquence, bearing, and sense of humor of the judge in his account after what he had been told about Orson Hyde.

In spite of the curse, and destruction by floods, in widespread parts of Carson County the landscape would remain beautified by Mormon trademarks: roses blooming and poplar trees spiring.[21]

In Springtown in early 1862 Orson kept his normal pace. He made arrangements in March to ride to April general conference with one of the local bishops. But uncooperative weather might prevent his attendance, he wrote to Brigham Young, March 29, adding that "in consequence of . . . snowstorms, mud, frost and water, our spring's work falls in the rear. . . . Last Saturday I hauled manure upon my garden, wheels sunk in [mud] almost to the axletrees. Improved every minute to make garden so as to be ready for conference. . . . I do want some garden, trees, shrubbing &c. . . . Last night we had a strong snow storm. Sheep to shear and send off with the herd, fence to make, garden to plant, carrots to sow. . . . [I]f I should not get there at the beginning of the conference, don't think I have apostatized, neither scold me any harder than you think I deserve." Orson asked Mary Ann to read this letter before he sent it off, and her comment caused him to add a marginal note: "My wife tells me that it may be inferred that you have scolded me some times more than I deserved; but I don't mean any such thing. You will understand me I think."

In spite of his concerns he was able to attend conference. In one session he expressed his gratitude for the gospel by comparing it to eating luscious ripe peaches. In a later session he said of the meetings that "all things that have been done feel like a balm to my soul."[22]

In domestic matters, 1862 brought a notable change to the Hyde family. Orson moved Ann Eliza to Springtown. Marinda would miss Ann Eliza, but she preferred staying in the City with her friends and comfortable home. Ann Eliza's four year old Charles and two year old George would add spice to life in the log dwelling in Springtown. Mary Ann had excitedly prepared. Ann Eliza later admitted that when she first viewed Springtown at a distance, from "Moroni Hill," during the move, her heart sank at the few houses and few trees. But she adjusted willingly.[23]

By now Orson had became well acquainted with the people of Sanpete. Also, they had grown at ease and trusting with him. An example of this trust occurred the summer of 1862, an extraordinary event on an ordinary day:

Orson had traveled in a horse-drawn conveyance a short distance beyond Mount Pleasant one afternoon when a galloping rider, alongside, waved and shouted for the apostle to stop. Orson responded. The man motioned back to the cluster of homes and breathlessly asked Elder Hyde to return to Mount Pleasant. The little daughter of his neighbor, Nathan Staker, he panted, had drowned. Someone saw Elder Hyde drive through town, he explained further. At Brother Staker's request the rider had come to "overtake you and ask you to return and administer to the child." Orson turned around, sped townward, and in the Staker yard stepped down.

In the two-room log home he looked into distraught faces wet with tears. Nathan Staker's anguished countenance instantly registered relief. Soaked and unmoving Eliza Jane, eighteen months old, lay on a bed. Nathan, stretching out his hands, spoke. "Administer to my little girl," he pleaded, "and call her back to life."

In silent compassion Orson turned his attention to the child. Gently his fingers touched the small wrist, cold on contact. No pulse. Leaning over, he rested his ear on her damp chest. No heartbeat. Straightening, he looked at the weeping father and mother and asked tenderly, "How long was the little girl in the water?"

Nathan pulled his watch from his pocket and studied it. "It's just about an hour since I went to the orchard," he said desolately, "and I suppose she followed me." Frantic searching, by the Stakers and then neighbors too, finally revealed toddler Eliza Jane at the end of the apple orchard in the full irrigation ditch. To revive the motionless child the rescuers tried many procedures, to no avail.

Orson shook his head sadly. "I am very sorry, Brother and Sister Staker," he said, "but I have examined your baby thoroughly, and she is dead." He paused. Then, referring to the use of priesthood power to restore life, he explained, "It isn't pleasing in the sight of the Lord that we should try to bring back our dead after he has called them home."

"Elder Hyde," Nathan Staker appealed, "I have always tried to bow to the will of the Lord in all things, and am willing to do so now, but one thing troubles me very much. Soon after our little girl was born a year and a half ago, we took her to Bishop Seeley to give her a blessing and a name. I gave her that blessing myself." Emotion almost overcame the young father. "I distinctly remember," his words quavered, "that I promised her that she should grow to womanhood and become a mother in Israel. I sincerely believe that such promises made by the authority of the priesthood will be fulfilled, but now......." His voice broke off, and his work-worn hands reached out in helpless quest.

Orson looked into eyes full of trust and humility. After a silent quest he said, "In that case, I will ask God to restore your little girl to life again, and if that promise you gave to her was made in the spirit of faith and righteousness, she shall live again to fulfill it."

Orson rested his hands gently on the head of the lifeless child, and he commanded, in the name of the Lord, that her spirit return from the world beyond death and reunite with her body.

The next day a lively Eliza Jane played with her homemade toys. Eventually she became a mother, a grand-mother, and a great-grandmother, living a "life of love, devotion, and self-denial."[24]

In contrast to dramatic occurrences, Orson's duties required mostly persistent effort. Regarding land, he noticed that many people acquired more property than they needed. Thus they over-burdened themselves with labor and worry in crop and stock management, ditch-digging, and fence-building. The absorption with land often caused neglect in acquiring home comforts. Orson's repeated preachings about being sensible in these matters had brought only moderate change. With thousands upon thousands of acres available, great temptation existed to use them.[25] Another matter Orson took seriously was appointing, and recommending to Brigham Young, brethren to hold local leadership positions and fulfill assignments. He tried to follow inspiration. Occasionally events brought personal complications; July 30, 1862, Orson wrote to Brigham Young: "Pardon mistakes or blunders. I write by candle light without glasses, having lost them."[26]

One assignment that President Young gave to Orson, first in the spring of 1861, was to send men and teams back toward the Missouri River to bring immigrating poor Saints to Utah. This required great exertions on Orson's part, with Sanpete's scarcity of teams and wagons. But his preaching prevailed, and the farmers who stayed at home shared the remaining teams. In 1862 Orson reported the year's resulting blessings: "[In Sanpete] we managed to put in a little grain, but a great deal of it grew without our doing anything to it ourselves, and thus the Lord blessed us . . . with a rich reward for what we had done towards the gathering of his people."[27]

When Orson departed from home early in December, 1862, to attend the Legislature, he left Ann Eliza expecting a baby the next month. He returned two weeks past the event. The baby boy had arrived January 15, "after 'Early Candlelight.'" And what an evening! Outside, about four feet of snow almost covered the picket fence around the yard. After her summons the faithful midwife, Mrs. George Brough, made it through the snow. Inside the Hyde home warmth prevailed. In the stone kitchen at the back of the house, the assigned person kept the stove well stocked with wood. A "pitch pine wood" fire blazed in the big fireplace in the "front room," to heat, through the opened door, the adjoining north bedroom. In this room the midwife counseled and soothed Ann Eliza during her labor. Young Charles and George were entertained elsewhere. Later, for her professional services, Orson gave Mrs. Brough one sheep, a payment "better than gold."

Orson decided to name this new son in honor of his own most beloved personal friend, the Prophet Joseph Smith. As he had done with his other children, Orson gave this infant a priesthood blessing. Head bowed and eyes closed, holding the baby in his hands, Orson officially pronounced little Joseph's name upon him and invoked favors.[28]

While Ann Eliza had been expecting this child, Orson sought household help. At a social in the Springtown meetinghouse he saw a young woman with Brother Lauritz Larsen and his wife. They introduced her, and Elder Hyde liked her soft-spoken and kind manner. Julia Thomene Reinert, from Denmark, had just recently arrived, the only member of her family in the

Church. She spoke mostly Danish. Orson invited her, with translation help from the Larsens, to come to the Hyde home to live and work. She accepted.

At first communicating primarily with smiles, Julia learned quickly to perform the tasks asked of her. Her efficiency and her cooperation pleased Mary Ann and Ann Eliza. In addition, she added a new spark to dinner table conversations, soon communicating well in her limited English and learning to pronounce js and vs. As Julia's language skills increased, the family learned about this young woman, age twenty, with the square face, clear complexion, and alert blue eyes. In Aalborg, the parish of her July 13, 1842, birth, she had received an excellent education "in a Danish School under special tutors and also . . . [in] a select private school for young ladies."

Julia's parents opposed the Latter-day Saint doctrines taught by missionaries in Aalborg, but Julia and two girlfriends secretly sought out the elders and accepted their instruction. Julia's unheralded baptism occurred at night. Then Julia yearned to travel to Zion, but she lacked necessary funds. A friend gave her financial aid, and she devised a plan. Her mother—having agreed that Julia could visit her brother, hospitalized in Copenhagen with a war injury—helped her pack "some of her best clothing and necessary articles." Allowed only a brief moment with her brother, afterward Julia sailed from Copenhagen with a company of Saints, leaving her beautiful Denmark. Part way across the plains of the United States she wrote a letter to her parents and informed them of what she had done. After her September 23 arrival in Salt Lake City, an acquaintance invited her to Springtown.

When Orson had returned home from the Legislature, early in 1863, he brought with him three pieces of beautifully woven fabric—lovely, soft, silky alpaca wool from South America. He presented the fabric, enough for a dress each, to Mary Ann, Ann Eliza, and "Miss Reinert." The women's pleasure pleased him. He liked the extra light in Julia's eyes when he handed her the identical quality of gift he gave to Mary Ann and Ann Eliza.[29]

In April 1863 Orson traveled to Salt Lake City to attend general conference. In a pre-conference meeting in the Bowery, from Brigham Young he received correction to his preaching. Orson's remarks gave Joseph Smith too much personal power, separate from the priesthood. President Young spoke after him and defined the powers more clearly. Orson, grateful for the President's counsel, said in a conference address, "I know that our religion is true. . . . God has spoken from the heavens through his servants in the last days, and . . . [Brigham Young] is the mouthpiece of the Most High, ready to instruct, to correct and to impart the principles of eternal life to every inquiring soul."[30]

Brigham Young invited Orson to accompany members of the Presidency and the Twelve on a visit to southern Utah, the "Cotton Mission." In 1861 Orson had participated in the enterprise, under Brigham Young's direction, of assigning families to move to this southern area and raise cotton.[31] The plans of the visiting group included travel through Sanpete on the way.

After conference Orson returned home to prepare. April 25, the travelers arrived in Springtown. "Presidents Young and Kimball," the company scribe wrote, "halted before the residence of Elder Orson Hyde, who, with his usual blandness of manner and a countenance which betokened a good heart, received his distinguished guests and welcomed them to the hospitality of his home. His house is of hewn logs, one and a half stories, with a stone kitchen. His corrals, yards and sheds are substantial, neat and orderly, and I discovered he is making an effort to raise quite a variety of fruit. Here [in Springtown] Presidents Young and Kimball, Elders John Taylor, Geo. A. Smith and Lorenzo Snow spoke to the people under the bowery, encouraging them to diligence in every improvement for the comfort and happiness of themselves and families. There are several good adobie buildings here. After dinner we rolled rapidly along a descending road to Manti, eighteen miles distant, passing through Fort Ephraim."[32]

For the next several days the traveling group, Orson included, preached in Sanpete towns and then continued south. In every settlement enthusiastic Saints greeted the visitors with joy (and often with banners and singing), fed them abundantly, listened to them preach, and gave them the best accommodations available. As the company entered their southern destination, Saint George, "the new and delightful home of about fifteen hundred Saints," the scribe recorded, "[w]e passed under a flag that waved proudly, . . . the product [cotton] of the soil over which it now floated." Further advertising the success of the mission, a "bale of cotton was also raised to the top of the flag-staff as the Presidency advanced, while bunches of cotton yarn, carded and spun here, were suspended at its base." The guests were "invited to the homes of old friends, endeared by the associations of past years."

Many area meetings and meals later, the travelers began their return: three hundred miles for Orson, more than four hundred miles for the people from Great Salt Lake City. The scribe wrote that the trip had "done incalculable good to the settlements. The presence of the Presidency and a portion of the Quorum of the Twelve, coupled with their words of encouragement, have roused up the energies of the people and enkindled a desire for enterprise and improvement."[33]

Orson's first public priority after arriving home was the Thistle Valley–Spanish Fork Canyon road. Orson's second summer in Sanpete Valley, 1861, the new road had been worked enough that loaded teams traversed it successfully, but the next spring, 1862, high waters washed out sections, preventing wagon use. Now, in May 1863, Orson took Bishop Jones of Fairview with him and they studied the route through to Spanish Fork, traveling a portion of it several times as they worked out changes. The next week about sixty men began repairs and modifications. Three weeks later the road was passable, and work continued.[34]

One of Orson's perpetual duties involved water problems. Local bishops worked with disputes among neighbor farmers, and Orson mainly dealt with disagreements between neighbor communities, when both villages wanted more water than streams supplied. Sometimes men diverted streams back and forth. Water conflicts lacked happy solutions. Orson tried diligently to make judgments according to the total picture, yet, no matter what he ruled, some people disagreed with him, considered him unfair. Never did all individuals concur, and some would carry resentments for years. Orson could only do his best.[35]

Orson sincerely tried to overcome his own problems too. In recent months Brigham Young had invited him to conscientiously work to eliminate his addiction to tobacco. June 28, 1863, Orson reported: "I have chewed no tobacco for 3 or 4 months—Smoked not a particle for one month, Snuffed but one pinch in a week—So you see I am trying to accept your invitation, and wind the 'pesky' thing off." Time proved his success.[36]

In the Hyde household Julia Reinert continued to fit well, and Orson asked her to marry him. She consented. They said their eternal wedding vows in Salt Lake City, August 29, 1863. If the age span between his fifty-eight and her twenty-one caused Julia any concerns, she resolved them to become a forever part of Orson's family.[37]

For October 1863 conference Orson made the trip to Great Salt Lake City and in December again left Springtown to attend the Legislature. Before his December departure he thought carefully about the operations of his home and farm. Wanting them to continue efficiently, he wrote out detailed instructions for his hired man:

Instructions to Mr. Welsh

1st make fires in fire-place & stove, then bring water for breakfast.

2nd Shovel & sweep away snow from about the door when necessary.

3rd Feed every head of stock before breakfast.

4th At the ringing of the bell, come in to prayers and breakfast.

5th After Breakfast, bring water for the women if they need, [then] milk the cows, after which feed them carrots.

5th Water horses, bull &c.

6th Feed sheep hay at noon, and plenty of cut carrots.

7th Give the stock a little hay at noon,- none, however, to waste.

8th feed the sheep small carrots and tops whenever you can.

9th Watch the scab on the sheep, and apply the ointment when necessary.

10th At all vacancies, chop wood for stove and fire-place.

11<u>th</u> Take care of all your tools, and keep the stable & stack yard tidy—

12<u>th</u> Feed, milk, bring in wood for night and morning before dark.

13<u>th</u> look carefully after the lambs when they come, and give the sheep plenty of carrots, so that they will give plenty of milk.

By strict attention to the above, and whatever else may be necessary, in the proper time and season thereof, you will merit a good name and secure a corresponding reward.

Good <u>hours</u> should be observed, not much joking, no profanity But good order and decorum observed, and respect will beget respect, and respect godliness, and godliness immortality and eternal life.

Orson Hyde[38]

Back in Sanpete, along with his Church responsibilities Orson oversaw military activities. County militia commandant, Colonel R. N. Allred, reporting musters and recommendations for new officers in March 1864, wrote to his commanding officer: "I . . . will consult Elder Hyde, as I have done in all my former movements."

A big event in the Hyde home in 1864 was the May 5 birth of Julia's first child. The baby, a girl, Orson and Julia named Mary Ann.[39]

In the spring of 1864 Sanpete Valley saw a major transition. Orson had felt growing concern about challenges caused by the great rise in population. The solution to over-settlement and increased water problems might be to ask families to move, starting new settlements south of the present Sanpete ones, up the Sevier River. Orson had discussed the situation with Brigham Young. President Young and others had then visited Sanpete in November 1863, and the President's own observations agreed with Orson's. During the 1863-1864 winter, around the valley, Orson and the bishops preached, "calling" some families and encouraging others to prepare to move. In early spring, families, livestock, and wagons began wending their way south from Sanpete to begin new communities along the upper Sevier.

Orson visited the Sevier River settlements in May—an excursion of eight days over rough roads and non-roads—accompanied by Bishop Kearns of Gunnison. The two men encountered varied adventures, held meetings, inspected "location[s] and premises, condition of things temporal and spiritual," Orson tells, "[and] we gave them the best instructions that circumstances would prompt and the spirit of the Lord inspire." They appointed leaders for the groups, and they met with friendly Indians, Bishop Kearns interpreting. "A good spirit prevailed. . . ," Orson reported about the trip. "Crops in every new settlement, though limited of necessity, are healthy and vigorous. . . . [W]hen I came home, my tongue was tired, my mind was tired — my body was tired; but after 24 hours of intermittent sleep, I was all right again."[40]

Reducing the population failed to eliminate all community problems, however. People's selfish acts brought censure from Orson, and they appealed to Brigham Young, claiming prejudice and unfair treatment by Elder Hyde.[41]

The biggest challenge in Sanpete, especially with many able men now moved, was getting in the tremendously large harvest. In the midst of this summer 1864 labor, Orson received official censure. Severe chastisement from President Young reached him by letter. Orson had sent less than the requested number of delegates from Sanpete to a convention. Lament burned his soul, upon reading the letter, for his unthinking act in considering Sanpete's overwhelming harvest work more important than an authoritative directive. Orson felt that he must ask forgiveness in person. However, trusting his pen more than his voice, he composed an introductory explanation to take with him. "First and foremost," he wrote, "I acknowledge the justice of your letter and the rebuke which it contained; I most sincerely regret the responsibility that I took. The thought never occurred to me that I understood better what was wanted than you and the other brethren; Still, the shape the question is now in, forbids any special evasion of the force of your letter."

He detailed his actions regarding delegates to the convention and went on. "Can you forgive me?" he pleaded. "Will you forgive? I ask it. I am sorry that I have done as I have—I have done wrong! — sinned against you and the brethren; . . . and for ought I know, a veto may have been passed upon me, still I hope not. I pray not so. Where could I go? . . . This Kingdom is all I live for. I have no hope anywhere else. With all my errors, stumblings and sins, I love this cause of God and them who honor it. I kiss the hand that applies the rod, especially in this case."

Ignoring the hurrying harvest season, Orson made a trip to Great Salt Lake City. After his session with Brigham Young, Orson's gratitude overflowed. He would try harder, again, to heed counsel rather than be caught up in worldly pressures.[42]

The same summer, 1864, President Young invited Orson to again accompany Church leaders on a journey to the southern settlements. Orson did, in September, and savored the excursion.[43]

In October of 1864 Orson tried to resign from the Legislature, feeling burdened by the "constant care and watchfulness" required of him in Sanpete. But Brigham Young replied that "you had better not resign your seat; we want you there."[44]

This autumn the Hyde family increased by another wife. Elisabeth Josephine Galli, of a spiritual nature, exchanged vows with Orson on October 15, 1864, in the Endowment House. Elisabeth had been born February 14, 1840, in Guendlischwand, Lauterbrunnen, Bern, Switzerland. When a young woman she listened to the Mormon missionaries and accepted baptism, as did her family. She arrived in Utah in October 1862. Elisabeth, called Lizzy, now spoke English fairly well, but Orson enjoyed practicing German with her.[45]

As well as the changes to his home of adding new wives, Orson's son Alonzo sometimes came to take his turn helping on the farm. At such times Frank lived in Salt Lake City to assist their mother, Marinda.

Orson thought much about Marinda and felt sad that he could do so little for her. In a letter to Brigham Young, October 29, 1864, he asked a favor: "Should Marinda be inclined to take boarders this fall and winter, and if you think her health will permit her to do so, I would be very thankful if you would use a little influence to procure some [boarders] for her of <u>the right stripe</u>, – such also as will pay her. She has been to some expense in furnishing her house for that purpose. By this business, she can help herself to live comfortably, and somewhat relieve me: but if her health is not adequate to the care and labor necessary for that business, by no means do I wish her to engage in it." Marinda took in boarders.[46]

Varied activities continued. In the fall of 1864, President Young asked Orson to call more families to the Sevier settlements. Orson did and in early November again visited the fledgling towns. He "found them generally well, hard at work, building Log Houses, 'Dugouts' and wheat bins, and making all other necessary preparations for winter consistent with their condition." Before traveling to Great Salt Lake City for the Legislature, Orson wrote to George A. Smith, December 3: "I have been forced to neglect my own affairs at home until my entire crop is froze in which is carrots but perhaps they will thaw out in the spring, yet I need them much this winter for feeding." In January 1865 the Legislature created the counties of Sevier and Piute from Sanpete, giving Orson Church jurisdiction over three counties.[47]

In the Rocky Mountains, Zion had grown by thousands of new arrivals, and diligent work had brought widespread favorable conditions. In December 1864 Orson raised a warning voice. "Many of us know," he declared in a Salt Lake Tabernacle sermon, "what it is to be in the very depths of poverty and privation; and we now seem to have advanced into a measurable prosperity, in order that we may be proved and tried in another manner, . . . whether we are able to abide prosperity as well as adversity."

After the Legislature adjourned, Orson returned home, February 1865, to other problems. "Measles are quite general amongst children in several of our settlements," he narrated, "especially in Springtown, and my family are almost worn out with care and anxiety day and night. Also, our youngest [Julia's nine month old Mary Ann] met with an accident by falling on the hot hearth on her cheek, a severe burn, and teething at the same time renders it almost impossible to heal the wound. Measles also setting in, it is extremely trying to the little thing, yet we hope, by the blessing of God to save her."[48] Little Mary Ann recovered.

Interwoven with the numerous other facets of Sanpete living, Indians played a constant, but changeable, part. One minute, in a little wickiup village near a settlement, Indians might seem peacefully going about their business, and then, the next minute, the squaws pack wickiups and everything else onto horse-drawn travoises. In a couple of hours the troupe heads elsewhere. When near settlements, Indian and white children and youths played and sported together, many becoming fast friends, sharing games and words. Some Indians learned a fair amount of English. Most Indians learned enough to beg for food. One minute, any given Indian might seem congenial, the next minute uneasy and agitated. A few settlers throughout the valley mastered the Indian dialects and acted as interpreters, an invaluable service. Any incident that seemed threatening to the Indians might lead to an altercation.[49]

One minute, adult Indians exchanged goods, bringing rawhide, buckskin, lariats, and moccasins to trade for food and clothing. The next minute Indians begged for flour or beef. Occasionally Indians killed cattle. Generally, however, to avert such slaughter, the settlers gave food to the natives. Brigham Young had long preached that feeding Indians was better than fighting Indians.[50] In spite of friendly relations, though, Indian habits remained foreign and often repugnant to whites. Cleanliness was alien to their culture, as was knocking on doors. They simply walked into homes unannounced. They also peered through windows, noses flat against the glass.

Orson became well acquainted with local chiefs Sanpitch and his nephew Jake Arapeen. Sanpitch, tall and well proportioned, with long nose and chin, contrasted with Jake, about five feet five inches in height, "shaped like an inverted post with his long braided hair . . . touching the [ground] as he walked." Each possessed a hawk nose. Jake's "heavy shaggy eye-brows" overshadowed deep eyes. After Orson arrived in the valley in 1860, Jake Arapeen was the first chief who visited him. In good English Jake extended friendship to this new local leader of the settlers.

Utah Indians functioned as many tribal groups, with no strong central authoritative leader. A brother of Sanpitch, Chief Wakara (or Walker), in 1849 had invited Brigham Young's people to settle in Sanpete Valley. Later, when the wagons, livestock, and families continued coming, displacing his own people, he became hostile and waged bitter war against settlers farther north. He died in 1855.[51] Orson extended courtesy and respect to Sanpete's nomadic inhabitants, and he received the same in return. As he observed personalities, he developed total trust in no Indian, but he continually tried to be fair.

The Indian situation was paradoxical. The Saints knew that the Almighty had guided Brigham Young to these extensive mountain valleys and continued to inspire Saints to come. Yet, these same valleys had been home to fathers of the Indians for generations, back to the Lamanites of Book of Mormon times. For centuries they had roamed at will, had gathered seeds and roots and berries, had used the wildlife, large and small, for food and clothes. The whites tried to change this nomadic people, to domesticate them, thinking that all they needed was to be taught to farm. These efforts failed. Beyond Indian comprehension was whitemen's practice of living and working on one piece of land year after year. To the Indians the entire valleys belonged to all of them—not one spot of land, but the whole land, the whole valleys, the canyons, the mountains.

Problems arose. Whites cleared and plowed fields where before Indians had gathered natural foods. Whites confiscated the streams that previously teemed with fish, food for the Indians, and with beaver, from which the Indians procured hides to barter with white traders in exchange for desired goods. Sometimes settlers cheated Indians and treated them with contempt, treachery, or deceit.[52]

As Orson became better acquainted with the local natives, sub-chief "Indian Joe" exasperated him more than did most. Early in December 1861, Joe asked Orson to tell the people of Fountain Green and Moroni to furnish him a beef. Orson replied negatively, reminding Joe that he begged strong enough to shame any ten decent Indians. Orson continued, "What, do you mean to beg beef of us, when you, Indians, a few years ago, drove off all our cattle and horses? If you had not done that, we might now have had an ox for you; but as it is, we have little or no beef for ourselves. We have not oxen enough to raise wheat for you and for us—not cows enough to give milk for our Squaws and papooses; and now, after stealing all our cattle and driving them away, you come and ask us for an ox. I shall not tell the Bishops to give you one. We give you bread and flour every day, and potatoes often, and you must kill Shoekum [rabbits[53]] for your meat."

Then, during Orson's December 1861 and January 1862 sojourn in Salt Lake City, Joe visited the Sanpete bishops and told them that Elder Hyde said they must give him a beef. They refused, fully aware of his strategies.

In February, Joe again visited the Hyde home. He wanted Orson, in a public meeting, to beg for him. Orson indeed discoursed publicly about the situation. Joe attended. "I spoke my mind freely to the people," Orson narrates. "I told the people that I gave more bread to the Indians every day than my own family consumed, and that I had not sent one of them away empty; but that they were dissatisfied with the 'peap captain' because he did not give it to them by the sack full. This I could not do if I would; and would not if I could. I told the people to feed them bread during the winter as much as would keep them alive, or kill them; and told the Indians when it was warm they must go to work and they should be paid for it; but if they did not work, they would all die. . . . I told Indian 'Joe' that he need not ask me to beg for him, for I should not do it — that I did not want to see him, for he had lied about me to the Bishops."

March 1, Orson reported to Brigham Young about this speech, stating that it "made quite a sensation amongst the Indians here. Shall I modify my position with them or not? They are a heavy tax upon all the people of this valley." Orson continued, saying that in spite of recent promises of the Indian agent in Salt Lake City to send clothing, blankets, and other items to the Sanpete natives, nothing had come. Orson's heart ached for the natives, but also for the Saints. He said to President Young that the Indians "are, truly, a poor miserable race. We truly have no cattle for them, yet we have given them many, also sheep. The people here are poor. They work hard and live hard, most of them. For clothing they are short; and for beds and bedding shorter. Their old adobie houses and sheds half melted down, look sorry. Yet we are rich and feel well, and intend to respond to every official call so far as it is in our power. But we do think that these Indians, after being nursed and pampered in their idleness for ten years, ought now to work or starve.

"Should you see any thing wrong in my views or instructions, in relation to the Indians, I should be very glad for you to put me right."[54]

President Young replied, "The Indians in your region are, as you state, 'a poor, miserable race,' for which reason, and for many other reasons that you are acquainted with, prudence counsels that they be dealt with on our part in the mildest, most forbearing, and liberal manner that the circumstances and relative conditions of both parties will permit."

In mid May, Orson's frustration with Indians spilled over again. Near Moroni, Brother Hambleton saw his sheep purposefully attacked by an Indian boy and dog. Brother Hambleton shot the dog. In retaliation, Indians afterward killed five head of cattle and left them on the ground. Orson detailed this to Brigham Young and added, "[The Indians] are generally sour, because they can get no [gun]powder of us. They get not enough food to gormandize and gorge themselves with. They say we dare not kill them nor harm them. They interpret our forbearance into cowardice. It looks rather hard, after feeding and clothing the miserable scamps, to have our cattle shot down, and we tantalized. . . . If Heaven require[s] us to bear with this, their conduct, we will try still to do so; but it is grievous to nature."[55]

Indian relations continued about the same for the remainder of 1862, but in the spring of 1863 hostilities increased in various parts of Utah Territory, with animosity against emigrant trains and soldiers. Brigham Young wrote a letter to several Indian chiefs, sent it to Orson, and asked Orson to have it read to them by an interpreter. The President reminded the natives, "We have fed you for many years and given you clothing and always been your friends and treated you kindly; but we cannot feed you and be friends to you unless you stop making war on the whites. . . . If you do make war on the whites, and determine to interrupt the mail coaches and the peaceable emigrants you may be assured sudden vengeance will follow you, and you will soon be chastised in a terrible manner, . . . for such conduct can not and will not be endured." Brigham Young had met with the chiefs during his recent excursion south, and had hoped the discussions would solve problems, but such had not happened.

Orson engaged an interpreter to carry and read the letter, but he lacked confidence that even a letter from "the Mormon Chief" would quell ravages. Orson reported this to the President June 21, 1863. "The Indians are very much determined to kill every gentile whom they see, and every soldier," Orson said. "How they will take your letter to them, I cannot say, but am a little apprehensive they will regard it as a threat. There are about 500 warriors now here. They hope to draw the soldiers out after them. The late killing of the mail coach driver and a passenger was done with a view to provoke the soldiers to following them to where there would be a heavy force of Indians, possibly in ambush. Your letter will go to them tomorrow, and be communicated by a faithful and competent interpreter. . . . They seem to entertain no feelings of hostility towards us at present, but in view of the possibility of a sudden change in their feelings, I concluded the brethren this day to have their arms and ammunition ready. . . . I shall use all the influence in my power with the Indians to have them cease their depredations upon the whites, and have instructed the brethren here to do the same. The Indians say Gentiles have covers on their wagons. Mormons should have no covers."

A week later Orson reported to Brigham Young again: "I have not heard from the Indians since your letter was read to them, having been away on the line of the new road, yet I think they are inclined to heed it, at least in a good degree for Indians."[56]

By the summer of 1864 the United States government passed enactments to remove the Indians from Sanpete northeast to a huge reserved area in Uinta Valley. Orson thought this a good idea. June 10, 1864, he reported to Brigham Young that the "Indians are quite troublesome of late. . . . They say that they intend to have all the beef they want, and ride horses. Two of our Brethren were in the Kanyon day before yesterday, and an Indian shot at them—range quartering, brushing the whiskers of both of them. This they probably did because they considered their hunting ground about to be infringed upon, as the brethren shot at were exploring a route for a road to the timber and poles. I care not how soon the Government removes them to Uinta Valley. They have killed only two or three head of cattle as yet that we know of. We are taking every measure to protect our stock that we reasonably can take. . . . Crops look remarkably well, especially wheat and oats throughout this entire region." However, Orson continued, "if the Indians shoot at us in the Kanyons, our improvements must cease, or we must have an Indian war. We are holding on for the present to see which way the tide will flow."[57]

Brigham Young answered Orson's letter on June 18. "In regard to the Indians," he said, "you are aware that we are settled upon their lands, (which materially interrupts their success in hunting, fishing, &c)." He reminded

Orson that the Book of Mormon predicted hardships for the Indians and also told of "the designs of the Almighty in their behalf; for these reasons it behooves us to exercise towards them all possible kindness, liberty, patience and forbearance on our part. Of course duty requires every one to keep a consistently vigilant watch upon their stock and other property, and also upon the natives. And inasmuch as we occupy their lands, as before stated, it is but right for us to give the well-behaved a horse or an ox now and again, and otherwise feed and help them as circumstances and a correct view of our respective conditions may require. The Lord who has decreed the regeneration of that race, giveth us seed time and harvest, the rain, the mountain streams, and all our increase, and being ever kind and liberal to that class of his children, so long as their conduct is not outrageous and unbearable, seems to us to be pleasing in His sight."

A few weeks later, July 30, 1864, Orson reported gratefully to President Young that "Our Indian matters or anticipated troubles with them are all blown by. Peace reigns in our valley for which I feel thankful to God."[58]

Aside from Indian relations, general events in early spring 1865 consisted of building projects, farm work, and valley developments. "We held meeting, for the first time, this morning in our new meeting house in this place," Orson reported from Springtown March 26, 1865. "A nice floor tongued and grooved finished– Stand and pulpit completed, windows handsomely cased &c. &c." In the same report Orson voiced concern that many people in Sanpete had sold their seed wheat even when admonished by Church leaders to retain it. He wondered if the Lord would bless their harvest after they were disobedient. "I fear more a disobedience to counsel than the late snows, frost and mud," he said. Big Sanpete news in early April was the solicitation of subscriptions from local citizens to construct the Deseret Telegraph line into the valley. This received enthusiastic response.[59]

Orson traveled to April general conference and enjoyed his few days in the City.[60] He began his homeward journey with no expectation that hostilities loomed formidably in Sanpete.

... *afflictions*. . . . *(1865–1867)*

> *. . . afflictions . . . thou shalt*
> *have many; but endure them. . . .*
> —Doctrine and Covenants 24:8

DEVASTATING news met Orson in mid April 1865 while on his way home after general conference. Before he reached Nephi, to cross the mountains east over into Sanpete Valley, a messenger told him that in Sanpete natives had stolen livestock and killed men. Astonished, appalled, Orson hastened on to Nephi and found Bishop Bryan, the whites' Indian interpreter and contact person. The bishop said that he had just seen Chief Sanpitch. Reassuringly, but unconvincingly, Sanpitch declared that he "had not heard of the outbreak, but expected it," adding that "he would send word to 'Joe' to have no hand in it."

Orson had little trust in Sanpitch's words, and less in Joe's. This feeling deepened after he left Nephi the morning of April 13. "When about two miles up Salt Creek Kanyon," he explains, "I met Sanpitch wrapped in his Buffalo robe, and on seeing me, he [quickly left the road], laid off his robe and displayed full Indian uniform, apparently very tired as though he had traveled some distance, and sat down. He was probably [previously] posted out at some distance to receive his nightly runners and give orders, and be about the settlements in the daytime to allay suspicion. These were my impressions when I saw him."[1]

Orson's team sped over the mountain road and into Sanpete Valley. At Fountain Green, Orson met an express messenger from Salina, many miles to the south. After brief consultation, Orson asked someone to write a hasty note for him to Brigham Young. (In recent years a tremor in Orson's hands had grown progressively more shaky, and other people now wrote most of his letters.) "Two o'clock afternoon," he dictated, ". . . I learn that quite an Indian war [has been] inaugurated. The Indians have possession of [Salina] Kanyon and [are] about one hundred strong. And the snows being so deep on the mountains and Kanyons, it is difficult to head them. A few have probably gone ahead with the stock stolen from Salina, Gunnison, & Manti, while the balance remain near the mouth of the Kanyon ready for fight."[2]

Driving directly to Fort Ephraim, Orson arrived a little after sundown. His team would feed and rest while he investigated. He learned no causes "more than ordinary" on the part of the settlers. The Indians, it seemed, simply decided to "get 'mad.'" Three days before, April 10, about fifteen or sixteen Indians wantonly shot down a young man hunting cattle in a canyon south of Manti. The same warriors, apparently, rode farther south to Salina Canyon and that evening shot down two more cattle-hunting men. One of these, Barney Ward, had been valuable to the Sanpete settlers in dealing with the Indians. Orson and Barney had enjoyed a long association, Barney being the Indian interpreter for Fort Supply a decade before.

The night of Barney's murder, fifty to one hundred warriors drove off livestock of Salina and Gunnison grazing together. Colonel Allred promptly, April 11, raised a large force (eighty-four men, Orson learned later) from the local militias and, April 12, pursued the thieves and animals up narrow Salina Canyon. An Indian ambush stopped the pursuers, and during the retreat Indians killed two whites. To Orson, some men expressed censure toward Colonel Allred for entering Salina Canyon. Though Orson also felt that the action may have been unwise, in a lengthy dispatch to the brethren in camp outside the canyon he withheld reproof, not wishing to discourage Brother Allred or his men.

Finally, at three o'clock in the morning, April 14, he arrived home in Springtown. His son Frank was absent, having responded to Colonel Allred's hasty call for troops. Orson slept fitfully and then dictated a report to Brigham Young. He also assessed the situation. "To all appearance," he said, "there is a move made by the Indians for a general campaign against us. We know not what point to guard and consequently we are guarding all points best we can. Almost every horse in the county is pressed into service, general anxiety and excitement prevail, plowing and seeding are necessarily neglected, . . . and on the whole, things look a little gloomy. I could wish I was a military man just now, but as I am not I have but little confidence in myself, yet I feel to exert the best and wisest influence I can. There is a little difference of feeling here in relation to the policy to be acted upon. Some say that you told the Indians . . . if they killed any more of our men, you would wipe them out. . . . [O]thers are on the conservative order: negotiate, &c. The Indians manifest great hostility by mutilating and cutting in pieces the unfortunate victims of their cruelty, and it seems difficult to get at them in any way but by force. Yet I know your general policy in relation to the Indians. . . .

"If, now, under these circumstances, you have any counsel or help for us, we need it. . . . God bless you and us too."[3]

The next day, April 15, Orson reported briefly to President Young that a "friendly" Indian stated that Black Hawk—another area chief known to the settlers—had gone to General P. Edward Conner "some time ago and made it all right for him, Black Hawk, to help kill the Mormons." General Conner commanded about seven hundred federal troops stationed at Camp Douglas, east of Salt Lake City. Filling his official assignment to guard mail routes and telegraph lines, he had shown no great friendship toward the Saints. Orson felt that the Indian move was likely underhanded, an effort to implicate Conner in the Sanpete troubles, but Brigham Young should be informed of developments. Orson ventured that the claim was just one of the "thousand tales and rumors . . . continually afloat.

"The main body of the Indians are yet in the Kanyon, [supposedly]," Orson's note went on, "and the brethren are guarding the mouth."

Orson added a postscript: "Perhaps I did Sanpitch injustice as I learn that he is gone to our camp, and recommends, in case peace cannot be made, to whip them out, and he proposes to take his men and help to do it, by going round and heading them: Still for this he wants Barney Wards two daughters, saying that Barney promised [he could have] them . . . after he, Barney, died."

Two days later, April 17, Orson received an express answer from Brigham Young. "When we were down there," President Young confirmed, in reply to Orson's query, "we promised the Indians, if they wantonly killed the brethren, as soon as we could get hold of them, we would use them up." Clarifying instructions, he sent to Orson a copy of his directive to Colonel Allred written April 14, cautioning him not to rush into danger, to watch the Indians strictly, to "be so vigilant that they can do no further damage," and to retain any offending Indians who came into the settlements. This had arrived too late.

"The course which has been taken in fighting and killing the Indians," Brigham Young continued, "has tied my hands." Orson read this with dismay. The President had obviously heard false rumors. No Indians had been killed. "How can we use up the guilty Indians, or ask for them to be given up," the letter went on, "without the Indians turning round and asking us for the whites who have killed Indians to be given up in return. . . .

"It is no time for us to have an Indian war on our hands;" the letter went on, "better for us to feed them and give them such necessaries as they may want than to fight them." Brigham Young's disappointment became more pronounced as he commented about communities' failures to follow former instructions to build strong protective forts.

President Young ended his letter "With love to yourself and the Saints and praying the Lord to give You the necessary wisdom to discharge every duty which devolves upon You in a manner to work out salvation for Israel." A postscript, containing an inference to the past actions of some Sanpete settlers selling their wheat against counsel, also fueled his exasperation that the actions of a few had such great effect upon so many.[4]

In Sanpete a careful calm evolved, and the militia members came home. Frank told a harrowing tale. During the troops' push up Salina Canyon, Frank's horse became one of the "killed or wounded." Frank tackled the steep narrow trail on foot, and soon, for stability and assistance, held to the tail of an advancing horse. This seemed his only security, but the pace exhausted him. Just as he felt he could go no farther, but must let go and rest, leaving his fate to angry Indians, the man on the horse pointed and yelled back to him, "Get that mule." Frank looked.

There stood a mule, its feet tangled in its bridle reins, its rider having been thrown or shot off. Frank let go of the horse's tail and scrambled to the mule, but he had no knife to cut the reins. Another man, seeing his plight, stopped his horse, took his knife from his belt, and handed the knife to Frank. Suddenly, howling Indians almost upon them, guns cracking, and bullets whining, the militia members spun around in full retreat. Only miracles kept the horrendous volley of Indian bullets from killing all of the whites and their mounts. Frank had never before been so grateful for a ride. As the assault lessened, and the riding slowed, a man came alongside Frank and asked him what he had done with the knife. Frank reached into his pocket. Holding out his hand he said, "Are you the man who let me take this knife? It saved my life." Frank learned later that the mule had thrown its owner, Jens Sorensen of Fort Ephraim, and the Indians killed him in Salina Canyon. Another white also died.

Though the Indians seemed bent on destruction, they too had compassion. Chief Sanpitch, two days after the Salina Canyon battle, appeared in Gunnison at night and reported that the two bodies in the canyon could be safely retrieved. Sorensen's body had been mutilated, but not that of young William Kearns. The whites learned that when the Indians realized they had killed Bishop Kearns' son, an old friend of younger days with whom they had shared much playing and hunting, they set the body next to a rock and around it wove a willow mesh to protect it from wolves.

As days passed, Orson gleaned additional details of the recent villainy. Some Sanpitch Indians declared that they "knew of this outbreak being in contemplation six weeks before it took place."

April 23, Orson wrote to Brigham Young and explained further about Sanpitch. The chief, soon after the Salina Canyon murders, "went to see Bishop Kearnes and told the Bishop that Barney Ward promised him (Sanpitch) his daughter or daughters upon his death. Sanpitch then proposed to lend his aid to negotiate . . . a peace on condition that he have the girl or girls according to promise. If Ward ever made him any such promise," Orson continued, "it is singular that he should limit the fulfillment of it to the time of his death. . . . I cannot learn that [Ward] ever mentioned any such thing to any one, not even to his daughters. . . . My conclusions are, therefore, these: Ward never promised Sanpitch his daughter. But he wanted one or both of them, and contrived this spurious and artful tale. . . . [He] set Jake, Black Hawk and Tapaddy to kill Ward, and also some others to cover his mischief: and as a reward . . . told them to drive off all the stock they could into the

Kanyon. . . . Then he, as the faithful ally of the Mormons, would offer to make peace on condition that the girl or girls were given to him. . . . This is the way the Book of reason reads to me. I may not read it correctly, but you can draw your own conclusions, not forgetting that the time of conference was hit upon for its execution when many of our Bishops were absent."[5]

Analysis of past events indicated that an Indian broil had been in the making before April. In March the behavior of the Sanpete Valley Indians, especially those encamped near Manti, had become insolent and extremely demanding toward the townsfolk. After several weeks of this, bands led by Joe and Black Hawk met with interpreters April 9 in Manti for a powwow. Joe's band accused Black Hawk's band of stealing cattle, and Black Hawk gave no denial. Sharp words ensued, Joe claiming Black Hawk had done wrong. Also, Orson was told, one of the Manti interpreters, John Lowery, "had a little quarrel with an Indian or two." This "was foolish," Orson felt, "not only foolish, but wicked. This however did not load the gun, but might have been the match in part to fire it off. I do not know. No man has the right to do any thing likely to involve the whole people in war by redressing a personal wrong. That is, this is my opinion." The thefts of cattle and killing of whites, begun soon after the heated Manti pow-wow altercations, were done by Black Hawk and his warriors. Black Hawk, of dauntless bearing, was intelligent and handsome, a natural leader.

In Orson's same April 23 letter he commented to Brigham Young about Sanpete residents killing Indians:

> You say that the course which has been taken in fighting and killing the Indians has tied your hands. . . . I cannot now call to mind the killing of a single Indian, good, bad or indifferent since I have been in this county. . . . [M]y heart leaped into my mouth on reading that paragraph in your letter. . . . I speak my feelings to you only; yet against your words, I shall not rebel.
>
> If any Indian has been killed here, he was of that class that you ordered . . . never to be allowed to pass out of our lines. We have fed and clothed them, and they have slaughtered and eaten our cattle at the same time, especially the later part of this winter and fore part of spring and we have not killed them, nor attempted to 'till they began to kill us: and if every red skin in that Kanyon had been killed, I cannot feel that we should have exceeded the limits of your instruction.
>
> We deplore an Indian war at any time, but it appears unavoidable when they, by their acts, inaugurate it. I have tried to be cautious, and have instructed our Bishops and people to be so, about taking any step to cause a friction between us and the Indians. My test, borrowed from you, is "cheaper to feed than fight them." Yet it is not cheap to feed them.

"But the war is over for the present," Orson continued. "The Indians are gone, and our troops are ploughing, and sowing wheat. God grant that their pursuits may not be soon again interrupted."[6]

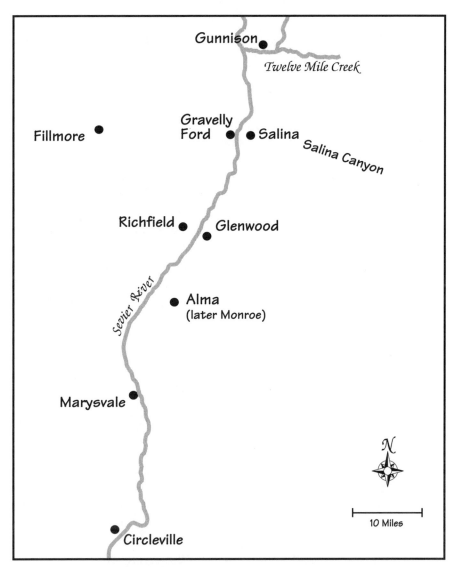

Black Hawk War area south of Sanpete Valley.

During the next few weeks the people felt secure in the Sanpete peace and disregarded many specific instructions about caution.

Then, May 25 Indians killed one Sanpete man, May 26 a family, and May 29 another man. Things happened so fast it seemed that Orson hardly talked with one messenger before more news arrived. May 29 he dictated a letter to Brigham Young to be sent by express rider. He told briefly of the killings and added, "not a friendly Indian in this country that I know of or have any reason to believe. Some have come in occasionally professing friendship but were spies. I have given instructions to capture every Indian that is seen and can be got hold of, and those that cannot be captured to be shot if within range. Those that are captured to be tied fast so that they will not rest very easy, and kept safely in some cellar 'till further orders. . . . I cannot see my Brethren shot down by the poor devils that we have fed and clothed without doing something to repel such aggressions. I do not wish to expose our men unnecessarily, yet too great caution emboldens the enemy and makes him haughty and confident of success. If we fight him he can but kill us. If we let him alone he is pretty sure to do it. In my opinion, vigorous, decided and effective measures are necessary, and immediate action seems to be imperatively demanded. We are raising forces to march to night in pursuit of the murderous villains. I hope I go not contrary to your mind when you know the circumstances; at least, I do not wish to. We wish to act like men and protect our wives and children, our homes and our substance. This war is on a scale that cannot well be kept within ourselves."

The next day, May 30, with no one around having time to write for him, Orson penned another letter to President Young and told his concerns about a conference planned for the next week in Spanish Fork with the President, Indians, and the Indian agent, Colonel Irish. "I can but express my unqualified opinion of the consumate hypocracy, deception, and villany of Sanpitch and Joe," Orson wrote. "Jake is an open Enemy, likewise Black Hawk. They are reckless desperadoes.

"I shall be at that conference if I can," Orson continued, "but for fear I may not be able to, I write you this note. I feel a great reluctance in taking the responsibility of conducting these difficulties with the Indians knowing that censure [from Brigham Young] is swift on the track of error. But as yet, none have fallen by acting upon my counsel. Yet circumstances are such that it has seemed to me necessary to adopt some measures a little stronger than those heretofore acted upon by us. I could wish that we had the [telegraph] wires in running order, so that I could ask you in relation to every movement. I have rec'd no word from you since the 16th of April last. It is not safe to go for a load of wood, to mill, or for a cow, ox or horse. To be penned up this way, has forced us into measures a little beyond the limits of your policy. It is trying. We have minute men out in various directions. . . .

"I am aware," Orson admitted, "if we take any Indian prisoners, the settlement where they may be imprisoned must be well guarded. With sincere prayer to God day and night, I am acting upon my best judgment, wisdom and skill, and trust in God that he will overrule my acts and movements for the best good. But to take the responsibility of the lives of my brethren, makes me tremble. But I do not feel that way towards the Indians. We have fed and treated them kindly, in the main, all the day long for the last five years."

Orson signed his name, and later added a postscript: "The boys have all returned this evening safely, having chased about 15 Indians high up into the mountains east of Springtown. . . .

"It is possible that Joe may not be so bad as I have considered him. But he has rec'd in his camp runners from the Enemy. He has not been seen about here for several weeks. I do not believe there is an innocent Indian in these regions. If there are any, they have gone away."[7]

After Orson had written his May 30 letter he received one from Brigham Young written May 13 (mails were notoriously slow getting to Sanpete). The President admonished watching "Sanpitch and the other Indians . . . so that they may not have it in their power to take any advantage of our brethren when they are not suspicious of danger. . . . When they see Indians prowling about, and they have reason to think that they are after nogood, they should endeavor to get hold of their leaders and keep them in custody." President Young asked Orson to appoint "bro. Warren S. Snow [of Manti] to take charge of the men who shall be on duty for this purpose and to manage this business."

Brigham Young received Orson's express letters of May 29 and 30, about the additional murders, and answered May 31. Orson was not surprised to read of the President's "feelings of great regret" at the news. Nor was Orson surprised at the President's astonishment at men lacking caution and "running foolish risks." Again he recommended constant and vigilant guarding.

"I expect to start on Monday next to the Indian Farm on Spanish Fork," Brigham Young added, "in company with the Superintendent of Indian affairs, Col. Irish, to have an interview with the Chiefs of the various bands in relation to the disposal of their lands to the United States. Government is desirous of affecting a treaty with them for the extinguishment of their title to their lands in this Territory. They have requested Col. Irish to solicit my aid in this matter."

The President also told Orson that arrangements had been made for Church meetings in "Payson on Saturday and Sunday, June 10th and 11th."[8]

Circumstances kept Orson from the Spanish Fork conference, but he attended the Payson meetings. He learned that the Indian conference had proceeded without serious problems. The Indians received many presents, and several chiefs agreed to leave the Sanpete area and move northeast to the Uinta Basin. Here, according to promises, the United States government would provide generously for them. The main leader of the attending Indians was Chief Tabby, a brother of Wakara and Sanpitch. Black Hawk ignored the conference.

Discussing matters again with President Young and the other brethren in the group strengthened Orson. He would continue his public exhortations, emphasizing that "to be always prepared for danger is the most certain way of always avoiding it."[9]

A month later, Tuesday, July 11, Brigham Young and company received a warm welcome from Orson Hyde and the other settlers in Sanpete. For a week the visitors traveled around, investigating the Indian situation, holding meetings, and encouraging the people. Music provided by local bands and "choirs of sweet singers" added pleasantness in each place. This rejoicing contrasted with the underlying apprehensions. President Young and the others promoted constant vigilance. The fourth day, Friday, news arrived that punctuated these admonitions. Indians had killed two men in areas near Sanpete.

Saturday began two days of meetings in a bowery in Manti. In the first session, excitement ensued with the discovery that many in the congregation carried loaded guns (a part of their vigilance). In a brief interlude, men carried out the guns and stashed them with an appointed guard. The meeting continued. Brigham Young announced that the newly-chosen commander of the Sanpete military district, Col. Warren L. Snow, should take fifty well-armed men to find and punish the Indians who had recently offended.

The next day, Sunday, July 16, in the Manti meetings, President Young strongly exhorted the people to maintain strict military strength and discipline, to act forcibly against problem Indians. The President also talked of the blessings resultant from righteous living. The farmers had stopped work in their fields to come to the meeting to hear counsel. A copious rain fell during the proceedings, inspiring one man to comment that because of their obedience "the Lord watered [our] broad acres abundantly from the heavens." As a result of the observations of the visiting Church leaders, Elder Orson Hyde received commendation for his "efficient presidency."

Peace, however, eluded attainment. July 18, two days after the departure of Brigham Young and his company, a mountain valley encounter between the Sanpete troops and Indians tragically left more than a dozen innocent Indians dead and one soldier wounded. The next week, in obvious retaliation, Indians attacked a village on the Sevier, killing two horses and wounding a settler.[10]

In spite of broad-scale apprehensions, many aspects of daily living continued in their customary cycle. June 1, the members of the Hyde family had welcomed the birth of Ann Eliza's fourth child, Maria Louisa, a daughter after three sons. August 12, Lizzy gave birth to her first child, also a daughter, Luella Minerva.[11] This would be nice to have daughters the same age.

Orson was also courting another addition to the family. He had been impressed by an attractive young woman in Fort Ephraim, cheerful Sophia Margaret Lyon, from Denmark.[12] Eventually Sophia agreed to become Orson's bride in October. They would travel to Salt Lake City at conference period for the ceremony.

In the meantime, Indians kept the forefront of news. Another battle, September 21, after militiamen had pursued Indians to a mountain valley, left a few Indians dead, and three Sanpete men wounded—including their commander, Warren Snow. This prompted a change of course in October. A directive arrived from Brigham Young,

"I[n] view of settling the Indian difficulties . . . which have resulted in the shedding of the blood of the Saints," Brigham Young stated, "we have deemed it wise and expedient to adopt another line of policy. . . . [I]f we continue to fight them . . . the probabilities are that many valuable lives may be lost in war operations.

"The plan we now propose to adopt," President Young's counsel continued, "is to stop fighting altogether, and as soon as possible establish communication with the disaffected Indians and endeavor to make peace with them by means of presents. For this purpose we shall soon send down a quantity of goods. Brother Dimick B. Huntington is going over immediately to Camp Floyd to find Sanpitch, and he will send directly to the Indians with whom we wish to treat, and inform them of our wishes. . . .

"We have learned," the letter went on, "that the brethren of Sanpete and up the Sevier are much exasperated against the Indians because of their mean and cruel actions; and feel like slaughtering them indiscriminately; but such a course would be most injudicious and cruel, and will never do. . . ."

The President expressed concern for the wounded brethren and requested "continued vigilance." He closed with "love and praying the Lord to bless and preserve you. . . . Your Brother Brigham Young."[13]

Orson, knowing that he had "warned and forewarned every settlement time and again to keep their horses up, to be armed and equipped with every necessary means of defense," felt that a brief absence by him would probably have no effect on the consternations of Sanpete. He, therefore, carried out his plan to travel to Salt Lake City, arriving October 5. A respite from Indian concerns would be good.

In the City Orson indeed received rejuvenation by mingling with friends and participating in general conference. Then, in the sacred atmosphere of the Endowment House, October 10, radiant Sophia became his bride.[14] The rest of this day was occupied by an exhilarating Zion's Camp reunion—dinner, speeches, and dancing.[15] October 16, Orson and party arrived home.

Orson visited Fort Ephraim the next day, October 17, and any of his residual joviality of the former week suddenly changed to horror. Chaos dominated Ephraim. Just before Orson arrived, he was told, about thirty or forty Indians, led by Black Hawk in person, made a sudden dash upon the settlement, coming almost directly into town. Howling marauders rushed into a field where a man, his wife, and a young girl were digging potatoes. All three met ruthless death. Swiftly the Indians drove off about one hundred cattle and horses, and at the mill they murdered another man. In the canyon, while speeding livestock ahead of them, the hostiles killed two more men. Where were Ephraim's watchmen? Where were the ready arms and ammunition and the saddled horses that President Young and Elder Hyde had repeatedly admonished prepared in every Sanpete community?

Terror brought obedience. The devastated citizens of Ephraim immediately changed their ways. In large armed parties men traveled to get wood. Sizable groups worked in the fields. A company of cavalry guarded grazing horses and cattle. Conscientiously men manned the lookout tower in town, to give warning of attacks.[16]

While Orson had been in Salt Lake City in October, Chief Sanpitch sent a request to Black Hawk to bring his band to Manti and agree to a treaty with government officers. Black Hawk declined. He replied, according to the Indian news carrier who delivered the message, "that he would fight until overcome or death ensued." The attack on Fort Ephraim apparently confirmed this. But the many variations in Black Hawk's actions seemed terribly inconsistent to whites. He and other Indians, scores of them, still appeared at Sanpete homes of white friends and ate offered meals, nothing being said about hostilities. In another vein, Black Hawk appeared to be reveling in his successes against whites. Increasing numbers of warriors flocked to his cause, apparently interested in gaining horses, cattle, and other goods for themselves.[17]

Orson received an express message that in Circleville, the extreme southern Sevier settlement, November 6, Indians killed three men. Orson decided he should visit the Sevier area and try to lift spirits and increase diligence. He left home November 11 and returned November 19. "I visited and preached to every . . . settlement," he narrates, ". . . traveled two hundred and fifty miles and preached eleven times. . . . [I] slept only about ten hours during the entire trip. . . . We traveled most of the day, preached a part of the night, talked and counseled most of the balance of the night [in each community]. . . . [I met] hearty welcome [from] the Saints."

He afterward reported to Brigham Young the greatest problem he found: "In consequence of our Indian troubles a number of families [had] left Circleville and returned to Ephraim, Mt. Pleasant, and Moroni. Their chief reasons were that the place was too weak to successfully repel Indian attacks, leaving the settlement still weaker. By way of comfort to those who wished to remain, and to check any further disposition to leave, I told them I should send back those that had left them or cut them [the departees] off from the church — that they were safer in Circleville than they would be in any other part of this region provided they would stand to their post."[18]

Meanwhile, in the Hyde home, the log dwelling crowded, everyone worked at adjusting. The household now consisted of Orson; five wives: Mary Ann, Ann Eliza, Julia, Lizzy, and Sophia; and six children: Ann Eliza's Charles (age seven), George (five), Joseph (three), and Maria (new); Julia's

Mary Ann (two); and Lizzy's Luella (new). Orson's wives provided an international atmosphere: Mary Ann from England, Ann Eliza born in Illinois, Julia a native of Denmark, Lizzy from Switzerland, and Sophia also from Denmark. Ann Eliza's son Joseph later told that his father would have had a Welsh wife too, but she declined.[19]

At convenient times Sophia, as had the other wives before her, told her background. In her native Copenhagen, Denmark (where she was born February 6, 1847), her mother had been baptized a Latter-day Saint when Sophia was small. After Sophia's baptism, at age ten, the children in her school taunted and teased her because of her "strange" religion. To save her sensitive daughter this misery, Sophia's mother hired a tutor, Mrs. Veneholm. Eventually Sophia hired out to care for the children of others. When almost fourteen, she gained employment to live in a home and care for a baby.

The following spring a phenomenal experience changed her life. She heard a voice, from seemingly the air, and the voice pronounced, "You can go to Zion." Traveling to Zion was a family dream, but lack of funds prevented it. Sophia heard the voice state the same words three times and immediately asked her employer permission to visit home. The woman granted two hours. Sophia never returned.

Her mother became as startled as Sophia when told what had happened, but she acted in faith, and, though ill, accompanied Sophia to the harbor and found Latter-day Saints about to leave. A stranger overheard them making inquiries and paid Sophia's passage in gold. When Sophia told her story to Orson, he remembered warmly that gold miraculously came to him from a stranger when he needed passage assistance on his way to Jerusalem. After boarding ship, Sophia surprisingly found her former tutor, Mrs. Veneholm, who watched out for her during their journey. Sophia's parents and sister traveled to Utah the next year, and the family settled in Ephraim.[20]

Sanpete seemed peaceful when Orson left in mid December 1865 for his stay in Salt Lake City to attend the Legislative Assembly, and the following weeks became a respite of varied activities. The Hyde home across the street from the Temple Block had naturally become more Marinda's than Orson's during these last few years of much separation, but Orson savored catching up on news and reacquainting himself with his "city" family.

January 8, honored to be asked, Orson offered the dedicatory prayer for Salt Lake City's beautiful new red sandstone City Hall. His words overflowed with thankfulness for the bounteous blessings of the Saints, and he prayed for aid from heaven for the preservation of the building. He also prayed for the guidance of the Holy Spirit in all the deliberations that would take place there.

Funds in the Territorial Treasury had increased over the years, a blessing to Orson January 19: "[Appropriated] To Orson Hyde, for moneys expended in running the boundary line between Utah and California, in 1855, and to compensate him for three months services in running said line, five hundred dollars."[21]

In Sanpete during early 1866 Indians caused no major outbursts, though Indians killed settlers in southern Utah. During winter months Sanpete's Indians remained beyond snow-barricaded canyons feasting upon cattle raised by whites. When weather warmed, however, General Snow arrested nine Indians in Nephi and jailed them in Manti in mid March. These included two chiefs, one of them Sanpitch. Orson attended April conference in Salt Lake City.[22]

After returning to Springtown, Orson received the news that Black Hawk and his warriors, April 13, had killed herdsmen and stolen cattle between Glenwood and Salina. This deepened Orson's already anxious concerns about conditions in the small Sevier River settlements. He had heard that the settlers had been so busy raising shelter and food that they only haphazardly obeyed caution instructions. Orson sent advice for the Salina and Glenwood settlers to move their families to Richfield, a larger town, "until the arrangements now in operation for their protection are more fully developed." They obeyed this counsel, women and children moving, men staying to finish the Glenwood fort.[23]

Observation revealed that Black Hawk's raiders were gaining admirable fit-outs as the spoils of their expeditions, or as trades from spoils of their expeditions. Black Hawk himself—in addition to feathers, colorful paint and ornaments on body, weapons, and horse—now sported silver rosettes on his horse's bridle, fancy spurs, and straps of sleigh bells.[24]

Apprehensive events increased. April 14 the jailed Indians in Manti managed to get free. The guard killed three, and others escaped to the mountains west. A posse pursued and brought the escapees down. The dead included Chief Sanpitch, killed April 18. April 22, Indians attacked Fairview, north of Springtown, killing one guard and wounding another.

Developments indicated that several Indian tribes, both north and south of Sanpete, had begun "uniting for the purpose of using us up," Orson wrote to George A. Smith on April 26. ". . . we are threatened with extermination. I feel anxious in this case but I cannot say that I have any fears, for I have determined to do the best I can and leave the event with an overruling Providence. Many are fearful and some are leaving. . . . [M]y only fears are that I may not give proper counsel, not being a military man."[25]

The regular spring assignment of outfitting men to travel east for immigrants seemed especially difficult this year. But enough volunteered. When the Springtown "boys" departed, Orson prophesied that the immigrants would have the cholera and that many would die, and he added, "If you boys will go and do right, not one will have the cholera." Months later, when the men returned home, they related that, indeed, the immigrants died by the dozens, and, though the teamsters "were with them day and night, waiting on them, not one boy took this disease." Samuel Allred, one of the teamsters confirmed, "Elder Hyde could not have explained this clearer if he had of been present."[26]

May 1 an Epistle arrived from Brigham Young with instructions that paralleled and augmented what Orson had been preaching. Small settlements should be abandoned. Every settlement should have at least 150 efficient men. Any activities outside forts should be done in groups, with armed guards. "When settlements are abandoned," President Young detailed, "measures should be taken to bury the house-logs and fence poles, to prevent their destruction by Indians." In the year since hostilities erupted, the President reminded, many people had failed to obey counsel in these matters. He also reminded that Indians are human beings. Nevertheless he was sending a command of fifty men from the city to strengthen defenses and thus discourage attacks. Orson traveled around to settlements and read the proclamation to the people.

Various developments kept things lively. In the few days before Brigham Young's letter arrived, Indians killed settlers in Marysvale to the south and Fairview to the north. After the letter, Orson's family and the other residents of Springtown, having less men than President Young specified, sadly began to abandon their homes and move eleven miles south to Fort Ephraim.

May 6, 1866, the fifty promised Salt Lake County troops arrived in Manti, also fifty more from Utah County. General Daniel H. Wells and other Territorial Military men directed them. May 8 the commanding officers visited Orson Hyde. May 20 Orson, temporarily living in Ephraim, replied to a letter from George A. Smith:

> I am glad to hear you prophesy in the name of the prophets of old, that peace shall be restored to our district. Our families are all removed from Springtown with the great bulk of our effects, stock, &c., & all housed in Ephraim, but to bury our poles, posts, and houselogs will require as much time as it will to bury the slain at the battle at Armageddon; to wit 6 months [7 months, Ezekiel 39:12], but we shall do the best we can, & we are going to work to fortify this town, considering that the life is of more value than posts or poles for the present.
>
> To increase the guards around the stock, horses, sheep & cattle, travel to & fro to water our grain, to build forts and fortifications, is more than any but Saints can endure; yet all are cheerful & hardly a murmuring word expressed; we feel to do all that is in our power to carry out the instructions contained in the Epistle [from Brigham Young] and trust in the Mercy of God for the balance. For the last 2 weeks Genl. Snow has been absent up the Sevier River, no fresh outbreaks of Indians here, & I am sorry to learn that there are any in Utah County. . . .[27]

All things considered, the Indians had reason to be upset. The United States government had failed to meet the agreements of supplies and advantages for the natives made by the Indian Agent in the treaty of the previous year, causing severe hunger. The rash acts and lack of respect by some of the whites fostered distrust, the indiscretion of a few causing the suffering of many. Brigham Young attempted to keep peace, and would undoubtedly have succeeded if the settlers had followed his counsel. May 18 he sent another letter to various Indian chiefs, trying to reconcile differences.[28]

Additional to the consuming Indian concerns, other items received Orson's attention. May 20–the Hyde family being newly settled in cramped quarters with many others in the rock school house in Fort Ephraim–Julia gave birth to her second baby, a boy. She and Orson named him William Arthur.[29] May 26 Orson received a letter from Brigham Young requesting "about Twenty Barrels of good Tar" from the Sanpete tar pits to cover the cloth on the roof of the new Tabernacle in Salt Lake City. Orson answered the next day, May 27. "It will afford us much pleasure to furnish the Tar which you require," he said, "if circumstances will at all permit. Our men are mostly employed in guarding herds and towns at present. We have very high water to contend with. In short there can be little or no freighting done at present hence to the city. Our mountain streams are rampant and a perfect sea of water between this place and Moroni. We could now give employment to one hundred additional laborers in this town to quarry and haul rock to fortify ourselves against our enemies. There seems to be so much to do, that we hardly know what to do first. One half of our Springtown men are at that place taking care of the crops one week, and half the next while the half that remain here are providing for their families guarding stock &c." In Springtown the men slept on the floor of the new adobe meetinghouse, in the center of their rock fort.[30]

Peace proved shortlived. June 10 an Indian raid on the upper Sevier left a man and a boy dead, with cattle and horses taken. Fortunately, the next day militia troops happened to be in the right place at the right time to intercept the livestock-driving Indians. This was at Gravelly Ford on the Sevier River, and a fierce battle ensued. Defeat almost came to the whites, but they shot many Indians before their ammunition ran out. They began a retreat at about the same time as troops appeared in the distance. Faster retreated the Indians. One of the wounded Indians, though the whites were unaware at the time, was Black Hawk.

Another of the wounded Indians was a daring, fine-looking chief who had become prominent in the raids. The exploits of his band rivaled Black Hawk's for ferocity. The Sanpete settlers knew not his name, as he had grown up elsewhere. Because he rode a magnificent white horse at the Gravelly Ford battle, he became known as the White Horse Chief.[31]

Unfortunately, hostilities continued. A young white, in retaliation for the June 10 murder of his father, on June 23 killed a friendly Indian. Indians killed a man in Thistle Valley June 24, and June 26 another settler lost his life in a battle at Spanish Fork. The first of July found refugees from the fartherest south Sevier settlement, Circleville, being added to the "guests" in Fort Ephraim. Fort-building activities increased at Fairview, Mount Pleasant, and Fountain Green.[32]

Then a new challenge arose: supplying beef for the troops defending Sanpete. Each settlement had been asked for a share of cattle, and several Ephraim men refused to comply. Orson, appalled, preached. "I told the people," he reports, "that God knew we had the beef, and I knew it, and they knew it, and that General Wells knew it, and that by such withholding they would cause General Wells to bid them good-bye and go home with his men and leave us and our stock at the mercy of Captain Black Hawk and that I could not blame him for so doing." It seemed to Orson "that they would rather our enemies would eat their beef than our friends who fight for us; and I told them so, and if they did not look out they would have the priviledge of seeing it. . . . I further told the people that our expeditions against our enemies must not fail for want of beef or for any thing else that we could supply, that it was a matter of life and death with us." Orson's concern for their covetousness grew more intense when his preaching had little effect. Some generously offered their cattle, but others continued to balk.

Finally Orson instructed the army commissary to go directly to the Ephraim common herd and get what he needed, recording an accurate description of the animals chosen. Then, when herders drove the selected animals into town, some owners refused to give theirs up. Orson instructed a second selection. "This operation," Orson narrates, "caused one man to come down, of some influence, . . . and said he had come to examine the cattle and see if any of his were in the number, and if so, he was going to take them out, and that he would shoot any man that attempted to prevent him—that such proceedings were high robbery." These actions intensified Orson's concern for these people who called themselves Saints, realizing that "their strong attachment to their stock" and their land, their worldly things, were "the curse of Sanpete."

Three weeks later, Orson's preaching to the Ephraim settlers became realized as prophetic. In a night raid, July 27, Indians drove away 150 head of stock from the Manti-Ephraim common herd. Troops pursued, but failed to recover.[33]

A few days previous, July 24, the Springtown families had returned to their homes. Displaced Sevier settlers came to Springtown too, to strengthen forces. All stayed nights in the cabins they had built close together around a central city block. Inside the large square of cabins the children played and men answered musters. Portholes bored and hacked in the backs of the cabins provided safe spots from which to shoot at any attacking Indians. Being close, again, to their crops and herds (though carrying rifles while tending) made life easier.

Summer and fall passed with no more Indian depredations. Apparently the Manti-Ephraim cattle had satisfied the natives' winter food preparation needs in their mountain retreats. However, the Sanpete settlers continued guarding. Rains helped provide a bounteous wheat, oats, and hay harvest. Orson attended October general conference. Eventually mountain snows, preventing Indian travel, gave Springtown settlers an increased sense of security, and they moved from the fort back to their own lots.[34]

Orson's main occupation the remainder of October, and continuing in November and December, he tells, was the "establishment of our Telegraph line—the getting of poles from the Kanyon and setting the same." Also, even with "not . . . very good" health, he made his regular preaching rounds of the county. In addition he "lectured long and loud upon the subject of Schools, education and the paying up of arrearages for newspapers and of continuing their subscription list &c &c."

Important family events transpired too. Lizzy's second child, her first son, was born December 7, 1866 and named Orson. Orson and Marinda's daughter Delia married Nathan Ellis, a Jewish merchant in Salt Lake City. Sons Frank and Alonzo received mission calls to England. This winter Frank would serve as a message carrier in the Legislative Council.[35]

Orson's health improved such that he traveled to Salt Lake City before the December 10 organization meeting of the Legislature. Big news to end the year came from Manti: on December 28 the telegraph line opened to that settlement.[36]

Legislative sessions past, Orson arrived back in Sanpete, February 6, 1867. Soon he received a request from the people on the upper Sevier, "with anxious eye and prayerful hearts," that he visit them. They wanted to maintain their communities, but feared an Indian-forced abandonment later in the year. Should they move and plant crops elsewhere?

Orson made travel plans and arrangements, by letters and by verbal messages sent with men going south up the Sevier. He also sought guidance from Brigham Young, by letter, February 12. In the meantime, Orson energetically encouraged the people of Ephraim and Springtown to build walls around their towns. This met with good response. In Springtown, work was to begin February 11, but storms caused delays.[37]

February 21, the weather good, Orson set out with his light wagon, his fine team, and instructions from Brigham Young. February 24, he and Bishop Kearns left Gunnison. Twelve armed men escorted them to Glenwood, Alma, and Richfield. The group even attended a dance in Richfield. At crowded meetings in each Sevier settlement Orson or another man read President Young's instructions and left a copy. The President had sent explicit words about completing forts, traveling in groups, keeping constant sentinels, having men always ready for defense, and guarding cattle. "If they faithfully comply with these requirements," Brigham Young added, "they can stay; but if the Settlements are going to be weakened, it would be wisdom for them to evacuate, for they are none too strong now." From Richfield, with a new escort of six men, Orson's group crossed the mountain pass and proceeded to Scipio, then on to Fillmore.

Orson arrived home after two weeks. Upon halting his wagon in the yard, family members soon greeted him. Someone noticed a replaced horse in his team. Orson told a heartwarming story. His original horse had performed fine at first, but became sick and died. Donations from generous Saints and the kindness of Brother James Ivie of Scipio, on the return trip, provided him a new one.

Orson felt enthusiasm about the attitudes he had encountered on this trip. The Saints had been "so eager to hear preaching" that they "turned out enmasse—hardly a man or woman left at home." Also, Orson noted, "every settlement seemed to have a most excellent choir, and they sang as though they meant it, indicating great improvement in the science of music."

Orson reported to the newspaper, March 7:

> I hear many rumors about Indian depredation to be committed upon us this spring,—that when the snow is gone the Indians are all going to get mad, east, west and south. . . .
>
> Last year we kept from three to five hundred men constantly on duty to operate against the Indians at our own expense and charges; this was a heavy tax upon our settlements, yet we have borne it and murmured not, besides the year before we had some two hundred on similar duty most of the season. In all we have killed about one hundred of them and they about sixty of us. . . . We intend to do our best to defend ourselves and protect our property, leaving the issue with an over ruling Providence.[38]

Orson composed another letter to the *Deseret News*, March 12, as an advertisement for "competent Teachers" to serve in Sanpete. "We would like young or middle aged men of good character," he stated, "not particular whether they are Jews or Gentiles, if they are morally upright men whose orthography and pronunciation are correct—who can pass an examination in reading, writing, geography, arithmetic and grammar. Qualifications in other branches would not be the least objectionable, but a good practical knowledge of the foregoing branches will be strictly necessary. . . . A few competent female teachers could also find situations here."[39]

In March, Orson pleasingly observed that Sanpete settlers, generally, prepared diligently for the upcoming season, but Indians struck sooner than expected. March 19 they attacked Glenwood, killing one man and driving off stock. March 21, between Glenwood and Richfield, they killed a man, his wife, and an accompanying friend's daughter.[40] Orson cringed to learn that, contrary to counsel, these three people had been traveling with no armed escort. Why, why, why did some people refuse to listen and obey?

March 24, Orson conducted a rewarding council in Ephraim of the Sanpete Bishops, Presidents, and principal military officers (except General Snow, who was ill). The group decided to call into active service upwards of one hundred men for defense and protection, allotted variously to the communities. They should have the best horses and each man be armed with breech-loading guns and two revolvers. Also, each town was assigned to take care of itself, and yet a confederation was effected by means of signals wherever practicable. The armed force of each place should go daily with the stock, then bring them up nights and corral them under a good guard. Other men should be ready to defend their own settlement and to co-operate with the regular soldiers if needed.

The next morning Orson attended the meeting in Ephraim where the proposal was presented. At the request for fifteen volunteers, around forty fine hardy young men stepped forward. Orson expected the same success in all the settlements, making readiness a fact.

The same day, March 25, before he left Ephraim for home, Orson sent a short note to Brigham Young asking "the privilege of using the tithing Oats in Sanpete Co. for Supply of the horses & mules of the standing army in said County."[41]

March 27, an express rider from the nearest telegraph station brought a message from Brigham Young to Orson Hyde: "If you think it wisdom to stay on account of Indian difficulties [instead of coming to general conference in April], it will be well to stay. . . ." The telegraph had been a boon since it began operating in Sanpete a few months before.

Orson immediately dictated a letter in reply. He told about the strengthening of Sanpete's military force and then commented about things personal. "My labors, since the Legislature," he told, " have been unceasing by day and by night. I have become billious and for the last four weeks have had little or no appetite and for the last two weeks it has snowed about every night and frozen very hard, and it has likewise snowed almost every day and thawed. Very high water is inevitable. The roads are so bad that it took me three long hours to come from Ephraim yesterday with as good a team as there is in the county and only two [people] in the vehicle. I have made every calculation to go to conference and it would please me very much to attend; but considering my rather poor health, I do not feel that I can endure the journey with the present state of the roads. . . .

". . . I find," he added, "that I have arrived at an age where constant labor and toil affect me more than they once did when younger. It is now apparently in the very dead of winter, and I don't know that I can keep my stock alive. I am pretty sure I cannot if the weather does not break soon. Yet it is all right. The hand of God is in it all." Orson ended his letter with a prayer that "the choice blessings of Heaven rest upon you and upon all Israel and especially upon beleagured Sanpete."[42]

Five days later, April 1, Orson received an urgent telegram from Brigham Young: "Richfield, Alma and Glenwood move to Gunnison or elsewhere as people choose. Pace will be sent with men. Will give you particulars by letter." Orson definitely would not be going to conference. Sanpete needed him.

The "particulars by letter" came, and they portrayed grave concern. The Church Presidency had "learned of the designs and probable power of Black Hawk and his band . . . the least of them sufficiently hostile," and gave instructions. All "settlements on the Sevier above Gunnison" should be evacuated. "Your settlements through Sanpete should take hold and help move them and take care of their property, houses and fences.

"To prevent the Indians from burning or destroying property the brethren can scatter their house logs and fences and cover them with dirt and they can take with them their doors, window frames &c of adobe houses. . . .

"We wish you to go to Gunnison," the directions to Orson continued, "and see that as many of the brethren who are willing to stop at Gunnison are provided with land as it is desirable to strengthen that point, and they must build a good fort there, and live within it. . . .

"If necessity arise, to prevent suffering of any from hunger they must be helped from the tithing. But we wish the tithing Oats and Barley especially reserved for the horses of the command to be sent with Gen. Pace; those of Sanpete must keep their own animals."

General Pace would "take military charge the present season, and will also have a company of fifty men from other locations to act in concert with the forces of Sanpete. . . . General Snow will be relieved from the command for the present . . . owing to his ill health. . . .

"We regret very much," the letter went on, "that the brethren have to be broken up as it keeps them poor, and it is brother Brigham's feelings to wish he could be there and share with the brethren in their greatest difficulties as formerly; and we feel to bless them and counsel them to . . . not give up the ship: bye and by they shall be blessed in return for all the sufferings and all the difficulties which they now are called upon to pass through. . . .

"Be fervent in Spirit & faithful in duty, and seek for the Spirit of Revelation that ye be not destroyed or injured by your enemies. . . ."[43]

In spite of his poor health Orson began carrying out instructions. He traveled to Gunnison[44] to induce the cooperation asked by the Presidency, and he discussed with others how to best bring families from the upper Sevier. He arrived home the evening of April 8, and afterward, late, received a telegram delivered to him from Manti, sent by Brigham Young: "Do not wait for Pace. Detail strong guard to accompany teams to help people down."

Orson consulted with his neighbor in Springtown, R. N. Allred, Colonel of the Sanpete First Regiment. They worked out "General order No. 1" and an efficient plan to distribute it to the settlements early the next morning. Their "order," dated April 9, began with a call for sixty horse and mule teams and the numbers of these that should come from each Sanpete community. Other details included:

> Also an equal number of mounted guard from each settlement, with provisions and forage for six days; and on no account will the animals be permitted to be turned out loose to graze by day or by night.
>
> The place of rendezvous will be the east bank of Sanpitch [River], between twelve mile creek and Gunnison: there to be in readiness to move off up the Sevier early on Friday morning April 12th. Order of travelling made known at that place. Teamsters and guard must be well armed and equip'd. General Stock drive postponed until those settlements are removed. An efficient guard should be stationed South of Manti to prevent Stock ranging in that direction. Diligence and a prompt and energetic compliance with this order are expected and required. . . .
>
> Those who can get waggon covers, take them along for hauling grain. Let the settlements have their things packed, and in readiness—— Doors and windows taken out and ready for removal. Log cabins thrown down and scattered. If Alma can move and camp at Glenwood, say, by Saturday noon, they will facilitate the operation. Richfield may have to lie over for the present; yet the Authorities of the Sevier settlements must judge of the ability of sixty teams coupled with their own strength to haul away the entire mass at once.
>
> Signed: By order of Prest. Orson Hyde.
> R. N. Allred Col. 1st Reg.

Response for teams and wagons, to help families move, far exceeded Orson's initial request for sixty. "I sent in all one hundred and seventy two teams & sixty mounted guard," Orson reported to Brigham Young April 21, "to aid in the removal of the three settlements on the Sevier; many of those teams performed a second trip, and I suppose that all will be at Gunnison by tomorrow night. The Sevier [River] is getting up so as to be difficult & somewhat hazardous crossing, but no serious accident has yet occurred, to my knowledge. There seems to be no rebellious spirit amongst the people, but [they] were sorrowful to have to leave their homes."

One settler, James B. Morrison, who was a boy at the time of the exodus, later remembered "the long string of teams coming in from the north to assist the settlers to remove, the general turmoil in getting loaded; the handling of the livestock — cattle, sheep, hogs grouped in their kind with youths and men detailed to handle them . . . the killing of the pet cats, rather than leaving them to their fate . . . [and] swimming the pigs across the swift, swollen river at Gravelly Ford. . . ."[45]

Sanpete folks found places for the about 200 families from the Sevier. Many had lost their teams and other stock and had no means to purchase replacements. "Ephraim, Springtown and Mt. Pleasant took them in," Orson praises, "gave them city lots and land in their fields, and generally free of charge, consequently this course brought the bulk of the new settlers that remained in Sanpete to the[se] three places. . . . North Bend, Moroni, and Fountain Green all had some from the Sevier; but Ephraim had the most." Ephraim's population swelled to nearly three hundred families, almost double Manti's about one hundred fifty-five. To produce enough food for the next winter, Orson counseled the people of Ephraim to clear five hundred more acres and plant it in wheat and oats.

The members of the Hyde household felt gratitude that they had not been required to move. Sophia, however, expected her first baby, and in the midst of all the uncertainties stayed with her parents in Ephraim for a while. The baby, a boy, was born in Ephraim, April 21. This baby received the name Brigham Young Hyde.[46]

April 28, Orson left for Manti and there conferred with the Territorial Militia Commander, General Daniel H. Wells. May 1, the official transfer of command of the Sanpete Military District was made from General W. S. Snow to General W. B. Pace. Nearly two weeks later Orson traveled to Nephi, pleased to mingle with Brigham Young's company returning from Southern Utah. Orson spoke in one of their Nephi meetings.

When several weeks passed without an Indian raid, the diligence of the Sanpete settlers seemed to be paying off. But quiet ended. June 1, near Fountain Green, in the north part of the valley, a man was killed and another wounded while herding stock. June 2, two men were killed at Twelve Mile Creek, in the south of the valley. June 5, Orson sent a letter to George Q. Cannon for Brigham Young.

Brigham Young answered June 11. "The news which we have heard from San Pete has been very saddening," he lamented. "We agree with you that had proper caution been used, Fountain Green need not have suffered the loss of their Stock, and circumstances might have been different in other respects. Oh, that the people would live So near to the Lord that they could have the revelations of His Spirit with them continually that they might be warned of every danger and be able to guard against Surprise! We have had experience enough and the people have been taught sufficiently to understand this; but they are careless, and nothing but bitter experience, apparently, is able to teach them the necessity of caution and vigilance. Why cannot the people understand that it is their privilege to have revelation about their Stock, and about their own lives when threatened by Indians, as well as to have revelation on any other point. . . ?"

Aside from Indian concerns, President Young wrote of a pleasant prospect: "I am intending to start for Cache and Bear Lake Valleys about the beginning of September, and would be pleased to have your company on the trip. If you can make it at all convenient to come you should be here by the first of September."

June 15, Orson thanked Brigham Young for his "kind and interesting letter of the 11ᵗʰ Inst. [that] came to hand this evening" and expressed gratitude for the President's invitation, adding, "If the Lord will I will do myself the honor to be in your train."[47]

June 30, Orson dictated a report for the *Deseret News*: ". . . We are not much troubled by Indians just at present. We are about as well organized for protection and defence as we well can be, in my judgement, yet it requires constant labor to keep the organization in working order; and if there is a day's lull or slackness on our part, the Indians seem to know it. The more diligent and faithful we are, the more danger there is of settlements in other valleys, who may not be so much on their guard, being visited by the redskins. . . .

"Our mail comes regularly twice a week;" the report continues. "'Wash' [the mailman] makes good time, Indians or no Indians. . . . Our papers are a treat to us." The newspapers came by mail. Orson was especially pleased that he could read them without glasses.

As Orson dictated he felt impressed to share with readers the enlightening epilogue to what had been a heartrending experience:

> You will recollect that early last spring a man and his wife with the daughter of a neighbor, while going from Richfield to Glenwood, were killed by Indians when near the latter place. Sometime after this sad occurrence, the mother of the young girl that was killed had a dream, or night vision, in which the girl appeared to her mother accompanied by the woman. The girl said to her mother: "Do not mourn or feel bad for me, for I would not come back to the earth if I could." The mother of the girl then asked the woman where her husband was, that was killed at the same time. She answered: "We have not seen him since our spirits left their bodies." The husband was cut off from the Church for misconduct a short time before. They said to the mother that Louis Lund was going to be sent on a mission soon, and he would take care of them. A few days after this dream Louis Lund, of Fountain Green, was shot by the Indians. . . .[48]

July 4, Orson conducted a convention in Fort Ephraim with the Sanpete bishops and other leaders. Troops from Salt Lake and Utah counties would soon leave, necessitating increased local military activities. One decision directed that every morning at sunrise a muster and roll call would be held in each settlement, all men required to attend.[49]

Toward the end of July, Orson received details from Brigham Young about the planned trip north, beginning September 2. The President also mentioned that he and others would be in Provo August 24 to dedicate a new meetinghouse.

Orson answered August 9, thanking Brigham Young for the information. Regarding the Sanpete Indian situation he told that "Indian fires are seen on the mountains around us, but we keep steadily along, herding, guarding and watching, with some praying and trusting a little in the Lord."[50]

Four days later, shattering events stunned the Hyde family and everyone else in Springtown. All spring and summer the ten specially-chosen Springtown "Minute Men," always on duty, had guarded, scouted, and in general watched over the settlers. The morning of August 13 something ran amiss. Twenty men, with teams and wagons, left to put up hay about six miles southwest of town. Unexplainably, no scouts preceded them. Instead, the minute men guarded the cowherd, coming toward the meadows behind the hay wagons. Suddenly, gunshots rang out and arrows flew. One surprised hay team driver lay dead; another had an arrow in his back (he died later); a third had been shot through the ear. Some minute men shot at Indians; others galloped to sound the alarm in town and to summon help from Mount Pleasant and by telegraph there from Fort Ephraim. Minute men and militia riders from the two places arrived and joined the Springtown men in pursuit of the Indians. The natives had a head start, driving into the mountains twenty-eight horses stolen from the herd and the hay teams. The settlers recovered a few horses and thought they killed several Indians.[51]

Vigilance increased, and daily routine returned.

The next week Orson managed to get to Provo to meet with Brigham Young and others at the dedication of the new meeting house. "At 6 o'clock this morning," Saturday, August 24, wrote the scribe of President Young's group, "the President and company were on the road traveling towards Provo [from where they had stayed in American Fork]. After a beautiful drive we reached a Provo bridge. . . . We were preceded into Provo City by a mounted escort in uniform, and by the strains of a good brass band, and a martial band. Elder Orson Hyde, from Sanpete, standing in the street hat in hand, bowed his welcome. The schools were out in their best, all seeming delighted to greet the President and his friends. . . ." During the next two days Orson spoke in two meetings and offered a prayer in one, pleased to be with Brigham Young and other friends whom he had last seen many months before. From Provo he traveled to Salt Lake City.

In the city Orson read an incredible item in the August 28 *Deseret News*, under the caption "Black Hawk." Indian Superintendent Head had come to town the week before from the

Uinta Reservation, where he had met and had a talk with the notorious Black Hawk, who came there with his family, unattended by his warriors. Black Hawk said he has 28 lodges under his sole control; and that he is assisted by 3 Elk Mountain chiefs, who have each 10 or 12 lodges with them. These Indians are scattered along the settlements, he avers, from the north of Sanpete County to the southern settlements, watching opportunities to make raids. He expressed a desire for peace; said he could control and would be answerable for his band; and believed he could get the others with him, as they all looked to him as the head chief. He would try and get them all together at some point, perhaps Uinta, to have a talk with Col. Head; but it would take some time to do this, as they are so scattered. As an earnest of his sincerity, he stated that he had made a covenant, when he commenced to fight, that he would not have his hair cut, and he had talked strong of Tabby and Kan-osh who had theirs cut like white men; but now that he was going to have peace, he wished to have it cut, and requested the Superintendent to shorten his locks for him, which was done after finding that he was anxious to have it so. The savage was saucy at the opening of their interview, but finally toned down, and talked reasonable before they got through.[52]

This was an encouraging, but almost unbelievable, development. Did peace with Indians wait over a near horizon?

When Orson had traveled from Springtown to Provo, before coming to Salt Lake City, he brought with him Ann Eliza and their twenty-one month old daughter, Maria Louisa. Maria had been ill. Mother and daughter remained with friends to visit while Orson continued on. He planned, after his trip north with Brigham Young, to bring them to Salt Lake City for general conference. But the plans changed. Before Orson left for the northward excursion he received a devastating telegram: Maria died August 31. Ann Eliza needed counsel. In August weather the body needed immediate burial. Trying to express his tender sadness in just a few words, his responsibilities requiring his stay in the City, Orson telegraphed a return reply:

> Salt Lake Aug 31
>
> Dear Ann Eliza Hyde
> I learn that I shall not hear that Sweet voice lisping Pa
> any more
>> Bury her and I will pay
>
> Orson Hyde

Maria received burial in Provo.[53] Now, regrettably, Ann Eliza and Lizzy no longer had daughters the same age to grow up together.

During the miles and days of the trip north that began September 2, his heartache relegated to private thoughts, Orson shared official duties and pleasures with his treasured friends of the Presidency, the Twelve, and the others in President Young's company. The brethren, including Orson, preached in settlements along the way, always graciously received and hosted. Their route took them along the Wasatch mountains, over mountains into Cache Valley, north in this valley, and over mountains into Bear Lake Valley. They returned south along beautiful blue Bear Lake, then over more and higher mountains for two days in snow storms to Blacksmith Fork and Huntsville, through spectacular Ogden Canyon, and back to Salt Lake City on September 17. During the entire excursion, discussions lifted spirits. In one of their meetings, however, President Young and the Twelve disappointingly replaced Amasa M. Lyman, who had apostatized. They chose as a new apostle, Joseph F. Smith.[54]

Orson enjoyed the trip, but thoughts strayed to Black Hawk. Would he truly keep his recent vows? Would other Indians, like the White Horse Chief, follow his example?

. . . *no more thine enemy.* . . . *(1867–1872)*

> *And again, verily I [the Lord] say unto you, if after thine enemy has come upon thee . . . , he repent and come unto thee praying thy forgiveness, thou shalt forgive him, and shalt hold it no more as a testimony against thine enemy.*
>
> —Doctrine and Covenants 98:39

UPON Orson's return to Salt Lake City from the Bear Lake trip that lasted from September 2 to September 17, 1867, he learned that Indians had killed another man in Sanpete. But this murder seemed an isolated incident, with no necessary role for Elder Hyde. He remained in the city for conference.

October general conference, in the nearly completed Great Tabernacle, proved to be a momentous experience. The huge structure with the incredible domed roof accommodated thousands of people and was crowded when meetings began October 6. People's faces registered wonder as they entered and as they looked at the pipes for the organ, 750 installed of the 2,000 designed. Brigham Young conducted the first meeting and offered the opening prayer. He expressed bounteous gratitude for the "steady perseverance and faithfulness" of all workers in their herculean efforts. An overpowering good feeling pervaded the massive hall. Heber C. Kimball delivered the opening address and augmented the rejoicing spirit. He projected his words intensely, that people in the mammoth room might hear. "I have seen a great many people assembled out of doors," he said, "but I have never seen so many in one house before. . . . [T]he Lord is here," his further words soared, "the God of Abraham, Isaac, and Jacob. I wish that your eyes were opened, that you could behold the angels who are here." About heavenly beings, Heber added, "When President Young, myself, Elders Hyde and Pratt, were anointed and ordained, the angels of the Lord were present, and were seen by the brethren. Joseph [Smith], John [the Beloved], and other angels are with us now. How then should we feel?"[1]

Asked to speak in the afternoon, Orson desired a continuing high spiritual tone, and, so that listeners could hear, he too spoke as loudly as possible. He began by echoing President Kimball's sentiment, saying that the size of the assemblage made him feel small. And he affirmed sacred events, giving details about "the voice of the Lord from heaven" speaking to the Twelve in 1847 in Hyde Park, Iowa, directing that "President Brigham Young be the

mouthpiece of God and the leader and guide to this people henceforth."
Orson also said that "there are those now within the sound of my voice who
were not in the house where we were, but in the adjoining houses some two
or three hundred yards distant, who can rise up in this congregation and testify that the earth shook and trembled, and that men, women, and children
ran out of doors supposing it was an earthquake." Brigham Young was truly
magnifying his sacred calling, Orson proclaimed.[2]

Several weeks after his return to Springtown, Orson and his neighbors
exulted in the finishing of their telegraph line while still pursuing their pre-
cautionary routine of guarding and scouting. Fortunately for the settlers, the
Indians feared the "magic" lines and evaded them. November 25, Orson Hyde
sent, to President Brigham Young, the first message on the line with "Best
respects to Israel's Chief."[3]

Orson's winter sojourn in the City, 1867-1868, lasted longer than in previous years, as the Legislature met through most of February. One notable
Legislative act officially changed the name of Great Salt Lake City to Salt
Lake City. Orson enjoyed participating in a new Church activity this winter—
a School of the Prophets for Church leaders and other selected brethren, patterned after the school of the same name held years ago in Kirtland, Ohio.[4]

As years had passed, Orson's Salt Lake City home became increasingly
different from his Springtown home. In Springtown small children dominated
the scene. Here in the city only one child—ten year old Zina—remained with
Marinda. Marinda's eight grandchildren in the Salt Lake City area, Laura's
and Emily's children, reciprocated the obvious affection she showed them.
They delighted in coming to Grandmother's peaceful and orderly home, eating her delicious unsalted butter on "wonderfully good" warm bread, and
consuming her scrumptious cookies. Orson enjoyed these treats too. He
wasn't usually around to eat from her strawberry patch in the spring, but he
heard about the marvelous berries. One thing the Salt Lake City and Springtown Hyde homes had in common was their celebrations when letters arrived
from Frank and Alonzo, on their missions in England. February 6, this year,
Marinda received the call as Relief Society President of the Seventeenth Ward.
She would be an expert leader for the benevolent activities of the neighborhood women.[5]

Orson arrived home in Springtown in early March and found Indian
matters quiet. He also found, because of the calm, great eagerness among
former upper Sevier settlers to return to their homes in time for spring plowing and planting. Brigham Young had approved Orson's feelings that returns
should be made with great caution. Only the men should go, and only in
armed groups of at least fifty. By March 24 one outfit had readied itself, and
Orson counseled the group to go quietly.[6]

A few days before, March 19, a telegram had arrived from Brigham
Young stating that Bishop Bryan from Nephi would soon accompany Indian

Joe to Sanpete and that a friendly gathering should be held. Joe had been gone for nearly three years, ever since he escaped from a guard in Manti by throwing his buffalo robe over the guard's head and running. Now he dare not return without a white escort. Orson, though recuperating from a severe cold, and tired, March 29, received Joe and other Indians. They had come to "meet," they said, to agree on peace. In spite of muddy roads, Orson sent messages to all the Bishops in the County that the Indian conference would be tomorrow in Mount Pleasant.

Orson conducted the volatile March 30 meeting with Indian Joe, three other Indians, the Sanpete bishops, and interpreter Bishop Bryan of Nephi. Heated words from both sides eventually evolved into friendliness, and at length the Indians promised that their immediate tribes would cease molestations. They had no control over some natives though, they said, and these might continue stealing cattle. To reward the Indians' promises, Orson and the bishops decided to give them one thousand pounds of flour, to be delivered to their camp.[7]

With this pow-wow the local Indian situation began to change costume. Some natives who once rampaged in war-paint, with blood-curdling yells, guns or tomahawks or bows and arrows in hand, became dignified natives seeking "peace," they said, in exchange for presents.

Orson attended April general conference. The new organ in the Tabernacle provided glorious music. In the immense building the speakers shouted their messages, but many people still could not hear. One of the subjects Orson touched during his sermon, April 7, was home manufacture. To illustrate his point he pleasurably told that the suit of clothes he wore had been made by his own family. They spun the thread, wove the cloth, cut out the pattern, and sewed the seams.[8]

In Salt Lake City Orson received devastating news from Sanpete. Indians attacked the men returning up the Sevier River, killing two and wounding a third. The group retreated to Gunnison, and the leader, Frederick Olsen, telegraphed Orson asking what they should do. Orson telegraphed back, telling them to pitch in at Gunnison and raise crops. Orson and Brigham Young discussed the situation, and the President had no objections to Orson's actions or to his feeling that no more settlers should try to return up the Sevier this season.

On his way home, Orson preached in settlements that any people from the Sevier should stay where they were for the present, put in crops, and do the best they could. Obviously the Mount Pleasant agreements with a few Indians had not brought lasting peace.[9]

The next couple of months contained varied activities. April 19, Orson and the Sanpete Bishoprics—in spite of the great challenge of a shortage of teams and provisions—arranged for enough outfits to help bring in the poor from the railroad terminus (a shorter trip each year, as the railroad progressed westward). May 10, at the organization of the Springtown Relief Society, Mary Ann became its first President; initially the Springtown sisters held meetings once a month. In May Orson "had a bad foot, caused by an attempt to destroy a corn on my toe," but it recovered. Also in May, grasshoppers devoured many acres of wheat, but the settlers' heroic attempts—beating them, burning them, and drowning them—maybe saved enough grain for the people. And word came that Brigham Young wanted men to bring teams and help construct the railroad, now progressing west of Fort Laramie.[10]

Monday, June 22, 1868, a telegram brought the sad news that Heber C. Kimball had passed away as the result of a stroke suffered ten days before. The funeral would be Wednesday. Because of the difficulties in trying to attend, Orson sent telegram messages, Tuesday, to the Sanpete County Bishops requesting their "congregations to meet to-morrow at 2 o'clock p.m., and offer up their prayers and condolence in behalf of the bereaved family, as a tribute of respect to the memory of the illustrious dead."

Heber had been the second apostle in seniority in the Church, and his death gave Orson this position, with the overwhelming possibility of eventual selection as President of the Church. At age sixty-five—his health declining, his handwriting shaky, his stamina decreasing—Orson tried not to think of what *might* be. Through natural means the Lord would choose the President, and whomever the Lord chose the Lord would support.

Orson's regular duties continued. He talked at the Springtown memorial service for President Kimball. He sympathized with Sanpete families who lost men in a drowning accident on the Green River on their way to bring Saints to Zion. He discoursed and danced at the Fourth of July celebrations in Fort Ephraim. He made his rounds of the settlements, held meetings, preached, and conversed about problems. And he wrote for the newspaper.[11]

After the April Indian attack on the men returning up the Sevier, no further immediate depredations came, and apprehensions about Indians slowly diminished. Then, May 30, Manti settlers grew concerned when Indian Joe's company of five or six wigwams settled into camp nearby. Two days later, June 1, Indians stole fifteen horses from Fairview. June 3, in the night, Indian Joe succeeded in returning nine of them. Joe appeared to be trying to help the settlers. In Fountain Green friendly Indians accepted provisions. The second week in June, Indians drove off more Sanpete cattle and horses. In July, lamentably, a Sanpete settler shot and wounded a native who proved to have been friendly. Soon Indians rode into Ephraim, July 11, and drove away horses and cattle.[12]

The end of July and first week of August, with visiting military officers, Orson traveled to several Sanpete settlements. He helped with inspections and musters, and implored the people to continue diligent in guarding and watching. These activities had progressively grown more difficult, with disheartened families moving away, and with many brethren absent building the railroad to earn means to buy food to replace what the grasshoppers had devoured.[13]

The Indians seemed to be mellowing. The August 11 newspaper revealed that in Coalville, many miles north of Sanpete, Indians had assured the bishop of peace, and he gave them a beef. In Fairview now, the whites felt safe because revered, peaceful old "Sow-e-et," with two or three squaws, had taken up residence. And Joe still kept his "lodges" in Sanpete. Previous to departing on an early August hunting trip he pledged the Fairview settlers safety during his absence, which materialized. In Nephi, August 18, the newspaper told, "citizens were honored with a visit from So-we-at . . . and his tribe, including all his warriors," on horseback. After negotiations with Bishop Bryan, and "a preach from [Indians] Joe and Dick," the visitors received presents and agreed to "a good peace and a long peace." The next day "they moved to Payson to pay a visit to the citizens of that place."[14]

The newspaper reported a more significant Indian conference, in Strawberry Valley, Uinta Reservation, August 19, conducted by "Col. F. H. Head, Superintendent of Indian Affairs, and Major Dimick B. Huntington, Indian interpreter." Black Hawk attended this "big talk" and had apparently been faithful to the treaty he signed last year when he asked that his hair be cut. The current dialogue was principally with "Aug-a-vor-um, Tam-a-ritz and Sow-ah-point, chiefs of the Shub-er-ech Indians," the newspaper account narrated. The report continued that after a long "'talk' with these chiefs . . . a treaty was concluded, which Major Huntington believes they will observe; but our brethren in the settlements who are exposed to their incursions will do well to . . . keep themselves ever ready . . . [for] Indian attacks."[15]

A surprise development of this peace meet was learning the identity of the fearsome "White Horse Chief." Tam-a-rits (Tam-a-ritz) was his name, and the She-ba-retch (Shub-er-ech) his tribe. The She-ba-retches ranged primarily in southeastern Utah,[16] but Black Hawk's successes apparently enticed them to try for their own Sanpete battle spoils.

Three baby boys joined the Hyde family in a five-month period during 1868, the third being Melvin Augustus, born to Ann Eliza on September 6. The earlier two were Julia's Hyrum Smith born May 23, and Lizzy's Odean Horatio born July 24. This brought the number of children in Orson's home to eleven, the eldest being Ann Eliza's ten year old Charles.

In early September, Sanpete citizens eagerly anticipated a visit by President Brigham Young and company. Each town prepared special festivities, including band music, singing, processions, displays, and feasts. September 19, Orson and several others traveled Salt Creek Canyon, spent the night in Nephi, and then accompanied President Young and the others back over the same road. Sanpete residents rejoiced in many gatherings September 21 through September 24. September 23, between meetings in Springtown and Fort Ephraim, the guests ate at Orson's home. In Fort Ephraim Brigham

Young organized a School of the Prophets for the south section of Sanpete County.

September 26, shocking news of another Indian attack rumbled through Sanpete. A raid on Fairview netted the natives eighteen horses. Two settlers lay dead. Orson wondered what more he could do to stop such behavior.[17]

Orson attended the October 1868 general conference, pleased to be part of a singular occurrence—the presence of all of the Quorum of the Twelve. The last time the entire Council had been together was more than thirty-two years before, in Kirtland, Ohio. Only three of the original group remained— Brigham Young, Orson Hyde, and Orson Pratt. At the present conference, George A. Smith received the calling to replace Heber C. Kimball in the First Presidency, and Brigham Young, Junior, became a member of the Twelve.[18]

Sanpete military units remained alert. In October a three-day "Grand" drill of the County Militia transpired at "Camp Hyde" near Ephraim. Orson and others addressed the troops their third day, October 21, praising their "discipline, arms, and equipment."

In mid October, Zion's Co-operative Mercantile Institution opened for business in Salt Lake City. Like Church leaders in other areas, Orson advised the Sanpete communities in setting up their branch "co-op" businesses.[19]

November 1, at his home, Orson received unexpected visitors, the Ute Indians "Tah-be-u-ner, Un-gitz-rib and Tah-rue-good." Handing him their "papers" from the interpreter at the Uinta reservation, which showed them "well recommended" as "men of influence," they wanted a "big talk" and to make a "big peace." By law Orson had no authority to sign an official treaty with them. The Government exercised exclusive jurisdiction over treaties, and no Government officers were around. Rather than upset his visitors, Orson decided that no harm would result from a good talk among the Indians and the local brethren, that the Government would not be jealous at this type of action. He had on hand, in the loft of his two-story log home, government supplies for Indians, and he also had some funds for their assistance. Orson summoned Springtown's interpreter, Jackson Allred, and the Sanpete bishops to a conference with the Indians November 3.

At the "big talk" the Indians declared that they wanted pay for the killing of Sanpitch and the men who were with him, and they wanted this pay in horses, beef-cattle, blankets, guns, ammunition, flour, tobacco, shirts, and other articles of clothing. Orson and the bishops thought this pretty big pay, and countered, Orson reported afterward,

> that we felt very differently towards them from what we should if we had begun the war; but the war was begun by them; they had stolen our horses and cattle, and had killed our men, women and children. They did not like to admit that they began the war; but, after a little conversation, and the introduction of testimony, they did admit it. We told them

we had nothing to give them for the killing of Sanpitch and his men; that they were in prison, and if they had remained there quietly, they would no doubt have been alive and with them to-day; but as they broke jail and attempted to escape they were shot down by the guard, they not being able to capture them without.

We told the Indians that it was the laws of the land to shoot down any prisoner that attempted to escape from prison, if he could not be captured without; that if the Mormons had been in prison and attempted to escape, they would have been shot down just as Sanpitch and his men were; hence, we told them we had nothing to give them for the killing of those prisoners; but we told them we would make them a present of something before they left; that we wanted peace, and that we always wanted it, and never wanted war. We told them that they owed us more than they could ever pay; consequently we would ask them for nothing. We told them they had taken our horses and our cattle, and we had none to give them: we had plenty of guns and ammunition and intended to keep them—that the grasshoppers had eaten up our wheat and therefore had not much flour; but we would, nevertheless, still show them favor, as they were inclined for peace. So we gave them two hundred dollars in money and divided it among them (by their own request), according to their rank and influence, sending fifty dollars of it to Tabby [at the Uinta Reservation], and ten hundred pounds of flour with other smaller presents, such as shirts, tobacco, etc.

They appeared highly satisfied, and said they were not lying to us; that no more of our men would be killed by the Indians, and after seeing our order in council and the union of sentiment among us, they lamented that they had not captains as we had. They said they would tell Tabby and all the Indians that I was a father to the Mormons and also to the Indians. Two of our brethren, Jackson Allred, our interpreter, and Reuben, his brother, accompanied them to their camp near the head of Spanish Fork [Canyon], and were there treated in the most friendly manner by all the Indians, and finally parted with them with the strongest assurances of peace and good will.[20]

November and December found Orson traveling around the county, as usual, preaching. He also attended the School of the Prophets in Ephraim, and relaxed at parties. In early December, with the weather cooperating, Orson and thirteen other brethren spent three days investigating and planning the course of a canal to drain thousands of acres west of the Sanpitch River. There hay would be raised.[21]

Orson resided in Salt Lake City for the 1868-1869 Legislature sessions. January 19 he underwent surgery. With assistance from brandy and chloroform a doctor removed the second toe from his right foot, frozen years before. Orson also received sad news of the death in Springtown, January 22, of his and Sophia's son, Brigham Young Hyde, age twenty-one months.[22]

Back in Sanpete, after the Legislature, Orson's days remained full. News came that communities to the south suffered Indian raids March 1. This gave Orson and his neighbors apprehensions. However, guarding and watching had long ago become routine, and all aspects of crop raising—grubbing, plowing, sowing, irrigating, and fencing—also continued. And Orson encouraged folks in their co-operatives. Some settlements did better than others, having more commodities to exchange. April 16, Sophia gave birth to a baby boy, a comfort after the loss of her son in January. She and Orson named the baby Oscar Waldemar.[23]

Utah's big event in May was the completion of the transcontinental railroad. The rails from the east joined the rails from the west May 10, north of the Great Salt Lake at Promontory. No longer would immigrants to Utah and other parts of the Great West need to spend months on the trail. No longer would men, teams, and wagons be called east to help them. Merchandise of all kinds could readily be shipped east or west. And trips to the east or west and back could be accomplished with ease. A great day had dawned.

Indian developments received their own newspaper space, the following in late May:

> "BLACKHAWK" IN THE CITY.—Major Dymock B. Huntington, Indian Interpreter, informs us that, on the evening of Friday last [May 21], he had a visit from the notorious Chief, "Black Hawk.". . . "Black Hawk" said he was sent by the Pi-edes, who live on Gunnison's Trail and the Spanish trail, west of Green River. They want peace, and "Black Hawk" said he would have them all,— men, women, and children in Gunnison in one moon, so that the Indian Superintendent, Col. Head, and he, Dymock, might go and have a talk with them. He says they will not want to come to Gunnison, because they have nothing but horses they have stolen from the "Mormons" to ride on; they would rather meet a distance from the settlement. . . . The Pi-edes see what presents the Shib-er-ech Indians, living north of Spanish trail and west of Green River, have got by being peaceful, and they are anxious to reap similar benefits themselves.
>
> "Black Hawk" says Tab-by-Uner has lately stolen six horses from the vicinity of Payson and taken them East to trade them off; and he thinks more vigilance is necessary in that neighborhood.

Chief Tab-by-Uner's actions were distressing. At Springtown last November he had solemnly agreed not to kill whites. On the other hand, he hadn't agreed not to steal horses.

Orson traveled to Salt Lake City in late May 1869, primarily to make arrangements to reprint his *Voice from Jerusalem*, the previously published letters about his journey to the Holy Land. Saints had shown interest in this, and Orson could find good use for the profits. Mary Ann accompanied him, as did his six year old son, Joseph. Mary Ann would remain in the Salt Lake Valley to promote the book and to handle orders.[24]

Also, Orson came to the City for a purpose not so pleasant, the extraction of his teeth. June 4, "I had all my teeth drawn and slept none that night," he tells. "Next day, left for home — rode all day and all night in the stage [Joseph with him]. Preached in Nephi Sunday Morning after attending Sabbath School and speaking to the children. In the evening preached at Fountain Green, and at ten o'clock Monday morning preached at Moroni; came home in the evening almost jaw broken and chop fallen, jaded out, sick and went to bed. There and thereabouts I remained for three or four days [his sore mouth causing strange sounds, particularly making s into th], until I thought I could thay, 'telegraph poles,' and started for Manti." In Manti he needed to say "telegraph poles," and many other words, while conducting a meeting about repairing the telegraph poles.[25]

A letter from Mary Ann, in Salt Lake City, arrived June 22. She told about her activities, and she expressed concerns regarding what else she should do and whom she should see. Orson answered immediately. Mary Ann wouldn't mind the tremble of his hand:

> Springtown June 22, 1869
>
> My Dear Mary,
>   Your welcome note of 20th Inst came to hand this evening. We were all glad to hear from you. You must take care of yourself; that is, your health. You have my cordial consent to go where you please and visit whomever you will. You must not worry about us, except you should send us a little medicine. Raise the money for the printer, then get yourself a good large family stove after your own heart. Next I want a good new wagon that will bear up 2,500[lb] fitted complete for a span of horses. Then you may talk of callicoes &c. &c. according to your own judgment and discretion. Supply your own wants after paying the printer or after having raised the means for that purpose. Lizzy has just got shoes made by Bro Davies for Orson & Luella [Lizzy's children]. When we really need any thing, I will ask you to get it.

Orson continued, telling about the family:

> Sophia's boy is well: But Lizzie's is weakly. She went to Manti to day with the mail to consult Sister Snow on his condition. I fear about our being able to raise little "Odin Horatio [Lizzie's eleven-month-old]." We will do all we can for him, and leave the issue with the Lord. All the rest of us are usually well.

Mary Ann had finished by writing across her letter. Orson commented:

Could you not afford paper to write a letter without crossing your lines at right angles? My dear girl, buy yourself some paper and a few stamped envelopes, and let us hear from you often. Every child, wife and chick wants to hear from you; and I, more.

Mary Ann had asked what she should do if Orson's former wife Martha sought to see her. "Will Martha seek an interview with you? Hardly!" Orson replied. "Poor woman! Her pride and stubborn will have proved disasterous to her, coupled with unbridled jealousy. Please send her Ten dollars and a pamphlet when printed."

Orson encouraged Mary Ann to enjoy herself:

If you feel embarrassed in the city to canvass for the Book, you can go into the country for a change whenever you wish. I give you the entire season for enjoyment, best you can, in the line of duty; not but that we all want you at home, and miss you very much: But you have been measurably secluded from society for a long time, and with me, you have experienced the excitement and horrors of a vexatious and bloody Indian war. Our society here is good. It is just such as we have made: But should "Auld acquaintance be forgot?" The old wine is said to be best, except when a man takes a new wife, you know. But after all, the faithful old wife is the anchor; the new, the sail. I thank Sister Clara Young for contributing to your comfort and enjoyment. God bless her, and all others who show you favor. Let me be what I may, I know that you are worthy, and I want you to enjoy yourself. I have my own views and feelings. They are mine, not yours: So visit where and whom you will.

Telling her of general news, Orson went on,

We have plenty, but it is a little dry living just now. Things are not just in the right shape: but I suppose every body is dry sometimes. I sold the Indian heifer for $38= Sister Morrison of Mt Pleasant sent me a note Sat. last containing $10= from the relief society for books. The people here offer me constantly their fifty cents for books, but I have not taken them, but tell them to keep their money till the books come. I cannot write, and cannot be bothered with taking names &c.

Our crops look remarkably well. Gardens tolerably well. One case of small pox at Mt Pleasant. I am invited to deliver an oration here on the 5th and to attend a party in the evening. Shall I dance with the "gals?" My toe is getting better at the very thought of a dance. I used to dance as well as I could write, but now my dancing and writing are about alike. The former, however, is rather better.

I have nothing more but nonsense now to write, so I'll stop.

My kind love to all our good friends in the city. I pray you accept the strongest assurances of devoted good will and love for your blessed self—Amen

Your affectionate Husband

Oh! All the wives and children send love by the bushel, or would if they were not fast asleep in bed. Good bye for the present. God bless you, all night.

Orson Hyde

After Orson had signed off twice, he thought of more things he wanted to say to Mary Ann. Now he understood why she had written across the lines of her letter. Because he had complained about that, he wrote in his margins:

So many Mary Ann Hydes in the city, I put my name on the envelope to distinguish

I got plenty of Ink pouches at the city. This is made from it.

Don't show this letter. It is written so badly

When your letter is read in any of the Wards, you would do well to be present, and receive your subscriptions then and there. Many persons would subscribe under such circumstances who would not spend the time to hunt you up at another place.[26]

In Mount Pleasant, June 28, 1869, an unexpected visitor, tall Black Hawk, approached Orson Hyde. Thin, obviously unwell, Black Hawk wore a wide buckskin belt around his abdomen to protect the festering bullet wound that had plagued him since the battle at Gravelly Ford in 1866. He retained his intense dignity, however, and his "straight as an arrow" stature. To Orson he announced his readiness for the peace meet he had requested of Dimick Huntington "one moon" ago. Many Indians had gathered for the occasion—thirty warriors "with their squaws and papooses numbering in all from seventy-five . . . to a hundred"—and they were impatient. Accustomed to this typical Indian behavior, and in spite of grim thoughts of "peace or war, life or death" galloping across his consciousness, Orson spoke calmly. He assured the Chief he would promptly set up a pow-wow.

Orson hurried to the Mount Pleasant telegraph office and dictated urgent words to Colonel Head, Territorial Indian Superintendent. A conference must be held as soon as possible. Orson and Black Hawk had agreed upon "Fort Ephraim as the place." Earlier, Black Hawk had suggested Gunnison for this meet, but Fort Ephraim seemed better; the Indians had special trust in Ephraim's bishop, Canute Peterson.[27]

Government officials in Salt Lake City responded speedily. Other duties occupied Colonel Head, but Dimick B. Huntington would come. During the next few days the Indians remained nervous.

Saturday, July 3, at the Bowery near the stone school house inside sturdy stone Fort Ephraim, conference members gathered. The setting provided its own reminders of warfare. The guard, stationed in the bastion of the two-and-a-half-acre fort, watched in all directions with his spy glass for suspicious signs near or far. Should the herdsmen with the stock, a few miles to the west, notice anything alarming, as a signal they would light fire to a readied pile of brush.

The conference began about noon, Orson Hyde presiding, Dimick B. Huntington interpreting. Nearby sat other brethren, including Bishops Johnson and Peterson of Ephraim. Around crowded "about a hundred Shib-er-ech and Pi-ede Indians." Heaven had already heard Elder Hyde's fervent pleadings for guidance, and with great care he chose his words. He expressed thankfulness to all, Indians and whites, for their efforts to attend the pow-wow, and he told of his hope for peace.

When beginning the proceedings, Orson's apprehensions still held sway in his mind, especially because with Black Hawk came Tam-a-rits, the dreaded White Horse Chief.[28] However, as Tam-a-rits and other chiefs talked, Orson sat almost unbelieving. Their manner had changed. Previously, defiance had been the initial behavior of the natives. Maybe Tam-a-rits truly honored his peace commitment of last year, 1868, the same as Black Hawk had honored his of 1867. The presence of these two perhaps strengthened chances of peace. "Five of the principal [Indian] men spoke . . . ," the reporter of the meeting penned, "expressing themselves very humbly and penitently over their past bad deeds, and asking what they must do to be saved. 'Black Hawk' said that for four years they had had no heart, but now they had got heart, eyes and ears, and could both see and hear. They agreed to protect the settlers, and give them warning when mischief was threatened by marauding Indians, and also agreed to bring in all Indians they could who are still marauding and bent on mischief. . . . During the conversation the Indians wanted to know who was making bad medicine and killing all the rabbits in the valley, as they are dying off in great numbers. Bro. Huntington informed them it was a disease among them." At the end of the long "big talk," Orson gave the concluding remarks, his inner feelings much more calm than at the beginning.

For ensuing festivities, the whites and guests walked to a big lawn, sat in a circle, and passed the peace pipe around. If this brought pangs to any of the brethren, none let on. Next, the Indians exulted loudly when handed presents: blankets, bright calico, tobacco, and other items. So pleased were they with their blankets of black, blue and red, they wrapped the colorful layers around themselves on this hot day. The parley adjourned.[29]

The next day, in Manti, Black Hawk, his brother Mountain, and Tam-a-rits attended church services, accompanied by interpreter Jack Allred. Black Hawk spoke to the congregation, telling that "he had buried the hatchet and meant to keep it buried. He had found his heart and it was good." He also told, speaking for those with him, that the Indians would live in peace from now on, adding that they had come to Sanpete, and especially to Manti, at the direction of President Brigham Young, to declare this peace at the place where the war began. After the meeting, Manti leaders "had a talk with [the Indians] and treated them kindly, and good feelings prevailed."

Black Hawk manifested loyalty to a previous oath when in Gunnison he visited Bishop Kearns, whom he had respected for years. He reminded the bishop that in peaceful times he had promised protection to the Kearns family. Then, in 1865, Indians killed the bishop's son, Black Hawk's good friend, in Salina Canyon. Black Hawk offered his own life to pay for the misdeed. Bishop Kearns refused the suggestion and affirmed no resentment.[30]

Black Hawk and company visited other Sanpete communities also, declaring peace and asking forgiveness. The many people who had known the chief previously were struck by his thinness and ill appearance, and as well by his sincerity.[31]

The Indians seemed in no hurry to leave Sanpete, and days passed. They *liked* the generous kindnesses of the settlers. "The Indians are excitable," Orson narrates, "and there is something up with them every day, and almost every hour in the day. They want many things, and indeed there is no end to their wants, and to preserve peace, they have got to be handled with much wisdom, skill, and care. They monopolize the time of two, or three, or us almost wholly, and though peace has been made with them, they are very restless, and uneasy, and the least breath excites them."[32]

Finally, to induce the natives to depart, Orson invited the whole visiting group to a "farewell" banquet on his premises in Springtown.[33] Orson's son Joseph, seven years old at the time, later recollected the excitement and solemnity of this

> general rendezvous where the chiefs congregated, together with their squaws, papooses, horses and wigwam or wickie-up equipment, and where great preparations had been made for the feast. No less than four steers were barbecued, with the accompanying foods to satisfy the Indians.
>
> Against a lilac tree, close to the entrance of the house, the Indians stacked their fire-arms, bows and arrows, as a token of their peaceful intentions. Well do I remember this occasion, although very youthful: all the splendid-looking Indian Chiefs, nicely dressed, with silver medals and metallic dressings, their appearance, their size and their actions. There was old Tabaunah, Jake Aropeen, Black Hawk, White Horse Chief, Old Joe, and Unganutherum and others.
>
> After the feast was over, and the talk, and the distribution [from the loft of our home] to the Indians of boxes of bar-lead, from which bullets were made, sacks of brown sugar, caddies of tobacco, bolt after bolt

of blue denims, bolts of "hickory" shirting, and other standard necessities, the mid-afternoon preparations began for the going away of the Indians. They would travel to the north and east crossing the mountains eastward, en route to the Reservation.

When the body of the Indians had taken leave, their Chiefs assembled in the big front room of the log house, and Mother [Ann Eliza] and Father stood there as farewell hosts. With Indian pride did they file in, shaking hands and bidding good-by.[34]

While the "sensational news" of the Ephraim peace meet traveled around Sanpete, a new problem arose: hordes of grasshoppers. Though they devastated some fields, mostly oats and barley, Sanpete crops were bounteous this year. Gratefully, during August, the farmers realized a good wheat harvest.[35]

Orson's 1869 summer included much in addition to Indian gatherings and grasshoppers and harvest. He enjoyed July 4 and July 24 celebrations. He attended the School of the Prophets in Ephraim and a second one in Mount Pleasant. (These continued until October 1872.[36]) He preached. And he had concerns about mining, resettling the upper Sevier, merchants, and a smallpox outbreak. Orson's health, he tells, "was never better: But I am getting clumsy. My toe now serves all right. It annoys me very much to get stiff and clumsy, but I can't help myself. This year, my knees, for the first time, falter in running up a ladder upon a high hay rick, but I believe neither heart nor tongue falters. My hand trembles, but I write this by lamp light without glasses."[37]

As summer weeks passed, Orson missed Mary Ann, still in Salt Lake City. Prompted by a disconcerting dream, he wrote to her, "My Dear Mary," August 27:

> Strange to say, but last night for the first time, I dreamed of you. I saw you in a clump of beautiful fruit trees, and you were high up in the very extremity of their branches, picking and eating grapes or berries. I looked to see what you stood upon, but could discover nothing but the frail twigs and their still frailer leaves. Presently, you rose above the trees alltogether and said, "I am going. You will never see me more except in this condition. Come quick." and you ascended out of sight. I know not that the dream means any thing, but if it does, and you go, I trust and pray that your journey will be heavenward; and if I go, I hope to take the same road. But your early departure will be interdicted if my faith can prevail. You are the anchor of my earthly hopes and comforts; for if you ever lied to me or deceived me in any thing vital or trivial, I do not know it. Consequently you have my unlimited confidence in all our relations in life.
>
> I want to live yet many years (if the Lord is willing) to fight the Devil, and do all the good I can — raise up my young family, and teach them the ways of life, and I want you to help me. . . .

Our folks are all in bed and sleeping, yet they all send their love to you and Emily [Orson and Marinda's married daughter], and I too.

Telling the local news, Orson added,

Our extensive harvest is nearly or quite all cut and in the shock but the hauling of it in for stacking is much retarded by daily showers of rain. Bro Musser was surprized beyond measure at the magnitude of our grain crops. It will not yield in threshing so bountifully as was expected in consequence of the grasshoppers; but we shall have plenty. I hope none of our friends will contract for oats & barley, relying on Sanpete for aid to fill them, for those crops are almost a total failure here. Many pieces are not cut at all, for they will not pay for harvesting.

Orson ended his letter to Mary Ann with, "Now God bless you – Good night. Your affectionate husband Orson Hyde."[38]

The next week Orson received sad telegramed news that another person he cherished, Ezra T. Benson, had passed away. Their friendship stretched back many years. Especially, Elder Benson had been a great strength to Orson in Kanesville, Iowa. September 5, as "President of the Twelve Apostles," Orson sent instructions to Quorum members: "It would be pleasing to me if the remaining apostles would wear crape on the left arm in all their public ministrations for forty days after the death of our highly esteemed friend and brother as a token of our commingled respect and sorrow for the departure of our much loved Ezra."[39]

September brought rewards to Orson. September 13, the reprint of his booklet about his Jerusalem mission came off the press. September 21, at a fruit and vegetable fair in Moroni, he received praise for the "very fine 'Excelsior' oats and 'Imperial Gage' plums" he had raised and exhibited.

About the time Orson traveled to Salt Lake City for October conference, Indians stole thirty horses from Fairview. But, the owner had left the grazing herd unattended, a great enticement to the natives. A few weeks later, news came of a raid in a southern community. In general, however, the Indians were definitely less aggressive than formerly.[40]

In December, Orson learned, Black Hawk embarked on an impressive endeavor, with permission from military authorities. In each community where he and his warriors had committed depredations, from Saint George in southern Utah, to Payson, north of Nephi, he explained his change of heart and sought good will. This venture extended the Sanpete peace-meets of July. Interpreter M. J. Shelton accompanied the chief on this "march" from Saint George more than three hundred miles to the Uinta Reservation.

From town to town, along Black Hawk's "peace path," different settlers escorted him. This showed honor to him and also provided protection in case persons might seek harmful retaliation for past deeds. In each place he told that he knew he soon would die and wished first to be "at peace with the pale faces."[41] The newspaper gave details of his stop in Parowan:

> On the 16th instant [December], we had a big visit from Black Hawk, his brother, Mountain, and quite a number of his band. Black Hawk and Mountain talked to the people in the meeting house in the evening, bro. Shelton, from Beaver, being the interpreter. Black Hawk made great declarations of friendship and said he wanted a big peace, a strong peace and a long peace. . . . He said that he wished to see the settlements on the Sevier River established again, and promised that they should not be disturbed by the Ute Indians.—Black Hawk's consumptive look [gaunt and thin] and hollow cough indicate that he cannot last long.
>
> His brother Mountain, a thoughtful and intelligent looking Indian, then addressed the meeting, and said that he had always told the Indians, when they wanted him to join their raids, that he would not go, for he had horses to ride, and when he wanted anything to eat he could kill deer and rabbits, and [he] always advised the Indians to stay at home. The Indians present testified to the truth of what he said. He told them that they had stolen hundreds of cattle and horses, and they were poorer now than ever, and they always would be poor while they continued to steal. . . . He says he does not want to shed the blood of any body, but wants all to live till God wants them to die.
>
> . . . The people had to furnish them the usual amount of beef, biscuits and flour, and they went on their way rejoicing.[42]

Orson's 1869-1870 winter proceeded. In November, thinking about how the Lord had increased the water supply to bless the Saints, he wrote an article about it. In part he said, "This land is naturally barren and worthless, except to hold the world together and run the railroad over, but God hath blessed it for our sakes." In early December, painful erysipelas (streptococcus infection) caused head swelling and fiery red bumps, which slowed Orson's pace for a short period. He recovered, attended meetings, preached, served in the Legislature (for a time as temporary president of the Senate), wrote articles, and enjoyed festive occasions. January 10 he participated in celebrating the completion of the branch railroad from Ogden to Salt Lake City.[43] February 14 he paid off William C. Staines the equity Staines had accrued in the Hyde Store lot in the City. Afterward Orson signed the property over to his son Frank, as security only. Orson would retain the rents, which amounted, after expenses, to about one thousand dollars a year.[44]

Back at home—in "Spring City," the name having been changed from Springtown during the winter—Orson's preaching and writing activities continued, and the Hyde family, March 19, 1870, welcomed another baby boy, Nathan, son of Lizzy. In Church matters, March 16, Orson had followed instructions from his superiors and organized a High Council in Manti to help supervise Sanpete. This would ease his burdens.[45]

During the early part of 1870, while Orson had sojourned in Salt Lake City, he and Marinda reached a major decision. With Orson so far away most of the time these past ten years, Marinda led an independent life. This winter she had been, unaccountably to Orson, tearful and despondent. Orson longed to assuage the turmoil obviously pulling her apart. She finally admitted that though she loved Orson and yearned to give him no hurt, her sealing to Joseph Smith for eternity had caused her to think increasingly of him and yet to feel this might be wrong. The subject of divorce at length surfaced.

Marinda, the sweetheart of Orson's young manhood, loved his wives Mary Ann and Ann Eliza, but hardly knew Julia, Lizzy, and Sophia, or his young children. With five devoted women to look after him, he received excellent care. Moreover, though pained by a sense of loss, Orson comprehended Marinda's love for the Prophet Joseph. Orson loved Joseph Smith, too, with all his heart. Discussion, sincere prayer, and consultation with Brigham Young, led to the agreement for Orson and Marinda to rescind their vows to each other.

Back in Sanpete County, Orson applied for the divorce, which was granted April 25. This decree, however, received no publicity. Orson and Marinda remained friends, but when in Salt Lake City Orson would stay with his daughters Laura or Emily. Delia and her husband had moved to California. The following October 7, for one dollar, Orson deeded the home on North Temple Street to Marinda.[46]

Spring general conference had been moved from April to May, allowing time to finish construction of a balcony gallery around the inside of the domed Tabernacle. This provided seating for many more people. And, Orson discovered May 5 at conference, the gallery improved the acoustics. People could hear speakers better than before.[47]

In Spring City, Orson felt good about the situation of his family. They had 50 acres of improved land, and the farm value was $700. The worth of farming implements and machinery was $150. Livestock, total value $1600, consisted of 2 horses, 12 milk cows, 20 other cattle, and 108 sheep. The farm produced, during the year ending June 1, 1870: 20 tons of hay, 65 bushels of spring wheat, 10 bushels of Indian Corn, 150 pounds of wool, 150 bushels of potatoes, 280 pounds of butter, and 250 pounds of cheese. Also, by 1870, Orson had provided a second home for part of his family; in it Julia and her children resided.[48]

The summer of 1870 found Indians again in Sanpete. May 18, in Manti, Orson and other local leaders met with about twenty from the south who came for a meeting. The "talk" resulted in peace agreements. A few days later trouble in the north of the Valley resolved itself. Indian–white relations remained good. Orson explained to Brigham Young, in a letter June 21, how it worked: "[The Indians] are very importunate; and it is give, give, all the time. They want to have a big talk every time they come round, and make big peace which amounts to little else than a demand for beef and flour."

In early August, surprisingly, two or three hundred Indians, with near-to-death Black Hawk, appeared in Spring City. They camped on the edge of town, having heard, they said, that Brigham Young and Dimick Huntington would meet with them here and bring presents. Orson wrote a hurried letter to President Young, August 9, giving particulars, but no "big meet" materialized. The President had planned a trip to the southern settlements, with Dimick Huntington in the group, but the agenda contained no travel in Sanpete. August 19, Black Hawk, almost a skeleton, camped near Manti with his band. The following Sunday, Orson Hyde and Black Hawk's brother, Mountain, preached peace and good will in a Manti meeting. The next weekend Orson and several Sanpete bishops rode over Salt Creek Canyon and met in Nephi with southbound Brigham Young and his company.[49]

In September, Black Hawk and his group moved their gear out of Sanpete Valley over the Salt Creek Canyon route. In the canyon the wasted chief and five of his warriors, all on horses, asked food of a settler herding sheep. The man, though apprehensive, gave them a sheep and also shared his campfire. That evening Black Hawk confided, "You need not be afraid any more. I am sick of blood. Look at me, the great chief. Brigham Young told me if I shed the Mormons' blood I would wither and die. I am going up to see the great chief, Brigham, once more and then I am going to the place where I was born, to die."

September 23, Indians indeed met Brigham Young and party, near Payson during the President's return north. Mountain and Joe, representing Black Hawk, reported that Black Hawk lay dying, encamped at Spring Lake Villa, three miles south of Payson.

Four days later the newspaper printed a telegram, from a settler at Spring Lake Villa, telling that the chief had passed away the previous night, September 26. A letter printed September 30, about the death, also mentioned that "[Joe] wants me to tell Brigham and Bro. Hyde not to let the Green river Indians have any powder, for they lie and steal, and they must be watched or they will take more horses this fall."[50]

Indian Joe's concern about natives stealing horses "this fall," proved not a problem. This was fortunate, as on September 15 the federally-appointed governor disbanded the Utah Militia. In 1870 the worst local devastation came from grasshoppers destroying crops.[51] The grasshopper invasion caused settlers to feel gratitude for last year's ample harvest to tide them over.

Hyde activities in 1871 kept their usual pace. Ann Eliza gave birth to daughter Flora Geneva January 2, 1871. The next month, sadly, the family buried Lizzy's son Nathan. He died February 22, age eleven months.[52] Orson continued to travel: to Salt Lake City, around Sanpete, and to neighboring counties. And he continued to compose articles for newspapers. July 18, 1871, Julia gave birth to another son, David Victor. [53]

July witnessed other good things in Sanpete: new meeting houses in Ephraim and Mount Pleasant, grain flourishing, and little damage from grasshoppers. Fairview settlers had met in a fine new meetinghouse for some time. Manti had a new tabernacle. Another evidence of Sanpete progress was three-times-a-week mail.[54]

The Indian situation in 1871 proved generally "peaceable and friendly." At the beginning of the year Orson had requested—in sermons, in a circular to the Sanpete bishops, and in an article to the *Deseret News*—that settlers refrain from hunting and killing the deer in the mountains. Indians had pointed out to him that the white men had farms and mines, while the hunting ground was the natives' only resource.[55] In July, in the mountains east of Spring City, local Indians stopped a band of other Indians from coming and marauding. Sanpete residents felt special gratitude for this help, because Acting-Governor George A. Black, June 30, had added more stringent military restrictions. Citizens could not legally organize to defend themselves or do anything that demonstrated military strength.[56]

In September 1871 Orson received the *Salt Lake Tribune (Weekly)* of September 16, accompanied by an envelope and stamp, but no message. Upon reading an article in this newspaper about the right of succession to the Presidency of the Church in case of the death of President Brigham Young, Orson became annoyed at how his own name had been used. The *Tribune* was anti-Mormon in sentiment. Orson ignored the implied invitation to reply. Instead he dictated a letter to George A. Smith:

> I wish here to say that no person living or dead ever heard me express the wish, desire or intention to reach after that exalted position [President of the Church], neither did I ever give place to the faintest or strongest wish or desire for that station even in my secret thoughts and meditations in case a vacancy should occur. I cannot help what the Tribune says or publishes. Right or wrong, I have my own opinion with regard to a successor of Prest. Brigham Young, and that opinion I expressed to Major Powel [John Wesley Powell] in conversation with him a few weeks since in which he raised the question as to the successorship to lead the Church. I told him that the just and pure in heart amongst the Saints had unmistakeable evidence of the calling of God of our present leader after the death of Joseph Smith. It was clearly manifest on whom the mantle of the martyred Prophet fell. And when it became necessary to appoint a successor, God would point out the man by unmistakeable evidences of his selection, and that it became no aspirant to seek for that position, [also] that I rested perfectly easy with regard to the matter and advised every body else to leave God's business in his

own hands. I suppose some have imagined I would seek for that station if I outlived President Young, but such thoughts are vain and groundless. They may exist in the minds of some, but they never existed in my mind at any period of my life.

I feel the infirmities of age creeping upon me, and if I can only magnify and honor my present position, I will therewith be content.[57]

Orson read the newspapers with sadness at how relentlessly federal officials in Salt Lake City pursued provocations against the Saints. The animosity would soon be personal.

Saturday, October 28, in his usual white shirt, Orson was working in the field near his log home when a son brought a disturbing message. The hired girl from the James A. Allred home, across the road from the Hyde dwelling, had informed that two United States Marshals were at Allred's. Stephen Allred, James' son, thought they were after Elder Hyde and, while tending the visitor's horses, asked the hired girl to give the warning. Orson's son Joseph later told that "Father immediately made his way down into the willows, and from there down into the canal creek, where the country was heavily studded with big cottonwood trees, birch, willows and thick under-brush, and there remained until nightfall, when contact was made with his friends, and in the middle of the night, by arrangements met a friend with a good span of mules and wagon on the main road, and was driven across Sanpete valley to the little town of Wales, where none but the Welsh people lived, and knowing them to be the staunchest of the staunch and fearless friends, entrusted his safety in their hands." The marshals telegraphed a message back to Salt Lake City that Elder Hyde eluded them after a chase of six miles.[58]

Orson eventually learned that the warrant for his arrest was based on the charge of murder. Back in May 1854 a man had met death on the way to Fort Supply with Orson Hyde's company. Now, as harassment, Orson was accused of ordering the demise.

"The following morning," Orson's son Joseph continues, telling about the attempted arrest, "a young fellow by the name of Nephi Reese [in Wales], led the way into a certain cave in the rocks on the mountain side, close to the town, and there with comfortable bedding and food stuffs, that were frequently replenished by his good Welsh friends, [Orson lived for varying periods during the winter. From the cave, that he called Fort Lookout, he] remained in full view of the valley and the approaching of every stranger who might enter into the town of Wales or thereabouts, having for his use . . . [his] spy glass . . . , and by a set of signals arranged . . . with old Sister Reese (mother of Nephi), as either Navy or Army battle signals. The signal flag, however, of Sister Reese, was given in the form of one, two, three, or four white sheets strung on the clothes line on the west side of her house in full view from Fort Lookout."[59]

"The Hounds are after me day and night," Orson said by letter to Brigham Young on November 10 during a secretive sojourn in Ephraim, "and I fear, they will be after you — I would rather be shot three times than you once. Look sharp. . . . God be with you." Indeed Brigham Young had "Hounds" after him too, but he had departed for southern Utah before issuance of the warrant. After his return to Salt Lake City, while waiting for trial on various charges of misconduct, he lived under house arrest for months.[60]

Orson occasionally attended priesthood gatherings, through the cautious help of friends. In addressing a meeting January 25, 1872, he emphasized calmness and seeking spirituality, one phrase being, "When anger arises, wisdom is dethroned." February 20, to a scribe with him at Fort Lookout, he composed a letter asking another man to resolve a difficulty in one of the settlements. During this disquieting period another child came into his family, a son to Sophia, March 16, named Sterling Washburn.[61]

Eventually Orson received word, after action of the United States Supreme Court, of the dismissal of the federal charges that had sent him and others into hiding, some into prison, and Brigham Young into house arrest.[62] Orson again lived at home. And again he traveled openly.

Unlike the previous year, when the Indians had been generally peaceable, 1872 brought complications. During the winter and into the spring, the settlers "fed and clothed the Indians that usually stay about on our borders," Orson detailed to Brigham Young, May 23, and continued, "They have been quite a tax upon us, and I have just given them between two and three hundred dollars worth of blankets, shirts and flour; and now there are in the neighborhood of two thousand, said to be, on our borders and approaching us with the expectation of quartering upon us by way of forced loans. Their Chiefs say they are all very friendly and very hungry and they may kill and eat our cattle in spite of all [the chiefs] can do to prevent it. They want sugar and Coffee by the sack and no end to the flour and beef.

"Our people here have had many calls and drafts, and every cord has been pretty well strained. I fear that under the garb of friendship, [the Indians] may provoke hostilities by exacting more than we can give. I yet have a little means to buy some of our own chiefs coats, pants &c &c."

The two thousand destitute Indians indeed thronged into the valley, just as Orson had heard they would. Two days of missionary meetings in Mount Pleasant, June 1 and 2, attended by people from many Sanpete settlements, developed into Indian meetings also. Orson announced that he had "appointed Bishop W. S. Seely to look after Indian matters in the north part of the county, and Brother Cox, of Manti, in the southern part." Several chiefs of various tribes attended the sessions, declaring friendship and peace. Orson exhorted the Saints to be kind to the gathering natives.

A few days afterward, June 5 and 6, the Indian Agent from Salt Lake City, Col. G. W. Dodge, met in long council with Indian representatives at

Fairview. The natives told that in many ways the agents at the Uinta Reservation had cheated them and not met their needs. The Indians had traveled to Sanpete to "visit [our] friends, the Mormons, to exchange friendly greetings, and trade with other Indians; to worship the Great Spirit near the resting place of [our] fathers; and to receive compensation for the use of [our] lands, now occupied by Mormons and miners." Agent Dodge asked the bishop of Fairview "to issue to them 4000 pounds of flour and 2,500 pounds of beef." He also gave them "ammunition and a few articles of clothing." The Indians desired to remain in Sanpete a few "moons," but Colonel Dodge thought he convinced them—with promises to supply future wants—to depart.[63]

The Indian situation seemingly about to be resolved, Orson traveled to Salt Lake City at the invitation of Brigham Young and accompanied the President and other Church leaders by train north to Brigham City. Orson enjoyed the two days of spirited meetings, June 8 and 9, and pleasant conversations with his brethren in between. Many months had passed since he had experienced this privilege.

Back in Salt Lake City, June 9, a sudden night crisis—a medical attack that left him incapacitated—caused those around Orson to think the apostle's days of mortal service were about to end. The next day he rallied, only to relapse. The summoned doctor thought he probably had apoplexy (a stroke). Within days, however, recovery began and progressed rapidly. Within two weeks he traveled home to Spring City.[64]

Indian events in Sanpete had been unnerving during Orson's absence. Though most of the natives remained peaceable, some occasionally stole cattle or horses. Particularly had stealing increased on the Sevier. Then, June 16, Indians killed a young man near Gunnison. Begging had become an extremely burdensome tax on several settlements, the Indians having ignored the directions of Agent Dodge to depart. Authorities in Sanpete and Sevier counties again strongly preached vigilance. That the unruly Indians might not be emboldened by success, settlers should carefully guard herds and travel in groups. Agent Dodge issued another departure order June 20, but the wandering visitors ignored it too.[65]

July 1, after a council of government officials in Salt Lake City, Agent Dodge telegraphed to Sanpete that he had permission for military assistance. Then, to judge if troops were needed, he came again to various settlements and held Indian meets, insisting on departure. The Indians declared that they had no food on the reservation. Dodge promised to provide it and made arrangements. Local officials, including Orson Hyde, in their own meetings supported the Agent, and, to Indians in the meetings, urged compliance.[66]

Orson's intense exasperation with the Indians, and grave concern about the overwhelming challenge they had been for seven years, caused his frustrations to sometimes come across to outsiders in a more negative way than he intended.[67] People who merely visited Sanpete had no concept of what a long and suffocating, frightful burden the natives had been, with fearsome potential for worse. To the unknowing, Orson's rigid stance seemed unkind. People around him, however, knew of his patience, his fairness, his personal sacrifices, his great exertions for the benefit of both whites and Indians. The Indians, too, respected him highly.

Finally, in mid July, Agent Dodge issued official instructions to the Sanpete bishops to cease giving provisions to the natives. This caused worsened conditions.[68] Many Indians became "arrogant, domineering, and dictatorial, . . . assumed finally the air of . . . conqueror towards a subjugated community." They entered homes at all hours and demanded women to cook for them. They begged to the point of being impudent robbers brandishing weapons.[69] Raiders, August 6, ran off stock from the Spring City meadow. Attackers' bullets and arrows, August 10 near Fairview, wounded one herder and killed another. More stock was taken. Chief Tabby, August 12, sent word to the bishops that he could no longer control his men, though he did move his company out of Sanpete Valley into Spanish Fork Canyon.[70]

August 13 the bishop of Fountain Green telegraphed Agent Dodge asking for troops, saying that the Indians "are no longer friendly. As soon as you gave orders not to feed them they began to get mad. . . ." As one observer wrote, "From all reports these Indians are in a starving condition, and hunger will make savages of even the gentle." Chief Tabby sent to the whites a declaration that he would take his people no farther, adding that "they can die now [of starvation] as well as any time."[71]

Troops eventually arrived. They included one hundred infantrymen and three companies of cavalry, under the command of General Henry A. Morrow. On the way, at Springville, August 21 and 22, General Morrow had promised provisions and signed a treaty with Tabby and several other chiefs, representing two thousand natives. A concourse of Indians departed for the Uinta Reservation. Then the General deployed his troops in sections, some to guard Sanpete settlements and some to scout for Indians still in the mountains, believed to be hostile. General Morrow camped at Mount Pleasant on September 1. Early that morning, before traveling to Mount Pleasant, the General and his mounted soldiers had first come to Spring City and consulted with Orson Hyde, Orson's son Joseph relates. They "camped in . . . our calf pasture, about 150 yards north of the log house."[72]

Five days later, September 6, the General received dispatches from his scouts that Chief Tabbyuna, White Horse Chief, and others would arrive that night and would "talk." General Morrow invited Orson and other local leaders to meet the next day with these chiefs who represented about one hundred Indians. At the council, September 7, the General listened patiently to the Indians' grievances. Most of them were valid. He presented the government's view. He said that if Indians remained in the area, his soldiers would stay as long as necessary to protect the settlers, because Indian promises to cease depredations had been broken. After a few hours of discussion, Indians and whites signed a treaty. Then General Morrow asked President Hyde to give a concluding speech. The report of the council states:

> . . . President Orson Hyde said in substance, that he was very glad that the Indians had had this interview with general Morrow; that whatever the general had promised them would be made good. . . . As for the Mormons, he was free to say that the recent events in this valley had changed their feelings toward the Indians. For kindness they had received nothing but unkindness . . . , and they felt it would be better for both the Indians and the whites that the former should go at once to their reservations. . . . [E]ven if the feelings of the people were otherwise, the government had decided that the Indians could not remain, and they must therefore go. The Utes had expressed great love for the Mormons; but said he, "If you did not steal our horses, why did you let others steal them?" He had not such hard feelings towards the Indians that he would not forgive them, and he desired to part from them on terms of friendship; but . . . the law . . . must be obeyed.
>
> Tabbyuna and the other chiefs listened with the greatest attention to elder Hyde, and the decided and emphatic manner in which he addressed them, and the decision which he came to, seemed to impress them very strongly. They shook hands with him and said they had promised to go, and they would keep their words. This was the end of the council.
>
> General Morrow gave the Indians orders for the purchase of sufficient provisions to supply them to the reservation. . . .

Thus Orson Hyde signed the final government treaty with Indians involved in the Black Hawk War—this time Tabbyuna, Ungitsib, White Horse Chief, and Comahpitch—and he gave the final address at the final government council.[73]

In the next few weeks, however, nothing seemed final. Horses were still being sought that had been stolen between the signing of the Springville and Mount Pleasant treaties. Also, stealing of livestock continued as Indians lingered in the valley. Two Indians shot at a traveler. And soldiers patrolled. "Excitement is the order of the day and guarding the order of the night," a Spring City resident narrated September 12. Then, from Spring City, September 26, Orson sent a telegram to Salt Lake City: "The Indians are upon us. Several horses were stolen last night. This morning a man was shot off a load of lumber and his little boy wounded in the hip and wrist. . . ." The man died. This, time disclosed, was the final casualty of the long-term conflict.

General Morrow commented: "I think I may say with truthfulness that there is not another American community in the nation which would have endured half the outrages these people have endured, before rising up as one man to drive out the savage invaders at the point of the bayonet."[74]

Though no more casualties resulted from Indian attacks, the next spring, 1873, marauding Indians harassed the upper Sevier settlements. In June, Church leaders sent George W. Bean, Indian interpreter, and other men, over the mountains to the southeast. Chief Tabbyuna accompanied them as "guide & peace-maker." In Fish Lake Valley the Chief arranged a meet with a dozen or so area Indians.

This pow-wow became a hallowed experience for every person involved, a fitting benediction—guided by the Great Spirit—to the past many years of "peace-meets." George Bean later wrote about it. "After supper," he detailed, "we arranged all present in a circle and proceeded to consider the object of our visit to this region. I . . . described to some extent the wisdom . . . of our leaders and their great desire to benefit and cultivate a reciprocal Spirit towards the remnants of this land. Then our Peace maker Tab-i-oonah arose and repeated much of my remarks. . . . [A]s he talked the good Spirit came over him and his countenance shone as white and clear as an angel's seemingly, and while in his greatest fervor of testimony in behalf of Prest. Young & our people the ground where we were quaked and shook to the plain observance of all present; and the spirit of Interpretation rested upon every one, so that I had no need to repeat any of his discourse which lasted 30 or 40 minutes.

"Thus," George Bean continued, "a special manifestation appeared in our favor on this mission. . . . [It] sealed a ratification of friendship with our people and this little band which has never since been violated."[75]

Another thought-provoking development, after the Black Hawk War, involved learning more about the White Horse Chief, Tam-a-rits, who became known as She-na-ba-wiken or She-nav-egan. He visited Sanpete Valley occasionally, and he confided in a white friend the account of his change of course back in 1868. The settler retold it. This shift from seeking bloodshed and lawlessness to promoting peace came, he said, as the result of a soul-stirring event. After a battle Tam-a-rits returned to camp and slept. "[S]o profound was the slumber," the settler's retelling goes on, "that he lay as if dead for three days and nights, giving no signs of life. When he awoke he was a changed man, and said that he had been in the last fight in which he would ever engage. He told the other Indians that he had been to the Great Spirit; that the Great Spirit had given him back his heart; and told him to be at peace with all, and to fight no more."[76]

. . . daily walk. . . . (1872)

> *. . . this shall suffice for thy daily walk, . . . support . . . thy family. . . ; speak freely to all; yea, preach, exhort, declare the truth, even with a loud voice, with a sound of rejoicing. . . ! Pray always, and I will pour out my Spirit upon you, and great shall be your blessing—yea, even more than if you should obtain treasures of earth. . . .*
>
> —Doctrine and Covenants 19:32, 34, 37, 38

ORSON'S son Joseph, called Joe, in later years recalled that in 1872, at the age of nine, "I was converted into a messenger boy for Father." Being Orson's close companion, Joe gained profound admiration for his father and later wrote of this fondness and respect:[1]

> We boys always addressed him as "Father," while the hired men always addressed him as "Mr. Hyde." In his absence, though, we generally spoke of him as "the Governor," he having told us of an incident in his traveling upon a foreign vessel, wherein the captain of the same, with its officers, saluted him with this peculiar "Governor." Doubtless his personality and superb carriage of body were responsible for this nom de plume.
>
> He was spoken of locally as "The Old Elder." Truly he was an "Old Elder," because wherever he went his very personality emanated superiority and authority. Yet gentlemanly courtesy, politeness of manner and perfection of speech were his outstanding characteristics. His faultlessness of English, and expression in usage of the same, has to my humble judgment never been excelled.[2]

"Neat and wholesome," Joe continues, "in addition to a good hat, he always wore a white shirt and cravat [tie, or neckpiece], with his clothes thoroughly accustomed to being brushed." Joe's younger sister Geneva mentions that their father "Always wore a white shirt. Aunt Mary [Orson's wife Mary Ann] made them. Have heard it said he could stand more cold weather than any person they ever knew. Always in his shirt sleeves." Joe adds,

> During the last thirty years of his life, he wore a short stubby beard about half to three-quarters of an inch in length. Occasionally he had

his beard trimmed, and we always took notice of the event from the fact that he was usually more sharp and exacting than when his beard was in a state of normalcy![3]

Father was very dignified and respectful to his superiors in the Church and his co-members of the apostleship, and to local officials in the priesthood, even to the Ward Teachers, also to officers in the civil government and general walks of life. He always referred to Brigham Young as "President Young," and to fellow apostles as "Elder Heber C. Kimball, Elder John Taylor, Elder Wilford Woodruff, etc."

Once, after the saints had arrived in the valley, President Young jocosely drew attention to the apostle's politeness and gentility. Father's explanation was that while in Europe, and in Washington, D.C., and Philadelphia, known as he was as "Reverend," he naturally gravitated to society of intellectual kind. As was customary in Europe particularly, he wore a top hat (stove pipe), and in society whose custom was frequent salutation, he sometimes humorously described the situation by saying that a new hat of this kind would last but a very, all too short, time, for the reason that it was literally doffed off and on so often.

When in counsel with his brethren—visiting apostles, bishops of wards, and representative men of the various settlements, in line of his labors—the outstanding feature of his general thought was, "Now brethren and men, what is the best for this territory? What then is best for this county, and, too, what is the best for this and that settlement?" Not what is the best policy for us to pursue for personal satisfaction, gain or pride.[4]

While sitting upon the stand he always sat erect, as was his bodily carriage when walking naturally. Whenever entering a Church or hall, wherein the congregation was assembled, it was easily discernible that he himself was the occasion, just from his walk and dignity of carriage, with his head aloft. In preaching, his gestures, like the true and complete orator that he was, reflected the emphasis of the point or points he was making.

Like every man in the ministerial career, he at times was masterful, while at others he was simply mediocre or passive. In later years his delivery of speech was not so pleasant as when in his prime, for the reason that his voice became a little husky. However, no one listening to the orator apostle was ever known to go to sleep on him, nor did "that tired feeling" urge them to go outside of the building.

One of his customs, when having preached a sermon that family members heard, upon returning home he asked his family, "Well, what did you think of the sermon today?" He was usually informed, "Oh, it was very very good." Continuing, he often remarked, "Well, is that all you have to say?" Whereupon, on one occasion as I recollect, the answer was, "Oh yes, the sermon was good, of course, but it was only Orson Hyde, it was not the apostle." On other occasions similar to this the answer was, "Oh, Mr. Hyde, your sermon today was glorious, powerful and divine. It was the apostle speaking today." [His wives called him Mr. Hyde.][5]

When Father was absent from home on the Sabbath Day, preaching in the neighboring settlements, on his return of a Sunday evening he would exact of us to tell him who had spoken that day in our church, and what the speaker or speakers dwelt upon, so as to make sure that we were complying, not only in physical presence, but in spirit, with that which he had established as our duties to attend church and Sabbath school.

With Orson's desires for a pleasant and upright atmosphere, "in a moral way he simply would not have a hired man on his premises who would engage in vulgar or smutty expressions, much less profanity," Joe relates, and continues,

> As to his employees, likewise to us older boys, he never commanded or dictatorially ordered us to do any certain thing, but always said in this manner, "Now boys, you may, if you will, do so and so." Thus was his general order of directing, though it was distinctly understood by one and all that his directions and orders given in this way should be carried out to the very letter. Unless something was unusually out of line in the work engaged in, no argument or opposition was ever offered.[6]

A great-granddaughter, Villa Fenton Barrow, narrates that though family members obeyed him, they sometimes used ingenuity in doing so:

> After [Great] Grandmother [Marinda] and [Great] Grandfather [Orson] separated, when Orson came to Salt Lake he stayed with my grandmother, his daughter, Laura. One night he was apparently in a bad mood. Something was said about Mother [Lavilla] and Aunt Ella going to a party, a ward dance, and he said,
>
> "I don't think the girls should go." He gave no reason. Oh, Mother and Aunt Ella felt badly, and Grandmother tried to reason with him, but, "Nope." They didn't want to disobey him. He finally said, "Well, if they were my girls they could go to the party, but they would go in their nightgowns."
>
> Grandmother winked at the girls, and they went upstairs. They got out their prettiest nightgowns, which WERE pretty, hand embroidered like a lot of their things were, and Grandmother came out with a beautiful sash for each one. The girls put on their long nightgowns, put their sashes around, tied beautiful bows, puffed the sleeves, put on their jewelry, and got themselves all prettied up. Grandfather didn't see them, but

away they went to the party, the way Grandfather said they should. They had a wonderful time. Nobody noticed that they were in nightgowns. When they came home Grandfather was still up, and he saw them. He looked at them for a few minutes, dumbfounded that they had bested him, and started to laugh. He said, "If I had girls like that I don't know what I'd do with them."[7]

About home circumstances, Joe states,

For those times his family never was in need, and in fact enjoyed some of the luxuries. He was a liberal host and a magnificent provider of the necessities of life. Notwithstanding the grass-hopper war, and the shortage of foods, he managed some way to always have "a good table." He made a specialty of a good and plentiful garden, with a variety, incident to the climate, of all the edibles and fruits, which in connection with good beef and plenty of hams and bacon, made his table one of joy and satisfaction in those "hard and trying times."

Joe's younger brother Oscar concurs:

Father had a good rock granary and smoke house for curing meat for his large family, and when he died our bins were full of wheat. He had other homes and property and a ten acre farm, also a thirty acre farm. Father was a good provider and seemed to have plenty of crops, cattle and sheep. My boyhood home in Spring City was a happy one, time for play, making flutes and whistles from willows; in the Spring hunting black bird's nests in the green meadows with my brothers and boy chums.

Daughter Luella "always spoke of life in the Hyde home as being without friction," her son Adrian Hess explains. "One wife had charge of the cooking, one the care and cleaning of the house, another, care of the children, others in educating the children and sewing. Whether or not these jobs were rotated I do not know."[8]

Orson's wife Mary Ann summarizes the Sanpete period:

My husband married three young wives after settling in Sanpete Co., and for several years we lived together until the offspring became so numerous we were compelled to have separate homes. He attended the Legislature in Salt Lake City and was frequently there on business, so that his time was divided. We always had a joyful time on his return, for he was very happy in his family and called them together night and morning for prayer. Mr. Hyde frequently questioned his children on their studies, the elder ones on grammar. He required us to attend faithfully to family prayer in his absence, which was adhered to.

Orson's granddaughter, Maude Hyde Anderson, writes that "Grandpa was a very busy man in Church and civic affairs. . . , and grandma always said how humble he was. He was a kind and devoted husband and father. His wives and children had much love and respect for him."[9] Joe adds,

> His most cheerful and lively home moments were generally exhibited at the table, or during meal hours, when with the family he told funny anecdotes amid some little laughter. While around the home fire of an evening (said home fire was a big open fire-place in a log house), he taught and schooled us boys in the rudiments of English speaking, language properly delivered. Here too he instructed his sons in common social etiquette. He showed us proper posture; to take correct positions when standing; the accepted salutation of the right arm or hand in saying "How do you do?"; and in meeting with a lady to give a respectful bow, with the head bared, of course. He strongly encouraged all those old time niceties that went to establish the possessor as being well bred. He likewise coached us in our lessons preparatory for school work the following day, and frequently gave us examinations on the subject matter.
>
> The correct speaking of the English language was the standard of speech in the home, even at the table at meal times. When any member of the family, inclusive of hired men or girls, asked for a second helping, or for the passing of some food dish, if improperly spoken the request was not complied with until the "English" was corrected. The person received all the time and guesses he might desire, but to have it right he must, before receiving the benefits desired.[10]
>
> I remember Father's fairness. Having five wives, whenever he procured the necessary dress for one, that meant four additional dresses, so that each wife would have a new dress, and all be treated and blessed alike. The order of the children, however, was on the basis of actual needs, and if any partiality at all was shown it was on the basis of seniority of age.
>
> In providing the family with shoes for the Winter (in the Summer time we went bare footed), to ascertain the sizes, he had each child or big boy stand up with their heels against the mop-board of the big room. He measured along-side of the foot with a straight currant sprout to the extreme end of the toes, where he cut the currant stick. He numbered each sprout according to the age of the child, thus making no mistake as to which shoe was for a certain child.[11]

Son Joe tells of Orson's fairness in another way. When he returned from Carson County in 1856 he still owed his friend Gideon Wood the $7,000 that Gideon had loaned him to build his sawmill. This weighed on Orson's mind, but Gideon said, "Brother Orson, you don't owe me a dollar; I forgive you the debt." Years passed, and Orson acquired property with John E. Reese in Sanpete County that became a profitable coal mine. The mine sold, and Joe relates what happened next: "On receiving his portion of the sale money from Bishop Reese about 3 p.m. one afternoon, the following morning with horses & 'light wagon' Father drove to Springville, Utah, about 65 miles, and gave the $7,000 to his good generous friend Gideon Wood."[12]

The Indians, too, considered Orson Hyde their friend. An example of this involved daughter Mary Ann. On one occasion when she was six or seven years old, she tells, "while members of the Hyde family were traveling . . . between Ephraim and Spring City," and had almost reached home, she "spied some flowers by the way and being a lover of the beautiful, left the 'coach' by permission, to gather some while the company continued on a short distance. While assembling my flowers I felt the strong arms of an Indian about me, who immediately made off with me. When the company arrived in town, I was not with them. An alarm was given and a frantic search began." Mary Ann informed the captor Indian that she was "Orson Hyde's 'papoose.' Thereupon he signalled his band of followers and I was immediately returned to my family who by that time were in a state of great excitement."[13]

Augmenting all this, son Joe comments that Orson Hyde's "finest and choicest efforts, emanating from a child-like, implicit faith in his God, was easily discernible when engaged in prayer." Saying more about prayer, Joe continues:

> The curriculum of our home was established first on prayers night and morning. The family, the hired men, the hired women, and all in the home and about the farm and yard were expected and did appear at the ringing of the bell for prayers, as faithfully as they did for their meals.

Luella, two years younger than her brother Joe, adds,

> During the early years of my childhood I can think of no incident which impressed me with greater pleasure than did the hour of prayer in our home, where my father, five wives, 12 or 15 children, with the hired help, knelt in family prayer around the hearthstone night and morning.[14]

CHAPTER 26

. . . *unto the end.* . . . *(1873–1878)*

> *Hearken, O ye who have given your names to go forth to proclaim my*
> *gospel, and to prune my vineyard. Behold, I say unto you that it is my will*
> *that you should . . . labor with your might. . . . And again, verily thus*
> *saith the Lord, let my servant Orson Hyde . . . proclaim the things which I*
> *have commanded . . . ; and inasmuch as [he is] faithful, lo, I will be with*
> *[him] even unto the end.*
>
> —Doctrine and Covenants 75:2-3, 13

ORSON'S 1873 course saw a slightly slowed pace. His responsibility to the Territorial Legislature had ended, but he visited Salt Lake City in January, also for April conference and for October conference.[1] February 2 and 8, sadly, the Hydes lost to "spotted fever . . . two promising little boys": William Arthur (five years old, mother Julia) and Melvin Augustus (three years old, mother Ann Eliza). Orson's health was generally good, "tho I have to act with much prudence and care."[2] April 23, his son Ernest Godfrey was born to Lizzy. In December, a visit by Brigham Young to Sanpete was a banner occasion. He announced, in Ephraim, December 4, that within two years a Temple would be commenced in the county.[3]

The next year, 1874, witnessed the births of two of Orson's children and the death of one. March 20, Julia's Aurelia Fiducia was born, and June 14, Sophia's Royal Justus. Royal proved to be the family's last child. Royal's birth softened Sophia's heartache from the death of her two year old Sterling several weeks before, April 1. Deaths of children saddened everyone in the household.

Upon returning home from the cemetery, after mournfully watching Sterling's little coffin lowered into the ground, Orson had walked into Sophia's room and sat in a chair near her table. Quietly he rested his head on his arm. Several minutes passed as unusual thoughts came into his mind. Raising his head, he looked over at Sophia, and said, "I thought my heart would break when I laid that child away. But, Sophia, you shall have Sterling again in this life."

An unbelieving expression crossed his wife's face. Though she had heard, she asked, "What did you say?"

"You shall have Sterling again in this life." He gave no further explanation and saw that the words mystified her. But her countenance softened.[4]

A significant Church development in 1874 was introduction of the "United Order." This was a revived and modified system of sharing work and commodities in local groups, patterned after principles directed by Joseph Smith in earlier days as part of the "Law of Consecration." Following impressions from the Spirit that the Saints needed increased unity and benevolence, Brigham Young had begun the "United Order" movement in Saint George during the winter by organizing several units.

Orson, in a sermon February 8, 1874, in Salt Lake City, had voiced his own apprehensions about the Saints becoming too caught up in personal interests. "I remember once, in Nauvoo," he said, "when we felt ourselves happy and fortunate if we could get half a bushel of meal to make mush of, the Prophet Joseph Smith, talking to some of us at the house of brother John Taylor, said—'Brethren, we are pretty tight run now, but the time will come when you will have so much money that you will be weary with counting it, and you will be tried with riches;' and I sometimes think that perhaps the preface to that time has now arrived. . . . [M]any Saints . . . are laboring to acquire wealth; and the kingdom [of God] . . . has become a secondary consideration."[5]

In spring general conference sessions the United Order was the main topic presented. Unable to attend, from "clumsiness and feebleness of body," Orson afterward read the sermons in the newspaper. "I know that the 'United Order' into which all true Saints are about entering," he expressed, "is of the Lord; and I hail it as a God send." April 18 and 19, Orson attended meetings in Nephi where Brigham Young, John Taylor, and others expounded United Order principles. In the next couple of weeks, Orson preached on the subject in Fountain Green, Ephraim, and Manti. The reactions he received pleased him, the "majority and better class of the people" manifesting readiness.[6]

And yet, Orson's past experience gave him reservations about sharing and cooperation. Even though the principles were God-ordained, would leaders of groups get caught up in their own authority and abuse their privileges? In 1846, Orson and Elders Taylor and Pratt had been sent to regulate the Joint Stock Company in England. Its directors had greatly hindered Church functions in that land by using "joint" funds for their personal interests. Would present leaders be able to direct matters unselfishly for the good of all? But, the Lord apparently had a purpose for trying it now, and Orson felt that he personally must do everything he could toward its success.

The latter part of May, Elders Orson Pratt and John Taylor came to Sanpete and organized communities in the United Order. Orson assisted somewhat. At home his assistance was about the same—somewhat. "I take my chair daily," he tells, "and go into the garden and sit down and instruct the boys how to apply themselves at gardening which is about all that I am able to do."[7]

During the summer Orson's health improved, and he preached around Sanpete. During meetings in Mount Pleasant, September 12 and 13, he delivered several sermons. A report contains:

At 10 a.m. [the second day] the general congregation began to pour in, filling the house to overflowing, seeking every available place to listen to the instruction. Bro. Hyde preached a sermon, with the vigor, force and eloquence of former years. . . . [He] wound up by a hearty endorsement of the New Order. . . .

[Toward the end of the afternoon meeting] . . . Bishop Seeley . . . moved— "That as a people we here give an expression of our sentiments and good will to Prest. O. Hyde, who, for near sixteen years, has labored with the zeal of an Apostle, has traveled, labored, counselled, and advised the people of this county . . . , has done them all the good that lay in his power, and has thereby secured to himself our faith our prayers, and our confidence." The motion was unanimous.[8]

In late November, Orson, wife Mary Ann, and son Joe followed Brigham Young and others to Saint George. Here the Hydes remained for several weeks. Reasonable health allowed Orson to take part in discussions and meetings, and to address congregations.

Church leaders discovered, sadly, disappointments with some of the Saint George area United Order units that had been organized the previous winter. Lack of cooperation, jealousies, and other problems had caused hard feelings and waste. Orson's hope grew dimmer that this program would be "the crowning blessing of this dispensation."[9]

Returning home in late December, Orson held meetings in settlements along the way, reaching Gunnison on December 31. That evening "a violent cold" beset him, but the next morning, January 1, 1875, he preached about magnificent possibilities of the United Order. He "gave practically a two-hour's discourse," son Joe recounts, "carrying his audience above the clouds with his splendid oratorical and descriptive powers. He declared to the Saints the absolute glory and desirableness possible when each person loved his neighbor as himself, and would share and share alike—no rich, no poor, all struggling for the good of the whole, individualism consecrated into a corporate firm. The people were simply breathless in complete wonderment and understanding of what would ensue from the consecration of their earthly all to this, the great project, as beautifully illustrated and made plain."

Immediately following the Gunnison meeting, "at the very height of mule speed," Orson describes, they traveled on to Manti to a prearranged meeting, but his cold by now made him miserable. A large congregation had gathered.

Orson's Manti address in essence became a continuation of his morning discourse, but rather than words telling glorious possibilities, they revealed the realities of mortality. And his words matched his physical condition—distressed. One man who listened, Jens Weibye, summarized the speech in his journal. "Prs. Orson Hyde," he wrote, ". . . said that Prs. G. A. Smith in St. George said to him, that we will have to go slow with the United Order because it is a very difficult principle to get to work well. The United Order in St. George and other settlements is about broke up, and he (Orson Hyde) does not think that any one has got rich in [it] . . . but poor. . . . Some have no bread to eat. Twenty acres of potatoes in one settlement have not been dug . . . , and some of their wheat rotted in the field, because they could not be united to haul it home, and save it, and have bread to eat. . . . Prs. Orson Hyde compared the United Order with a premature child."

Joe's description of the same meeting states that his father "proceeded to demolish the beautiful structure which he had builded during the morning session. Not only did he demolish it in argument and fervor, but showed that it was now humanly impossible. And in conclusion he put on the capstone, in his most splendid and efficacious manner of speech: 'It is prematurely born, and I prophecy in the name of my Maker that it will die in failure.'"

After the meeting Orson felt too ill to travel. Two days later, on the way to Spring City, "Aunt Mary Ann," Joe narrates, "in talking the [Manti meeting] over with Father, remarked tremblingly, 'Oh, Mr. Hyde, I fear for you. I feel that you have given cause for a severe rebuke to be called upon your head. Oh, Mr. Hyde, I am sick and distressed in my soul.' Whereupon Father replied, talking slowly, as if measuring every word he uttered, 'Mary, the people should know, and they really want to know, the truth, and as Jehovah is my witness, that which I have said, and explained to the people, is Heaven's truth.'"

A few days afterward, January 6, 1875, realizing that his words truly might have been misconstrued, Orson wrote an explanation to James Wareham in Manti. He preceded the explanation with an apology:

> My health is very much improved since my return home. . . . I wish you to personally apologize to Bishop Moffitt for me. It was my intention to call on him and ascertain concerning his health; but being extremely fatigued and sick with cold, I felt unable to walk to his house, and when I arrived at Manti I was a more fit subject for the bed than for the stand or pulpit and I hope he will not consider it any marked unkindness in me in not calling on him.
>
> I think some of the people of your place got a wrong impression with regard to my ideas respecting the "United Order." I was so upset with cold that I cannot tell what I said, but I will tell you now what I meant to say: That some thought that the "Order" was prematurely introduced, and that it, like a child forced into the world before its time, was not apt to prosper, but that I would not say that it was introduced

before its time; but be this as it may, the workings of the United Order in St. George, for reasons better known to others, than to me, has proved so nearly a failure that I can hardly call it by any other name. . . . This however, does not impeach the truth of the Order but its conduct and management. Nor do I wish to impeach the honesty and integrity of its officers, but it shows a want of a proper understanding and ability to carry out the principle.

If I failed in my remarks to embody the foregoing, this is the way I intended to be understood.[10]

The "premature child" talk worked on Orson's mind, and in Manti, January 29 and 31, he apologized in public meetings, retracting statements of January 1. He declared that he had not intended to say that the program had come prematurely. If people applied themselves properly it could be a success. He recommended that they start slowly, one major project at a time, learning as they progressed.[11]

Orson traveled around the county somewhat. "My general health is very good," he stated February 15, but he had difficulty getting "about much on account of my weight, stiffness and slight infirmities," his usual complications. In April he journeyed to Salt Lake City for general conference.[12]

In meetings connected with the April 1875 conference, Church leaders, including Orson, discussed seniority among the apostles and decided to make changes. The changes involved Orson Hyde, Orson Pratt, John Taylor, Wilford Woodruff, and George A. Smith (counselor to President Young). Elders Taylor and Woodruff, and President Smith, had served faithfully since their ordinations as apostles, whereas Elders Hyde and Pratt had each withdrawn from activity for a period. When restored to full fellowship these two had been reinstated in their original places. Their positions, their brethren and they now decided, should be based on the dates of their restoration. This put Orson Hyde after, instead of before, John Taylor, Wilford Woodruff, and George A. Smith. The change received no public explanation. Rather, in conference on Saturday, April 10, at the time for sustaining officers, George Q. Cannon (counselor to President Young) merely read the names of the Quorum of the Twelve in revised order. The sustaining vote was affirmative.[13]

The seniority change brought Orson relief. At age seventy his mind and spirit remained lively, but physical energy waned. While living in Sanpete he had been unable to function as effectually as he should have as president of the Twelve. John Taylor, on the other hand, the new president, lived in Salt Lake City, in good health. The will of the Lord had been accomplished, and Orson thought the conference vote ended the matter.

He returned to Spring City and resumed his leadership role among the people he knew so well. He preached and he resolved problems.[14]

Sunday, June 20, found him in Nephi to accompany Brigham Young and party on a tour of Sanpete County. Orson offered the closing prayer in the morning Nephi meeting. Monday the group reached Moroni. In Tuesday's meeting in Mount Pleasant, George Q. Cannon mentioned a letter by local David Candland, published in the *Salt Lake Herald*. Candland complained about Mormon Indian policy and about taxes. The tone of the letter upset President Young, and when he spoke he read the letter and commented very derogatorily of the writer. Then, disturbed, he turned his forceful remarks into an apparent attack on Orson Hyde. "Brother Orson Hyde is not fit to be an apostle, no more than David Candland, and he [Candland] is not more fit than a mule. Brother Hyde had not the Spirit, or he would have seen the United Order."

Immediately Orson realized that Brigham Young had been told about the "premature child" speech. But had the President been told about Orson's apologies and his efforts to clarify hasty words? This didn't matter. Once again, Orson served as Brigham Young's whipping boy, a role to which he had become accustomed—not comfortable, but accustomed. President Young was making a point about obedience and diligence by giving a tongue-lashing, with Orson's back taking the stripes.

Thundering on, President Young referred to the realignment in the Quorum of the Twelve. Perception came to Orson that Brigham Young thought Elder Hyde *wanted* to be president of the Church, that Orson was upset about the change in seniority made two-and-a-half months before. With effort, Orson continued to sit quietly. Then shock touched him as President Young scoffed: "Why even Elder Hyde's oldest son has come pussying around me, and saying that his father had been misrepresented." After the meeting Brigham Young and Orson Hyde "had a long talk." Orson truly understood why the President warned him to be more careful.

During meetings the next day, still in Mount Pleasant, Brigham Young disfellowshiped David Candland. Then he talked about the United Order. He also asked Elder Hyde to speak. Orson rose ponderously from his seat. Leaning on his cane, with deliberate steps he walked to the pulpit. He spoke calmly and politely, his voice husky with age. Gone was the clarion sound of former times, but his words carried well. Orson admitted that he had been "very unwise to have said anything" against the United Order. "I don't want to refer to my chastisement yesterday," he added. Then he continued, in substance saying, "Brothers and Sisters, I have been here for all these years, have labored with you, and you have had knowledge of my everyday walk and conversation. . . . As for myself, and in reply to President Young, I have nothing to say, but inasmuch as the President has made reference to my son in particular, having come pussying, as the President says, in favor of his father about action concerning the Twelve apostles at Conference, all I have to say is [and raising his voice and his hand upwards], in the name of Jesus Christ, God bless that boy!" Then he sat down.

Spontaneously the people rose to their feet. As a unit they shouted, "Amen!" Brigham Young's "Amen" seemed louder than anyone else's. The desired effect had been gained. Whether or not President Young had planned it this way, the course of events at the Mount Pleasant meetings had rallied the whole congregation in unity.

As members of the Hyde family rode home in their wagon, the clopping of the team's hoofs seemed louder than usual. Orson said nothing about what had transpired. Yes, Brigham Young at times rode rough-shod over the feelings of others, but he accomplished the Lord's work, and he did it in a fraction of the time required by anyone else. He was God's mouthpiece on earth. Orson loved him and respected him, would be obedient to his counsel whether stinging or sweet. Order reigned in the Kingdom of God, and this frontier of occasional chaos required an iron-tongued leader. Though President Young's methods hurt at times, Orson could withstand the reproof, and he knew that the President recognized this. The earlier tendency of Orson's to disobedience, that had been shed in tears of anguish during and after his soul-stretching ordeal of 1838, still lay buried on the prairies of Missouri.

Beside Orson, on the driver's seat of the wagon, rode his son Joe, twelve years old, too young to comprehend what had happened. He had yet to learn about the complexities of obedience. He had not sat in meetings of the Twelve and heard the strong direct language that flowed. He had not the experience to know that apostles were fully aware that they were mortal. They disagreed in discussions, often vigorously so. The Lord used strong men, not weak men, as his personal servants, his leaders on earth. But these men, apostles of the Lord Jesus Christ, had no doubt that Brigham Young was God's earthly representative. They carried no doubt that though he, like they, manifested faults, he was the *prophet*. If they followed his official mandates the results would be good.

Arriving home that late afternoon, the sun low in the sky, Orson walked directly to his bedroom and closed the door. This being unlike his established habit, a hush fell upon the family.

Son Joe tells that after the sun had gone down, the bedroom door opened. His father looked as though he had been asleep. Joe watched as Orson walked over and rang the bell for the customary evening household ritual of "prayer time." Then, Joe tells, "leading in prayer himself, and commencing in the usual terminology of family prayer, Father made a direct departure on this occasion. . . . Never before in my recollection did he emphasize and pray so earnestly for divine wisdom to be showered upon President Young, with the hope that heavenly order and decree, nay, heavenly and divine pleasure would be made manifest to the President, and through him to the people. . . . Father concluded by saying, 'Oh, God, assist us one and all to follow the admonitions of Thy servant, and enable us to endure faithfully to the end, for Thy name's honor and glory.'"

Expecting his father and Brigham Young now to treat each other with disdain, Joe looked on incredulously the following morning. "At about ten o'clock," Joe narrates, "as President Young and his party, a long train of carriages, drove down to our old log home, Father stepped out to meet him, and as the President alighted from his carriage he greeted Father by putting his arms around him. In twenty minutes the apostle, with his conveyance, had joined the train and was speeding south to Manti."[15]

On the way to Manti the group stopped in Ephraim to investigate a possible temple site and potential rock for its walls. Ever since President Young announced in 1873 that Sanpete would have a temple, Sanpete residents had been eager for specific plans. In Manti the company walked around again, at what locals called "the Temple block," on a hill already a rock quarry. The next day, at a meeting in Ephraim, Brigham Young asked for a vote about the temple site. Orson said that he personally favored the Manti location, in spite of it being "hard climbing," but he voted for "where the Lord directs." The Manti stone quarry received the most votes. This, President Young stated the next day, was the Lord's choice.[16]

This day, Saturday, June 27, 1875, Brigham Young announced and also explained a needed reformation among Church members as part of the United Order. Fourteen rules, of the basic way Saints should live, had been drawn up for compliance by Church members wishing to receive the blessing of rebaptism. Sunday, in the ample creek east of the Ephraim meetinghouse, Orson Hyde was the first to be immersed, baptized by Daniel H. Wells. The wording of the baptismal prayer contained the phrases: "for the remission of your sins and renewal of your covenants, with a promise on your part to observe the rules of the United Order which you have heard read." Orson stepped out of the water and sat down. Brigham Young rested his hands on Orson's head and confirmed him, sealing upon him "former washings and anointings and ordinations." Six other apostles received the same privileges. George Q. Cannon required two immersions, when part of his arm floated out of the water the first time. As weeks and months passed, local leaders and members also made commitments and received rebaptism.

During this trip around Sanpete, Brigham Young had apparently noticed the conveyance Orson drove. At one point the President put his arm around Elder Hyde's shoulders and said, "You are too old a man to ride in a 'lumber wagon,' and you shall have something better."[17]

Orson's 1875 activities remained much the same as in previous years. And, to his pleasure, Brigham Young indeed began arrangements for him to receive a new carriage, sending Orson notice of this soon after his arrival back in Salt Lake City.[18]

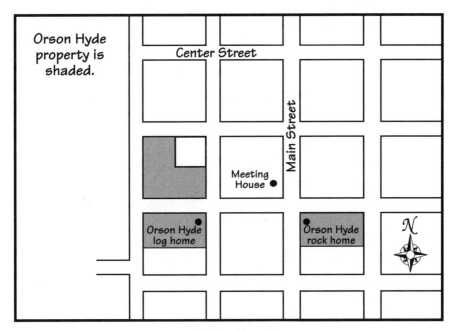

Spring City.

A major change for the Hydes this summer was some family members, including Orson, moving into their newly-completed impressive rock home. Built of cream-colored limestone, it stood two-and-a-half stories tall. The basic dimensions were thirty-two feet across the front and nearly thirty-one feet front to back, with walls twenty inches thick. Facing west on Main Street, a block directly east of the log home, this house replaced the original dwelling on the lot. In the half basement, spring water provided cool storage; the water came into the basement through a pipe on the south side near the front wall, ran along in a shallow cement ditch and out the front near the other side, an arrangement similar to that in the basement of the log home. Two full floors each contained four rooms. The main floor had a lean-to on the back, nine feet wide and twenty feet long. The floors contained random-width boards. In the main rooms the rich brown finish on the window and door casings had been hand-grained with stiff feathers. The staircase, in the center of the home, angled several times, with landings, as it ascended to the attic floor.[19]

In September, 1875, Orson preached in Salt Lake City at the funeral of his friend, George A. Smith. In his remarks Orson described Elder Smith as "a noble man of God, . . . whose voice we have listened to with so much pleasure."[20]

In late November, Orson's new carriage arrived from Brigham Young. And a splendid conveyance it was! Eli Day, a resident of Mount Pleasant, describes it as "a large, beautiful two seat, white topped buggy," and adds,

"Orson Hyde . . . used it in all his travels after that. I believe it was the best buggy that had ever been owned in Sanpete Co. up to that time. It was in O. Hyde's family many years after his death."

December 10, 1875, Orson and Julia's youngest child died, not yet two years old. "We have just buried our lovely little daughter, Aurelia Fiducia, and feel her loss," Orson wrote to Brigham Young, December 13, "a sore affliction; but God is just, right and merciful."

Regarding children, Orson had preached earlier in the year, "It is very pleasing to me to call my wives and children together in the morning and to spend a few minutes in giving them a few words of kindly instruction. I have practiced it until it is as much of a pleasure to me as it is to eat my breakfast when I have a good one, and I feel lost without it. . . . What are we here [on earth] for but to raise up children and endow and qualify them for future usefulness?

". . . Our children are entrusted to our care and management, and unless we do our best to cultivate and improve them, . . . we [have no] right to be the agents in bringing their spirits from the realms of day to earth."[21]

In the July 28, 1876, *Deseret Evening News* an item brought memories to Orson. Sidney Rigdon had died July 14 in Friendship, Allegheny County, New York. The article said that he had "unwaveringly adhered to his original" statements about the Book of Mormon.

In 1876 several Sanpete units of the United Order reverted back to co-operatives or otherwise discontinued. Not only had some unwise management and selfishness caused problems, but in many instances insufficient resources limited success in spite of diligent effort.[22]

September 24, 1876, Orson presided at a conference in Ephraim, and in his address to the multitude of Saints from all around Sanpete County he appealed for help. He told them that his health prevented him from acquiring adequate means for his household. He detailed some of his yearly cash costs: $300 for hired help, $100 for shoes for his family, and $100 for his children's school bill. Afterward people shared generously.

During the closing weeks of 1876, the near completion of the temple in Saint George prompted increased emphasis on the temples being built in Salt Lake City, Logan, and Manti. Sanpete folks responded well to appeals from Orson and the bishops for pledges of assistance for the Manti Temple. This came—in labor, grain, and some money.[23]

The 1877 April general conference had been scheduled to convene in Saint George and would include dedication of the completed temple. Orson left home March 14 to attend. Mary Ann accompanied "him on this long journey over the mountains—where the roads were nothing short of trails in some places, and mud hub deep in other places, storms of snow and sleet in the last of March, and some sunshine as well—," son Joe relates, "and I was the teamster and messenger boy. Our visit extended over about a month, while domiciled at the home of Richard and Elizabeth Price Bentley (Mrs. Bentley being the only living sister of Aunt Mary Ann Price Hyde).

"I," Joe continues, "was not present with Father in the temple when he first saw the baptismal font, in the shape of a bowl on the backs of twelve cast iron oxen, but it has been reported that on beholding the same, in silent adoration, and upon leaving the room, he came walking out to where the laborers were, tears streaming down his face, tears of joy, remarking as he wiped the same away from his cheeks, 'Thank God, I have been permitted to again behold a temple baptismal font.'"

Joe tells also of a memorable day involving personal blunders:

> Accompanying Father to lunch with President Young, in his home, the food thus provided was enticing to me, a boy fourteen and a half years of age. The thinly sliced dried beef with buttered hot biscuits simply over-powered me. After the first helping had been consumed, President Young, noticing that I had already made a "clean up," being a genuine lover of humanity, and particularly to see a hundred percent boy eat, noticed that I was ready for more. The grand old President himself passed the plate containing more of such splendid eats to me, saying, "Joseph, please — have — some — more." I helped myself very liberally, and proceeded to devour the same. Now the real tragedy is to come. Not being yet thoroughly satisfied with the two helpings I had already absorbed, looking up, I asked President Young for another helping of the same good eats, which he graciously gave me.
>
> The second and climaxing social error on this day, was at a dinner given by Mrs. Bentley, to which a number of apostles and their wives were invited, and other guests. Being seated at the table next to Father's right arm, in my clumsy boyish fearless manner, somehow my hand contacted with Father's cup of chocolate, garnishing one fifth of practically the whole table spread.
>
> This day brought to Father more blushes and real embarrassment than he had experienced for many a day. That evening just before retiring to bed, while on the upper veranda of the Bentley home, the apostle proceeded to give to his son a lecture on etiquette, which in effect was a whole course or curriculum in the small space of about thirty minutes. Can I ever forget it?[24]

Though Joe added spice to events, Orson enjoyed his 1877 stay in Saint George. He preached in the local Tabernacle March 25. He met with his brethren many times, "rejoicing before the Lord." In the Temple, April 5, the day before conference officially began, he spoke to a large congregation. "I have not language, my brethren and sisters," he said, "to express the feelings and emotions of my heart on coming into this Temple yesterday morning" after all preparations had been made for its dedication. "I will sum up in short by saying, that the sentiments of my heart were, Thank God for such a place in which to worship and to reverence his high and holy name." In part of Orson's talk he spoke of things personal, saying that he wished he could do more for the kingdom of God and adding, "I labored with my hands until I reached my seventieth year, when I had to cease working; and for the last two years I have not been able to do anything, not even to cut a stick of wood or fetch a bucketful of water. But I feel thankful that my health is as good as it is, and that I have lived to see this day, and to behold this elegant structure reared to the honor of our God. . . . [M]any of us now, after these many years of toil, have to struggle with the going down sun of our earthly existence. . . . But while we remain let us struggle on, and continue the good fight of faith until we are called home."[25]

Later in the month, after Orson's return to Spring City, Brigham Young and others, on their way home, stopped in Sanpete Valley to dedicate the Manti Temple site. Hundreds of people, including Orson, joined the President on Wednesday, April 25, in Manti, in spite of the "stormy cold afternoon," Orson's son Joe tells. "Together with the President's caravan, we drove up to the brow of the hill, and while the snow was falling," Brigham Young knelt and dedicated the spot for construction of the Manti Temple. He admonished the people to commence work the following Monday. They did.[26]

In July another progressive event occurred: Brigham Young came and organized the Sanpete Stake. He selected a Stake President and numerous other officers. Orson was pleased that local leaders would assume many of the duties that had been his. The following week Erastus Snow and Orson traveled to Richfield and organized the Sevier Stake.[27]

August 27, unexpected sad word arrived that Brigham Young was seriously ill. Telegrams urged the Saints to pray for him, privately, in prayer circles, and in meetings. They did, anticipating his recovery. But, August 29, a hot oppressive day, a telegram brought the shocking news of his death! Orson stared in disbelief at the words on the paper in his hand. "We were startled, stunned, and in fact nearly overwhelmed," son Joe relates. The living Brigham Young had been as much a part of their lives as their own hands. Orson said simply, "Now the greatest tree in the forest of God has fallen." To his wives, with a distant look of sadness, recalling indications that Brigham Young thought Orson desired the Presidency, Orson confided, "President Young knows now [looking upon us from his present vantage point], if he never knew before, that I never wanted his place."

For this busy "haying time," Orson gave instructions to the hired men, and he and Mary Ann prepared to attend the funeral. Leaving home that Thursday evening, Joe took them in the family carriage to the railroad terminus, York Station, twenty miles beyond Nephi. They arrived by train in Salt Lake City early Friday evening.[28]

Mourning enshrouded the Saints, disbelief the common sentiment. Multitudes thronged into the city, and crowds readied the Tabernacle for services. The next day, as a gentle rain settled the dust, thousands lined up, entered the domed building, and walked respectfully past the open flower-adorned coffin of their revered leader. Betokening love and admiration, flowers, greenery, and drapes of black festooned the hall.

Beginning early Sunday morning, a resplendent sun in the sky, thousands more admirers filed past the coffin of "Brother Brigham." Brigham Young had given his heart and his soul, his all, to the Church and the Saints. At the Sunday afternoon funeral services the speeches and music, heartfelt, matched the glorious weather outside. Orson offered the benediction, expressing gratitude and respect, praying that "all the saints here assembled . . . may feel to renew our energies . . . , that when the time comes when we shall be called hence, we may be prepared and qualified to . . . behold our leaders and join with them in songs of praise to God and the Lamb. . . ." Following the funeral Orson participated in the impressive procession to Brigham Young's grave site in the private Young family plot east and north of the Tabernacle.

Two days afterward Orson met with a solemn group of his brethren. "[T]he two counselors of President Young," the report of the meeting tells, "and ten of the Twelve Apostles,—two of the Twelve, brothers Orson Pratt and Joseph F. Smith being absent in England—held a meeting, and waited upon the Lord. With humble, contrite, and saddened hearts we earnestly sought to learn His mind and will concerning us and His Church. The Lord blessed us with a spirit of union, and condescended to reveal to us what steps we should take. Elder John Taylor, the senior Apostle, and who has acted as the President of the Twelve, was unanimously sustained in that position. With the same unanimity, also, it was voted that the Quorum of the Twelve Apostles is the presiding Quorum and authority in the Church. . . . [T]he two Counselors of President Young—Presidents John W. Young and Daniel H. Wells—were unanimously sustained as one with [the Twelve], counselor[s] to [the Twelve], and associated in action with the Twelve Apostles."[29]

Orson returned home, then a few weeks later he traveled again to Salt Lake City for October 1877 general conference. Part of the conference included a "solemn assembly," where the authorities of the Church were sanctioned in their positions by the voting of priesthood quorums in turn and then the voting of the general congregation. Orson also participated in other meetings for two weeks. In one of these the brethren decided to allocate $1,500 a year to the members of the Twelve who needed assistance. This included Orson.[30]

Back in Sanpete he ignored, as best he could, his slowing physical abilities. After he spoke in a meeting in Manti, November 4, a settler who had not seen him for a long period, John Pulsipher, wrote: "It was good to hear [Elder O. Hyde preach] again. A good faithful man he has been—begins to look old."[31] Concerns continued to receive Orson's attention, as he traveled, preached, and consulted.

Orson missed attending April 1878 conference because of infection in his legs that for several weeks caused running sores and swelling. In August, in his own yard, Orson oversaw the construction of a fine granary. Built of the same rock as his house and other sturdy outbuildings, the granary contained two stories and measured seventeen feet by twenty-three feet.[32]

In October he attended general conference and delivered—"with great force and freedom"—the opening address. During his several days in Salt Lake City he "felt particularly joyful and animated, . . . was buoyant and cheerful," in private conversations as well as in public meetings.[33]

When Orson returned from the City, and as he resumed preaching around Sanpete, he felt grateful to come home each time to his supportive family. In day to day living, family members made no complaints about their material lacks. Food was adequate this fall: sixty bushels of wheat for flour for bread for a year, and their beef and pork and vegetables that they raised. Only minimal clothes were on hand for the children, the youngest now four years old. Cash had not stretched for new shoes or boots for anyone. But the family's health remained good, and love abounded.[34]

Over the years Orson had pondered the many avenues of progress in the Lord's work, reading with particular interest of developments among the Jews, a subject close to his heart. After his apostolic pleadings with the Lord on the Mount of Olives in the Holy Land in 1841, changes came. During the following decades many European countries passed laws in favor of Jews, and Jewish hopes of returning to the land of their fathers materialized. "Zionism" blossomed and flourished. In 1862 Moses Hess published a notable book about it. Progress would continue, Orson knew.[35]

Orson preached in Mount Pleasant, November 3, 1878. He had been sick for four days, then felt better for a day, and this next day functioned quite well. Desiring "all to hear and to understand, especially those who may not be fully conversant with the English language," he spoke slowly and carefully. He talked of the progress of the Church and of the eventual downfall of its enemies, and he stated, "We are now living in the days of a 'marvelous work and a wonder.'" He prophesied about the "great rush of people [that will come] to the Saints in the last days [for succor]." With fervor he admonished his beloved friends to prepare for the future, to heed the words of the Lord.

In conclusion he declared, "I will here say to you my brethren and sisters and to the Saints generally: Set your houses in order. . . . Let the blood of the covenant be freely sprinkled [figuratively] on your door posts and lintels—[evidenced by] a deep-rooted union exist[ing] in your hearts and practiced in your lives. Devote yourselves to earnest prayer in secret and in your families, and allow not the cries of the poor to reach the ears of Jehovah against you. Omit not the duty of patronizing every institution of learning among the Saints, whether day or evening schools, or Sunday schools. Defeat not the designs of the Almighty by fooling away the fruits of the earth, knowing that we are placed here, not to do our own will, but the will of him by whose goodness we live; and we should be willing to be used in doing good, [in] building temples [and] places of education and in learning to manufacture what we need. . . ." Looking lovingly around the Mount Pleasant congregation he knew so well, he closed with these words: "Now, my brethren and sisters I bless you, in the name of the Lord Jesus Christ. Amen." Time showed this to be Orson's last public address.

By the following Saturday, November 9, Elder Orson Hyde had become "dangerously ill." Telegrams conveyed the news to distant children, requesting those that could come to his bedside to do so.[36]

But he rallied, and November 18 he rejoiced when President John Taylor, and Elders Orson Pratt, Erastus Snow, and Joseph F. Smith, visited him. With these cherished friends pleasant and reminiscent conversation ensued.

A few days later Dr. Heber J. Richards arrived in Spring City, sent by President Taylor to administer possible professional assistance to ailing Elder Hyde. The doctor's kind manner comforted, but he could do little. He observed that Orson had "no affliction as sickness goes, but his vital organs have become so honeycombed in fat that he is gradually smothering, and in my opinion will finally smother to death, not being able to breath."[37]

As family members arrived, each expressing affection in his or her own way, Orson's thankfulness abounded. This compensated for the many earlier years of his life when he essentially had no family. This also lifted the depressive mood that more frequently in late months had seemed to override his thoughts unbidden.

With his daughter Mary Ann, fourteen years of age and old enough to understand heartache, Orson shared a few quiet moments that all of her life would remain precious to her. He told Mary Ann he realized that his recent melancholy had been interpreted by some as disappointment because his position in the Twelve had been changed. Such was untrue, he emphasized. Rather, he had felt weighed down in mind for his own regrettable act of forty years ago, in the fall of 1838 when he "let [the Prophet] Joseph down." He repeated details, telling of the great kindness of Heber C. Kimball, Hyrum Smith, and Joseph Smith in that somber period. Orson told his daughter that he was dying of a *broken heart*, that for these many years he had carried "this great burden of sorrow and grief because of signing the affidavit with Thomas B. Marsh." However, he added, "I have only myself to blame, because it was done at a time when I was without the Spirit."[38]

Orson spent most of November 27 sitting or reclining. He walked a little, however, "across the floor from his couch to his rocking chair," son Joe relates, "when he scarcely had breath with which to speak."

The next day, November 28, destined as his last, Orson dictated a letter to President Taylor. Joe describes that this required extreme effort, "while pulling for breath and perspiration rolling off from his manly forehead." Briefly Orson told John Taylor about his worsening "pain and distress." He also expressed a prayer to "the Lord to bless the Quorum." His humor shone through too, when he referred to the restrictions placed upon his diet by the recent visit of the doctor from Salt Lake City: "My appetite is very poor, and rendered doubly so by the late mission of Dr. Richards to Sanpete County." Hoping for renewed energy he closed: "Shall be highly gratified to hear of your prosperity and listen to any suggestions that you may be pleased to make to me. Affectionately, Yours in the Gospel, Orson Hyde."[39]

About noon a man on a horse rode into the yard. Orson's eyes lit up with pleasure when, as Joe relates, "his dear old constant friend William Price, brother-in-law," entered the room. William had "come on horseback over sixty miles to see his old pal, encountering the severest of severe weather." Joe, in his usual capacity as errand boy, was "in and out of the room to wait upon the occasion as best I could when so ordered."

Orson said little as he lay on his couch. He seemed content to have loved ones near. Then, for a short time, he sat up. Next, Joe narrates, "he simply yielded all, and his last words spoken on earth were, 'Let me lie down. I must give up.'"

"My older brothers," Joe continues, "together with Bishop Frederick Olsen, assisted him in lying down. They comfortably placed his head on the pillow, but before his feet and legs could be placed on the couch (he was a very heavy man), the death gurgle was heard in his throat, and the great apostle had now gone the way of all flesh, on the 28th day of November, 1878."

A few moments before, Mary Ann had sent a telegram to President John Taylor: "Bro. Hyde has taken worse and is failing fast." Now she sent another: "Prest. Hyde breathed his last at 6 o'clock." His age was seventy-three years, ten months, and twenty days.

Forty-seven years had passed since the fretful night in Ridgeville, Ohio, when the "golden Bible" began to be a beacon rather than a stumbling block in the life of the red-haired preacher, Orson Hyde. In that period his hair had turned to auburn and then to sandy gray, and he had become a patriarch to wives and children, a leader of men, a friend of angels, a true servant of God. Now he had entered a new environment, fresh and vibrant, another realm in which he would continue his service as the Olive Branch of Israel.

A singular occurrence, observed by several people individually, marked the glorious welcoming passage of Orson Hyde's spirit into the sphere beyond death. A neighbor girl, Sarah Justesen, was helping in the Hyde home when she heard what sounded like tissue paper rattling under the window. Curious, she walked outside. She heard overhead a choir singing gloriously in the heavens. The choir seemed to be passing over. The singers were so close that Sarah recognized the separate voices. For another neighbor, C. G. Larsen, something unusual outside his home caught his attention. He opened his door. Overwhelmed by what he saw, he felt it so sacred he never spoke of the details. Orson's son Charles, with others in the field irrigating, heard the same sublime choral rendition as had Sarah.[40]

The day after the death of Apostle Hyde, the *Deseret News* announced his passing. A long article told of his devotion to the Lord's work. His missions were outlined in Ohio, the eastern states, Missouri, New England, England twice, and Jerusalem. His work as an editor was praised, both for the *Millennial Star* and the *Frontier Guardian*. His leadership of the Saints at Council Bluffs received applause and also his role in colonizing Carson County and Sanpete County. "Elder Hyde," the article continued in a personal tone, "was a man of great natural ability, and by industrious application had acquired a good education, which, with his great and varied experiences and extended travels, rendered him a powerful instrument in the hands of God for the defence and dissemination of the gospel and the building up of the latter-day work. He leaves a numerous family and a host of faithful friends who mourn their separation from one of the great men of Israel, an Apostle of the latter-day dispensation. His voice has been heard in many lands. It is now hushed in death. But he has gone to join his brethren of the Holy Priesthood behind the vail, who will welcome his coming with joy, and, freed from the infirmities which enfeebled him in his later years and all the weaknesses of mortal flesh, he will again, and with greater power than ever, proclaim the glad tidings of great joy, finding a wider sphere for his labors than the whole of this earthly globe can afford.

"The funeral," the article continued, "will take place at Spring City, Sanpete, on Sunday at noon. . . ."

In England the news of Orson Hyde's death arrived by "telegraphic dispatch from Salt Lake City . . . late on the evening of Nov. 29th." The *Millennial Star* published a lengthy article about him. Part of it stated: "In his younger years especially, he was noted for his powerful eloquence, which is even to this time a matter of remark among people still living in this country who knew him in his ministry in this land."

Orson's death also received notice in Seymour, Connecticut, his childhood habitation, where his mother had passed away. "ORSON HYDE, One of the Mormon Twelve apostles, . . . died in Utah Thanksgiving Day," the local *Seymour Record* published. The obituary outlined Orson's life, and added that he was "an eloquent speaker and fluent writer. . . . His brother Abijah is still living in Quaker Farms [neighboring Seymour]."[41]

The day of Orson's funeral in Spring City, Sunday, December 1, 1878, was "extremely cold," with a shining sun and a blue sky. In every direction, from near and far, carriages, wagons, horses, and people jammed the streets by eleven o'clock. The hundreds of people milled about, dressed in their warmest clothes. Just after eleven o'clock men carried the casket of Orson Hyde from his home and into the meeting house. Appropriate black mourning cloth had been draped on the stand in the front of the chapel. Sweet strains of organ music wafted faintly to the friends lining up to step inside and walk past the casket of their beloved leader. Seeing his serene face and his closed eyes, they spoke of his diligence, recalled his personal acts of kindness and concern for them, and marveled again at his numerous abilities. Many shed tears, sad that in mortality they could no longer feel reverently honored as "The Elder" removed his top hat and bowed in friendship. The line continued for nearly two hours.

The funeral services began at one o'clock, an hour after scheduled. Many people waited outside because the little meeting house held only a fraction of them. Inside, Orson's survivors sat in front, facing the stand. Among these were Orson's five wives, his twelve living sons, four of his seven living daughters (the others unavoidably absent), and many of his nineteen grandchildren.

Two apostles, Wilford Woodruff and Erastus Snow, had traveled to Spring City to bid their brother farewell. President Taylor and the other brethren of the Twelve were too far away handling other duties. Wilford Woodruff conducted the funeral. After the opening hymn by the choir, the opening prayer, and another choir hymn, Elder Woodruff stood to speak. His countenance conveyed a sweet peace, almost a look of joy, as he surveyed the crowded room. He asked pardon of his listeners, "if I do not manifest as much mourning as the occasion seems to demand." His eyes gazing above and beyond the congregation, he explained the reason for his elation: "The vision of my mind is opened to behold both sides of the veil." He saw the "first Elders of this Church, with the Prophet Joseph at their head, . . . now rejoicing, the heavens also, with the prophets of every age and generation, at the birth of brother Hyde into the spirit world."

Elder Woodruff reminded his audience of the uniqueness of the man they now honored. "Elder Hyde was one of the First Quorum of the Twelve Apostles of this dispensation," he said. "There have been other quorums of Apostles: among the Nephites [recorded in the Book of Mormon], on this Continent; and in all probability among the people of Enoch; as well as in the days of the Savior in Jerusalem; but only a few more, if any, than a hundred have occupied this important position among the many millions of men that have been upon the earth, from the foundation of the world. Brother Hyde is among that number."

Orson Hyde "has filled his mission;" Elder Woodruff declared, "he is safe and free, and has accomplished his warfare successfully, has been true and faithful unto death. . . . The Lord chose brother Hyde to be an apostle. . . . His mission to Jerusalem alone is sufficient to hand his name down in honor to future generations." Elder Woodruff gave a long and inspiring discourse. He reminded his listeners to be faithful to their own callings and duties that they might again associate with their lately-departed friend "in the blessings of the Father's kingdom, worlds without end."

Elder Erastus Snow also addressed the congregation. "I was sixteen years of age when I first made the acquaintance of Elder Hyde," he said. "Elder Hyde came with the apostles through New York and the eastern States in 1835, the first summer after the Twelve was organized. They held a conference at my father's house. The Twelve were then all together. Now there remains but one living of that number who has continued faithful—Brother Orson Pratt. One-half of that number magnified their calling. . . .Whatever mistakes they made, they took the first opportunity to rectify, and were forgiven. . . ." Continuing his uplifting address, Elder Snow reminded the congregation that at death the weaknesses of the righteous pass away, and that the spirit enters "a new estate that can properly be compared to a new birth. This causes friends to rejoice as much or more than at the birth of our natural bodies." Because of these truths, Elder Snow admitted, "I wept for joy today . . . at contemplating the glorious destiny awaiting my faithful brother." Elder Snow spoke for some time of the triumph of the resurrection. He closed by expressing his desire "that the family of Brother Hyde and all present will so live, as he has done, as to be counted worthy to receive the keys, powers and blessings of immortality and eternal lives."

The choir sang "Let Us Sing as We are Marching to our Home." Elder Woodruff pronounced the benediction.

An impressive procession made its way to the Spring City cemetery. Riding in one hundred and twenty carriages and other vehicles were: the brass band, the Spring City choir, the casket of Elder Orson Hyde, Elders Woodruff and Snow, the family and relatives, the presidency of the stake, the high council, bishops and counselors, patriarchs, seventies, high priests, elders, Aaronic priesthood holders, and the general public. Following the vehicles came "many horsemen and footmen." A serene atmosphere warmed hearts in this vast group, "a general gathering of Sanpete County."

The report adds: "After the remains of our beloved brother, President Orson Hyde, were securely deposited, surrounded by his wives, children and grandchildren, and innumerable friends, the dedicatory prayer [seeking protection and sanctity for the gravesite] was offered by Elder Erastus Snow. Elder Wilford Woodruff then expressed his thanks to all for the respect they had shown their departed brother, and invoked in brief and touching terms the blessings of Heaven upon the family and friends who remained behind. After which the choir sang, 'There's a Beautiful Home for Thee.'"

Orson's son Joe's most precious moment of the occasion came, he tells, "while the older sons, and hired men, much beloved, lowered Father into the grave. I stood at the head of the same. The thought that came to me then, and has ever been with me, when reduced to language is simply, 'Father, I will see you again.'"[42]

EPILOGUE

AND what of Apostle Orson Hyde as decades passed after his mortal mission? One of his callings, when ordained an apostle of the Lord Jesus Christ, the Messiah, was that he would be as the Three Nephites. Divine power changed the bodies of the Three Nephites that they might remain on earth, the same as had happened to John the Beloved. They would be privileged to "bring the souls of men unto me [Christ], while the world shall stand," to "be among the Gentiles, and the Gentiles shall know them not," to "be among the Jews, and the Jews shall know them not," to "minister unto all the scattered tribes of Israel, and unto all nations, kindreds, tongues and people, and . . . bring out of them unto Jesus many souls." They would be "as the angels of God. . . . Therefore, great and marvelous works shall be wrought by them . . . before [the] judgment day." Orson died a natural death, thus became unlike the Three Nephites in this regard. But what missions would he oversee from beyond the veil, or walking on earth as an angel unawares, to prepare people to "Come unto Christ"? He served as the first missionary of the Latter-days to bear faithful testimony of the Master in the Netherlands, in Germany, along the Danube River, in Constantinople, and in Jerusalem. Later the Prophet Joseph Smith assigned him a mission to Russia. Would these areas be among his fields of labor?[1]

APPENDIX ONE

Was Orson Hyde a Jew?

"ORSON Hyde was a Jew, wasn't he?" many people ask, obviously expecting an affirmative answer. They expect an affirmative answer because they see casual statements to this effect in Church literature and in public literature.

As the Hyde family genealogist, I smile when asked about Orson Hyde's Jewish connections and then decide quickly if the questioner wants the long answer or the short answer. If the short answer seems enough, I say, "No evidence of Jewish ancestry has been found."

This rarely satisfies, and the next question is, "Then why do I hear that he was a Jew?" Now the long answer is in order. If the questioner and I are in my home we walk into the study and I pull down books from the shelves. While turning pages I relate some background: that Orson Hyde was born in 1805 in Connecticut, baptized into The Church of Jesus Christ of Latter-day Saints in 1831 in Ohio, and chosen one of the original Latter-day Twelve Apostles in 1835.

We look at Volume 4, page 375, of Joseph Smith's *History of the Church*. While in London, on his way to Jerusalem to dedicate that land for the return of its scattered children, Orson composed a letter of introduction to the "Rev. Dr. Solomon Hirschell, President Rabbi of the Hebrew Society in England." Written in June of 1841, the letter contained the following: "About nine years ago [thus in about 1832], a young man with whom I had had a short acquaintance [Joseph Smith], and one, too, in whom dwelt much wisdom and knowledge—in whose bosom the Almighty had deposited many secrets, laid his hand upon my head and pronounced these remarkable words—'in due time thou shalt go to Jerusalem, the land of thy fathers, and be a watchman unto the house of Israel.'" I point out that this "land of thy fathers" seems to have started the whole speculation.

The next book I open is Volume 2 of Brigham H. Roberts' *Comprehensive History of The Church*, written in 1930, long after Orson Hyde's 1878 death. On page 45 we read, "Elder Hyde it appears was a descendant of the tribe of Judah." I point out particularly the "it appears." The cited source is the 1841 letter where Orson's blessing is quoted as having "thou shalt go to Jerusalem, the land of thy fathers."

Twenty years later, in 1950, Joseph Fielding Smith compiled his *Essentials in Church History*. We see that on page 259 (of the 1971 edition) he stated that "Elder Orson Hyde was of the house of Judah." Again the letter to Rabbi

Hirschell was used as the authority, and this author left out the "it appears" that B. H. Roberts included in his narrative.

LeGrand Richards, writing in 1954 in *Israel! Do You Know?*, repeated in his own words the declaration of Joseph Fielding Smith: "In preparation for the gathering of the Jews, the Prophet Joseph Smith . . . sent Elder Orson Hyde, a descendant of Judah, . . . on a mission to Jerusalem" (1973 edition, page 194).

Then, to confuse the issue, we look at Hubert Howe Bancroft's *History of Utah*, published in 1889. A footnote on page 773 states: "In 1840 [actually 1841] he [Orson Hyde] went to Jerusalem, where he held service at the mount of Olives, and consecrated the holy land, being appointed to this duty by the prophet, who declared him to be of the house of Judah." No qualifiers appear in this statement, indicating that possibly during his lifetime people thought of Orson Hyde as a Jew.

Setting the books aside, my questioner and I discuss the three main points that my research has revealed regarding Orson Hyde's ancestry:

First, what lineage did his patriarchal blessing give to Orson? This is unknown, because his first patriarchal blessing apparently has not survived to the present. A second blessing survives, given by Joseph Smith, senior, but it has no lineage. Patriarchal blessings have been found for four of Orson's children, with lineages as follows: Zina, none given; Mary Ann [White], "Ephraim"; Hyrum, "seed of the first born in Israel"; and Oscar, "Abraham."

Second, what has genealogical research revealed about Orson Hyde's forebears? I have traced about three-fourths of his ancestral lines to the New England immigrants. They were mostly from England, and I found no Jews among them. However, one-fourth of his ancestors, the progenitors of his mother's father, remain unknown.

Third, what did Orson, himself, know about his family? In his 1841 letter to Rabbi Hirschell he stated that he was not "able by any existing document or record, to identify [myself] with your nation." Orson knew little about his ancestry, according to the statements of his son, Joseph S. Hyde, in a newspaper article, "Genealogy: The Hyde Family," in *The Salt Lake Herald-Republican*, May 2, 1915, Section 1, page 4. Orson's mother died when he was seven years old, and his father gave him into the care of a guardian, resulting in him growing up outside family circles.

Apostle Orson Hyde prayed on the Mount of Olives in October of 1841, dedicating the Holy Land for the return of the seed of Abraham, Isaac, and Jacob, "its rightful heirs . . . who come home with a spirit of grace and supplication." During his homeward journey he remained in Germany for several months in 1842 and finished writing a book that he translated into the German language. Published for the purpose of introducing the gospel to the German people, the book's English title is *A Cry from the Wilderness: A Voice from the Dust of the Earth*. In recent years, this book has been translated back into English. In it Orson wrote of himself (English typescript, page 81): "I am not a Jew, neither am I a son of a Jew; but I am a friend of the Jews."

In a meeting of the Orson Hyde Foundation that I attended, during the period of gathering donations for the Orson Hyde Memorial Garden on the Mount of Olives (finished in 1979), the subject of Orson Hyde's possible Jewish ancestry came up. Elder LeGrand Richards, president of the foundation, made the remark that he formerly thought that Orson Hyde was a Jew, but he had almost changed his mind. Orson's 1842 statement was pointed out to him, which he gratefully received. After that, if anyone asked him about Orson's lineage, he gave them a copy of Orson's own words that he was "not a Jew. . . ."

As my questioner and I discuss Orson Hyde's alleged Jewish progenitors we agree that the tradition is based on a statement so broad as to fit vast millions of earth's people. If we with origins in Europe, America (Indians), the Middle-East, and other areas could trace all of our ancestral lines far enough we would find "fathers" who lived in "the land of Jerusalem."

People continue to ask, "Was Orson Hyde a Jew?"

I continue to answer, "No evidence of Jewish ancestry has been found."

APPENDIX TWO

Location of Hyde Park in Iowa

In 1846 a small cluster of dwellings in western Iowa received the name Hyde Park, in honor of Orson Hyde. Its inhabitants were a few of the Latter-day Saints who had arrived at the Missouri River as part of the mass exodus from persecutions in Nauvoo, Illinois. The "Hyde Park" area ceased to be a community sometime after the 1852 departure from Iowa of most of the Saints. During the decades that followed, the settlement's location became lost to historians. The site's primary significance is that here the Lord directed the Council of the Twelve to confer upon Brigham Young the presidency of the Church.

At "Hyde's Camp," James Allen Browning wrote in his autobiography, his father's family, Orson Hyde's family, and others built their log cabins. The location lay "some 7 miles So. of" Miller's Hollow. Miller's Hollow later became Kanesville and then the city of Council Bluffs. The "little burg" of Hyde's Camp, Browning added, was "situated in a large hollow, hard by springs of excellent water."[1] Another resident, Richard Bentley, described the location of "Hyde's Park" as "six miles east of Council Point on the Missouri River, and thirteen miles south of Kanesville."[2] Bentley's estimate of thirteen miles south from Kanesville is too far, unless he came a very round-about route over and around the many ridges of the area. William Appleby, in his journal entry for December 2, 1847, said that his group "arrived at Council Point about 2. O'clock P.M. Thence to Elder O. Hydes Camp, about 6 miles back from Council Point."[3]

Since the writing of these descriptions, the Missouri River has changed course, obliterating Council Point, but old maps have its location. In studying old maps and new maps together, plus other records, the site of Hyde Park proves to be southwest of the present Dumfries Post Office.

Orson Hyde moved his family from Hyde Park to Kanesville in March or April 1848. After he left, Benjamin K. Bullock received appointment as the leader of "Hydes Park Branch."[4] On an early sketch map of the beginnings of the Mormon sojourn in western Iowa, drawn by a Church member, Benjamin K. Bullock is shown settled a mile or two north of Orson Hyde.[5] Bullock apparently moved south, because the location of Bullock's Grove, named after him, and where he lived from 1850–1852, has been positively learned.

In 1987 my husband and I traveled to Council Bluffs for research. In the Pottawattamie County Engineers office, Engineers Charles E. (Gene) Hales and Carroll J. Jensen gave us kind and painstaking assistance in examining many documents. Original survey notes, made August 1851 to April 1852, show that on the survey line between Sections 25 and 26 of East Lewis Township (74 North, Range 43 West), the surveyors walked northward. They "entered Bullocks grove" one-fourth mile ("20 chains") into the Section, thus one-and-one-fourth miles north of the Mills County line. They left the settlement more than three-quarters of a mile farther north (total distance: 65 chains). Bullock's Grove, they wrote, "contains 5 Residents [i.e. dwellings] and about 70 acres improvement and in part held in common by the Residents." Aerial survey maps show this area to be a sloping wide ridge. This is obviously the location of Orson's fields.

The owner of the Hyde Park land, when we visited in 1987, was Henry Brandt. His mother, ninety years old, had lived in the area since age fifteen. She told us that when she came, trees covered the sloping ridge field beyond her present home. This field is what the original surveyors identified as Bullock's Grove. Mrs. Brandt had been told that Henry Plumer, her grandfather (adopted), settled on the land in 1851.[6] East of the field is a hollow with springs. Mr. Brandt informs that the springs have always been in the same place and have never, to his knowledge, been dry.

To compile the 1850 Federal Census of Pottawattamie County, the census taker apparently started at the county line and walked north through Bullock's Grove. He found the following families in sequence: 8. Benjamin Bullock, 9. John Riggs (son-in-law of Benjamin Bullock), 10. William Price and his sister Mary Ann (she a wife of Orson Hyde), 11. Charles Price (brother-in-law of Orson Hyde), 12. Luke Johnson (brother-in-law of Orson Hyde).

The 1851 Iowa State Census, Pottawattamie County, has, in the following order: Benjamin Bullock, Benjamin K. Bullock (son of Benjamin), Joseph Bardsley, Thomas Giles, Mr. Plummer (with wife and infant), William Price, Charles Price.

The 1852 Iowa State Census has the following, in order: Henry Plumer, David Lachlin, Mariah Ilder, William Price, Chas. Price, Benjamin Bullock.

The cited records indicate that Hyde Park became Bullock's Grove, which in turn became the Plumer Settlement, and then part of the extensive Plumer farm. Perhaps, however, in the early period the hollow remained Hyde Park and the ridge Bullock's Grove.

APPENDIX THREE

Orson Hyde's Estate

THE inventory of Orson Hyde's estate, after his death, lists the household items of each of his wives separately. Living quarters were reasonably furnished with stoves, bedsteads, lounges, bureaus, bedding, tables, chairs, cupboards, wash stands, boxes, a writing desk, sewing machines, a washing machine (with hand crank), tubs and water pails, churns, kettles (including a large copper one), kitchen utensils, mirrors, and clocks.

Farming implements, in their places in the sturdy rock farmyard buildings, included "Two Scythes & Snaths [scythe handles] & One grain Cradle, Two Augers, One Draw Knife, One Grub Hoe, Two Garden Hoes, One Pick, Two three tine forks, Two L. H. Shovels, Three Spades, One Rake, Two Axes, [and] Six Barrels." The barrels served as containers to store water and also as a place to settle out sediment from ditch water, that it could be used for washing clothes and other purposes. Orson's farm machinery amounted to "One Wagon, One Harrow, Two Ploughs, [and] One Feed cutter." Orson's fine carriage reposed in its stall, ready for his "splendid team of young traveling horses" to be buckled into the harness that matched the carriage. Other animals included ten cows, several heifers and calves, eight pigs, a crippled pony, and nearly two hundred sheep. A portion of the tall timber hay barn, attached to the commodious rock stable on the lot with the rock home, held ten tons of hay.

Orson's real estate in Spring City, independent of that earlier deeded to his wives, totaled thirty-two and one-fourth acres, worth, with structures, $886.87½. He also owned a small lot in Saint George, a gift in 1874 from George A. Smith. Orson had anticipated possibly building a winter home near the Saint George Temple.

The estate contained additional minor assets. From the days Orson used oxen he had an "Ox Yoke & bows" and "Two Ox Chains." He also had "Two thousand ft Lumber," a gun, and a few other items. He owned shares in the co-op stores in Spring City and in Provo, total worth $25.00. His personal belongings comprised: "Clothing . . . very much worn, One Bible, One Doctr & Covenant, [and] One Websters Abridged Dictionary."[1]

Decisions about division of the property resulted in Mary Ann receiving Orson's Bible, and Ann Eliza owning his other two books. Two utilitarian kettles became the four-way property of Ann Eliza, Julia, Lizzy, and Sophia. Years before, Orson had given Ann Eliza the compass he carried to Jerusalem, a treasure that she showed lovingly to grandchildren.[2]

Mary Ann and friend Frederick Olsen, Spring City's Bishop, were appointed to administer Orson Hyde's estate. Mary Ann wished to own a team, but Orson's spirited horses intimidated her. As estate administrator, she applied, March 26, 1879, to "sell one span of horses, because . . . [they are] restive and unsafe." She wanted "to use the means arising from such sale in the purchase of . . . a safer pair." She received permission, and eventually, May 13, 1880, sold Orson's team, exchanging them for a different horse and for cash to pay debts.[3]

APPENDIX FOUR

Wives

SOURCES and explanations for genealogical information are in Myrtle Stevens Hyde, *Orson Hyde Genealogy*, Vol. 1 (1997), at the Family History Library, Salt Lake City, Utah.

Sources for the period before Orson's death can be found by consulting the present book's index.

1. Marinda Nancy Johnson

Marinda Nancy Johnson: daughter of John Johnson and Alice (Elsa) Jacob; born 28 June 1815 Pomfret, Windsor, Vermont; married 4 September 1834 Kirtland, Geauga, Ohio (divorced 1870); died 24 March 1886 Salt Lake City, Salt Lake, Utah; buried Salt Lake City.

1. Nathan Hyde: b. 1835 Kirtland; d. 1835 Kirtland.

2. Laura Marinda Hyde: b. 21 May 1837 Kirtland; m. 30 May 1856 Aurelius Miner, Salt Lake City; d. 10 Aug. 1909 Salt Lake City.

3. Emily Matilda Hyde: b. 13 Dec. 1839 Nauvoo, Hancock, Illinois; m. 25 Dec. 1854 George Ogden Chase, Salt Lake City; d. 6 Dec. 1909 Salt Lake City.

4. Orson Washington Hyde: b. 9 Nov. 1843 Nauvoo; d. 23 Nov. 1843 Nauvoo.

5. Frank Henry Hyde: b. 23 Jan. 1846 Nauvoo; m. (1) Mary O'Neal, (2) 18 Jan. 1876 Marcia Amelia Hanks, Salt Lake City; d. 28 June 1908 Salt Lake City.

6. Alonzo Eugene Hyde: b. 28 Feb. 1848 Hyde Park (in what is now East Lewis Township), Pottawattamie, Iowa; m. (1) 15 Dec. 1870 Annie Maria Taylor, Salt Lake City, (2) 9 Mar. 1883 Ellen (Ella) Amelia Wilcox, Salt Lake City; d. 14/15 June 1910 Salt Lake City.

7. Delia Annette Hyde: b. 28 Dec. 1849 Kanesville (now Council Bluffs), Pottawattamie, Iowa; m. 1866 Nathan Ellis; d. 25 Dec. 1907 Battle Creek, Calhoun, Michigan.

8. Heber John Hyde: b. 10 Nov. 1852 Salt Lake City; d. 11 Nov. 1853 Salt Lake City.

9. Mary Lavinia Hyde: b. 10 July 1854 Salt Lake City; d. 29 Jan. 1855 Salt Lake City.

10. Zina Virginia Hyde: b. 23 Apr. 1858 Salt Lake City; m. 8 Jan. 1897

Joseph Bull, Salt Lake City; d. 24 Feb. 1939 San Francisco, San Francisco, California.

Marinda—tall and slender, with natural grace—undoubtedly captivated Orson's heart when he first met her in 1831. A pretty hazel-eyed girl of sixteen, she lived with her family in Hiram, Ohio, neighboring Kirtland, when Orson gave up school teaching and returned to Kirtland to investigate Mormonism. She became Orson's bride three years later.

Marinda provided steadfast support to her husband through his numerous short missions and while he served major missions to England and to the Holy Land, also during his period outside the Church. Consistently she manifested sterling devotion to the Gospel. Her trials increased her sympathy for others and developed her leadership skills.

With her husband and children she shared homes both humble and commodious in many places: Kirtland, Ohio; Far West, Missouri; Howard County, Missouri; Iowa Territory; Nauvoo, Illinois; Hyde Park, Iowa; Kanesville, Iowa; and Salt Lake City, Utah. In each location her excellent housekeeping skills added comfort.

A regal and competent woman, always well-groomed and attractive, she bestowed love and affection to those around her. After Orson and wife Mary Ann, then later wife Ann Eliza, moved from Salt Lake City to settle in Spring City, Marinda devoted her energies to her children and grandchildren, church, and community. She served as Relief Society President of her ward for seventeen years. She helped found the Deseret Hospital in Salt Lake City.

Marinda passed away in 1886 after a difficult illness, age seventy.

Sources about Marinda for the period after Orson's death:

1. Journal History, 13 January, 19 February (p. 4) 1870, 24 March (pp. 2–3) 1886.

2. Winifred Miner Stone and Florence Miner Slusser, "Marinda."

3. *Deseret News*, 31 March 1886 (p. 176).

4. See also *Woman's Exponent* 12:25; 14:165, 179, 181; 26:173–174; 37:1.

2. Martha Rebecca Browett

Martha Rebecca Browett: daughter of Thomas Browett and Martha Puller; born 5 June 1817 Tewkesbury, Gloucestershire, England; married February or March 1843 Nauvoo, Hancock, Illinois (divorced 1850); married (2) 9 December 1850 Thomas McKenzie, Kanesville (later Council Bluffs), Pottawattamie, Iowa (divorced); died 30 October 1904 Salt Lake City, Salt Lake, Utah; buried Salt Lake City.

1. Adella Marie Hyde: b. Apr. 1850 Kanesville; d. July 1850 Kanesville.

Martha met Orson after his December 1842 return to Nauvoo from the Holy Land, and she became his bride within a few months. Her tidiness and industry impressed him. As time passed, however, her exactness and her difficulty accepting hardships, together with Orson's overwhelming duties that gave him little time to meet her needs, caused a rift in their relationship, and they parted while living in Kanesville, Iowa. Martha remained with the Church and traversed the plains to Utah. Her second marriage met the same fate as her first, but she stayed in Salt Lake City.

"Being an expert seamstress and tailoress," a friend wrote of her, "she sewed for the wealthy women of Salt Lake. . . . Hours, days and years of constant sewing and strain became too severe . . . and she lost completely the sight of her eyes. She was blessed with wonderful friends and neighbors and . . . never wanted for the necessities of life. She lived her last 30 years confined to her room but she was gentle, kind and alert. She lived to be 86 years of age and died of infirmities."

Source about Martha for the period after Orson's death:

1. Arvilla Greenwood, "Steamer Trunk," *Our Pioneer Heritage* 19 (1976): 442–443.

3. Mary Ann Price

Mary Ann Price: daughter of William Price and Mary Ann Price; born 5 June 1816 Lea, Hereford, England; married 20 July 1843 Nauvoo, Hancock, Illinois; married (1) 30 June 1836 Thomas Price, Lea; died 16 June 1900 Salt Lake City, Salt Lake, Utah; buried Spring City, Sanpete, Utah.
1. Urania Hyde: b. 15 Aug. 1846 Hyde Park (in what is now East Lewis Township), Pottawattamie, Iowa; d. 27 Aug. 1846 Hyde Park.

Mary Ann, from England, married Orson Hyde in Nauvoo in 1843 as his third wife. Steady and gentle, of medium height and attractive features, she possessed a spiritual nature. She grew to love and respect Orson's wife Marinda. An increasing strength to her husband, Mary Ann accepted her role as a background person in Nauvoo and western Iowa. Her only child, born soon after the family's arrival in western Iowa, lived a mere twelve days.

While Orson supervised Carson County (in what later became western Nevada) Mary Ann was the only wife with him. Also, she accompanied him to Sanpete County and helped establish their roots in Spring City. She welcomed later wives and helped mother their children. The children affectionately called her "Ma Hyde." This title came partly because of the initials of her name.

For years after Orson's death Mary Ann lived in the Spring City rock home. At first, Julia, Sophia, and their children resided with her. Sophia moved to Provo in 1882, and Julia remained.

In 1879, Mary Ann received the calling as Sanpete Stake Relief Society President. She had served as the Spring City Ward Relief Society President for eleven years. In her new responsibility she traveled all over Sanpete County, visiting each Relief Society unit twice a year to encourage and advise. Over the years a notable feature of her addresses became her use of a God-given gift from Nauvoo days, speaking in tongues, with gratitude for the privilege.

Some winters she spent months in Saint George doing temple work and visiting, staying with her sister, Elizabeth Bentley. During one visit an accident seriously injured her hip. Doctors told her that she would likely never walk again. But prayers and priesthood blessings, coupled with Mary Ann's faith and diligent exercising, brought her a miraculous, though slow, recovery.

Mary Ann passed away in 1900, in Salt Lake City, age eighty-four, after enduring a long illness. She had lived for some time at 430 East Seventh South with the family of Julia's daughter Mary Ann and husband Herbert White. Her obituary told of the great help she had been to her husband, of her devotion as a Relief Society president, and of the love Orson's children felt for her. Funeral services were held in the Second Ward and also in Spring City, before she was "laid to rest in the Spring City cemetery at the side of her husband."

Sources about Mary Ann for the period after Orson's death:
1. Mary Ann Hyde autobiography.
2. Oscar W. Hyde, "Biography," 3.
3. Adrian H. Hess to Myrtle S. Hyde, 10 December 1979, 2.
4. "Sanpete Stake, historical records and minutes," under Relief Society.
5. *Woman's Exponent*: 9:99, 111; 11:109, 189-190; 12:92, 94, 119; 13:55; 14:101; 15:22, 74, 79; 16:31, 116, 142; 17:46, 94; 18:184-185; 20:118; 22:22, 130; 25:13, 30, 85; 26:173-174; 29:11.
6. Polk, *Salt Lake City Directory*, 1899, 435, 875.
7. "Death of Mrs. Mary A. P. Hyde," *Deseret Evening News*, 16 June 1900, 3.

4. Charlotte S. Quindlin

Charlotte S. Quindlin: daughter of William Quindlin and Jemima —; born 22 August 1802 Lower Pensnack, Salem, New Jersey; married 21 November 1852 Salt Lake City, Salt Lake, Utah (separated); married (1) — Johnson; died 3 December 1881 Mount Pleasant, Sanpete, Utah.
No children.

Charlotte's first marriage ended by her husband's death or by divorce, and she eventually associated with the Hyde family as a "domestic" in their Kanesville, Iowa, home. She trekked across the plains to Utah with them in 1852. Two years older than Orson, she became his bride soon after arriving in Utah. The marriage, however, proved unsatisfactory before 1856, and Brigham Young granted a "separation" in 1859.

The "move south" in 1858 took Charlotte to Sanpete County, where she lived first in Fort Ephraim and then in Mount Pleasant. She resided the remainder of her life in Mount Pleasant, not remarrying after her separation from Orson. "Aunty Hyde" to the town's little school children, she taught them for many years. She died at age seventy-nine.

Sources about Charlotte for the period after Orson's death:
1. "Died," *Deseret News (Weekly)*, 14 December 1881 (p. 736).
2. Hilda Madsen Longsdorf, *Mount Pleasant*, 75–76.

5. Ann Eliza Vickers

Ann Eliza Vickers: daughter of James M. Vickers and Hannah Maria Daley; born 26 January 1841 Big Neck Prairie, Madison, Illinois; married 12 March 1857 Salt Lake City, Salt Lake, Utah; died 4 May 1923 Spring City, Sanpete, Utah; buried Spring City.
1. Charles Albert Hyde: b. 13 May 1858 Springville, Utah, Utah; m. (1) 17 Aug. 1882 Sarah Ellen Justesen, Salt Lake City, (2) 30 Apr. 1909 Stella West; d. 10 May 1923 Springville.
2. George Lyman Hyde: b. 16 Mar. 1860 Salt Lake City; m. 26 Apr. 1883 Jennie Davis, Salt Lake City; d. 1 Apr. 1940 Springville.
3. Joseph Smith Hyde: b. 15 Jan. 1863 Spring City; m. 20 July 1887 Janette Louise Acord, Salt Lake City; d. 27 Feb. 1944 Salt Lake City.
4. Maria Louisa Hyde: b. 1 June 1865 Spring City; d. 31 Aug. 1867 Provo, Utah, Utah.
5. Melvin Augustus Hyde: b. 6 Sep. 1868 Spring City; d. 8 Feb. 1873 Spring City.
6. Flora Geneva Hyde: b. 2 Jan. 1871, Spring City; m. 28 Dec. 1892 Joseph Alexander Justesen, Manti, Sanpete, Utah; d. 17 July 1953 Spring City.

Ann Eliza—five feet four inches tall, with large brown eyes and lustrous brown hair—endeared herself to Orson and his older wives when she became Orson's bride in 1857 at the age of sixteen. Kind and soft-spoken, she was also already skilled in homemaking arts. Her family had been friends with Orson ever since his schoolteaching days in Ohio.

When Orson and Mary Ann moved to Sanpete County in 1860, Ann Eliza had a young son and a new baby. She remained in Salt Lake City with Marinda for two years.

She welcomed new brides into the family the same as she had been welcomed, and the five Sanpete wives learned to cooperate well under the gentle, but structured, guidance of their revered husband. Before Orson's death the sturdy log home became Ann Eliza's, and she remained there for many years.

Energetic and warm-hearted, she had numerous interests, first among them her children and then her grandchildren, but also tending her garden; washing, dying, and carding wool; quilting quilts; knitting stockings and shawls; and braiding rag rugs. In 1879 she received the calling as Second Counselor to the Spring City Relief Society President and served well.

Ann Eliza lived out her life in Spring City, eventually moving three blocks east from her log home into a "nice little modern brick home" near her son Charles. Charles' son Barney, born in 1898, "as a lad" lived "just over the fence" and gained fond memories of his soft-spoken, jolly, and precise grandmother.

A "devoted Latter-day Saint and . . . great reader of the scriptures," narrates granddaughter Maude Hyde Anderson, every "Sunday found [Ann Eliza] . . . in her place on the front row in the chapel." At home "she had a place for everything and everything in its place." In "her well-kept garden [she] raised all kinds of flowers and herbs, . . . vegetable[s], . . . berry bushes, and fruit trees. She had a few hives of bees to supply the family with honey. As a child, I thought there was nothing quite so delicious as Grandma's Pottawatomie plumb preserves made with honey, spread generously on her good home-made bread and butter. . . . She was a wonderful cook. She always raised some chickens to supply eggs and 'chicken and dumplings' for the family. She raised a few ducks also."

Widow Ann Eliza's brown eyes closed permanently in 1923. She had reached age eighty-two.

Sources about Ann Eliza for the period after Orson's death:

1. 1880 Census Spring City, household 89.

2. Florence J. Anderson to Myrtle S. Hyde, 14 September 1979.

3. Geneva Hyde Justesen to Romania Hyde Woolley, 11 October 1946, Romania Woolley Collection.

4. Barney Hyde to Myrtle S. Hyde, 14, (answer to) 22 September 1979.

5. Maude Hyde Anderson, "Ann Eliza Vickers Hyde."

6. *Improvement Era* 26 (1923):764.

6. Julia Thomene Reinert

Julia Thomene Reinert: daughter of Thomas Wessing Reinert and Barbara Kirstine Hjorth; born 13 July 1842 Aalborg, Aalborg, Denmark; married 29 August 1863 Salt Lake City, Salt Lake, Utah; married (2) William Blain; died 16 May 1919 Salt Lake City; buried Spring City, Sanpete, Utah.
1. Mary Ann Hyde: b. 5 May 1864 Spring City; m. 7 Jan. 1886 Herbert Addison White, Spring City; d. 5 Apr. 1938 Salt Lake City.
2. William Arthur Hyde: b. 20 May 1866 Ephraim, Sanpete, Utah; d. 2 Feb. 1873 Spring City.
3. Hyrum Smith Hyde: b. 23 May 1868 Spring City; m. Elizabeth Schofield; d. 23 Oct. 1943 Ogden, Weber, Utah.
4. David Victor Hyde: b. 18 July 1871 Spring City; m. 29 Nov. 1899 Mary Ann Davis, Salt Lake City; d. 1 Nov. 1951 Santa Monica, Los Angeles, California.
5. Aurelia Fiducia Hyde: b. 20 Mar. 1874 Spring City; d. 10 Dec. 1875 Spring City.

Quiet blue-eyed Julia became a part of the Hyde household soon after her autumn 1862 arrival in Spring City from Denmark when she accepted Elder Hyde's invitation to move in and assist with housework. Gentle and competent, several months later she accepted his invitation to stay permanently.

After Orson's 1878 death his Danish widows, Julia and Sophia, remained in the new rock home with Mary Ann. In 1881, President John Taylor requested Julia's daughter Mary Ann to learn telegraphy and re-establish a telegraph office in Spring City. Mary Ann learned this skill, then operated in the rock home.

In course of time, quiet widow Julia remarried. Neighbor Sarah Blain died March 10, 1880. Eventually widower William Blain courted Julia, and she said her second wedding vows. Julia again became a widow when William Blain passed away July 6, 1897. Julia resumed the surname Hyde.

After her second widowhood, Julia resided beside the creek in a small adobe and frame dwelling a block southeast of Ann Eliza's brick home. She tended a few chickens and a modest garden. Various young family members helped cut wood, gather eggs, and water the garden. "Having become an expert in needlework in her native land," daughter Mary Ann narrates, "she filled many requests, made by Z.C.M.I. for lady's silk hair nets and was noted far and near for her excellence in cooking and other household attainments. She was very active in the work of the Relief Society and was Treasurer of that organization for Sanpete Stake. Her religion to her was paramount to all else."

Julia became deaf, but functioned well in her small home. Her little dog "Prina" (Danish pronunciation; others called the dog Prinie)—white with black and brown spots, short hair, short ears, short tail—assisted her. When a visitor knocked, "Prina" grabbed Julia by the skirt and pulled her to the door to answer it.

In October 1918 Julia's health grew poor, and seven months later she died at her daughter Mary Ann's home in Salt Lake City, age seventy-six.

Sources about Julia for the period after Orson's death:
1. Mary Ann Hyde autobiography, 5.
2. 1880 Census Spring City, household 101.
3. Florence Anderson to Myrtle S. Hyde, 24 September 1979.
4. Kaye Watson, *Under The Horseshoe*, 39, 40, 41, 111.
5. "Pioneers Construct Own Telegraph Lines," *Heart Throbs of the West* 1 (1939):184-185.
6. Luella Hyde Hess paper.
7. The date of Julia's marriage to William Blain has not been found. Julia does not appear on William Blain (born 1839) family group records, Patron's Section, Family History Library. Neither does her Blain marriage appear in Hyde family records. Probably she married him only a few years, or maybe months, before his 1897 death. In Sanpete County Land Records, "Spring City Townsite Abstracts," 1:72 (1884) and 1:71 (1886) her last name is Hyde. July 13, 1897, seven days after her second husband's death, she quit-claimed, as Julia T. Blain, Blain property to William's son (Deed 40:525-526). April 9, 1898, she received a share of William Blain's estate as his widow (Deed A18:491-493). In 1906 she was listed as "Julia T. Hyde, now Blain" ("Abstracts," B:88). Subsequent land records list her as Julia T. Hyde, indicating that she resumed the name Hyde.
8. Barney Hyde to Myrtle S. Hyde, late September 1979, June 1980, 13 May 1983 (p. 3).
9. Mary Ann H. White, "Julia T. Reinart Hyde."
10. Morgan Hyde White, interview, 1984.
11. Morgan Hyde White to Myrtle S. Hyde, 9 December 1984.
12. Morgan Hyde White, *Autobiography*, 55.
13. "Mrs. Julia T. Hyde Dies at Advanced Age," *Deseret Evening News*, 19 May 1919, 2.

7. Elisabeth Josephine Gallier

Elisabeth (Lizzy) Josephine Gallier: daughter of Peter Galli and Magdalena Haesler; born 14 February 1840 Guendlischwand, Gsteig, Bern, Switzerland; married 15 October 1864 Salt Lake City, Salt Lake, Utah; died 17 March 1920 Farmington, Davis, Utah; buried Spring City, Sanpete, Utah.
1. Luella Minerva Hyde: b. 12 Aug. 1865 Spring City; m. 24 Apr. 1901 David Hess, Logan, Cache, Utah; d. Jan. 1939 Farmington.

2. Orson Hyde: b. 7 Dec. 1866 Spring City; unmarried; d. 10 June 1946 Salt Lake City.

3. Odean Horatio Hyde: b. 24 July 1868 Spring City; m. Marie Hiller; d. 27 Nov. 1927 Salt Lake City.

4. Nathan Hyde: b. 19 Mar. 1870 Spring City; d. 22 Feb. 1871 Spring City.

5. Ernest Godfrey Hyde: b. 3 Apr. 1873 Spring City; d. 2 Feb. 1889 Salt Lake City.

When Elisabeth, called Lizzy—tall and efficient and spiritual—became a member of Orson's Spring City household in 1864, the number of wives in the home became four. Children already numbered four. Lizzy had arrived in Utah two years previously, as part of a family of faithful Church members from Switzerland.

When first a widow, after Orson's death, Lizzy continued in her own home, near Ann Eliza's. Six years later she and her three children moved to Salt Lake City, where her daughter Luella had secured a teaching position. Leaving, however, was difficult. Spring City held a special place in their hearts. "The inhabitants of my childhood home[town]," Luella later wrote, "were composed for [the] most part of Mormons of the 'Good Old Fashioned Kind,' . . . [with] simplicity and frugality in all things[,] with love & charity for each other. A neighbor's happiness, my happiness. A neighbor's sorrow, my sorrow."

In Salt Lake City, Lizzy struggled to stretch her means for her family's needs, and in 1900 she and her three children (none yet married) moved several miles north to the farming community of Farmington. Lizzy continued her domestic activities, always persistent at daily chores. She prepared scrumptious pork sausage. She cured delicious ham and bacon. She dried fruit. She made cheese and pickles. She fermented sauerkraut. She dyed rags, tore them into strips that she and her daughter sewed together, wound the strips into balls that a neighbor family wove into carpet, and enjoyed the look and feel of the carpet. Lizzy's daughter gave birth to Lizzy's only grandchild who reached adulthood, Adrian Hess.

Lizzy passed away in Farmington in 1920. She had suffered a stroke four years before, which left her an invalid. After her stroke, grandson Adrian says, "[m]y mother cared for her in our home until her death. . . . During the time she was confined to her . . . rocker, she [lost] the [English] language [reverted to her Swiss-German] & became very hard to understand." She passed away at the age of eighty years, and was transported lovingly to Spring City for burial.

Sources about Lizzy for the period after Orson's death:
1. 1880 Census Spring City, household 87 [surname Hoyt, in error].
2. Adrian Hess to Myrtle S. Hyde, 8, 15 November 1979.

3. Luella Hyde Hess paper.

4. Elizabeth J. Hyde to Wilford Woodruff, 21 December 1897, HDC.

5. Polk, *Salt Lake City Directory* 1899:435, 1900:380.

6. Morgan Hyde White, *Autobiography*, 40, 42.

7. Elizabeth [Lizzy] Hyde obituary, *Deseret Evening News*, 18 March 1920 (which states that her death age was seventy-six—Lizzy had been confused about her age since young womanhood).

8. Spring City Cemetery.

8. Sophia Margaret Lyon

Sophia Margaret Lyon: daughter of James Martin Lyon and Susannah Olmstead; born 6 February 1847 Copenhagen, Copenhagen, Denmark; married 10 October 1865 Salt Lake City, Salt Lake, Utah; married (2) 18 September 1885 Sven Wilhelm Fogelberg, Logan, Cache, Utah (divorced); died 25 March 1932 Salt Lake City; buried Spring City, Sanpete, Utah.

1. Brigham Young Hyde: b. 21 Apr. 1867 Ephraim, Sanpete, Utah; d. 22 Jan. 1869 Spring City.

2. Oscar Waldemar Hyde: b. 16 Apr. 1869 Ephraim; m. 11 Feb. 1892 Estella Strong, Manti, Sanpete, Utah; d. 25 Dec. 1935 Salt Lake City.

3. daughter Hyde: b. about 1871 Ephraim or Spring City; d. about 1871 Ephraim or Spring City.

4. Sterling Washburn Hyde: b. 16 Mar. 1872 Spring City; d. 1 Apr. 1874 Spring City.

5. Royal Justus Hyde: b. 14 June 1874 Spring City; d. 25 June 1893 Denver, Arapahoe, Colorado.

Sophia, a diminutive (five feet tall) bride in 1865, at age eighteen, added her own effervescent sparkle to the Hyde home. She and Orson shared the unusual experience of receiving gold from a stranger for journeys—his to the Holy Land, and hers from Denmark to Utah.

After Orson's death Sophia's cheerfulness served her well. For three-and-a-half years she and her children remained in Spring City, living congenially in the rock home with Mary Ann, Julia, and Julia's children. Assisting Sophia was a young Swedish girl, Agnes E. Jack, whom Sophia had "adopted." In 1882 Sophia moved to Provo that her son Oscar could attend the Brigham Young Academy. She took in boarders, even purchased a home and lot. Among her welcome boarders, over the years, were several of Orson's children who attended the Academy.

In 1885 she married Wilhelm Fogelberg, music instructor at the Academy. However, after a few years, and two new babies (the second died at age eighteen months after a fall from his highchair), the marriage became unbearable for Sophia. Wilhelm's threats sent her into hiding with friends.

Her unfortunate situation contributed to rebellion in her son Royal, and he ran away to Denver, where he met an untimely death.

Though Sophia's second marriage brought sadness to her, her first son by this marriage became her comfort and strength. At his birth, in family discussion about what the baby's name should be, Sophia liked the suggestion that helper Agnes offered, that he be named Sterling after Sophia's baby boy who had died thirteen years before. Wilhelm agreed, and Sterling the baby became. Days passed before Sophia recalled words that her first husband, Orson Hyde, had uttered the day he and Sophia laid her first Sterling in a tiny grave. Sophia now remembered the love in Orson's manner when he said to her, "Sophia, you shall have Sterling again in this life."

Sophia resumed the surname Hyde. From 1907 until her death, she lived in a small home at 20 West North Temple, far back from the street north of the Temple block. This was just east of where Marinda had lived, and where Marinda's son Alonzo's family still lived. A long path, under trees, led guests to her welcoming door. Still cheerful, energetic, and generous, Sophia enjoyed having her home everyone's home; she continually had guests. Son Sterling remained with her. She suffered a stroke in 1930, and Sterling devotedly cared for her. Her sunny disposition remained, in spite of her limitations. She died at her home two years later, 1932, age eighty-five.

At Sophia's funeral her bishop, Nicholas G. Smith, praised her life of cheerfulness and service, and he also praised the accomplishments of the family to which she belonged. "I pray," he continued, ". . . [that] the spirit of Orson Hyde [and his work] may go down to the generations yet to come; with faith in God and in His Church, and a willingness to devote everything they have in the world to this great cause. . . ."

Sophia received burial in the Spring City Cemetery, in the cluster with Orson, Mary Ann, Ann Eliza, Julia, and Lizzy. Still living, of Orson's thirty-three children were Marinda's Zina; Ann Eliza's George, Joe, and Geneva; Julia's Mary Ann, Hyrum, and David; Lizzy's Luella and Orson; and Sophia's Oscar. Sophia's death brought to a close, in his family, the earthly lives of the generation of Orson Hyde. But Orson Hyde's legacy would live on.

Sources about Sophia for the period after Orson's death:

1. Mary Ann Hyde autobiography, 5.
2. 1880 Census Spring City, household 101.
3. Florence Anderson to Myrtle S. Hyde, 24 September 1979.
4. Oscar W. Hyde, "Biography."
5. Utah County Deed Abstracts, Block 14, Plat B (Sophia purchased, 26 October 1883).
6. Sterling Fogelberg, "Sophia."
7. 1900 Census, Provo, Utah, Enumeration District 163, sheet 21.

8. Logan Temple Sealings, 18 September 1885 (for time only).

9. *Woman's Exponent* 16 (1888): "Notes By The Way," 116, "Correspondence," 192.

10. Sophia Hyde to Wilford Woodruff, 1892, HDC.

11. "Sorrowful News," *Deseret Evening News*, 26 June 1893, 4.

12. Polk, *Salt Lake City Directory* 1908:566.

13. Stella Miller interview, 1979.

14. Barney Hyde to Myrtle S. Hyde, 17 December 1984.

15. Villa Barrow interview, 3 (filed with papers about Orson's first wife, Marinda).

16. "Sophia funeral," 6, 9, 13.

17. Sophia Hyde obituary, *Deseret Evening News*, 25 March 1932, sec. 2, 5.

BIBLIOGRAPHICAL ESSAY

About Orson Hyde's Journals

PEOPLE ask repeatedly if Orson Hyde kept journals. He apparently kept several, but only one is known to exist, that of his 1832 mission with Samuel Smith.[1] In 1837, Heber C. Kimball copied from another of Orson's journals when they served together on a mission in England.[2]

But misfortune seems to have ended the practice. Two of Orson's sons, Joseph and George, and granddaughter Romania Hyde Woolley, said that his journals were lost in a river. Joseph named it as the Mississippi; George called it a "large" river; Romania identified it as the Missouri in 1846. Combining the accounts: Orson Hyde and Parley P. Pratt, hastening, "took passage aboard a flat boat, laden with wood." The "skip, or boat, got into a whirl pool and capsized." Orson had "kept a very close diary [diaries] on his travels and mission work . . . until" his "collections, letters, writings, scrap books, etc., were deposited" in the river. The men had to "swim for their lives. Both being good swimmers—and with a protecting hand of a kind Providence—they made it," landing "right under some heavy embankments."[3]

Because these family accounts agree that a river swallowed several of his diaries, along with other papers, the accident likely occurred during a move of household goods, rather than when Orson was traveling. The year 1846, given by Romania, seems a probable time, during one of Orson's crossings of the Missouri River. He and Parley P. Pratt had been asked to leave hastily for a mission to England. Before leaving, Orson took his family and belongings back to the east side of the river. He may have done this in several trips and on one of them lost his papers.

Letters to Wives

The only original letters found, written by Orson to his wives, are those to Mary Ann. Undoubtedly he wrote to the other wives also, but those messages were apparently not saved.

About Sources and Interpreting Sources

During the years that this book about Orson Hyde has been one of my primary endeavors, I have felt intense gratitude to numerous authors and editors. Their efforts have made mine easier. They published the results of their diligent efforts in compiling historical information that relates to my project. Many items would have been undiscovered without their help.

However, regarding certain aspects of the life of Orson Hyde, an unfortunate situation has arisen over the decades. Probably it evolved innocently. Some authors apparently build their own views almost solely on foundations laid by others, and occasionally those foundations have serious, but unobvious, defects. A graphic example of what can result from this practice is seen in perceptions about Orson Hyde. Authors have noted that Brigham Young and Orson had differences of opinion. This is true. But, some authors have incorrectly used this fact as a whole foundation or have built upon other authors' assumptions. As years passed, this practice gave Orson the reputation of a maverick (a rebel, a dissenter, a nonconformist). This reputation has come in error. As part of this, a legend has grown that Brigham Young and Orson Hyde not only had differences of opinion but feuded about them. Again, the basic truth has been amplified merely by opinion, or by authors building "facts" upon the incorrect premises of others.

No primary document found substantiates that Orson purposely dissented from Brigham Young or that the two feuded. Yes, Brigham Young corrected Orson (and many others), sometimes severely, but Orson *never* retaliated. A feud requires combatants. Orson accepted the corrections. Though a difficult accomplishment at times, self-control won out.

Brigham Young used Orson Hyde's blunders to assist other people in understanding correct principles. President Young knew Orson's faith to be strong enough to withstand criticism of actions, and Orson understood the President's methods. Because of these things, caution has been used with the interpretations of other authors, especially when these interpretations are disparaging or seem to lack faith in God. Orson Hyde, an Apostle of the Lord Jesus Christ, had implicit faith in God, and reason implores that his book reflects this same attribute.

For reaching conclusions, documents have been sought that were made at the time of the happenings and by the people involved. What people said at the time should generally have more basic understanding of an issue in its context than later interpretations. When consulting articles and books by others, where sources have already been evaluated, I have tried to use extra care in being objective about the conclusions. Many times the conclusions have promoted further inquisitiveness, exploration, and verification. In another positive aspect, other authors' bibliographies and source notes have been a valuable help in sleuthing. Thank you, authors, for your research, your presentations, your source notes, and your bibliographies! May mine, as well, serve others.

The challenge of composing a biography is to try to capture the twinkle in the eye, the laughter in the voice, and the tear on the cheek without having the privilege of seeing, hearing, or touching these in the inanimate written sources. Obviously, all historical writers will at times err regarding this. Writers cannot perceive and describe completely the meaning of words portrayed when they were fresh, when all background emotions and circumstances were a natural part of the scene. While attempting to interpret past events, I have tried to err on the side of compassion rather than on the side of condemnation, and I take full responsibility for all interpretations. In spite of good intentions and extensive study, errors, both of fact and of understanding, have undoubtedly slipped into Orson Hyde's story. For these mistakes I apologize. All effort has been toward depicting his life accurately.

ACKNOWLEDGMENTS

I heard the expression from somewhere that "it takes a village to rear a child." Likewise, it has taken a village of people–many people, with many attributes–to provide what has been needed for this book. To the entire village I express my gratitude.

From early in the endeavor, I thank my predecessors in researching and writing about Orson Hyde: Marvin S. Hill for his Master's thesis, and Howard H. Barron for his biography. I checked all of the source notes in the works of these two men and built upon their foundations, using my own conclusions.

A good number of Orson Hyde's descendants, and also relatives of his wives, have assisted. Three of Orson's grandsons–Barney H. Hyde, Morgan H. White, and Adrian H. Hess–were wonderfully cooperative in answering questions and delving into their memories. Villa Fenton Barrow also shared remembrances. Marjory Hyde Eldredge and Stella Frisby Miller provided valuable records. Additional documents were graciously furnished by Dorothy S. Rogers, Jane Buckmiller, LeRoi Bentley, Lucille P. Jacob, Florence J. Anderson, Melva G. Mitchell, Joyce Hooker, Aleene LaBaron, and others. Thank you all, ever so much.

For use of the most extensive collection of Orson Hyde material, adequate gratitude cannot be expressed. Orson's granddaughter, Romania Hyde Woolley, gathered and preserved many family items and assisted her father, Orson's son Joseph, to record his memories. All of this was generously shared with me by her daughter, Virginia Woolley Quealy. Thank you, thank you, Virginia.

Many librarians and archivists gave kindness and helpfulness. Among these are the staffs of libraries at the University of Utah and Brigham Young University, and the staffs of archives at the Utah State Historical Society, the Utah State Archives, the Nevada State Archives, the County Engineers' office in Council Bluffs (Iowa), the Salt Lake County offices, and the Sanpete County offices. A special thanks has been earned by the personnel, over many years, of the Historical Department of The Church of Jesus Christ of Latter-day Saints; they have been kind, helpful, patient, informative, and consoling. My thankfulness abounds.

Special accolades of praise are due Charles W. (Bill) Stuart, the teacher-writer of marvelous knowledge who gave me prodigious time and patience during three years of consultation before his death in 1985. I also thank his widow Betty for her interest.

Other friends, too, have been of treasured aid. Sherman Young was instrumental in starting me on the Orson Hyde path that led to the village of helpers. Jeffrey Kahn in the beginning gave me great encouragement. Mark Martin kindly gave me books that had been his about the Jews. Lawrence Miner and his then wife Kisty helped with research. Everett L. Cooley shared valuable insights into the process of creating books. Madelyn Player and I enjoyed sharing Iowa research. Elaine Speakman was generous with Johnson information. Gail Holmes gave valuable suggestions. Carolyn Mollinet read my drafts, giving me the advantages of her knowledge of grammar and composition. LaVal Spencer's reading of the drafts and expert comments became a decided asset to progress. Margaret (Peggy) Chapple, by reading and pondering and discussing, gave marvelous encouragement. Calvin Stephens, whose exceptional knowledge of doctrine and history he willingly imparted, read two drafts of the book and offered excellent counsel. My gratitude is immense.

My sister, Nelean Meadows, has been a continuing support. She has read and commented and has inspired confidence. Thank you, Nelean.

Most of my children, and the choice partners they married, read parts of the book and were helpful. Daughter Marilyn (Cook) saw me through to the end, reading and re-reading. Son Steve, in the final stages, scrutinized carefully. Thank you all.

Numerous persons have assisted just by being interested in my pursuit. This has been strengthening.

Thanks, too, go to Linda Taylor at Agreka Books for her expertise and to Bryan Baker of Quality Impressions for maps and for technical help.

Heartfelt thanksgiving goes to my husband, for believing in me and for rendering marvelous support and patience.

Regarding various facets of the project, I feel that I should acknowledge that guidance from spiritual realms has been perceived. And, all along, with Orson I have laughed, and I have wept. For these rewarding experiences I express reverence.

Many other people deserve personal gratitude. I thank you too. When I entered the village of this endeavor many of the inhabitants were unfamiliar. I feel deeply grateful for new friends made and new horizons reached because of the interest and assistance given.

ABBREVIATIONS

THE following abbreviations are used in the Notes and in the Bibliography to reference people, manuscripts, publications, and record repositories. The sources here listed have short citations; full citations appear in the Bibliography.

BE	A. Jenson. *Biographical Encyclopedia.*
BoM	The Book of Mormon.
BY	Brigham Young.
BYA	L. J. Arrington. *Brigham Young.*
BYC	Brigham Young Collection. HDC.
BYL	Brigham Young Letterbook. BYC.
BYOJ	Brigham Young Office Journals. BYC.
BYUL	Harold B. Lee Library, Brigham Young University, Provo, Utah.
BYUS	*Brigham Young University Studies.*
CFW	O. Hyde. *A Cry from the Wilderness.*
CHC	B. H. Roberts. *Comprehensive History.*
D&C	Doctrine and Covenants.
DEN	*Deseret Evening News.* (See DN.)
DN	*Deseret News.* Title varies: *Deseret News (Weekly), Deseret Evening News.*
DNW	*Deseret News (Weekly).* (See DN.)
EnA	*Encyclopedia Americana.*
ETB	Ezra T. Benson.
FG	*Frontier Guardian.*
FG&IS	*Frontier Guardian and Iowa Sentinel.*
FHL	Family History Library of The Church of Jesus Christ of Latter-day Saints, Salt Lake City, Utah.
GAS	George A. Smith.
GASC	George A. Smith Collection. HDC.
GCM	General Church Minutes.
HC	J. Smith. *History of The Church.*
HCK	Heber C. Kimball.
HCKK	S. B. Kimball. *Heber C. Kimball.*
HCKW	O. F. Whitney. *Heber C. Kimball.*
HDC	Library-Archives of the Historical Department, The Church of Jesus Christ of Latter-day Saints, Church Office Building, Salt Lake City, Utah. (Materials used and quoted by permission.)
HOH	Historian's Office. "History of the Church." HDC.
HOJ	Historian's Office Journals. HDC.
HSD	Hosea Stout. *Diary.*
JD	*Journal of Discourses.*
JFSE	J. F. Smith. *Essentials in Church History.*

JH	Journal History.
JI	*Juvenile Instructor.*
JS	Joseph Smith.
JSH	J. S. Hyde. "Orson Hyde."
JSHG	J. S. Hyde. "Hyde Genealogy," *Utah Genealogical and Historical Magazine* 4.
JT	John Taylor.
JTP	John Taylor Presidential Papers. HDC.
LDS	The Church of Jesus Christ of Latter-day Saints.
MA	*Latter Day Saints' Messenger and Advocate.*
MAPH	Mary Ann Price Hyde.
MAPHA	Mary Ann Price Hyde. "Autobiography."
MFP	J. R. Clark. *Messages of the First Presidency.*
MS	*The Latter-day Saints Millennial Star.*
MT	Minutes of Tabernacle meetings, Salt Lake City.
OH	Orson Hyde.
OHH	O. Hyde. "History of Orson Hyde."
OP	Orson Pratt.
OPE	B. England. *Orson Pratt.*
OPJ	O. Pratt. *Orson Pratt Journals.*
PH	Daughters of Utah Pioneers. *Our Pioneer Heritage.*
PHCM	Pottawattamie High Council Minutes.
PPP	Parley P. Pratt.
PPPA	*Autobiography of Parley Parker Pratt.*
RWC	Romania Jeannette Hyde Woolley Collection. HDC.
T&M	O. Hyde. *Travels and Ministry.*
TPH	Daughters of Utah Pioneers. *Treasures of Pioneer History.*
TS	*The Times and Seasons.*
USA	Utah State Archives. Salt Lake City, Utah.
USHS	Library and Archives of the Utah State Historical Society, Salt Lake City, Utah.
UUL	Special Collections, Marriott Library, University of Utah. Salt Lake City, Utah.
WB	*The Western Bugle.*
WE	*Woman's Exponent.*
WNNP	W. N. Nordgren. Papers. HDC.
WR	Willard Richards.
WRP	Willard Richards. Papers. HDC.
WW	Wilford Woodruff.
WWC	M. F. Cowley. *Wilford Woodruff.*
WWJ	W. Woodruff. *Wilford Woodruff's Journal.*

NOTES

To save space, because the sources are extensive, a few devices have been employed:
1. Letter symbols are used. These are identified in the Abbreviations list preceding.
2. Shortened versions are used. Full citations of these are in the Bibliography.
3. Some note numbers seem strangely placed in the text. This is because many of them pertain to several items, each note covering everything since the previous note.

Quoted items appear as in the originals unless otherwise stated in notes.

CHAPTER 1   . . . *a marvellous work and a wonder. . . . (1805–1831)*

[1] JSH, 8 (dialogue condensed), 97; OHH, DN, 5 May 1858 (parts used in this chapter reprinted MS 26 [1864]:742-744, 760-761); Geneva Justesen to Romania Woolley, 11 October 1946, RWC.

[2] *History Lorain County*, 157-167; JSH, 5, 7; OHH.

[3] Photographs of Orson Hyde.

[4] OHH; JSH, 7, 8, 97; BoM, 1830 printing; Woodward, "Reminiscences," 191.

[5] OHH (punctuation modified slightly).

[6] JSH, 99 (modified to dialogue).

[7] OHH; JSH, 4 (modified to dialogue); BYOJ, 10 December 1861 (p. 323).

[8] OHH (condensed, and punctuation modified slightly); "Pioneer Times," Hadden Scrapbook, 8.

[9] The Wheeler farm was Kirtland Tract 1, Lot 8: Geauga County Deeds 19:61 and Lake, *Atlas*, 47; OHH; JSH, 4-5.

[10] OHH (punctuation modified).

About Nathan Wheeler's family: Geauga County Probate Records D:19; Geauga County Deeds 18:272; Campbell, Sharpe, and Basset, *Seymour*, 591.

The "quarter cent" was in mills. In circulation were mills, tokens worth fractions of a penny, one mill being one-tenth of a cent. Mill tokens were still used (for tax) during the childhood of the author.

[11] OHH; the Newell foundry was on Mentor Tract 1, Lot 101: *History Geauga and Lake Counties*, 251, and Lake, *Atlas*, 31; EnA, s.v. "Iron and Steel Industry in the Western Hemisphere" by John W. W. Sullivan, "Massachusetts": Saugus Ironworks Restoration.

[12] OHH (punctuation modified slightly); EnA, s.v. "Textile Machinery" by Nathaniel M. Mitchell; Cowley, "Abigail Gloyd Hyde."

[13] OHH (punctuation modified); *Painesville Telegraph*, 13 May (p. 3), 29 December (p. 3) 1826; EnA, s.v. "Potash" by H. I. Smith, "Pearl Ash." Orson may have clerked in two locations for Gilbert and Whitney, their earlier small store and the new corner one (see "Kirtland. A Boy's Recollections," Hadden Scrapbook, 13).

[14] OHH; Cochran and Cochran, *Captives*, 68, 69; McKiernan, "Sidney Rigdon," 13, 16-17; Hayden, *Disciples*, 186, 192.

[15] OHH; *History Geauga and Lake Counties*, 35, 61.

[16]   OHH; Hayden, *Disciples*, 184, 191, 197; Wickham, *Pioneer Women* 1 (1896):101; JSH, 5.

[17]   OHH (modified slightly, part to present tense); JSH, 8 (punctuation modified slightly); Woodward, "Reminiscences," 191.

[18]   "Kirtland. A Boy's Recollections," Hadden Scrapbook, 13; Geauga County Deeds 12:627; OHH; HC 1:188.

[19]   OHH; JSH, 10; OH lecture, 6 October 1854, JD 2:81.

[20]   Genesis 9:8-9, 12:7, 19:1, 32:30; Exodus 3:2; Daniel 6:21-22.

[21]   Genesis 6:13-16; Exodus 7-11; 1 Kings 17; Isaiah; Jeremiah; Ezekiel.

[22]   Johnson family records; Tullidge, *Women*, 403-404; Luke Johnson, "History," MS 26 (31 December 1864):834; Hayden, *Disciples*, 250-251.

[23]   Stocks, "Book of Mormon Publishing," 37; OHH.

[24]   In this explanation all information is in the Book of Mormon unless otherwise stated. Specific quotations have their own notes.

[25]   See 2 Kings 17:13-15; 2 Chronicles 36:15-16; Jeremiah 26:18, 20.

[26]   OHH; Hayden, *Disciples*, 196-197.

[27]   HC 1:2, 206, 5:210; PPPA, 45-46; "Joseph Smith, The Prophet," *Young Woman's Journal*, December 1905, 548-558; Hatch, "Joseph Smith," 65-73; OHH.

[28]   This narrative generally follows Orson Hyde's 1842 account of the life of Joseph Smith, published in CFW, 6-15. However, Orson Hyde and his friends borrowed written words from one another at will, added and deleted as they chose, and published the results as their own. Part of Orson Hyde's was first published by Orson Pratt in 1840 in *Interesting Account of Several Remarkable Visions. . .* , 3-14 (in OPJ, 466-473). Part of it was first published by Oliver Cowdery in 1835 in MA, volumes 1, 2. Orson Hyde added a few comments of his own. These three writers associated closely with the Prophet and talked with him about details of his life. Careful comparison has been made with the sources Orson Hyde used and also with Joseph Smith's own 1838 account, published as Joseph Smith–History, in The Pearl of Great Price. The following notes show the earliest published sources of quoted (and some unquoted) material.

[29]   JS–History, v. 17.

[30]   OP, *Interesting Account*, 5.

[31]   Malachi 4:5.

[32]   Isaiah 11:12.

[33]   Cowdery, MA 1:157, 2:197-199 (punctuation modified slightly). Regarding Joseph Smith's vision see also L. Smith, *Joseph Smith*, 81.

[34]   Cowdery, MA 2:198-199.

[35]   HC 4:537.

[36]   JS–History, vv. 66, 67; L. Smith, *Joseph Smith*, 138-141.

[37]   "The Testimony of Three Witnesses," and "The Testimony of Eight Witnesses," BoM; D&C 17:3-4; L. Smith, *Joseph Smith*, 152.

CHAPTER 2   *. . . saints [and] walk. . . . (1831-1832)*

[1]   McConkie, *Doctrine*, 667.

[2]   OHH, DN, 5 May 1858 (parts used in this chapter reprinted MS 26 [1864]:760-761, 774); HC 1:215; "The Way It Looks Today," *Ensign*, January 1979, 32; D&C 20:

73-74; Mosiah 18:8-10, BoM.

Orson later recollected his baptism date as October 30, 1831 (OHH). Joseph Smith's record has it as the "first Sunday in October" ("History of Joseph Smith," TS 5 [1 April 1844]:481), which was October 2. This date is obviously correct. Orson was a member of the Church before October 10, as this chapter shows.

3   JS–History vv. 68-69, 72, 72 footnote, Pearl of Great Price.

4   OHH; JS–History v. 70; D&C 20:38, 43, 107:3-4; HC 1:40 footnote.

5   OHH; "History Smith," TS 5:481-482 (punctuation modified slightly).

6   OHH.

7   *Far West Record,* 15-16, 19-21, 23-26; HC 1:219, 238, 245; JH, 26 October 1831 (credentials of Emer Harris, one of the committee).

8   *Far West Record,* 26, 27; "The Way It Looks," *Ensign,* January 1979, 38,39; Johnson family records; HC 1:226 (note), 227, 229; D&C 57:2-3, 68:1, 6, 7, 11-12; BYOJ, 14 April 1862 (pp. 361-362). The revelations of the Lord explain "the congregations of the wicked" as people not acquainted with His voice (D&C 84:49-53) (see also Brewster, *Encyclopedia,* 97).

9   OHH; "Joseph Smith, The Prophet," *Young Woman's Journal,* December 1905, 551; Woodward, "Reminiscences," 191; JH, 13 December 1831 (Hyrum left Kirtland this day for another mission, so he and Orson had already returned).

10   HC 1:242-243; JH, 31 December 1831; OPJ, 11-12; PPPA, 62; D&C 75:3-4, 13; OH, 1832 journal, 21 October 1832.

11   Rigdon, *Appeal,* 2nd Edition, preface; OH to JS, 15 June 1841, TS 2 (1 October 1841):552-553 (reprinted HC 4:375). The preface to Sidney's revised *Appeal,* dated 11 July 1840, was written by Orson Hyde. He stated that Joseph Smith gave him the blessing about Jerusalem "near eight years ago." Eight years before July of 1840 was July of 1832. In that month Orson had been gone from the Kirtland area since a few days after the 25 January Amherst conference. The conference was the *nearest* time that the Prophet could have given him the blessing. In Orson's June 1841 letter he quoted the Jerusalem part of his blessing and said that Joseph Smith pronounced it "about nine years ago."

12   OH, 1832 journal; S. Smith, 1832 journal. These two journals are used without specific source references, except for quotes not identified in text. Knapsacks are assumed. Samuel carried one on a previous mission (HC 7:218). Necessities included a change of clothing (OPJ, 12) and probably a blanket.

13   HC 7:222; JH, 11 May 1870; OHH; Rollins, "Life," 2.

14   D&C 75:19-20.

15   Quote from OH journal, 1 April 1832.

16   Hill, *Buffalo,* 267, 269, 271; quote from OH journal, 8 April 1838.

17   OHH (order changed, and typesetter's error corrected).

18   Sharpe, *Seymour,* 77; Jones, *Brewster* 1:297-298.

19   Quotes from OH journal, 6-8 June 1838 (punctuation modified slightly).

20   Vedder, *Greene County.*

21   Hyde family records; "Orson Hyde," *Seymour Record,* 19 December 1878, 2; 1810 Census, Derby, Connecticut; Sharpe, *Seymour,* 59; Joseph S. Hyde to George L. Hyde, 15 June 1920, RWC (order rearranged, number spelled out, punctuation modified slightly).

²² Quote from Smith journal, 12 June 1832 (spelling modified slightly).
²³ Visit to Boston by author.
²⁴ Quote from Smith journal, 22 June 1832.
²⁵ Quote from Smith journal, 28 June 1832 (spelling modified slightly).
²⁶ Quote from Smith journal, 2 July 1832.
²⁷ Early 12th Ward L.D.S. Records, Salt Lake City, 11; Records of Emer Harris (who baptized Vienna, 12 July 1831, and was in Kirtland at the time); Tullidge, *Women*, 441.
²⁸ OHH.
²⁹ Spelling and punctuation are modified slightly in these OH journal quotes.
³⁰ North, *North*, 135-136; OHH (parts of dialogue modified slightly); Scales, *Strafford County*, 222; quotes from Smith journal, 15 September 1832; OH journal, 16 September 1832.
³¹ Quote from OH journal, 25 September 1832.
³² Quote from OH journal.
³³ Quotes from OH journal, 25 September, 21 November 1832.
³⁴ Quotes from OH journal, 4 December 1832.

CHAPTER 3   *. . . prepare. . . . (1832-1834)*
¹ HC 1:261-266, 272; L. Smith, *Joseph Smith*, 223, 224 (notes).
² D&C 84 (quotes are from vv. 14-16, 6, 12, 18, 24, 26), 88 (quotes are from vv. 1, 2, 70, 74, 77, 81, 82, 127, 137); HC 1:316; Woodford, "Revelations," 29.
³ HC 1:317; D&C 88:138; Brewster, *Encyclopedia*, 50.
⁴ D&C 57:1-3; HC 1:315-321.
⁵ HC 1:297 (and note), 322-323; O. Peterson, "Schools," 17-18; Backman, *Heavens Resound*, 264-266; "The Way it Looks Today," *Ensign*, January 1979, 34, 35; Arlen Clement to Myrtle S. Hyde, 11 February 1985.
⁶ HC 1:323; O. Peterson, "Schools," 26; D&C 27:2.
⁷ D&C 88:78-79, 118, 122; O. Peterson, "Schools," 19-22.
⁸ Zebedee Coltrin testimony, Spanish Fork high priests meeting, 5 February 1878, 99; D&C 89; O. Peterson, "Schools," 16, 24, 28; BY remarks, 8 February 1868, JD 12:158; OH to BY, 3 July 1855, BYC.
⁹ HC 1:334-335; O. Peterson, "Schools," 29; Kirtland Council, 16-17; Salt Lake School of the Prophets, 3 October 1883, 60 (modified to dialogue).
¹⁰ HC 1:340; OHH, DN, 12 May 1858 (parts used in this chapter reprinted MS 26 [1864]:776, 790); Kirtland Council, 15.
¹¹ OH to BY, 27 February 1859 (modified to dialogue) (gives amount as $280, but recalled years later), BYC; D&C 95:1-3; JSH, 11; HC 2:336 (has amount as $275, recalled in 1835).
¹² HC 1:125, 334, 353, 444.
¹³ HC 1:353, 400; JH, 23 July 1833; Coltrin diary (spelling and punctuation modified).
¹⁴ HC 1:417, 407, 372-376; Church Educational System, *Church History*, 130-132.
¹⁵ HC 1:376, 390-395, 398-399, 411-412, 454; L. Smith, *Joseph Smith*, 225.
¹⁶ HC 1:417, 450; OHH; Knight, "Journal," 71.
¹⁷ HC 1:410-415; Knight, "Journal," 79; D&C 100:13-14.

[18]   OH to Editors, 8 November 1833, "The Outrage in Jackson County, Missouri," and OH to Editor, December 1833, *Evening and Morning Star* 2 (December 1833):118-120; HC 1:423-438, 446; OHH (modified to dialogue).

[19]   HC 1:418, 453, 454 (part modified to dialogue); D&C 58:3-4, 101:1, 4, 5, 76, 77, 93.

[20]   HC 1:475, 2:2-3, 28-32, 34-35, 39-40; D&C 102:2, 3, 103:22, 27, 30, 35.

[21]   HC 1:127, 2:40 (note), 44, 48-49; OPJ, 41; PPPA, 109.

[22]   OH, "I am going to the Valley, and shall I take the Guardian?" FG, 6 February 1850, 2; Hammond, "Prayer," 89 (which has the experience as on Orson's way to Jerusalem, in error).

[23]   WWJ 1:9; Launius, *Zion's Camp*, 47 (this has the amount Orson collected, from "Register of Funds received for Zion's Camp," at HDC); HC 2:50, 52, 61 (amounts Joseph Smith collected before the trek began, including what Orson brought), 64 (marchers' personal funds), 51 (by April 19 the Prophet had decided to go to Zion).

[24]   HC 2:62-63 (and note).

CHAPTER 4   *. . . to Zion . . . a wife. . . witnesses. . . .* *(1834-1835)*

[1]   HC 2:61, 63-65, 67 (note), 152; WWJ 1:9; OHH, DN, 12 May 1858 (parts used in this chapter reprinted MS 26 [1864]:790-791); L. Taylor, *Andrus*, 8-10; OH to BY, 27 February 1859, BYC.

[2]   HC 2:64-65, 67 (and note), 68, 69, 71; OPJ, 40-41; HCKW, 41, 45, 48, 51; Andrus and Andrus, *Prophet*, 48; WWC, 40.

[3]   HC 2:70 (modified to dialogue), 71-73; JH, 10 October 1866, 2 (modified to dialogue).

[4]   HC 2:76, 80, 82-83, 92; OH speech, 4 July 1853, JD 7:109; HCKW, 48; Andrus and Andrus, *Prophet*, 48; L. Taylor, *Andrus*, 10.

[5]   HC 2:87-89, 94-95, 100-103; PPPA, 115, 116; OHH; Hancock, "Life," 145 (spelling and punctuation modified). Parts of first three sources modified to dialogue.

[6]   PPPA, 116; Andrus and Andrus, *Prophet*, 21.

[7]   JSH, 104.

[8]   HC 2:104-106; HCKW, 53-55; WWC, 42.

[9]   HC 2:99-100, 103-104.

[10]   HC 2:108, 121-122; HCKW, 55; D&C 105:9-10, 14, 16, 19.

[11]   HC 2:112, 114 (quote rearranged), 119-120, 182 (note); OH speech, 4 July 1853, JD 7:109-110; WW discourse, 12 December 1869, JD 13:158.

[12]   GAS, "The Return to Kirtland," *The Instructor* 81 (1946):287-288, 295, 320-323, 327.

[13]   Stone and Slusser, "Marinda"; HC 1:363; Perkins, "Divided," 54.

[14]   OH discourse, 8 February 1874, JD 17:12; Stone and Slusser, "Marinda."

[15]   HC 1:261-264; Barrow interview.

[16]   Weston N. Nordgren to Romania Woolley, 15 February 1948, RWC; CHC 2:101. For a similar occurrence see Huntington diaries 1:12, 14. See also "Funeral Services of Sister Elizabeth A. Whitney," DEN, 17 February 1882, 3, col. 2, and "Correction," DEN, 18 February 1882, 2, col. 3.

[17]   OHH; Geauga County, Ohio, Marriages, 1834.

[18] HC 2:144, 147, 151, 161, 165, 167, 172, 175, 176. Sometime while in Kirtland, Orson also participated in the brotherhood of the Masonic Order (from Nauvoo [Illinois] Lodge Petitions, by which he applied for transfer from the Meridian Orb Lodge No. 10, Painesville, Ohio [near Kirtland]).

[19] HC 2:181, 182; John 15:13-14, 16. See Exodus 12:5; Colossians 1:12-20.

[20] HC 2:184, 185-187, 297; D&C 18:26-28, 37-38; BE 1:75, 76, 77, 82, 88, 91; HCKW, 17; Hayden, *Disciples*, 215.

[21] "History of Joseph Smith," MS 15 (26 March 1853):206 (order of quotes changed) (modified version in HC 2:189-190); 3 Nephi 28:4-9, 27-29, 31, BoM.

[22] HC 2:194-198 (condensed, order changed, and punctuation modified slightly); Matthew 10:1-20; S. Kimball, *Potter's Wheel*, 207.

[23] HC 2:200, 209; BY, "History," MS 25 (18 July 1863):455-456; OH, W. E. M'Lellin, Clerks, to O. Cowdery, Editor, 8 March 1835, MA 1 (March 1835):90; D&C 107:23, 24, 30.

[24] HC 2:219-220. Thomas B. Marsh thought he was thirty-five years of age, thus born in 1799 and two weeks older than David W. Patten. Vital Records, however, show his birthday to be November 1, 1800 (*Vital Records of Acton, Massachusetts*, 81), making him almost a year younger than Elder Patten. (This situation is mentioned in Church Educational System, *Church History*, 154.)

[25] HC 2:222-225, 238, 240, 241-242; BY, "History," MS 25:456; OH and M'Lellin to Cowdery, March 1835, MA 1:90; McLellin, *Journals*, 171-196; HCK discourse, 28 September 1856, JD 4:107.

[26] HC 2:240-241, 252, 283, 372-373, 375; Jessee, *Writings*, 136; McLellin, *Journals*, 196.

[27] JSHG, 60.

[28] HC 2:335 (see 299 also).

[29] HC 2:300-301, 302, 307-310 (about Joseph Smith's actions in vexing situations see 293, 294-297).

[30] HC 2:333-338.

[31] HC 2:346-347; Johnson family records; Blessings of Orson and Marinda Hyde, HDC.

CHAPTER 5   *. . . Elijah. . . . (1836)*

[1] HC 2:318, 320, 355-356, 363, 376; *Berlitz Hebrew*, vi-ix; Helen Mar Whitney, "Life Incidents," WE 9 (1881):131; Jessee, "History," 444.

[2] HC 2:382-383.

[3] HC 2:355, 356, 385-386, 396, 397, 406, 429; Orson Hyde to Professor J. Seixas, 31 March 1834 (spelling modified slightly), UUL.

[4] Lundwall, *Temples*, 7; Backman, *Heavens Resound*, 142, 149, 150, 157, 159; BYA, 51; "Speech Delivered by Heber C. Kimball," TS 6 (15 July 1845):972.

[5] HC 2:410-428 (some capitalization added to quoted material); Lundwall, *Temples*, 13, 22; "The Way It Looks Today," *Ensign*, January 1979, 46-48; D&C 109.

[6] HC 2:430-432 (quote modified to dialogue).

[7] HC 2:434-436; D&C 110. No record has been found that tells what the congregation did while Joseph Smith and Oliver Cowdery prayed at their pulpit. Traditionally,

at that period, during the sacrament the assembled Saints listened to sermons. Perhaps the meeting ended after all present had received the sacrament.

[8] Ricks, "Kirtland Temple," 483-486; Ausubel, *Jewish*, 324-329.

[9] See Isaiah 11:11, Jeremiah 31:10, and Ezekiel 37:21.

[10] Genesis 22:18, 48:20; Jeremiah 31:9; Hosea 9:16, 17, 14:8; Zechariah 10:6-8; D&C 133:30-34, 110:12.

[11] Malachi 4:1-2, 5-6; Ezekiel 37:11-14; WW remarks, 5 September 1869, JD 13:327; HC 6: 251-252.

CHAPTER 6   *. . . nations, and isles afar off. . . . (1836-1838)*

[1] HC 2:436; OH to Editor, 4 May 1836, MA 2 (April 1836):29.

[2] OHH, DN, 12 May 1858 (parts used in this chapter reprinted MS 26 [1864]:791-792); Oliver Cowdery to Editor, 3 August 1836, MA 2 (September 1836): 373; HC 2:463.

[3] Scadding and Dent, *Toronto*, 170; OHH; PPPA, 151, 152, 156-157; JSH, 16A:5.

[4] See D&C 25:1, 65:2, 5, 6.

[5] OH, "A Prophetic Warning," MA 2 (July 1836):342-346 (punctuation modified slightly) (reprinted in Toronto, August 1836; reprinted, with minor revisions, as *A Timely Warning*, Kirtland, 1837, Preston, England, August 1837, and Manchester, England, 1840); OHH; PPPA, 151-152, 159, 165.

[6] WWJ 1:108, 109; HC 2:467-468, 470-472; Backman, *Heavens Resound*, 314-315; Adams, "Chartering," 472.

[7] R. K. Fielding, "Economy," 341; WWJ 1:110; Geauga County Court of Common Pleas, V:449. No records have been found that disclose what the store sold.

[8] Adams, "Chartering," 472-474; HC 2:468, 470-473; WWJ 1:120; Backman, *Heavens Resound*, 315-317; K. Anderson, *Kirtland*, 197; Hill, Rooker, and Wimmer, "Economy," 468.

[9] Backman, *Heavens Resound*, 317-324; HCKW, 99; BE 1:91; Ames, "Journal," [November] 1836, 1837; HC 2:469, 478-479, 487-488 (and notes), 509-510; "Discourse by Wilford Woodruff," MS 57 (30 May 1895):339-340; GAS discourse, 15 November 1864, JD 11:11; Corrill, *History*, 27.

[10] Geauga County Deeds 23:449, 450, 451. The home next east of the Whitney Store has for years been considered Orson Hyde's. This is in error. Orson's two properties were across the road west of the store and southeast from the store across the road on the south.

[11] This interpretation is the author's regarding Orson's later comment that he had disagreed with Joseph Smith "about the printing business" ("Much interest and anxiety. . . ," *Painesville Telegraph*, 9 June 1837, 2). No extant records indicate involvement by Orson with the Church press, or any other press, so apparently he was merely contemplating.

[12] Ames, "Journal," 1837; HC 2:487-488, 509-510, 5:412; PPPA, 168; OPE, 48-51; Backman, *Heavens Resound*, 323-325; "President Young's Trip North," MS 30 (26 September 1868):626; "Discourse Woodruff," MS 57:339-340; Helen Mar Whitney, "Life Incidents," WE 9 (1881):178. See D&C 112:12-13.

[13] Geauga County Court of Common Pleas T:53; "Much interest. . . ," *Painesville Telegraph*, 9 June 1837, 2 (part modified to dialogue); HC 2:485; *History Geauga and*

Lake Counties, 250, 251; PPPA, 128; Kennedy, *Mormonism,* 157-158; "To Sidney Rigdon," *Painesville Telegraph,* 26 May 1837, 3; Firmage and Mangrum, *Courts,* 55-56.
[14] Claim is made in HC 2:490, that Orson Hyde asked Joseph Smith for forgiveness because of being caught up in speculation. However, the buying of property or goods and trying to sell them for a huge profit seems to have been only a minor part of Orson's problem. Orson Hyde wrote to his wife from England, 14 September 1837, that "Whoever comes here for loaves and fishes will realize their expectations as much as our Kirtland speculators" (*Elders' Journal* 1:20). His wording suggests that he felt his problems had not come as a speculator. The editor of HC may have been unaware of Orson's testimony against Joseph Smith at the Newell [State of Ohio] versus Smith hearing. Heber C. Kimball later spoke kind words about Orson and this trying Kirtland period (JD 6:65).
[15] S. Kimball, *Potter's Wheel,* 4 (modified to dialogue); "The Way It Looks Today," *Ensign,* January 1979, 42; Helen Mar Whitney, "Incidents," WE 9:186 (partly modified to dialogue); HCKW, 105. A good example of Joseph Smith's forgiving nature is in HC 2:297.
[16] HC 2:489; HCKW, 2, 6, 9, 13; JSHG, 60; OH to Marinda Hyde, 14 September 1837, *Elders' Journal* 1 (1837):20.
[17] Firmage and Mangrum, *Courts,* 55-56; Grandison Newell to Editor, *Painesville Telegraph,* 30 June 1837, 3; "The Mormon Persecutor," *Painesville Telegraph,* 6 July 1837, 2.
[18] HCKW, 109; BE 1:53-55; J. Fielding, "Diary," 3.
[19] HCK, OH, and WR, "Mission," MS 1 (April 1841):289; HCK to sons, 20 November 1864, MS 27 (4 February 1865):76; HCK to Vilate Kimball, 27 June 1837, HDC.
[20] Kouwenhoven, *New York,* 190-195; JSH, 99; "Mission," MS 1:289-290; PPPA, 163; HCKW, 111. That *A Timely Warning* was printed in Kirtland is concluded because Orson's tract printed in Canada was called *A Prophetic Warning.*
[21] "Mission," MS 1:289-290; HCK to Kimball, June 1837, HDC; WR journal, 23, 24, 25, 29 June 1837; J. Fielding, "Diary," 5; Manuscript History of British Mission, 5 October 1837; HCK to David P. and Charles S. Kimball, 27 July 1863, JH, same date.
[22] HCK to Kimball, June 1837, HDC; WR journal, 1 July 1837; OH to Marinda Hyde, 18 [20] July 1837, MA 3 (August 1837):550-551; HCKW, 117-118; Manuscript of Mission, 20 July 1837.
[23] Lewis, *Topographical,* 3:104-107, 109-111; 1831 Census Liverpool; HCKW, 119.
[24] HCKW, 118; WR journal, 20 July 1837; OH to Hyde, 18 [20] July 1837, MA 3:550-551 (order rearranged).
[25] HCKW, 121; Lewis, *Topographical,* map and named places; OH address, 17 October 1846, MS 8 (15 November 1846):118-119.
[26] "Mission," MS 1:290-291; J. Fielding, "Diary," 6; Family group record, John and Rachel Fielding, Archives, FHL (for age of James); HCK to Vilate Kimball, 2 September 1837, *Elders' Journal* 1 (1837):4; JFSE, 170 (photograph); HCKK, 47; HCKW, 124-128.
[27] HCKW, 129-132; J. Fielding, "Diary," 7-8; HCK to Kimball, September 1837 (includes quote from OH journal), *Elders' Journal* 1:4-5 (part modified to dialogue); JSH, 14-15. See also: JD 3:229, 4:2-5; JH, 16 Dec 1860, 4.

[28] HCKW, 135; HCKK, 48; Allen, Esplin, and Whittaker, *Mission*, 35.

[29] "Alexander Neibaur," 53-54.

[30] HCKW, 137-139; S. Kimball, *Potter's Wheel*, 11.

[31] Manuscript of Mission, 12, 20 September 1837; HCKW, 152, 156; OH, *Timely Warning*, 19 August 1837.

[32] OH to Marinda Hyde, 14 September 1837, *Elders' Journal* 1 (1837):19-22 (order changed).

[33] J. Fielding, "Diary," 12-13; Manuscript of Mission, 12 September 1837.

[34] Manuscript of Mission, 12 September, 5 October, 14 November 1837; J. Fielding, "Diary," 12; HC 2:243-251, 3:336.

[35] Manuscript of Mission, 14 November 1837.

[36] HCKW, 153; Manuscript of Mission, 8, 12 October, 14 November 1837; J. Fielding, "Diary," 11.

[37] Manuscript of Mission, 14 November 1837; OH to Marinda Hyde, 16 November 1837, added to end of HCK to Vilate Kimball, 12 November 1837, HDC.

[38] OH to WR, 7 December 1837, WRC; CFW, 86 (quote changed to present tense); HCKW, 173-174, 178, 188-190; Manuscript of Mission, 14 February, 9 April 1838.

[39] This number is Orson's estimate as recorded in OHH.

[40] HCKW, 190-194; Manuscript of Mission, 9 April 1838.

[41] Backman, *Heavens Resound*, 325-349; CHC 1:396-407; J. Fielding, "Diary," 18; Marinda Hyde obituary, JH, 24 March 1886.

[42] HCKW, 199-200, 202, 111-112. Heber gives the date of arrival as May 22; Orson says May 21 in OHH. Probably "home" for Marinda was with her parents during Orson's absence. Possibly rent from a home on the property Orson bought in early 1837 helped maintain her while he was gone.

CHAPTER 7   *. . . sorrow. . . . (1838–1839)*

[1] HCKW, 202-203; HC 2:528-529, 3:1; L. Smith, *Joseph Smith*, 241-243, 247; Perkins, "Divided," 57.

[2] Geauga County Deeds 26:487, 488; HCKW, 203; Geauga County Court of Common Pleas V:499. Orson probably also paid his share of the debt that came due in June as payment of the business loan from Eliphalet Boynton to Jacob Bump, Edmund Bosley, and himself. The money was due "one year from June 1837." Eliphalet Boynton sued for payment June 8, 1838. November 6, 1838 "plaintiff discontinue[d] his suit" and was ordered to pay the court costs.

[3] Tullidge, *Northern Utah*, Appendix, 177; HCKW, 203; Helen Mar Whitney, "Closing Paragraph of Life Incidents," WE 10 (1881):9; "Erastus Snow," 301; CHC 1:422, 424-425.

[4] HC 2:522, 3:14, 16-17; JFSE, 569; *Far West Record*, 190; D&C 115:4, 118:4, 6.

[5] OHH, DN, 12 May 1858 (parts used in this chapter reprinted MS 26 [1864]:792); A. Blair, "Massacre," 66; HC 3:41-42, 56, 58, 69, 74, 75, 78, 81, 85. See also Durham, "Battle," 36-61.

[6] OH to BY, 30 March 1839, BYC.

[7] *Far West Record*, 203-206; HC 3:55-86.

[8] BY remarks, 6 September 1857, JD 5:212, 210; E. Smith, *Lorenzo Snow*, 30-31; "Erastus Snow," 301 (Erastus Snow, with the Heber C. Kimball group, said that they

"arrived at Far West . . . the day Thomas B. Marsh's wife was being tried for stealing a pint of [cream] strippings." He gave the date, from memory, as August 8, but the group arrived July 25 [Whitney, "Incidents," WE 10:9]). See also GAS discourse, 6 April 1856, JD 3:283-284; HCK remarks, 12 July 1857, JD 5:28-29; Thomas B. Marsh remarks, 6 September 1857, JD 5:206-209.

9   OH to Sidney Rigdon, 21 October 1844, *Prophet*, 9 November 1844 (part modified to dialogue).

10   HC 3:162, 163; HCKW, 212, 244; *Document, Disturbances*, 57; Thomas B. Marsh remarks, 6 September 1857, JD 5:207; Thomas B. Marsh to Lewis and Ann Abbott, 25 October 1838, JS Collection, Letter Book 1837-1843, 18.

11   HC 3:165; JT, *Succession*, 10; Corrill, *History*, 39; Thomas B. Marsh, "History of Thomas Baldwin Marsh," MS 26 (1864):360, 406 (part modified to dialogue); 1840 Census, Bonne Femme Township, Howard County, Missouri (lists Thomas's children); Marsh to Abbott, 1838, JS Collection, 18.

12   CHC 1:462-463, 500-505; *Document, Disturbances*, 57-59.

13   Marsh to Abbott, 1838, JS Collection, 18, 19; OH to Lewis and Ann Abbott, 25 October 1838, added to Marsh to Abbott, 19 (paragraphing added); Oliver Olney to OH, 5 February 1843, Olney Papers, document 44.

14   HC 3:168-173, 176, 182 (part modified to dialogue).

15   OH to Bro. Pierce, 30 May 1844, *Prophet*, 8 June 1844; Marsh to Abbott, 1838, JS Collection, 18, 19; Johnson family records (Marinda's sister, Alice Olney, and her husband Oliver, were also in Richmond).

16   Wetmore, *Gazetteer*, 77-79, 86; *History Howard and Cooper Counties*, 241-242. The exact location of the Marsh-Hyde residence in Howard County is unknown. In March 1839 Orson wrote to Brigham Young and asked that mail be sent to New Franklin, Howard County, which is two miles from the Missouri River. The 1840 census lists Thomas and his family in Bonne Femme Township, Howard County, about twenty-six miles from the river. Thomas feared the Mormons finding him (JT remarks, 9 August 1857, JD 5:115), thus Orson may have suggested that mail be sent to a post office some distance from their residence.

17   HC 3:175, 178, 183-192, 205-215, 4:56-70; HCKW, 216-217; PPPA, 214.

18   OH to BY, 1839, BYC. See L. Davis, *Why Me?*, 60-74, for insight into the steps involved in overcoming major tribulation.

19   HC 2:195-196; WWJ 2:198-199; OHH.

20   J. Stout journal, 11 (modified to dialogue). For more about the curse of Cain (which is what Orson called the punishment) see Matthew 12:31; John 17:12; Revelation 20:10; Alma 40:13, BoM; D&C 76:31-37, 43-46; Moses 5:23-24, 29-31, Pearl of Great Price.

21   OH to BY, 1839, BYC; OH to PPP, 30 January 1842, T&M, 19; HC 3:257; J. Stout journal, 11.

22   CHC 1:487, 515; HCKW, 223, 246; OH to BY, 1839, BYC; HCK to Joseph Fielding, 12 March 1839, J. Fielding, "Diary," 36.

23   OHH; OH to Bro. Pierce, *Prophet*, 8 June 1844 (modified to dialogue); HCKW, 238, 239; JFSE, 587; JH, 23 February 1859.

24   Jessee, *Writings*, 374, 381, 382 (order changed). When this letter was first published in Nauvoo in April 1840 (TS 1:82-86), the names of most of the apostates were left

out, probably because a few of them had by then returned to the Church. At the letter's second printing (HC 3:226-233) editor B. H. Roberts quoted it as "Marsh and 'another,'" possibly because of his admiration for Apostle Hyde.

For additional references to the buffetings of Satan, which can evidently be for long or short duration, depending on the repentance of the individual, see: D&C 104:9-10; HC 3:384; McConkie, *Doctrine*, 108; L. Smith, *Joseph Smith*, 223; *Far West Record*, 176.

25 HCKW, 244 (modified to dialogue); OH to BY, 1839 (modified to dialogue), BYC.

26 For example: Ames, "Journal." In England, meanwhile, Joseph Fielding reacted with grief and astonishment at news of Orson Hyde's fall, then with exultation at his repentance (J. Fielding, "Diary," 30-31, 32, 36).

27 OH to BY, 1839, including outside of folded letter (see Psalm 84:10 [doorkeeper], and Luke 15:11-32 [prodigal son]), BYC; *History Lee County*, 347, 377, 439-440.

28 Thomas B. Marsh remarks, 6 September 1857, JD 5:206-207.

29 HC 3:283-284, 3:327, 344, 345; J. Fielding, "Diary," 36; CHC 2:3-4; HCK, "Journal and Record," Book 94C, 103; OHH.

30 OHH; WWJ 1:339-340; OH to William Smith, 22 June 1847, BYC (see Leviticus 4:22-26, about sin offerings); HC 3:349; CHC 2:8-12; map of Illinois.

31 Tyler, "Recollections," 27:491. The present author has added "Hyde" in the space where Tyler's recollection has a blank for the name Joseph Smith used. The cited particulars fit only Orson Hyde. Daniel Tyler obviously knew this, but for some reason apparently felt the story had more power without the name.

32 WWJ 1:339-341 (punctuation and spelling modified); HC 3:382-385, 4:1-2.

33 JT, *Succession*, 21. About Peter's denial see Matthew 26:33-34, 69-75; Mark 14:29-30, 66-72.

CHAPTER 8   *. . . toward Jerusalem. . . . (1839-1841)*

1 HC 4:12 (heading should read October 5th, 6th, and 7th); OHH, DN, 12 May 1858 (parts used in this chapter reprinted MS 26 [1864]:792); HCKW, 262-263.

2 WWC, 109; BYA, 74-76; PPPA, 294; BE 1:87, 92.

3 Emma Smith to JS, 6 December (1839) (the letter has no year in its date; someone has erroneously added 1840), JS Collection, Letterbook 1837-1843, 115; Youngreen, *Emma*, 24, 115; Map of Nauvoo Historic Sites; "A History of the Persecution. . . ," TS 1 (September 1840):165 (statements dated 26 October 1839).

4 Smith to JS, 1839, JS Collection, 115; OH to Bros. Smith & Robinson (editors), 4 March 1840, TS 1 (March 1840):71-72 (punctuation slightly modified).

5 Vilate Kimball to HCK, 2 February 1840, addenda by OH, HDC; JSHG, 60; HCKK, 66; OHH.

6 OH to Rabbi Solomon Hirschell, 15 June 1841, TS 2 (1 October 1841):553 (reprinted in HC 4:376) (punctuation is from the King James version of the Bible); J. Fielding, "Diary," 105; OH, Preface to revised Rigdon, *Appeal*, iii-iv.

7 McConkie, *Doctrine*, 188; HC 2:200; D&C 124:128; HCK discourse, 6 April 1857, JD 5:22.

8 OH, Preface to revised Rigdon, *Appeal*, iv; OH to Hirschell, TS 2:553; J. Fielding, "Diary," 105 (part modified to dialogue).

9   HC 4:89, 105, 106, 109 (parts modified to dialogue); OHH.

10   TS 1 (April 1840):86-87 (punctuation slightly modified; spelling retained) (reprinted HC 4:112-113); Stone and Slusser, "Marinda"; "Grandmother Miner"; "Laura Hyde Miner"; OH, Preface to revised Rigdon, *Appeal*, v.

11   HC 4:39, 47; composite of OH, Preface to revised Rigdon, *Appeal*, iv, and CFW, 82.

12   OH to Bro's Smith & Robinson, 28 April 1840, TS 1 (June 1840):116-117; BE 1:92; "Conference Minutes," TS 3 (15 April 1842):761-762 (quoted part modified to present tense).

13   OH, Preface to revised Rigdon, *Appeal*, vi; HC 4:123-125, 201; OH to Editor, 7 July 1840, TS 1 (July 1840):156-157; "Conference Minutes," TS 3:762.

14   OH to Editor, July 1840, TS 1:156-157; EnA, s.v. "Zionism," by Isidore Abramowitz; D&C 109:61-64.

15   HC 4:128-129; E. Robinson to Editor, 16 July 1840, TS 1 (July 1840):155, 156; "Conference Minutes," TS 3:762; OH to Editor, July 1840, TS 1:157; OH statement regarding John E. Page, undated, WNNP, Box 4 Folder 3 (changed to present tense).

16   OH letter, 28 September 1840, TS 2 (1 November 1840):204-205; Wilkinson, Autograph album, first entry; J. Young, *Philadelphia* 2:106-107, 113, 133; "Alexander Neibaur," 53; Lorenzo Barnes to Bro's. Smith & Robinson, 5 May 1840, TS 1 (June 1840):117; George J. Adams to Brothers Robinson and Smith, 7 October 1840, MS 1 (March 1841):275; "Conference Minutes," TS 2 (15 November 1840):215-216; Appleby journal, 33, 34.

17   "Conference Minutes," TS 2 (1 February 1841):306; OH to PPP, 13 April 1841, MS 1 (April 1841):309; Orcutt, *Derby*, 238, 242; 1800 Census, Oxford, Connecticut (Orson's father, Nathan Hyde, living next door to brother Daniel); Oxford, Connecticut, Deed 6:440; Sharpe, *Seymour*, 59, 77; Campbell and Sharpe, *Seymour*, 197; "Orson Hyde," *The Seymour Record*, 19 December 1878.

18   TS 2:273-288 (notice to Elders Hyde and Page on 287); John E. Page to the President and Council of the Church, 1 September 1841, JH, same date; OH to JS, 17 April 1841, TS 2 (15 July 1841):483.

19   "Conference Minutes," TS 3:762; OH to PPP, 22 November 1841, MS 2 (January 1842):132.

20   "Beck Family Biography," 1, RWC; Morris, *Prophecies*, 301-302; JSH, 21a; Page to President, etc., 1 September 1841, JH; John S. and Mary Beck Davis to Milton Beck, 14 December 1948, RWC; 1840 Census, Freehold Township, New Jersey.

21   OH to PPP, April 1841, MS 1:307-309; George J. Adams to Editor, 21 April 1842, TS 3 (15 June 1842):826; J. Fielding, "Diary," 105-107.

22   J. Fielding, "Diary," 107; Lewis, *Topographical* 3:229, 231-233; PPP, 303, 310, 311, 462.

23   BY, "History," MS 25 (26 December 1863):819 (first printed DN, 10 March 1858); OH to PPP, April 1841, MS 1:308 (modified to dialogue); E. England, *Brigham*, 35-37, 90, 91; CHC 5:514; J. Fielding, "Diary," 49, 70.

24   WWJ 2:77-78; BY, "History," MS 25:819; J. Fielding, "Diary," 110; OH to JS, April 1841, TS 2:483; William Miller to BY and HCK, 15 August 1841, TS 3 (15 November 1841):597.

25   Miller to BY and HCK, August 1841, TS 3:597; WWC, 122; Lorenzo Snow to BY,

etc., 26 May 1841, TS 2 (15 September 1841):543, 544; George J. Adams to PPP, 22 June 1841, MS 2 (July 1841):36–37; Adams to Editor, April 1842, TS 3 (15 July 1842): 826; OH [still in Bedford] to PPP, 3 June 1841, MS 2 (June 1841):24.

26 OH to Hirschell, TS 2:552–554 (whole letter reprinted HC 4:372–379).

27 OH to JS, 15 June 1841, TS 2 (1 October 1841):551, 554; CFW, 84.

28 OH to JS, 17 July 1841, TS 2 (15 October 1841):570–572 (paragraphing and punctuation modified).

29 Historisch, *Rotterdams*, 225; OH to JS, July 1841, TS 2:570–571 (spelling modified slightly). Orson Hyde's Rotterdam publication was the first L.D.S. tract in a foreign language; no copies have been found.

30 CFW, 83–84; OH to JS, July 1841, TS 2:571; OH remarks, 8 October 1863, JD 10:261–262 (punctuation modified slightly).

31 OH to JS, July 1841, TS 2:571–573 (punctuation modified slightly).

32 *Encyclopædia Britannica*, s.v. "Regensburg"; EnA, s.v. "Bavaria" by Edgar Alexander; JSH, 22, 23; OH to PPP, 30 August 1841, MS 2 (October 1841):93.

33 EnA, s.v. "Danube" by Ferdinand Lane, "Vienna" by Egon Kaskeline; OH to the Brethren of the Twelve, 1 January 1842, T&M, 11.

34 EnA, s.v. "Danube," "Vienna," "Budapest" by Joseph Kövágó, "Belgrade," "Galati"; OH to the Twelve, January 1841, T&M, 12; OH remarks, 1 April 1855 (spelling modified slightly), MT.

35 EnA, s.v. "Black Sea," "Bosporus" by Lewis V. Thomas, "Istanbul (formerly Constantinople)" by Lewis V. Thomas; OH to Twelve, January 1842, T&M, 7 (no copies of his French communication have been found); OH remarks, April 1855, MT.

36 EnA, s.v. "Marmara, Sea of," "Dardanelles" by Lewis V. Thomas, "Aegean Sea," "Izmir."

37 EnA, s.v. "Lebanon" by Philip K. Hitti; OH to PPP, 20 October 1841, T&M, 23–24 (spelling modified slightly).

38 OH to the Twelve, January 1842, T&M, 14 (paragraphing changed).

39 OH to PPP, October 1841, T&M, 23–24 (order rearranged, and punctuation modified slightly); "Lectures on the Holy Land," *The Ogden [Utah] Junction*, 30 August 1871, 2; JH, 23 February 1873, 8, 9.

CHAPTER 9   *. . . he shall come and pray. . . . (1841–1842)*

1 OH to the Brethren of the Twelve, 1 January 1842, TS 3 (15 July 1842):847, 850–851 (excerpts from this letter reprinted HC 4:495–499), and addenda to PPP, in T&M, 16 (punctuation modified slightly); David Roberts paintings of Jerusalem and environs, 1839, reproduced in Roberts, *The Holy Land*.

Orson's own account is augmented by the Syrian Mission records of "The American Board of Commissioners for Foreign Missions," microfilm reel 538 as follows: Mr. Whiting's given name (frame 7, etc.); turmoil of war, and Whitings have four little girls (frames 153, 252, 430, 573); after staying in Bethlehem for a few months the Whitings moved back to Jerusalem early in October 1841, to a "commodious" home in the northwestern part (frame 820).

2 OH to Twelve, January 1842, TS 3:847; OH to PPP, 22 November 1841, MS 2 (January 1842):133 (letter reprinted HC 4:454–459); Obituary of Charles Gager, *New*

Haven Palladium, 26 March 1842; Syrian Mission records noted in source 1, microfilm reel 538: about convents where visitors in Jerusalem lodge (frame 98).

3   OH to Twelve, January 1842, TS 3:848-850 and MS 2:167-168; OH to PPP, T&M, 16. Parts modified to dialogue.

4   OH to PPP, November 1841, MS 2:133; "Book of Mormon land, Guatemala, is dedicated," DN, *Church News*, 2 November 1991, 3-4; Hammond, "Prayer," 89.

5   National Geographic, *Bible Times*, 350; OH to Twelve, January 1842, TS 3:851; Acts 1:9-12; Zechariah 14:4.

6   Berrett, *World of Bible*, 264-272; OH to Twelve, January 1842, TS 3:851 (spelling of "Kedron" changed to Kidron; modified to present tense); WWJ 2:194; OH to PPP, November 1841, MS 2:132 (modified to present tense). (John E. Page never left the United States.)

7   OH to PPP, November 1841, MS 2:133-135.

About the "stranger in Philadelphia," near the end of the prayer, John F. Beck wrote, 22 November 1924: "My father, Joseph Ellison Beck, born 1810, was the man who sent the purse of gold to Elder Orson Hyde. . . . [In 1847 Beck and his wife were baptized by a Mormon elder (Archives, FHL).] Father . . . always had prayers in his family, and always paid his tithing. . . . He had fourteen children. . . . He always had plenty for his family, and loaned breadstuff to scores who were in want. He did not become rich, but always had money laid aside for a time of need. I have heard the prayer Elder Hyde offered up in his behalf, and am a witness that every feature of it was wonderfully fulfilled" (Morris, *Prophecies*, 302).

8   OH to PPP, November 1841, MS 2:135; Genesis 31:44-52; Joshua 4:1-9, 24:26-27.

9   OH to Twelve, January 1842, TS 3:851, 852; National Geographic, *Bible Times*, 295; Berrett, *World of Bible*, 278; Roberts, *Holy Land* (1-19 shows the Pool of Shilom [Siloam] as it appeared when Orson saw it); CFW, 80-81.

10   OH to PPP, November 1841, MS 2:135; OH to Twelve, January 1842, TS 3:851-852 (punctuation slightly modified); Book of Commandments, 19 (Section 7, verses 2-3); Exodus 4:16-17, 7:9; HCKW, 115.

11   D&C 6:28. Also see Deuteronomy 17:6; Matthew 18:16; 2 Corinthians 13:1; 2 Nephi 11:3, BoM.

12   OH to PPP, November 1841, MS 2:135; "Madame Lydia von F. Mountford," *Relief Society Magazine*, February 1921, 72, 74, 75.

13   Hayward family records.

14   OH to PPP, November 1841, MS 2:133; "American Board of Commissioners," microfilm reel 538: frame 251, 31 December 1841, death of Mr. Gager in Egypt (frame 251), and 28 December 1841, lack of doctors (frame 820); EnA, s.v. "Nile" by Ferdinand C. Lane, "Damietta," "Cairo"; OH discourse, 19 January 1873, JD 15:305.

The Consul's report has the date of death a day different than does Orson's report. The following was published in the *New Haven Palladium*, 28 March 1842:

Department of State, Washington, March 26, 1842.

Information has been received at this Department, from the U.S. Consul for Alexandria, in Egypt, of the death at Cairo, on the 16th of November last, of the Rev. CHARLES GAGER, late of Connecticut.

In conformity with the provisions of the law, the Consul has taken possession of the effects of the deceased, and has transmitted an inventory of the same
to the Department.

[15] EnA, s.v. "Nile," "Alexandria"; "American Board of Commissioners," reel 537:
Alexandria in 1834, frames 279-302; OH to PPP, November 1841, MS 2:132, 135-
136; OH to Brethren and Sisters at Nauvoo, 17 January 1842, T&M, 16, 18; OH to
Marinda Hyde, 21 December 1841, TS 3 (2 May 1842):776-777 (order changed, and
paragraphing added); EnA, s.v. "Trieste" by Henry Paolucci.

[16] OH to Twelve and postscript to PPP, January 1842, from three sources: TS 3:847,
MS 2:168-169, T&M, 15-16 (order changed in these); Alice Olney obituary, TS, 1
August 1841.

[17] OH to Brethren and Sisters, January 1842, T&M, 16-19; OH to PPP, 30 January
1842, T&M, 19; PPP to the Publishers of the Times and Seasons, 19 March 1843, TS
4 (15 April 1843):162; MS 2 (April 1842):189, 3 (August 1842):80.

[18] CFW, 82, 85, title page of original and of English translation; OH to PPP, 24
April 1842, MS 3 (May 1842):15; JSH, 22, 23; Marinda Hyde, quoted in Tullidge,
Women, 405; OH to PPP, 10 August 1842, MS 3 (September 1842):96.

Inquiry to the Archivist in Regensburg, for searches about Orson Hyde, brought
the response that civil records of 1841 and 1842 became lost during World War II.

[19] CFW, 82-83.

[20] CFW, quotes from 36-37 (also see Luke 8:17), 30-31.

[21] CFW, 80, 37.

[22] CFW, 82; JSH, 22-23; "Items of News," MS 3 (September 1842):96.

[23] "Church Emigration," 1842, Fifteenth and Sixteenth Companies; Drennan, "Haslam," 2; OH to JT, n.d., TS 4 (1 February 1843):90; "Elder Orson Hyde. . . ," *The
Wasp*, 17 December 1842, 2.

Orson's method of travel from Saint Louis to Nauvoo in 1842 is unknown; both
"light draught boat" and "by land," apparently on horseback, are mentioned in
"More River Distress," *The Wasp*, 17 December 1842, 2.

[24] OH to JT, 1843, TS 4:90.

[25] HC 4:467 (Joseph Smith apparently received the revelation a few days before
writing it down, as Wilford Woodruff mentioned its contents November 30, 1841
[WWJ 2:140]). For comments about Marinda in May 1841, months before the struggles that led to the revelation, see Appleby journal, 63-64.

Ebenezer Robinson, in "Items Of Personal History Of The Editor," *The Return*,
September 1890, 324-325, tells of Marinda moving in. In *The Return* of October 1890,
346-347, Robinson makes unjust claims. Possible explanations for these are in Noall,
Intimate Disciple, 273, 276-278, 288, 308, 312, 314, 610-611.

CHAPTER 10   . . . *Martha and Mary. . . . (1843)*

[1] JSH, 39; MAPHA, 1; BY remarks, 6 April 1868, JD 12:194; BY discourse, 9 August
1868, JD 12:262; OP discourse, 7 October 1869, JD 13:194.

[2] MAPH sketch, RWC; Bentley, "True," 176-177; MAPHA, 2, 6 (partly modified
to dialogue); MAPH, "A Woman's Testimony," WE 12 (1884):169.

[3] Geneva Hyde Justesen to Weston Nordgren, 15 September 1951, WNNP, Box 1
Folder 2; Diocese of Gloucester Marriage Licenses, 1836, microfilm, FHL; Lea,

Hereford, Parish Registers, 1836, microfilm, FHL; 1841 Census Sollers Hope, 6; William Price and Mary Ann Price family group record, Archives, FHL.

[4]   MAPHA, 1-2; MAPH to Joseph C. Bentley, 16 March 1897, RWC; MAPH, "Testimony," WE 12:169.

[5]   Weston Nordgren to David V. Hyde, 15 September 1951, 3, WNNP, Box 1 Folder 4; Weston Nordgren, "Workbook 2," notes after 252, WNNP, Box 2 Folder 2; MAPH, "Testimony," WE 12:170; Bentley, "True," 176; MAPH to Bentley, 1897, RWC; MAPHA, 2.

[6]   MAPH to Bentley, 1897, RWC; William Price and Mary Ann Price family group record, Archives, FHL; "Mary Ann P. Hyde was born. . . ," RWC.

[7]   MAPHA, 2; JSH, 95; MAPH to Bentley, 1897, RWC.

[8]   MAPHA, 2; D&C 112:30-32, 128:18, 132:1, 3-6, 35, 45; Acts 3:21; CHC 6:227.

[9]   D&C 132:3-6; Helen M. Whitney, *Plural Marriage*, 53.

[10]   D&C 132:51, 62.

[11]   MAPHA, 2-3 (partly modified to dialogue); JSH, 39.

[12]   D&C 132:37-39.

[13]   Jacob 2:23-30, BoM. See also D&C 132:63.

[14]   Joseph F. Smith discourse, 7 July 1878, JD 20:26-27; Amasa M. Lyman remarks, 5 April 1866, JD 11:208; OP discourse, 1869, JD 13:192-193; WWJ, 5:563.

[15]   MAPHA, 3 (partly modified to dialogue).

[16]   Helen M. Whitney, *Plural Marriage*, 53; J. F. Smith discourse, 1878, JD 20:29. See also Erastus Snow discourse, 24 June 1883, JD 24:164-165.

[17]   HCKW, 321-328; BY remarks, 14 July 1855, JD 3:266. See also JT discourse, 9 April 1882, JD 23:64.

[18]   JSH, 39-40 (part changed to first person); MAPH to Bentley, 1897 (part modified to dialogue), RWC.

[19]   MAPHA, 3; OH to Martha Browett, 1859, RWC; Thelma Holbrook, "Martha," 195 (which has her birth date in error as 22 June 1818); Tewkesbury Parish Registers, baptisms 1825, microfilm, FHL.

[20]   Joseph F. Smith, *Atonement and Marriage*, 74; Tullidge, *Women*, 405.

[21]   MAPHA, 3 (sentence order partly changed); Faulring, *Joseph Smith*, 396; Joseph F. Smith, *Atonement and Marriage*, 74; Tullidge, *Women*, 405. See also "Sanpete Stake," WE 12 (1884):119; "Sanpete," WE 15 (1886):22; "Juab Stake," WE 15:80. (That Martha lived in the Hyde home, along with Mary Ann, is assumed.)

[22]   Genesis 38:8; Matthew 22:25-28.

[23]   Widtsoe, *Joseph Smith*, 234.

[24]   Smith, *Atonement and Marriage*, 69.

[25]   Widtsoe, *Joseph Smith*, 234, 240. For an example of this see HCKK, 97-98 and 109-110 n. 15 (Helen Mar Whitney sealed to Joseph Smith for eternity), 310 (Presendia Huntington sealed to Joseph Smith for eternity the same day married to Heber C. Kimball for time).

[26]   "Funeral Services of Sister Elizabeth A. Whitney," DN, 17 February 1882, 3; "Correction," DN, 18 February 1882, 2; OP discourse, 1869, JD 13:193. Another example of sealing for eternity only: Hulda C. T. Smith, "To My Children And Grandchildren," *The Nauvoo Journal* 4 (1992):3-8.

[27]   See D&C 98:14, 101:4, 124:55, 132:51.

[28] Under some conditions the Lord revokes commands; see Genesis 22:12 and D&C 56:4-6. Obedience is also tested; see HCKW, 321-328 and OP discourse, 20 May 1855, JD 2:14.

[29] Faulring, *Joseph Smith*, 396; Lee, *Mormonism Unveiled*, 147; Olney, *Absurdities*, 16. On 1 May 1869 Marinda signed her own affidavit about her sealing to Joseph Smith; she stated that the ordinance was performed "– May 1843" by Brigham Young, witnesses Eliza Maria (Partridge) Lyman and Emily Dow (Partridge) Young (Joseph F. Smith Affidavit Books 1:15 [second copy 4:15]). Apparently Marinda's memory of the date was inaccurate; the date in Faulring was recorded at or near the time of the procedure.

[30] HC 5:200, 207, 256, 272, 290, 293.

CHAPTER 11   *. . . many things. . . . (1843-1844)*

[1] HC 5:207 (etc.), 255; CHC 2:101; Minutes of the Council of Twelve, 20 January 1843, HDC, in OPE, 84-85; WWJ 2:213.

[2] OH to JT, TS 4 (1 February 1843):91; Nauvoo Land Book A, Hotchkiss Purchase, Block 101, Lot 4; Map of Nauvoo. In 1843 both Carlin and Hyde referred to the same street (City Council, 74, 86, 212, etc.).

[3] HC 5:232, 265, 285, 312, 461, 470, 484, 537, 6:105, etc.; Nauvoo City Council Proceedings, 1841-1845, HDC.

[4] HC 5:277-279.

[5] OH to Martha Browett, 1859, RWC; HC 5:303, 317, 318, 323-326 (parts modified to dialogue); BY discourse, 8 March 1857, JD 4:266.

[6] HC 5:120, 252-253, 293, 317, 367; JSH, 27 (modified to dialogue).

[7] HC 5:8, 46, 121-122, 139, 270, 271, 280-281, 314-316, 327-329, 339, 345, 6:47; Jedediah M. Grant remarks, 12 October 1856, JD 4:151; OH, *Speech 1845*, 24.

[8] HC 5:302, 322, 366-367, 417.

[9] "Recommendatory," TS 4 (1 June 1843):218; HC 5:417, 488, 6:41; WR journal, 10 June 1843.

[10] HC 5:453, 488, 491.

[11] HC 5:448-452, 474, 485; WWJ 2:256.

[12] Faulring, *Joseph Smith*, 396; HC 5:354; "Laura Hyde Miner."

[13] Measured by Jim Kimball, Salt Lake City, during visit to Nauvoo, 1985; Photographs of home; Stone and Slusser, "Marinda," 2. A wing was later added to the back of the home.

[14] OH, *Speech 1845*, 24-25. Joseph Smith likely said this in a Sabbath meeting on August 13. The statements fit his announcement at that time of withdrawing personal fellowship from Sidney Rigdon. (A short synopsis is printed in HC 5:532; see also 5:553, 6:47-49.)

William Hyde wrote in his journal that "on one occasion I heard Joseph Smith say that he had carried Elder Rigdon on his back long enough, and then turning to the Twelve said that if they did not help him at that time in shaking him off, the time would come when they would have it to do, and that without his, Joseph's, assistance" (William Hyde, *Journal*, 12). William Hyde was away from Nauvoo on a mission at the time of the April 1843 conference. He returned in mid June and left again September 23 for another mission. Joseph Smith was absent when William returned, and until the end of June. Orson Hyde was gone most of July and possibly in early August (See HC 5:553) and left again August 17, returning in mid October. All three—Joseph Smith, William Hyde, and Orson Hyde—were in Nauvoo on August 13. Most of the Quorum of the Twelve were then gone on their eastern states mission; none of those apostles recorded the prophecy.

15   HC 5:367, 537, 6:11, 39, 41.

16   The Twelve had all returned by November 8 (*Nauvoo Neighbor*, 8 November 1843); JSHG, 60; HC 6:82.

17   "Trial of Sidney Rigdon," TS 5 (15 September 1844):651; HC 6:98.

18   HC 5:2.

19   "History of Brigham Young," MS 26 (1864):312, 326-327 (for further background see 2 Peter 1:1-11); "Trial Rigdon," TS 5:651 (punctuation modified slightly).

20   HC 6:xxxv-xxxvi, 40, 119-124.

21   HC 6:81, 83, 84-88.

22   HC 6:88, 100, 144-145. Orson was in Nauvoo on December 2 ("History Young," MS 26:311) and gone before December 5. He probably traveled to Saint Louis.

23   HC 6:124-132.

24   HC 6:32; OH to Thomas Ward, 20 January 1844, MS 4 (March 1844):175 (punctuation modified slightly).

25   HC 6:63, 64-65, 155-160, 187-189, 210-211, 231-232; CHC 2:202-207.

26   HC 6:221, 222 (modified to dialogue), 223, 7:550.

27   "Trial Rigdon," TS 5:651; OH remarks, 6 October 1869, JD 13:180; JH, 12, 19 March 1897; JSH, 31; WWJ 2:455; "Sanpete Stake," WE 18 (1 May 1890):185 (modified to dialogue); George Q. Cannon discourse, 5 December 1869, JD 13:49; WW discourse, 12 December 1869, JD 13:164; George Q. Cannon discourse, 29 October 1882, JD 23:362-363.

28   OH to BY, 14 March 1844 (in error, HC 6:263 has Orson Hyde in Nauvoo March 13; perhaps the scribe meant Orson Pratt), BYC; HC 6:224, 229, 334-340.

29   HC 6:274-277, 282, 283, 347; *Nauvoo Neighbor*, 3 April 1844; Nauvoo City Council, 186-187, 204 (Councilmen were paid for attendance and fined for unexcused non-attendance. The first six months Orson was fined $5.00. The second six months he was paid $1.00, which interprets that during the second period he attended about half the time.); OH to the Brethren in Nauvoo, 9 June 1844, JH, 4 (punctuation modified).

30   HC 6:286 (which has typographical error of 14 April for 4 April), 369-370; S. Kimball, *Potter's Wheel*, 64; Junior League, *Washington*, 124-125, 177; OH to Brethren, 9 June 1844, JH, 2-4 (parts modified to present tense and augmented for clarity).

31   HC 6:371-372, 373; Junior League, *Washington*, 177; Esler, *Presidents*, 20-21.

32   HC 6:373, 375; EnA, s.v. "Douglas, Stephen Arnold" by Jay Monaghan.

33   OH to Brethren, 9 June 1844, JH, 5; OH to John E. Page, 6 May 1844, McQuown Papers; OH to the Brethren in Nauvoo, 30 April 1844, JH, 1, 3, 4.

34   HC 6:341; OH to Bro. Pierce, 30 May 1844, *Prophet*, 8 June 1844 (punctuation and spelling modified slightly).

35   OH to Brethren, 9 June 1844, JH, 1, 2, 4, 5; HC 6:369, 376, 392; OPJ, 214.

36   OH to the Brethren in Nauvoo, 11 June 1844, JH, 3 (modified to dialogue, punctuation modified slightly).

[37] OH, "Communications," *Prophet*, 29 June 1844.

[38] HC 7:132. Orson Spencer first published the June 27 afternoon experiences of the Twelve. Orson Hyde and others apparently told him what had happened to them before he published ("Night of Martyrdom," MS 9 [15 February 1847]:54). In the next published account of the feelings of the Twelve that day ("History of Joseph Smith," DN, 23 December 1857, p. 1, col. 4) only the following are mentioned: Brigham Young, Orson Pratt, Heber C. Kimball, Lyman Wight, and Wilford Woodruff. A subsequent account of the "History of Joseph Smith," published MS 24 (20 September 1862):600, is the one quoted in HC 7:132.

[39] HC 7:159, 210; "Trial Rigdon," TS 5:649; Elisha H. Davis statement (punctuation added) (assignment to Connecticut is in HC 6:336); JSH, 28 (modified to dialogue), 29; WWJ 2:419.

[40] OH remarks, 6 October 1869, JD 13:181; MS 5 Supplement (August 1844):14.

[41] WWJ 2:423-428 (spelling and punctuation slightly modified); OH, *Speech 1845*, 11; "Trial Rigdon," TS 5:649 (modified to present tense); BE 1:99; JFSE, 567; HC 7:133, 236.

[42] HC 7:148, 200, 209, 211; William Hyde, *Journal*, 11; E. Watson, *Brigham Young*, 175, 176.

[43] HCKW, 340; B. Roberts, *John Taylor*, 114-119; OH, *Speech 1845*, 36; OH discourse, 3 November 1878, JD 20:98; "Letter from Orson Hyde," FG, 2 May 1849, 1; Andrus and Andrus, *Prophet*, 151.

Particulars of the martyrdom and causes are contained in HC 7. A detailed account that has been attributed to Orson Hyde is printed in FG, 27 June 1849, and in *Liahona, The Elders' Journal* 12 (30 June 1914):12-14. This article was actually penned by Orson Spencer and first published in MS 9 (15 February 1847):54-56, 103-104.

[44] OH sermon, 3 January 1858, JD 6:153.

CHAPTER 12   *. . . foundation of apostles. . . . (1844-1846)*

[1] HC 7:213, 221-222, 249; MAPH, "A Remembrance of Joseph the Prophet," and "A Tribute of Love," WE 19 (1 October 1890):61 and 24 (1 May 1896):148.

[2] OH, *Speech 1845*, 7, 11, 12; "More Revelations," TS 5 (15 December 1844):742; "Continuation of Elder Rigdon's Trial," TS 5 (1 October 1844):661.

[3] McKiernan, "Sidney Rigdon," 16-17; OH to Editor, TS 5 (15 December 1844):739; OH to Editor, 16 September 1844, reprinted in *The Prophet*, 2 November 1844, from the *People's Organ*.

[4] OH, *Speech 1845*, 12; Call, "Journal," 29; "Trial," TS 5:663.

[5] OH, *Speech 1845*, 13 (order changed in last paragraph). For more about this episode with Sidney Rigdon see HC 7:223-242.

[6] "Trial," TS 5:649-650 (punctuation modified).

[7] E. Watson, *Brigham Young*, 176; CHC 5:513-515; Spencer and Harmer, *Brigham Young*, 16-18; HC 7:248-249.

[8] HC 7:249, 326; Park, "Nauvoo," 24; OH to E. Robinson, 19 September 1844, *The Return*, April 1890, 253. (See also BY sermon, 6 April 1853, JD 1:134-135, about the apostleship.)

⁹ HC 7:254; composite of OH remarks, 6 October 1869 and OH discourse, 5 April 1877 (modified slightly for dialogue), JD 13:181, 19:58; "Memorial Anniversary," WE 17 (1888):46 (Mary Ann's account of this event).

¹⁰ A few of the other Saints who saw the transfiguration are mentioned in CHC 2: 418.

¹¹ S. Kimball, *Potter's Wheel*, 83; GAS, "My Journal," *The Instructor*, 83:370-371; OH *Speech 1845*, 15, 16-17, 18 (paragraphing changed).

¹² "Trial," TS 5:647, 686, 687 (punctuation modified); OH to Editor, 16 September 1844, *The Prophet*, 2 November 1844.

¹³ OH to Editor, September 1844 (modified to dialogue), *The Prophet*, November 1844; HC 7:270; OH to Brethren, 12 September 1844 (spelling modified slightly), BYC.

¹⁴ OH to Brethren, September 1844, BYC; Sidney Rigdon to Editor, and OH to Editor, September 1844, reprinted in *The Prophet*, 2 November 1844, from the *People's Organ*; OH to Robinson, 1844 (punctuation modified), *The Return*, April 1890, 253.

¹⁵ OH, "Sidney Rigdon," *The Prophet*, 9 November 1844; "Conference Minutes," TS 5 (15 November 1844):718-719.

¹⁶ OH to BY, 29 December 1844, BYC; W[illiam] W. Phelps, "The Answer," TS 5 (1 January 1845):758, 759, 761.

¹⁷ OH to Joseph L. Heywood, 22 January 1845, HDC; HC 7:363; OH to BY, 18 February, 6 March 1845, BYC; "Superstition," *St. Louis New Era*, 25 February 1845, in Clifford Stutz, "St. Louis Newspaper Clippings"; OH to Newel K. Whitney, 27 February, 5 March 1845, Newel K. Whitney Papers.

¹⁸ BYA, 119; HC 7:377, 378; "Speech Delivered by Heber C. Kimball," TS 6 (15 July 1845):970-971, 973.

¹⁹ "Extract of a Letter from Elder Orson Hyde," MS 6 (1 July 1845):26; HC 7:275, 350-360, 365, 375-376, 387, 388, 399, 408; CHC 2:468-471; BYA, 122-123; OH to Editor, *Nauvoo Neighbor*, 28 May 1845.

²⁰ GAS, "My Journal," *The Instructor* 83 (1948):418, 419; "The Cap-stone of the Temple," *Nauvoo Neighbor*, 28 May 1845; HC 7:417-418, 430-431; "Extracts of Letters from Nauvoo," MS 6 (1 November 1845):153; CHC 2:473; Helen Mar Whitney, "Scenes in Nauvoo. . . ," WE 11 (1883):169-170.

²¹ "Letters," MS 6:153-154; Proverbs 25:11.

²² "Speech of Elder H. C. Kimball, Delivered June 1st 1845," TS 6 (1 August 1845): 987, 988.

²³ HC 7:426, 427; *New-York Messenger*, 30 August 1845, 67, quoted by E. Watson, "The Nauvoo Tabernacle," 420; "Speech Of Elder Orson Hyde, Delivered Sunday, June 15, 1845," TS 6 (15 August 1845):1001-1005 (punctuation modified).

²⁴ N. G. T. (OH) to Sylvia H. Thomas (MAPH), 1845, RWC.

²⁵ *New-York Messenger*, 2, 9, 16 August 1845, 37, 45, 52 (reprinted HC 7:427).

²⁶ OH to MAPH, 1845 (some paragraphing added; a sentence about the children has been moved from one paragraph to another).

²⁷ *New-York Messenger*, 16 August 1845, 52 (another of Orson's articles was published 23 August, 60).

²⁸ OH to Whitney, 24 August 1845, quoted by E. Watson, "The Nauvoo Tabernacle," 418; *New-York Messenger*, 13 September 1845, 84; OPJ, 548.

29   OH to BY, 11 September 1845, Philip Blair Family Papers; *New-York Messenger*, 13, 20 September 1845, 85, 93; HC 7:482.

30   HC 7:437-438, 445, 456; S. Kimball, "Nauvoo Temple," 976.

31   HC 7:440-450, 456-477, 482; CHC 2:519; Hansen diaries, 1845; Joseph L. Heywood to Sarepta, 6 October 1845, Heywood Collection.

32   HC 7:447, 481; Helen M. Whitney, "Scenes," WE 11 (1883):186.

33   Hypothetical statements based on: HC 7:454-455, 488-541; S. Kimball, *Potter's Wheel*, 156, 158.

34   HC 7:539, 541; S. Kimball, "Temple" 1963, 975, 978, 979.

35   HC 5:2, 6:98, 7:541-542; Call, "Journal," 34.

36   Nauvoo Temple Records; HC 7:544, 547, 548, 565, 581.

37   HC 7:549-551, 553-554, 557.

38   HC 7:566; Nauvoo Temple Records.

39   HC 7:558, 560, 567; JSH, 10; Rollins, "Life," 16.

40   OH, "Letter from Nauvoo—Course of the Mormons," *New-York Daily Tribune*, 5 February 1846, furnished by Marjory Hyde Eldredge (great-granddaughter of Orson Hyde), Salt Lake City, Utah; HC 7:569; JT, "Address to the Saints in Great Britain," MS 8 (15 November 1846):113.

41   JSHG, 60 (year erroneously given as 1845).

42   HC 7:578, 580, 602; JFSE, 331; Helen M. Whitney, "Scenes," WE 12 (1883):77.

43   JH, 8 February 1846; HC 7:581, 582, 584, 602, 603; PPPA, 340; Bentley, "True," 179.

44   HC 7:585, 586; Barrows, "Journal."

45   CHC 3:45; HC 7:585-586; Bentley, "True," 179; Helen M. Whitney, "Scenes," WE 12:82.

46   CHC 3:40-41; HC 7:343, 377, 379, 383, 417, 419, 460, 483, 542, 568, 582-583, 602; BE 1:96; OH to BY, 10 March 1846, BYC.

47   OH to BY, 28 February 1846, BYC; Hancock County, Illinois, Bonds and Mortgages 2:328.

48   HC 7:586, 602, 604; OH to BY, 10 March 1846, BYC; photograph of Luke Johnson, PPPA, facing p. 123; Johnson family records; JH, 8 March 1846.

49   OH to BY, 10 March 1846, BYC; BY to Joseph Young, 9 March 1846, JH, same date.

50   HC 7:326 (Truman Angell was a son of the James Angell who in 1832 had befriended missionaries Samuel H. Smith and Orson in Providence, Rhode Island); CHC 2:429, 528-530; OH to BY, 10 March 1846, BYC; Western Historical Society, *History St. Clair County*, 350.

51   OH, *He that hath ears to hear. . .*, (reprinted MS 7 [15 May 1846]:157-158 [spelling modified slightly]). Orson penned a letter to Brigham Young about this, 16 March 1846, on the reverse side of one of the printed copies, HDC. One Saint's reaction is in Haight journal, 24.

52   OH to BY, 27 March 1846 (part changed to dialogue), BYC.

53   Scott diaries, 1846, 2 (modified to dialogue); OH report, JH, 18 June 1846 (parts modified to dialogue).

54   OH to Thomas Ward, 5 April 1846, MS 7:156-157; JH, 8 April 1846.

55   WWJ, 3:38, 39, 41; OH to BY, 22 April 1846, BYC; CHC 3:2.

[56] BY to OH, 21 April 1846, BYC.

[57] Kane, "Mormons," 129-130; WWJ, 3:41; JH, 30 April 1846 (punctuation modified); Scott diaries, 1846, 8 (modified to dialogue); "Letter from Ursalia B. Hastings Hascall," *Nauvoo Journal* 5 (Spring 1993):13.

[58] Cannon, "History," JI 7 (1872):139; D&C 124:31-32; WWJ, 3:42-47 (speeches reconstructed from the hurried journal notes); WWC, 320.

[59] BY to OH, 21 April 1846, BYC; CHC 3:48-50; L. Cook, *Kingsbury*, 98-103; B. Roberts, *John Taylor*, 170.

[60] Kane, "Mormons," 130; Council of the Twelve to OH and WW, 30 April 1846, BYC.

CHAPTER 13   *. . . labours, journeyings. . . . (1846–1848)*

[1] WWJ 3:47-49; JH, 17 June 1846; OPJ, 351; Bentley, "True," 179-180.

[2] Kane, "Mormons," 116, 117; EnA, s.v. "Iowa" by Leland L. Sage, Erma Plaehn, and Herman Nelson; MAPH to Joseph C. Bentley, 1897, RWC; Early Ecclesiastical Minutes Collection, Mount Pisgah, 4 June 1846, HDC; "Eliza R. Snow: From Her Diary," PH 17:358; OPJ, 351, 354, 355, 357, 360; JH, 17-19 June 1846; CHC 3:51, 55; Helen Mar Whitney, "Travels," WE 13 (1884):182.

[3] JH, 18, 19 June 1846; Kane, "Mormons," 163, 164; "Extracts from Orson Pratt's Private Journal," MS 12 (1 January 1850):3; Bennett, *Mormons Missouri*, 48; Bentley, "True," 180; Browning autobiography; original map, Manuscript History of Kanesville. (See Appendix Two.)

[4] CHC 3:65, 76-80; JH, 1, 2 July 1846; OH, "Letter from Nauvoo—Course of the Mormons," *New-York Daily Tribune*, 5 February 1846; JT Correspondence, Box 1, Book 1, 64, 2 July 1846; HSD, 178; Bennett, *Mormons Missouri*, 68.

[5] WWJ 3:58; CHC 3:76; Kane, "Mormons," 130-132 (punctuation slightly modified).

[6] JH, 12, 13 July 1846; Kane, "Mormons," 132-133; OPJ, 550; Hansen diary, summer 1846; map, Manuscript Kanesville; *Hymns*, 55 ("Down by the River's Verdant Side"); Helen M. Whitney, "Travels," WE 13:10.

[7] JH, 16 July 1846; Tyler, *Battalion*, 124; OH, "Mr. Springer's Speech," FG, 21 March 1849; OH, "State of Deseret," FG, 31 October 1849; OH, remarks, 25 January 1863, JD 10:81. The last quote is a composite.

[8] JH, 16 July 1846; OH to Brethren, MS 8 (15 October 1846):91; WWJ, 3:59.

[9] WWJ 3:59: "Grandmother Miner"; OH to Samuel Brannan, 5 September 1846, HDC; ETB to Wm. Huntington and C. C. Rich, 21 July 1846, HDC; Bennett, *Mormons Missouri*, 61-66.

[10] "Diary of Lorenzo Dow Young," 145-146; Helen M. Whitney, "Travels," WE 13:18; Horace K. Whitney journals 1:43, 2:7; OH to BY, 7 August 1846, BYC.

[11] Helen M. Whitney, "Travels," WE 13:10; Bentley, "True," 179-180; Lucille P. Jacob to Myrtle S. Hyde, 1980; Price daughter, "Wm. Price"; Bradshaw, "Richard and Elizabeth Bentley," 8, 9, 10; OH to Brannan, September 1846, HDC.

[12] PPPA, 345; JH, 4 August 1846; William Hyde, *Journal*, 17; OH to BY, 7 August 1846 (order rearranged somewhat) ("flummeries" are items of little worth), BYC.

[13] "For the satisfaction. . . ," "Copy Of A Letter. . . ," MS 8 (15 October 1846):94; OH to Brannan, September 1846, HDC; JT to [Orson] Spencer, 13 March 1847, MS

9 (1 June 1847):162; PPPA, 346; OH to BY, 22 October 1846 (partly modified to dialogue), BYC; "General Conference at Manchester," MS 8 (15 November 1846):118.

[14] OH to BY, 22 October 1846, BYC; OH to the Brethren [in England], 15 October 1846, and "Circular," MS 8 (15 October 1846):90-92; PPPA, 346; "Conference," MS 8:119.

[15] MAPH to Joseph Bentley, 1897, RWC; JSHG, 60; OH, "Lines By Orson Hyde To His Wife," MS 8 (1 November 1846):106 (the omitted parts tell of persecutions to the Church).

[16] OH to Brethren, October 1846, MS 8:92; PPPA, 346; OH to BY, 22 October 1846, BYC; Huntington, "Diaries," 1:79-80.

[17] OH, "The Joint Stock Company," MS 8 (1 November 1846):102-103; OH, "Notices," MS 8 (20 November 1846):143.

[18] JT to Spencer, 13 March 1847, MS 9:161; Andrew Cahoon to Reynolds Cahoon, 8 February 1847, HDC; OH, "Farewell Address," MS 9 (15 January 1847):25; CHC 3:127; "Notices," MS 9 (1 February 1847):48; PPPA, 354.

[19] OH, "Important From America," MS 9 (1 January 1847):13; (Editor's name) MS 9 (1 February 1847):48; OH, "Letter To The Editor," MS 9 (15 February 1847):59; HC 7:370; "Notices," MS 9 (15 January 1847):32; "Notices," MS 9 (15 February 1847):64; — Lyon [identity unknown], "Impromptu," MS 9 (1 April 1847):111-112.

[20] OH to [Orson] Spencer and [Franklin D.] Richards, 7 April 1847, MS 9 (15 June 1847):177; OH to [Orson] Spencer, 30 May 1847, MS 9 (15 August 1847):243.

[21] PPPA, 357-358; B. Roberts, *John Taylor*, 185-189; OH to Orson Spencer, 30 May 1847, MS 9 (15 August 1847):243; OH to William Smith, 22 June 1847, BYC; PHCM, 1.

[22] CHC 3:147; WWC, 260; OPJ, 381; Bennett, *Mormons Missouri*, 68-69 (Florence, Nebraska, eventually occupied the same site and was later absorbed by Omaha); "Thomas Jefferson Sutherland, and the Saint Joseph Gazette," FG, 27 June 1851; BY to OH, PPP, and JT, 6 January 1847, MS 9 (1 April 1847):97. Also see HSD, 222; Helen M. Whitney, "Scenes," WE 13 (1885):115, 139.

[23] Cannon, "History," JI 18 (1883):213-214, 237; OH to Spencer, May 1847, MS 9:244; OH remarks, 7 October 1860, JD 8:237; OH discourse, 8 February 1874, JD 17:7; Kane, "Mormons," 115-116.

[24] Bentley, "True," 180-181; BY remarks, 7 October 1860, JD 8:197.

[25] OH to BY, 22 April 1848, BYC; HC 5:139, 255. See also D&C 103:24-25; 124:93. Brigham Young alluded to this type of discipline, as recorded by Hosea Stout (HSD, 192-193 [and footnote], under dates 12 and 13 September 1846, also 208-209). A curse pronounced by Hyrum Smith is recorded TS 4:183.

[26] HSD, 258-259, 261; B. Roberts, *John Taylor*, 188; OH to Nathaniel Felt, 21 June 1847, BYC; Ward, *Winter Quarters*, 148-149, 170, 308 (note 9); PHCM, 40, refers to a meeting of the same type.

[27] OH to Felt, June 1847, BYC; HSD, 244, 262 (and footnote), 263, 264; Helen M. Whitney, "Scenes," WE 14:82; OH to Bishop [Newel K.] Whitney and the Council, 22 June 1847, JH, same date.

[28] OH to Spencer, 5 August 1847, MS 9 (15 September 1847):274; PHCM, 39-43, 65; OH discourse, 8 October 1854, JD 2:65.

29 OH to Spencer, August 1847, MS 9:273-274; CHC 3:104-121, 357-370; HSD, 268; Tyler, *Battalion*, 197, 198, 201; PHCM, 54-55; OH discourse, 8 October 1854, JD 2:65; Bentley, "True," 180.

30 PHCM, 63-65 (quotations adapted to first person); OH to Orson Spencer, 7 October 1847, MS 9 (15 December 1847):375.

31 OH to BY, 22 April 1848, BYC; WWJ 3:288; Cannon, "History," JI 18:327; WW to Orson Spencer, 24 April 1848, MS 10 (15 June 1848):186; Thomas Bullock to Orson Spencer, 4 January 1848, MS 10 (15 April 1848):117-118.

32 WWJ 3:290; OH to BY, 12 November 1847, BYC; OH to WR, 27 November 1847, WRP; Appleby journal, 186, 188 (spelling modified slightly).

33 CHC 3:305-306; WWJ 3:290-294; BY to Orson Spencer, 23 January 1848, MS 10 (15 April 1848):114.

34 Bathsheba Smith autobiography, 19; WWJ 3:294-295 (partly adapted to dialogue and spelling modified slightly); Ruth Rust recollection, WNNP, Box 5 Folder 6; GCM, 5 December 1847; Helen M. Whitney, "Scenes," WE 13:139; BY remarks, 7 October 1860, JD 8:197 (adapted to dialogue); OH remarks, 7 October 1860, JD 8:234 (In these remarks Orson Hyde made two errors of dates: that this meeting of the Twelve in Hyde Park occurred in February of 1848 [actually 5 December 1847], and that the sustaining of Brigham Young as President of the Church took place in Conference the following April [actually 27 December 1847]. In the 1860 assemblage where Orson related the sublime events associated with the reorganization of the Presidency, Brigham Young spoke after him, talked glowingly of the truth of what Elder Hyde had said, and added details [JD 8:194, 197]); OH remarks, 6 October 1867, MT, recorded by David W. Evans; HC 7:249; Bentley, "True," 180-181. See also Cannon, "History," JI 18 [1883]:237, who said that the "mind of the Lord had been obtained."

35 WWJ 3:295; HC 7:622; JH, 6 December 1847, 1-6.

36 BY to Spencer, January 1848, MS 10:114; Foote autobiography 1:106; Appleby journal, 194; Charles Allen (historical architect and builder) to Robert Schulze, 2 October 1995, copy possession author; Bentley, "True," 181; Thomas Bullock drawings of Tabernacle, HDC; Thomas Bullock notes, December 1847, copied by Richard E. Bennett, HDC; GCM, 24-27 December 1847; Minutes by Robert Campbell for the Seventy, 24-27 December 1847, HDC.

37 WWJ 3:299-301; HSD, 292-293; BY to Spencer, January 1848, MS 10:115; OH remarks, 7 October 1860, JD 8:234; CHC 3:317-318; Appleby journal, 194.

38 OH to GAS, 8 December 1847 (Orson planned to leave the next day), GASC; JH, 23 January 1848, 2; OH to BY, 28 December 1847, BYC; GCM, 25 December 1847 (punctuation added).

39 JH, 6, 9 December 1847, 18 January, 14 February 1848; OH to GAS, December 1847, GASC; Appleby journal, 199; OH to BY, 15 February, 22 April 1848, BYC; HOH, 1848, 7; WWJ 3:322; JSHG, 60.

40 OH to GAS, December 1847, GASC; Bathsheba Smith autobiography, 20-21; WWJ 3:295; JH, 24, 25, 27 (pp. 5-9, 10) March 1848.

41 JH, 6 (pp. 1, 7-9), 8 April 1848; OPJ, 360; Cannon, "History," JI 18 (1883):361.

42 The last known letter of Orson Hyde from Hyde Park is dated February 15, 1848. Marinda's baby was born February 28, obviously in Hyde Park. Wilford Woodruff

dined with Orson on April 15 after a meeting in the Kanesville Log Tabernacle, and that same afternoon he traveled to another place, indicating that Orson lived near the Tabernacle (WWJ 3:344). April 22, Orson wrote two letters to Brigham Young from Kanesville (BYC); nothing in these indicates that Orson was not at home. Probably he moved to Kanesville in early April.

[43] 1850 Census, Pottawattamie County, Iowa, 64; Charles Price family group record, Patrons Section, Archives, FHL.

[44] Simons, drawing titled "Elder Orson Hydes residence on Washington Ave. Council Bluffs"; "Trek Revived by Mormons," *World Herald* [Omaha], 18 July 1946; "Hyde Did Much. . . ," *Nonpareil*, 5 February 1953; Babbitt, *Council Bluffs*, 83; Stimson, "Overland Journey," 404, 405; "This Was Council Bluffs," *Nonpareil*, 5 March 1953; *History of Pottawattamie County*, 72, 86, 87; Field and Reed, *History Pottawattamie*, 6, 16, 33; Browning autobiography.

[45] Early survey records and maps in Pottawattamie County Engineers Office, Council Bluffs, Iowa; OH to Nathaniel Felt, 12 April 1848, JH, same date; PHCM, 235.

[46] WWJ 3:347-351; HSD, 311-312; JH, 2, 3 June 1848; "Pioneer Journal," *Utah Genealogical and Historical Magazine* 30:11; Stimson, "Overland Journey," 408.

[47] OP, "President Orson Pratt's First General Epistle," MS 10 (15 August 1848):242; JH, 2 (p. 16), 5 (pp. 1-2) October 1848.

[48] OH, "Letter from Orson Hyde" from the *Missouri Republican* of 19 September 1848, reprinted FG, 2 May 1849, 1; GAS to OP, 20 October 1848, MS 11 (1 January 1849):14; OH to William Martindale, 23 October 1848, Martindale Papers; OH to HCK, 5 April 1849, JH, same day; OH to WR, 12 April, 1 June 1849, WRP; OH to BY, 13 July 1849, BYC.

[49] MAPHA, 3; Bennett, *Mormons Missouri*, 198; OH to Martha Browett, 1859, RWC; WWJ 3:353-356; Woodruff, *Leaves*, 88.

[50] WWJ 3:356-358; OH to HCK, 5 April 1849 (punctuation modified), JH, same date; OH to Editors of the *Missouri Republican*, 19 September 1848, reprinted FG, 2 May 1849; OH to WR, 26 April 1850, WRP; OH to HCK, 5 April 1849; OH to GAS, 8, 22 July 1848, BYC; OH to Friends and Brethren, 8 July 1848, JH, 2 October 1848, 7; WW to Orson Spencer, 21 August 1848, MS 10 (15 October 1848):316.

[51] OH to HCK, 5 April 1849, JH, same date; GAS to BY, 9 October 1848, JH, same date; Appleby journal, 232.

[52] JH, 2 October 1848, 3; Wight, *Address . . . and appeal. . .* ; OH, *To The Saints Scattered Abroad–Greeting*, reprinted MS 10 (15 October 1848):317-319 (spelling modified slightly). Lyman Wight was disfellowshipped at the October 1848 conference in Kanesville (MS 10:12) and excommunicated in December 1848 by the Church authorities in Salt Lake City (JFSE, 572).

[53] Examples of this practice are given in JH, 17 January 1848, 2.

[54] JH, 2 October 1848, 7, 10; Testimony of Orson Hyde, House of Representatives, 42; "Cincinnati Type Foundery," FG, 7 February 1849; GAS to BY, 9 October 1848, JH, same date; GAS and Evan M. Greene to BY, 15 October 1848, JH, same date, 5; GAS, etc., to BY, etc., 2 October 1848, JH, same date, 10.

[55] Two letters, published 19 and 21 September 1848 in the *Missouri Republican*, were reprinted in the FG 2 May 1849; OH to HCK, 5 April 1849, JH, same date; Schmidt,

"Election Contest," 34-127; OH to Brethren, 20 May 1849, BYC. A version of the story is in *History of Pottawattamie County*, 22-25.

56 GAS to BY, 2 October 1848, JH, same date, 10; GAS to OP, 20 October 1848, MS 11 (1 January 1849):13.

57 JH, 3 July, 2 October (p. 14), 5 October (p. 3) 1848; intensive study of advertisements in FG (for site locations).

58 GAS to OP, 20 October 1848, MS 11:12-13; JH, 5 October 1848, 2-3; OH, GAS, and ETB (clerk Robert Campbell) report, 15 March-5 April 1849, 1, BYC.

59 GAS to OP, 31 October 1848, MS 11:14 (part adapted to dialogue); Woodward, "Reminiscences," 192; OH, GAS, and ETB report, March-April 1849, 4-5 (punctuation modified), BYC; OH to BY, 10 March 1846, BYC; PHCM, 116-117; GAS, etc., to BY, etc., 2 October 1848, JH, same date, 4; D&C 124:91-95; R. Miller journal, 5 November 1848 (modified to dialogue); OH to WW, 10 [or 11] November 1848, WNNP, Box 4, Folder 3; Reuben Miller to Henry Sabey, 16 November 1848, HDC; WW to OP, 26 December 1848, MS 11 (1 February 1849):43; Gunn, *Oliver Cowdery*, 205-209; Greenhalgh, *Oliver Cowdery*, 74; "Last Days of Oliver Cowdery," DN, 13 April 1859 (p. 48).

60 Nathaniel Felt to OP, 16 November 1848, MS 11 (1 January 1849):15.

61 Lucius N. Scovil to OP, 11 December 1848, MS 11 (15 February 1849):54; CHC 3:361-366; GAS and ETB to OP, 20 [30] December 1848, MS 11 (5 February 1849): 52-54 (order rearranged) (the date of this letter is printed as December 20, but it tells about a Christmas party on December 25, so the date is likely December 30.)

CHAPTER 14   *. . . gold. . . . (1848-1850)*

1 OH, GAS, and ETB (clerk Robert Campbell) report, 15 March-5 April 1849, 28, 35, 36, BYC; Browning autobiography; OH to WR, 12 April 1849, 5, WRP; R. C. [Robert Campbell], "Fulfillment Of Revelation And Prophecy," JI 16 (1881):51-52 (parts modified to dialogue, and paragraphing changed) (the author gives the date of this incident as December 1849, but it was 1848).

2 Bentley, "True," 181; "The Latest Arrival Of Winter Goods" (advertisement), FG, 7 February 1849.

3 OH, GAS, and ETB report, March-April 1849, 29, BYC; "Appeared at Last!" "To Our Readers," FG, 7 February 1849.

4 FG, original at Utah State Historical Society; "To Our Farmers," "Outfitting for the Valley and Gold Region," "To the Saints in Iowa," "There is a Preacher. . . ," "Subscribe for the Guardian," FG, 21 February 1849.

5 D&C 68:12; OH to MAPH, 27 February 1849, RWC.

6 "No mail here. . . ," "Not Gone Yet," "Did You Curse the Whisky Seller!" (paragraphing modified slightly), FG, 7 March 1849; OH, GAS, and ETB report, March-April 1849, 30, BYC.

7 "Chunks of Gold. . . ," FG, 21 February 1849; Stone, *Men*, 111; "The Gold Region and Gold Fever," FG, 7 February 1849; WW to OP, 26 December 1848, MS 11 (1 February 1849):43; "Council Bluffs," FG, 21 March 1849; "Conference Minutes," FG, 18 April 1849 (modified to dialogue).

8 "First Boat This Season," "New Goods. . . ," "Gold Seekers," "We learn that between 600. . . ," "Wanted at this Office," FG, 18 April 1849; "Gold Adventurers,"

FG, 2 May 1849; "We are most agreeably. . . ," FG, 16 May 1849; "The Knoxville Company. . . ," FG, 30 May 1849; OH to BY, 16 May 1849, BYC.

[9] "We will publish. . . ," "The following are what names. . . ," FG, 2 May 1849; Bentley, "True," 181; OH to BY, 7 May 1849, BYC; "Store And Warehouse For Sale" (advertisement), FG, 3 April 1850; "Business is lively. . . ," FG, 16 May 1849.

[10] "Kanesville Market," FG, 7 February, 18 April, 30 May 1849; PHCM, 235; Campbell, "Fulfillment," JI 16:52; "Backing Out," FG, 16 May 1849.

[11] "California Emigrants," FG, 30 May 1849; OH to BY, 20 May 1849, BYC.

[12] OH to BY, 23 May 1849, BYC; GAS, ETB, and OH to President Young and Council, 7 May 1849, BYC.

[13] "Attention, Second Train!!," FG, 13 June 1849; "Emigrants for the Salt Lake should get over the Missouri. . . ," FG, 27 June 1849; "Conference Minutes," FG, 2 May 1849; "Some few disaffected spirits. . . ," FG, 27 June 1849; "Camp near Buyou Lake. . . ," FG, 11 July 1849; "The Last Train," FG, 27 June 1849; "The Last Train," FG, 25 July 1849.

[14] OH to BY, 3 July 1849 (paragraphing modified), BYC. Apparently more than one Indian was killed.

[15] "Special Conference," FG, 25 July 1849; OH to WR, 28 April, 1 June 1849, WRP; OH to GAS, 17, 23 July 1849, GASC; "Brighamites and Hydeites," FG, 27 June 1849; "Salt Lake," FG, 8 August 1849; "Try the Spirits," FG, 14 November 1849.

[16] OH to BY, 13 July 1849, BYC; OH to Friends, 30 April 1849, WRP.

[17] "Music," FG, 8 August 1849; "Music," FG, 22 August 1849; Early Ecclesiastical Minutes Collection, Kanesville, 22 July 1849, 4 November 1849; PHCM, 166-167; Pottawattamie High Council (Local Unit) Tithing Record, 23-27. The Tabernacle was standing in December 1849 (JH, 11 December 1849, p. 11) and was probably torn down in the spring of 1850, as no later mention of it has been found.

[18] "Saturday Last," FG, 5 September 1849.

[19] Various advertisements, FG.

[20] R. Johnson, *J.E.J.*, 1, 104, 105, 107, 210 (on page 105 the statement is made that J. E. Johnson arrived in Kanesville in April 1848, but page 104 has the reproduction of a document showing him in business in Nauvoo in February 1849; he may have visited Kanesville in 1848, but he apparently became a resident in 1849); location of Johnson's store from intensive study of advertisements in FG; "More Gold Discovered! . . ." (advertisement), FG, 19 September 1849; various advertisements, FG.

[21] Orson was in Kanesville September 8 ("A Day of Rejoicing") and gone before September 19 ("Our Editor has left. . . ,"), FG, 8, 19 September 1849; "Returned," FG, 17 October 1849 (no document has been found to prove that this is when Mary Ann returned, but it is the most likely time); William Price family group record, Patrons Section, Archives, FHL; "The following letter. . . ," FG, 2 May 1849; OH to GAS, 23 July 1849, GASC; PHCM, 174.

[22] "Desmoines Mail," "Misunderstanding," FG, 17 October 1849; "Request," FG, 14 November 1849; "Weather," FG, 12 December 1849.

[23] Erastus Snow report and Curtis E. Bolton journal, JH, 11 December 1849, 11, 19-21; "Letter from John Taylor," FG, 9 January 1850; BY, HCK, WR, "Second General Epistle," FG, 26 December 1849 (reprinted MS 12 [15 April 1850]:118-122; reprinted MFP 2:30-37); "Prepare for the Valley," FG, 9 January 1850.

[24] BY, HCK, and WR to OH, 16 October 1849, FG, 26 December 1849 (reprinted MS 12 [15 April 1850]:124-125; reprinted MFP 2:37-39); WR to OP, 14 January 1850, MS 12 (14 February 1850):62; "Epistle," FG 26 December 1849; JH, 4 July (p.3), 11 December 1850; HC 4:416-417.

[25] "Letter from John Taylor," FG, 9 January 1850; "The First this Season," FG, 26 December 1849; PHCM, 185, 192, 205; JSHG, 60 (the Annette in her name most often appears in family records as Ann; her father's probate record lists her as Delia Annette); OH to Martha Browett, 28 February 1859, RWC.

[26] "The Closing Year," FG, 26 December 1849; Pottawattamie High Council, 152; "Adjourned Conference," FG, 29 May 1850; "Wine," FG, 20 February 1850.

[27] House of Representatives, 47; "Reported for the Guardian," "Stolen," FG, 3 April 1850; "The Stolen Harness Returned," FG, 17 April 1850.

[28] "Conference Minutes," FG, 1 May 1850; D&C 87:3; "Grievances!" FG, 1 May 1850; "Conference," FG, 20 February 1850.

[29] "Gold Seekers," FG, 1 May 1850; Langworthy, *Scenery*, 17-19; Stimson, "Overland Journey," 405; "Kanesville Market," FG, 20 March, 3, 17 April 1850; OH to Brethren [BY, etc.], 22 April 1850, BYC; House of Representatives, 47:44; "Californians," FG, 1 May 1850; McKinstry diary, 15 May 1850; various issues of FG, spring 1850.

[30] Morgan H. White records; OH to Martha Browett, 1859, RWC.

[31] OH to BY, HCK, and WR, 25 April 1850, BYC; OH to Brethren, 26 April 1850, BYC; OH to BY, 27 April 1850, BYC.

[32] "Do You want to Sell Your Farm?" FG, 6 March 1850; "Seed Corn, &c.," FG, 17 April 1850; "Now is the Time," "He that neglects. . . ," FG, 1 May 1850.

[33] "The Season," FG, 29 May 1850; "Signs of the Weather and of the Times," FG, 15 May 1850; R. C. [Robert Campbell], "A Miraculous Shower of Rain," JI 16 (1 June 1881):130; WWJ 3:550, 551; "Bow of Promise," FG, 15 May 1850; HC 6:254; "President Orson Pratt. . . ," MS 12 (15 July 1850):216; "Conference," FG, 15 May 1850.

[34] "Conference Minutes," FG, 1 May 1850; "Conference," FG, 15 May 1850; "Adjourned Conference," FG, 29 May 1850 (parts modified to dialogue); Hammond, "Prayer," 89 (part modified to dialogue); Campbell, "Shower," JI 16:130 (part modified to dialogue); WWJ 3:551-555 (parts modified to dialogue). References to Elijah and rain: 1 Kings 8:35; 17:1; 18:1-2, 45.

[35] "The Season," "Arrivals," FG, 29 May 1850; "Emigration," FG, 12 June 1850; "Prepare for the Valley," FG, 9 January 1850; "Tithing," FG, 1 May 1850; WWJ 3:551-552.

[36] "News Expected by the Horn Telegraph," FG, 12 June 1850; BY to OH, 13 April 1850, BYC; "Wants," FG, 27 November 1850; OH to BY, 27 April 1850, BYC; "One Number More," FG, 9 January 1850; OH to BY, etc., 25 April 1850, BYC.

[37] "August Election," "Counsel," "Think of These Things," "Remember the Printer," "Emigration," "Schools," "Estray Animals," "Any person that. . . ," FG, 26 June 1850.

CHAPTER 15   *. . . deserts and mountains. . . . (1850)*

[1] "The Fourth of July," FG, 10 July 1850.

[2] "Grey Pony" (advertisement), FG, 4 April 1851; Robert Campbell (en route from Salt Lake Valley, who later went by Robert Lang Campbell to distinguish himself

from the Robert Campbell who was in 1850 living in Kanesville [JH Index Card]) to Editors of The Frontier Guardian, 7 July 1850, FG, 24 July 1850 (reprinted MS 12 [1 October 1850]:301); J. E. Johnson diary, 18 July 1850 (wagons), J. E. Johnson Papers (cited letters, following, included in papers); "To complete our outfit. . . ," FG, 10 July 1850.

³   "State of Deseret," "Deseret," FG, 31 October 1849; "Deseret," FG, 17 April 1850; Isaiah 2:2; Micah 4:1; EnA, s.v. "Utah" by Leonard J. Arrington.

⁴   J. E. Johnson to Editors, 14 July 1850, FG, 4 September 1850; H. Miller journal, June 1857; Johnson diary, 6-7 June 1850; J. E. Johnson to Mother, Harriet, Hannah, & friends, started 9 July 1850.

⁵   Johnson diary, 6-10 July 1850; Johnson to Mother, etc., started 9 July 1850; "From Elder Orson Hyde to Editor," 11 July 1850, FG, 21 August 1850.

⁶   Composite of: Johnson diary, 12-14 July 1850; J. E. Johnson to Editors, 14 July 1850, FG, 4 September 1850. Punctuation modified.

⁷   Johnson diary, 15-18 July 1850; J. E. Johnson to friends, started 18 July 1850; J. E. Johnson to Editors, 10 January 1850 [means 1851], FG, 22 January 1851.

⁸   Johnson diary, 19-20 July 1850; Hall family records; JH, 31 December 1850, Supplement, 20.

⁹   Composite of: Johnson diary, 22-24 July 1850; J. E. Johnson to friends, started 23 July 1850.

¹⁰   Johnson diary, 25-27 July 1850; J. E. Johnson to friends, started 26 July 1850.

¹¹   EnA, s.v. "Asa Whitney [1797-1872]."

¹²   OH to Brother Mackintosh, started 30 July 1850, FG, 2 October 1850 (rearranged to make the account chronological; capitalization and paragraphing modified).

¹³   Johnson diary, 9-15 August 1850.

¹⁴   Johnson to Editors, 10 January 1851, FG, 22 January 1851; "Elder Orson Hyde arrived. . . ," DN, 17 August 1850 (p. 97); Henry Atkinson Stine journal, JH, 11 August 1850, 2; WWC, 313.

¹⁵   Gilbert Belnap's document, JH, 17 September 1850, 4; Johnson to Editor, 29 January 1851, FG, 7 February 1851; Stine journal, JH, 11 August 1850.

¹⁶   BYA, 169; "Returned," FG, 27 November 1850.

¹⁷   OH to Editor, DN, 14 September 1850 (p. 106); J. E. Johnson, "Correspondence of the Frontier Guardian, No. 2. . . ," FG, 7 February 1851; author observation; GAS and ETB to OP and F. D. Richards, 29 September 1850, MS 13 (15 January 1851):23, 24; CHC 3:280-282, 4:13; "Fourth General Epistle of the Presidency," FG, 11 December 1850; WWC, 317.

¹⁸   Langworthy, *Scenery*, 90; PH 8 (1965):432-438; OH sermon reconstructed from abbreviated MT minutes by Thomas Bullock, 18 August 1850.

¹⁹   OH, "Public Dinner," FG, 8 January 1851 (modified to singular person); "Capt. Stansbury and suite. . . ," DN, 31 August 1850 (p. 95).

²⁰   "Presidents Young and Kimball. . . ," DN, 31 August 1850 (p. 95); "President Young and his associates. . . ," DN, 7 September 1850 (p. 103); Utah Historical, *Ogden*, 21-25; Manuscript History of Weber Stake; JH, 16, 17, 21 September 1850.

²¹   JH, 30 August 1850; "The Board of Regents. . . ," DN, 7 September 1850 (p. 103); GAS and ETB to OP and Richards, September 1850, MS 13:23; "Fourth General Epistle," FG, 11 December 1850.

[22] "Minutes of the General Conference. . . ," FG, 27 November 1850 (a typesetter's error corrected); "Fourth General Epistle," FG, 11 December 1850; JH, 28 September 1850.

[23] "Elder O. Hyde. . . ," DN, 31 August 1850 (p. 95); "Fourth General Epistle," FG, 11 December 1850; JH, 11 September 1850; OH sermon reconstructed from abbreviated MT minutes by Thomas Bullock, 24 September 1850.

[24] "Returned," FG, 27 November 1850; BY to OH, 28 July 1850 (mechanics and capitalization modified), BYC.

[25] OH to Editor. (For part of his letter Orson paraphrased a prophecy in Isaiah 35:1.)

[26] GAS and ETB to PP and Richards, September 1850, MS 13:24; (Pottawattamie) High Priest Quorum Minutebook 1848-1851, 37 (number seven spelled out).

[27] John Brown journal, JH, 18 November 1850; J. E. Johnson, "Now We'll Pass O'er Half the Nation Council Bluffs Our Destination," J. E. Johnson Papers (in the quotes from this poem, punctuation and capitalization are modified for ease in reading) (the poem contains 428 lines, the last ten of which have many faded words; about one-third of the poem is published in R. E. Johnson, *J. E. J.*); "Wheat," FG, 25 December 1850; WWJ 3:576; J. E. Johnson, "Return From The Valley," FG, 21 March 1851.

[28] "Reception of President Orson Hyde and Company," FG, 11 December 1850.

CHAPTER 16   *. . . gain and loss. . . . (1850-1852)*

[1] OH to First Presidency, 29 December 1850, BYC; Morgan H. White records.

[2] "Reception of President Orson Hyde and Company," "Adjourned Conference," FG, 11 December 1850.

[3] OH to Presidency, 29 December 1850, BYC; "Wants," FG, 27 November 1850; "Wood," FG, 11 December 1850 (punctuation modified slightly); "Storage, Forwarding, and Commission Business," FG, 27 November 1850 and each issue afterward; "To Salt Lake Emigrants," FG, 25 December 1850 (spelling modified slightly).

[4] "Their Children," TPH 5 (1956):462; Stimson, "Overland Journey," 406; OH to Martha Browett, 1859, RWC; JH, 20 (pp. 1, 2), 27 (p.1) April 1848, 22, 24 (p. 1), 28 (p. 5) October 1849, 26 February (p. 2), 21 April (p. 3) 1850; Thomas McKenzie officiated at marriages published in the FG 10 July, 4 September, 2 October 1850; "Obituary," FG, 4 September 1850; 1850 Census Pottawattamie County, Iowa (as of 1 June 1850), dwelling 188; "Married," FG, 11 December 1850.

[5] "Woman's Rights Convention," FG, 11 December 1850; "Infallible Signs," FG, 11 December 1850; "Kanesville Academy," FG, 25 December 1850; "Grandmother Miner."

[6] 1850 Census, Pottawattamie County, Iowa, 142; Temple Index Bureau, Charlotte Quindlin; 1860 Census, Mount Pleasant, Sanpete County, Utah; "Died," DNW, 14 December 1881 (p. 736).

[7] OH to Presidency, 29 December 1850, JH; "Letter From the Editor," FG, 8 January 1851; Bee autobiography, 9; (Pottawattamie) High Priest Quorum Minutebook 1848-1851, 41.

[8] "Fire in Kanesville," "Emigration," FG, 7 February 1851; "Fire," FG, 21 February 1851; "Sarah Beriah Fiske Allen Ricks," PH 11 (1968):135, 143.

[9] "Conference Report," FG, 2 May 1851 (partly modified to dialogue).

[10] "Emigration," FG, 16 May 1851 (printer's error corrected); "Attention," FG, 18 April 1851; "The Last Company," FG, 13 June 1851; "District Clerk's Office Moved," FG, 27 June 1851; "Summary of News, &c.," FG, 11 July 1851; "Treaty," "Oysters," FG, 27 June 1851; "Friend Guardian," FG, 11 July 1851.

[11] "Summary of News, &c.," FG, 11 July 1851; "Letter from Elder Orson Hyde," FG, 22 August 1851; 1851 State Census, Pottawattamie County, Iowa; Bee autobiography, 9-10; "Something New, Editors turned Prophets," FG, 25 July 1851.

[12] "Highly Important. . . ," FG, 22 August 1851; "Recovered Property," FG, 14 November 1851; "Letter from Elder Orson Hyde," FG, 22 August 1851; Carrington, "Travel Diary 29 June to 17 Aug, 1851" (contains a daily account of this journey), Carrington Papers; "President Orson Hyde. . . ," DN, 19 August 1851 (p. 308); "Sixth General Epistle," MS 14 (15 January 1852):19 (reprinted MFP 2:81).

[13] JH, 17 August-23 September 1851; WWJ 4:52-55, 58-59; "Minutes of General Conference. . . ," FG, 28 November 1851 (reprinted MS 14 [1 February 1852]:35); Lewis Abbott and Ann Marsh Archive Record, FHL; JT remarks, 9 August 1857, JD 5:115; BY remarks, 6 September 1857, JD 5:207.

[14] "Home Again," FG, 14 November 1851 (modified to first person); JH, 23 September 1851; "Highly Important. . . ," FG, 6 February 1852; "Epistle," MS 13 (15 September 1851):279; "Sixth General Epistle," MS 14:23; JH, 3 May 1852, 2-3.

[15] "Indian Treaty," "Home Again," FG, 14 November 1851 (parts modified to first person).

[16] "Emigration," FG, 3 October 1851; "Recovered Property," FG, 14 November 1851 (partly changed to first person).

[17] "Highly Important. . . ," FG, 22 August 1851 (partly changed to first person and to dialogue); OH to Presidency, 29 December 1850, JH.

[18] Composite of: "Home Again," "Pay the Printer," FG, 14 November 1851 (changed to first person).

[19] "The Weather," FG&IS, 20 January 1853; ETB to BY, 15 November 1851, JH, same date; MFP 2:94; "Special Conference," FG, 12 December 1851; "Great Salt Lake City. . . ," FG, 14 November 1851; ETB to GAS, 12 March 1852, JH, same date.

[20] "Corn and Hay," "Wanted," "Things to be Remembered. . . ," "Pottowatamie County For Sale," FG, 14 November 1851; "To our Subscribers, Patrons, and Friends," FG, 26 December 1851; "Have You Forgotten?" FG, 9 January 1852 (modified to first person); "Reminiscence," FG, 14 November 1851.

[21] "Horses, Mules, Oxen, Cows, &c., for Crossing the Plains," FG, 14 November 1851; "Wanted Immediately," FG, 6 February 1852; "Pay the Printer," FG, 28 November 1851; "Have You Forgotten?" FG, 9 January 1852; "Wanted Immediately," FG, 13 June 1851.

[22] ETB to BY, 15 November 1851, JH; "Beet Sugar in Utah," WB, 9 June 1852.

[23] "Wanted at this Office," FG, 12 December 1851; "Public Meeting," FG, 9 January 1852; "House Room," FG, 22 August 1849.

[24] "To our Subscribers. . . ," "Gratifying," FG, 26 December 1851; JH, 9 March 1852; OH to BY, 27 May 1852, BYC; ETB to BY, 16 March 1852, JH, same date; "Cold Weather," FG, 23 January 1852.

[25] "Read," FG, 9 January 1852; "Conference Minutes," FG&IS, 22 April 1852; "Prospects of the Church," FG, 4 April 1851.

26 "Pursuant to previous notice. . . ," FG, 26 December 1851; "Public Meeting," FG, 9 January 1852; "Read," FG, 9 January 1852; Hillman autobiography and journal, 37-39.

27 Genesis 1:27; Acts 6:55-56; Hebrews 1:1-3; "A few thoughts on hearing a Sermon," FG, 23 January 1852.

28 "Wholesale Only," FG, 9 January 1852; "Hymn Books," FG, 23 January 1852; "Guardian Office," FG, 20 February 1852.

29 D&C 89:8.

30 Mortgage, Pottawattamie County Deeds A:70-71 (printed in *History of Fremont County, Iowa*, 405-406, and in *History of Mills County, Iowa*, 387-388); "Valedictory," FG, 20 February 1852; "Mr. Editor," FG&IS, 8 April 1852.

Orson's press, affectionately called "Old Guardy," had earned many meals for Orson's family. What lay ahead for it? In just nine months it would change hands again. October 19, 1852, Jacob Dawson advertised the property and press for sale, "the ill health of my family requiring my undivided attention" ("Printers, Take Notice!" [advertisement] FG&IS, 21 October 1852). The purchaser was Dawson's friend, A. C. Ford, who became editor of the *Guardian and Sentinel* November 18, 1852. After six more months Mr. Ford terminated publication of the newspaper and sold the office and materials, stating that he had "not received a sufficient amount of patronage to warrant its continuance" ("Last Notice," FG&IS, 12 May 1853). Joseph E. Johnson, still an enterprising citizen of Kanesville (name changed to Council Bluffs), next owned "Old Guardy." He used it to print several newspapers in various locations and eventually had it hauled to the Rocky Mountains, where it again stamped out newspapers. The last known resting place of this printing press was in storage in Salt Lake City. Someone apparently removed it and sold it for metal salvage (Rufus D. Johnson, *J.E.J.*, 183-186).

31 ETB to GAS, March 1852 (punctuation modified slightly); ETB to BY, March 1852 (punctuation modified slightly).

32 "Mormons the Apocalyptic Frogs," *Savannah Sentinel*, 6 March 1852.

33 William Simpson to OH, 16 March 1852, OH to Simpson, 16, 18 March 1852, and Simpson to OH, 23 March 1852, *Savannah Sentinel*, 3 April 1852; OH to Editor, 2 April 1852, and OH to Simpson, 24 March 1852, WB, 28 April 1852; "Bugle Office" (advertisement), WB, 5 May 1852; Matthew 24:7.

34 "We give place. . . ," FG&IS, 4 March 1852; "Anti-Mormon Meeting in Fremont County, Iowa," *Savannah Sentinel*, 6 March 1852; "The Judgeship," FG&IS, 11 March 1852; "History of the Judgeship," FG&IS, 18 March 1852; "The Judgeship Again," A. C. Ford to [Editor] Dawson, 20 March 1852, and H. D. Johnson to Editor, FG&IS, 25 March 1852.

35 OH, "The question to be settled. . . ," FG&IS, 4 March 1852; "Affidavits of Orson Hyde & G. W. Harris," Orson Hyde to Editor, "Libel," FG&IS, 11 March 1852; "Slander," WB, 19 May 1852.

36 "Ignatius" to Editor, WB, 19 May 1852.

37 "Election of District Judge," FG&IS, 4 March 1852; "Unscrupulous Villainy and Locofoco Trickery!" FG&IS, 1 April 1852; "Judge of the 6th Judicial District," WB, 26 May 1852; *History Fremont County*, 387; OH to Guardian and Sentinel, 27 May 1852, FG&IS, 28 May 1852.

[38] "Highly Important," FG&IS, 28 May 1852; Jedediah M. Grant to BY, 13 May 1852, JH, same date; "Utah Appointments," FG&IS, 11 June 1852; "The Tables Turning," MS 14 (12 June 1852):249.

[39] "Emigration," FG&IS, 13 May 1852; "Kanesville Again," "Our Country," WB, 19 May 1852; ETB to BY, 13 May 1852, JH, same date; "The Times," WB, 26 May 1852.

[40] Henry C. Brandt to Myrtle S. Hyde, November 1987; *History of Pottawattamie County*, 337, and Biographical 147-148; 1851 Iowa State Census, Pottawattamie County (Plumer family listed next door to William Price).

[41] "Attention, The Hand Cart Trains," WB, 19 May 1852; "Rendezvous, First Mormon Company," FG&IS, 20 May 1852.

[42] "Arrivals," WB, 26 May 1852; "Salt Lake," WB, 16 June 1852; "Claim And Property Agent," WB, 26 May 1852.

[43] OH to the Council of the Twelve, 27 May 1852, BYC (part of this is in JH, same date); "Our regular Packet. . . ," WB, 30 June 1852; "Kanesville as it Was and Is," "Disgraceful Assault," WB, 16 June 1852; "Outrage upon Elder Hyde," FG&IS, 18 June 1852.

[44] Henry L. Southworth to WR, 21 June 1852, JH, same date.

[45] ETB to BY, 1 July 1852, JH, same date; "Fourth of July," "Orson Hyde," WB, 7 July 1852.

[46] "Davy" to Editor, 31 May 1852, WB, 2 June 1852; "Western Iowa," FG&IS, 15 April 1852 (population figures before Saints left).

[47] "Most Delicious," WB, 16 June 1852; Hammond, "Prayer," 89.

[48] J. R. Perkins, *Battalion*, 14, 15. Orson's was not the last Mormon wagon to leave town; a few left in the next two days ("Already Gone," WB, 7 July 1852).

Orson Hyde's printing office stood for eighteen more years. *The Council Bluffs Weekly Nonpareil* of July 29, 1870, 3, has the following (found by Elaine Speakman, Mount Pleasant, Utah):

The hand of Progress has played sad havoc with the landmarks of Mormon occupation of these beautiful bluffs. One by one they have been laid low, until now they are by no means a distinguishing feature of the city. Those that still remain are so disguised with "modern improvements" as to be scarcely recognizable by those who knew them in their pristine glory. Chief among those remaining, and not thus defiled, we may mention "Nebraska Hall", next to the Bryant House, and the store now occupied by Charles Butterfield, corner of Broadway and Madison streets. This latter will be known to us but a short time, for already the brick are being hauled for a building that is to supplant it. The old logs are to give way to brick and mortar, and a more sightly store is to take the place of the former headquarters of Orson Hyde, the Mormon Apostle. . . .

CHAPTER 17   *. . . went our way. . . . (1852)*

[1] "Orson Hyde," "Oh, Dear!" WB, 7 July 1852; G. Harris journals, 85 (he in the fifth Ten); Mortensen, *Carling*, 49 (he in the third Ten); A. Miller, "Henry Miller," 6; JH, December 1852 Supplement, 20th Company.

[2] Williams autobiography; JH, December 1852 Supplement; MAPH to Joseph C. Bentley, 16 March 1897, RWC; Mortensen, *Carling*, 51; William Mason and Sarah Wright family group record, Patrons Section, Archives, FHL.

[3]   Cowley reminiscences; Bee autobiography, 1, 9–11 (punctuation modified slightly).

[4]   Mortensen, *Carling*, 49; G. Harris journals, 85–86; Jonathan E. Layne account, JH, 27 September 1852, 1, 2; "Friend Dawson and Ford," FG&IS, 23 July 1852; "Letter from the Editor," WB, 9 June 1852.

[5]   Browning autobiography (he in the second Ten); Bee autobiography, 12–13 (punctuation modified slightly).

[6]   Mortensen, *Carling*, 49; Harris journals, 86–87; "Grandmother Miner" (changed to first person, with slight punctuation modification).

[7]   G. Harris journals, 87–88; Bee autobiography, 13–14 (punctuation slightly modified); "Letter from Thomas Bullock," MS 10 (15 April 1848):116–117; Mortensen, *Carling*, 50; Browning autobiography.

[8]   Bee autobiography, 15 (punctuation modified slightly); Mortensen, *Carling*, 50.

[9]   "Grandmother Miner"; James Byars Carter, "Disease and Death in the Nineteenth Century: A Genealogical Perspective," *National Genealogical Society Quarterly* 76 (1988): 295; G. Harris journals, 91 (teamster's name inadvertently recorded as John Mason); Mortensen, *Carling*, 51; MAPH to Bentley, 1897, RWC; Williams autobiography.

[10]   G. Harris journals, 91, 92, 94; Clayton, *Emigrants' Guide*, 11; Mortensen, *Carling*, 51; "Laura Hyde Miner."

[11]   Mortensen, *Carling*, 50–51; G. Harris journals, 90–94; Layne account, JH, 27 September 1852, 3; Clayton, *Emigrants' Guide*, 12, 23; Bee autobiography, 15–16 (punctuation modified slightly).

[12]   Bullock, MS 10:117; Mortensen, *Carling*, 51, 52; G. Harris journals, 94, 95.

[13]   G. Harris journals, 87–88, 95–96, 100; Mortensen, *Carling*, 50, 52; Clayton, *Emigrants' Guide*, 13; Bathsheba Smith autobiography, 25 (spelling modified slightly); Layne account, JH, 27 September 1852, 4; Browning autobiography.

[14]   Bee autobiography, 16–17; Layne account, JH, 27 September 1852, 4; Mortensen, *Carling*, 52; G. Harris journals, 95–96 (spelling modified slightly) (Orson's comments adjusted to dialogue); Browning autobiography.

[15]   Mortensen, *Carling*, 52; G. Harris journals, 96, 98; Clayton, *Emigrants' Guide*, 14–17; Bullock, MS 10:117; Layne account, JH, 27 September 1852, 4; author observation.

[16]   John Brown account, JH, 2 November 1852; author observation; Clayton, *Emigrants' Guide*, 19–20; G. Harris journals, 101; Franklin D. Richards to Samuel W. Richards, 30 September 1852, JH, same date; Langworthy, *Scenery*, 81–83; Bee autobiography, 17–18.

CHAPTER 18   *. . . build. . . . (1852–1855)*

[1]   Bee autobiography, 18–19; Cowley reminiscences.

[2]   "Minutes of Conference, 1852," DN, 18 September 1852, 4.

[3]   CHC 4:13–16, 54; "Tabernacle," FG&IS, 20 May 1852; "Minutes of the General Conference . . . October 1852," MS 15 (5 March 1853):149–150.

[4]   Mortensen, *Carling*, 55; OP discourse, 29 August 1852, JD 1:53–66; JSHG, 60; Temple Index Bureau: Charlotte Quindlan.

[5]   Angell journal, 29 November 1852; Salt Lake County Deed Abstracts, Book A-2: 94; JSH, 41; photograph of home. Orson's home was undoubtedly built in two segments. His son Joseph recalled being told by Orson that Marriner W. Merrill

shingled it. Marriner W. Merrill arrived in Utah in September of 1853 (Nibley, *Stalwarts*, 96), so could not have shingled Orson's home in late 1852 or early 1853. Probably he shingled the second section.

6   G. Harris journals, 104 (spelling and punctuation modified); scriptures: 1 Thessalonians 5:2, 2 Peter 3:10, Matthew 24:30, Revelation 1:5-7.

7   JH, 27 November 1852; WWJ 4:154-181; (Editorial), MS 15 (30 April 1853):281 (modified to dialogue); "New Year's Day Visit. . . ," MS 15 (2 July 1853):427-428.

8   JH, 14, 17, 21 January, 7 February 1853; "Prosperity of Utah County, Utah Territory," MS 14 (11 December 1852):668.

9   WWJ 4:195-198 (spelling modified slightly), 208-213; BE 1:334-335; OH prayer, 6 April 1853, JD 2:47-49; "Minutes of the General Conference. . . ," MS 15 (16 July 1853):449.

10   "Minutes of General Conference. . . ," DN 30 April 1853; "Prosperity," MS 14:668; "Deseret," MS 15 (30 April 1853):286; L. Brown, *Journal*, 35; WWJ 4:198; JH, 12, 14 (p. 2), 18 February 1853; "Ninth General Epistle," MFP 2:113; CHC 3:396-400; "News from Utah and the Plains," WB, 7 July 1852; "We understand that the Sugar company . . . ," DN 27 November 1852; "Notice to the Public," OH, "Sugar and Oil, Vinegar and Spirits," DN, 5 March 1853.

11   BYOJ, 25 March, 11, 23 April 1853; Harris journals, 109; "General Conference. . . ," DN, 30 April 1853; "Epistle," MFP 2:113; "Sugar Beet Seed," DN, 19 March 1853; Angell journal, 12, 22 April 1853.

12   OH to BY, 4 May 1853, BYC; BYOJ, 20 April 1853; Angell journal, 25 April 1853; JH, 16 June 1853; Charles L. Schmalz, "The Failure of Utah's First Sugar Factory," *Utah Historical Quarterly* 56: (1988):41.

13   JH, 18 June 1853; "There are a few score. . . ," DN, 28 May 1853; "Ploughs Again! The Last Chance!!" (advertisement) DN, 10 July 1853; JSH, 42 (modified to dialogue).

14   OH to BY, 23 July 1853, BYC; JH, 1 August 1853; Pottawattamie County Deeds A:70-71.

15   Gowans and Campbell, *Fort Supply*, 9-11; "General Conference," DN, 15 October 1853; J. Brown, *Autobiography*, 304-305 (changed to present tense).

16   J. Brown, *Autobiography*, 305-306 (partly modified to dialogue); "Green River Expedition," DN, 1 December 1853; Gowans and Campbell, *Fort Supply*, 30; Green River Company Journal, 2; *Portrait, Genealogical and Biographical of Utah*, 477; WWJ 4:225.

17   "C. Allen," 137; Green River Company Journal, 10 (Orson probably traveled with a companion or companions, but no record found so states), 11, 25, 33-37 (spelling and punctuation modified); Gowans and Campbell, *Fort Supply*, 3, 5, 29; J. Brown, *Autobiography*, 306-309; Sanderson, "Diary," 90; "We learn that Elder Hyde returned. . . ," DN, 15 December 1853, 3.

18   JSHG, 60.

19   Chamberlin, *University*, 17-44, 568; "The Regents of the University," DN, 24 November 1853; "Laura Hyde Miner"; HSD, 508-511; OH to BY, 4 October 1853, BYC; JH, 31 January 1854.

20   HOJ 16:230-231; L. Brown, *Journal*, 48; Gowans and Campbell, *Fort Supply*, 27-28; Green River Company Journal, entries during winter 1853-1854.

21 "Flour For Sale," DN, 16 February 1854, 3; HSD, 507; WWJ 4:254-255; L. Brown, *Journal*, 50; JFSE, 565.

22 Autograph book of Martha S. Heywood.

23 "Green River Men, Attention!" DN, 30 March 1854; J. Brown, *Autobiography*, 309-312; HSD, 514-516 (for details about Orson Hyde possibly practicing law in Green River County, see OH to BY, 2 May 1854, BYC; BY to OH, 6 May 1854, BYL 1:527); Green River Company Journal, 32; "C. Allen," 137; I. Bullock diary, 8 May 1854.

24 HSD, 516-518; J. Brown, *Autobiography*, 313 (modified to present tense); I. Bullock diary, 10 May 1854; Sanderson, "Diary," 97-98 (quoted portion changed to dialogue); Green River Company Journal, 38.

25 OH to Albert Carrington, 31 May 1855, DN, 27 June 1855; Pulsipher diaries, 32; HCK to William Kimball, 29 June 1854, MS 16 (7 October 1854):633; OH to BY, 30 July 1856, 7, BYC; JSH, 45; Salt Lake County Deed Abstracts A-2:70; MT 19 February, 5 March, 16 April, 18 June (and others) 1854.

26 OH address, 4 July 1854, JD 6:367-371 (see 2 Nephi 10:11, 13, BoM).

27 Green River Company Journal, 40, 41, 46; Sanderson, "Diary," 90; J. Brown, *Autobiography*, 314-346; I. Bullock diary, 13 May-6 June 1854; Price, "Wm. Price," 4.

28 "Cash Paid," DN, 7 September 1854, 3; HCK to Kimball, MS 16:633; "Foreign Intelligence," MS 17 (27 January 1855):56; advertisements, DN, summer 1854; JSHG, 60; Olsen, "Aurelius Miner," 272-273; Nicholson, *Martyrdom*, 120-121.

29 OH discourse, 24 September 1854, JD 2:112-120 (quoted parts are from 114, 117, 120) (punctuation modified slightly) (JD identifies this discourse as being delivered in 1853, in error; it first appeared in print in DN, 5 October 1854, properly dated); OH lecture, 6 October 1854, JD 2:81-82.

30 JH, 10-18, 26 October 1854; author observation; OH address, 4 July 1854, JD 6:370; "Foreign Intelligence," MS 16 (8 July 1854):425; JSH, 56-57; O. Whitney, *Utah* 4:668.

31 OH to BY, 2 October 1855, 8, BYC; "Honor to Whom Honor," DN, 26 October 1854; "Bowery," DN, 9 November 1854; "Teacher's Certificates," DN, 23 November 1854; A. C. Brower to Editor, 23 December 1854, DN, 4 January 1855.

32 Price, "Wm. Price," 4; Archive Record, George Ogden Chase, FHL; BY to OH, 17 January 1855, BYL 1:826.

CHAPTER 19   *. . . westward. . . . (1855)*

1 BY to OH, 17 January 1855, BYL 1:826 (punctuation and spelling slightly modified); OH to BY, 17 January 1855, BYC.

2 "Notice to all Emigrants," DN, 3 August 1854, 3, and following issues; HSD, 546, 547; JH, 18, 19 January 1855; OH lecture, 22 January 1855, JD 6:371-376.

3 HSD, 549, 550; JH, 19 January 1855; MT, 21 January 1855 and following weeks, specifically 11 March; WWJ 4:302; OH to BY, 8 February 1855, BYC.

4 JSHG, 60, which has June instead of January; Salt Lake City Cemetery Records, January 1855; Olsen, "Aurelius Miner," 273.

5 "Complimentary," DN, 11 April 1855; WWJ 4:303 and following.

6 OH, "The Mormons," DN, 14 March 1855; JH, 7, 27 April 1855, 5 May 1855; MT, 29 April 1855.

[7]   MT, 6, 13 May 1855 (punctuation added); HSD, 554-555; JH, 30 April 1855.

[8]   OH to BY, 27 April 1856, 2, BYC. Brigham Young granted Charlotte's official "separation" from Orson in 1859 (divorce and separation papers, BYC).

[9]   HSD, 555; "Departure," DN, 30 May 1855; OH to Albert Carrington, 31 May 1855, DN, 27 June 1855.

Whereas Stout gives the date of departure as May 15, the DN has May 16. The practice was, as here presented, to camp near home the first night (or several nights) for practice. Presented this way, both dates are accurate.

[10]   JH, 9 December 1856 (this is a report of the mission, written in December 1856, and it gives the number of guards as 35; HSD, 555, written at the time, says the guards numbered 25.); Bentley, "True," 182.

[11]   BY to OH, 7 May 1855, BYL 2:140-143; JH, 8 May 1855; OH to BY, 3 July 1855, BYC; "Departure," DN, 30 May 1855; "The Hon. Orson Hyde & Company. . . ," DN, 30 May 1855; "From Israel Justus Clark's Journal," PH 7:164; "Autobiography of Gilbert Belnap," 47.

[12]   OH to Carrington, May 1855, DN 27 June 1855. Background information from author observation and Curran, *Fearful Crossing*, 53-65.

[13]   OH to BY, 19 June 1855, BYC.

[14]   Curran, *Fearful Crossing*, 31-46, 66-67, 86-102; Greeley, *Journey*, 270-272; author observation; OH to BY, 19 June 1855, BYC.

[15]   OH to BY, 19 June 1855, BYC; Curran, *Fearful Crossing*, 124-143, 176-184; author observation.

[16]   Curran, *Fearful Crossing*, 184-191; "The Carson River Country," *Western Standard*, 30 August 1856; OH to BY, 19 June 1855, BYC; Greeley, *Journey*, 278-279; Morgan, *Humboldt*, 199; author observation.

[17]   O. B. Huntington and C. A. Huntington to Editor, 27 November 1854, DN, 7 December 1854; Col. John Reese, "Mormon Station," *Nevada Historical Society Papers* 1:186-189; H. Van Sickles, "Utah Desperadoes," *Nevada Historical Society Papers* 1:190; JH, 30 June 1855.

[18]   Norton, *Life*, 321.

[19]   OH to BY, 19 June 1855, BYC. The boundary is explained in OH to BY, 30 September 1855, 4, BYC.

[20]   OH to BY, 3 July 1855, 1, BYC; J. Heywood diary, 1; JH, 21 July 1855, 1; Lillard, *Desert Challenge*, 155; author observation.

[21]   Yohalem, *"I remember. . . ,"* 26-27, 78, 90, 143, 145, 185, 190-191, 218; OH to BY, 3 July 1855, 1, BYC; Willis, *Sacramento County*, 5-12; J. Heywood diary, 1; OH to BY, 3 July 1855, 1, 3, BYC; JH, 1 August 1855, 4.

[22]   BY to OH, 7 May 1855, BYL 2:140-143 (spelling and punctuation modified slightly); Byington and Lewis, *San Francisco* 1:191, 205, 227, 251, 276-277.

[23]   OH to BY, 3, 15 July 1855, BYC; JH, 1 August 1855, 3, 4; J. Heywood diary, 1.

[24]   Willis, *Sacramento County*, 59; OH to BY, 15 July, 2 October 1855, BYC; OH to Albert Carrington, 9 September 1855, DN, 10 October 1855 (p. 248).

[25]   OH to BY, 15 July 1855, 1, 2, BYC; OH to Carrington, September 1855, DN, 10 October 1855.

[26] OH to Carrington, September 1855, DN, 10 October 1855; Merkley, *Biography*, 35; OH to BY, 30 September 1855, 2, BYC; JH, 15 August 1855; "Amasa Potter—1848," PH 18 (1975):168.

[27] Norton, *Life*, 11-12, 321, 324; OH to BY, 30 September 1855, 2-3 (punctuation modified slightly), BYC; George H. Goddard, "Boundary between California and Utah. Wagon Road Route," DN, 21 November 1855.

[28] OH to Carrington, September 1855, DN, 10 October 1855; OH to BY, 30 September 1855, 3-4, 6-7, BYC.

[29] Norton, *Life*, 321-323.

[30] JH, 30 September 1855, 9 December 1856; Bentley, "True," 182; OH to Carrington, September 1855, DN, 10 October 1855.

[31] JH, 1 August 1855; OH to Bros. Young, Kimball and Grant, 4 September 1855, BYC; Norton, *Life*, 321, 324.

[32] Goddard, "Boundary," DN, 21 November 1855; OH to BY, 30 September 1855, 4-5, BYC; OH to Carrington, September 1855, DN, 10 October 1855.

[33] OH to BY, 30 September 1855 (pp. 1, 5) (some writers have said that in his previous travels Orson saw the birthplace of Columbus, which is untrue), 29 October 1855 (p. 3), BYC; Miluck, *Genoa*, 39, 44-45.

[34] OH to BY, 30 September (p. 7), 2 October (pp. 3-4, 8) 1855, BYC; CHC 4:192; Ellison, *Carson County*, 317, 328, 329; Thompson and West, *Nevada*, 39.

[35] OH to BY, 29 October 1855, 1, 3, 4, BYC; BY to OH, 31 August 1855, BYL 2:332.

[36] OH to BY, 17 November 1855, 1, BYC; BY to OH, 29 September 1855 (BYL 2:385), 9 October 1855 (BYL 2:424).

[37] Thompson and West, *Nevada*, 333; JSH, 46.

[38] Norton, *Life*, 326; OH to BY, 17 November 1855, 1, 4 (punctuation modified slightly), BYC.

[39] OH to BY, 13 January 1856, 3-4, BYC; JSH, 47-48.

CHAPTER 20   *. . . Israel among the Gentiles. . . . (1855-1856)*

[1] OH to BY, 13 January 1856, 3-5, BYC; JSH, 47-49 (punctuation modified); Norton, *Life*, 327; JH, 9 December 1856. The account of Orson's mountain ordeal as recounted years later by his son Joseph, has impossibilities when compared with Orson's statements written at the time. Apparently Joseph's memories were used in *Utah Since Statehood* 3:707-708.

[2] OH to BY, 13 January 1856 (minor punctuation added), BYC; JH, 24 January, 9 December 1856; Oliver W. Hyde, Jr., M.D. interview; Jean Hilliard Vig, "She Was Frozen Solid," *Guideposts*, May 1995, 35-36; BY to OH, 30 October 1855, BYL 2:439-441.

[3] OH to BY, 25, 29 January 1856, BYC; Norton, *Life*, 327; JSHG, 62; HSD, 580, 581.

[4] BY to OH, 3 January 1856, BYC; OH to BY, 22 March, 11 May 1856 BYC; Merkley, *Biography*, 39-40.

[5] OH, "From Carson Valley," *Western Standard*, 22 March 1856, 5 April 1856.

[6] Ratay, *Pioneers*, 7, 17 (quoted by permission of the author).

7   "Orson Hyde vs. H. M. Hodgis, In Attachment," 29, 30 April, 1 May 1856, Carson County Probate Court; OH to BY, 20, 27 April, 8 August 1856, BYC.

8   OH to BY, 20, 27 April 1856, BYC. Orson may have been unaware that his store was running low in provisions (see HCKW, 405).

9   OH vs. Hodgis, and related papers, Carson County Probate Court; HCKW, 411; Call journal, 57; Bentley, "True," 183; OH to BY, 30 September 1855, BYC.

10 OH to BY, 11 May, 18 August 1856, BYC; Mack, *Nevada*, 158; Carson "Early Maps," 17, 37; Bentley, "True," 183.

11 Author observation; OH to BY, 2 July 1856, BYC; John Hyde, "From Wash-ho Valley," *Western Standard*, 12 July 1856 (some punctuation modified); JH, 12 December 1857, 1; "Andrew Jackson Stewart," PH 1 (1958):279; Amasa Potter, "Missionary Sketches," JI 6 (15 April 1871):63; John Hyde to Brother Cannon, 12 August 1856, *Western Standard*, 23 August 1856.

12 OH to BY, 30 July (p. 6), 18 August (p. 4), 28 September (p. 1), 12 October (p. 1) 1856, BYC; Bentley, "True," 184; Ratay, *Pioneers*, 127; Thompson, "Murdock," 88; Hunsaker journal, 23; John Hyde to Cannon, August 1856, *Western Standard*, 23 August 1856; "Stewart," PH 1:279.

13 OH to BY, 2 July (p. 2), 30 July (pp. 1-7 [part of p. 1 modified to dialogue]), 18 August (pp. 2, 3), 12 September (pp. 1-3), 12 October (p. 4-5), 18 October (p. 2) 1856, BYC; Thompson and West, *Nevada*, 40, 333; JH, 12 December 1857.

14 OH to BY, 30 July (p. 5), 8 August (p. 4) 1856, BYC. A newspaper account (DN, 3 September 1856, 5) states that the group from Carson arrived in Salt Lake City in July, but an item above it in the same column says August, which is correct.

15 JSH, 46, 47a; HSD, 571-574; "Death of a Veteran," DEN, 18 September 1890, 3. This last reference, Gideon Wood's obituary, states that he was baptized by Orson Hyde in February 1832, but Orson's mission to Florence was in November and December of 1831.

16 OH to BY, 30 July (pp. 7, 8), 8 August (p. 3) 1856, BYC; BY to OH, 29 May 1856, BYL 2:764; John Hyde to Cannon, August 1856, *Western Standard*, 23 August 1856.

17 John Hyde to Cannon, August 1856, *Western Standard*, 23 August 1856; JSH, 47; Price, "Wm. Price," 4; OH to BY, 18 August 1856, BYC; OH remarks, 21 December 1856, JD 4:214.

18 OH to BY, 18 August (p. 5), 12 September (p. 4), 28 September (p. 3) 1856, BYC; Hunsaker journal, 20; Carson, "Early Maps," 37, 38; Bentley, "True," 184.

19 OH to BY, 18 August (p. 5), 28 September 1856, BYC; Baker, *Baker Genealogy*, 25; Leonard Wines, "From Franktown, Washo Valley, Utah," *Western Standard*, 13 March 1857.

20 "From Carson Valley," *Western Standard*, 3 April 1857, 3; OH to BY, 12, 16 (pp. 1-2; punctuation modified), 18 (pp. 3-4) October 1856, BYC.

21 Price, "Wm. Price," 5; OH to BY, 12 (p. 4), 22 October, 4 November (p. 1) 1856, BYC; Wines, "Franktown," *Western Standard*, 13 March 1857; Bentley, "True," 184; "Carson Valley," *Western Standard*, 13 December 1856; Ratay, *Pioneers*, 121; Madison S. Hambleton to BY, about January 1857, BYC.

[22] OH to BY, 4 November 1856, BYC. November 3 is assumed; Orson says he will leave "tomorrow," and the letter was "Finished Nov. 4," which was apparently "tomorrow."

[23] BY to OH, 1 September 1856, BYL 3:47-50; OH to BY, 4 November 1856, BYC; OH to MAPH, 28 December 1856, RWC.

CHAPTER 21   . . . *edifying and chastisement.* . . . *(1856-1860)*

[1] "Elder O. Hyde. . . ," DN, 17 December 1856 (p. 325); WWJ 4:513; OH to MAPH, 28 December 1856, RWC; JH, 9 December 1856; JSH, 50-51; Price, "Wm. Price," 6.

Various dates are mentioned as the start of the journey, but November 5 seems most accurate.

Wilford Woodruff recorded that Orson said he came part way on the "Beckworth road." This is impossible; the Beckworth (Beckwith) Road was north of the Truckee River and took travelers west into California (Elliott, *Nevada*, 46, 47, 387). Probably Orson said, or meant to say, "Bidwell-Bartleson Road," which came close around the north tip of the Great Salt Lake (Leigh, *Nevada Names*, 35-36; D. Miller, *Utah Atlas*, Map 24). In the Ruby Mountains the Bidwell-Bartleson "road" crossed Harrison Pass and here was impassable by wagons. The north pass in the Rubys, the Secret Pass, was also impassable by wagons. Orson's group undoubtedly traversed Overland Pass, which was easy and smooth, on the Hastings Cutoff road, at the south end of the Ruby Mountains (Curran, *Fearful Crossing*, 77, 79).

The paragraph quoting Orson is a composite.

[2] BYOJ, 9 December 1856; OH to BY, 12 October 1856, 7, BYC; Olsen, "Aurelius Miner," 273.

[3] HCK discourse, 12 October 1856, JD 5:202; WWJ 4:445-446; CHC 4:119-126.

[4] Discourses by BY, HCK, Jedediah M. Grant, and Franklin D. Richards in JD 4:43, 44, 49, 53, 61, 63, 71, 74, 97, 108, 109, 117, 120, 129, 152, 153, 188, 203, 205; BY to OP, 30 October 1856, MS 19 (14 February 1857):98-99.

[5] WW remarks, 21 December 1856, JD 4:146; WWJ 4:476-477 (spelling modified).

[6] BYA, 154-155, 460n.7; Bancroft, *Utah*, 201, 204; Burton, *Saints*, 239.

[7] HOH, 1856, 1170-1172 (punctuation modified slightly); JH, 4 February 1857, 3-4; WWC, 370; BY to OP, 1856, MS 19:99; OH remarks, 21 December 1856, JD 4:213-215.

[8] HCK discourse, 21 December 1856, JD 4:138-145 (quoted part is on 141); WW remarks, 21 December 1856, JD 4:147; Franklin D. Richards discourse, 5 October 1856, JD 4:118.

[9] OH to MAPH, 28 December 1856, RWC (order partly rearranged).

[10] WWJ 4:522-523.

[11] Job 5:17; Proverbs 3:11-12; Hebrews 12:6; Revelation 3:19; D&C 95:1, 101:5, 136: 31; BY discourse, 15 March 1857, JD 4:290; BY remarks, 19 June 1859, JD 7:191.

[12] BY instructions, 21 September 1856, JD 4:43; Jedediah M. Grant remarks, 21 September 1856, JD 4:50; HCK discourse, 28 September 1856, JD 4:106; WWJ 4:440, 458, 524. (The water was probably heated somewhat.)

[13] JFSE, 566; Burton, *Saints*, 241; BE 1:62-63.

[14] HSD, 610-612; MT, recorded by Leo Hawkins, 4 January 1857; Salt Lake County Deeds A:212-213; OH to Albert Carrington, 20 February 1857, Carrington Papers; OH sermon, early 1857, DN, 18 March 1857 (p. 10) (reprinted JD 4:262).

[15] JH, 4 February 1857, 3-4; OH discourse, 8 March 1857, JD 5:67-72.

[16] JSHG, 60; Barney Hyde to Myrtle S. Hyde, 30 October 1979; family group records of Moses Daley and sons-in-law Sidney Kent and James Vickers, Archives, FHL; 1850 census Davis County, Utah, households 180, 181; JSH, 47b; HC 2:400; M. Anderson, "Ann Eliza Vickers Hyde," 1-2; Endowment House Sealings C:104.

Note: The Endowment House records (C:96) contain another sealing for Orson Hyde in 1857, March 6, a week before his and Ann Eliza Vickers' marriage. The March 6 "bride" was Helen Melissa Winters. She seems, however, not to have actually become Orson's wife. She is in no Hyde family records. In the sealing record, Helen's birth is given as December 3, 1841, which indicates an age of fifteen years in March 1857. Other records have her birth year as 1844 (Endowment House endowments; family group records of Hiram Winters [born 1805] and of James Marion Francis Hickerson [born 1831], Archives, FHL). Apparently she was only twelve years old in March of 1857. Possibly her father wanted her married to his friend Orson Hyde, but when Orson learned her true age, plans changed. Brigham Young granted a cancellation of this sealing August 12, 1859 (HDC). Helen was eventually married in 1867 to James M. F. Hickerson and later to James Lawson. In the Winters and Hickerson family records, no mention is made of a marriage of Helen to Orson Hyde.

[17] "Minutes of the General Conference," DN, 15 April 1857 (p. 43); WWJ 5:46-47; BY discourse, 2 November 1856, JD 4:68 (nothing suggests new complaints against Hyde and Richards).

[18] HCK discourse, 19 April 1857, JD 4:365.

[19] "Excursion To Fort Limhi," DN, 10 June 1857 (p. 108); BY remarks 31 May 1857, JD 4:324-326, 348, 351, 352; CHC 4:8.

[20] OH remarks, 14 June 1857, JD 5:14-16.

[21] JH, 13 May 1857, from DN, 1 July 1857 (p. 133).

[22] JH, 31 July 1857 (weather); Endowment House Sealings C:234.

[23] JH, 12, 17 August 1857; HSD, 635; MAPH to Joseph C. Bentley, 16 March 1897, RWC; "From Carson Valley, Utah," *Western Standard*, 17 January 1857.

[24] OH discourse, fall 1857, JD 6:11-12 (first published DN, 30 December 1857); BY remarks, 19 July 1857, JD 5:56-57; CHC 4:200-205, 215, 236-246; OH discourse, August 1857, JD 5:144; Talmage, *House of the Lord*, 140.

[25] HCK remarks, 12 July 1857, JT remarks, 9 August 1857, Thomas B. Marsh remarks, 6 September 1857, JD 5:28-29, 115, 206-209.

[26] CHC 4:139-180; JSH, 74; *Encyclopedia of Mormonism* 4:966-968.

[27] CHC 4:266, 273-293; HOJ, 14 September 1857; OH discourse, 4 October 1857, JD 5:280, 281; OH discourse, fall 1857, JD 6:14; BY remarks, 25 October 1857, JD 5:352, 353.

[28] Mack, *Nevada*, 169-171.

[29] OH sermon, 15 November 1857, JD 6:57, 58.

[30] CHC 4:301; Weston Nordgren interview with Mrs. Maude Hyde Anderson (granddaughter of Orson Hyde), about 1947, WNNP, Box 3 Folder 1 (modified to dialogue). The date of this incident is unknown, as is the explanation of why a

squash was handy for Brigham Young to use. Orson's son Joseph related a similar story (JSH, 93-94).

[31] JH, 12 August 1857; Belle A. Gemmell, "Utah Medical History: Some Reminiscences," *California and Western Medicine* (San Francisco) 36 (January 1932) (reprint of article is in HDC); JSH, 50. The time of this operation is uncertain, but it occurred after August of 1857, when Doctor Anderson arrived in Salt Lake City.

[32] HSD, 649, 652, 679; OH sermon, 3 January 1858, JD 6:150-153.

[33] CHC 4:349-353, 360-361, 375-376; HOJ, 8, 18, 21 March 1858.

[34] JH, 5, 28 April, 2 May 1858; CHC 4:377, 380-383, 387-388, 399.

[35] CHC 4:386, 397-398; JSHG, 60; JSH, 51.

[36] Hal Knight, "Old N.Y. newspapers give rare glimpse of Church in pioneer days," DN, *Church News*, 22 August 1981, 5; CHC 4:447; JH, 4 July 1858, 6 February 1859 (p. 2) (modified to dialogue).

[37] CHC 4:452-471; JH, 24 September 1858 (pp. 1-2), 25 July 1858; "Army Supplies," DN, 29 December 1858 (p. 183); "Meetings For Worship," DN, 22 September 1858 (p. 126); WWJ 5: regular entries, summer 1858; OH to BY, 12 July 1858, BYC; BY to OH, 12 July 1858, BYL 4:290.

[38] Salt Lake County Tax Assessment Rolls, 1858, 17th Ward (perhaps between the two assessments Orson had butchered or sold one pig and two cattle); "Elder Orson Hyde...," DN, 6 October 1858 (p. 134). Wilford Woodruff's Journal for the summer of 1858 has many references to his own orchard work; Orson Hyde probably did about the same.

[39] OH, "Manufacture of Clothing, etc.," DN 3 February 1858 (p. 381); JH, 8 June 1857; "The Fair! The Fair!" DN, 22 September 1858 (p. 127); "List of Prizes," DN, 20 October 1858 (p. 144); "Deseret State Fair," DN, 13 October 1858 (p. 139).

[40] JH, 24 (p. 2), 26 September, 6, 7 October, 13 November (p. 4) 1858; "Meetings For Worship," DN, 22 September 1858 (p. 126).

[41] JH, 29 October-2 November 1858 (quotation modified to dialogue); Jenson, *Encyclopedic History*, 953.

[42] JH, 23, 30 September, 13 (pp. 1, 7), 29 November, 3 December 1858, 7 February 1859; CHC 4:452, 476, 5:78-80; WWJ 5:246, 298; HSD, 675, 679, 683, 685.

[43] "Kirkham's Grammar Wanted," DN, 1 December 1858 (p. 166); "Grammar Class," DN, 8 December 1858 (p. 172); Orton autobiography 1:12; OH address, 14 December 1858, JD 7:68-70; HSD, 675.

[44] WWJ 5:255, 285, 291-301.

[45] WWJ 5:219; OH to BY, 27 February 1859, BYC.

[46] Martha and Thomas had apparently separated by 1853. In the Salt Lake County Taxation Assessment Rolls for that year, he lived in the Twentieth Ward (p. 37), and she lived in the Ninth Ward (p. 6).

[47] OH to Martha Browett, 28 February 1859, RWC.

[48] "Tabernacle," DN, 18 May 1859 (p. 88) (modified to dialogue).

[49] WWJ 5:379; JH, 22, 24 (p. 1), 27 (p. 1) August 1859; "First Judicial District Court," DN, 7 September 1859 (p. 213).

[50] D. Johnson, *Springville*, 40-41; Mary Finley, *Springville*, 29-30; JH, 4 February 1857, 3-4; A. Johnson journal, 11 February 1857.

[51] WWJ 5:385; "Tabernacle," DN, 5 October 1859 (p. 245); OH speech, 2 October 1859, MT by G. D. Watt; JH, 3 September, 17 October 1859.

[52] JH, 18, 25 April, summer, 6 October 1859; WWJ 5:385; "Tabernacle," DN, 5 October 1859 (p. 245); OH remarks, 6 October 1859, JD 7:313-317.

[53] "Organization of the Cache Valley Settlements," DN, 30 November 1859 (order rearranged) (included in JH, 27 November 1859).

[54] "From the Late Capital," DN, 11 January 1860 (p. 357); "Minutes of a Conference," DN, 8 February 1860 (p. 392) (both speech excerpts modified to dialogue); "From San Pete County," DN, 1 February 1860 (p. 381); Madsen history, #27; JH, 20 January 1860; BYOJ D:30.

[55] OH remarks, 12 February 1860, JD 7:149-154; BYOJ D:41; JH, 15, 28 February 1860.

[56] JH, 27, 29 January, 5 April 1860; "Tabernacle," DN, 14 December 1859 (p. 328); WWJ 5:420-430 (see also 6:361, 363-364) (see D&C 41:2-5); OP remarks, 29 January 1860, JD 7:371-376; "Tabernacle," DN, 1 February 1860 (p. 380); "Through some inadvertency. . . ," DN, 22 February 1860 (pp. 401-402); BYOJ, 4, 5 April 1860; Minutes of a Meeting in the Historian's Office, 4 April 1860, BYC; BY remarks, 20 May 1860, JD 8:62.

[57] JH, 2 March 1860; CHC 4:538; BYOJ, 11 April 1860 (punctuation and wording modified slightly for clarity); MAPHA, 3-4 (spelling modified slightly); JSHG, 60.

CHAPTER 22   . . . *increase.* . . . *(1860-1865)*

[1] JH, 12 June 1860; OH to BY, 9 August 1860, BYC; MFP 2:43; JSH, 53.

[2] OH to BY, 17 June 1860, BYC; "Matters in San Pete County," DN, 20 July 1859 (p. 157); "San Pete County," DN, 30 May 1860 (p. 101); Lever, *Sanpete*, 11, 13, 17-24, 47, 49, 50, 52; "San Pete County Correspondence," DN, 27 July 1859 (p. 161); "From San Pete County," DN, 23 November 1859 (p. 301); Longsdorf, *Mount Pleasant*, 308-309.

[3] OH to BY, 17 June, 6 July 1860, BYC; JSH, 54; P. Cook, *Diary*, 73 (the home stood on the southwest corner of the lot where the Manti Temple was later constructed); BY to OH, 20 June 1860, BYL 5:538.

[4] "Obituaries," WE 10 (1 January 1882):117; 1860 Census, Mount Pleasant, Utah; Longsdorf, *Mount Pleasant*, 75-76, 260, 267, 273.

[5] OH to BY, 6 July, 7 August 1860, BYC; Mount Pleasant L.D.S. Ward Records, Record of Members 1858-1871, 11-12 (modified to first person); BYOJ, 20 July 1860.

[6] OH to BY, 9 August 1860, BYC; Salt Lake County Deed Abstracts A-2:231; Advertisements in DNW, with gratitude to W. Randall Dixon for his research: "Bassett & Needham," 27 April 1859 (p. 64), "Dissolution," 29 June 1859 (p. 136), "Rogers, Shropshire & Ross," 28 September 1859 (p. 240), "Thomas Taylor," 25 December 1861 (p. 208); Salt Lake County Taxation Assessment Rolls, 17th Ward (in 1864 [Appendix], 1865-1869, the store property was assessed separately, once as an entry in the 13th Ward, its location).

[7] Salt Lake County Deed Abstracts A-2:29, 31, 47, 61, 62, 84, 94 (and probably others).

[8] OH to BY, 6 July, 15 December 1860, BYC; author observation; JSH, 54; Barney Hyde to Myrtle S. Hyde, 10 December 1979 (p. 3), June 1980 (p. 3), 13 May 1983

(pp. 3, 4); "Springtown town site plotted Sept. 23rd, 1867," Spring City Ward Records, Book 1, no p. (after 154).

[9]   OH remarks, 7 October 1860, JD 8:232-234; WWJ 5:511, 517 (capitalization modified).

[10]   OH to BY, 6 July, 18 November, 17, 31 December 1860, 19 March, 22 June 1861; BY to OH, 19 November, 2 December 1860, BYL 5:635, 644; WWJ 5:554.

[11]   BY to OH, 1 December 1860, BYL 5:643; OH to BY, 15, 17 December 1860, 16 January, 24 October 1861; JSH, 54.

[12]   "Deseret," MS 25 (21 March 1863):187; Black to BY, 7 February 1861 (spelling and punctuation modified); Daniel H. Wells to Bishop W. S. Snow, 5 March 1861, BYL 6:716-717.

[13]   OH to BY, 19 March 1861, BYC.

[14]   WWJ 5:562-564; JH, 7 April 1861, 2.

[15]   OH to BY, 22 June, 24 October, 21 November 1861, 1 March 1862, BYC; BY to OH, 28 November 1861, BYL 6:48.

[16]   WWJ 5:606, 6:8-9, 82, 83, 94, 149-150, 200, 201, 206, 207; JH, 29 October, 18, 23 December 1861, 10, 14, 15, 24 December 1862, 25 January 1863, 9, 24 January, 12 December 1864, 15 January 1865; OH to BY, 30 January 1862, BYC.

[17]   WWJ 5:606, 614, 6:5; JH, 1 January 1862 (also see previous sources about attending Legislature); Hansen diaries, 2 December 1860; CHC 4:548; "Correspondence," MS 24 (8 March 1862):157-159; OH remarks, 25 January 1863, JD 10:82.

[18]   "A Timely Warning From An Apostle Of Jesus Christ," reprinted MS 24 (3 May 1862):273-275; *Utah Since Statehood* 3:709.

[19]   OH to MAPH, 8 January 1862, RWC.

[20]   OH to BY, 30 January, 1 March 1862, BYC.

[21]   For tremor example: OH to BY, 22 June 1861, BYC; Thompson and West, *Nevada*, 40-41; OH to BY, 1 March 1862, BYC; Mack, *Nevada*, 165-166; Miluck, *Genoa*, 62; Anderson and Branch, *Landslide Case*.

[22]   OH to BY, 29 March 1862, BYC; OH remarks, 6 April 1862, JD 10:47-49; OH remarks, 7 April 1862, JD 10:31-32.

[23]   Justesen, "Ann Eliza," 3. No documentation so far reveals the month in 1862 when Ann Eliza moved to Springtown. April seems most probable. No references have been found to Orson being in Salt Lake City in the summer of that year. He attended October conference, but apparently briefly. Ann Eliza's third child was born in Springtown the following January.

[24]   Alvin D. Day, "She Shall Live," *The Improvement Era*, January 1947, 23 (parts modified to dialogue).

[25]   OH to BY, 6 July 1860, 19 March 1861, BYC; Hansen diaries, 26 April 1861; OH discourse, 7 October 1862, JD 10:72-73.

[26]   OH to BY; 11 May, 30 July 1862, 30 July 1864, BYC; OH to GAS, 31 May 1864, GASC.

[27]   JH, 7 April 1861; OH to BY, 19 March 1861, 19 February, 29 March 1862, BYC; Lever, *Sanpete*, 54; Frantzen autobiography, 63-72; OH discourse, 7 October 1862, JD 10:71-73 (punctuation modified). The JD has another sermon of Orson's attributed to 7 October (10:112-113); it was probably delivered 8 October. Wilford Woodruff recorded that Orson Hyde spoke both days (WWJ 6:76).

[28] JSH, 54-55; Joseph S. Hyde to Romania Hyde Woolley, 15 January 1929, RWC.

[29] M. A. H. White, "Julia Hyde"; Barney Hyde to Myrtle S. Hyde, 30 October 1979; photograph of Julia; Morgan Hyde White interview, 1984. In some records Julia's surname is spelled Reinart. However, on a paper in her own handwriting (possession author, a gift from Julia's grandson Morgan Hyde White), also in her christening record in Aalborg, Denmark (St. Budolfi parish), and at her endowment, the spelling is Reinert.

[30] "Thurber," TPH 3:304; WWJ 6:108; OH remarks, 7 April 1863, JD 10:159.

[31] JH, 13 October 1861; OH to BY, 20 October 1861, 19 February 1862, BYC; Averett biography, 27-28; CHC 5:117.

[32] "America," MS 25 (23 May 1863):334; "Incidents of Travel. . . ," DN, 6 May 1863 (p. 353).

[33] "Incidents of Travel. . . ," DN, 6, 20, 27 May 1863 (pp. 353, 373, 379).

[34] D. Candland letter, Manti City, 29 May 1863, DN, 10 June 1863 (p. 400); OH to BY, 7, 28 June 1863, BYC; BY to OH, 2 July 1863, BYL 6:630. Further progress on the road was reported in "The Spanish Fork Road," DN, 26 August 1863 (p. 34).

[35] OH to BY, 22 June 1861, 7, 8, 21, 28 June 1863, BYC; Madsen history, 31, 46; BY to OH 15 June 1863, BYL 6:613; OH to GAS, 3 December 1864, GASC.

[36] OH to BY, 28 June 1863, BYC (by reply Brigham Young encouraged him [BY to OH, 2 July 1863, BYL 6:630]). For Orson's preaching the summer of 1863 see JH, 4 July, 23 August 1863; "Deseret," MS 25 (21 March 1863):187.

[37] Endowment House sealings, 29 August 1863.

[38] OH to BY, 20 October 1863, BYC; OH, "Instructions to Mr. Welsh," RWC. The carrots that Orson mentions in his instructions were probably the large-rooted type grown for stock feeding (EnA, s.v. "Carrot").

[39] JH, 20 May 1863, 2; R. N. Allred to General, 7 March 1864, Territorial Military, No. 754; JSHG, 61.

[40] Bean autobiography, 67-68; JH, 25 November 1863, 29 January 1864; "Larsen," TPH 6 (1957):204; Lever, *Sanpete*, 54; OH to GAS, 31 May 1864, GASC.

[41] OH to BY, 31 December 1860, 10 June 1864, BYC.

[42] BY to OH, 18 June (in this letter Brigham Young alludes to his "remarks published in this week' 'news'" [this was the publication, 15 June 1864, of a 15 May 1864 address in the Tabernacle; it also appears in JD 10:289-298]), 2 August 1864, BYL 7:224-226, 261; JH, 11 July, 8-10 August 1864; OH to BY, 30 July, 13 August 1864 (and note written on it), BYC.

[43] OH to BY, 30 July 1864, BYC; JH, 5, 7, 29 September 1864; WWJ 6:185-191 (on this trip a wife accompanied Wilford Woodruff; perhaps a wife accompanied Orson too); L. Brown, *Journal*, 157.

[44] OH to BY, 29 October 1864, BYC; BY to OH, 22 November 1864, BYL 7:360.

[45] Endowment House sealings, 15 October 1864; Christening Register of Gsteig bei Interlaken, Bern, Switzerland, IX:251, entry 35, searched by Paul Nielson (which has her birthdate as 14 February 1840; records of her family have 2 February 1844; the Endowment House record, at the time of her marriage, has 26 Feb'y 1845); JH, 24 September, 29 October 1862; OH to BY, 29 October 1864, 4, BYC.

Research has failed to reveal how Orson and Elisabeth met. After arriving in Utah she apparently lived with her parents in "Cottonwood," later Murray, several miles south of Salt Lake City ("History Peter Galli"). In some records, but not the original Swiss, Elisabeth's surname appears as Gallier.

[46] MAPHA, 4; OH to BY, 29 October 1864, BYC; Sloan, *Salt Lake City Directory, for 1869*, 95, 96, 103.

[47] OH to BY, 29 October, 12, 15 November 1864, BYC; OH to GAS, 3 December 1864, GASC; Lever, *Sanpete*, 54.

[48] OH remarks, 18 December 1864, JD 10:373; OH to BY, 13 February 1865 (punctuation modified slightly), BYC.

[49] J. Peterson, "Mormons, Indians," 50-52. For more background about the area Indians see Gottfredson, *Indian Depredations*, 19, 21, 30.

[50] Centennial, *Gunnison*, 41; BY remarks, 8 July 1863, JD 10:231-232.

[51] Dixon, *Peteetneet Town*, 100-102; JSH, 56-57; OH to BY, 6 July 1860, BYC; Centennial, *Gunnison*, 41-42 (this gives another name for Jake as Aug-o-vor-um, but Aug-o-vor-um was a Shub-er-ech chief [see "Indian Treaty," DEN, 22 August 1868, 3]). A personal glimpse of Wakara is printed in Alter, *Utah* 1:171-174.

[52] Dixon, *Peteetneet Town*, 101; D. Jones, *Forty Years*, 192-193; J. Peterson, "Mormons, Indians," 51; Papanikolas, *Peoples*, 27-28, 36. The Indians, however, had not always had plenty; see: JH, 24 March 1850, 16 February 1855, 25 June 1872, 2; Antrei and Scow, *Other Forty-Niners*, 127-140.

[53] Gottfredson, *Indian Depredations*, Supplement (in back of 1969 printing), 9.

[54] OH to BY, 1 March 1862 (some punctuation added), BYC.

[55] BY to OH, 8 March 1862, BYL 6:159-160; OH to BY, 11 May 1862, BYC.

[56] BY to OH, 15 June 1863, BYL 6:613; BY to Little Soldier, Kanosh, Tabby, Sowiette, and all the Chiefs connected with them, 15 June 1863, BYL 6:614; JH, 25 April 1863; OH to BY, 21, 28 June 1863, BYC.

[57] CHC 5:146; OH to BY, 10 June 1864, BYC.

[58] BY to OH, 18 June 1864, BYL 7:224 (spelling and punctuation slightly modified); OH to BY, 30 July 1864, BYC.

[59] OH to GAS, 26 March 1865, GASC; Lever, *Sanpete*, 54.

[60] JH, 6, 8 April 1865.

CHAPTER 23   . . . *afflictions*. . . . *(1865-1867)*

[1] OH to BY, 14 April 1865, BYC (written for OH and he signed [punctuation and spelling modified]); OH to Bishop Bryan (to be sent to BY), 26 April 1865, BYC.

[2] OH to BY, 13 April 1865 (spelling and punctuation modified), BYC.

[3] OH to BY, 14 (punctuation modified), 15 April 1865, BYC; Lever, *Sanpete*, 54 (Elijah B[arney] Ward); "Green River Expedition," DN, 1 December 1853; Centennial, *Gunnison*, 42-43; H. R. Merrill, "A Veteran Of The Black Hawk War," *Improvement Era*, November 1925, 59; Madsen history, 51, 52, 58.

[4] OH to BY, 15 April 1865, BYC; CHC 5:15-18, 30-31, 154; BY to OH, 16 April 1865, BYL 7:559.

Black Hawk has traditionally been identified incorrectly. The young Indian of the same name, later recalled by some Mormon settlers, was probably his nephew (J. Peterson, *Black Hawk War*, 42-47, 78–79).

[5] Gottfredson, *Indian Depredations*, 133-137; OH to BY, 23 April 1865 (punctuation modified slightly), BYC.

[6] Lever, *Sanpete*, 25-26, 54; Bean autobiography, 69; Warren S. Snow report, 6 November 1865, JH, same date; OH to BY, 23 April 1865 (order rearranged), BYC; Gottfredson, *Indian Depredations*, 335-338; J. Peterson, *Black Hawk War*, 43-46, 83.

[7] Lever, *Sanpete*, 55; OH to BY, 29 (some punctuation added), 30 May 1865, BYC.

[8] JH, 9 March 1863 (p. 3), 29 November 1864 (p. 3); BY to OH, 13 (spelling modified slightly), 31 May 1865, BYL 7:613-614, 657.

[9] CHC 5:145-149; WWJ 6:226-227; Gottfredson, *Indian Depredations*, 151-156; Coombs diary, PH 1:370; JH, 6, 7, 8, 10, 16 (pp. 3-4), 20 (p. 2), 21 June 1865; Bean autobiography, 65, 70.

[10] JH, 13, 14, 16, 19 July 1865; WWJ 6:234-236; Lever, *Sanpete*, 55; M. Johnson, "Life," 9; J. Peterson, *Black Hawk War*, 164-167.

[11] JSHG 60, 61. Provo Cemetery burial record, made nearer the time, has June, rather than November, as Maria Louisa's birth month; her mother was the informant.

[12] Fogelberg, "Sophia," 1, 5.

[13] Lever, *Sanpete*, 55; J. Peterson, *Black Hawk War*, 175-176; BY to OH, etc., 1 October 1865, BYL 7:745-748 (spelling modified slightly).

[14] OH to GAS, 29 October 1865, GASC; JH, 6-8 October 1865; OH remarks, 7 October 1865, JD 11:147-148; Endowment House Sealings, 10 October 1865.

[15] JH, 10 October 1865. Orson attended with "wife, and girl"; probably these were Marinda and Sophia. Also, this may indicate that Sophia worked in Orson's home as a "domestic" before their marriage.

[16] OH to GAS, 29 October 1865, GASC; OH to GAS, 18 October 1865, BYC; GAS to OH, 22 October 1865, JH, same date; M. Johnson, "Life," 10 (which has the date of the raid on Fort Ephraim as 10 September, in error).

[17] JH, 6 November 1865, 2; Josiah F. Gibbs, "Black Hawk's Last Raid—1866," *Utah Historical Quarterly* 4 (October 1931):108; O. Whitney, *Utah* 2:191.

[18] Lever, *Sanpete*, 55; OH to BY, 19 November 1865 (order changed and punctuation modified), BYC.

[19] JSH, 61. Another instance of a woman who did not become Orson Hyde's wife is explained in Jennifer L. Lund to Myrtle S. Hyde, 21 January 1997.

[20] Copenhagen LDS Branch Records; Endowment House Sealings, 10 October 1865; Fogelberg, "Sophia."

[21] JH, 17 December 1865, 1, 19 January (pp. 9-10) 1866; WWJ 6:263-265, 271 (Joseph Smith's vision is recorded in HC 2:381); "City Hall — 1866," PH 10:5-10.

[22] Lever, *Sanpete*, 56; Centennial, *Gunnison*, 43; JH, 14 (p. 5), 27 (p. 8) March, 5 April (p. 1) 1866.

[23] JH, 28 March (p. 2), 15 (pp. 3-4), 24 April 1866; Gottfredson, *Indian Depredations*, 185-187; GAS to General D. H. Wells, 2 April 1866, Territorial Military, No. 829; Lever, *Sanpete*, 56; J[ames] Wareham to OH, 25 April 1866, GASC; OH to GAS, 26 April 1866, GASC.

[24] JH, 28 March 1866, 2-3; Antrei and Scow, *Other Forty-Niners*, 142-143; "Bones of Black Hawk. . . ," DEN, 20 September 1919, 2:7; J. Peterson, *Black Hawk War*, 97.

[25] Lever, *Sanpete*, 56; Gottfredson, *Indian Depredations*, 187-189; OH to GAS, 26 April 1866, GASC.

[26] Virginia Osborne to Romania Woolley, 11 November 1931 (punctuation modified slightly), RWC; JH, 1 May, 11 August (p. 5) 1866.

[27] Lever, *Sanpete*, 56-57; BY to OH, etc., 28 April 1866, BYL 8:342-352 (the first part of this is printed in MFP 2:240-242); JH, 1 May 1866, 29 April 1866; Longsdorf, *Mount Pleasant*, 109; GAS to BY, Jr., 21 May 1866, MS 28 (30 June 1866):412; Dewey journal, 8 May 1866; OH (by a scribe) to GAS, 20 May 1866 (spelling and punctuation slightly modified), GASC (an edited version is in JH, 20 May 1866).

[28] Papanikolas, *Peoples*, 37-38; GAS to BY, May 1866, MS 28:412; JH, 21 May 1866; BY to Tabbey, Sowiett, Toquer-ona, Jim, Joe and Anthoro, 18 May 1866, BYL 8:419-422.

[29] Justesen, "Ann Eliza," 3; JSHG, 61.

[30] BY to OH, 16 May 1866, BYL 8:418; OH to BY, 27 May 1866, BYC; K. Watson, *Under The Horseshoe*, 15, 20.

[31] Lever, *Sanpete*, 57; Gottfredson, *Indian Depredations*, 201-203; Culmsee, "Black Hawk War," DN, 25 August 1934, 3:IV, Chapter XIII; J. Peterson, *Black Hawk War*, 268-274.

[32] Lever, *Sanpete*, 57. For more about the June 10 and June 23 episodes see JH, 2 (p. 3), 5 (pp. 1-2) July 1872; R. N. Allred to Gen'l Wells, 3 July 1866, Territorial Military, No. 898; Longsdorf, *Mount Pleasant*, 110; OH to Prest. D. H. Wells, 9 August 1866, Territorial Military, No. 1,542; Madsen history, 65.

[33] OH to Gen'l. D. H. Wells, 4 July 1866, Territorial Military, No. 903 (spelling and punctuation modified; order rearranged); Lever, *Sanpete*, 57. For Brigham Young's opinions at this time see JD 11:263-266.

[34] Peacock journals 3:44; Frantzen autobiography, 82-84; Rasmussen reminiscences; OH to Wells, 9 August 1866, Territorial Military, No. 1,542; WWJ 6:299; JH, 10 October 1866, 1-2; Frantzen autobiography, 84.

[35] BY to OH, 12 October 1866, BYL 9:191 1/2; OH to GAS, 16 November 1866, GASC; JH, 1, 12 (p. 2) December 1866; JSHG, 61; Brooks, *Jews*, 46, 52, 53, 58; 1870 Census, Ukiah, Mendocino County, California, 236, house 65.

[36] JH, 9 December 1866; WWJ 6:304 (in a talk by Orson, December 9, he said that every person who keeps celestial laws will receive crowns of glory that will be worth all the trials and hardships required to be worthy of them; later Brigham Young said each person would receive only one crown [JH, 9 October 1867]); Lever, *Sanpete*, 57. See also "Pioneers Construct Own Telegraph Lines," Daughters of Utah Pioneers, *Heart Throbs* 1 (1939):182-183.

[37] JH, 1, 3, 7 January, 3 (p. 1), 6 (p. 2) February, 1 March (p. 2) 1867; WWJ 6:317, 319-322; OH, "For the Deseret News," DEN, 29 January 1867 (p. 34) (also in JH, 20 January 1867); OH to BY, 12 February 1867 (modified to dialogue), BYC; R. N. Allred to General Wells, 7 March 1867, Territorial Military, No. 1,553.

[38] JSH, 61 ("light wagon"); OH to Editor DN, 7 March 1867, DN, 20 March 1867 (p. 94) (February 21 is assumed as the day he departed from home, because he left Ephraim February 22 and preached twice in Manti the same day); BY to OH, 21 February 1867, BYL 9:388; Weibye journal, 24-27 February 1867; Allred to Wells, 7 March 1867, Territorial Military, No. 1,553.

[39] DN, in JH, 12 March 1867.

[40] JH, 18, 20 March 1867; "Black Hawk Indian War," PH 9 (1966):230-231; Culmsee, "Black Hawk War," DN, 22 September 1934, 3:V.

[41] OH to BY, 25, 27 March 1867, BYC.

[42] Peacock journals 3:54; BY to OH, 27 March 1867, BY Telegram Letterbook, 1867, 148; OH to BY, 27 March 1867, BYC.

[43] BY to OH, BY Telegram Letterbook, 1867, 150; BY, HCK, and Wells to OH, 2 April 1867, BYL 10:96.

[44] Gunnison is assumed. Orson was in Manti April 8, on his way home, according to OH and R. N. Allred to Prests. Young, Kimball, and Wells, 9 April 1867, BYC.

[45] OH and Allred to Young, Kimball, and Wells, 9 April 1867, BYC; BY to OH, 8 April 1867, BY Telegram Letterbook, 1867, 151; Weibye journal, 2-16 April 1867; OH to BY, 21 April 1867 (punctuation modified slightly), BYC; James B. Morrison, quoted by Culmsee, DN, 22 September 1934, 3:V.

[46] OH to BY, 21 April, 7 December 1867, BYC; JSHG, 61 (this source gives the year of the birth as 1868, whereas family records, gathered by Morgan Hyde White, have 1867; the more consistent date is 1867).

[47] OH to General Wells, 29 April 1867, Territorial Military, No. 1,007; Lever, *Sanpete*, 58; WWJ 6:344; JH, 12 June 1867; Bean autobiography, 75; BY to OH, 11 June 1867, BYL 10:222-224 (mentions Orson's letter, which has not been found); OH to BY, 15 June 1867, BYC.

[48] OH to General Wells, 29 April 1867, Territorial Military, No. 1,007; OH to Editor, 30 June 1867, DN, 10 July 1867 (p. 222) (quotation marks added, order rearranged).

[49] Weibye journal, 20 June, 4, 15, 27 July 1867; "The Convention," *Sanpitcher*, 6 July 1867. For this period see also OH to GAS, 21 Jul 1867, GASC.

[50] OH to BY, 9 August 1867, BYC. The letter states that Orson intended to "bring up two of my wives. . . . One of them I expect to leave with her friends at Springville 'till near conference, and the other to accompany me on the trip north should their children be well enough to leave." One of these wives was Ann Eliza, subsequent records indicate.

[51] Gottfredson, *Indian Depredations*, 270-275; JH, 19 August 1867, 3; Frantzen autobiography, 85-87.

[52] JH, 24, 25 August 1867; WWJ 6:358-361; BY to Franklin D. Richards, 29 August 1867, MS 29 (5 October 1867):634; "Black Hawk," DNW, 28 August 1867 (p. 277).

[53] OH to BY, 9 August 1867, BYC; JSHG, 60; Telegram from OH to wife Ann Eliza, 31 August [1867], BYUL; Hiatt, *Provo Cemetery*, 162.

[54] WWJ 6:361-366; MS 29 (2, 9, 16 November 1867):689-695, 705-710, 721-726 (reprinted from DN) (has summaries of Orson Hyde's and others' sermons).

CHAPTER 24   *. . . no more thine enemy. . . . (1867-1872)*

[1] Lever, *Sanpete*, 58; WWJ 6:367-368; JH, 6 October 1867 (the report of Heber C. Kimball's words changed to first person).

[2] WWJ 6:368; JH, 6 October 1867; acoustics were poor in the Tabernacle at the time (JH, 7 April 1868); OH remarks, 6 October 1867, Meeting Minutes recorded by David W. Evans (order rearranged), HDC (in this sermon Orson mentioned his former erroneous teachings about the resurrection, and, in a following discourse, Brigham Young referred to the same).

[3] Culmsee, "Black Hawk War," DN, 29 September 1934, 3:viii; "Another Office," DNW, 4 December 1867 (p. 339).

[4] JH, 12, 19, 20, 24, 29, 30 January, 7, 10, 28 February 1868; WWJ 6:397; BY remarks, 8 December 1867, JD 12:116 (see also BY remarks, 8 February 1868, JD 12:157–159 and Joseph F. Smith remarks, 10 January 1869, JD 12:349).

[5] JSHG, 61, 62; Alonzo E. Hyde to OH, 20 March 1868, JH, same date (the sons undoubtedly also wrote to their mother); Stone and Slusser, "Marinda"; Manuscript History Seventeenth Ward, Relief Society section.

[6] JH, 28 February 1868; OH to BY, 24 February, 11, 18, 24 March 1868, BYC; BY to OH, 7, 28 March 1868, BYL 10:672, 744.

[7] Weibye journal, 19 March, 4 April 1868; "Interesting Indian News," JH, 30 March 1868; Peacock journals 3:29; Longsdorf, *Mount Pleasant*, 122.

[8] OH to BY, 24 March 1868, BYC; Weibye journal, 20, 22 March 1868; JH, 6, 7 April 1868. For an item about hearing in the Tabernacle see WWJ 6:406.

[9] Lever, *Sanpete*, 58–59; Weibye journal, 3, 6 April 1868; F. Olsen to OH, 7 April 1868, Territorial Military, No. 1,104; OH to BY, 20 April 1868, BYC.

[10] OH to BY, 20 April, 27 May 1868, BYC; K. Watson, *Under The Horseshoe*, 19; JH, 15 June, 9 July (p. 9) 1868; John R. Winder to Daniel H. Wells, 11 June 1868, Territorial Military, No. 1,570; Weibye journal, 27 May, 7 June, 19 July 1868.

[11] WWJ 6:411, 412; JH, 23, 24 June, 4 July (p. 9) 1868; OH to BY, 19, 20 July, 7 August 1868, BYC; Weibye journal has dates that Orson preached in Manti; Clipping from DN, in JH, 20 August 1868.

[12] John R. Winder to Daniel H. Wells, 11 June 1868, Territorial Military, No. 1,570; Weibye journal, 30 May, 1, 3, 7, 14 June, 11 July 1868; JH, 15 June 1868; Lever, *Sanpete*, 59.

[13] W. B. Pace to John R. Winder, 14 July, 6, 12 August 1868, Territorial Military, Nos. 1,130, 1,131, 1,573; Peacock journals 3:60; Weibye journal, 2 August 1868. (Conditions in Gunnison: "Gunnison," DEN, 4 August 1868.)

[14] "Correspondence, Echo City, Aug. 6, 1868," DEN, 11 August 1868, 2; Pace to Winder, 12 August 1868 (Military, No. 1,131); "Salt Creek. . . ," DEN, 24 August 1868.

This same month, in Ephraim, according to BE 1:362, a consultation of ten leading Sanpete area Indians with Bishop Canute Peterson (called by them "White Father") resulted in peace agreements. Contemporary evidence of the meeting with Canute Peterson has not been found; this reference perhaps is to the July 1869 pow-wow in Ephraim, which has been confused by Black Hawk War writers.

[15] "Indian Treaty," DEN, 22 August 1868, 3 (reprinted DNW, 26 August 1868); JH, 22 August 1868.

Orson F. Whitney (*Utah* 2:213), in his version of this conference, attributed to Aug-a-vor-um, probably inadvertently, the items about Tam-a-rits, which has led to confusion about these two chiefs for other writers.

Another confusion that has appeared in print is that Dimick B. Huntington and Orson Hyde conducted a major meeting with the Indians in Ephraim in August of 1868. The Ephraim peace meet convened in July 1869.

[16] "Indian Treaty," DEN, 22 August 1868, 3; Government Printing Office, *Report of the Secretary of the Interior*, 1868, 609, 612 (the Indian agent reported that Black Hawk had been farming industriously at the Uinta reservation); JH, 25 May 1869.

[17] JSHG, 60, 61; Weibye journal, 9, 23 September 1868; WWJ 6:426-432; JH, 18, 20, 23 September 1868; Lever, *Sanpete*, 59.

[18] WWJ 6:432, 433; JH, 6 October 1868 (order rearranged).

[19] Peacock journals 3:60, in JH, 25 October 1868; Lever, *Sanpete*, 59; OH to BY, 13 October 1868, BYC; BY to OH, 17 October 1868, BYL 11:89; Weibye journal, 24 October 1868.

[20] OH, "Springtown, Dec. 4, 1868. . . ," DNW, 16 December 1868 (p. 357) (slightly augmented, for clarity); Weibye journal says the meeting was held November 2; JSH, 58.

[21] Weibye journal, 8, 15, 28 November, 22, 24 December 1868; JH, 7 December 1868; "Manti," DEN, 14 December 1868 (in JH, 12 December 1868). More details about the possibility of the canal are contained in OH to GAS, 3 December 1869, GASC.

[22] WWJ 6:451, 456; JSHG, 61; JH, 12, 14, 15, 16, 18, 25 January, 4, 8, 9, 11, 12, 15, 16, 17 February 1869.

[23] Lever, *Sanpete*, 59; OH to BY, 2 April 1869, BYC; JSHG, 61 (this baby was born in Ephraim, probably at the home of Sophia's parents).

[24] CHC 5:241; WWJ 6:477; JH, 25 May 1869; JSH, 62-63.

[25] OH to Bro. Musser, 17 June 1869, BYC.

[26] OH to MAPH, 22 June 1869, RWC.

[27] OH to Antone Lund, 2 July 1869, transcript in WNNP, Box 4, Folder 3; Rogerson, "Black Hawk War," 3; Bate, *Hanks*, 65; OH to Supt. Head, 28 June [1869], Telegrams no date, BYC; BE 1:362 (see note 14, this chapter).

[28] "Indians at Fort Ephraim," DNW, 7 July 1869 (p. 261); C. L. Christensen observation, as told by Culmsee, "Black Hawk War," DN, 6 October 1934, 3:V; JH, 23 September 1868, 2.

[29] "Repentant Indians," DEN, 7 July 1869 (reprinted DNW, 14 July 1869 [p. 276]); C. L. Christensen observation, as told by Culmsee (see note 28).

Note: Both of Culmsee's accounts (DN, 6 October 1934, 3:V, and *Black Hawk War*, 149-151) have this conference confused with the peace-making in Strawberry Valley the previous year, except for the comments from C. L. Christensen (for more about Christensen see his obituary, *Salt Lake Tribune*, 28 November 1940, 21).

[30] Weibye journal, 4 July 1869; "Manti," DEN, 9 July 1869, in JH, 4 July 1869; Centennial, *Gunnison*, 41, 42 (the definite time of Black Hawk making this visit and offer is unknown; it is placed here as the likely period).

[31] Culmsee, *Black Hawk War*, 154. Culmsee has no dates for the visits to the Sanpete towns he mentions—Fountain Green, Spring City, and Fairview—and no other documents have been found that contain such dates. I have placed them in July because this seems the most likely time. The following December, Black Hawk's "peace march" began in Saint George, southern Utah. Spanish Fork was his destination before the Uinta Reservation (W. H. Dame to BY, 13 December 1869, Telegram, BYC). This route bypasses Sanpete Valley.

[32] OH to BY, 12 July 1869, BYC (punctuation and spelling modified slightly).

[33] A "farewell" feast is the author's interpretation of this event. Orson's son Joseph, who wrote about it, gave no date, and undoubtedly remembered a few of the particulars incorrectly in his recollection years later. A careful study of the Indian

events in Springtown seemingly leaves no other time for this gathering. The Ephraim treaty was July 3; Orson Hyde wrote to Brigham Young July 12 about the Indians' continuing demands; R. N. Allred stated July 18 that they had "left for their hunting grounds with good peace" ("Springtown," DEN, 21 July 1869).

[34] JSH, 55-58 (rearranged, condensed, and slightly augmented).

[35] Weibye journal, 4 July 1869; "Springtown," DEN, 21 July 1869; JH, 2, 5 July 1869; OH to BY, 11, 28 July, 6 August 1869, BYC; "Larsen," TPH 6 (1957):216-217.

[36] Weibye, 3rd Daybook, 108.

[37] JH, 24 July, 1 August 1869; Weibye journal, 15, 22 August 1869; OH to BY, 28 July, 6, 8 August 1869, BYC.

[38] OH to MAPH, 27 August 1869, RWC (part of the original letter has been cut off). For more about Sanpete's 1869 crops see JH, 22 October 1869.

[39] JH, 3 (p. 2), 5 (p. 4) September 1869.

[40] JH, 13, 21 (p. 4) September, 1, 11 October 1869; OH remarks, 6 October 1869, JD 13:179; Lever, *Sanpete*, 60.

[41] (All items mentioned in the text were not in the newspapers.) Clipping from DN in JH, 7 December 1869; Walker, *Diary Walker* 1:302; Culmsee, *Black Hawk War*, 153-155; W. H. Dame to BY (telegram), 13 December 1869, BYC; Gottfredson, *Indian Depredations*, 227-228; Operator for Black Hawk to BY (telegram), 28 December 1869, BYC; Rogerson, "Black Hawk War," 1-3; Fillmore Ward Minutes, 26 December 1869, in Millard Stake Minutes 1:60.

Reminiscent accounts of the Fillmore meeting appear in at least two places: Josiah F. Gibbs, "Black Hawk's Last Raid–1866," *Utah Historical Quarterly* 4 (October 1931):107-108, and "Black Hawk Indian War," PH 9 (1966):246-247. The latter account states that the meeting occurred in April 1870, in error. The Fillmore Ward Minutes agree in enough particulars to determine the correct date. Also, a telegram from Abram Hatch, in Heber City, to Brigham Young, 17 April 1870 (BYC), states that Black Hawk is at that time sick on the reservation. In the Fillmore meeting some response to Black Hawk was decidedly negative.

[42] Clipping from DN in JH, 22 December 1869.

[43] OH to GAS, 3 December 1869, GASC; Weibye journal, 25 December 1869; JH, 24 November 1869, 8, 9, 10, 27 January, 21, 22 February 1870; WWJ 6:518-519, 525, 526, 529.

[44] Salt Lake County Deed Abstracts A-2:231, lines 6, 10; Salt Lake County Deeds D:677; OH to JT, 8 October 1878, HDC. After three years Frank transferred title to Mary Ann Price Hyde for her security (Salt Lake County Deed Abstracts A-10:14, lines 23, 28).

[45] Lever, *Sanpete*, 60; JH, 9, 14, 15 March, 4 April 1870; Weibye journal, 9, 13, 16 March, 2, 7, 24 April 1870; CHC 5:225-229; JSHG, 60, 61.

[46] Morgan Hyde White interview, 27 September 1984; Sanpete County Probate A:37-38; Barrow interview, 1-2; Frantzen autobiography, 90; 1870 Census, Ukiah, Mendocino County, California, 236, house 65: OH to BY, 15 May 1870, BYC; James Jack (clerk for BY) to OH, 31 May 1870, BYC; Salt Lake County Deed Abstracts A2:94.

[47] Weibye journal, 20 March 1870; "Temple Square" and "Bring on the Lumber," *Improvement Era*, April 1967, 2, 9; OH discourse, 5 May 1870, JD 13:363-368.

[48] 1870 Census, Sanpete County, 87, 92, and Agriculture schedule; Weibye journal, 31 July 1870.

[49] Weibye journal, 17, 18, 21, 22 May, 18, 25 June, 19, 21, 23 August 1870; Peacock journals 3:66; OH to BY, 21 June, 9 August 1870, BYC; JH, 27, 28, 29 (p. 2) August 1870. An incident involving Black Hawk and Canute Peterson that probably occurred in August 1870 is contained in *The Instructor* 81 (1946):283-384.

[50] Mary Goble Pay, quoted in "Black Hawk Indian War," PH 9 (1966):247-248 (punctuation modified slightly); JH, 23 (p. 8), 26 September 1870.

[51] Lever, *Sanpete*, 60, 61; Weibye journal, 26 April, 31 July 1870; Peacock journals 3:66, 67; OH to BY, 9 August 1870, BYC.

[52] JSHG, 60, 61 (has Geneva's birthdate as 2 July; Geneva always celebrated it 2 January, which is undoubtedly correct). Regarding daughter Geneva, some records have her name as just Geneva, some have Geneva Flora, and her father's probate record has Flora Geneva.

According to a family record (possession Stella Frisby Miller, Salt Lake City), Sophia had a baby daughter that died soon. The record has her born "before Sterling." Sterling's birth occurred 16 March 1872, and Sophia's known son before that, Oscar, was born 16 April 1869. Thus 1871 fits for the birth of this unnamed daughter.

[53] OH to BY, 23 February, 6 March 1871, BYC; Weibye journal, 1, 25 January 1871; Peacock journals 3:68, 70; JH, 19 January, 5 February, 13 March (p. 2), 4, 6, 29 April, 15 June, 22 July, 10 September (p. 3) 1871; JSHG, 60, 61.

[54] Weibye journal, 13 September, 7-8, 17 October 1870; JH, 5 February, 4 April, 22 July 1871.

[55] JH, 26 December 1870, 3 January (p. 2), 6 April (p. 3) 1871; D. H. Wells to OH, 30 December 1870, 17 January 1871, BYL 12:470, 488; Weibye journal, 1 January 1871; "Brethren Don't Hunt The Deer," DEN, 3 January 1871.

Regarding mines, the 1871 newspapers have much about their development in Utah. About abundant silver being found "up and down the Sevier," Orson related his feelings to Brigham Young in a letter dated 6 March 1871 and to George A. Smith in a letter dated 11 March 1871.

Brigham Young agreed with Orson's views on mining and on hunting deer. He wrote, 15 March 1871 (BYL 12:592): "If the brethren kill the game, the Indians have as much right to complain of it as we have when the Indians kill our cattle."

[56] JH, 22 July 1871; CHC 5:331, 357-359.

[57] OH to GAS, 23 September 1871 (punctuation modified slightly), GASC. In the issues on microfilm at the Utah State Historical Society of the *Salt Lake Tribune (Weekly)*, 16 September 1871 is missing, thus the title and exact content of the troubling article are unfound.

[58] JH, 29 April 1871; JSH, 99-100; Justesen to Woolley, 11 October 1946, RWC; "The Mormon Trouble," *Utica Daily Observer*, 30 October 1871, in JH, same date; "The Recent Arrests," *Salt Lake Tribune*, 30 October 1871, 2.

[59] JH, 28 October 1871, 5, 6; JSH, 99-101 (punctuation modified slightly); HSD, 507n.5, 514-515; Dorius diary, 1871, 1.

[60] OH to BY, 10 November 1871 (punctuation modified slightly), BYC; CHC 5:382-415; Walker, *Diary Walker* 1:336; Bean autobiography, 78-79.

[61]   Hansen diaries, 18 November 1871, 11, 25 January 1872; OH to President James Wareham, 20 February 1872, USHS; JSHG, 61 (in some other records Sterling appears as Sterling Washington).

[62]   JH, 16 (p. 5), 23, 24, 25, 30 April 1872.

[63]   OH to BY, 23 May 1872, BYC (see also JH, 7 [p. 5], 18 February, 15 May 1872); JH 2 (p. 3) June, 16 September (p. 2) 1872.

[64]   JH, 8, 10, 11, 12, 21 June 1872.

[65]   JH, 10, 16 (p. 2), 17, 18 (p. 2), 19 (p. 2), 20 (p. 3), 21, 22, 24, 28, 30 June, 16 September (p. 2) 1872; Peacock journals 3:73. See also JH, 25 (p. 2), 26 June 1872.

[66]   JH, 1 (p. 2), 7 (p. 4), 9, 10 (p. 2), 14 (pp. 4, 5), 16 (p. 2), 17 (p. 3), 21 (pp. 3-4) July, 16 September (pp. 2-3) 1872. For more about the Indian situation in late June and early July see JH, 1 (pp. 2-3), 2 (p. 3), 3 (p. 2), 5, (p. 2), 6 July 1872.

[67]   Bean autobiography, 81.

[68]   JH, 20, 21 (pp. 1, 3-4) July, 16 September (pp. 2-3) 1872.

[69]   Henry A. Morrow to Geo. W. Dodge, 7 September 1872, JH, 16 September 1872, 2 (changed to present tense). See also JH, 22, 23, 27, 30 (p. 2) July, 4 (p. 4), 7 (p. 2), 20 (p. 3) August 1872.

[70]   JH, 9 (pp. 2, 3), 12 (p. 4), 13 (p. 2), 14 (p. 2), 15 (p. 2), 18 (p. 3) August 1872; OH to BY, 12 August 1872, BYC.

[71]   JH, 14 (p. 2), 15 (pp. 1, 2) August 1872.

[72]   JH, 14 (p. 2), 15, 16, 17, (pp. 2, 3), 18 (pp. 3, 4), 20 (pp. 1-3), 21 (pp. 2-3), 22 (pp. 1-2), 24 (p. 5), 26, 27 (p. 2) August, 7 (p. 5) September 1872; JSH, 58.

[73]   JH, 7 (pp. 1-5), 9, 10 (p. 3), 16 (pp. 2-3), 19 (pp. 2-3), 20 (p. 2) September 1872.

[74]   JH, 3 (p. 4), 7 (p. 5), 12, 19 (p. 2), 27 (p. 3) September 1872; Gottfredson, *Indian Depredations*, 306-313.

[75]   Bean autobiography, 82-85; Jex, "History," 10.

[76]   Gottfredson, *Indian Depredations*, Supplement, 4; C. L. Christensen observation, as told by Culmsee, "Black Hawk War," DN, 25 August 1934, 3:IV; Rob. W. Sloan, "She-na-ba-wiken. . . ," JI 18 [1883]:379.

CHAPTER 25   *. . . daily walk. . . . (1872)*

[1]   JSH, 1, 67. This 104-page manuscript is the primary source for chapter 25. Quoted material from it has been condensed, modified, and rearranged.

[2]   JSH, 97-98, 102.

[3]   JSH, 97; Geneva Hyde Justesen to Romania Woolley, 11 October 1946, 3 (punctuation modified slightly), RWC.

[4]   JSH, 102, 93, 67.

[5]   JSH, 94-95; MAPHA.

[6]   JSH, 96, 97.

[7]   Barrow interview, 1-2 (condensed).

[8]   JSH, 96-97; Oscar W. Hyde, "Biography," 1 (spelling modified slightly); Adrian Hess to Myrtle S. Hyde, 15 November 1979, 3 (condensed).

[9]   MAPHA, 4; M. Anderson, "Ann Eliza Hyde," 3.

[10]   JSH, 92a, 95, 99.

[11]   JSH, 96.

[12]   JSH, 47a.

[13] M. A. H. White, "Julia Hyde," 3 (changed to first person and punctuation modified).

[14] JSH, 94-95, 96a; Luella Hyde Hess paper, 3 (spelling and punctuation modified slightly).

CHAPTER 26   *... unto the end. .... (1873-1878)*

[1] JH, 5 August 1872 (p. 2), 2 April 1873; OH discourse, 19 January 1873, JD 15:310; OH discourse, 5 October 1873, JD 16:236.

[2] JSHG, 60 (61 has error for William's death date); Julia Hyde's record; OH to BY, 10 February 1873 (spelling modified slightly), BYC (O. Wendell Hyde, Jr., M.D. interview, 30 November 1994: "The disease sounds like meningococcal meningitis."); OH discourse, 7 April 1873, JD 16:13; "We are favored with. . . ," WE 1 (15 May 1873):186; JH, 29 June 1873.

[3] JSHG, 61 (Temple Index Bureau gives Godfrey as Ernest's second name and has April 3 as his birth date); Weibye journal, 4 December 1873; OH to BY, 5 December 1873.

[4] JSHG, 61; Fogelberg, "Sophia," 7.

[5] CHC 5:484-488; MFP 2:249-266; OH discourse, 8 February 1874, JD 17:5.

[6] JH, 18 April 1874; OH to BY, 1 May 1874, BYC; several speakers: JD 17:24-90; "Spring City . . . ," WE 3 (1874):18; OH to GAS, 15 May 1874, GASC.

[7] JH, 17 May 1874; Weibye, 3rd Daybook, 127; Dorius diary, May 1874; OPE, 255-256; OH to BY, 1, 31 May 1874, BYC.

Brigham Young's earlier concerns about "all things in common" are in JH, 7 August 1847, 9-10. Orson wrote apprehensions in 1848; see MS 10 (15 October 1848):317-319.

[8] Weibye, 3rd Daybook, 138; JH, 13 September 1874.

[9] Weibye, 3rd Daybook, 147, 150, 153; Bleak, "Southern Utah," 1874, 209; Walker, *Diary* 1:393-394; JH, 13 September, 14 December 1874, 5 January 1875.

[10] OH to GAS, 4 January 1875 (parts modified to dialogue), GASC; JSH, 67-68, 79-81 (modified and rearranged); Weibye, 3rd Daybook, 153-154 (punctuation and spelling modified); OH to James Wareham, 6 January 1875 (punctuation modified slightly), USHS.

[11] Weibye, 3rd Daybook, 166.

[12] OH to GAS, 15 February 1875, GASC; JH, 18 February, 6 April 1875; Weibye, 3rd Daybook, 171, 183.

[13] CHC 5:519-521; WWJ 7:224; "Annual General Conference," DNW, 14 April 1875 (p. 168). Note: John Taylor and Wilford Woodruff had previously been switched with each other, putting John Taylor first because he had been ordained first, rather than second because he was the younger (see JH, 6 April [p. 2], 7 October [p. 1] 1861).

[14] OH to BY, 20 April 1875, BYC.

[15] BY, Jr. journals 15:216-224, 16 (apparently the field notes for vol. 15): 3, 11-14, 18-21; JSH, 70-72, 82-83 (modified); Geneva Hyde Justesen to Romania Hyde Woolley, 11 October 1946, RWC; D[avid] C[andland], "Poor Sanpete," *Salt Lake Daily Herald*, 21 April 1875, 3 (see also JH, 21 April 1875; W. S. Seely, "Sanpete," *Salt Lake Daily Herald*, 22 April 1875, 3); Day autobiography, 39.

[16] BY, Jr. journals 15:224-225, 16:26; Weibye 3rd Daybook, 186-188; HCKW, 436.

[17] BY, Jr. journals 15:227-228, 231; Weibye, 3rd Daybook, 188-189, 191-195, 4th Daybook, 1; "Andrew Christian Nielson, Pioneer," PH 11 (1968):287; Gunnison Manuscript History, 95; Spring City Ward Records, 1875-1876; "Spring City," WE 4 (1876):130; Day autobiography, 39.

[18] OH to George Q. Cannon, 9 July 1875, BYC, Telegram Letterbooks, Box 10 Folder 2, 450; JH, 19 March (p. 6), 12 July, 22 August, 10 (p. 4), 16 (p. 2) December 1875, 5 March 1876, 16 February, 30 July (p. 3) 1877; Weibye, 4th Daybook, 54, 59, 69, 140, 146, 157, 169, 195, 5th Daybook, 1, 13; OH to BY, 5 July, 23 September, 31 December 1875, 19 March, 3, 17 October 1876, BYC; WWJ 7:250, 286; "Spring City," WE 5 (1876):26.

[19] OH to BY, 5 July 1875, BYC; measurements by author, 1986; comments by 1986 owner, Faye Sluga. Orson owned this lot by 1867 ("Springtown town site plotted Sept. 13th 1867," Springtown Record Book I, n.p., but several beyond 154), and because it was on Main Street in the central area of town it undoubtedly had a dwelling on it before he built the rock home; he was still residing in his log home in June 1875 (JSH, 71).

[20] JH, 5 September 1875, 1-2; Day autobiography, 39; OH to BY, 5, 8 (telegram), 10 (telegram) July, 25 October, 24 November, 29 December 1875 (punctuation modified slightly); BY to OH, 27 November, 1 December 1875, BYL 14:32, 37.

[21] JSHG, 61; OH to BY, 13 December 1875 (spelling modified slightly), BYC; OH remarks, 6 April 1875, JD 17:351-353 (paragraphing added).

[22] JH, 14 July 1876; Longsdorf, *Mount Pleasant*, 146-147; Dorius diary, 1876; Gunnison Manuscript History, 96.

[23] Weibye, 4th Daybook, 176; OH to James Wareham, 26 October 1876, USHS; MFP 2:280-281; OH to BY, 30 November, 17 December 1876, BYC.

[24] Weibye, 5th Daybook, 23; JSH, 72, 76-78 (rearranged, condensed, and modified).

[25] JH, 25 March, 5 April (pp. 2, 11) 1877; WWJ 7:341-343; Bleak, "Annals Southern Utah," 1877, 57-58; OH discourse, 5 April 1877, JD 19:57-60.

[26] Weibye, 5th Daybook, 38, 40, 43; JSH, 81 (modified slightly).

[27] Weibye, 5th Daybook, 52-53, 56-57; Longsdorf, *Mount Pleasant*, 152; Dorius diary, 1877; JH, 15 July 1877, 2; OH to BY, 22 July 1877, BYC; CHC 5:508.

[28] WWJ 7:370; Weibye, 5th Daybook, 69; JSH, 83-84; Geneva Hyde Justesen to Joseph S. Hyde, 24 January 1932, RWC; JH, 31 August 1877.

[29] CHC 5:509-511; Bancroft, *Utah*, 669-670; William W. Slaughter, *Life in Zion*, 64; "Funeral of President Brigham Young," DEN, 2 September 1877; MFP 2:300.

[30] Weibye, 5th Daybook, 77; JH, 25 September (p. 2), 5, 8, 20, 21 (p. 4) October 1877; WWJ 7:376-379. For financial assistance to the Twelve in 1878 see OH to JT 4, 18 February, 19 August, 8 October 1878, HDC.

[31] Weibye, 5th Daybook, 82; Pulsipher diaries 2:9 (punctuation modified slightly).

[32] JH, 6 (p. 3), 18 (pp. 4, 6), 25 (pp. 2-4) November 1877, 20 January, 16, 17 February, 3 (p. 8), 24 (p. 4) March, 17 (p. 8), 18 (pp. 2, 3), 25 (p. 3) May, 1 (p. 3), 16 (p. 3) July, 18 August, 6 (p. 2), 29 September 1878; WWJ 7:383, 394, 407, 415-416, 430; Weibye, 5th Daybook, 89, 95, 103, 116, 117, 120, 134; OH to JT, 17 December 1877, 4, 18, 25 February, 10, 13 March, 14, 21, 25 April, 8, 12 June, 10 July, 7, 19 August 1878; JSH, 85; measurements by author.

[33] JH, 5 (p. 4), 6 (partly modified to dialogue) October, 28 November (p. 2) 1878; "Territorial Convention," WE 7:76-77.

[34] Weibye, 5th Daybook, 137; OH to JT, 8, 23 October 1878, HDC; Inventory of the estate of Orson Hyde, Sanpete County Probates, Box A, Number 221; OH to George Hyde, 2 November 1878, possession Mariam Johanson, Midvale, Utah.

[35] WE 18 (1890):185, 20 (1892):103, 25 (1896):13; EnA, s.v. "Jewish History and Society – 18th Century to World War II," "Jewish History and Society – Zionism," "Palestine" by Christina Phelps Grant and revised by Farhat J. Ziadeh, "Jewish History and Society–Zionism" by Isidore Abramowitz. See: LeGrand Richards, *Israel! Do You Know?*; *Congressional Record [United States]*–Appendix, May 1955 (contains praise for Orson Hyde in Abraham J. Multer, "Mormons and Israel").

The above sources include the following details about what happened to Jews after Orson's death: By the 1880s Jews feverishly migrated to the area of their ancient origins. In 1896 Theodor Herzl published another book outlining the dream of a Jewish homeland. In 1897 Herzl convened a Zionism conference in Switzerland. In 1917 world Jewish news related to a prophecy Orson pronounced seventy-six years before, that England would have a major role in the gathering. Great Britain, under the military expertise of Gen. Edmund Allenby, freed Palestine from the Turks. The Balfour Declaration, November 2, 1917, in London, announced British avowal to achieve "the establishment in Palestine of a national home for the Jewish people." Thirty-one years later the independent State of Israel became a reality.

[36] OH to George Hyde, 2 November 1878, possession Mariam Johanson, Midvale, Utah; OH discourse, 3 November 1878, JD 20:97-101 (punctuation modified); JH, 10 (p. 4), 11 November 1878; Telegrams regarding OH, 6, 11 November 1878, Church Letterbooks, telegrams, Box 10, Folder 4, 680, 683, 685; Weibye, 5th Daybook, 138.

[37] Weibye, 5th Daybook, 139, 140; JH, 20 (p. 2), 22 (p. 3) November 1878; JSH, 86.

[38] Morgan Hyde White to Harold B. Lee, 9 October 1972, copy possession author (modified to dialogue); Morgan Hyde White interview, 27 September 1984.

[39] JSH, 86, 87; OH to JT, 28 November 1878 (minor punctuation added), HDC.

[40] JSH, 86-88 (modified); JH, 28 November 1878, 2; Notes, WNNP, Box 3 Folder 1.

[41] JH, 28 November 1878, 2-3; "Death of Apostle Orson Hyde," MS 40 (2 December 1878):760-762; "Orson Hyde," *Seymour Record*, 19 December 1878, 2.

[42] JH, 1 December 1878, 3-5 (parts modified to dialogue; punctuation modified slightly); JSH, 86-87 (modified); MAPHA, 4.

A poem written in tribute to Elder Orson Hyde, by J. H. Ward, appears in DEN, 24 January 1879, p. 3, col. 4, furnished by Aleene LeBaron (great-granddaughter of Orson), Heber, Utah.

Epilogue

[1] HC 2:189-190; 3 Nephi 28:4-6, 9 (end), 27-29, 30-32, BoM. See, about John the Beloved: D&C 7:3, 5, 6, 8; John 21:15, 16. See, about angels declaring the gospel: Alma 13:22-24, BoM.

APPENDIX TWO   **Location of Hyde Park in Iowa**
1   Browning autobiography.
2   Bentley, "True," PH 180.
3   Appleby journal, 186.
4   PHCM, 112.
5   Manuscript History of Kanesville, Iowa.
6   For more about Henry Plumer see *History of Pottawattamie County, Iowa,* 147–148 of Biographical Section.

APPENDIX THREE   **Orson Hyde's Estate**
1   JSH, 101; Inventory of the Estate of Orson Hyde, Sanpete County Probate Records, Box A, Packet 221; Barney Hyde to Myrtle S. Hyde, 30 October 1979, 7; OH to GAS, 5 September 1874, GASC.
2   Distribution of the Estate of Orson Hyde, 23 November 1881, Sanpete County Probates, Box A, Packet 221; Barney Hyde to Myrtle S. Hyde, 14 September 1979.
3   Sanpete County Probate Records: B:88, 92, 111; Box A, Packet 221, document of 15 January 1881 reporting sale.

Bibliographical Essay
1   Original at HDC.
2   *Elders' Journal* 1 (1837):4.
3   JSH, 27–28; George L. Hyde to Nephi L. Morris, 5 May 1921, Nephi L. Morris Papers; Romania Woolley note card in Virginia Quealy to Myrtle S. Hyde, 27 October 1986.

SELECTED BIBLIOGRAPHY
(Alphabetical)

SOURCES that are included in the Abbreviations list are repeated here with full citations.

Some of the abbreviations for repositories, periodicals, and collections are used in this section.

Source materials and drafts will be donated to the Library-Archives of the Historical Department, The Church of Jesus Christ of Latter-day Saints, Church Office Building, Salt Lake City, Utah.

Adams, Dale W. "Chartering the Kirtland Bank." BYUS 23 (1983).

[Allen] "Charles H. Allen." Daughters of Utah Pioneers, *An Enduring Legacy* 1 (1978).

Allen, James B.; Esplin, Ronald K.; and Whittaker, David J. *Men With A Mission: The Quorum of the Twelve Apostles in the British Isles, 1837-1841.* Salt Lake City: Deseret Book, 1992.

Alter, J. Cecil. *Utah: The Storied Domain.* 3 vols. Chicago and New York: The American Historical Society, Inc., 1932.

"American Board of Commissioners for Foreign Missions." Papers. Syrian Mission, microfilms 537, 538. Houghton Library, Harvard University, Cambridge, Massachusetts.

Ames, Ira. "Journal and Record of the Life & Family of Ira Ames." HDC.

Anderson, Frederick, and Branch, Edgar M. *The Great Landslide Case, by Mark Twain, with editorial comment.* Berkeley: The Friends of the Bancroft Library, University of California, 1972.

Anderson, Karl R. *Joseph Smith's Kirtland: eyewitness accounts.* Salt Lake City: Deseret Book, 1989.

Anderson, Maude Hyde (granddaughter of Orson Hyde). "History of Ann Eliza Vickers Hyde." Typescript. 1967. From Barney Hyde, Ephraim, Utah.

Andrus, Hyrum L., and Andrus, Helen Mae, comp. *They Knew The Prophet.* Salt Lake City: Bookcraft, 1974.

Angell, Truman O. Journal. HDC.

Antrei, Albert C. T., and Scow, Ruth D., ed. *The Other Forty-Niners, a topical history of Sanpete County Utah 1849-1983.* Salt Lake City: Western Epics, 1982.

Appleby, William. Journal. Typescript. HDC.

Arrington, Leonard J. *Brigham Young: American Moses.* New York: Alfred A. Knopf, 1985.

Ausubel, Nathan. *The Book of Jewish Knowledge.* New York: Crown Publishers, Inc., 1964.

Averett, George Washington Gill. Biography. Library of Congress Collection of Mormon Diaries. Microfilm. FHL.

Babbitt, Charles Henry. *Early Days at Council Bluffs.* Washington D.C.: Press of B. S. Adams, 1916.

Backman, Milton V., Jr. *The Heavens Resound: A History of the Latter-day Saints in Ohio, 1830-1838.* Salt Lake City: Deseret Book, 1983.

Baker, Amenzo White. *The Baker Genealogy and Collateral Branches.* Ogden, Utah: A. T. Hestmark, 1910.

Bancroft, Hubert Howe. *The Works of Hubert Howe Bancroft.* Vol. 26: *History of Utah, 1540-1886.* San Francisco: The History Company, 1889.

Barron, Howard H. *Orson Hyde: Missionary, Apostle, Colonizer.* Bountiful, Utah: Horizon Publishers, 1977. (The page 20 photograph is Orson Spencer rather than Orson Hyde.)

Barrow, Villa Fenton (great-granddaughter of Orson Hyde). Typescript of tape-recorded interview by author, 5 October 1978. Salt Lake City.

Barrows, Ethan. "The Journal of Ethan Barrows." *Journal of History.* Independence, Missouri: Herald Publishing House 15 (1922).

Bate, Kerry William. *The Ebenezer Hanks Story.* Provo, Utah: M. C. Printing, 1982.

Bean, George Washington. "Autobiography of George Washington Bean." HDC.

Bee, Richard. Autobiography. FHL.

Belnap, Gilbert. Autobiography. Library of Congress Collection of Mormon Diaries. Microfilm. FHL.

Bennett, Richard E. *Mormons at the Missouri, 1846-1852.* Norman, Oklahoma: University of Oklahoma Press, 1987.

Bennion, John. Journal. USHS.

Bentley, Richard. "True to the Faith." PH 18 (1975).

Berlitz Hebrew Phrase Book. New York: Grosset & Dunlap, 1974.

Berrett, LaMar C. *Discovering the World of the Bible.* Provo, Utah: Brigham Young University Press, 1973.

Blair, Alma M. "The Haun's Mill Massacre." BYUS 13 (1972).

Blair, Philip. Family Papers. UUL.

Black, William to Brigham Young, 7 February 1861. HDC.

Bleak, James Godson. "Annals of the Southern Utah Mission." HDC.

Book of Commandments, for the Government of the Church of Christ, organized according to law, on the 6th of April, 1830. Zion, Missouri: W. W. Phelps & Co., 1833.

The Book of Mormon. Translated by Joseph Smith, Jun. Palmyra, New York: E. B. Grandin, Printer, 1830 (590 pages); reprint ed., Salt Lake City: The Church of Jesus Christ of Latter-Day Saints.

Bradshaw, Hazel B. "The Family Life of Richard Bentley and Elizabeth Price Bentley." Typescript. From LeRoi Bentley, Salt Lake City.

Brandt, Henry. Council Bluffs, Iowa. Correspondence with author.

Brewster, Hoyt W., Jr. *Doctrine & Covenants Encyclopedia.* Salt Lake City: Bookcraft, 1988.

Brigham Young University Studies. Provo, Utah, 1959–

Brooks, Juanita. *History of the Jews in Utah and Idaho.* Salt Lake City: Western Epics, 1973.

Brown, James S. *Life of a Pioneer, being the Autobiography of James S. Brown.* Salt Lake City: Geo. Q. Cannon & Sons Co., 1900.

Brown, Lorenzo. *The Journal of Lorenzo Brown.* St. George, Utah: Heritage Press, 198-.

Browning, James Allen. Autobiography. HDC.

Bullock, Isaac. Diary. HDC.

Burton, Richard F. *The City Of The Saints, And Across The Rocky Mountains To California*. New York: Harper & Brothers, 1862.

Byington, Lewis Francis, and Lewis, Oscar. *The History of San Francisco*. 3 vols. Chicago-San Francisco: The S. J. Clarke Publishing Company, 1931.

Call, Anson, "Life Record and Journal of Anson Call." Typescript. From Mildred Maw, Ogden, Utah.

Campbell, Hollis A.; Sharpe, William C.; and Bassett, Frank G. *Seymour [Connecticut], Past and Present*. Seymour, Conn.: W. C. Sharpe, Publisher, 1902.

Cannon, George Q. "History of the Church." *Juvenile Instructor*, various issues.

Carrington, Albert. Papers. UUL.

Carson County, Utah Territory, "Early Maps, 1855-1860." Nevada State Archives.

Carson County, Utah Territory, Probate Court. Original documents. Nevada State Archives.

Census Records. Microfilm. FHL.

Centennial Committee. *Memory Book to Commemorate Gunnison Valley's Centennial*. Provo, Utah: Press Publishing Co., 1959.

Chamberlin, Ralph V. *The University of Utah, a History of Its First Hundred Years, 1850 to 1950*. Salt Lake City: University of Utah Press, 1960.

Church Educational System. *Church History in the Fulness of Times*. Salt Lake City: The Church of Jesus Christ of Latter-day Saints, 1989.

"Church Emigration 1831-1848." Typescript. HDC.

Clark, James R. *Messages of the First Presidency*. 6 vols. Salt Lake City: Bookcraft, 1965-1975.

Clayton, W[illiam]. *The Latter-Day Saints' Emigrants' Guide*. St. Louis: Mo. Republican Steam Power Press—Chambers & Knapp, 1848.

Clement, Arlen. Living Kirtland, Ohio. Correspondence with author.

Cochran, Louis, and Cochran, Bess White. *Captives of the Word*. Garden City, New York: Doubleday & Co., 1969.

Coltrin, Zebedee. Diary 1832-34. HDC.

Cook, Lyndon W. *Joseph C. Kingsbury, A Biography*. Provo, Utah: Grandin Book Company, 1985.

Cook, Phineas Wolcott. *The Diary of Phineas Wolcott Cook*. Brigham City, Utah: The Phineas Wolcott Cook Family Organization, Inc., 1980.

Corrill, John. *Brief History of the Church of Christ of Latter Day Saints, (Commonly called Mormons)*. St. Louis: For the author, 1839.

Cowley, Matthias F. "A Brief Sketch of the Life of Abigail Gloyd Hyde." Typescript. HDC.

——. Reminiscences. Typescript. HDC.

——. *Wilford Woodruff*. Salt Lake City: Bookcraft, 1964.

Culmsee, Carlton. *Utah's Black Hawk War—Lore and Reminiscences*. Logan, Utah: Utah State University Press, 1973.

——. "The Black Hawk War." DN, 1934, various issues.

Curran, Harold. *Fearful Crossing*. Las Vegas, Nevada: Nevada Publications, 1982.

Daughters of Utah Pioneers. *An Enduring Legacy.* 12 vols. Salt Lake City, 1978–1989.

—. *Heart Throbs of the West.* 12 vols. Salt Lake City, 1939–1951.

—. *Our Pioneer Heritage.* 20 vols. Salt Lake City, 1958–1977.

—. *Treasures of Pioneer History.* 6 vols. Salt Lake City, 1952–1957.

Davis, Elisha Hildebrand. Statement (handwritten). HDC.

Davis, Larry M. *Lord, Why Me? Understanding Adversity.* Salt Lake City: Hawkes Publishing Inc., 1982.

Day, Eli A. Autobiography. Typescript. HDC.

Deseret Evening News. (See *Deseret News.*)

Deseret News. Title varies: *Deseret News (Weekly), Deseret Evening News.* Salt Lake City, Utah (and Fillmore, Utah), 1850–

Deseret News (Weekly). (See *Deseret News.*)

Dewey, Albert. Journal. HDC.

Dixon, Madoline Cloward. *Peteetneet Town, A History of Payson, Utah.* Provo, Utah: Press Publishing Co., 1974.

Doctrine and Covenants. The Church of Jesus Christ of Latter-day Saints.

Document Containing the Correspondence, Orders, &c. in Relation to the Disturbance with the Mormons; and the Evidence Given Before the Hon. Austin A. King, Judge of the Fifth Judicial Circuit of the State of Missouri, at the Court-House in Richmond, in a Criminal Court of Inquiry, Begun November 12, 1838, on the Trial of Joseph Smith, Jr., and Others for High Treason and Other Crimes Against the State. Fayette, Missouri: Printed at the office of the Boon's Lick Democrat, 1841.

Dorius, Carl Christian Nikolai. Diary. HDC.

Drennan, Martha Gladys Haslam. "Biography of John 'S' Haslam." Typescript. HDC.

Durham, Reed C., Jr. "The Election Day Battle at Gallatin." BYUS 13 (1972).

Early 12th Ward L.D.S. Records, Salt Lake City. Microfilm. FHL.

Elders' Journal of the Church of Latter Day Saints. Kirtland, Ohio, 1837–1838.

Elliott, Russell R. *History of Nevada.* Lincoln, Neb.: University of Nebraska Press, 1973.

Ellison, Marion, comp. *An Inventory & Index to the Records of Carson County, Utah & Nevada Territories, 1855–1861.* The Carson Valley Historical Society, 1984.

Encyclopedia Americana. International Edition. New York, 1964.

Encyclopedia Britannica. 15th ed.

Encyclopedia of Mormonism. Edited by Daniel H. Ludlow. 4 vols. New York: Macmillan Publishing Company, 1992.

Endowment House Records. Microfilm. FHL.

England, Breck. *The Life and Thought of Orson Pratt.* Salt Lake City: University of Utah Press, 1985.

England, Eugene. *Brother Brigham.* Salt Lake City: Bookcraft, 1980.

Ensign. Salt Lake City: The Church of Jesus Christ of Latter-day Saints, 1971–

Esler, L. A. *Presidents of Our United States.* Chicago: Rand McNally & Co., 1941.

The Evening and the Morning Star. Independence, Missouri, and Kirtland, Ohio: The Church of Jesus Christ of Latter-day Saints, 1832–1833, 1834–1836.

Far West Record: Minutes of The Church of Jesus Christ of Latter-day Saints, 1830–1844. Edited by Donald Q. Cannon and Lyndon W. Cook. Salt Lake City: Deseret Book, 1983.

Faulring, Scott H., ed. *An American Prophet's Record: The Diaries and Journals of Joseph Smith.* Salt Lake City: Signature Books, 1989.

Field, Homer H., and Reed, Joseph R. *History of Pottawattamie County, Iowa.* Chicago: S. J. Clarke Publishing Co., 1907.

Fielding, Joseph. "Diary of Joseph Fielding." Typescript. FHL. (As was customary in some schools of the time, Joseph Fielding capitalized many nouns. These have been changed to lower case for clarity.)

Fielding, R. Kent. "The Mormon Economy in Kirtland, Ohio." *Utah Historical Quarterly* 27 (1959).

Finley, Mary J. Chase. *A History of Springville [Utah].* Springville: Art City Publishing, 1948.

Firmage, Edwin Brown, and Mangrum, Richard Collin. *Zion in the Courts: A Legal History of the Church of Jesus Christ of Latter-day Saints, 1830-1900.* Urbana and Chicago: University of Illinois Press, 1988.

Fogelberg, Sterling. "A Brief History of The Life of Sophia Margaret The Wife of Elder Orson Hyde." Typescript. From Stella Miller (great-granddaughter of Orson Hyde), Salt Lake City, Utah.

Foote, Warren. "Autobiography." Typescript. HDC.

Frantzen, John. Autobiography. 1889. HDC.

Frontier Guardian. Kanesville (Council Bluffs), Iowa, 1849-1852.

Frontier Guardian and Iowa Sentinel. Kanesville (Council Bluffs), Iowa, 1852-1853.

[Galli] "History of Peter Galli." From Melva G. Mitchell, Murray, Utah.

Galpin, Henry J., comp. *Annals of Oxford, New York.* Oxford, New York: Times Book and Jot Printing House, 1906.

General Church Minutes. HDC.

Geauga County, Ohio, Court of Common Pleas. Microfilm. FHL.

Geauga County, Ohio, Deeds. Microfilm. FHL.

Geauga County, Ohio, Marriages. Microfilm. FHL.

Gottfredson, Peter. *Indian Depredations In Utah.* 2nd ed. Salt Lake City: Private Printing, 1969. (This edition has Appendix and Index.)

Gowans, Fred R., and Campbell, Eugene E. *Fort Supply, Brigham Young's Green River Experiment.* Provo, Utah: BYU Publications, 1976.

"Grandmother [Laura Hyde] Miner's life." Ca. 1900. Handwritten. From Dorothy S. Rogers (great-granddaughter of Orson Hyde), Salt Lake City, Utah.

Greeley, Horace. *An Overland Journey, from New York to San Francisco, in the Summer of 1859.* New York: C. M. Saxton, Barker & Co., 1860.

Green River Company Journal, November 1853-July 1854. HDC.

Greenhalgh, Joseph Hyrum. *Oliver Cowdery: The Man Outstanding.* 2nd printing. Phoenix, Arizona: Clico Press, 1965.

Gunn, Stanley R. *Oliver Cowdery: Second Elder and Scribe.* Salt Lake City: Bookcraft, 1962.

Gunnison Manuscript History. Historical Record 1859-1891. HDC.

Hadden Scrapbook. Lake County, Ohio, Historical Society. Microfilm. FHL.

Haight, Isaac Chauncy. Journal. Typescript. UUL.

Hall family records. Natalie and Annette Ashton, submitters to Edgemont Sixteenth Ward Family History collection, 1997. From Joyce Hooker (great-granddaughter of Orson Hyde), Provo, Utah.

Hammond, F. B, Jr. "A Prayer, And Prophecy." *The Liahona* 1 (1907).

Hancock County, Illinois, Bonds and Mortgages. Microfilm. FHL.

Hancock, Levi W. "The Life of Levi W. Hancock." Holograph. HDC.

Hansen, Peter Olsen. Diaries. HDC.

Harris, Emer. Family records. From Janet Low, Ogden, Utah.

Harris, George Henry Abbot. Journals. Typewritten. HDC.

Hatch, Ephraim. "What Did Joseph Smith Look Like?" *Ensign*, March 1981.

Hayden, A. S. *Early History of The Disciples in the Western Reserve, Ohio.* Cincinnati: Chase & Hall, 1876.

Hayward, William. Family records. From Virginia Wheeler, Riverdale, Utah.

Hess, Luella Minerva Hyde. Paper, handwritten, copied by author in 1979 from original possession of Adrian Hyde Hess (grandson of Orson Hyde), Oakland, California.

Heywood, Joseph L. Collection. HDC.

Heywood, Joseph L. "Diary of Joseph L. Heywood." Typewritten. HDC.

Heywood, Martha S. Autograph book. HDC.

Hiatt, Mattie, comp. *Sexton's Records of the Provo Cemetery, 1849-1929.* 1930.

Hill, Henry Wayland, ed. *Municipality of Buffalo, New York.* New York and Chicago: Lewis Publishing Company, 1923.

Hill, Marvin S. "An Historical Study of the Life of Orson Hyde, Early Mormon Missionary and Apostle from 1805-1852." Master's thesis, Brigham Young University, 1955.

—; Rooker, C. Keith; and Wimmer, Larry T. "The Kirtland Economy Revisited: A Market Critique of Sectarian Economics." BYUS 17 (Summer 1977).

Hillman, Silas. Autobiography and journal. HDC.

Historian's Office. "History of the Church, 1839-[ca. 1882]." HDC. (Also called "History of Brigham Young.")

Historian's Office Journals. HDC.

Historisch Genootschap Roterodamum. *Rotterdams Jaarboekye 1967.* Rotterdam: W. L. & J. Brusse, 1967. From the Bibliotheca Rosenthaliana, University of Amsterdam.

History of Fremont County, Iowa. Des Moines: Iowa Historical Company, 1881.

History of Geauga and Lake Counties, Ohio. Philadelphia: Williams Brothers, 1878.

History of Howard and Cooper Counties, Missouri. St. Louis: National Historical Company, 1883.

The History of Lee County, Iowa, containing a History of the County, its Cities, Towns, &c. Chicago: Western Historical Society, 1879.

History of Lorain County, Ohio. Philadelphia: Williams Brothers, 1879.

History of Madison County, Illinois. Edwardsville, Ill.: W. R. Brink & Co., 1882.

History of Mills County, Iowa. Des Moines: State Historical Company, 1881.

History of Pottawattamie County, Iowa. Chicago: O. L. Baskin & Co., Historical Publishers, 1883.

Holbrook, Thelma. "Martha." PH 5 (1962).

House of Representatives. "Iowa Contested Election Case. Evidence." *House of Representatives Miscellaneous Documents.* 1st Session, 31st Congress, Document No. 47.

Hunsaker, Abraham. "Reminiscences and journal, 1842-1859." Typescript. HDC.

Hunter, Edward. Papers. BYUL.

Huntington, Oliver B. Diaries. Typescript. HDC.

Hyde, Barney (grandson of Orson Hyde), Ephraim, Utah. Correspondence with author.

Hyde family records. Possession of author.

Hyde, Joseph Smith. "Orson Hyde." (Manuscript dictated and revised by Orson Hyde's son, Joseph Smith Hyde, 1930-1931. Original typewritten copy, with author's notations, at UUL. HDC has carbon copy without some of the author's notations, RWC.)

——. "The Orson Hyde Genealogy," *Utah Genealogical and Historical Magazine* 4 (April 1913):59-64.

Hyde, Mary Ann Price. "Autobiography." Bancroft Library, University of California, Berkeley, 1880. (Quoted by permission.)

Hyde, Myrtle Stevens. *Orson Hyde Genealogy, Volume 1.* Monograph. Ogden, Utah: By the author, 1997. FHL.

Hyde, Oliver Wendell, Jr., M.D. Interviews by author.

Hyde, Orson. *A Cry from the Wilderness. A Voice from the Dust of the Earth* (translated by Justus Ernst). Frankfurt, Germany: By the Author, 1842. (German title: *Ein Ruf aus der Wüste. Eine Stimme aus dem Schoose der Erde. . . .*)

——. *"He that hath ears to hear, let him hear what the Spirit saith unto the Churches."* Broadside. Nauvoo, Illinois, 14 March 1846.

——. "History of Orson Hyde." DN 5, 12 May 1858; reprinted MS 26 (November, December 1864):742-744, 760-761, 774-776, 790-792.

——. "Journal of Orson Hyde [1832]." Typescript, BYUL. Original, HDC.

——. "Letter from Nauvoo - Course of the Mormons." *New-York Daily Tribune,* 5 February 1846. From Marjory Hyde Eldredge (great-granddaughter of Orson Hyde), Salt Lake City, Utah.

——. *A Prophetic Warning.* Toronto, August 1836. Library, Reorganized Church of Jesus Christ of Latter Day Saints, Independence, Missouri.

——. Publisher's Preface to *An Appeal To The American People. . . .* by Sidney Rigdon. Second Edition, Revised. Cincinnati: Shepard & Sterns, 11 July 1840.

——. *A Sketch of the Travels and Ministry of Elder Orson Hyde, Missionary of The Church of Jesus Christ of Latter-day Saints, to Germany, Constantinople and Jerusalem . . . compiled from his late letters and documents. . . .* Liverpool: Parley P. Pratt, 1842. Reprint ed., Salt Lake City: Deseret News Office, 1869.

——. *Speech of Elder Orson Hyde delivered before the High Priests Quorum in Nauvoo, April 27th, 1845, upon the course and conduct of Mr. Sidney Rigdon, and upon the merits of his claims to the presidency of the Church of Jesus Christ of Latter-day Saints.* City of Joseph [Nauvoo, Illinois]: printed by John Taylor, 1845.

——. *A Timely Warning.* Kirtland, Ohio, 1837. Reprinted Preston, England, August 1837.

Hyde, Oscar Waldemar. "Biography of the Life and Labors of Oscar Waldemar Hyde." Typescript. From Stella Frisby Miller (great-granddaughter of Orson Hyde), Salt Lake City, Utah.

Hyde, William. *The Private Journal of William Hyde [1818-1874].* Privately printed, 1974. Original at HDC. (William Hyde was a second cousin once removed to Orson Hyde, but the two men were unaware of this relationship during their lifetimes.)

Hymns. Salt Lake City: Church of Jesus Christ of Latter-Day Saints, 1948.

The Improvement Era. Salt Lake City, 1898-1970.

The Instructor. Salt Lake City, 1930-1970.

Jacob, Lucille P., Salt Lake City, Utah. Correspondence with author.

Jenson, Andrew. *Encyclopedic History of the Church of Jesus Christ of Latter-day Saints.* Salt Lake City: Deseret News Publishing Co., 1941.

——. *Latter-day Saint Biographical Encyclopedia.* 4 vols. Salt Lake City: Andrew Jenson History Company, 1901-1936.

Jessee, Dean C. *The Personal Writings of Joseph Smith.* Salt Lake City: Deseret Book, 1984.

——. "The Writing of Joseph Smith's History." BYUS 11 (1971).

Jex, William. "History of William Jex Written by Himself." HDC.

Johnson family records. From Elaine Speakman, Mount Pleasant, Utah.

Johnson, Don Carlos. *A Brief History of Springville, Utah.* . . . Springville: William F. Gibson, 1900.

Johnson, Joseph Ellis. Papers. UUL.

Johnson, Milas Edgar. "The Life Review of Milas Edgar Johnson." Typescript. HDC.

Johnson, Rufus David. *J.E.J. Trail to Sundown, Cassadaga to Casa Grande, 1817-1882.* Salt Lake City: Joseph Ellis Johnson Family Committee, 1961.

Jones, Daniel W. *Forty Years Among The Indians.* Salt Lake City: Juvenile Instructor Office, 1890.

Jones, Emma C. Brewster. *The Brewster Genealogy, 1566-1907.* 2 vols. New York: The Grafton Press, 1908.

Journal History. The Church of Jesus Christ of Latter-day Saints. HDC.

Journal of Discourses. 26 vols. London: Latter-day Saints' Book Depot, 1855-1886.

"Julia Thomene Reinert Hydes Record." From Morgan Hyde White (grandson of Orson Hyde), Hollywood, California.

Junior League of Washington. *The City of Washington: An Illustrated History.* New York: Alfred A. Knopf, 1985.

Justesen, Geneva Hyde (daughter of Orson Hyde). "Ann Eliza Vickers Hyde." 1948. RWC.

Juvenile Instructor. Salt Lake City, 1866-1929.

Kane, Thomas L. "The Mormons." MS 13 (1851).

Kennedy, J[ames] H[arrison]. *Early Days of Mormonism.* New York: Charles Scribner's Sons, 1888.

Kimball, Heber C. Journals. HDC.

Kimball, Stanley B. *Heber C. Kimball: Mormon Patriarch and Pioneer.* Urbana, Illinois: University of Illinois Press, 1981.

——. *On The Potter's Wheel. The Diaries of Heber C. Kimball.* Salt Lake City: Signature Books, 1987.

——. "Nauvoo Temple." *Improvement Era,* November 1963.

Kirtland Council Minute Book, 1832-1837. HDC.

Knight, Newel. "Newel Knight's Journal." *Classic Experiences and Adventures.* Third Section, 46-104. Salt Lake City: Bookcraft, 1969.

Kouwenhoven, John A. *The Columbia Historical Portrait Of New York.* New York: Doubleday & Company, 1953.

Lake, D. J. *Atlas of Lake and Geauga Counties Ohio.* Philadelphia: Titus, Simmon & Titus, 1874.

Langworthy, Franklin. *Scenery of Plains, Mountains and Mines . . . Upon the Overland Route to California. . . .* Ogdensburgh: J. C. Sprague, Book-Seller, 1855.

Larson, A. Karl, and Larson, Katharine Miles, ed. *Diary of Charles Lowell Walker.* 2 vols. Logan, Utah: Utah State University Press, 1980.

Latter Day Saints' Messenger and Advocate. Kirtland, Ohio, 1834-1837.

The Latter-day Saints Millennial Star. Manchester, Liverpool, London, 1840-1970.

Launius, Roger Dale. *Zion's Camp: Expedition to Missouri 1834.* Independence, Missouri: Herald Publishing House, 1984.

["Laura"] "Life of Laura Marinda Hyde Miner." Typewritten. From Lawrence A. Miner, Salt Lake City.

Lee, John D. *Mormonism Unveiled. . . .* St. Louis: Byran, Brand & Co., 1877.

Leigh, Rufus Wood. *Nevada Place Names, Their Origin and Significance.* Salt Lake City: Deseret News Press, 1964.

Lever, W. H. *History of Sanpete and Emery Counties, Utah.* Ogden, Utah: W. H. Lever, 1898.

Lewis, Samuel. *Topographical Dictionary of England.* 4 vols. London: S. Lewis and Co., 1845.

The Liahona, The Elders' Journal. Chattanooga, Tennessee and Independence, Missouri, 1907-1945.

Library of Congress Collection of Mormon Diaries. Microfilm. FHL.

Lillard, Richard G. *Desert Challenge. An Interpretation of Nevada.* Lincoln, Nebraska: University of Nebraska Press, 1942.

Longsdorf, Hilda Madsen, comp. *Mount Pleasant, 1859-1939.* Mount Pleasant, Utah: Mount Pleasant Pioneer Historical Association, 1939. Reprinted 1989.

Lundwall, N. B., comp. *Temples of the Most High.* Revised. Salt Lake City: Bookcraft, 1977.

Mack, Effie Mona. *Nevada, a history of the state from the earliest times through the Civil War.* Glendale, California: The Arthur H. Clark Company, 1936.

Madsen, Andrew. "The Personal History Of Andrew Madsen. . . ." Typescript, 1968. HDC.

Manuscript History of the British Mission. HDC.

Manuscript History of Kanesville, Iowa. HDC.

Manuscript History of Salt Lake City Seventeenth Ward. HDC.

Manuscript History of Weber Stake. HDC.

Martindale, William Addington. Papers. BYUL.

McConkie, Bruce R. *Mormon Doctrine.* 2nd ed. Salt Lake City: Bookcraft, 1966.

McKiernan, F. Mark. "The Voice of One Crying in the Wilderness: Sidney Rigdon, Religious Reformer 1793-1876." Ph.D. thesis, University of Kansas, 1968.

McKinstry, Byron N. "Excerpts from the Diary of Byron N. McKinstry." Typescript. Public Library, Council Bluffs, Iowa.

McLellin, William E. *The Journals of William E. McLellin 1831-1836.* Edited by Jan Shipps and John W. Welch. Provo, Utah: BYUS, and Urbana and Chicago: University of Illinois Press, 1994.

McQuown, Madeline R. Papers. UUL.

Merkley, Christopher. *Biography of Christopher Merkley.* Salt Lake City: J. H. Parry & Company, 1887.

Middleton, Jesse Edgar. *The Municipality of Toronto, A History.* 3 vols. Toronto: The Dominion Publishing Company, 1923.

Millard [LDS] Stake Minutes. HDC.

Miller, Arnold D. "The Life Story of Henry William Miller." Typescript. HDC.

Miller, David E. *Utah History Atlas.* David E. Miller, 1964.

Miller, Henry family records. From Arlene Taysom, Ogden, Utah.

Miller, Henry. Journal. HDC.

Miller, Reuben. Journal. HDC.

Miluck, Nancy C., ed. *The Genoa-Carson Valley Book.* Genoa, Nevada: Dragon Enterprises, 1961.

Minutes of Tabernacle meetings, Salt Lake City. HDC.

Morgan, Dale L. *The Humboldt: Highroad of the West.* New York and Toronto: Farrar & Rinehart, 1943.

Morgan, Nicholas G., Sr. "Pioneer Map, Great Salt Lake City." HDC.

Morris, Nephi L. Papers. UUL.

——. *Prophecies of Joseph Smith and their Fulfilment.* Salt Lake City: Deseret Book Company, 1931.

Mortensen, Elda P., ed. *Isaac V. Carling Family History.* Provo, Utah: J. Grant Stevenson, 1964.

National Geographic Society. *Everyday Life in Bible Times.* Washington, D.C.: National Geographic Society, 1967.

Nauvoo, Illinois, City Council Proceedings, 1841-1845. HDC.

Nauvoo, Illinois, Lodge Petitions, among papers of Nauvoo Restoration. HDC.

Nauvoo, Illinois, Trustees Land Book A. HDC.

Nauvoo Journal. Hyrum, Utah, 1989–

Nauvoo Neighbor. Nauvoo, Illinois, 1843-1845.

Nauvoo the Beautiful. Pamphlet, LDS, 1979.

Nauvoo Temple Records. FHL.

[Neibaur] "Alexander Neibaur." *Utah Genealogical and Historical Magazine* 5 (1914).

Nevada Historical Society Papers. Vol. 1. Carson City, Nevada: State Printing Office, 1917.

New Haven Palladium. The Beinecke Rare Book and Manuscript Library, Yale University, New Haven, Connecticut.

Nibley, Preston. *Stalwarts of Mormonism.* Salt Lake City: Deseret Book Company, 1954.

Nicholson, John. *The Martyrdom of Joseph Standing.* Salt Lake City: Deseret News Co., Printers, 1886.

Noall, Claire. *Intimate Disciple. A Portrait of Willard Richards, Apostle to Joseph Smith – Cousin of Brigham Young.* Salt Lake City: University of Utah Press, 1957.

Nonpareil. Council Bluffs, Iowa, 1857–

Nordgren, Weston Nephi. Papers. HDC.

North, Dexter. *John North of Farmington, Connecticut, and His Descendants.* Washington, D.C.: D. North, 1921.

Norton, L. A. *Life and Adventures of Col. L. A. Norton.* Oakland, California: Pacific Press Publishing House, 1887.

Olney, Oliver H. *The Absurdities of Mormonism Portrayed.* Hancock Co., Illinois, 1843.

—. Papers. HDC.

Olsen, Mabel M. "Aurelius Miner." PH 4 (1955).

Orcutt, Samuel. *The History of the Old Town of Derby, Connecticut, 1642-1880, with Biographies and Genealogies.* Springfield, Mass.: Springfield Printing Company, 1880.

Orton, Joseph. Autobiography. Library of Congress Collection of Mormon Diaries. Microfilm. FHL.

Oxford, Connecticut, Deeds. Microfilm. FHL.

Painesville Telegraph. Painesville, Ohio.

Papanikolas, Helen Z., ed. *The Peoples of Utah.* Salt Lake City: Utah State Historical Society, 1976.

Park, Babzanne. "Nauvoo Still 'The Beautiful.'" *Ensign,* March 1979.

Peacock, George. Journals. Typescript. HDC.

Pearl of Great Price. The Church of Jesus Christ of Latter-day Saints.

Perkins, J. R. *Mormon Battalion For Service Against Mexico Was Recruited Here."* Pamphlet, apparently privately printed, probably in 1932. Also published in *Nonpareil,* 24 July 1932.

Perkins, Keith. "A House Divided." *Ensign,* February 1979.

Peterson, John Alton. "Mormons, Indians, and Gentiles and Utah's Black Hawk War." Ph.D. dissertation, Arizona State University, 1993.

—. *Utah's Black Hawk War.* Salt Lake City: University of Utah Press, 1998.

Peterson, Olen Curtis. "A History of the Schools and Educational Programs of The Church of Jesus Christ of Latter-Day Saints in Ohio and Missouri, 1831-1839." M.A. thesis, Brigham Young University, Provo, Utah, 1972.

Polk, R. L. & Co. *Salt Lake City Directory.* Salt Lake City.

Portrait, Genealogical and Biographical Record of the State of Utah. Chicago: National Historical Record Co., 1902.

Pottawattamie County, Iowa, Deeds. Microfilm. FHL.

Pottawattamie High Council Minutes, 1846-1851. HDC.

Pottawattamie High Priest Quorum Minutebook 1848-1851. HDC.

Pratt, Orson. *Interesting Account of Several Remarkable Visions.* . . . Edinburgh: Ballantyne and Hughes, 1840. Reprinted Elden J. Watson, *Orson Pratt Journals.*

—. *The Orson Pratt Journals.* Compiled by Elden J. Watson. Salt Lake City: By the Compiler, 1975.

Pratt, Parley Parker. *Autobiography of Parley Parker Pratt*. Edited by Parley P. Pratt. 10th printing. Salt Lake City: Deseret Book Company, 1973.

Price, daughter of. "History of Wm. Price Known as Bishop Price." Typewritten. From Lucille P. Jacob, Salt Lake City, Utah.

The Prophet. New York City, 1844-1845.

Pulsipher, John. Diaries. Library of Congress Collection of Mormon Diaries. Microfilm. FHL.

Rasmussen, Peter. Reminiscences. HDC.

Raty, Myra Sauer. *Pioneers of the Ponderosa*. Sparks, Nevada: Western Printing & Publishing, 1973.

Relief Society Magazine. Salt Lake City, 1915-1971.

The Return. Davis County, Iowa, 1889-1900.

Richards, LeGrand. *Israel! Do You Know?* 8th printing. Salt Lake City: Deseret Book Company, 1973.

Richards, Mary Haskin Parker. *Winter Quarters: the 1846-1848 life writings of Mary Haskin Parker Richards*. Edited by Maurine Carr Ward. Logan, Utah: Utah State University Press, 1996.

Richards, Willard. "Journal." HDC.

——. Papers. HDC.

Ricks, Stephen D. "The Appearance of Elijah and Moses in the Kirtland Temple and the Jewish Passover." BYUS 23 (Fall 1983).

Rigdon, Sidney. *An Appeal To The American People: Being An Account Of The Persecutions Of The Church Of Latter Day Saints; And Of The Barbarities Inflicted On Them By The Inhabitants Of The State Of Missouri*. Cincinnati: Glezen and Shepard, 1840. (See Hyde, Orson, for data about revised issue.)

Riser, George Christian. "Life's story of George Christian Riser." Typewritten. HDC.

Roberts, B[righam] H[enry]. *A Comprehensive History of the Church of Jesus Christ of Latter-day Saints*. 6 vols. Revised. Provo, Utah: Brigham Young University Press, 1965.

——. *The Life of John Taylor*. Salt Lake City: Bookcraft, 1963.

Roberts, David. *The Holy Land*. London: Terra Sancta Arts, 1982.

Rogerson, Josiah. "The Ending Of The Black Hawk War In Utah." Typescript. HDC.

Rollins, James Henry. "The Life of James Henry Rollins as dictated to his daughters." Copied by Ada Long, Las Vegas, Nevada, 1949. HDC.

Roylance, Ward J. *Utah: A Guide To The State*. Revised and Enlarged. Salt Lake City: A Guide to the State Foundation, 1982.

Salt Lake County Deeds. County offices.

Salt Lake County Tax Assessment Rolls. Microfilm. FHL.

Salt Lake School of the Prophets, 1883. From Calvin Stephens, Morgan, Utah.

Salt Lake Tribune. 1871-

Sanderson, Henry Weeks. "Diary." Typescript. HDC.

Sanpete County Deeds. County offices.

Sanpete County Probate Records. County Offices.

Sanpete Stake, historical records and minutes. HDC.

Sanpitcher. A handwritten newspaper. HDC.

Scadding, Henry, and Dent, John Charles. *Toronto: Past and Present: Historical and Descriptive.* Toronto: Hunter, Rose and Company, 1884.

Scales, John. *History of Strafford County, New Hampshire and Representative Citizens.* Chicago: Richmond-Arnold Publishing Co., 1914.

Schmidt, Louis B. "The Miller-Thompson Election Contest." *The Iowa Journal of History and Politics* 12 (January 1914).

Scott, James Allen. Diaries. HDC.

The Seymour Record. Seymour, Connecticut, 1871– From Yale University Library.

Sharpe, W. C. *History of Seymour, Connecticut, with Biographies and Genealogies.* Seymour, Conn.: Record Print, 1879.

Shurtleff, Stella Cahoon, and Cahoon, Brent Farrington. *Reynolds Cahoon and His Stalwart Sons.* Salt Lake City: Paragon Press, 1960.

Simons [Simmons], George. Drawings of early Council Bluffs. Council Bluffs Public Library.

Slaughter, William W. *Life in Zion: an intimate look at the Latter-day Saints, 1820-1995.* Salt Lake City: Deseret Book Company, 1995.

Sloan, E. L., comp. *The Salt Lake City Directory and Business Guide, for 1869.* Salt Lake City: E. L. Sloan & Co., 1869.

Smith, Bathsheba Wilson Bigler. Autobiography. HDC.

Smith, Eliza R. Snow. *Biography and Family Record of Lorenzo Snow.* Salt Lake City: Deseret News Company, Printers, 1884.

Smith, George A. Collection. HDC.

Smith, Joseph. Collection. HDC.

—. *History of The Church of Jesus Christ of Latter-day Saints.* Edited by Brigham H. Roberts. 7 vols. 2nd ed., revised. Salt Lake City: Deseret Book Company, 1951.

Smith, Joseph F. Affidavit Books. HDC.

Smith, Joseph Fielding. *Blood Atonement and the Origin of Plural Marriage.* Salt Lake City: Deseret News Press, 1905.

—. *Essentials in Church History.* 24th ed. Salt Lake City: Deseret Book Company, 1971.

Smith, Lucy Mack. *History of Joseph Smith By His Mother.* 2nd ed. Salt Lake City: Bookcraft, 1958.

Smith, Samuel H. "Journal [1832]." HDC.

[Snow] "Apostle Erastus Fairbanks Snow." PH 6 (1963).

"Sophia Margaret Hyde . . . Funeral Ceremonies." Typescript, 1932. From Stella Frisby Miller (great-granddaughter of Orson Hyde), Salt Lake City, Utah.

Spanish Fork high priests meeting, 1878. From Calvin Stephens, Morgan, Utah.

Spencer, Clarissa Young, and Harmer, Mabel. *Brigham Young at Home.* Salt Lake City: Deseret Book, 1961.

Spring City L.D.S. Ward Records. FHL.

Standley, Michael. "Michael Standley Tells His Own Story." PH 10 (1967).

Steward, Julian H. "Aboriginal and Historical Groups of the Ute Indians of Utah: An Analysis." *American Indian Ethnohistory: California and Basin Plateau Indians.* New York and London: Garland Publishing Inc., 1974.

Stimson, Fancher. "Overland Journey to California by Platte River Route and South Pass in 1850." *Annals of Iowa.* Third Series 13 (1921).

Stocks, Hugh G. "The Book of Mormon, 1830-1879, A Publishing History." M.L.S. thesis, University of California at Los Angeles, 1979.

Stone, Irving. *Men to Match My Mountains.* Garden City, New York: Doubleday & Co., Inc., 1956.

Stone, Winifred Miner, and Slusser, Florence Miner (granddaughters of Orson Hyde). "Life of Nancy Marinda Hyde." Typewritten. From Jane Buckmiller (great-grand-daughter of Orson Hyde), Salt Lake City, Utah.

Stout, Hosea. *On the Mormon Frontier: The Diary of Hosea Stout.* Edited by Juanita Brooks. Salt Lake City: University of Utah Press, Utah State Historical Society, 1964.

Stout, Joseph Allen. Journal. Typewritten. HDC.

Stutz, Clifford. "St. Louis Newspaper Clippings." HDC.

Talmage, James E. *The House of the Lord.* Salt Lake City: Bookcraft Publishers, 1962.

Taylor, John. Correspondence. UUL.

——. Presidential Papers. HDC.

——. *Succession in the Priesthood. A Discourse by President John Taylor, Delivered at the Priesthood Meeting, held in the Salt Lake Assembly Hall, Friday Evening, October 7th, 1881.* Privately printed.

Taylor, Leone Andrus, comp. *Milo Andrus, Junior - The Man and His Family.* Provo, Utah: J. Grant Stevenson, 1971.

Temple Index Bureau. FHL.

Territorial Military Records. USA.

Thirtieth Quorum of Seventies Records. HDC.

Thompson, George A. "Advancing The Mormon Frontier: The Life and Times of Joseph Stacy Murdock, Pioneer, Colonizer, Peacemaker." HDC.

Thompson and West. *History of Nevada, 1881.* Reprint ed. Berkeley, Calif.: Howell-North, 1958.

The Times and Seasons. Nauvoo, Illinois, 1839-1846.

Tullidge, Edward W. *Tullidge's Histories, (Volume II) containing the History of all the Northern, Eastern, and Western Counties of Utah; also the Counties of Southern Idaho. Biographical Appendix.* Salt Lake City: Edward W. Tullidge, 1889.

——. *The Women of Mormondom.* New York: [Tullidge and Crandall],1877.

Tyler, Daniel. *A Concise History of the Mormon Battalion in the Mexican War, 1846-1847, by Sgt. Daniel Tyler.* Salt Lake City: By the Author, 1881.

——. "Recollections of the Prophet Joseph Smith." *The Juvenile Instructor.* 27 (1892).

U.S. House of Representatives. "Iowa Contested Election Case." *31st Congress, 1st Session, Miscellaneous Document No. 47.* Washington, D.C.: Government Printing Office, 1850.

Utah Genealogical and Historical Magazine. Salt Lake City, 1910-1940.

Utah Historical Quarterly. Salt Lake City, 1928-

Utah Historical Records Survey WPA. *A History of Ogden.* Ogden, Utah: Ogden City Commission, 1940.

Utah Since Statehood. 4 vols. Chicago-Salt Lake City: S. J. Clarke Publishing Co., 1919-1920.

Vedder, J. Van Vechten, comp. *History of Greene County [New York].* By the County, 1927.

Vital Records of Acton Massachusetts to the Year 1850. Boston: New England Historic Genealogical Society, 1923.

Walker, Charles Lowell. *Diary of Charles Lowell Walker.* Edited by A. Karl Larson and Katharine Miles Larson. Logan, Utah: Utah State University Press, 1980.

The Wasp. Nauvoo, Illinois, 1842–1843.

Watson, Elden Jay, comp. *Manuscript History of Brigham Young, 1801–1844.* Salt Lake City: The Compiler, c. 1969.

——. "The Nauvoo Tabernacle." BYUS 19 (Spring 1979).

Watson, Kaye C., ed. *Life Under The Horseshoe.* Spring City, Utah: Spring City Corporation, 1987.

Weibye, Jens Christian Andersen. Journal. HDC.

The Western Bugle. Kanesville, Iowa, 1852–1853.

Western Historical Society. *History of St. Clair County, Michigan.* Chicago: A. T. Andreas & Co., 1883.

The Western Standard. San Francisco, California. 1856–1857.

Wetmore, Alphonso. *Gazetteer of the State of Missouri.* St. Louis: C. Keemle, 1837.

White, Herbert Addison. "Autobiography of Herbert Addison White." Typewritten. From Morgan Hyde White (grandson of Orson Hyde), Hollywood, California.

White, Mary Ann Hyde (daughter of Orson Hyde). "A Brief History of Julia T. Reinart Hyde." Typewritten. Morgan Hyde White (grandson of Orson Hyde), Hollywood, California.

White, Morgan Hyde (grandson of Orson Hyde). *An Autobiography.* Bountiful, Utah: Family History Publishers, 1986.

——. Family Records. Hollywood, California. Copies possession author.

——. Interviews.

Whitney, Helen Mar. "Life Incidents." WE, various issues.

——. "Scenes and Incidents at Winter Quarters." WE, various issues.

——. "Scenes in Nauvoo after the Martyrdom of the Prophet and Patriarch." WE, various issues.

——. *Why we Practice Plural Marriage.* Salt Lake City: Juvenile Instructor Office, 1884.

Whitney, Horace K. Journals. HDC.

Whitney, Newel K. Papers. BYUL.

Whitney, Orson F. *History of Utah.* 4 vols. Salt Lake City: George Q. Cannon & Sons Co., 1904.

——. *Life of Heber C. Kimball.* 9th ed. Salt Lake City: Bookcraft, 1979.

Wickham, Gertrude Van Rensselaer, ed. *Memorial to the Pioneer Women of the Western Reserve.* 5 vols. By the Woman's Department of the Cleveland Centennial Commission, 1896–1924.

Widtsoe, John E. *Joseph Smith, Seeker After Truth, Prophet of God.* Salt Lake City: Deseret News Press, 1951.

Wight, Lyman. *An Address by way of an abridged account and journal of my life . . . with an appeal to the Latter Day Saints, scattered abroad in the earth. . . .* Austin, Texas, 1848.

Wilkinson, Susan Hough Conrad. Autograph album. HDC.

Williams, Electa C. Briggs. Autobiography. HDC.

Willis, William L. *History of Sacramento County, California.* Los Angeles: Historic Record Company, 1913.

Woman's Exponent. Salt Lake City, 1872–1913.

Woodford, Robert J. "How the Revelations in the Doctrine & Covenants were Received and Compiled." *Ensign.* January 1985.

Woodruff, Wilford. *Leaves From My Journal.* Salt Lake City: Juvenile Instructor Office, 1882.

——. *Wilford Woodruff's Journal 1833–1898.* Edited by Scott Kenney. 9 vols. Midvale, Utah: Signature Books, 1983–85.

Woodward, William. "Reminiscences of Elder Orson Hyde." JI 35 (1900).

Woolley, Romania Jeannette Hyde. Collection. HDC.

Yohalem, Betty. *"I remember . . ." Stories and pictures of El Dorado County pioneer families.* Placerville, California: Chamber of Commerce, 1977.

Young, Brigham. Collection. HDC.

——. Letterbook. BYC.

——. Office Journals. BYC.

Young, John Russell, ed. *Memorial History of the City of Philadelphia From its First Settlement to the Year 1895.* 2 vols. New York: New York History Company, 1898.

Young, Lorenzo Dow. "Diary of Lorenzo Dow Young." *Utah Historical Quarterly.* 14 (1946).

The Young Woman's Journal. Salt Lake City, 1889–1929.

Youngreen, Buddy. *Reflections of Emma, Joseph Smith's Wife.* Orem, Utah: Grandin Book Company, 1982.

INDEX

LOCATIONS (towns, etc.) in the United States are listed under their states.

Locations in Canada, England, Scotland, Europe, and the Eastern Mediterranean are listed under these designations.

Major lakes are listed together.

Major rivers are listed together.

Aaron, 18, 142

Abbott, Ann, 99–101, 279

Abbott, Lewis, 99–101, 279

Abraham, 12, 32, 69, 70, 113, 117, 123, 129, 138, 139, 141, 156

Acord, Janette Louise, 500

Adam, 12, 32, 220

Adams, George J., 120–122, 165

affidavit, 100, 102, 103

Allen, Charles, 39

Allen, (Capt.) James, 207

Allen, Sarah, 276

Allred, Jackson, 443, 444, 449

Allred, James, 48

Allred, James A., 457

Allred, (Col.) R. N., 404, 413, 414, 432

Allred, Reuben, 444

Allred, Samuel, 425

Allred, Stephen, 457

Alma, 13

Amos, 113

Amy, Dustin, 236

Anderson, Maude Hyde, 467, 501

Anderson, (Dr.) Washington F., 377

Andrus, Milo, 4, 45, 266

angel(s), 12, 36, 48, 58, 66–69, 73, 99, 156, 199, 202, 376, 438, 484–485, 488

Angell, Harriet (Jacques), 27

Angell, James, 27, 535n.50

Angell, Truman, 198, 306, 309

Angell, William, 27

animals, 48–49, 245, 380, 389, 390, 403–404, 427, 429, 432, 454, 494, 495

anointing and blessing, 66

apostasy, 74, 372

apostate(s), 42, 96–97, 99–100, 104, 167, 172, 178, 197–200, 202, 252, 525n.24

apostle(s), 57–60, 63, 103, 105, 111, 113, 117, 135–136, 140, 142, 169, 176, 217, 219, 267, 390, 471, 473, 475; *see also* Quorum of the Twelve Apostles

Appeal to the American People, An, 107, 112

Appleby, William, 220, 318, 492

Army, United States, 374–377, 379, 380, 387

Aug-a-vor-um, Indian Chief, 442, 560n.51, 564n.15

Babbitt, Almon W., 201, 285

Baker, Simon, 360

Bancroft, Hubert Howe, 366, 490

baptism(s), 17–18, 73, 88, 122, 135, 140–141, 327, 370, 476

Bardsley, Joseph, 493

Barrow, Villa Fenton, 465

Bean, George W., 462

Beck, Joseph Ellison, 120, 528n.7

Bee, Richard, 276, 278, 294–296, 298–300, 305

Benson, Ezra T.: apostle, 211; Hyde Park, 221; Iowa, 227, 233, 243, 279, 281, 285, 290; Salt Lake City, 307, 312, 382; travels, 386–387; died, 452

Bentley, Elizabeth (Price), 237, 294, 355, 359, 479, 499

Bentley, Frank, 359
Bentley, Richard, 206, 212, 217, 219,
    221, 237, 238, 294, 328, 341, 352,
    355, 359, 396, 479, 492
Bible, 4, 9–10, 12, 20, 32, 322
Bigler, (Bishop) –, 369
Bigler, (Governor) –, 333, 335, 337
Black, (Acting-Governor) George A.,
    456
Black, William, 393
Black Hawk, Indian Chief, 413, 415,
    416, 418, 419, 421, 422, 424, 426,
    427, 431, 435–437, 442, 445, 448,
    449, 450, 452–453, 455, 564n.16,
    565n.30, 565n.31, 566n.41, 567n.49
Black Hawk Indian War:
    1865: beginning, 412; Salina Can-
    yon, 413–415; previous develop-
    ments, 415–416; killings, 417; Span-
    ish Fork Conference, 419; killings,
    420; battle 421; attack on Fort Eph-
    raim, 421; battle, 421; attack on
    Fort Ephraim, 421; attack on Cir-
    cleville, 422
    1866: attack between Glenwood and
    Salina, 424; attack on Fairview, 424;
    attack on Marysvale, 425; attack on
    Fairview, 425; Springtown residents
    moved to Fort Ephraim, 425;
    troops from Salt Lake County and
    Utah County, 425; government
    failed to supply reservation Indians,
    426; raid on upper Sevier, 426; bat-
    tle at Gravelly Ford, with Black
    Hawk wounded, 426; White Horse
    Chief, 426; friendly Indian killed,
    427; men killed in Thistle Valley
    and Spanish Fork, 427; settlers left
    Circleville, 427; stock driven from
    Ephraim, 427; Brigham Young
    opinions, 562n.33; families return
    to Springtown, 427
    1867: attacks in and near Glen-
    wood, 429, 434; military plans, 430;
    more people leave upper Sevier,
    431, 432–433; military plans and

changes, 432, 433; attack near
    Fountain Green, 433; attack at
    Twelve Mile Creek, 433; attack near
    Springtown, 435; Black Hawk offers
    peace, 436; man killed, 438
    1868: Mount Pleasant conference,
    440; Indians attacked men returning
    to Sevier settlements, 440; horses
    stolen from Fairview, 441; settler
    wounded Indian, 441; livestock
    stolen from Ephraim, 441; peace
    assurance in Coalville, 442; Sow-e-et
    residing in Fairview, 442; peace
    meet in Nephi, 442; peace meet in
    Payson, 442, 564n.14; treaty at
    Uinta Reservation, 442; raid on
    Fairview, 443; military drill, 443;
    "big talk" in Springtown, 443
    1869: Black Hawk in Salt Lake
    City, 445; Black Hawk in Mount
    Pleasant, 448; peace meet in Eph-
    raim, 449; Black Hawk seeks peace
    in Manti, 449–450; Black Hawk
    seeks forgiveness in Sanpete com-
    munities, 450; banquet in Spring-
    town, 450–451, 565n.33; horses
    stolen in Fairview, 452; Black Hawk
    "peace march" from Saint George
    to Payson, 452– 453
    1870: "talk" in Manti, 454; Black
    Hawk in Spring City, 455; Black
    Hawk in Manti, 455; Black Hawk
    in Salt Creek Canyon, 455,
    567n.49; Black Hawk died, 455;
    governor disbanded Utah militia,
    455, 456
    1871: peaceable, 456
    1872: Indian demands, destitute
    Indians thronging Sanpete, 458;
    Mount Pleasant meeting, 458; Colo-
    nel Dodge holds council at Fair-
    view, 458–459; stealing, killing (near
    Gunnison), and begging, 459; mili-
    tary aid, 459; bishops to cease aid-
    ing Indians, 460; raids near Spring
    City and Fairview, 460; troops

arrived, 460; treaty at Springville, 460; council at Mount Pleasant and final treaty, 460–461; stealing, man killed, 461

Blain, Sarah, 502

Blain, William, 502, 503n.7

Blair Company, 260

blessing sick, 22

Boggs, (Gov.) Lilburn W., 102

Book of Commandments, 21, 39

Book of Mormon, 12–16, 23, 27–30, 82, 88, 99, 122, 147, 258, 323, 407, 411

Bosley, Edmund, 75, 76

Boynton, Eliphalet, 75

Boynton, John F., 58, 75, 77, 96

"boys, the," 212

Brandt, Henry, 493

Brandt, (Mrs.) —, 493

Brocchus, (Judge) P. E., 277, 278, 282

Brough, (Mrs.) George, 400

Browett, Daniel, 210, 233

Browett, Martha Rebecca, 274, 353, 383–385, 447, 556n.46; *see* Hyde, Martha Rebecca (Browett)

Browett, Mother (Martha), 211

Brown, James S., 311, 318, 320–321

Brown, John, 269–273, 301

Browning family, 207

Browning, James Allen, 207, 492

Bruce, (Major) —, 48

Bryan, (Bishop) —, 412, 439, 440, 442

buffalo, 260, 296

Bull, Joseph, 497

Bullock, Benjamin, 493

Bullock, Benjamin K., 492, 493

Bump, Jacob, 75, 76

Burton Academy, 9

Burton, Richard F., 366

Cahoon, Reynolds, 61, 64, 79

California: 169, 235, 325; Johnson Pass, 335, 343, 351; Placerville (Hangtown), 335, 338, 339, 343, 346, 347; Sacramento, 335, 337, 338, 343, 344; San Francisco, 335–337, 343

California Trail, 329–332, 335, 364

California-Utah boundary, 333, 334, 337–339, 342, 423

Campbell, Robert, 242, 255, 542–543n.2

Campbellites (Disciples), 3, 9, 10, 18, 22

Canada: Kingston, 60; Toronto, 72–73

Candland, David, 474

Cannon, George Q., 328, 336, 344, 351, 433, 473, 474, 476

canvas, 187, 190, 192

carding mill (machines, etc.), 7, 8, 308

Carlin, (Gov.) Thomas, 116

carrots, 559n.38

Carson County and Valley, 324, 325, 333–335, 337, 338, 341, 343, 345, 349–352, 354, 355, 357, 358, 360, 361, 374–376, 396, 397; *for Carson County period see* Hyde, Orson

Carter, —, blacksmith, 236

Carter, John S., 54

Catholics, 129, 135

cave, 457

Chadwick, —, tailor, 236

Chase, Emily ("Em"), granddaughter, 365, 369

Chase, Emily (Hyde), daughter, 365, 369, 439, 452, 454; *see* Hyde, Emily

Chase, George Ogden, 324, 369, 496

Chassan, (Mr.) —, 129

children, 478

cholera, 54, 244, 297, 424

Church of Christ, 73

Church of England, 135

Church of Jesus Christ of Latter-day Saints, The, 96

Civil War, 395

Clapp, Matthew, 9

Clapp, (Judge) Orris, 9

Clark, Hiram, 236

(Colorado): Pueblo, 219

Coltrin, Zebedee, 38

Columbus, 320, 552n.33

Comahpitch, Indian Chief, 461

common stock, 229-230

confirmation(s), 18, 89

Connecticut: New Haven, 175; Oxford, 5, 25, 119; Seymour, 119, 485; Woodbury, 25

Constitution, United States, 377, 378

Conner, (Gen.) P. Edward, 413

co-operatives, 443, 445, 470, 478

Cossers, (Mr.) –, 349

"Cotton Mission," 401

Coulson, George, 253

Council Bluffs, Iowa, 206, 207, 208, 212, 214, 216, 492

Council of Twelve, *see* apostles; Quorum of the Twelve Apostles

counterfeiters, 245

Cowdery, Oliver: assisted Joseph Smith, 18, 20; writings, 516n.28; Kirtland from Missouri, 38, 39; clerk, 42, 43; Assistant President, 57; helped choose apostles, 57-58; council, 60; purchased Hebrew textbooks, 66; Kirtland Temple dedication, 67; vision, 69; New York, 72; bank plates, 75; apostate, 96, 97, 99, 100, 198; return, rebaptism, and death, 231-233

Cowley, Matthias, 294, 296, 305

Cox, (Mr.) –, 458

credentials, 20, 113-116, 125, 170, 187

Cry from the Wilderness, 147, 170, 490-491

Cumming, (Gov.) Alfred, 379

Cutler, Alpheus, 252

Daggett, (Dr.) Charles D., 348-350

Daley, Almira, 371

Daley, Moses, 371

Daniel, 12, 16

David, 139, 156

Davies, (Brother) –, 446

Davis, Elisha H., 175-176

Davis, Jennie, 500

Davis, Mary Ann, 502

Dawson, Jacob, 284, 287-289, 546n.30

Day, Eli, 477

death, after, 268, 434, 486-488

debate, 72-73

dedication of land, 113, 135, 138, 140

Deity, 12-16, 58, 163, 204, 221, 283, 326, 327, 438

Denton, Solomon W., 77-79

Deseret, 258-259

Deseret Alphabet, 316

Deseret Theological Institute, 327

Desert, Great Salt Lake, 364

Devine, Susan, 210

Dick, Indian, 442

Disciples, *see* Campbellites

Doctrine and Covenants, 82, 163, 168

Dodge, (Col.) G. W., 458-460

Douglas, Stephen A., 172

Drewzes, 129

Drummond, (Judge) William W., 356, 357, 359, 360, 362, 366, 374

Dunklin, (Gov.) Daniel, 39-40, 49-50

Durfee, (Brother) –, 192

dust, shake, 24, 29, 141

Dustin, Seth, 338

earth, 327

Eastern Mediterranean: Aegean Sea, 128; Alexandria, 126, 143, 144; Beirut (Beyrout), 128, 129; Bosporus Strait, 128; Cairo, 143; Constantinople, 113, 126-129, 488; Damietta, 143; Dardenelles Strait, 128; Garden of Gethsemane, 136, 137; Isle of Patmos, 128; Jaffa (Joppa), 129, 131; Jerusalem, *see separate listing*; Mediterranean Sea, 129, 143, 144; Mount Lebanon, 129; Mount of Olives, *see separate listing*; Mount Zion, 142; Nile River, 143, 144; Palestine, 128, 129; Sahara Desert, 143; Sea of Marmara, 128; Smyrna (Izmir), 128; Syria, 126, 128-129; Turkey, 128, 129

Eckles, Judge, 385, 386

education, 246, 267, 275, 316, 323, 326, 327, 381, 429

Ein Ruf aus der Wüste. . . , 147

Elder, 18

election(s), 84, 225, 228–231, 250, 343, 358

Elias, 69, 70

Elijah, 12, 15, 43, 70, 71

Ellis, Delia (Hyde), 428, 454; *see* Hyde, Delia

Ellis, Nathan, 428, 496

emigrant rescue, 368

endowment (temple), 166, 193

Endowment House, 327, 373

England: 79–80, 117, 121–122, 124, 145, 148, 211, 213, 485; Bedford, 122; Cheshire, 215; Lea, 153; Liverpool, 82–84, 93, 121, 148, 213, 215; London, 113, 122–124; Manchester, 121, 122 213, 214; Preston, 84–93, 121, 215; Tewkesbury, 159;

Ephraim, 70

Ephraim (and Fort Ephraim), Utah, 323, 389, 390, 412, 421, 422, 425–428, 430, 433–435, 441–444, 448, 449, 451, 456, 458, 469, 470, 476, 478

Europe: Amsterdam, 113, 125; Arnheim, 125; Austria, 126, 395; Balkan Peninsula, 127; Bavaria, 126, 145–146; Belgrad, 127; Black Sea, 128; Budapest, 127; Bulgaria, 127; Frankfurt, 126, 147; Galatz (Galati), 127, 128; Germany, 116, 122, 123, 125–127, 488, 490–491; Holland, 124–125, 488; Italy, 395; Mainz (Mazenty), 126; Munich, 126; Prussia, 395; Ratisbon, 126; Regensburg, 126, 127, 145–147, 549n.18; Rotterdam, 124–125; Rumania, 127; Russia, *see separate listing*; Trieste, 144; Vienna, 127

Evans Company, 260

evil spirits, 15, 31, 86–87

extermination order, 103

Ezekiel, 12, 71

faith, 375–376

Father and Son, 14

Feed and Provision Store, *see* store, Orson Hyde's

Fielding, James, 81, 85, 86

Fielding, Joseph, 81, 83, 85, 86, 88, 91, 93, 525n.26, 577

fire, 276, 280

flag, 124

fleas, 340–341

Flint, (Justice of the Peace) –, 78–79

Fogelberg, Sterling, 506

Fogelberg, Wilhelm, 505–506

Foot Company, 260

Ford, A. C., 284, 287, 288, 546n.30

Fordham, Elijah, 81, 94

Fordham, (Mr.) –, 82

Fordham, (Mrs.) –, 81

Fort Ephraim, *see* Ephraim

Fort Supply, 313–321, 324, 375, 457; *see also* Green River Mission

Foster, Robert D., 172, 178

Fox, Jesse, 309

Fremont, J. C., 172

French language, 127, 128

"Frog Sermon," 286, 287

Frontier Guardian, The, 235–236, 241–242, 245, 247, 251, 256–257, 282, 284, 311

Gager, Charles, 133, 143–144, 528n.14

Galli, Elisabeth Josephine, *see* Hyde, Elisabeth (Lizzy) Josephine (Galli)

gathering of Israel, 15, 68, 70, 73–74, 113, 114, 123, 125, 135, 137, 571n.35

genealogy, 71

Genoa (Nevada), 343–345, 348, 351, 352, 355, 360

Gentiles, 58, 70, 73–74, 113, 123, 238, 253, 276, 283, 287, 292, 308, 327, 328, 344, 374, 488

German book, Orson's, 147

German language, 126, 127, 162, 322

Gilbert & Whitney store, 8, 515n.13

Gilbert, Sidney, 7, 10, 11, 39, 40

Giles, Thomas, 493

Goddard, George H., 338, 339, 343

gold, 120, 233, 423
gold country, 335
Gold Rush to California, 235, 238,
    240-243, 251, 253, 255
gold seekers, 329, 332, 350-352, 375
Golden Bible, 3, 4, 10, 12, 56, 142, 484
Gooch, John, 235, 257
Goodson, John, 81-83, 86, 89, 91
Gould, John, 39-41
grain, 36
grammar, 327
Grant, Jedediah M., 279, 281, 317, 365,
    369
Graves, Peter, 393
Green River Mission, 311-314, 318,
    319, 550n.23; *see also* Fort Supply
Gunnison, (Lt.) –, 265

Hales, Charles E. (Gene), 492
Hall, Edward, 260
Hall, Nancy, 260
Hall, Sarah, 260
Hambleton, (Brother) –, 409
Hancock, George, 338
Hanks, Marcia Amelia, 496
Harris, Emer, 518n.27
Harris, Martin, 57
Haslam, James, 375
Hayward, William, 142
Head, (Superintendent and Colonel) F.
    H., 435, 442, 445, 448
healing, 12, 22, 73, 187, 260
Heaven, 15
Hebrew language and school, 63, 64,
    66, 67, 322
Hedlock, Reuben, 213, 214
Herrick, (Mr.) –, 343
Hess, Adrian, 466, 504
Hess, David, 503
Hess, Moses, 482
Heywood, (Marshal) Joseph L.,
    328-330, 335, 337, 341, 343
Heywood, Martha S., 317
Hickman, William, 243-244, 253
Higbee, (Mr. and Mrs.) –, 178
High Council, 42, 216, 218, 244, 246,

    248, 249, 257
High Priest, 19
Hiller, Marie, 504
Hirschell, (Rev. Dr.) Solomon, 122-
    123, 489, 490
Hodges, John, 227, 238
Hodges, Lavinia (Price), 227, 237-239,
    247
Hodgis, H. M., 352, 354
Hollister, (Brother) –, 183
"the holocaust," 123
Holy Land, 138, 145; *see* Eastern Medi-
    terranean
Holy Spirit (Holy Ghost, Spirit of the
    Lord, etc.), 16, 17, 18, 19, 22, 33,
    35, 58, 83, 84, 91, 103, 105, 113,
    115, 120, 158, 210, 212, 221-223,
    228, 234, 239, 242, 243, 249-252,
    254-255, 423, 462, 483
Hosanna shout, 68, 186, 203
Hosea, 70, 123
Humphrey, (Judge) –, 80
Hunter, Edward, 218, 248, 256
Huntington, Dimick B., 421, 442, 445,
    448, 449, 455
husbands, 146
Hyde, Abijah, brother, 5, 25, 145, 485
Hyde, Adella Marie, daughter, 251,
    272, 385, 497
Hyde, Alonzo Eugene, son, 224, 275,
    293, 328, 365, 369, 388, 406, 428,
    439, 496, 506
Hyde, Ami, brother, 5, 145
Hyde, Ann Eliza (Vickers), wife: mar-
    ried 372; met Mary Ann; children
    born, 379, 388; Salt Lake City, 389,
    391, 395; Springtown, 398, 558n.23;
    child born, 400; Springtown, 401;
    child born, 420; at home, 422, 423;
    child died, 436; child born, 442,
    455; and Indians, 451; named, 451;
    child died, 469; property, 494;
    family and history, 500-501
Hyde, Asahel, brother, 5, 25, 145
Hyde, Aurelia Fiducia, daughter, 469,
    478, 502

Hyde, Barney, grandson, 501
Hyde, Brigham Young, son, 433, 445, 505
Hyde, Charles, brother, 5
Hyde, Charles Albert, son, 379, 388, 398, 400, 422, 442, 485, 500, 501
Hyde, Charlotte (Quindlin) (Johnson), wife: married, 306; adjustments, 309; separated, 328, 551n.8; Mount Pleasant 390; history, 499–500
Hyde, daughter, 505, 567n.52
Hyde, David Victor, son, 456, 502
Hyde, Delia (Adelia Annette), daughter, 248, 275, 293, 299–300, 328, 365, 369, 388, 428, 496, 542n.25; *see* Ellis, Delia (Hyde)
Hyde, Elisabeth (Lizzy) Josephine (Galli), wife: married, 405; child born, 420; at home, 422, 423; child born, 428; at home, 436; child born, 442, 453; activities, 446; named, 454; child born, 469; property, 494; family and history, 503–505, 559n.45
Hyde, Emily Matilda, daughter, 112, 115, 166, 184, 189, 206, 293, 298, 324, 350, 496; *see* Chase, Emily (Hyde)
Hyde, Ernest Godfrey, son, 469, 504, 569n.3
Hyde, Frank Henry, son, 195, 206, 219, 237, 239, 275, 293, 297, 328, 365, 369, 388, 389, 390, 393, 394, 406, 413–415, 428, 439, 453, 496, 566n.44
Hyde, Geneva Flora (or Flora Geneva), daughter, 455, 463, 500, 567n.52
Hyde, George Lyman, son, 388, 398, 400, 423, 500, 508
Hyde, Harry, brother, 5
Hyde, Heber John, son, 306, 315, 496
Hyde, Horatio, brother, 5
Hyde, Hyrum Smith, son, 442, 490, 502
Hyde, John, missionary, 355
Hyde, Joseph Smith, son, 400, 423,
446, 457, 460, 463–468, 471, 472, 475, 476, 478–480, 483, 484, 487, 490, 500, 508, 579
Hyde, Julia Thomene (Reinert), wife: married, 403; child born, 404; at home, 422, 423; child born, 426, 442; own home, 454; child born, 456; child died and child born, 469; child died, 478; property, 494; family and history, 502–503, 559n.29
Hyde, Laura, sister, 5,
Hyde, Laura Marinda, daughter, 80, 92, 94, 95, 99, 101, 105, 112, 115, 166, 184, 206, 293, 295, 297, 298, 316, 328, 496; *see* Miner, Laura (Hyde)
Hyde, Lizzy, *see* Hyde, Elisabeth Josephine (Galli)
Hyde, Luella Minerva, daughter, 420, 423, 446, 466, 468, 503, 504
Hyde, Maria, sister, 5
Hyde, Maria Louisa, daughter, 420, 423, 436, 500, 561n.11
Hyde, Marinda Nancy (Johnson), wife: described, 21, 55; friend, 45; history, 55–56, 496–497; married, 56; farewell, 60; child born and died, 61; mended, 62; meeting and blessing, 64–65; at home, 72; Canada, 73–74; child born, 80; property, 76, 95, 523n.42; farewell, 81; letter, 84, 89–91; at home, 93, 95, 166; Missouri, 96–105; Illinois, 111; ill, child born, 112, 115; asleep during vision, 114; letters, 144, 146; revelation for, 149–150, 529n.25; met Mary Ann, 155–157; accepted Martha and Mary Ann, 159; sealed to Joseph Smith, 159–161, 373, 531n.29; property, 162, 197; adjustments, 163, 165–166; child born and died, 166–167; Kirtland, 177–178, 182, 184; Nauvoo, 184; named, 189; temple, 193, 194; child born, 195; ill, 196; recovering, 197, 198; Nauvoo to Council Bluffs, 206; Hyde Park, 214, 224; child born,

224; Kanesville, 225, 237, 239, 244, 247, 258, 275, 278, 384; child born, 248; plains, 293, 299; Salt Lake City, 305, 309, 315, 319; child born, 306, 321; child died, 326; at home, 328; missed, 342; letter, 350; at home, 365, 369, 374; washing, 371; baby born, 379; stayed Salt Lake City, 388, 389, 391, 395, 398; boarders, 406; at home, 423, 428, 561n.15; Relief Society President, 439; divorce, 454; family, 496–497; home, 506

Hyde, Martha Rebecca (Browett), wife: married, history, 159, 497–498; adjustments, 163, 165–166; Nauvoo, 179, 181, 189, 197; temple, 193, 194; Nauvoo to Council Bluffs, 206; Hyde Park, 214; Kanesville, 225, 237, 239, 244, 247, 258; jealous, 227–228, 249, 268–269; child born, 251; child died, 272; unhappy, 272–273; divorced and married Thomas McKenzie, 274; family, 497; *see* Browett, Martha Rebecca

Hyde, Mary, wife of Asahel, 25

Hyde, Mary Ann (Price), wife, described, 153; history, 153–155, 498–499; met Hydes, 155–157; fasting, prayer, answer, 158; married, 159, 165; family, 166; adjustments, 165–166; Nauvoo, 179, 181; letter, 187, 188–190; temple, 193, 194; Nauvoo to Council Bluffs, 206; child born and died, 211, 214; Hyde Park, 225; Saint Louis, 227–231, 237, 244, 247, 541n.21; letter, 237–239; Hyde Park, 247, 258, 278, 493; plains, 294, 297, 300; Provo, 306; Salt Lake City, 309; trip south, 322; at home, 328; missed, 342; Genoa, 344–346, 349, 350, 352–354; Wassau Valley, 355, 362, 363, 364, 371; letter to, 367–370; Salt Lake City, 374, 379; Sanpete, 388, 389,

390; Springtown, 391, 393, 395, 398, 401, 422, 423; Relief Society President, 439; Salt Lake City, 446; letters to, 446–448, 451–452; property, 566n.44; sewed, 463; about Orson, 466; Saint George, 471; concerned, 472; Saint George, 478–479; Salt Lake City, 480; telegrams to John Taylor, 484; property, 494–495; family, 498; letters, 508

Hyde, Mary Ann, daughter, 404, 406, 468, 483, 490, 502; *see* White, Mary Ann (Hyde)

Hyde, Mary Lavinia, daughter, 321, 326, 496

Hyde, Melvin Augustus, son, 442, 469, 500

Hyde, Nathan, father, 5, 526n.17

Hyde, Nathan, brother, 5

Hyde, Nathan, son, 61, 496

Hyde, Nathan , second son of name, 453, 455, 504

Hyde, Odean Horatio, son, 442, 446, 504

Hyde, Orson, described, 3, 4, 96, 267, 339, 340, 342, 430, 451, 484, 485; ancestors, 490; youth, 5–6, 18, 119 *Kirtland, Ohio, period:* Campbellite pastor, 3, 4, 10, 371; foundry worker, 7; carding, 7, 8; store clerk, 7–8, 11; laborer, 8–9; education and religion, 6, 9; memory, 10, 322; schoolteacher, 10, 57, 62; studied Mormonism, 11–16; writing of, 516n.28; baptized, 17, 517n.2; confirmed, 18; ordained Elder, 18; peace, 19; church clerk, 19; ordained High Priest, 19; "committee of six," 20, 22; rebuke, 20; witnessed Book of Commandments, 21; revelations about, 21–22, 23; mission Ohio, 22; mission eastern states, 23–31; School of the Prophets, 33–36; church clerk, 34, 37, 41, 42, 66; spoke in tongues, 34; teacher 34, 37; mission Pennsylvania, 36-37; preparing for marriage, 37; Kirtland Temple cornerstone, 37-38; mission Missouri, 38-40; revelation about, 40; High Council, 42; mission New York, 42-44; angel visited, 43-44; Zion's Camp, 45-55; courtship, 55-56; married Marinda Johnson, 56-57; School of Elders, 57; Mason, 520n.18; apostle, 57-59; clerk to Twelve, 59; mission eastern states, 59-61; censured, 60-61, 62; dealings with store, 61; Hebrew language project, 63, 64, 66, 67; meeting and blessing, 64-65; Kirtland Temple dedication and meetings, 67-69; mission Ohio, 72; mission New York and Canada, 72-74; published tract, 73; bank charter, 75; business partnership, 75; property, 76, 95, 521n.10; printing, 76, 78, 521n.11; confused, 77-78; court, 78-79, 522n.14; repented, 79-80; mission to England, 80-94; Kirtland, 95, 523n.2

Missouri and Iowa period: to Missouri, 95-96; Far West, 96-99; Richmond, 99-102; affidavit, 100; Howard County, 102-107, 524n.16; schoolteacher, 103; not excommunicated, 107-108; Iowa, 107-111; repentance, 103-109; privileges restored, 109-110

Nauvoo (Commerce), Illinois, period: Commerce, 111; full fellowship, 111; Cincinnati, 112; vision, 112-114; Nauvoo to New York City, 115-120; New York City to England, Holland, and Germany, 120-125; first L.D.S. tract in foreign language, 527n.29; Germany to Jerusalem, 127-131; Jerusalem, 131-143; prayer on Mount of Olives, 137-140; Jerusalem to Germany, 143-146; Germany, 146-148; Germany to Nauvoo, 148-149; met Mary Ann Price, 155-157; married

Martha Rebecca Browett, 159; married Mary Ann Price, 159, 165; was taught, 160-161; to Springfield, 162; City Council, 162, 170; house, 162, 165, 166, 531n.13; travels and meetings, 163-166; admired, 165; mission Illinois, 165; mission eastern states, 166; Nauvoo, 166-170; Washington, D.C., Philadelphia, 170-174; Boston, New York City, Connecticut, 174-177; Kirtland, 177-178; Nauvoo, 179-183; Kirtland and back, 183-184; "the olive branch of Israel," 184; Saint Louis and Nauvoo, 184-187; east for canvas, 187-191; preparing to leave Nauvoo, 191-198; in charge at Nauvoo, 198-205; revelation to, 199-200; Nauvoo to Council Bluffs, 206

Iowa period: Council Bluffs and area, 206-212; England, 210-215; editor, 215; Hyde Park, 216-225; Kanesville, 225, 538-539n.42; east, 227-231; newspaper, 235, 284, 546n.30, 547n.48; attorney, admitted Iowa Bar, 250; across plains and back, 258-271; Kanesville, Saint Louis, and 1851 trip to Utah, 272-292; farewell, 292, 547n.48; family to Utah, 293-301

First Salt Lake City, Utah, period: married Charlotte Quindlin (Johnson), 306; Legislative Council, 306, 316; home, 306, 548-549n.5; University Regent and Chancellor, 307, 316; attorney, 307, 310, 311, 317; Green River Mission, *see*; store, *see*; sugar manufacture, *see*; Grammar School, 326-327

Carson County (Nevada) period: assigned, 325-326; travel to, 328-332; investigations, 332-335; trip to San Francisco and back, 335-337; boundary, 338-339; Mormon Station, 340-343; Genoa, 343; court,

344, 345; Sierra Nevadas, 346–349; exploration, 350–352; new settlers, 354, 355–360; court, 356–357, 360; sawmill, *which see*
Second Salt Lake City, Utah, period: from Carson County, 364–365; reformation, 365-367, 370, 372–373, 374; married Ann Eliza Vickers, 371–372; trip to Salmon River, 372–373; meetings, preaching, service 374–379, 380–383; moved south and returned, 379–380; grammar course, 381, 385; hiding from arrest, 385–386; travels, 386–387; to move to Sanpete, 387–388
Sanpete, Utah, period: moved, 389–390, 557n.3; duties, 390, 393; Springtown, 391; Civil War prophecy, 395; "Curse," 396–397; raises child from dead, 398–399; married Julia Thomene Reinert, 400–401, 403; trip southern Utah, 401–402, 405; instructions to hired man, 403–404; censure and reply, 405; married Elisabeth Josephine Galli, 405; Indians, 406–411; beginnings of Black Hawk War, 412–419; married Sophia Margaret Lyon, 420, 421; war (*see* Black Hawk Indian War) and other things, 420–435; about celestial crowns, 562n.36; trip north, 435–437; in first meeting in new tabernacle, 438–439; toe removed, 444; letters from Jerusalem mission reprinted, 445, 447, 452; teeth extracted, 446; Marinda divorce, 454; as successor to Brigham Young, 441, 456–457, 480; hiding from government officials, 457–458; personality and actions, 463–468; United Order, 470–476, 478; seniority changed, 473; new carriage, 476–478; new home of rock, 477, 570n.19; Saint George, 478–480; Brigham Young's death and funeral, 480–481; last trip to

Salt Lake City, 482; last public address, 482–483; ill, 483–484; died, 484; funeral and burial, 485–487; after death, 488
Miscellaneous: "Was Orson Hyde a Jew?" 489–491; estate, 494; journals, 508; letters to wives, 508; reputation, 509; not his wives, 342, 423, 555n.16, 561n.19; photograph, 574 (Barron)
Hyde, Orson, Memorial Garden, xi, 491
Hyde, Orson, son, 428, 446, 504
Hyde, Orson Washington, son, 166–167, 496
Hyde, Oscar Waldemar, son, 445, 466, 490, 505
Hyde, Royal Justus, son, 469, 505, 506
Hyde, Sally, mother, 5, 348
Hyde, Sophia Margaret (Lyon), wife: married, 421, 561n.15; Springtown, 422, 423; child born, 433; child died, 445; child born, 445; named, 446, 454; child born, 567n.52; child born, 458; child born, 469; property, 494; family and history, 505–507
Hyde, Sterling Washburn, son, 458, 469, 505, 568n.61
Hyde, Urania, daughter, 214, 498
Hyde, William, distant relative, 531–532n.14, 580
Hyde, William Arthur, son, 426, 469, 502, 569n.2
Hyde, Zina Virginia, daughter, 379, 388, 439, 490, 496
Hyde Park (Hyde's Camp), Iowa, 207, 211, 216, 217, 220, 221, 225, 228, 258, 278, 438–439, 492–493

Idaho: Fort Limhi, 373; Goose Creek, 329; Salmon River, 372
Ilder, Mariah, 493
Illinois: Carthage, 169, 176, 178; Chicago, 166; Columbus, 116; Commerce (afterward Nauvoo), 108,

109, 111, 115; Jacksonville, 117; Lima, 115, 168; Morley settlement, 192; Nauvoo, *see separate listing*; Quincy, 106–108, 115, 116, 163, 183; Ramus, 163; Shokoquon, 163; Springfield, 112, 117, 162

Indian(s): 194–195, 266, 279, 280, 297, 322, 323, 329, 333, 350, 560n.52, 567n.55; Black Hawk War, 412–462 (*see also specific names*); Cheyenne, 279; on Humboldt, 358, 359, 362, 364; Omaha, 206, 218, 225, 277, 278; Otoe, 206; Pawnee, 244, 253, 270, 278, 280; Pi-ede, 445, 449; Pottawattamie, 206, 207, 225, 227; Sanpete Valley, 389, 390, 393, 404, 406–411; Shoshone, 311–312, 314–315, 318–321; Shib-er-ech, 442, 445, 449; Ute, 259, 453, 461; Washoe, 352, 358, 361

Indiana: 112; Indianapolis, 48, 117; Pleasant Garden, 117;

Ingalls, Captain, 328, 330, 334

"Instructions to Mr. Welsh," 403–404

Iowa: 106, 107, 201, 202, 204, 206, 228, 230–231; Big Pigeon, 285, 286; Browning's settlement, 258; Bullock's Grove, 258, 278, 289, 492–493; Burlington, 228, 229, 230; Carterville, 244; Council Bluffs, *see separate listing*; Council Point, 241, 242, 246, 492; Dumfries Post Office, 492; Garden Grove, 205, 206, 228; Grand River, 202; Hyde Park, *see separate listing*; Indian Creek, 219, *see also* Kanesville; Kanesville, *see separate listing*; Keokuk, 247; Miller's Hollow, *see separate listing*; Montrose, 109; Mosquito Creek, 210; Mount Pisgah, 206, 211, 228; Point-aux-Poules, 207; Sugar Creek, 196, 197; Trader's Point (Trading Point), 207; *for Iowa period see* Hyde, Orson

Irish, (Colonel) –, 418, 419

iron foundry, 7

Isaac, 70, 138, 141, 156

Isaiah, 12, 113, 376

Ivie, James, 429

Jack, Agnes E., 505

Jacob (Israel), 12, 70, 138, 140, 141, 156

Jacobs, Henry, 100

Jacques, Vienna, 27, 28

Jake Arapeen, Indian Chief, 407, 415, 418, 450, 560n.51

James, 18

Jehovah, 69, 70, 134, 135

Jensen, Carroll J., 492

Jeremiah, 12, 113

Jerusalem, xi, 12, 13, 23, 33, 68, 113, 114, 117, 120, 123, 129, 131–132, 135–141, 145, 486, 488, 527–528n.2

Jerusalem, Voice From, reprinted, 445, 447, 452

Jethro, 32

Jew(s), xi, 58, 70, 73–74, 88, 114, 117, 120, 122, 123, 125, 127, 128, 135, 137, 141, 145, 162, 276, 287, 482, 488, 489–491, 571n.35

Joe, Indian Sub-chief, 408, 412, 416, 418, 439–442, 450, 455

John (New Testament), 18, 57, 129, 438, 488

John the Baptist, 18

Johnson, Aaron, 249

Johnson, (Bishop) –, 449

Johnson, Charlotte (Quindlin), wife: "domestic" 275, 278; plains, 293, 299; married, 306; *see also* Hyde, Charlotte (Quindlin) (Johnson)

Johnson, (Dr.) –, 236

Johnson, Elsa, 20, 178

Johnson, John, 20, 32, 55, 76, 95, 101, 178

Johnson, Joseph E. ("J.E."), 246–247, 256, 259–261, 269, 271, 290, 541n.20, 546n.30

Johnson, Justin, 21

Johnson, Luke: friend, 20, 21, 55; apostle, 58; disgruntled, 77; court, 79; dissenting, 95, 99; removed from

Twelve, 96; Kirtland, 178; Nauvoo, rebaptized, 197–198; Council Bluffs, 211; Hyde Park, 224, 493

Johnson, Lyman E.: friend, 20, 21, 55; married 56; apostle, 57–58; store, 76; disgruntled, 77; dissenting, 95, 99; removed from Twelve, 96; Richmond, 96, 97

Johnson, Marinda Nancy, *see* Hyde, Marinda Nancy (Johnson)

Johnston, (Col.) Albert Sidney, 379

Joint Stock Company, 213, 215, 470

Jones, (Bishop) –, 402

Joseph (Old Testament), 12, 70, 142

Joshua, 51, 140

Judah, tribe of, 33, 113, 118

Judas, 199

judge, 277, 287–290

Justesen, Joseph Alexander, 500

Justesen, Sarah, 484–485

Justesen, Sarah Ellen, 500

Kane, (Col.) Thomas L., 208–210, 224, 225

Kanesville, Iowa: 226, 231, 233, 234, 241, 242, 246, 248, 271, 282, 291, 292, 492; Hyde Street, 231, 281; Indian Creek, 226, 231; Main Street, 231, 281; mercantile, 231, 235, 236, 246–247, 251, 291, 292; Miller's Hollow, *see separate listing*; Music Hall, 246, 248, 277

Kan-osh, Indian Chief, 436

(Kansas): Fort Leavenworth, 207, 208, 212

Kearns, (Bishop) William, 404, 415, 428, 450

Kelley, Joseph, 256, 258, 259, 261, 273

Kennedy, James H., 78

Kimball, Heber C.: apostle, 58; described, 60, 80; steadfast, 77; blessing, 79–80; mission England, 80–94; Kirtland, 95; Missouri, 96, 104–106, 483; Illinois, 108, 483; England, 111, 121; letter, 112; plural marriage, 157; admired, 165;

eastern states, 173, 174, 176, 177; assistant to Brigham Young, 181; named, 184; wrote, 187; Hyde Park, 221, 224; counselor to Brigham Young, 222; Utah, 265, 266, 307; in dream, 337; reformation, 365–367, 370; trip north, 372; trip southern Utah, 402; speech, 438; died, 441

Kimball, Helen, 96

Kimball, (Sister) –, 265

Kimball, Vilate, 92, 93, 112

Kinkaid, –, merchant, 263

Kinney, (Judge) J. F., 250, 321, 323

Kirtland, 6, 42, 74, 78, 95, 177–178, 184; *for Kirtland period see* Hyde, Orson Kirtland Bank, 75–77, 93

Kirtland Temple, 37–38, 42, 57, 62, 66–70, 95

Lachlin, David, 493

Lakes: Bigler (Tahoe), 335, 339, 343, 346; Erie, 3, 24, 60, 81, 178; Ontario, 72

language, 125, 126, 326, 401, 405, 467

Larsen, C. G., 485

Larsen, Lauritz and wife, 400

Latter-day Saints, 44, 148

law, 357

Law, William, 172, 178

Law, Wilson, 172, 178

Legislature, Utah Territory, 369, 371, 377, 381, 395, 400, 403, 405, 406, 423, 428, 439, 444, 453, 469

Little, Jesse, 207

Livingston, –, merchant, 263

Lord, The, 87, 113, 147; *see also* Messiah, Savior

Louisiana: New Orleans, 148

Löwenstam, Emanuel Joachim, 124–125

Lowery, John, 416

Lund, Louis, 434

Lyman, Amasa M.: apostle, 162; discussed, 177; Hyde Park, 221; Utah, 267, 269, 307; excommunicated, 437

Lyon, Sophia Margaret, wife, 420, 423; *see* Hyde, Sophia Margaret (Lyon)

Mackintosh, (Brother) –, 257
Maine: 60; Kennebunkport, 30; Lyman, 30, 31; Portland, 30; Saco, 30
Malachi, 15, 66, 70
Mamreov, (Mr.) –, 142
Manti, Utah, 322, 323, 389, 390, 393, 412, 416, 420, 424, 425, 428, 431–433, 440, 441, 446, 449, 454, 456, 458, 470–473, 476, 480, 481
Manti Temple, 469, 476, 478
Marlette, (Mr.) –, 337
marriage, eternal, 155–157, 160
marriage, plural, 156–157, 160, 194, 228, 252, 269, 306, 384
Marsh, Elizabeth, 99
Marsh, Thomas B.: friend, 23, 27; apostle, 58–59, 520n.24; Missouri, 98–102, 105, 107, 279, 483, 524n.16; Salt Lake City, 375
Marsh, wife of Thomas B., 524n.8
Maryland: Baltimore, 173, 176
Mason, William, 294, 297
Massachusetts: 60; Boston, 23, 27-28, 31, 165, 166, 174–176, 190, 191; Georgetown, 190; Lowell, 191; Salem, 190
McKenzie, Maria, 274
McKenzie, Thomas, 274, 354, 383, 384, 544n.4, 556n.46
meat, 35–36
Melchizedek, 18
Merkley, Christopher, 338, 345
Merrill, Marriner W., 548–549n.5
Merritt, –, lawyer, 236
Messiah, 13, 57, 69–71, 73–74, 115, 123, 125, 488; *see also* Lord, Savior
Methodists, 9
Militia(s), Utah Territory, 374–375, 379, 413, 414, 418, 420, 421, 425–427, 429–433, 441, 443, 455, 456, 459, 460
Millennial Star, 215

millennium, 71
Miller, Daniel F., 250
Miller, Henry W., 256, 258, 259, 261, 271, 273, 293, 299, 300
Miller Company, 293–301, 306
Miller's Hollow, Iowa (became Kanesville), 219–221, 223, 225, 291, 492
Miner, Aurelius, 321, 326, 365, 369, 496
Miner, David, 25
Miner, Ella, 465
Miner, Laura (Hyde), daughter, 365, 369, 439, 454, 465
Miner, Lavilla, 465
Miner, Sally (Hyde), sister, 25, 145, 321, 365
mining in Utah, 567n.55
Missouri: 42, 168; Big Blue, 40, 41; Boonville, 41; Caldwell County, 101; Chariton County, 50; Clay County, 50, 51, 53; Di-Ahman, 98, 100, 105; Far West, 96–106; Fishing River, 51, 52; Gallatin, 97, 100; Glasgow, 275; Haun's Mill, 103; Howard County, 102, 103, 107; Independence, 21, 33, 38–41; Jackson County, 45, 47, 50–53; Jefferson City, 40, 49, 50; Liberty, 50, 104, 105; New Franklin, 107; Paris, 49; Ray County, 50, 52, 53; Richmond, 50-52, 96, 97, 99, 101–104; Richmond Landing, 96; Saint Joseph, 241; Saint Louis, 95, 96, 149, 169, 183–185, 188, 190, 219, 223, 224, 229–231, 247, 275, 276, 290, 532n.22; Salt River, 49; *for Missouri period see* Hyde, Orson
Mitchell, (Major) -, 207, 218, 219
M'Lellin, William E.: friend, 21; apostle, 58–59; censured, 60–62; Hebrew course, 67; persecution, 32, 38–41; removed from Twelve, 96
mob violence, *see* persecutions
Moffitt, (Bishop) –, 472
Mormon, 13
Mormon Battalion, 207, 208, 210–212,

219, 233, 240

Moroni, 13, 15, 16, 320

Morrison, James B., 432

Morrison, (Sister) —, 447

Morrow, (Gen.) Henry A., 460, 461

Moses, 12, 13, 32, 51, 57, 69, 70, 74, 142, 156

Mott, (Mr.) —, 343, 349

Mount of Olives, xi, 120, 136–137, 140, 391, 482, 490, 491

Mount Pleasant, Utah, 389, 390, 398, 422, 427, 433, 435, 447, 448, 451, 456, 458, 460, 471, 474, 475, 482, 483

Mountain, an Indian, 449, 453, 455

Mountain Meadows Massacre, 375

Mountford, (Madame) Lydia, 142

"move south," 379, 381, 390

music, 67–68, 92, 246, 484–485

Musser, (Brother) —, 452

Nauvoo, Illinois, 115, 119; 149, 162–163, 168, 179, 185–187, 191–192, 196–198, 202, 204, 212, 217, 229, 230, 470; *for Nauvoo period see* Hyde, Orson

Nauvoo City Council, 532n.29

Nauvoo Temple, 119, 164, 184–186, 192–194, 196, 198, 201–204, 233

(Nebraska): Bellevue, 218; Chimney Rock, 297; Fort Kearney, 260, 270, 280, 295; Loup Fork River, 270, 278, 294; Platteville, 271; Salt Creek, 271; Scott's Bluff, 260; Winter Quarters (later Florence), 216, 218, 220, 225–227, 293, 294, 537n.22

Needham, —, merchant, 237

Neibaur, Alexander, 88

Nephi, 13

Nephites, Three, 58, 488

(Nevada): 343, 376, 396, 397; Carson County and Valley, *see separate listing;* Carson River, 332; Daggett Pass, 335, 343; Eagle Valley, 351, 355; Fallon, 332; Franktown, 359,

360, 363, 364, 397; Genoa, *see separate listing;* Humboldt Mountains, 329; Humboldt River, 329–331, 364; Jack Valley, 355; Mormon Station, 325, 332, 335, 337, 340, 341, 343; Opir, 397; Pilot Peak, 364; Ragtown, 332; Reno, 352; Ruby Mountains, 329, 364, 554n.1; Ruby Valley, 364; Steamboat Springs, 355; Truckee (Trucky) River and Valley, 337, 352, 355, 364; Walker River Valley, 337; Washaw (Wassau, Washoe) Valley, 337, 351, 352, 354, 355, 359, 363, 396, 397; Wassau (Washoe) Lake, 351, 352, 355, 397; "the Wells," 329

New Hampshire: 60; Great Falls, 28–29; Peterboro, 190

New Jersey: 118; Freehold Township, 120

New Testament, 73, 74, 148

New York: 60; Albany, 31, 177; Avon, 42; Buffalo, 24, 60, 72, 81, 177; Catskill, 25; Erie Canal, 81; Fredonia, 24; Hempstead, 190; Lake Skaneatelas, 25; New York City, 81, 94, 119, 120, 175–177, 190, 213, 214, 216; Niagara Falls, 72; Oxford, 25; Palmyra, 13; Rochester, 81; Utica, 31

Newell, Grandison, 7, 77–80

Newfoundland, 82

Noah, 12

North, Laura (Hyde), sister, 28–29, 145

North, William, 28–29

Norton, L. A., 338–342

Ohio: Amherst, 22; Burton, 9; Cincinnati, 117, 118, 120, 184, 229, 230; Columbus, 75; Dayton, 117, 120; Elyria, 3, 10, 22; Fairport, 60, 81, 178; Florence, 3, 10, 11, 22, 45, 371; Franklin, 117; Hiram, 17, 20, 32, 55; Hudson, 67; Kirtland, *see separate listing;* Mansfield, 45; Mentor, 7, 9, 77; Milton, 120; Orange,

19; Painesville, 8, 77, 78; Ridgeville, 3, 10, 484; Thompson, 38; Wellsville, 95

Old Testament, 148, 259

Olive Branch of Israel, 184, 215, 484

olive trees, 136, 137

Olney, Alice (Johnson), 64, 146

Olney, Oliver, 64, 106, 146

Olsen, (Bishop) Frederick, 440, 484, 495

O'Neal, Mary, 496

Oregon, 169, 170, 172, 351

Pace, (Gen.) W. B., 431, 433

Page, John E.: apostle, 97; not to England, 111; Nauvoo to Ohio, 114–120; stayed in United States, 528n.6; absent, 164; Boston, 166; named, 184; disfellowshipped, 197; apostate, 198; excommunicated, 211

Parish, Warren, 77–79

Parrish, William and family, 385, 386

Partridge, Edward, 39

Passover, 70

Patriarch, 64

patriarchal blessing(s), 64–65, 490

Patten, David W., 58, 59, 68, 102, 520n.24

Paul, 128

pearl ash, 8–9

Pennsylvania: Elk Creek, 37, 38; Philadelphia, 118, 120, 166, 172, 188, 190, 224, 229; Pittsburgh, 191; Springfield, 24

Perpetual Emigrating Fund, 248, 255, 267, 269, 272–273

persecution(s), 22, 27, 28, 32, 38–41, 42, 93, 95, 97, 98, 101–102, 104, 105, 167–169, 178, 191, 192, 282, 283, 287–289, 305

Peter, 18, 74, 110

Peterson, (Bishop) Canute, 448, 449, 564n.14, 567n.49

Phelps, William W., 38, 40, 184, 193

Plumer, Henry, 289, 493

Plumer Settlement, 493

Porter, (Commodore) —, 129

potash, 8–9

Powell, (Major) John Wesley, 456

Pratt, Mary Ann, 121

Pratt, Orson: writings, 516n.28; mission New York, 42; Zion's Camp, 47; apostle, 58; disgruntled, 77; New York City, 94; England, 111; excommunicated and rebaptized, 162; travels, 163; Washington, D.C., 168, 170–171; Boston, 176; New York City, 177; named, 184; wrote, 185, 187; New York City, 190, 191; Council Bluffs, 206; Hyde Park, 221; England, 226; Kanesville, 253, 255; Echo Canyon, 301; sermon, 306, 381; Washington, D.C., 307; surveying, 334; doctrine, 387; named, 438, 443; United Order, 470; seniority changed, 473; England, 481; Spring City, 483; last of original Twelve, 487

Pratt, Parley P.: Zion's Camp, 49, 50; apostle, 58; Canada, 72–74; persecuted, disgruntled, 77; jail, 103, 104; England, 111, 121, 122; letter, 129; publication, 154; England, 144–146, 159; Nauvoo, 166, 377; named, 184; New York City, 190; England, 211–215, 470, 508; westward, 216–218; Salt Lake City, 306, 307, 312; killed, 373

Pratt, Thankful, 72, 74

Presidency, First, 220–223, 227, 248, 326, 365, 366, 381, 387, 394, 441, 443, 456–457, 480, 483, 538n.34

Price, Charles, 225, 237, 238, 294, 369, 493

Price, Elizabeth, 238

Price, Elsa, 237, 238, 369

Price, Emily, 189

Price, Emma, 154, 155

Price, Martha, 369

Price, Mary Ann, *see* Hyde, Mary Ann (Price)

Price, Mother, 155, 206, 211, 212

Price, Thomas, 153, 154
Price, William, 206, 212, 217, 219, 225, 237, 238, 278, 294, 300, 306, 313, 321, 324, 353, 355, 359, 362, 363-365, 369, 387, 396, 484, 493
priesthood, 18, 32, 70-71, 135, 167, 232, 401
printing office, 227, 231
printing (press), 224, 226-230, 235, 281, 290
Probate Judge, 325, 344, 345, 350, 354, 357, 359, 362, 363
Prophetic Warning, A, 73, 81
prophet(s), 113, 142, 177
Provo Canal and Irrigation Co., 307
Provo Manufacturing Co., 307
Pulsipher, John, 481

Quorum of the Twelve Apostles, 57-59, 62, 68, 96, 97, 109, 121-122, 140, 162-167, 164, 165, 169, 177, 179-181, 185-187, 192, 193, 196, 205, 207-211, 220-223, 247, 307, 366, 367, 381, 382, 387, 388, 437, 438, 443, 452, 474, 475, 481, 486, 487, 531-532n.14, 532n.16, 533n.38; *see also* apostle(s)

rabbi, 122-125
railroad, 263, 316, 441, 442, 445, 453
rainbow, 253, 255
Reese brothers, 332, 333
Reese, Enoch, 325
Reese, (Col.) John, 325, 333, 343, 349
Reese, John E., 468
Reese, Nephi, 457
Reese, (Sister) —, 457
reformation, 365, 367-370, 373-374
Reinert, Julia Thomene, 400-401; *see* Hyde, Julia Thomene (Reinert)
repentance, 20, 61, 64, 103-107
resurrection, 13, 82, 563n.2
revelation(s), 12, 18-19, 21, 23, 32-33, 35-36, 73, 134, 148, 374, 433
Rhode Island: Providence, 27-28
Rich, Charles C., 247, 307

Richards, Franklin D.: 215; apostle, 247; Salt Lake City, 307; return from Europe, 367; Salt Lake City, 369, 372; trip, 372
Richards, (Dr.) Heber J., 483, 484
Richards, LeGrand, 490, 491
Richards, Willard: mission England, 81, 83, 86-87, 91-93; apostle, 97; England, 111, 121; at martyrdom, 178; named, 184; assistant to Brigham Young, 181; Hyde Park, 221; counselor to Brigham Young, 222; Kanesville, 225; Utah, 267, 307; died, 317
Rigdon, Sidney: Campbellite preacher, 9, 10; joined Mormons, 10; to Missouri, 11; baptized Orson, helped confirm him, 17-18; Church leader, 20; persecuted, 32; School of the Prophets, 35; Counselor to Joseph Smith, 37; Justice of the Peace, 57; council, school in Kirtland, 60-61; Kirtland Temple dedication, 67-68; New York, 72; bank, 75; letter, 78; blessing, 79; Missouri, 97-100, 103; Quincy, 108; Commerce, 109; book, 112, 118; discontented, 164, 166, 531n.14; Pittsburgh, 177; Nauvoo, 179-180, 182-183; excommunicated, 183; leaves, complains, 183, 184; died, 478
Riggs, John, 493
rights, 199
Rivers: Danube, 126-128, 488; Delaware, 118; Elkhorn ("Horn"), 227; Hudson, 25; Mersey, 83; Mississippi, 49, 95, 106, 108, 148, 188, 196, 197, 206, 229, 247; Missouri, 53, 96, 201, 202, 206, 207, 212, 214, 216, 219, 247, 271, 292; Ohio, 95, 184, 188; Piscataqua, 30; Platte, 227, 259-261, 270, 271, 279, 293, 298, 300; Rhine, 124, 125, 395; Ribble, 88
Roberts, Brigham H., 489
Robinson, Ebenezer, 149, 529n.25

Robinson, (Capt.) George D. W., 238
Robinson, George W., 112
Robinson, Jane (Sutch), 238
Robinson, W. H., 292
Rocky Mountains, 216, 231, 258, 265
rod, 142
Rollins, James H., 194
Rose, Jacob, 396, 397
Rose, (Mrs.) Jacob, 345
Russell, Isaac, 81, 83, 86, 88, 93, 94
Russia, 117, 165, 488

sacrament, 34–35, 319, 520–521n.7
sacrifice, 108
Saint George Temple, 478, 479
Saints, 17, 344
Salt Lake, Great, and Valley of the,
    220, 243, 258, 263–265, 269, 279,
    301, 306, 439
Salt Lake City, Great, 263–265, 279,
    305–306, 321, 359, 379, 391, 393;
    for two Salt Lake City periods see
    Hyde, Orson
Salt Lake Temple, 307–308, 375, 394,
    478
Sanpete Valley, and County, 322, 371,
    386–388, 389, 393, 398, 400, 412;
    for Sanpete period see Hyde, Orson
Sanpitch, Indian Chief, 407, 412, 414,
    415, 418, 419, 421, 422, 424, 443,
    444
Satan, 14–16, 62, 80, 103–105, 117,
    135, 142, 167, 185, 199, 282, 286
Satan, buffetings of, 105, 183, 525n.24
Savior, 13, 36, 69, 136–137, 141, 306;
    see also Lord, Messiah
sawmill, Orson Hyde's, 351, 354, 355,
    358–363, 374, 396
Schofield, Elizabeth, 502
School of the Elders, 57
School of the Prophets, 33–35, 439,
    443, 444, 451
Sconce, (Colonel) –, 52, 53
Scotland: Edinburgh, 215
sea, 5, 81–83, 92, 94, 121, 124, 128,
    144, 148, 213, 216

Seeley, (Bishop) –, 399, 458, 471
Seixas, Joshua, 67
Semple, James, 170–173
Sevier River settlements, 404, 406, 422,
    425–429, 432, 433, 439, 440, 451,
    453, 462
Shelton, M. J., 452, 453
Sherman, Charles S., 133
Sherman, Lyman, 105
Sides, R. D., 396, 397
Sierra Nevada Mountains, 324, 331,
    332, 335, 336, 339, 340, 346–347,
    351, 352
Simons, (Mr.) –, 134
Simpson, (Rev.) William, 283, 286, 287
slavery, 38
Smith, Bathsheba, 221, 222
Smith, (Capt.) –, 278
Smith, Emma, 16, 32, 34, 36, 56, 111
Smith, George A.: Kirtland Temple
    dedication, 68; England, 111;
    named, 184; Hyde Park, 221, 222;
    Iowa, 227, 229, 232, 233, 237, 243;
    Utah, 267, 269, 307; trip southern
    Utah, 402; letters, 406, 424, 425;
    counselor to Brigham Young, 443;
    letter, 456–457; Saint George, 472;
    seniority changed, 473; died, 477;
    gift, 494
Smith, Hyrum: preached, 20; mission
    Ohio, 22; letter, 34; mission Penn-
    sylvania, 36; Kirtland Temple cor-
    nerstone, 38; Zion's Camp, 49;
    council, 60; New York, 72; blessing,
    79; Missouri, 96, 98, 103; counselor
    to Joseph Smith, 96, 232; Quincy,
    108, 483; Commerce (afterward
    Nauvoo), 109, 162, 169; martyred,
    175–176, 178, 179
Smith, Joseph, Jr.: leader of Mormons,
    10; to Missouri, 11; powers of, 12;
    history, 13–16, 24, 56, 147, 232,
    320; writings, 516n.28; returned
    from Missouri, 14; described 14, 47,
    54, 155; helped confirm Orson, 17,
    18; conference, 19; revising Bible,

20; "President of the High Priesthood," 22–23; revelations to, 21–23; blessed Orson, 23, 123, 517n.11; Boston, 31; tarred, 32, 56; moved to Kirtland, 32; revelation to, 32–33; spoke in tongues, 34; School of the Prophets, 33, 34–36; requests money, 37; chooses counselors, 37; Kirtland Temple cornerstone, 37–38; persecuted, 42; letter, 43; Zion's Camp, 45–55; directed choosing of twelve apostles, 57; met with Twelve, 59, 62; court case, 60; council, 60, 61; discusses letter, 63–64; Hebrew school, 66; Kirtland Temple dedication and meetings, 67–71; New York, 72; bank in Kirtland, 74–75; against speculations, 76–78; lawsuit and hearing, 78–79; blessing, 80; about evil spirits, 87; advise, 90; Missouri, 93, 95, 96, 98–100, 103, 104; instructions, 105; Quincy, 108, 483; Commerce, 108–109, 111, 114; letters, 116–117, 119, 122–124, 126–127, 146; revelation to Marinda, 149–150; in Hyde home, 155–157; and Mary Ann Price, 158; teaches, 159–160; Nauvoo activities, 162–169, 488; candidate for President of the United States, 169, 170, 173, 176, 178; memorial to U.S. government, 170–174; defended, 172, 175; martyred, 175–176, 178, 179; teachings, 180–181, 187, 193–195, 217, 229–230, 253; mantle of, 181–182, 456; remembered, 362; and constitution, 378; Orson proxy, 373; and priesthood, 401; after death, 438, 486; Marinda's feelings, 454; about Law of Consecration and about wealth, 470
Smith, Joseph, Sr., 38; 64–65
Smith, Joseph F.: apostle, 437; England, 481; Spring City, 483
Smith, Joseph Fielding, 489

Smith, (Col.) Lockwood, 250
Smith, (Bishop) Nicholas G., 506
Smith, Samuel H., 23–31, 179
Smith, Sylvester, 48
Smith, William: 50; apostle, 58; mission eastern states, 60; privileges, 63; rumors false, 64; not England, 111; named, 184; excommunicated, 197
snails, 128
snakes, 48, 87
Snow, Erastus: apostle, 247; Salt Lake City, 307; Sanpete, 480, 483; Orson's funeral, 486–487
Snow, Lorenzo: apostle, 247; Salt Lake City, 307, 367, 369, 370; trip southern Utah, 402
Snow, (Sister) —, 446
Snow, (Col. and Gen.) Warren L., 419, 420, 424, 425, 430, 431, 433
Snyder, John, 81, 83, 91
soldiers, 323, 327, 328
Solomon, 156
Sorensen, Jens, 415
Sow-ah-point, Indian, 442
Sow-e-et, Indian Chief, 442
speculations, 75, 76, 90
Spencer, Orson, 215, 533n.38, 533n.43, 574 (Barron)
Spring City, Utah, *see* Springtown; 453, 460, 461, 485; *see also* Hyde, Orson, *Sanpete period*
Springtown, Utah, 389, 391, 393, 398, 411, 424–428, 433, 435, 450, 453; *see* Spring City; *see also* Hyde, Orson, *Sanpete period*
Squash, Indian Chief, 323
"squash sermon," 377
Staines, William C., 371, 391, 453
Staker, Eliza Jane, 399
Staker, Nathan, 398, 399
Staker, (Sister) —, 399
Stansbury, (Capt.) Howard, 265
State Fair, 381
Steptoe, (Col.) —, 323, 328, 330, 334
Stiles, (Judge) George P., 328–330, 335,

337, 338, 341–343, 357
stones, stacked, 140, 142
store, Orson Hyde's, 319, 321, 323, 327, 345, 353, 358, 371, 391, 453
Strong, Estella, 505
Stout, Hosea, 219
Stout, Joseph Allen, 104
Strang, James J., 198, 199, 202
stranger in Philadelphia, 120, 139
Stutsman, –, merchant, 291
sugar manufacture, 282, 290, 308, 309
survey(ing), 338–340, 343, 344, 351, 352, 354
Sutch, Jane, 238

Tabby, Indian Chief, 419, 436, 444, 460
Tabbyuna, Indian Chief, 443, 445, 450, 460–462
tabernacle, adobe, Salt Lake City, 305–306, 323, 380–382, 394
tabernacle, log, Kanesville, 221, 223, 225, 231, 234–235, 246, 291, 292, 541n.17
tabernacle, Nauvoo, 187, 191
tabernacle, new domed, Salt Lake City, 426, 438, 440, 454, 481, 563n.2
Tam-a-rits, Indian Chief (*also called* White Horse Chief), 442, 449, 462, 564n.15
Tapaddy, Indian Chief, 415
tar, 426
Ta-rue-good, Indian Chief, 443
taxes, 380-381
Taylor, Annie Maria, 496
Taylor, John: apostle, 97; statement, 110; England, 111, 121; at martyrdom, 178; Nauvoo, 181, 470; named, 184; Council Bluffs, 209; England, 211–215; westward, 216–218; Kanesville, 247, 248; England, 282; Kanesville, 290, 291; Salt Lake City, 307, 380, 381, 394; trip southern Utah, 402; United Order, 470; seniority changed, 473, 569n.13; President of Twelve, 481; Spring

City, 483; letter, 484; messages, 484, 486; request, 502
teacher(s), *see* education
teeth extracted, 446
telegraph, 395, 411, 414, 428, 430, 439, 440, 446, 480, 483–485, 502
Temple Block, 326, 327, 380
temple ordinances, 71, 167
temple store, Kirtland, 61–64
Texas, 170, 197, 229
Thacker, –, slave, 345
Thompson, William, 250
Thorington, W. B., 343, 349
Thorp (Hyde), Sally, mother, 5; *see also* Hyde, Sally
Timely Warning, A, 81, 89, 94
tithing, 236–237, 252
tobacco, 35, 36, 284, 337, 344, 345, 350 382, 403
tongue, govern, 378
tongues, gift of, 34, 66, 68, 69
Townsend, James, 344, 351, 354, 355
Twain, Mark, 397
Twelve Apostles, *see* Quorum of the Twelve Apostles
Tyler, (Pres.) John, 170, 171, 173–174

Unganutherum, Indian Chief, 450
Un-gitz-rib, Indian Chief, 443, 461
United Order, 470–474, 476, 478
University of the State of Deseret, 266–267, 307, 315, 316, 377, 381
Utah Bar, 326
Utah Territory, 259, 325, 328; Alma, 428, 431, 432; Bear Lake, 437; Bear River, 329, 373; Big Canyon Creek, 309; Big Cottonwood, 309; Big Mountain, 316–318; Blacksmith Fork, 437; Brigham City, 386, 459; Cache Valley, 386, 437; Camp Floyd, 380, 385, 387; "Camp Hyde," 443; Circleville, 422, 427; Coalville, 442; Echo Canyon, 301; Ephraim (Fort), *see separate listing*; Fairview (formerly North Bend), 389, 424, 425, 427, 442, 443, 452,

456, 459, 460; Farmington, 381;
Fillmore, 386, 393, 429; Fish Lake
Valley, 462; "Fort Lookout," 457,
458; Fountain Green, 389, 408, 412,
427, 433, 434, 441, 446, 460, 470;
Glenwood, 424, 428, 430–432, 434;
Goshen, 387; Grantsville, 323–324;
Gravelly Ford, 426, 433; Gunnison,
389, 412, 415, 428, 431, 432, 440,
445, 450, 459, 471; Huntsville, 437;
Jordan River, 264, 322, 380; Manti,
see separate listing; Marysvale, 425;
Moroni, 389, 408, 409, 422, 426,
433, 446, 452, 474; Mount Nebo,
322; Mount Pleasant, *see separate
listing*; Mount Timpanogos, 322;
Nephi (also Salt Creek), 322, 412,
424, 433, 442, 446, 455, 470, 474;
North Bend (later Fairview), 389,
391, 433; Ogden, 266, 386; Ogden
Canyon, 437; Parley's Canyon, 309;
Parowan, 453; Payson, 419, 442,
445, 452, 455; Promontory, 445;
Provo, 306, 308, 309, 322, 380, 381,
435, 436; Richfield, 424, 428–432,
434, 480; Saint George, 402, 452,
470–473, 478, 479, 494; Salina, 412,
424; Salina Canyon, 412–414; Salt
Creek (also Nephi), 322, 323; Salt
Creek Canyon, 322, 389, 412, 442,
455; Sanpete Stake, 480; Sanpete
Valley, and County, *see separate listing*; (Great) Salt Lake City, *see separate listing*; Salt Lake County, 434;
Sanpitch River, 432; Scipio, 419;
Sevier River, 426, 432; Sevier River
settlements, *see separate listing*; Sevier
Stake, 480; Spanish Fork, 418, 419,
427; Spanish Fork Canyon, 390,
391, 402, 444, 460; Spring Lake
Villa, 455; Springtown, *see separate
listing*; Springville, 379, 386, 391,
460; Sugarhouse, 309; Thistle Valley, 427; Twelve Mile Creek, 432;
Uinta Basin and Indian Reservation, 410, 419, 436, 443, 444, 459,
460, 564n.16; Utah County, 434;
Utah Lake, 322; Utah Valley, 371,
386; Wales, 389, 457; Wasatch
Mountains, 264; Weber River, 263,
301; Willow Creek (Willard), 381;
York Station, 480

Veneholm, (Mrs.) –, 423
Vickers, Ann Eliza, 371–372; *see* Hyde,
Ann Eliza (Vickers)
vision(s), 36, 69, 73, 86, 88, 89, 91,
104, 113–114, 128–129
Voice From Jerusalem, A, 146
Voorhis, –, merchant, 237, 291

Wakara (Walker), Indian Chief, 407,
419
Wallace, (Captain) –, 48
War of the Revolution, 320
Ward, Elijah Barney, 312, 315, 413–
415
Ward, J.H., poem 571n.42
Ward, Thomas, 213, 214
Wareham, James, 472
Washakie, Chief, 314, 318, 320–321
Washington, D.C., 170–174, 229
water, 403, 453
Weibye, Jens, 472
Wells, Daniel H., 371, 372, 394, 425,
427, 433, 476, 481
Welsh, (Mr.) –, 403
Wentworth, (Mr.), 172
Weymouth, Simeon, 30–31
Wharton, (Capt.) –, 280
Wheeler, Nathan, 5–6, 18, 515n.10
Whiskey, 239–240
White, Herbert Addison, 499, 502
White Horse Chief, Indian, 426, 437,
449, 450, 460, 461, 462; *see* Tam-a-
rits
White, Mary Ann (Hyde), 499, 502,
503
Whiting, George B., 132, 133, 527n.1
Whitmer, David, 57, 97, 99, 100, 233
Whitmer, John, 97
Whitney, Asa, 263

Whitney, N. K. & Co., 8, 11, 34, 194

Whitney, Newel K., 7-8, 10, 32, 38, 43, 76, 79, 95, 182, 190, 211, 267, 268

Wight, Lyman: apostle, absent, 164; Washington, D.C., 173-174; Albany, 177; named, 184; Texas, 197; apostate, 229, 231; excommunicated, 230, 539-540n.52

Wilcox, Ellen Amelia, 496

Williams, (Dr.) —, 236

Williams, Frederick G., 37, 38, 43, 96

Willis, —, young man, 346, 349

wine, 35, 249

Winters, Helen Melissa, 555n.16

witnesses, 16, 142-143

women, 274, 317

Wood, Gideon, 358, 467, 468, 553n.15

Woodruff, Wilford: Zion's Camp, 54; apostle, 97; meeting, 109; England, 111; east, 173; Boston, 175, 176; Albany, 177; England, 181, 197; named, 184; Nauvoo, 202-204; Hyde Park, 221; eastward, 226, 228; Kanesville, 253, 255, 256; Salt Lake City, 307, 367, 369, 370, 385; pruned, 391; seniority changed, 473, 569n.13; Orson's funeral, 486-487

Woolley, Romania Hyde, 508

Wooster, Nathan, 6

Word of Wisdom, 35

Wyckoff, A. J., 345

(Wyoming): 219; Bear River, 263; Big Sandy River, 263, 270; Black's Fork, 301; Deer Creek, 299; Fort Bridger, 263, 270, 301, 311, 313, 375; Fort John, 298; Fort Laramie, 219, 261, 270, 298; Fort Supply, *see separate listing*; Green River Mission, *see separate listing*; Independence Rock, 261, 301; Laramie River, 298; South Pass, 262, 263, 301; Sweetwater River, 262, 262, 300, 301; Wind River Mountains, 301, 320

Young, Brigham: apostle, 58; described, 60, 121, 181, 184; mission eastern states, 60; Kirtland Temple dedication, 68; steadfast, 77; Missouri, 104, 105; letter, 106-107; Iowa, 109; England, 111, 121-122; plural marriage, 157; east, 173; Boston, 175, 176; Albany, 177; Nauvoo, 180-186, 190-196; Iowa, 196-198, 200-201, 204; Council Bluffs, 206, 207, 209-211; letter, 212, 213; westward, 216, 219; Miller's Hollow, 221; President, 222, 223-225, 438-439, 492, 538n.34; westward, 226-228; letters, 243, 252, 256; Utah, 264-269; letters, 275, 281, 285; leader, 306-311, 314-316, 319, 323, 324; new counselor, 317; trip to Manti, 322; letters and instructions, 325, 327, 328, 333-338, 341-346, 349-351, 353, 354, 357-363; methods and actions, 365-367, 370, 372; new counselor, 371; trip north, 372-373; officiates, 373; instructions and actions, 374-377; averting war, 379, 380; instructs and directs, 381, 382, 386-388; house Manti, 390; instructions and letters, 393-398, 400; correction by, 401; trip southern Utah, 402, 405; instructions, 403, 404, 406; censure by, 405; letter, 406; and Indians, 407-411; war (*see* Black Hawk Indian War), 412-416, 418-422; visits Sanpete, 419-420; war (cont.), 425, 426, 428-433; about celestial crowns, 562n.36; trip south, 433; in Provo, 435; trip north, 434, 435, 437; new tabernacle; war (cont.), 439, 440; railroad, 441; in Sanpete, 442-443; Salt Lake City, 443; consultation, 454; war (cont.), 450, 454, 455; Nephi and Payson, 455; successor, 456; letter, 458; Brigham City, 459; chided Orson, 464; Sanpete, 469; United Order, 470, 569n.7; Saint George, 471; Sanpete 474-477; carriage, 476, 477; letter, 478; lunch,

479; Manti Temple site, 480; organized Sanpete Stake, 480; died, 480; funeral, 481; methods, 509
Young, Brigham, Jr., 443
Young, Clara, 447
Young, John W., 481
Young, Joseph, 196–198, 203

Zechariah, 70
Zion, 21, 33, 34, 38–45, 105, 113, 122, 140, 142, 148, 210, 308, 374, 406
"Zionism," 482, 571n.35
Zion's Camp, 45–55, 57
Zion's Co-operative Mercantile Institution, 443

Edinburgh, Scotland

Amsterdam, Netherlands

Preston, England
Manchester

Rotterdam, Netherlands
Arnheim, Netherlands

Frankfurt, Germany
Regensburg, Germany

Liverpool
Bedford

London

Mainz, Germany

Trieste, Italy

N